Rampart Nations

New Perspectives on Central and Eastern European Studies

Published in association with the Herder Institute for Historical Research on East Central Europe, Marburg, Germany

Series Editors
Heidi Hein-Kircher, Head of Academic Forum
Eszter Gantner, Research Associate
Peter Haslinger, Director, and Professor for East Central European History at Justus-Liebig-University, Giessen

Decades after the political changes that accompanied the fall of the Soviet Union, the history and cultures of Eastern Europe remain very important for understanding the challenges of today. With a special focus on the Baltic states, Poland, the Czech Republic, Slovakia, and Hungary, *New Perspectives on Central and Eastern European Studies* investigates the historical and social forces that have shaped the region, from ethnicity and religion to imperial legacies and national conflicts. Each volume in the series explores these and many other topics to contribute to a better understanding of contemporary Central and Eastern Europe.

Volume 1
Rampart Nations: Bulwark Myths of East European Multiconfessional Societies in the Age of Nationalism
Edited by Liliya Berezhnaya and Heidi Hein-Kircher

Rampart Nations
Bulwark Myths of East European Multiconfessional Societies in the Age of Nationalism

Edited by
Liliya Berezhnaya and Heidi Hein-Kircher

First published in 2019 by
Berghahn Books
www.berghahnbooks.com

© 2019, 2022 Liliya Berezhnaya and Heidi Hein-Kircher
First paperback edition published in 2022

All rights reserved. Except for the quotation of short passages
for the purposes of criticism and review, no part of this book
may be reproduced in any form or by any means, electronic or
mechanical, including photocopying, recording, or any information
storage and retrieval system now known or to be invented,
without written permission of the publisher.

Library of Congress Cataloging-in-Publication Data

Names: Berezhnaya, Liliya, editor. | Hein-Kircher, Heidi, 1969– editor.
Title: Rampart Nations: Bulwark Myths of East European Multiconfessional
  Societies in the Age of Nationalism / edited by Liliya Berezhnaya and Heidi
  Hein-Kircher.
Description: New York: Berghahn Books, 2019. | Series: New Perspectives on
  Central and Eastern European Studies; volume 1 | Includes bibliographical
  references and index.
Identifiers: LCCN 2018053684 (print) | LCCN 2018058014 (ebook) | ISBN
  9781789201482 (ebook) | ISBN 9781789201475 (hardback: alk. paper)
Subjects: LCSH: National characteristics, East European. | Groupidentity—
  Europe, Eastern. | Ethnicity—Europe, Eastern. | Religious pluralism—
  Europe, Eastern. | Nationalism—Europe, Eastern. | National security—
  Social aspects--Europe, Eastern.
Classification: LCC DJK26.5 (ebook) | LCC DJK26.5 .R36 2019 (print) |
  DDC 947—dc23
LC record available at https://lccn.loc.gov/2018053684

British Library Cataloguing in Publication Data

A catalogue record for this book is available from the British Library

ISBN 978-1-78920-147-5 hardback
ISBN 978-1-80073-435-7 paperback
ISBN 978-1-78920-148-2 ebook

https://doi.org/10.3167/9781789201475

Contents

List of Illustrations   vii

Acknowledgments   ix

A Note on Transliteration and Toponyms   x

Part I. Background

Introduction Constructing a Rampart Nation: Conceptual Framework   3
Liliya Berezhnaya and Heidi Hein-Kircher

Chapter 1 The Origins of *Antemurale Christianitatis* Myths: Remarks on the Promotion of a Political Concept   31
Kerstin Weiand

Part II. (De-)Sacralizing and Nationalizing Borderlands

Chapter 2 Not a Bulwark, but a Part of the Larger Catholic Community: The Romanian Greek Catholic Church in Transylvania (1700–1850)   61
Ciprian Ghisa

Chapter 3 Securitizing the Polish Bulwark: The Mission of Lviv in Polish Travel Guides during the Late Nineteenth and Early Twentieth Centuries   81
Heidi Hein-Kircher

Chapter 4 Ghetto as an "Inner *Antemurale*"? Debates on Exclusion, Integration, and Identity in Galicia in the Nineteenth and Early Twentieth Centuries   103
Jürgen Heyde

Chapter 5 Holy Ground and a Bulwark against "the Other": The (Re)Construction of an Orthodox Crimea in the Nineteenth-Century Russian Empire   125
Kerstin S. Jobst

Chapter 6 Bastions of Faith in the Oceans of Ambiguities: Monasteries in the East European Borderlands (Late Nineteenth–Beginning of the Twentieth Century) 146
Liliya Berezhnaya

Chapter 7 "The Turkish Wall": Turkey as an Anti-Communist and Anti-Russian Bulwark in the Twentieth Century 186
Zaur Gasimov

Part III. Promoting *Antemurale* Discourses

Chapter 8 Why Didn't the *Antemurale* Historical Mythology Develop in Early Nineteenth-Century Ukraine? 207
Volodymyr Kravchenko

Chapter 9 Translating the Border(s) in a Multilingual and Multiethnic Society: *Antemurale* Myths in Polish and Ukrainian Schoolbooks of the Habsburg Monarchy 241
Philipp Hofeneder

Chapter 10 Mediating the *Antemurale* Myth in East Central Europe: Religion and Politics in Modern Geographers' Entangled Lives and Maps 262
Steven Seegel

Chapter 11 Bulwarks of Anti-Bolshevism: Russophobic Polemic of the Christian Right in Poland and Hungary in the Interwar Years and Their Roots in the Nineteenth Century 293
Paul Srodecki

Chapter 12 Defenders of the Russian Land: Viktor Vasnetsov's *Warriors* and Russia's Bulwark Myth 319
Stephen M. Norris

Part IV. Reflections on the Bulwark Myths Today

Chapter 13 *Antemurale* Thinking as Historical Myth and Ethnic Boundary Mechanism 347
Pål Kolstø

Chapter 14 Concluding Thoughts on Central and Eastern European Bulwark Rhetoric in the Twenty-First Century 374
Paul Srodecki

Index 396

Illustrations

Figures

Figure 6.1. Cartoon, "Galician Pilgrims Travelling Abroad," *Zerkalo* 15, no. 27 (May 1882): 4. Photo by Liliya Berezhnaya.   158

Figure 6.2. Iulian Butsmaniuk, mural in the Church of the Sacred Heart of Jesus in Zhovkva, featuring Bohdan Khmelnytskyi, Ivan Vishenskyi, Ivan Mazepa, Halshka Hulevichyvna, 1932–1939. Wikimedia Commons, public domain.   164

Figure 6.3. Iulian Butsmaniuk, mural in the Church of the Sacred Heart of Jesus in Zhovkva, featuring the Brest Union and the heroes of the Cossack Times, 1932–1939. Wikimedia Commons, public domain.   165

Figure 11.1. Polish recruitment poster dated 1920. The text reads: "To Arms! Save the Fatherland! Remember well our fate." Wikimedia Commons, public domain.   300

Figure 12.1. Viktor Vasnetsov, *Bogatyri*, 1898. Photograph by anagoria. Wikimedia Commons, public domain.   322

Figure 12.2. Viktor Vasnetsov, *Kreshcheniie Rusi*, 1896. Special stamp to commemorate the 1,025th anniversary of the Christianization of Rus by the Russian Post, Publishing and Trade Centre "Marka," 2013. Design of the souvenir sheet by A. Moscovets. Scanned by Dmitry Ivanov. Wikimedia Commons, public domain.   328

Maps

Map 10.1. Map of Poland during the reign of King Jan Sobieski, published on the 200th anniversary of the Defense of Vienna, 1883. Map by J. Szpetkowski. Wikimedia Commons, public domain.   263

Map 10.2. Geological and special map of the Kingdom of Saxony, 1878. Map by Albrecht Penck. Reprinted from Albrecht Penck, *Geologische Spezialkarte des Königreich Sachsen* (Leipzig: Giesecke & Devrient, 1878). 267

Map 10.3. German ethnic and cultural lands, 1925. Map by Albrecht Penck. Courtesy Cornell University, PJ Mode Collection of Persuasive Cartography. 269

Map 10.4. Military-political map of Poland, 1916. Map by Eugeniusz Romer. Courtesy Library of Congress. Retrieved 14 June 2018 from https://blogs.loc.gov/loc/files/2017/01/Figure-1.jpeg. 271

Map 10.5. The Ukrainian territory in Europe, 1914. Map by Stepan Rudnytskyi. Reprinted from Stepan Rudnyts'kyi, *Ukraina und die Ukrainer* (Berlin, 1915). 275

Map 10.6. Ukraine in its ethnographic borders, 1920. Map by Stepan Rudnytskyi and Heorg von Hasenko. Courtesy Harvard Map Collection, Harvard Library. 277

Map 10.7. Ethnographical map of Hungary, based on population density, 1919. Map by Count Pál Teleki. Reprinted from Count Pál Teleki, *Magyarország néprajzi térképe a népsűrűség alapján* (Budapest: Magyar Földrajzi Intézet, 1919). 281

Acknowledgments

The idea of this book is the result of the cooperation between the Cluster of Excellence "Religion and Politics in Pre-Modern and Modern Cultures" at the University of Münster and the Herder Institute for Historical Research on East Central Europe—Institute of the Leibniz Association in Marburg. It was cofinanced by the SFB/TRR 138 "Dynamics of Security."

We would like to thank these institutions for their financial and organizational support.

A Note on Transliteration and Toponyms

For transliterating the Cyrillic alphabet into Latin, we chose the BGN/PCGN romanization system, developed by the United States Board on Geographic Names and by the Permanent Committee on Geographical Names for British Official Use. For purposes of simplification, we have omitted apostrophes for ъ and ь.

Toponyms in multiethnic Eastern Europe differ in spelling from language to language. For example, the Western Ukrainian city of L'viv was officially called Lemberg in German during the Habsburg monarchy from 1772 until 1918, while under Polish rule and control it was Lwów, and in Soviet times and in the Russian language it is Lvov. As the spelling of a toponym varies from one (national) perspective of analysis to another, we decided to use only the common English spelling—in this case Lviv, for example—to make it simpler to read the text. We introduce the cities' spelling in the respective languages of the region only at the first mention of the toponym in each chapter.

PART I

Background

INTRODUCTION
Constructing a Rampart Nation
Conceptual Framework

Liliya Berezhnaya and Heidi Hein-Kircher

Nowadays, images of fences, walls, bastions, and fortresses are popular metaphors in the political sphere. They polarize and divide societies into ideological camps as we can observe in contemporary Europe. The old topos of Europe as a fortress has been reintroduced in numerous forms in the media and has once again found its way into various political agendas, for example in the present Polish and Hungarian right-wing governments.

Bulwark myths, otherwise called *antemurale* myths, are widespread in East European countries today but also have a tradition dating back to early modern times. Such myths contain several components:

> The claim of a perennial menace caused by an "Other" as enemy on a territorial or cultural basis. . . ; the call to defend, not only oneself, but also one's own people against the threat of the "Other". . . ; the claim of being chosen to defend a higher or greater entity, of which one is a part.[1]

They also contain the claim of a civilizing mission. The *antemurale* myth is often instrumentalized, not only against foreign enemies but also in order to mobilize and unite the community inside the bulwark.

During the nationalizing processes in nineteenth-century Eastern Europe, bulwark myths gained particular importance in the southern and western borderland territories of continental empires, mainly today's Poland, Hungary, and Ukraine but also in neighboring states. Being a "rampart nation" was one of the main motifs in national claims to be part of Europe. *Antemurale* mythology was also crucial for the creation of national identity and coherence in Eastern European borderland societies.

Our volume deals with bulwark (*antemurale*) myths as securitizing and spatial myths in East European border regions in the age of nationalism, focusing on their definition, how they functioned and were spread, and the key figures and groups who played a role in their dissemination. Despite the obvious popularity of these narratives in European history, historiography has not yet paid enough attention to bulwark myths in modern Eastern European history. Above all, transnational studies have until recently ignored the field of political myths in multiconfessional and multiethnic East European regions, although a few comparative studies provide incentives for further research.[2]

The very notion of "transnational history," other than being a possible alternative to dominant national narratives, remains quite vague. Some identify it as an umbrella term for historical debates, whereas others give a rather open definition: transnational history deals with the "people, ideas, products, processes and patterns that operate over, across, through, beyond, above, under, or in-between polities and societies."[3] Notably, transnational history goes further than comparative history, as it suggests tracing interaction and transfer not only between direct neighbors but also between entities and institutions far away from the borderline.[4] Urban and religious history is particularly fruitful for these purposes.

In particular, present-day Ukraine exemplifies contact and conflict regions in Eastern Europe. Recently, the collection of articles by Philipp Ther and Georgiy Kasianov[5] described a way in which transnational history could be used by historians dealing with Ukrainian borders and contact zones. Importantly, such an approach allows placing Ukrainian history within the general European context. While advocating Ukraine as a laboratory of transnational history "that deliberately transcends the boundaries of one culture or country," Ther and Kasianov suggest focusing on agents of cultural exchange.[6] Notably, the recent collection of articles edited by Serhii Plokhy on the outlook of historical writing in post-Soviet Ukraine contains a section on the "transnational turn" and goes beyond the cultural focus. Its contributors elaborate on, among other things, military history, cartography, art and Jewish studies as possible "transnational fields" of Ukrainian historiography.[7]

This is indeed relevant, not only to Ukrainian history but also to the neighboring territories.[8] Moreover, the application of transnational history—with its emphasis on agents of *antemurale* rhetoric—in combination with the study of political myths offers an unusual and rather new perspective. Our book, which can neither cover the whole geographical range nor address all possible thematic affiliations, aims to bridge this research gap at least partly.

In this introduction, we shall first dwell upon the general definition of political myth, then highlight the features of bulwark myths as securitizing and spatial myths, and finally outline the history of *antemurale* myths in modern Eastern Europe as reflected in the structure and the major conclusions of this book.

Political Myths: General Definitions

Bulwark myths belong to the category of the so-called political myths. These are simplifying and meaningful narratives in which the mental frame of reference is based on a set of prior assumptions. Myths always delineate "an eternal fight between the good and the evil,"[9] between "Self" and "Other." In contrast to religious myths, they do not necessarily have a transcendental component. A political myth thus refers to a politically constituted community and interprets its origins and character. In order to achieve this goal, it constitutes an emotionally charged narration that constructs the past quite selectively, stereotypically idealizing past and present.[10] According to Peter Niedermüller, it "purges the memory symbolically" and becomes a "collective autobiography."[11] The semantic structure makes a political myth changeable, which is necessary in the long run. Thus, the mythical narration could be varied and also adapted to the audience.[12] Through its message, a political myth provides the community with orientation that it also shapes at the same time. It paraphrases and verifies modes of behavior and values by means of this functionality. Hence, a political myth explains existing collective problems and designates binding goals for the community.[13]

Because of its function in providing sense and orientation, political myths are an inherent element of a political system. To put it briefly, they are "narratives, that is, stories that deal with the origins, the sense and the historical mission of a political community so as to enable orientation and options for action."[14] Moreover, they are important elements of cultures of memory and provide a unifying storyline for "imagined communities."[15] In showing historic achievements and heroes, political myths explain why one should be a member of this or that community. Hence, they contribute mainly to the self-confidence of a political association, being "the narrative foundation of the symbolic order of a community."[16]

These myths possess conveying, legitimizing, and integrating functions and contribute to the coherence of the society. Their communicative and mobilizing mission proves to be of great importance when the community undergoes phases of collective uncertainty, for example during political, economic, and social crises, when it experiences deficiencies regarding integration, identity, and legitimization.[17] Because of these functions, it becomes clear why political myths give a heroic account of merits and tell of the successful defense of the community against various dangers. This historic achievement provides the feeling of security.

Each political community has its own myths. According to George Schöpflin, difficulties in categorizing political myths are caused by the nature of myth itself. Its function is to construct coherence; therefore, "different myths receive emphasis at different times to cope with different challenges."[18] Whereas the individual myth's narration depends on historical context, political myths share common characteristics. Most of them give an account of the origins of the community. Additionally, myths deal with transfiguration, authentication, and/or a catharsis. Each community has a certain repertoire of political myths that can be adjusted to the collective needs and activated if there is a need for articulated collective identity, coherence, cohesion, or legitimation. The case of the Jewish ghetto, discussed by Jürgen Heyde (Leipzig) in this volume, demonstrates that through the erection of "inner walls," society itself can be aggregated by excluding national and religious Others.

John Armstrong labeled the most constitutive myths as "mythomoteurs" that help to define group identities in relation to the polity, which they already did in premodern times. A mythomoteur "arouses intensive affect by stressing the individuals' solidarity against an alien force, that is, by enhancing the salience of boundary perceptions."[19] When the conditions within a society are perceived as threatened and insecure, concepts of danger become virulent.[20]

This mosaic of myths is implemented in a society through elements of memory and political culture, such as political rituals and festivities, symbols, and memorials that nonverbally paraphrase the mythical narrative. This helps to present political myths as first-order truths that "cannot be perceived to be inventions."[21] However, it is also possible to communicate the general story verbally, for example through various media that are aptly discussed in the individual chapters of this book (e.g., historical texts, schoolbooks, maps, travel guides, but also theatrical performances, songs, and so on).

Such forms of media are assumed to be "objective" and communicate values through a normative mythical "story." This issue is highlighted in many contributions in this volume: Volodymyr Kravchenko (Edmonton) scrutinizes it using the example of Ukrainian and Russian historiography; Liliya Berezhnaya (Münster) demonstrates the role of Ukrainian monasteries in the formation of political myths; Kerstin Weiand (Frankfurt) addresses the issue in the writings of Renaissance and Baroque authors and in the documents of Imperial Diets; Zaur Gasimov (Istanbul) highlights the story of émigré politicians; and Paul Srodecki (Kiel/Ostrava) examines the interwar Catholic Right and the contemporary press as the key agents in the myth-making process. These and other contributions reveal that the texts popularizing bulwark myths were often produced in political and academic milieus. From the late Middle Ages on, various historians, politicians, Church hierarchs, and later also journalists were actively involved in the formation and dissemination of bulwark rhetoric.

Importantly, there were many other influential intermediaries that helped to transfer *antemurale* myth to the lower layers of society in the age of nationalism. This becomes clear by looking at schoolbooks in Philipp Hofeneder's (Graz) contribution and at travel guides from Heidi Hein-Kircher's (Marburg) chapter. Besides these, maps and painted artworks were also crucial in this process, to name just a few examples discussed by Steven Seegel (Greeley, CO) and Stephen M. Norris (Oxford, OH). Both genres, maps and paintings, promoted the popularity of the bulwark mythical narrative, providing it with visual attributes. For instance, Seegel argues that modern mappers (Polish, Ukrainian, Hungarian, and German) often regarded themselves as public servants and scientific experts; maps were a form of graphic media deployed by geographers as historical actors, who often presupposed Europe's uniqueness.

In contrast, Norris focuses on the *longue durée* "life" of a single painting, Viktor Vasnetsov's famous *Bogatyri* ("Warriors," 1898) in Russian/Soviet cultural memory. For Norris, Vasnetsov's painting, frequently popularized in the press, on postage stamps, on cigarette cases, and on postcards, functioned as an expression of a bulwark myth while it was used as means to call for unity. In this way, visualized *antemurale* mythical narration was used for the consolidation of a society.

Bulwark Myths as Securitizing and Spatial Myths

Bulwark myths have two important distinctive features as political myths. First, they interpret heroic performances in securing a community faced with a great threat that came from outside. This surmounted threat, the "evil," is a point of reference for present and future times. Through focusing on a past threat, which is interpreted quite selectively in favor of the group, a threat for present and future times is derived. This bulwark mission becomes a promise to the members of the community to protect them, their values, and their faith against threats that are coming or will come from outside the bastion. At the same time, the narrative of the heroic defense, of being a rampart, is invoked in order to incite the community to future heroic performances. The implication is that the community will only be saved by following the bulwark myth's message. So, a bulwark myth quite heavily distinguishes between community members and nonkinsmen, the Other. It describes a threat scenario and a process of creating security as one of managing the threat.[22]

If a threat to the community is indicated, the necessary answer is the promise to secure the community. Thus, we can understand "security" as a discursively communicated political notion of value and of societal order to which political myths and particularly bulwark myths contribute.[23]

This is most prominently demonstrated in Weiand's chapter. Military phrasing has adhered to bulwark rhetoric from its very beginning. Renaissance authors were already using the *antemurale* metaphor to underline the impression of an isle under siege, of inner peace and outer war. The idea of an existential threat to the community shielded by a bulwark linked European borderland peripheries with the core of the Holy See.

The securitizing mythical narratives often deal with both the threat and the ways to overcome it. The example of the "Turkish wall" against the (Russian/Soviet) Communist danger, introduced in Gasimov's chapter, makes clear the mobilizing potential of the bulwark myth. Gasimov's study is also paradigmatic for understanding the common mechanisms of the *antemurale* myth's functioning on both sides of the historical Christian/Muslim border.

Second, bulwark myths clarify which territory belongs to the community. They are thus spatially oriented narratives, defining a specific claimed territory that should be defended. Through such a narrative, they create a specific idea of a space. The imagined territory acquires a symbolic function and represents a community. Thus, bulwark myths as myths of space can function as emotional glue.[24]

Contested borderland regions are a particular focus of the myths of space in general and of the bulwark myths in particular. These narratives are particularly prevalent in multiethnic regions where a specific territory has been claimed. Pål Kolstø (Oslo) points out in this context that *antemurale* myths constitute a special case of a boundary-creating mechanism relying to a large extent on civilizational thinking. Because it belongs to a greater civilization, the in-group is defined as superior to certain adjacent groups. Focusing on the national states in Eastern Europe (Georgia, Ukraine, and Russia), Kolstø asks how the *antemurale* myth can play out in situations in which two groups belong to the same Christian confession. In these cases, he concludes, power differentials are just as important as civilizational perceptions for the construction of *antemurale* myths, and stronger and more resourceful groups (nations, ethnic groups) tend to downplay differences while the smaller and less resourceful group will emphasize the differences.

Bulwark myths as myths of space function as narrative "border posts," if we understand space as a cognitive construct functioning as a base for the community.[25] Hence, these myths define and justify the claims on the collective territory. This observation fits Georg Simmel's classical definition that, "the boundary is not a spatial fact with sociological consequences, but a sociological fact that forms itself spatially."[26]

The role of a bulwark myth in modern societies is not necessarily limited to the creation of meaning. Often, these myths provide the basis for the sacralization of political ideologies. Contemporary historiography argues that, despite various manifestations of secularization in economic and cultural spheres (like the "nationalization" of Church property in nineteenth-century Western Europe), the "symbiosis of religious and national" remained intact in ideological and mental spheres.[27] In the modern period, myths were above all an important instrument of the sacralization of nation/empire/multistate entities and also of the nationalization of religion.[28]

Many of the authors of this book, with the help of *antemurale* mythology, have been able to trace the theme of the sacralization of nation/empire and the nationalization of religion. It is analyzed in Norris's text, which describes the transformation of sacralized Russianness into secular Sovietness. It is also scrutinized in Seegel's chapter on maps as a modern tool to sacralize and instrumentalize the past, and in Hein-Kircher's case study, which reveals how the Polish rampart Lviv was stylized as a martyr for Western Christianity. But the role of *antemurale* myths in the process of sacralization within modern nations and empires is presented most vividly in the chapters by Berezhnaya, Kerstin Jobst (Vienna), and Srodecki.

Berezhnaya's study compares the history of three Ukrainian monasteries—the Orthodox Pochaiv Holy Dormition Lavra (Volhynia), the Greek Catholic Nativity Monastery in Zhovkva (near Lviv), and the Orthodox Holy Dormition Monastery (the Crimea). Despite denominational differences, the leadership of these three monasteries shows the same pattern in interpreting the challenges of nationalism. The dissemination of national and imperial ideology with religious overtones occurred with the help of new mass media, actively used by Church hierarchs in political propaganda. It was enhanced by the notions of a "true faith," a "national Church," and the new "nationalized" images of enemies.

This "mutual conditioning" between religion and nation as social systems of interpretation is based on political mythology. For some experts, like Anthony Smith, nationalism itself is a product of a hybridization between "the earlier religious myth and the nationalist ideal."[29] Others pay attention to how threats to the national identity are mythologized and sharpen the sense of us and them. As Srodecki discusses in his chapter on East European Catholic Right movements, thanks to that hybridization, bulwark myths in interwar Poland and Hungary stylized both countries as the most important bastions of European freedom and Christian civilization against "godless Bolsheviks."

It is the borderland situation, the feeling of a "contested frontier," that determines the specificity of the religious-national bond: "The political conflict is likely to have superimposed upon it a sense of religious conflict, so that national identity becomes fused with religious identity."[30] The case of Crimea, discussed by Jobst, is perhaps one of the most striking. The absorption of the Crimea into the Russian collective memory was not only a result of organic colonization but a much more complex and multifaceted process of unification. It was accompanied by the ideology of the sacralized and nationalized empire that actively grew on the basis of the bulwark myth and the topos of the Crimea as the cradle of Russian civilization.

One case study in this volume looks at an opposite development: the way the *antemurale* rhetoric was secularized in the twentieth century. As demonstrated by Gasimov, the role of religion in the development of the idea of the Turkish wall was just secondary. Both the exiled intellectuals and their Turkish counterparts were able to combine laicism with Turkish nationalism by developing the idea of an anti-Communist bulwark. In this way, the Turkish rampart nation differed from most European projects on *antemurale*, demonstrating parallels with the contemporary Soviet model.

In public perception, bulwark myths are often mixed with other political myths like that of the "Golden Age" (glorious past) or of common origin.[31] In the taxonomy of political myths provided by George Schöpflin, *antemurale* myths are placed in the category of redemption and suffering. They could also be situated among the myths of territory, civilizing mission, or national character. The third option contains some contradictions: the *antemurale* myth postulates the inclusion of a single ethnic group into a broader community that is presumably more culturally developed.[32] By narrating a heroic achievement of the border community, this myth also claims this community to be an equal part of the core community, which in turn brings it into contradiction with the myth of national character, also quite popular among the borderland communities. The topos of a civilizing mission inherent in bulwark myths suggests a possible resolution to this dilemma. On the one hand, the bulwark myth narrates how the given borderland society defends itself and the core communities. On the other hand, it claims a mission of bringing the communities living on the other side of the "bulwark" the advantages and privileges of a presumably higher and culturally more developed civilization.

In this way, the notion of a civilizing mission, having been a constitutive part of imperial and colonial discourses since the second half of the nineteenth century, also contributes to the popularization of bulwark myths. Yet, several other aspects of its use are important here. The general definition of the civilizing mission refers to the conviction that one's own society has the right and the duty to intervene in less developed societies in order to promote more progress there.[33] Four basic components are inherent to such a definition: the idea of progress, the idea of the superiority of one's own society, the notion that the civilizing society is able to reach the highest level of civilization, and, finally, the conviction that progress in other societies can be accelerated through intervention.[34] This secular definition of a civilizing mission, however, is deeply rooted in the old concept of Christian mission, which did not disappear with the rise of modernity. As the studies of bulwark myths reveal, the general idea of progress and civilization is often enriched here by messianic overtones and the notion of moral progress (as, for instance, demonstrated in Seegel's study of the 1883 Polish map). It is associated with Divine Providence and religious conversions.[35]

Another consistent feature of bulwark myths is the constant reference to common places of memory. Our book provides a variety of examples of East European *antemurale* places of memory. These include historical personalities (e.g., the Polish King Jan III Sobieski in Hein-Kircher's study) and events (e.g., the "Miracle on the Vistula" and the "Red Terror" in Srodecki's chapter) and sacral places (e.g., Pochaiv Holy Dormition Lavra and Crimea) and artifacts (Vasnietsov's "Warriors" and Butsmaniuk's frescoes in western Ukrainian Zhovkva).

These are symbols that serve as building blocks of political myths, including the bulwark ones. As formulated by George Schöfplin, "Reference to symbols could be quite sufficient to recall the myth for members of the community without needing to return to the ritual."[36]

Generally, cultures of memory consist of various historically and culturally variable practices and concepts. They (re)produce a certain image of the past in the collective memory and transform it into the present. Moreover, they produce suggestive interpretive patterns and imagined traditions that are used as a message for the respective society. In this way, the culture of memory is potently charged with political myths.[37]

In sum, bulwark myths are an interpretation of the historic achievements of a society and its territorial shape. At the same time, they not only claim a territory but also define the society's relation to its territory. Bulwark myths quite paradigmatically demonstrate the interrelation between identity formation and territorial claims. They also provide legitimacy to the "borders in the mind."[38] As a result, one can find bulwark myths where it is necessary to strengthen identity and culture, to define a society in demarcating it from Others and to imagine a territory.[39]

Bulwark Myths in Modern Eastern Europe

These narrative strategies are often to be found in East European history, and they contribute to the imagination of Eastern Europe in a specific way. As discussed in Weiand's chapter, the concept of *antemurale christianitatis* emerged in the high Middle Ages against the background of the Mongol raids and reached its peak between the late fifteenth and seventeenth centuries, particularly during the anti-Ottoman wars.[40] The notion of being a bulwark against the Muslim threat was widespread in early modern Croatia, Hungary, and Venice; the Polish-Lithuanian Commonwealth; and the lands of the Habsburg monarchy.[41]

From the very beginning, the (self-)definition of *antemurale* was mostly limited to the Catholic lands. Territories dominated by the Eastern Rite believers—such as Serbia, Muscovy, Rhodes, and Crete—were granted this title by the Holy See only with certain reservations. Although typical for the Christian-Islamic border, *antemurale* myths can also be found in the regions where different Christian faiths meet. Here, the extrapolation "civilization/barbarism" is often enriched with thoughts about the "true faith." In this way, the *antemurale* myth is used as a source of legitimation for different kinds of missionary activities (religious, political, and cultural), perhaps with the only exception being the Transylvanian case Ciprian Ghisa (Cluj) discusses in this volume.

The *antemurale* rhetoric is by no means a prerogative of East European elites and media. However, *antemurale* myths acquired particular relevance and meaning in East European frontier zones. By frontier zones, we mean the territories that are situated along the southern, southwestern, and western borders of the former Russian Empire, encompassing the lands of modern-day Ukraine and the Black Sea region. These lands have been contested since antiquity, and they have contributed to the growth of the Byzantine, Ottoman, Habsburg, and Russian empires as multiethnic and multifaith communities. For some, these territories, with regard to their historical legacies, fit the category of the so-called mesoregions,[42] or even "borderland-type civilizations" (e.g., the Black Sea region, the so-called East European borderland including Belarus and Moldova),[43] or, more traditionally, East Central Europe, otherwise defined as New Central Europe.[44]

It is remarkable, though, that many of these regional attempts to reconsider European geography within the so-called spatial turn combine the positively charged borderland's "pluralistic image" with the narratives of "victimization" and "resistance." The concept of the "frontier civilization" as a precondition of the democratic development in post–Cold War Europe also found its promoters.[45] Clearly, such methodological approaches "are neither harmful nor innocent. Imagined spaces on mental maps can be ascribed not only as 'spaces of perception,' but also as 'spaces of action.'"[46]

Although we are aware of the shortcomings of regionalization in modern historical writing,[47] we define the geographical focus of our volume as mesoregional. Our book deals mostly with the lands of modern Ukraine and its neighbors (Polish, Hungarian, Romanian, Russian, Habsburg, and

Ottoman lands) in the age of nationalism. This includes border regions as well as some of the so-called core imperial areas (e.g., Russian in Norris's and Kolstø's chapters and Ottoman/Turkish in Gasimov's text). The mesoregional approach permits looking "at de-territorialized yet not timeless units of analysis by way of intra-regional and inter-regional comparison in order to identify clusters of *longue durée*-like structural markers."[48] We are also fully aware of terminological intricacies in this sense (Ukraine and its many neighbors did not have sovereignty in this period and, thus, had no clearly defined state borders). Still, it is on the one hand fruitful to start from the classical view of *antemurale* rhetoric as the prerogative of Catholic countries. On the other hand, our approach allows us to introduce various multiconfessional and multiethnic perspectives on the whole region beyond the narrow scope of specific national discourses.

Recent historiography emphasizes that "mesoregion" is an analytical category, not an ontological one. As Diana Mishkova and Balázs Trencsényi argue in their latest book, "Regions thus do not emerge as objectified and disjointed units functioning as quasi-national entities with fixed boundaries and clear-cut lines between insiders and outsiders, but rather as flexible and historically changing frameworks for interpreting certain phenomena."[49]

We assume that Eastern Europe as a mesoregion could be described in terms of multilayered, complex interactions of the steppe, of Rus, Polish, Habsburg, Russian, Ottoman imperial, and Soviet traditions.[50] We are aware that—with reference to long and intensive research debates—some of our authors (e.g., Seegel and Srodecki) could not follow the geographical term "Eastern Europe" and define these territories more concretely as East Central Europe, which includes German territories, or Central Europe, which also encompasses Austrian lands.

Whether called Eastern, Central, or East Central Europe, these were the lands of "several nested geographies,"[51] at the same time being "a contact zone possessing a quite differentiated spectrum of social and cultural phenomena."[52] Mary Louise Pratt defines contact zones as social arenas in which cultures "meet, clash, and grapple with each other within spaces of asymmetrical power relations."[53] These territories could otherwise be called a communication region that is characterized by dense internal interaction and multiple cultural practices and experiences.[54]

The logic of the *antemurale* functioned on both sides there. For the local population, living on a front line required both cooperation and confrontation with close neighbors. In the case of danger, bulwark rhetoric was often in use, while the logic of cooperation across the border emerged in peaceful times. This region was seen both as a bulwark and as a bridge. Border conflicts gave rise to the formation of semi-independent military units, such as the Ukrainian Cossacks, who were often portrayed as frontiersmen defending the Orthodox faith, the Ukrainian nation, or the Russian Empire.[55] The boundary between Christian and Islamic cultures, which is rooted in history, also influenced various interdependent debates about civilization, barbarism, religious missions, and self-identification with the role of a "chosen people" (e.g., as defenders of faith or culture) in the region.[56]

Since the nineteenth century, the mythic narrative of bulwarks has undergone considerable change due to the rise of nationalism and the transformations of political borders. *Antemurale* myths have therefore experienced a revival as modern rampart nations were born. Recent statements by East European politicians and journalists, as analyzed in Kolstø's chapter and Srodecki's concluding remarks on the legacies of the *antemurale* rhetorics at the end of the book, show that ancient topoi of a chosen people and the civilization/barbarism divide remain intact today. Since the beginning of the twentieth century, anti-Islamic rhetoric has sometimes been replaced by a sharp anti-Russian/Soviet vocabulary.

This is aptly demonstrated in several case studies in this volume, particularly in those of Kolstø, Gasimov, and Srodecki. Political myths of *antemurale*, due to their semantic flexibility, are essential elements of national ideologies. A certain chain effect has been crucial in this respect. Despite the obvious "dividing function" of bulwark myths, many national traditions in the region have been determined in their modern (i.e., mainly nineteenth-century) development by the inclusion of mirroring images of the enemy from the other side of the border. Since the nationally motivated and accelerated enhancement of bulwark narratives in the nineteenth century, they have become an important source of legitimation for the ideologies of nation-states and empires in the region. Consequently, they are deeply engraved in today's national consciousness.

One focus of our book rests upon the *longue durée* processes in national consciousness from the end of the eighteenth century until World War II. In the historical literature, this period has been given the name of "the age of nationalism." It is generally supposed that this time witnessed the rise of nationalism, which became a generally recognized sentiment molding public and private life. However, such a universal definition is questionable. In the abovementioned region, the expression of nationalism had different forms. Some scholars define an "Eastern type of nationalism" as ethnic, as opposed to "Western nationalism," which they say was a civic one. Hans Kohn, who coined this typology around World War II, described ethnic nationalism as inherently backward, while civic (political) nationalism was allegedly progressive.[57] The critique of such assertions concerned mostly the equation of nation and state, which in some East European cases is rather problematic. The often postulated equation of nation and modernity also does not seem to work in Eastern European contexts in the "long" nineteenth century.[58]

However, the most critical point deals with the dichotomy between nation-state and empire. For decades, historians have seen empires, in contrast to nation-states, in the, "tradition of negativity, which perceived social reality through a framework defined by the characteristics of the modern world of nation-states and its historicity. Empire within this old trend has been defined as the opposite and the subordinate: a historical archaism before the advent of the age of nationalism."[59]

Instead, we opt for a more balanced solution: one should not sharply oppose the nationalization of empires to the formation of nation-states during the long nineteenth century.[60] Both processes took place in the region; both were legitimized by bulwark myths. The examples discussed by Kravchenko and by Ghisa in this book demonstrate this statement *ex negativo*. Kravchenko and Ghisa raise the issue of historical contexts that prevent the spread of bulwark rhetoric. In Kravchenko's article, these were territorial divisions that prevented the formation of *antemurale* mythology.

Early nineteenth-century Ukrainian territories were often perceived as "lands-in-between" suffering from "fatal geography." Because Ghisa describes a rather peaceful coexistence in eighteenth- and early nineteenth-century Transylvania, one can presume that this particular situation was also the reason for the absence of the *antemurale* rhetoric. A "confessional security" could indeed prevent the feeling of threat and in this way hinder the dissemination of bulwark rhetoric in confessional polemics. For the Greek Catholic elites in Transylvania, the only apparent danger was that coming from inside, as the Orthodox threat. Although the rhetoric of belonging to the greater and more civilized Roman Catholic community was quite popular at the time, bulwark mythology did not find fertile ground in Transylvania. From these counterexamples, we can assume that a threat scenario from outside is one of the absolute prerequisites for the formation and popularization of bulwark myths.

The second focus of our book is on a synchronic perspective, allowing the tracing of reciprocal transfers and multisided national and interconfessional ideological competition and the intertwining of mythical narratives. The emphasis on transfers and the media of myth making allows us to apply the approach of transnational history to our subject. One of our key arguments is that, since the late Middle Ages, the main agents of *antemurale* mythology's dissemination in Eastern Europe have been transnational actors. This is apparent in the studies of Weiand, Gasimov, and Seegel: whether in the case of Renaissance theologians, historians and diplomats, or modern émigré politicians and cartographers, these were all the stories of transnational lives, contacts, and careers. Our book is the history of transfers and borrowings that demonstrate how *antemurale* rhetoric, colored with the stains of separation and delineation, has always been popularized by transnational actors.

In this book, we have scrutinized the peculiarities of *antemurale* rhetoric's application to various national and imperial ideologies and the respective processes of "mental mapping" in the region. We thus decided to focus on two important aspects: the abovementioned role of *antemurale* mythology in the (de-)sacralization and nationalization of borderland regions and the major forms, media, and actors of *antemurale* discourses. Our volume is hence organized in four parts: Background (Part I), (De-)Sacralizing and Nationalizing Borderlands (Part II), Promoting *Antemurale* Discourses (Part III), and Reflections on the Bulwark Myths Today (Part IV).

After an introduction by Berezhnaya and Hein-Kircher and a historical reframing presented by Weiand in Part I, all chapters of Part II deal with the (de-)sacralization and nationalization of the Eastern European borderlands. As explained above, Ghisa's chapter provides a counterexample and demonstrates that the denominational Othering functioned only within the ethnic community and not outside of it. As he discusses the early stage, it seems that this process embossed the further development of the national movement of the late nineteenth and twentieth centuries. Hein-Kircher explains then, that due to the negative image of the Ruthenians/Ukrainians, the Polish *antemurale* topos picked up the denominational differences between these groups and lead finally to a legitimization of the national conflict within the city of Lviv and Galicia and to a de-sacralization of the *antemurale* topos.

In the next chapter, Heyde explains the inner-Jewish discussions on excluding or integrating the Jews mainly in postemancipational times in Galicia. One important finding is, like that of Ghisa, that innergroup conflicts using religious arguments also lead to the erection of inner walls. The same phenomenon is discussed in Berezhnaya's chapter, which demonstrates that through religious *antemurale* argumentations, nationalizing processes lead to national differentiations. Gasimov's chapter concludes the section by showing through the Turkish case—the imagination of an anti-communist and anti-Russian bulwark—that *antemurale* rhetoric does not necessarily lead to the sacralization of the nation. (De-)sacralization and nationalization of the Eastern European borders are hence highly entangled, possessing legitimizing and coherence-giving functions.

Part III is consecutively dedicated to the promotion of these discourses. At first, Kravchenko discusses why the *antemurale* myth had not developed in Ukraine during the first half of the nineteenth century. He concludes that, because of the late nation-building process, the promotion of *antemurale* thinking became possible only when the Ukrainian national movement began to build its own national space at the beginning of the twentieth century. Hofeneder and Seegel explain in their chapters how seemingly "neutral" media, such as schoolbooks and maps, were used as key instruments for the dissemination of rampart myths and the construction of a national space that excluded Other ethnic and national groups.

The following chapters of Srodecki and Norris discuss the *longue durée* aspects of the lives of myths. Srodecki focuses on the new anti-Bolshevik narrative that emerged after World War I in Hungary and Poland, while Norris discusses the varying perceptions of one painting that represents the Russian founding myth from the nineteenth century until the first decade of the twenty-first century. To sum up the findings of this part, the promotion of *antemurale* myths could be carried out by different media, but they have to narrate the myth's message verbally, visually, or even ritually.

The consequences of this promotion and implementation of bulwark myths in contemporary Eastern European historical consciousnesses are analyzed in Part IV. Kolstø focuses on the boundary-making *antemurale*, emphasizing their cultural and denominational differences, but concludes that they mostly refer to power relations. Srodecki's chapter discusses the emergence of today's *antemurale* rhetoric. The contemporary bulwark myth is experiencing a revival and is often used to legitimize and sharpen political conflicts in the region. It appears to be grounded on the historical legacies of the nineteenth and twentieth centuries discussed in this book. Rampart myths have not yet lost their political impact on Eastern European rampart nations.

Our book demonstrates that *antemurale* rhetoric arises from the need of the border society to differentiate itself from a religious (confessional)/ethnic/national/civilizational Other when faced with a real or perceived threat. In modern Eastern Europe numerous actors took part in the dissemination of *antemurale* mythology: political and religious leaders, intellectuals, artists, cartographers, and journalists. As they crossed multiple state and regional borders to popularize threat scenarios, they became real protagonists of transnational history. In the age of nationalism, these actors used various media to reach an audience from schoolbook maps, newspapers, and paintings to historical texts, sermons, and political manifestos.

In a way, by legitimating lines of division, *antemurale* propagators have all worked against borderland traditions of coexistence and cross-border cooperation. By the end of the nineteenth century, as the traditional imperial orders of the Romanovs, Habsburgs, Ottomans, and Hohenzollern gradually waned, nationalizing discourses using *antemurale* rhetoric became dominant. These communicators of *antemurale* rhetoric often used various religious and secular sites of memory in this mesoregion for the popularization of *antemurale* mythology within the framework of nationalist or imperial ideologies. Because this rhetoric was an effective weapon with high mobilizing potential, it was particularly attractive for the opposing sides during World War I. By the end of the war, East European borderlands had indeed become "bloodlands."[61]

Our book is intended to provide a stimulus for further transnational studies of myth making in this East European mesoregion and to supply historical background knowledge for understanding the revival of bulwark mythology in contemporary Eastern Europe. It includes examples of Jewish and other non-Christian *antemurale* mythology in order to enrich scholarship on bulwark myths. However, our book cannot cover the whole geographical spectrum—for instance, Moldova is only touched on, while the Baltic lands are entirely missing from this book. The sample case studies use various methodological approaches (from art history to theology, with most chapters concentrated at the crossroads of political, social, and religious history) and introduce the diversity of bulwark myths, while also revealing their common foundations.

Nevertheless, our volume does not encompass a systematic or complete investigation of bulwark rhetoric in the region. Several questions remain to be answered: How is the use of bulwark mythology in political and religious ideologies to be distinguished from its abuse? Were there any differences between denominationally homogeneous areas and those that were mixed? Can we find any specifically confessional aspects in bulwark mythology? How did the panmovement ideologies (e.g., pan-Slavism) influence transformations in the *antemurale* myths? Although some questions remain to be answered, our book gives an overview of the way bulwark myths contributed to the "historization" of borderland communities. It also reveals how these myths were, and today still are, appropriated by national movements to demarcate themselves from other denominational and ethnic groups.

Liliya Berezhnaya is a research associate at the University of Amsterdam and a visiting professor at KU Leuven in the Faculty of Theology and Religious Studies. She is the author of *Die Militarisierung der Heiligen in Vormoderne und Moderne* (2020), *Iconic Turns: Nation and Religion in Eastern European Cinema Since 1989* (2013; co-edited with Christian Schmitt), and *The World to Come: Ukrainian Images of the Last Judgment* (2015; co-authored with John-Paul Himka).

Heidi Hein-Kircher earned her M.A. and her Ph.D. (East European history, modern history, political sciences, and Yiddish) from Heinrich Heine-University in Düsseldorf. In 2018, she earned her habilitation degree at Philipps University in Marburg. Since 2003, she has been on the research staff of the Herder-Institute for Historical Research in East Central Europe in Marburg, Germany, and since 2009 she has been the head of department "academic forum." In her research, she focuses on political and cultural myths in East Central Europe and on urban history of the nineteenth and twentieth centuries in East Central Europe, especially on Lviv in the nineteenth century.

Notes

1. A. Lawaty, "The Figure of 'Antemurale' in the Historiography," in *East and Central European History Writing in Exile 1939–1989*, ed. M. Zadencka, A. Plakans, A. Lawaty (Leiden: Brill, 2015), 363. See also the contributions of Volodymyr Kravchenko, Liliya Berezhnaya, and Pål Kolstø in this volume.
2. *The Palgrave Dictionary of Transnational History* does not contain any entry on political or other types of myths. On political myths in comparative perspective, see M. Flacke, ed., *Mythen der Nationen: Ein europäisches Panorama* (Berlin/München: Koehler und Amelang, 1998).
3. A. Iriye and P.-Y. Saunier, "Introduction: The Professor and the Madman," in *The Palgrave Dictionary of Transnational History* (New York: Palgrave Macmillan, 2009), xviii. Transnational history is also often described in terms of postnational, postcolonial, and polycentric studies: I. Tyrell, "Historians and the Nation State," in *The Palgrave Dictionary of Transnational History*, ed. A. Iriye and P.-Y. Saunier, 486–95; K.K. Patel, "Transnational History," in *European History Online (EGO)* (Mainz: Institute of European History, 2010), retrieved 20 October 2016 from http://www.ieg-ego.eu/patelk-2010-en.
4. On the potential and limitations of applying transnational history methodology to the study of borderlands, see J. Cañizares-Esguerra, "Entangled Histories: Borderland Historiographies in New Clothes?" *The American Historical Review* 112, no. 3 (2007): 787–99.
5. G. Kasianov and P. Ther, eds., *A Laboratory of Transnational History: Ukraine and Recent Ukrainian Historiography* (Budapest/New York: Central European University Press, 2009).
6. P. Ther, "The Transnational Paradigm of Historiography and Its Potential for Ukrainian History," in Kasianov and Ther, *Laboratory of Transnational History*, 86.
7. Contributors include Andrea Graziosi, George O. Liber, Mark von Hagen, Hiroaki Kuromiya, Steven Seegel, Yohanan Petrovsky-Shtern, and Mayhill C. Fowler, in S. Plokhy, ed., *The Future of the Past: New Perspectives on Ukrainian History* (Cambridge, MA: Harvard University Press), 97–276. See also, A.V. Wendland, "*Randgeschichten*? Osteuropäische Perspektiven auf Kulturtransfer und Verflechtungsgeschichte," *Osteuropa* 58, no. 3 (2008): 95–116; Wendland, "Ukraine

transnational: Transnationalität, Kulturtransfer, Verflechtungsgeschichte als Perspektivierungen des Nationsbildungsprozesses," in *Die Ukraine: Prozesse der Nationsbildung*, ed. A. Kappeler (Köln and Wien: Böhlau Verlag, 2011), 51–66.
8. H.G. Haupt and J. Kocka, eds., *Comparative and Transnational History: Central European Approaches and New Perspectives* (New York and Oxford: Berghahn Books, 2009).
9. Y. Bizeul, "Theorien der politischen Mythen," in *Politische Mythen und Rituale in Deutschland, Frankreich und Polen*, ed. Y. Bizeul (Berlin: Duncker & Humblot, 2000), 17.
10. H. Hein-Kircher, "Überlegungen zu einer Typologisierung von politischen Mythen aus historiographischer Sicht—ein Versuch," in *Politische Mythen im 19. und 20. Jahrhundert in Mittel- und Osteuropa*, ed. H. Hein-Kircher and H.H. Hahn (Marburg: Verlag Herder Institut, 2006), 408–10.
11. P. Niedermüller, "Der Mythos der Gemeinschaft," 6. *Kakanien revisited*, retrieved 15 August 2016 from http://www.kakanien-revisited.at/beitr/fallstudie/PNiedermueller1/?alpha=n.
12. H. Hein-Kircher, "Deutsche Mythen und ihre Wirkung auf Europa," *Jahrbuch für öffentliche Sicherheit* 8 (2016/2017): 529–40; R. Zimmerling, *Mythen in der Politik der DDR: Ein Beitrag zur Erforschung politischer Mythen* (Opladen: Leske + Budrich, 2000), 13; H. Hein-Kircher, "The Influence of Political Myth on Historical Consciousness and Identity as Factors of Mentality," in *From Mentalities to Anthropological History: Theory and Methods*, ed. B. Klich-Kluczewska and D. Kałwa (Kraków: Historia Iagellonica, 2012), 103–20.
13. K. Knabel, D. Rieger, and S. Wodianka, "Einleitung," in *Nationale Mythen—kollektive Symbole: Funktionen, Konstruktionen und Medien der Erinnerung*, ed. K. Knabel, D. Rieger, and S. Wodianka (Göttingen: Vandenhoeck & Ruprecht, 2005), 9.
14. H. Hein-Kircher, "Zur 'mythischen Lesart der Wirklichkeit': Wirklichkeitskonstruktionen, Funktionen und Verflochtenheit politischer Mythen in der Erinnerungskultur," in *Deutsch-Polnische Erinnerungsorte*, vol. 4: *Reflexionen*, ed. H.H. Hahn and R. Traba (Paderborn: Schöningh, 2013), 134–35.
15. B. Anderson, *Imagined Communities: Reflections of the Origin and Spread of Nationalism* (London: Verso, 1983).
16. H. Münkler, *Die Deutschen und ihre Mythen* (Berlin: Rowohlt Berlin Verlag, 2009), 15–16.
17. F. Becker, "Begriff und Bedeutung des politischen Mythos," in *Was heißt Kulturgeschichte des Politischen?*, ed. B. Stollberg-Riliniger (Berlin: Duncker & Humblot, 2005), 129–48.
18. G. Schöpflin, "The Functions of Myth and a Taxonomy of Myths," in *Myths and Nationhood* (New York: Routledge, 1997), 35.
19. J. Armstrong, *Nations before Nationalism* (Chapel Hill: University of North Carolina Press, 1982), 9.
20. See also the contribution of Pål Kolstø in this volume.
21. A. Smith, "Myths of National History in Belarus and Ukraine," in *Myths and Nationhood*, ed. G. Hosking (New York: Routledge, 1997), 183.
22. Thus, bulwark myths should also be regarded as a securitizing discourse, which could offer a promising new perspective for further research on political myths. In regard to securitization discourses relating to "threat design" and "threat management," see T. Balzacq, S. Léonard, and J. Ruzicka, "'Securitization' Revisited: Theory and

Cases," *International Relations* 2015, doi: 10.1177/0047117815596590, retrieved 16 July 2016 from http://journals.sagepub.com/doi/abs/10.1177/0047117815596590. These conceptual reflections are inspired by the collaborative project SFB/TRR 138 "Dynamics of security."

23. G.L. Mosse, *The Nationalization of the Masses: Political Symbolism and Mass Movements in Germany from the Napoleonic Wars through the Third Reich* (Ithaca/London: Cornell University Press, 1996).

24. H. Hein-Kircher, "Überlegungen zur Ausprägung und Funktion von Raummythen," in *Deutschlands östliche Nachbarschaften: Eine Sammlung von historischen Essays für Hans Henning Hahn*, ed. E. Dmitrów and T. Weger (Frankfurt a. M.: Lang Verlag, 2009), 105–20.

25. "Each community willing to consolidate itself aims at creating and securing places." P. Haslinger and K. Holz, "Selbstbild und Territorium: Dimensionen von Identität und Alterität," in *Regionale und nationale Identitäten: Wechselwirkungen und Spannungsfelder im Zeitalter moderner Staatlichkeit*, ed. P. Haslinger (Würzburg: Ergon Verlag, 2000), 24–25.

26. G. Simmel, "The Sociology of Space," in *Simmel on Culture: Selected Writings*, ed. D.P. Frisby and M. Featherstone (London: Sage, 1997), 142. See also H. Medick, "Grenzziehungen und die Herstellung des politisch-sozialen Raumes: Zur Begriffsgeschichte und politischen Sozialgeschichte der Grenzen in der Frühen Neuzeit," in *Literatur der Grenze—Theorie der Grenze*, ed. R. Faber and B. Naumann (Würzburg: Königshausen & Neumann, 1995), 211–24.

27. G. Krumeich and H. Lehmann, "Nation, Religion und Gewalt: zur Einführung," in *"Gott mit uns": Nation, Religion und Gewalt im 19. und frühen 20. Jahrhundert* (Göttingen: Vandenhoeck & Ruprecht, 2000), 1.

28. See M. Schulze Wessel, "Einleitung: Die Nationalisierung der Religion und die Sakralisierung der Nation im östlichen Europa," in *Nationalisierung der Religion und Sakralisierung der Nation im östlichen Europa* (Stuttgart: Franz Steiner Verlag, 2006), 7–14; M. Falina, "Svetosavlje: A Case Study in the Nationalization of Religion," *Schweizerische Zeitschrift für Religions- und Kulturgeschichte* 101 (2007): 505–27; H. Lehmann, "Die Säkularisierung der Religion und die Sakralisierung der Nation im 20. Jahrhundert: Varianten einer komplementären Relation," in *Religion im Nationalstaat zwischen den Weltkriegen 1918–1939*, ed. H.-Chr. Maner and M. Schulze-Wessel (Stuttgart: Franz Steiner Verlag, 2002), 13–27; P.F. Sugar, *East European Nationalism: Politics and Religion* (Brookfield: Ashgate, 1999); R. Vulpius, *Nationalisierung der Religion: Russifizierungspolitik und ukrainische Nationsbildung 1860–1920* (Wiesbaden: Harassowitz Verlag, 2005); H.-G. Haupt and D. Langewiesche, "Einleitung," in *Nation und Religion in Europa: Mehrkonfessionelle Gesellschafen im 19. und 20. Jahrhundert*, ed. H.-G. Haupt and D. Langewiesche (Frankfurt a. M.: Campus Verlag, 2004), 11–23.

29. A.D. Smith, "Ethnic Election and National Destiny: Some Religious Origins of National Ideals," *Nations and Nationalism* 5, no. 3 (1999): 332. See also Smith, *Myths and Memories of the Nation* (Oxford: Oxford University Press, 1999).

30. A. Hastings, *The Construction of Nationhood. Ethnicity, Religion, and Nationalism* (Cambridge: Cambridge University Press, 1997), 190.

31. Schöpflin, "Functions of Myth," 29; A.D. Smith, "The 'Golden Age' and National Renewal," in *Myths and Nationhood*, ed. G. Hosking and G. Schöpflin (New York: Routledge, 1997), 36–59.

32. Armstrong, *Nations before Nationalism*; Armstrong, "Myth and History in the Evolution of Ukrainian Consciousness," in *Ukraine and Russia in Their Historical Encounter*, ed. P.J. Potichnyj, M. Raeff, J. Pelenski, and G.N. Zekulin (Edmonton: Canadian Institute of Ukrainian Studies Press, 1992), 125–39.
33. J. Osterhammel, "The Great Work of Uplifting Mankind: Zivilisierungsmission und Moderne," in *Zivilisierungsmissionen: Imperiale Weltverbesserung seit dem 18. Jahrhundert*, ed. B. Barth and J. Osterhammel (Konstanz: UVK-Verlags-Gesellschaft, 2005), 363.
34. On debates on colonial, global, and transnational history in the context of the civilizing mission, see U. Hofmeister, *Die Bürde des Weißen Zaren: Russische Vorstellungen einer imperialen Zivilisierungsmission in Zentralasien* (Stuttgart: Steiner, 2018). On the civilizing mission in general, see D. Olstein and S. Hübner, eds., "Preaching the Civilizing Mission and Modern Cultural Encounters," special issue *Journal of World History* 27, no. 3 (2016); J.P. Daughton, *An Empire Divided: Religion, Republicanism, and the Making of French Colonialism, 1880–1914* (Oxford: Oxford University Press, 2004); H. Fischer-Tiné, *Colonialism as a Civilizing Mission* (London: Anthem, 2004); A.L. Conklin, *A Mission to Civilize: The Republican Idea of Empire in France and West Africa, 1895–1930* (Stanford: Stanford University Press, 1998).
35. J. Tazbir, "The Bulwark Myth," *Acta Poloniae Historica* 91 (2005): 73–97; P. Kolstø, "Introduction: Assessing the Role of Historical Myths in Modern Society," in *Myths and Boundaries in South-Eastern Europe*, ed. P. Kolstø (London: Hurst, 2005), 20; C. Delsol, J. Nowicki, and M. Maslowski, eds., *Mythes et symboles politiques en Europe centrale* (Paris: Presses Universtaires de France, 2002), 95–162.
36. Schöpflin, "Functions of Myth," 20.
37. Hein-Kircher, "Zur 'mythischen Lesart,'" 133–34.
38. P. Haslinger, ed., *Grenzen im Kopf: Beiträge zur Geschichte der Grenze in Ostmitteleuropa* (Frankfurt a. M.: Lang Verlag, 1999).
39. With regard to Eastern European imagined regions, see L. Wolff, *Inventing Eastern Europe: The Map of Civilization on the Mind of Enlightenment* (Stanford: Stanford University Press, 1996); T. Snyder, *The Reconstruction of Nations: Poland, Ukraine, Lithuania, Belarus, 1569–1999* (New Haven: Yale University Press, 2003); I.B. Neumann, *Uses of the Other: "The East" in European Identity Formation* (Minneapolis: University of Minnesota Press, 1999); T. Zarycki, *Ideologies of Eastness in Central and Eastern Europe* (London: Routledge, 2014).
40. See also, P. Srodecki, "Antemurale-Based Frontier Identities in East Central Europe and Their Ideological Roots in Medieval/Early Modern Alterity and Alienity Discourses," in *Collective Identity in the Context of Medieval Studies*, ed. M.A. Malaníkova and R. Antonín (Ostrava: University of Ostrava, 2016), 97–120.
41. P. Srodecki, *Antemurale Christianitatis: Zur Genese der Bollwerksrhetorik im östlichen Mitteleuropa an der Schwelle vom Mittelalter zur Frühen Neuzeit* (Husum: Matthiesen Verlag, 2015); W. Fritzemeyer, *Christenheit und Europa: Zur Geschichte des europäischen Gemeinschaftsgefühls von Dante bis Leibniz* (München: R. Oldenbourg, 1931); J. Tazbir, *Polska przedmurzem chrześciańskiej Europy* (Warszawa: Twój Styl, 2004); J. Armstrong, "Myth and History in the Evolution of Ukrainian Consciousness," in *Ukraine and Russia in Their Historical Encounter*, ed. P.J. Potichnyj, M. Raeff, J. Pelenski, and G.N. Zekulin (Edmonton: Canadian

Institute of Ukrainian Studies Press, 1992), 125–39; Kolstø, *Myths and Boundaries*; U. Borkowska, "The Ideology of 'Antemurale' in the Sphere of Slavic Culture (13th–17th Centuries)," in *The Common Christian Roots of the European Nations*, vol. 2: *Written Contributions*, ed. Pontificia Università Lateranense (Florence: Le Monnier, 1982), 1206–21.

42. S. Troebst, "Introduction: What's in a Historical Region? A Teutonic Perspective," *European Review of History—Revue européenne d'Histoire* 10, no. 2 (2003): 173–88. Mesoregion as a geographical description is derived from the *mesoregão* dividing the Brazilian federative states into smaller geographical units. The application of that concept to Eastern Europe aims to highlight the peculiarities of the Eastern European (former imperial) borderlands.

43. L. Titarenko, "Teorii pogranichia," *Zhurnal sotsiologii i sotsialnoi antropologii* 2, no. 67 (2013): 28–48.

44. S. Plokhy, "Nova Skhidna Ievropa: geopolitychna prymkha chy istoriohrafichna znakhidka?" Retrieved 20 October 2016 from http://www.historians.in.ua/index.php/doslidzhennya/550-serhii-plokhiy-nova-skhidna-yevropa-heopolitychna-prymkha-chy-istoriohrafichna-znakhidka.

45. N. Kovalchuk, "Kordonna tsivilizatsiia: osnova rozvytku demokratii v Ukraini," *Osvita rehionu: politologiia, psychologiia, komunikatsiia* 4 (2009): 100–104; L. Berezhnaya, "View from the Edge: Borderland Studies and Ukraine, 1991–2013," in *The Future of the Past: New Perspectives on Ukrainian History*, ed. S. Plokhy (Cambridge, MA: Harvard University Press, 2016), 41–68.

46. F.B. Schenk, "The Historical Regions of Europe: Real or Invented? Some Remarks on Historical Comparison and Mental Mapping," in *Beyond the Nation: Writing European History Today* (Sankt-Peterburg: Zentrum für Deutschland und Europastudien, 2004), 22. Schenk refers to the publications of Maria Todorova in which she objected to the concept of "historical regions" (ibid., 22–23).

47. See K. Verdery, "Post-Soviet Area Studies?" *Newsnet: News of the American Association for the Advancement of Slavic Studies* 43, no. 5 (2003): 7–8; quoted from O. Ieda, "Regional Identities and Meso-Mega Area Dynamics in Slavic Eurasia: Focused on Eastern Europe," in *Emerging Mesa-Areas in the Former Socialist Countries, Histories Revived or Improvised*, ed. K. Matsuzato, Slavic Eurasian Studies no. 7 (Sapporo: Slavic Research Center, Hokkaido University, 2005), 21fn. 5.

48. S. Troebst, "Meso-Regionalizing Europe: History Versus Politics," in *Domains and Divisions of European History*, ed. J.P. Arnason and N. Doyle (Liverpool: Liverpool University Press, 2010), 79.

49. D. Mishkova and B. Trencsényi, "Introduction," in *European Regions and Boundaries: A Conceptual History* (New York: Berghahn Books, 2017), 3.

50. K. Matsuzato, "Preface," in *Emerging Mesa-Areas in the Former Socialist Countries, Histories Revived or Improvised*, Slavic Eurasian Studies no. 7 (Sapporo: Slavic Research Center, Hokkaido University, 2005), 7–18. See also A. Graziosi, "Viewing the Twentieth Century through the Prism of Ukraine: Reflections on the Heuristic Potential of Ukrainian History," in *The Future of the Past: New Perspectives on Ukrainian History*, ed. S. Plokhii (Cambridge, MA: Harvard University Press, 2016), 99–100.

51. Y. Hrytsak, "On Sails and Gales, and Ships Sailing in Various Directions: Post-Soviet Ukraine," *Ab Imperio* 1 (2004): 252.

52. N. Yakovenko, "Early Modern Ukraine between East and West: Projecturies of an Idea," in *Regions: A Prism to View the Slavic-Eurasian World: Towards a Discipline of "Regionology,"* ed. K. Matsuzato (Sapporo: Hokkaido University, 2000), 50; V. Kravchenko, "Ukraine: History Confronts Geography," in *The EU's Eastern Neighbourhood: Migration, Borders and Regional Stability,* ed. I. Liikanen, J.W. Scott, and T. Sotkasiira (London/New York: Routledge, 2016), 45.
53. M.L. Pratt, "Arts of the Contact Zone," *Profession* 91 (1991): 34.
54. W.E.J. Weber, "Die Bildung von Regionen durch Kommunikation: Aspekte einer neuen historischen Perspektive," in *Kommunikation und Region, Forum Suevicum: Beiträge zur Geschichte Ostschwabens und der benachbarten Regionen,* vol. 4, ed. C.A. Hoffmann and R. Kiessling (Konstanz: UVK, 2001), 58–59; S. Rohdewald, D.A. Frick, and S. Wiederkehr, "Transkulturelle Kommunikation im Großfürstentum Litauen und in den östlichen Gebieten der Polnischen Krone: Zur Einführung," in *Litauen und Ruthenien: Studien zu einer transkulturellen Kommunikationsregion (15.–18. Jahrhundert)* [Lithuania and Ruthenia. Studies of a Transcultural Communication Zone (15th–18th Centuries)] (Wiesbaden: Harrassowitz Verlag, 2007), 7–33.
55. L. Berezhnaya, "'Kazacki bastion' 17 veka—vzgliad snaruzhi i iznutri," in *Religion und Integration im Moskauer Russland. Konzepte und Praktiken, Potentiale und Grenzen. 14.-17. Jahrhundert Forschungen zur osteuropäischen Geschichte 76,* ed. L. Steindorff (Wiesbaden: Harassowitz Verlag, 2010), 269–97; J. Bürgers, *Kosakenmythos und Nationsbildung in der postsowjetischen Ukraine,* Konstanzer Schriften zur Sozialwissenschaft, vol. 71 (Konstanz: Hartung-Gorre, 2006); S. Plokhy, *The Cossack Myth: History and Nationhood in the Age of Empires* (Cambridge: Cambridge University Press, 2012).
56. A.D. Smith, *Chosen Peoples: Sacred Sources of National Identity* (Oxford: Oxford University Press, 2003); A. Mosser, *"Gottes auserwählte Völker": Erwählungsvorstellungen und kollektive Selbstfindung in der Geschichte* (Frankfurt a. M.: Lang Verlag, 2001); Zarycki, *Ideologies of Eastness.*
57. H. Kohn, *The Idea of Nationalism: A Study in Its Origins and Background* (New York: Macmillan, 1944).
58. G. Schöpflin, "Ethnic and Civic Nationalism (Hans Kohn's Typology)," in *Encyclopaedia of Nationalism,* ed. A.S. Leoussi (New Brunswick/London: Transaction Publishers, 2001), 60–61.
59. I. Gerasimov, S. Glebov, J. Kusber, M. Mogilner, and A. Semyonov, "New Imperial History and the Challenges of Empire," in *Empire Speaks Out: Languages of Rationalization and Self-Description in the Russian Empire,* ed. I. Gerasimov, J. Kusber, and A. Semyonov (Leiden: Brill, 2009), 3–4.
60. See J. Burbank and M. von Hagen, "Coming into the Territory: Uncertainty and Empire," in *Russian Empire: Space, People, Power, 1700–1930,* ed. J. Burbank, M. Von Hagen, and A.V. Remnev (Bloomington: Indiana University Press, 2007), 2.
61. T. Snyder, *Bloodlands: Europe between Hitler and Stalin* (New York: Basic Books, 2010).

Bibliography

Anderson, B. 1983. *Imagined Communities: Reflections of the Origin and Spread of Nationalism.* London: Verso.
Armstrong, J. 1982. *Nations before Nationalism.* Chapel Hill: University of North Carolina Press.
———. 1992. "Myth and History in the Evolution of Ukrainian Consciousness." In *Ukraine and Russia in Their Historical Encounter*, ed. P.J. Potichnyj, M. Raeff, J. Pelenski, and G.N. Zekulin, 125–39. Edmonton: Canadian Institute of Ukrainian Studies Press.
Balzacq, T., S. Léonard, and J. Ruzicka. 2015. "'Securitization' Revisited: Theory and Cases." *International Relations.* doi: 10.1177/0047117815596590. Retrieved 16 July 2016 from http://journals.sagepub.com/doi/abs/10.1177/0047117815596590.
Becker, F. 2005. "Begriff und Bedeutung des politischen Mythos." In *Was heißt Kulturgeschichte des Politischen?*, ed. B. Stollberg-Riliniger, 129–48. Berlin: Duncker & Humblot.
Berezhnaya, L. 2010. "'Kazacki bastion' 17 veka—vzgliad snaruzhi i iznutri." In *Religion und Integration im Moskauer Russland: Konzepte und Praktiken, Potentiale und Grenzen. 14.-17. Jahrhundert Forschungen zur osteuropäischen Geschichte 76*, ed. L. Steindorff, 269–97. Wiesbaden: Harassowitz Verlag.
———. 2016. "View from the Edge: Borderland Studies and Ukraine, 1991–2013." In *The Future of the Past: New Perspectives on Ukrainian History*, ed. S. Plokhy, 41–68. Cambridge, MA: Harvard University Press.
Bizeul, Y. 2000. "Theorien der politischen Mythen." In *Politische Mythen und Rituale in Deutschland, Frankreich und Polen*, 15–39. Berlin: Duncker & Humblot.
Borkowska, U. 1982. "The Ideology of 'Antemurale' in the Sphere of Slavic Culture (13th–17th Centuries)." In *The Common Christian Roots of the European Nations*, vol. 2: *Written Contributions*, ed. Pontificia Università Lateranense, 1206–21. Florence: Le Monnier.
Burbank, J. and M. von Hagen. 2007. "Coming into the Territory: Uncertainty and Empire." In *Russian Empire: Space, People, Power, 1700–1930*, ed. J. Burbank, M. Von Hagen, and A.V. Remnev, 1–29. Bloomington: Indiana University Press.
Bürgers, J. 2006. *Kosakenmythos und Nationsbildung in der postsowjetischen Ukraine, Konstanzer Schriften zur Sozialwissenschaft.* Vol. 71. Konstanz: Hartung-Gorre.
Cañizares-Esguerra, J. 2007. "Entangled Histories: Borderland Historiographies in New Clothes?" *The American Historical Review* 112, no. 3: 787–99.
Conklin, A.L. 1998. *A Mission to Civilize: The Republican Idea of Empire in France and West Africa, 1895–1930.* Stanford: Stanford University Press.
Daughton, J.P. 2004. *An Empire Divided: Religion, Republicanism, and the Making of French Colonialism, 1880–1914.* Oxford: Oxford University Press.
Delsol, C., J. Nowicki, and M. Maslowski. 2002. *Mythes et symboles politiques en Europe centrale.* Paris: Presses Universitaires de France.
Falina, M. 2007. "Svetosavlje: A Case Study in the Nationalization of Religion." *Schweizerische Zeitschrift für Religions- und Kulturgeschichte* 101: 505–27.
Fischer-Tiné, H. 2004. *Colonialism as a Civilizing Mission.* London: Anthem.
Flacke, M., ed. 1998. *Mythen der Nationen: Ein europäisches Panorama.* Berlin and München: Koehler und Amelang.

Fritzemeyer, W. 1931. *Christenheit und Europa: Zur Geschichte des europäischen Gemeinschaftsgefühls von Dante bis Leibniz.* München: R. Oldenbourg.
Gerasimov, I., S. Glebov, J. Kusber, M. Mogilner, and A. Semyonov. 2009. "New Imperial History and the Challenges of Empire." In *Empire Speaks Out: Languages of Rationalization and Self-Description in the Russian Empire,* ed. I. Gerasimov, J. Kusber, and A. Semyonov, 3–32. Leiden: Brill.
Graziosi, A. 2016. "Viewing the Twentieth Century through the Prism of Ukraine: Reflections on the Heuristic Potential of Ukrainian History." In *The Future of the Past: New Perspectives on Ukrainian History,* ed. S. Plokhii, 97–118. Cambridge, MA: Harvard University Press.
Haslinger, P., ed. 1999. *Grenzen im Kopf: Beiträge zur Geschichte der Grenze in Ostmitteleuropa.* Frankfurt a. M.: Lang.
Haslinger, P. and K. Holz. 2000. "Selbstbild und Territorium: Dimensionen von Identität und Alterität." In *Regionale und nationale Identitäten: Wechselwirkungen und Spannungsfelder im Zeitalter moderner Staatlichkeit,* ed. P. Haslinger, 15–38. Würzburg: Ergon Verlag.
Hastings, A. 1997. *The Construction of Nationhood: Ethnicity, Religion, and Nationalism.* Cambridge, UK: Cambridge University Press.
Haupt, H.-G. and J. Kocka, eds., 2009. *Comparative and Transnational History: Central European Approaches and New Perspectives.* New York and Oxford: Berghahn Books.
Haupt, H.-G. and D. Langewiesche. 2004. "Einleitung." In *Nation und Religion in Europa: Mehrkonfessionelle Gesellschafen im 19. und 20. Jahrhundert,* 11–24. Frankfurt a. M.: Campus Verlag.
Hein-Kircher, H. 2006. "Überlegungen zu einer Typologisierung von politischen Mythen aus historiographischer Sicht—ein Versuch." In *Politische Mythen im 19. und 20. Jahrhundert in Mittel- und Osteuropa,* ed. H. Hein-Kircher and H.H. Hahn, 408–10. Marburg: Verlag Herder Institut.
———. 2009. "Überlegungen zur Ausprägung und Funktion von Raummythen." In *Deutschlands östliche Nachbarschaften: Eine Sammlung von historischen Essays für Hans Henning Hahn,* ed. E. Dmitrów and T. Weger, 105–20. Frankfurt a. M.: Lang Verlag.
———. 2012. "The Influence of Political Myth on Historical Consciousness and Identity as Factors of Mentality." In *From Mentalities to Anthropological History: Theory and Methods,* ed. B. Klich-Kluczewska and D. Kałwa, 103–20. Kraków: Historia Iagellonica.
———. 2013. "Zur 'mythischen Lesart der Wirklichkeit': Wirklichkeitskonstruktionen, Funktionen und Verflochtenheit politischer Mythen in der Erinnerungskultur." In *Deutsch-Polnische Erinnerungsorte,* vol. 4: *Reflexionen,* ed. H.H. Hahn and R. Traba, 134–35. Paderborn: Schöningh.
———. 2016/2017. "Deutsche Mythen und ihre Wirkung auf Europa." *Jahrbuch für öffentliche Sicherheit* 8: 529–40.
Hofmeister, U. 2018. *Die Bürde des Weißen Zaren: Russische Vorstellungen einer imperialen Zivilisierungsmission in Zentralasien.* Stuttgart: Steiner.
Hrytsak, Y. 2004. "On Sails and Gales, and Ships Sailing in Various Directions: Post-Soviet Ukraine." *Ab Imperio* 1: 229–54.

Ieda, O. 2005. "Regional Identities and Meso-Mega Area Dynamics in Slavic Eurasia: Focused on Eastern Europe." In *Emerging Mesa-Areas in the Former Socialist Countries: Histories Revived or Improvised*, ed. K. Matsuzato, 19–42. Slavic Eurasian Studies no. 7. Sapporo: Slavic Research Center, Hokkaido University.

Iriye, A. and P.-Y. Saunier. 2009. "Introduction: The Professor and the Madman." In *The Palgrave Dictionary of Transnational History*, xvii–xx. New York: Palgrave Macmillan.

Kasianov, G. and P. Ther, eds. 2009. *A Laboratory of Transnational History: Ukraine and Recent Ukrainian Historiography*. Budapest and New York: Central European University Press.

Knabel, K., D. Rieger, and S. Wodianka. 2005. "Einleitung." In *Nationale Mythen—kollektive Symbole: Funktionen, Konstruktionen und Medien der Erinnerung*, 9–16. Göttingen: Vandenhoeck & Ruprecht.

Kohn, H. 1944. *The Idea of Nationalism: A Study in Its Origins and Background*. New York: Macmillan.

Kolstø, P., ed. 2005. *Myths and Boundaries in South-Eastern Europe*. London: Hurst.

———. 2005. "Introduction: Assessing the Role of Historical Myths in Modern Society." In *Myths and Boundaries in South-Eastern Europe*, ed. P. Kolstø, 1–34. London: Hurst.

Kovalchuk, N. 2009. "Kordonna tsivilizatsiia: osnova rozvytku demokratii v Ukraini." *Osvita rehionu: politologiia, psychologiia, komunikatsiia* 4: 100–104.

Kravchenko, V.V. 2016. "Ukraine: History Confronts Geography." In *The EU's Eastern Neighbourhood: Migration, Borders and Regional Stability*, ed. I. Liikanen, J.W. Scott, and T. Sotkasiira, 36–49. London/New York: Routledge.

Krumeich, G. and H. Lehmann. 2000. "Nation, Religion und Gewalt: zur Einführung." In *"Gott mit uns": Nation, Religion und Gewalt im 19. und frühen 20. Jahrhundert*, ed. G. Krumeich and H. Lehmann, 1–6. Göttingen: Vandenhoeck & Ruprecht.

Lawaty, A. 2015. "The Figure of 'Antemurale' in the Historiography." In *East and Central European History Writing in Exile 1939–1989*, ed. M. Zadencka, A. Plakans, and A. Lawaty, 360–74. Leiden: Brill.

Lehmann, H. 2002. "Die Säkularisierung der Religion und die Sakralisierung der Nation im 20. Jahrhundert: Varianten einer komplementären Relation." In *Religion im Nationalstaat zwischen den Weltkriegen 1918–1939*, ed. H.-Chr. Maner and M. Schulze Wessel, 13–27. Stuttgart: Franz Steiner Verlag.

Matsuzato, K. 2005. "Preface." In *Emerging Meso-Areas in the Former Socialist Countries: Histories Revived or Improvised*, 7–18. Sapporo: Slavic Research Center, Hokkaido University.

Medick, H. 1995. "Grenzziehungen und die Herstellung des politisch-sozialen Raumes: Zur Begriffsgeschichte und politischen Sozialgeschichte der Grenzen in der Frühen Neuzeit." In *Literatur der Grenze—Theorie der Grenze*, ed. R. Faber and B. Naumann, 37–51. Würzburg: Königshausen & Neumann.

Mishkova, D. and B. Trencsényi. 2017. "Introduction." In *European Regions and Boundaries: A Conceptual History*, 1–12. New York: Berghahn Books.

Mosse, G.L. 1996. *The Nationalization of the Masses: Political Symbolism and Mass Movements in Germany from the Napoleonic Wars through the Third Reich*. Ithaca and London: Cornell University Press.

Mosser, A. 2001. *"Gottes auserwählte Völker": Erwählungsvorstellungen und kollektive Selbstfindung in der Geschichte.* Frankfurt a. M.: Lang Verlag.
Münkler, H. 2009. *Die Deutschen und ihre Mythen.* Berlin: Rowohlt Berlin Verlag.
Neumann, I.B. 1999. *Uses of the Other: "The East" in European Identity Formation.* Minneapolis: University of Minnesota Press.
Niedermüller, P. 2016. "Der Mythos der Gemeinschaft." *Kakanien Revisited.* Retrieved 15 August 2016 from http://www.kakanien-revisited.at/beitr/fallstudie/PNiedermueller1/?alpha=n.
Olstein, D. and S. Hübner, eds. 2016. "Preaching the Civilizing Mission and Modern Cultural Encounters." Special issue *Journal of World History* 27, no. 3.
Osterhammel, J. 2005. "The Great Work of Uplifting Mankind: Zivilisierungsmission und Moderne." In *Zivilisierungsmissionen: Imperiale Weltverbesserung seit dem 18. Jahrhundert,* ed. B. Barth and J. Osterhammel, 363–426. Konstanz: UVK-Verlagsgesellschaft.
Patel, K.K. 2010. "Transnational History." In *European History Online (EGO).* Mainz: Institute of European History. Retrieved 20 October 2016 from http://www.ieg-ego.eu/patelk-2010-en.
Plokhy, S. 2012. *The Cossack Myth: History and Nationhood in the Age of Empires.* Cambridge: Cambridge University Press.
———. 2016a. "Nova Skhidna Ievropa: geopolitychna prymkha chy istoriohrafichna znakhidka?" Retrieved 20 October 2016 from http://www.historians.in.ua/index.php/doslidzhennya/550-serhii-plokhiy-nova-skhidna-yevropa-heopolitychna-prymkha-chy-istoriohrafichna-znakhidka.
———, ed. 2016b. *The Future of the Past: New Perspectives on Ukrainian History.* Cambridge, MA: Harvard University Press.
Pratt, M.L. 1991. "Arts of the Contact Zone." *Profession* 91: 33–40.
Rohdewald, S., D.A. Frick, and S. Wiederkehr. 2007. "Transkulturelle Kommunikation im Großfürstentum Litauen und in den östlichen Gebieten der Polnischen Krone: Zur Einführung." In *Litauen und Ruthenien: Studien zu einer transkulturellen Kommunikationsregion (15.–18. Jahrhundert)* [Lithuania and Ruthenia: Studies of a Transcultural Communication Zone (15th–18th Centuries)], 7–33. Wiesbaden: Harrassowitz Verlag.
Schenk, F.B. 2004. "The Historical Regions of Europe: Real or Invented? Some Remarks on Historical Comparison and Mental Mapping." In *Beyond the Nation: Writing European History Today,* 15–24. Sankt-Peterburg: Zentrum für Deutschland und Europastudien.
Schöpflin, G. 1997. "The Functions of Myth and a Taxonomy of Myths." In *Myths and Nationhood,* 19–35. New York: Routledge.
———. 2001. "Ethnic and Civic Nationalism (Hans Kohn's Typology)." In *Encyclopaedia of Nationalism,* ed. A.S. Leoussi, 60–61. New Brunswick and London: Transaction Publishers.
Schulze Wessel, M. 2006. "Einleitung: Die Nationalisierung der Religion und die Sakralisierung der Nation im östlichen Europa." In *Nationalisierung der Religion und Sakralisierung der Nation im östlichen Europa,* ed. M. Schulze Wessel, 7–14. Stuttgart: Franz Steiner Verlag.
Simmel, G. 1997. "The Sociology of Space." In *Simmel on Culture: Selected Writings,* ed. D.P. Frisby and M. Featherstone, 137–86. London: Sage.

Smith, A.D. 1997. "Myths of National History in Belarus and Ukraine." In *Myths and Nationhood*, ed. G. Hosking and G. Schöpflin, 36–59. New York: Routledge.
———. 1997. "The 'Golden Age' and National Renewal." In *Myths and Nationhood*, ed. G. Hosking and G. Schöpflin, 36–59. New York: Routledge.
———. 1999. "Ethnic Election and National Destiny: Some Religious Origins of National Ideals." *Nations and Nationalism* 5, no. 3: 331–55.
———. 1999. *Myths and Memories of the Nation*. Oxford: Oxford University Press.
———. 2003. *Chosen Peoples: Sacred Sources of National Identity*. Oxford: Oxford University Press.
Snyder, T. 2003. *The Reconstruction of Nations: Poland, Ukraine, Lithuania, Belarus, 1569–1999*. New Haven: Yale University Press.
———. 2010. *Bloodlands: Europe Between Hitler and Stalin*. New York: Basic Books.
Srodecki, P. 2015. *Antemurale Christianitatis: Zur Genese der Bollwerksrhetorik im östlichen Mitteleuropa an der Schwelle vom Mittelalter zur Frühen Neuzeit*. Husum: Matthiesen Verlag.
———. 2016. "Antemurale-Based Frontier Identities in East Central Europe and Their Ideological Roots in Medieval/Early Modern Alterity and Alienity Discourses." In *Collective Identity in the Context of Medieval Studies*, ed. M.A. Malaníkova and R. Antonín, 97–120. Ostrava: University of Ostrava.
Sugar, P.F. 1999. *East European Nationalism: Politics and Religion*. Brookfield: Ashgate.
Tazbir. J. 2004. *Polska przedmurzem chrześciańskiej Europy*. Warszawa: Twój Styl.
———. 2005. "The Bulwark Myth." *Acta Poloniae Historica* 91: 73–97.
Ther, P. 2009. "The Transnational Paradigm of Historiography and Its Potential for Ukrainian History." In *A Laboratory of Transnational History: Ukraine and Recent Ukrainian Historiography*, ed. G. Kasianov and P. Ther, 81–114. Budapest: Central European University Press.
Titarenko, L. 2013. "Teorii pogranichia." *Zhurnal sotsiologii i sotsialnoi antropologii* 2, no. 67: 28–48.
Troebst, S. 2003. "Introduction: What's in a Historical Region? A Teutonic Perspective." *European Review of History—Revue européenne d'Histoire* 10, no. 2: 173–88.
———. 2010. "Meso-regionalizing Europe: History Versus Politics." In *Domains and Divisions of European History*, ed. J.P. Arnason and N. Doyle, 78–90. Liverpool: Liverpool University Press.
Tyrell, I. 2009. "Historians and the Nation State." In *The Palgrave Dictionary of Transnational History*, ed. A. Iriye and P.-Y. Saunier, 486–95. Basingstoke and New York: Palgrave McMillan.
Verdery, K. 2003. "Post-Soviet Area Studies?" *Newsnet: News of the American Association for the Advancement of Slavic Studies* 43, no. 5: 7–8.
Vulpius, R. 2005. *Nationalisierung der Religion: Russifizierungspolitik und ukrainische Nationsbildung 1860–1920*. Wiesbaden: Harassowitz Verlag.
Weber, W.E.J. 2001. "Die Bildung von Regionen durch Kommunikation. Aspekte einer neuen historischen Perspektive." In *Kommunikation und Region, Forum Suevicum: Beiträge zur Geschichte Ostschwabens und der benachbarten Regionen*. Vol. 4, ed. C.A. Hoffmann and R. Kiessling, 43–67. Konstanz: UVK.
Wendland, A.V. 2008. "Randgeschichten? Osteuropäische Perspektiven auf Kulturtransfer und Verflechtungsgeschichte." *Osteuropa* 58, no. 3: 95–116.

———. 2011. "Ukraine transnational: Transnationalität, Kulturtransfer, Verflechtungsgeschichte als Perspektivierungen des Nationsbildungsprozesses." In *Die Ukraine: Prozesse der Nationsbildung*, ed. A. Kappeler, 51–66. Köln and Wien: Böhlau Verlag.

Wolff, L. 1996. *Inventing Eastern Europe: The Map of Civilization on the Mind of Enlightenment*. Stanford: Stanford University Press.

Yakovenko, N. 2000. "Early Modern Ukraine between East and West: Projecturies of an Idea." In *Regions: A Prism to View the Slavic-Eurasian World: Towards a Discipline of "Regionology,"* ed. K. Matsuzato, 50–69. Sapporo: Hokkaido University.

Zarycki, T. 2014. *Ideologies of Eastness in Central and Eastern Europe*. London: Routledge.

Zimmerling, R. 2000. *Mythen in der Politik der DDR: Ein Beitrag zur Erforschung politischer Mythen*. Opladen: Leske + Budrich.

CHAPTER 1

The Origins of *Antemurale Christianitatis* Myths
Remarks on the Promotion of a Political Concept

Kerstin Weiand

The metaphor of a bulwark has influenced the political imagination in Eastern Europe for centuries. Literally, it constituted and maybe still constitutes alleged frontiers between civilization and barbarity, faith and heresy, liberty and despotism. It can be described as a semantic code that identifies the right side in the dichotomy of Self and Other, right and wrong, good and bad. To look at the bulwark metaphor as a semantic code, therefore, means to look at the emergence of this discourse and its semantic frame, which can be applied to various contexts. This differs slightly from *antemurale* myths, which are primarily to be studied in respect to individual manifestations.

There is no such thing as the bulwark myth, but there is a plurality of myths related to specific contexts. Focusing on how the bulwark metaphor emerged as a semantic code, however, can help us to understand how individual myths were interconnected with one another by semantic adaptations in interconnected spheres of communication. As a semantic code, the bulwark metaphor points beyond itself and has become an important part in the formation of collective identities and national self-consciousnesses. Not only did it enhance the national prestige and highlight the assumed own cultural, political, or religious superiority, but it also served as an argumentative reservoir for emphasizing particular demands. Of course, the meaning of the bulwark discourse transcends the sphere of Eastern European states. As an argumentative figure, it embraces not merely a national or regional but a truly European dimension. It can therefore be characterized as a national discourse and myth but also, as was recently suggested by Anne Cornelia Kenneweg, as a European *lieu de mémoire*.[1]

Kenneweg depicts the *antemurale* myth as a genuine national discourse that created a certain understanding of Europe.[2] This view coincides with the majority of *antemurale* historians arguing that the bulwark metaphor in Europe was largely furthered by Hungarian or Polish diplomats and intellectuals.[3] In this chapter, I suggest a reverse interpretation of the *antemurale* myth and its European dimension by stressing that the *antemurale* discourse was as much a European discourse as it was a deep influence on the development of premodern national identities in Eastern Europe, especially in Hungary and Poland.

Accordingly, the object of this chapter is twofold. In the first part, it will analyze the roots of this discourse in Europe: How was the bulwark metaphor implemented in European discourses? How did it become part of a shared European memory? In short, it attempts to trace the origin of *antemurale* as a semantic code back to fifteenth-century Catholic Europe by highlighting specific speaking situations and their context as well as their reception and long-term impact, because in that age the incentives were raised to promote *antemurale* as a political concept. This process itself reverberated in Eastern Europe and especially in the Catholic kingdoms of Poland and Hungary, where this concept became a "guidepost of political thought."[4] Here, the *antemurale* topos remained of utmost political importance until the twentieth century and even beyond.[5] Accordingly, in the second part, this chapter will provide an outlook on how the bulwark metaphor was received in Poland and Hungary and how it influenced the emerging of a premodern national identity in these countries.[6] The focus of this study, therefore, is on Catholic Europe, leaving aside Orthodox territories where the *antemurale* topos developed its own dynamics.

The Emergence of a European Discourse

The bulwark metaphor was in use well before the fifteenth century. However, in the second half of the fifteenth century, this metaphor gained a distinctive connotation.[7] The bulwark myth was closely linked to a set of metaphors that became topical. Next to *antemurale christianitatis*, the term *propugnaculum* (rampart) belonged to the myth, as did the terms *scutum, clipeus,* and *murus christianitatis*—the shield, or wall, of Christianity.[8] It has been correctly pointed out that these terms were in use well before the fifteenth century, that they were already being applied in diplomatic texts concerning the Mongol invasion in the first half of the thirteenth century[9] and in the Spanish Reconquista, the fight against the Muslims in Spain.[10]

However, reading the sources closely suggests that the early quotations did not represent a common concept or political idea. The terms were used in a rather ad hoc and unsystematic fashion. In Augustin Theiner's (1804–

1874) monumental source edition of Vatican documents concerning Poland and Hungary, the terms *antemurale* and *propugnaculum* can hardly be found at all before the mid-fifteenth century. In a letter written in 1414, Pope Gregory XII (1335–1417) calls on Emperor Sigismund (1368–1437) as *scutum fidei*; however, he did not refer to external dangers to the Christian faith but to inner-Christian conflicts.[11]

The metaphor *propugnaculum* could even be applied in a negative way. The enemies of the faith, for example, could be named as the ones who were building a bulwark against truth and religion, as when in 1246 Pope Innocence IV (1195–1254) advised Bela IV (1206–1270) of Hungary: "Princes must with virtue and power tame the heads of those who are proud against God and who erect an erroneous rampart against the Holy Roman Church on the subversion of the Christian faith."[12] As a political argument, its use was limited mainly to the Teutonic Order's description of itself.[13] Apparently, the meaning and use of bulwark metaphors were still open to various interpretations. From the middle of the fifteenth century onward, this rather unspecific, random use changed into what can be described as a shared European discourse describing the idea of a common Christian Europe defended against an infidel, heretical, or pagan aggressor from the outside.[14] In the following paragraphs, I will draw attention to some aspects within this multifaceted process by highlighting the political and institutional context, the influence of individual agents, and the role of rhetoric and media distribution.

The Political and Institutional Context

The political and cultural context of the mid-fifteenth century provided an important framework for the rise of the *antemurale* metaphor as a semantic code for a frontier between Christianity and Islam. This development was based on the debates following the capture of Constantinople by the Ottoman army under Mehmed II (1432–1481) on 29 May 1453.

From a strategic point of view, the capture of Constantinople was a realignment of the Ottoman boundaries with no direct power-related implications.[15] The Byzantine Empire had long been without major political significance. In fact, Christian forces had contributed decisively to its decline. After being seized and plundered by French and Venetian crusaders in 1204, Byzantium lost its status as an independent power in the East for decades, never totally recovering its strength.[16] Due to the weakening of the Byzantine Empire, the Ottomans captured the majority of the Empire's former territory by the end of the fourteenth century and rendered the emperor himself tributary to the sultan.[17]

The capital Constantinople remained an island surrounded by spheres of Ottoman influence. After the defeat of an allied Christian army in the Battle of Nicopolis in 1396, it was merely a question of time until Constantinople surrendered to the Ottoman forces. Due to the Mongol invasion under Timur (1336–1405) and his victory over the Ottoman forces in 1402, further expansions of the Ottomans in Europe were postponed and resumed under the young sultan Mehmed II in 1451. Although the existential threat was obvious, few efforts were taken to assist Constantinople. After the defeat of a Christian army at Varna in 1444, in which the king of Hungary and Poland, Władysław III (1424–1444), was killed, no efficient alliances against the Ottomans were formed. The hostilities and rivalries between the Byzantine Empire and European powers as well as the antagonism between the Orthodox and the Catholic Church remained dominant. The attempt to reunite the two Churches in the Union of Florence in 1439 failed due to the excessive demands of the Catholic side.[18]

Notwithstanding the obvious shortcomings in the organization of an effective alliance to assist the Byzantine Empire, news of the city being seized caused a shock in European countries, in the political elite as well as in the broader population.[19] More important than the strategic aspect of Constantinople was its cultural meaning as a common symbol of Christianity and its ancient heritage. The fall of the "second Rome" caused a common fear in Christianity and even affected those territories that were not particularly threatened by the Ottoman expansion.

The perception of an existential crisis among elites as well as common people influenced the political sphere. It led to intensified political communication and to a revaluation of common ideological patterns. The moment of this major political crisis formed the breeding ground for developing new patterns of meaning. The months following the capture of Constantinople saw an enormous increase in diplomatic correspondence and an intensification of diplomatic missions. In the center of these efforts to form alliances against the Ottoman expansion stood the Pope and the Roman Curia.[20] After the Patriarch of Constantinople fell into the hands of the infidels, Rome confirmed its claim to the single leadership in the Christian world. Papal legates were sent to various European courts, focusing, however, on the courts of the king of Hungary and the Holy Roman Emperor, who were supposed to play key roles in the defense against the Turks.

One of the results was the quest for multilateral communication platforms to form an alliance of European princes. In this context, three Diets of the Holy Roman Empire were conscripted, which were held in very quick succession in Regensburg, Frankfurt, and Wiener Neustadt in 1454 and 1455. Three Imperial Diets were held within one and a half years. The effort it took organizers and attendants to hold these huge assemblies provides insight into the contemporaries' perception of an existential crisis. The agenda consisted in forming an anti-Ottoman alliance and raising an imperial army.[21] However, the Imperial Diets did not function merely as a representation of the estates. Besides the estates of the Holy Roman Empire, numerous other European princes and sovereignties were summoned. Accordingly, the invitation list is quite impressive: Naples-Aragon, Castile, Portugal, France, England, Scotland, Denmark, Sweden, Norway, Poland, Bohemia, Hungary, Genoa, Florence, Venice, Milan, and several other Italian states and principalities.[22] Even though not all of them sent a delegation, the character of the Imperial Diets is obvious: they were meant to provide a platform for exchange and encounter on a European level.

The Rhetoric of *Antemurale*

The main purpose of the Imperial Diets was to bring together a Catholic alliance to stop the Ottoman forces or, even better, drive them back and free Constantinople.[23] Accordingly, the main aim of the Diets' speakers was to stress the importance of this alliance and to illuminate the danger to Christianity. The list of speakers in favor of an anti-Ottoman alliance was prominent. Among them were the most famous intellectuals of the time who excelled in both classical rhetorical knowledge and political influence at the courts of Europe.[24] Enea Silvio Piccolomini, later Pope Pius II (1405–1464) and at that time councilor of Emperor Frederick III (1415–1493); Cardinal Nicholas of Cusa (1401–1464), Prince-Bishop of Bressanone; Cardinal Giovanni di Castiglione († 1460), Bishop of Pavia; and the Hungarian councilor and bishop of Oradea, János Vitéz (1408–1472) were among them, to name only the most influential advocates.[25] Due to these speakers, the Diets were a show of great oratorical skills.[26]

The content of the speeches proved to be very similar. The speakers concentrated on the imminent threat to Hungary that, they declared, was just about to fall under Ottoman rule without the assistance of other European powers. They also urged the German princes in the name of the Pope and the emperor or—in the case of János Vitéz—in the name of the Hungarian king to take up arms and aid Hungary in its fight against the Turks. Their speeches differed, however, when it came to their semantic structure. For example, Giovanni di Castiglione asked his audience to "Think of the Hungarian Kingdom, of whose praise I cannot speak enough, which threw itself so often against so many calamities and dangers for the defense of the condition of Christianity. Its power, its uprightness, its battles, its overthrows meant peace for the rest of the world."[27] In a speech authored by Hungarian councilor Vitéz, the condition of Hungary is described even more dramatically[28]: "By objecting its own flanks, the remaining bodies and hearts of Christianity were secured. This concern and care to protect the faith and the faithful was left to my King by a hereditary law from his ancestors."[29]

Even though Giovanni di Castiglione and János Vitéz described the role of Hungary as defending Christianity against a non-Christian enemy, they did not apply any kind of bulwark rhetoric.[30] That leads to the conclusion that in 1454, when these speeches were performed, the metaphor of the bulwark as a political concept or semantic code had not yet fully developed. The speakers did not refer to the bulwark metaphor as a means to sum up their description of the role and function of Christian border states against Islam. Even though the terms may have been used before, they were not yet part of a common and shared imagination. This can be affirmed by the letters of John Hunyadi (1406–1456), the regent in Hungary.[31] In his letters, which played a crucial role in the consultation in Wiener Neustadt, Hunyadi reported the unstable situation concerning the defense of Hungary against the Turks and demanded military assistance from the emperor. Like Vitéz, he referred to the crucial role of Hungary without applying any kind of bulwark semantics: "The Turks are plotting to invade the Kingdom of Hungary and from there to obtain further Christianity."[32] As it appears, even though Hungary is described as a frontier state, the bulwark metaphor was not yet a compulsive part of Hungarian self-presentation.

In contrast to his fellow speakers, Enea Silvio Piccolomini, the emperor's councilor and one of the most eminent orators of his age, systematically drafted the bulwark-related metaphors as a rhetorical device for describing the situation and role of Hungary as a border state.

> More and more the virus creeps in. The Hungarians have been the shield of our faith, the wall of our religion. . . . If Hungary is defeated or by force joined with the Turks, neither Germany nor Italy will be safe and the river Rhine will not render the French secure enough.[33]

Apparently, Piccolomini's use of the bulwark metaphor is not incidental.[34] While it is lacking in all other speeches, Piccolomini not only refers to it constantly but also attributes it to the other speeches. János Vitéz did not use the bulwark metaphor himself, but Piccolomini refers to the Hungarian councilor's speech by using his own threefold formula of *murus, antemurale,* and *clipeus*[35]:

> Hungary is our shield as well as the wall and strongest rampart of our religion. If we do not protect this province, neither Italy nor Germany will be at peace. Neither will the river Rhine be able to protect France, nor will the Pyrenean Mountains be able to protect Spain.[36]

By referring to Germany, Italy, France, and Spain, Piccolomini shifts the view from a geographically defined level to a European level, thereby addressing all major European powers. However, the bulwark metaphor in Piccolomini's speeches was not only a rhetoric pattern but also an integral part of a larger argument concerning his concept of Europe. As such it aimed at a self-description of Europe rather than an ascription to Hungary. In the most famous of his Diet speeches, the "Constantinopolitana clades," performed on 15 October 1454 in Frankfurt, he combined the concept of Christianity and Europe in a programmatic way[37]:

> And, if we want to confess the truth, in many centuries before, Christian society had not suffered a greater disgrace. In former times, we were wounded in Asia or Africa, which means in foreign territories; but now, we are deeply distressed and forced to give way in Europe, which is our native land, in our very own house, in our home.[38]

The concept of Catholic Europe formed the nucleus of an intensified rhetoric of and an appeal to an asserted collective identity.[39] Geopolitical imagination as expressed in mythical or historical narratives helped define coherent spaces and create collective identities.[40] The emergence of collective identities is accompanied and provided by the drawing of mental borders.[41] In this sense, the bulwark metaphor was crucial: it underlined the impression of a beleaguered isle, of inner peace and outer war.[42] This proved to be important, as Piccolomini's Europe was largely defined by what was on the other side of this bulwark. The common rejection of the Ottoman enemy united Europe, according to the definition of Piccolomini, Europe thus being defined ex negativo by its Muslim counterpart. However, that was not always the case. In the fifteenth century, various opinions existed of how to classify the Ottoman Empire. Several theologians compared the Muslim religion with Christian heresy.

The name "Turks" was etymologically derived from *Teucri*, the citizens of the mythic city of Troy. According to a common opinion in fifteenth-century Europe, the Turks were identified with the Trojans of the *Iliad* and, therefore, within the common cultural heritage: many dynasties and nations, most importantly Rome itself, traced their origin back to Trojan fugitives. Piccolomini rejected this interpretation stridently, emphasizing the historical and cultural differences of the Turks[43]: "Not Asians by origin are the Turks, who they call Teucer, from whom the Romans derive . . . : the tribe of the Scythians came from the middle of Barbarian territory, an impure and disgraceful people that fornicates in every possible form of sexual intercourse."[44] Piccolomini further illustrates the fundamental difference of Ottomans and Europeans in his account of the capture of Constantinople. This account has become part of the European memory.[45]

Piccolomini employs three different categories structuring the Otherness of the Turks: (1) humanity, (2) religion, and (3) culture and learning.[46] First is humanity, that is, the inhumanity of the Turks as demonstrated by their cruelty against captured citizens:

> At that I shudder, that I loathe, that I detest: after the city was captured, the arms were laid down, the citizens were shackled, there was a severe ravage. Children were murdered in front of their parents, noblemen slaughtered like sacrificial animals, priests butchered, monks torn to pieces, nuns defiled, mothers and daughters-in-law ridiculed. Oh you miserable face of the city! Oh you unfortunate people! Oh you accursed Mohammed! Who can keep back tears while reporting things like these?[47]

Second is the Christian religion, that is, the impiety of the Turks as seen in their cruelty toward churches and saints:

> Our God's temples were delivered to their false prophet, the holy altars torn down, the bones of the martyrs and other saints who already reign with Christ fed to pigs or dogs. Statues were broken, pictures destroyed; and not even the image of the Mother of God, the Queen of Heaven, the glorious Virgin Mary was spared. Even the image of the crucified Christ was with much noise and even more derision taken to the camp, while drums and pipes preceded. For fun, it was pulled all over the place, spit on, polluted with excrements. Oh what an inexpiable sin! Oh what a disgrace of the Christian people! Oh what an eternal dishonor of our name![48]

Third is their ancient culture and education, that is, the illiterateness of the Turks as shown by their mistreatment of ancient texts: "He [the Turk] eats the flesh of horses, wisents and vultures, he serves his lust, he breaks down to his cruelty, he hates literature, he attacks science. I do not know who is able to sufficiently express his sorrow that learned and eloquent Greece fell into his hands."[49] To make sure his audience kept track of his argument, Piccolomini summarized the fundamental differences in education, law, humanity, and religion: "Do we doubt the justice of a war against these human monsters who do not care for any education, who do not observe any contracts, who thirst for our blood, who cannot get enough of slaughter, who pollute and banish all rites for our God?"[50]

In contrast to this image of "human monsters," Piccolomini drafts the picture of a common European identity above all existing conflicts. Piccolomini is sometimes seen as the father of a concept of Europe as a secular community of sovereign states.[51] This interpretation ignores the Christian framework of Piccolomini's concept: religion remained an integral and indispensable part of his concept of Europe. He referred to faith as the unifying element in various ways: Europe as *christiana societas*,[52] *christi-*

*ana communitas,*⁵³ *christiana gens,*⁵⁴ *christianus populus,*⁵⁵ and *respublica christiana nostra.*⁵⁶ In this context, the bulwark metaphor appeals to Europe as a defensive alliance and community of solidarity in a highly religious interpretation. The bulwark metaphor accompanied and emphasized Piccolomini's idea of Europe. It can be characterized as a metaphor of territorial as well as cultural and religious integration. Piccolomini put much effort into repeating his concept of Europe over and over again, thereby standardizing it in terms of semantics.⁵⁷ In this regard, Europe and the bulwark metaphor were concepts of persuasion constructing an identity and a common interest beyond political rivalries and conflicts.

This idea of Europe set the stage for bringing up and emphasizing the bulwark metaphor in the context of the Imperial Diets in the mid-fifteenth century. Piccolomini's use of the bulwark metaphor differed from previous use. By incorporating it into a greater ideological context, he loaded it with meaning, while he used it as a catchword by constantly repeating it.

Antemurale Christianitatis as a Career Enhancement

At this point, it is worth taking a closer look at the protagonist who emphasized the concept of the bulwark and the idea of a culturally and religiously united Europe, a Europe threatened from the outside by non-Christian aggressors. In 1454, Enea Silvio Piccolomini, who later ascended to the Cathedra Petri as Pope Pius II, was already looking back on a quite colorful political career.⁵⁸ The son of an impoverished aristocratic family of Siena, he became one of the most famous humanists by the middle of the century. He played a major role in the Council of Basel (1431–1449) and afterward had a career as a diplomat and councilor at the court of Emperor Frederick III. While still working for the emperor, he was appointed papal secretary and, finally, bishop of his hometown, Siena. When organizing the Imperial Diets of Regensburg, Frankfurt, and Wiener Neustadt, therefore, Piccolomini acted as a representative of both of the two universal powers in Europe, the emperor and the Pope.

The promotion of his concept of Europe and a European crusade has to be viewed in the light of his own career enhancement. In 1454, few people would have foreseen that Piccolomini was going to become head of the Church four years later. His curriculum vitae was somewhat crooked. Not only was he well known for his dubious lifestyle and famous as author of erotic bestsellers, but more importantly, by starting his career at the Council of Basel, he had backed the wrong horse.

In Basel, Piccolomini had become one of the leading figures of the council that questioned the Pope's status in the Church. He had even played an important role in the attempted deposition of Pope Eugene IV (1383–1447) in 1439. He was later reconciled with the Pope, but the blemish of his past remained. His further career, meaning the promotion to the cardinal hat and maybe even to the tiara, required substantial effort. In this regard, Piccolomini's Diet speeches against the Ottomans can be read as recommending himself. In front of a secular as well as an ecclesiastical elite, he proved his excellent rhetorical and humanist skills. At the same time, he presented himself as a *defendor fidei* and as an advocate of Christianity. This reinvention and branding of his own person distracted from his past and qualified him for higher tasks and duties. Taking into account his election to Pope only three years later, this self-marketing proved to be extremely successful.

Distributing a Rhetoric Concept

As pointed out above, the Imperial Diets were important as platforms for political communication reaching far beyond the borders of the Holy Roman Empire.[59] In the case of the three Imperial Diets held after the fall of Constantinople, almost all European states and princes were invited to join the assembly. The Imperial Diets, therefore, represented European political elites. The attendants were multipliers and ensured the dissemination of Piccolomini's speeches.[60] Piccolomini himself later described in his *Commentarii* that many attendants copied his speeches afterward.[61] Owing to their self-marketing character, Piccolomini himself was interested in spreading his speeches.[62] As a recommendation and as an example of his rhetorical excellence, he sent them personally to key figures he knew, many of them high-ranking ecclesiastical persons.[63] Piccolomini, however, was not alone in spreading his rhetorical agenda. Some of these key figures, for example Nicholas of Cusa (1401–1464), themselves became multipliers of Piccolomini's speeches within the humanist *res publica literaria*.[64]

Due to this multiple dissemination politics, there can even today be found at least forty-five manuscripts of Piccolomini's most famous speech in Frankfurt, most of them written at the time of the Diet or shortly afterward.[65] Never before were humanist speeches copied and transmitted in a similar number.[66] Piccolomini's words, and thereby his concept of Europe and the bulwark metaphor, found their way into reports and the correspondence of the delegates, furthering their distribution as well as their translation into the vernacular languages all over Europe.[67]

In addition to Piccolomini and the attendants of the Imperial Diets, a technical innovation proved to be crucial for the long-time reception of Piccolomini's concepts: the development of the printing press.[68] The new media created a public sphere transcending personal contact or physical presence. Piccolomini's speeches benefited from this. At a very early stage, they found their way into printed publications, thereby spreading beyond humanist circles and personal networks.[69] This distribution resulted in a European-wide circulation of Piccolomini's speeches. This was not due only to the convincing content of his speeches: the humanist interest in rhetoric and style furthered the reception and imitation of Piccolomini's speeches.[70] As a rhetorical model, they became prototypes for orations against the Turks, which developed as a genre in the following years.[71]

Piccolomini set the example by providing certain stereotypes—among them the bulwark metaphor—that were to become topical. By means of these orations against the Turks, they reached segments of society far beyond the intellectual and political elites and became part of a shared European knowledge and experience. As a result, the bulwark metaphor found its way into the vernacular languages, for instance, *antemuraglia* and *baloverde* in Italian, *rampart* in English, *vorpauw* and *gemeier* in German, *boulevert* in French.[72] However important Piccolomini's role was in furthering the implementation of the concept of *antemurale*, it should be viewed within the broader political and cultural context. As an orator as well as a thinker, Piccolomini was far from isolated. The success and broad resonance of his concepts can largely be credited to the fact that they were generally compatible with humanist ideas.

Various structural and cultural conditions furthered their acceptance: First, the network of a republic of letters provided the fast dissemination of Piccolomini's words and a communicative coherence. Second, the close connection among humanists between *eruditio* and *officium*, between literacy and political duty as councilors and secretaries, facilitated its implementation into political and diplomatic texts. Third, the emphasis on linguistic elegance and style caused a corresponding sensitivity to excellent phrasing. The Ottoman expansion and the siege of Constantinople was lively discussed within humanist circles, not least because of their self-conception as admirers of ancient literature. Dealing with the war against the Turks and the crusade, therefore, became a prominent theme in humanist literature.[73] This entailed the engagement with concepts of Europe and its frontier.[74] However successful Piccolomini's concept of *antemurale* was, he was not the first humanist dealing with this concept: as early as 1444—prior to the Battle of Varna—the Italian humanist Francesco Filelfo (1398–1481) had addressed King Władysław III as *Christianae Reipublicae propugnaculum*.[75]

The emergence of a bulwark metaphor is linked to the political context after the fall of Constantinople. However, its implementation as a semantic code for the frontier between civilization and barbarism, religion and heresy, despotism and liberty did not evolve accidentally. It was the result of a decisive politics of distribution, of the widespread humanist interest in rhetoric and crusades, and of the new medium of printing, which furthered a European public sphere. What became the nucleus of the evolving collective identity in Hungary, Croatia, and Poland was, in its beginning, closely connected to a broader concept of Europe as a religious, cultural, and geographical unity with a common interest in self-defense. Its distribution can also be described as a successful campaign to gain the papal throne. Of course, Piccolomini himself stood in a broader humanist rhetorical context. However, his stringent rhetorical repetitiveness and distribution channels surpassed earlier uses of this metaphor by far. As Pope Pius II, Piccolomini remained faithful to his rhetorical agenda.[76]

In his succession, the bulwark metaphor became an integral part of the papal public statements and of papal diplomatic missions.[77] From Leo X (1513–1521) to John Paul II (1978–2005), Popes and their legates used the bulwark metaphor as a semantic code to highlight the unity of Christian Europe and the leading role the Popes themselves claimed in it.[78] Piccolomini did not invent the bulwark metaphor, but his repetitive use of the bulwark metaphor alongside his concept of a religiously and culturally united Europe decisively contributed to the spreading of this imagery in the second half of the fifteenth century. This successful implementation was based on communication platforms such as the Diets of the Holy Roman Empire, the personal network of the *res publica literaria*, and the development of the printing press.

Piccolomini designed his rhetoric imagery against a background of a deep political and cultural crisis in Western Europe after the seizure of Constantinople. The implementation of the bulwark metaphor as a part of European discourses also affected political discourses in Eastern Europe. Even though the humanist concept of *antemurale* addressed an imaginative European res publica, it reverberated in regional identities. This is especially true for Poland and Hungary, where the *antemurale* myth played a crucial role in outlining a collective agenda and a sense of mission and in providing a source of political legitimation for centuries. Poland and Hungary can be described as major carriers of the *antemurale* myth.[79] Even though the reception of the *antemurale* myth differed chronologically—while it was firmly in use in Hungary by the end of the fifteenth century, the reception in Poland reached its height in the late sixteenth century[80]—it yielded similar results in both countries.[81] The second part of this chapter focuses on how this discourse helped to form premodern national identities in Poland and Hungary.

The Bulwark Myth in Poland and Hungary (Fifteenth–Eighteenth Centuries)

Early versions of bulwark rhetoric in Eastern Europe can be traced back to the Middle Ages.[82] Particularly in the thirteenth century, in the course of the Mongol invasion, the efforts of Poland and Hungary in resisting this invasion were highlighted. However, this was not used only to address foreign aggressors but also to characterize inner-Christian conflicts, particularly the struggle between the Teutonic Order and the Kingdom of Poland.[83] The sources in the first case, those dealing with the Mongol invasions, are mostly records from authors who were not Polish or Hungarian themselves.[84] In the conflicts with the Teutonic Order, the bulwark metaphor was used to legitimate the hostility of the Teutonic knights against Poland by labeling the country as an enemy of the Christian faith against whom the Teutonic Order erected a bulwark. In this context, the bulwark rhetoric played an important part in delegitimizing Polish political interests.[85] These few examples indicate that the bulwark metaphor was still open to a great range of interpretations, that it was not yet bound to a specific country or to a certain understanding.

Up to the fifteenth century, the bulwark metaphor was not an integral part of an emerging national consciousness or awareness in Poland and Hungary.[86] It had yet to become a semantic code or discourse pointing beyond itself, transporting definable normative values and anticipating certain estimations and political actions. This is underlined by the abovementioned orations at the Imperial Diets of Frankfurt, Regensburg, and Wiener Neustadt (1454–1455), which addressed the fragile situation in Hungary in the course of the Ottoman expansion without using bulwark metaphors.

This situation changed during the second half of the fifteenth century: from then on, political and intellectual elites in Hungary and Poland increasingly referred to their country as a bulwark. Hence, this chronologically correlates with the implementation of the European bulwark discourse promoted by Piccolomini.[87] This coincidence suggests that the implementation of a bulwark discourse in Eastern Europe cannot be interpreted as a geographically confined process but rather as part of a broader European process. Further indications support this assumption: regarding Poland, most references before the late sixteenth century cited by Janusz Tazbir and others were from non-Polish authors.[88]

The majority of early bulwark references in Hungarian and Polish self-descriptions refer to the diplomatic sphere. The bulwark metaphor was used in diplomatic correspondence with the papal or imperial court or in political speeches addressing a European rather than a national audience. In light of this genre, however, interpreting the bulwark rhetoric in these texts as part of a premodern national consciousness appears questionable. Focusing on diplomatic correspondence is hardly suitable to clearly distinguish between self-images and external images, as it often focused heavily on the recipient's assumed expectations to achieve one's objectives.

Besides the diplomatic correspondence, there are further indications that the strengthening of the bulwark discourse in Eastern Europe must be seen in a European context: multipliers of the bulwark discourse in Hungary and Poland themselves were part of a European network of political and intellectual elites. An important protagonist in the reception and strengthening of the bulwark metaphor in Hungary was the abovementioned János Vitéz, then Hungarian chancellor, humanist, and close correspondent of Piccolomini.[89]

After attending the Imperial Diets of 1554–1555, Vitéz began to use the bulwark metaphor more frequently as a Hungarian self-description. As he himself used the bulwark metaphor in his speeches at the Imperial Diets only to address Emperor Frederick III,[90] his inspiration might have derived from Piccolomini's concept of Europe and its bulwarks. After all, a manuscript copy of the Frankfurt Piccolomini speech was found in his library.[91] Until their estrangement in the late 1460s, Vitéz served as an educator, later as a close advisor to Matthias Corvinus (1443–1490), king of Hungary since 1458 and later king of Bohemia. Matthias Corvinus himself built his own monarchic representation around the idea of his role as *antemurale christianitatis*, thereby furthering the reception of the concept in Hungary.[92]

A close connection between European communication networks can also be traced for the second literary genre that highlighted the bulwark discourse as part of collective self-description: humanist national historiography.[93] From the end of the fifteenth century onward, it included the bulwark narrative, thereby incorporating it into collective memory. The authors of these texts were important multipliers of the bulwark discourse as part of premodern national identities. However, they were also part of a European communication network. One striking example is Callimachus Experiens (1437–1497), councilor of King Casimir II (1448–1528) and author of a historiographical account of King Władysław III (1424–1444), who had died fighting against the Ottomans at Varna in 1444. In this account, Callimachus depicted the heroized king as *antemurale christianitatis* and as a bulwark against the Ottoman invasion of Europe.[94] This account was more than a narration of a historical event and person; it outlined the position of Poland in the present and in the future. The name Callimachus was of course a pseudonym of the Italian Filippo Buonaccorsi, who had lived at the Polish court since the 1470s. Before arriving in Poland, he had spent several years in Rome as part of the humanist circle around Piccolomini.[95]

Polish historiographer Jan Długosz (1415–1480) also referred to the bulwark concept in his *Annales seu cronica incliti regni Poloniae* by describing an embassy of Pope Pius II Piccolomini. In his audience with King Casimir I (1016–1058), nuncio Hieronimus Lando, Bishop of Crete, addressed Poland as a bulwark against the Turks, as *christianitatis scutum* and as *christianae* *fidei murus et antemurale.*⁹⁶ The similarity to Piccolomini's threefold expression of *murus, clipeus,* and *antemurale* in his speeches and letters is striking.⁹⁷

These Latin works circulated on a national as well as a European level. However, they played a decisive part in implementing bulwark discourses in a nationwide discursive sphere. Due to their print publication, they reached a broader public. Several new editions attest to a wide interest. These historiographies provided certain narratives and stereotypes characterizing the nation and its historical fate or task. The attribution of a bulwark and its historical legitimation now appeared as an integral part of premodern national imagery. Without a doubt, this historiography played a decisive role in implementing the bulwark rhetoric in Polish discourses and as a formative part of developing a premodern national identity that reached levels of society far beyond the intellectual elite.

Until the sixteenth century, the Polish bulwark rhetoric had almost completely been limited to Latin texts, such as the abovementioned diplomatic texts and historiography.⁹⁸ This situation changed in the course of the sixteenth century, when the bulwark discourse became an important aspect of vernacular poetry, preaching, and literature.⁹⁹ While it originally addressed Latin-speaking elites in Europe as well as in Poland, it excluded the vast majority of the countries' inhabitants. Now, the *antemurale* discourse became part of broader public discourses.¹⁰⁰ Important anti-Ottoman orations such as the *Turcicae* of Krzysztof Warszewicki (1543–1603) were now translated into and printed in Polish.¹⁰¹

In the seventeenth century, the mental identification of *antemurale christianitatis* and the Polish nation permeated texts of various media, such as preaching, poems, newspapers, and diaries.¹⁰² Notably, poetry was an expression and a motor of strengthening the equation of the nation and its function as a rampart against the enemies of Christianity. Poetry such as that of Stanisław Grochowski (1542–1612), who addressed Poland in one of his poems: "Oh, the famous wall of Christian countries/The mighty bulwark sheltering from pagan powers."¹⁰³ This view helped to implement and further the idea of Poland as a chosen nation, the idea of a special union of God with the Polish people. As Poland served as a bulwark for the Christian faith, God himself was a bulwark for Poland:

> Therefore we should call upon God day in, day out
> To be our wall in need;
> And to shield the herd of His believers;
> And to be the Bastille for the paltry sheep.¹⁰⁴

The success of this discourse in a European communication network of political and intellectual elites as well as in vernacular poetry was based on its imagery and impressiveness.

Even more important was another aspect, however: despite its precise imagery, it remained open to interpretation and therefore adaptable to various situations and purposes. This aspect paved the way for its implementation in national discourses as well as its persistence up to the present day.

The development of the bulwark discourse and its implementation in patterns of a premodern national identity has to be seen against the backdrop of and the interaction with a European communicative sphere. However, this did not prevent the development of exclusionary bulwark discourses in Eastern Europe. Poland is an excellent example in this respect. The promotion of the concept of Europe and its bulwarks in the second half of the fifteenth century took place in the light of the Ottoman expansion and the seizure of Constantinople. It was hence an essentially anti-Turkish discourse. The adoption into premodern national discourses, however, shifted this image and perspective. The concept of a bulwark as used by Piccolomini not only stigmatized the Turks as religious Others but also highlighted their cultural, political and legal, ethnic, and historical Otherness. Accordingly, the identity on this side of the bulwark was implicitly characterized by religious, cultural, political, ethical, and historical homogeneity. This emphasis on various delimiting aspects as well as on the comprehensive homogeneity left room for new interpretations.

From a Polish perspective, it was not only the Turks who threatened the Polish bulwark. Farther neighbors were included in this discourse: Poland formed a bulwark not only against the Muslim Turks and Tatars but also against the schismatic and despotic Orthodox Muscovites and their heretical Protestant neighbors in Sweden and the Holy Roman Empire.[105] In this view, instead of one definable Other, the bulwark discourse formed multiple Others; instead of being the frontline of a homogenous Europe against foreign aggressors, Poland increasingly saw itself as a "beleaguered isle." The concept's meaning, originally designated to invoke European cohesion and solidarity, changed fundamentally in this context. As part of premodern national discourses, it increasingly provided a pattern for aggressive distinctiveness.[106]

Of course, the bulwark discourse could and did serve as an argument to achieve certain political goals, such as freedom from papal taxation. However, it cannot be reduced to its functional purpose. By shaping collective self-perception, it became a guiding basis for political actions. The perception of the nation as a besieged bulwark defined not only the attitude toward an assumed hostility of the surrounding neighbors. In Poland, it led to decisive antireformatory aspirations aiming at confessional homogeneity and at eliminating Protestant voices.[107] This happened against the backdrop of an increasingly messianic tone that underlay bulwark discourses.[108] Hence, it became the motor and expression of a messianic interpretation initiating and legitimating action taken against outer as well as inner enemies.[109]

Conclusion

Even though the term *antemurale* or *propugnaculum* was well in use before the fifteenth century, only in the second half of the fifteenth century did it become a compelling discourse and a semantic code. The implementation of this *antemurale* discourse can be described as a European process in two ways. First, the *antemurale* discourse itself developed within a European, transnational humanist public sphere. The diffusions of humanism[110] and the European humanist network were the preconditions for an increasing reception of *antemurale christianitatis* as a semantic code and political concept.

The implementation of the *antemurale* concept, therefore, can be described as a European act of communication against the backdrop of a pan-European humanist public. In addition to these structural and cultural aspects of its implementation, there was a second, substantial aspect underlining its European character: the discourse as it had been propagated by Piccolomini and others since the fifteenth century defined the European borders as a sharp line of demarcation against a hostile, religiously and culturally diverse alterity. It thus appealed to an imagined European integration, a shared European identity. This European discourse was received in the Kingdom of Hungary and later in the Polish-Lithuanian Commonwealth. Its inclusion in national discourses, however, developed its own dynamics and increasingly contravened its original meaning: as a cultural border, *antemurale* served to establish an early modern national identity and a distinctiveness that identified multiple enemies outside as well as inside the community. A concept originally designed to further the idea of European integration and consensus was thus able to develop a disintegrative and conflict-provoking impact.

Kerstin Weiand currently holds the position of lecturer in early modern history at the Philipps-University in Marburg, Germany. Her research focuses on papal crusading diplomacy in the sixteenth and seventeenth centuries. She has published monographs on the myth of Elizabeth I in Stuart England and the Landgraviate Hessen-Kassel during the Thirty Years War. She has also edited a volume on discourses of deficiency in the early modern political sphere.

Notes

1. A.C. Kenneweg, "Antemurale Christianitatis," in *Europäische Erinnerungsorte*, vol. 2: *Das Haus Europa*, ed. P. den Boeret, H. Duchhardt, and G. Kreis (München: Oldenbourg Verlag, 2012), 73–81.
2. Ibid.
3. See P.W. Knoll, "Poland as 'Antemurale Christianitatis' in the Late Middle Ages," *The Catholic Historical Review* 60 (1974): 381–401. According to M. Biskup, "No foreigner, only our own diplomacy strengthened the opinion of the Curia and Western Europe that Poland—consolidated in its faith—was a bulwark and shield of Christendom." Cited in J. Krzyżaniakowa, "Polen als antemurale christianitatis. Zur Vorgeschichte eines Mythos," in *Mythen in Geschichte und Geschichtsschreibung aus polnischer und deutscher Sicht*, ed. A. von Saldern (Münster: LIT, 1996), 141. Wictor Weintraub provides a different view when stating that the concept of *antemurale* was assigned to Poland by the West. W. Weintraub, "Renaissance Poland and *Antemurale Christianitatis*," *Harvard Ukrainian Studies* 3/4 (1979–1980): 921.
4. J. Pekacz, "Antemurale of Europe; from the History of National Megalomania in Poland," *History of European Ideas* 20 (1995): 419.
5. U. Borkowska, "The Ideology of 'Antemurale' in the Sphere of Slavic Culture (13th–17th centuries)," in *The Common Christian Roots of the European Nations*, ed. Pontificia Università Lateranense, vol. 2, 1206 (Firenze: Le Monnier, 1982); P. Srodecki, *Antemurale Christianitatis. Zur Genese der Bollwerksrhetorik im östlichen Mitteleuropa an der Schwelle vom Mittelalter zur Frühen Neuzeit* (Husum: Matthiesen Verlag, 2015), 11–16, 339–52; M. Morawiec, "*Antemurale christianitatis*. Polen als Vormauer des christlichen Europa," *Jahrbuch für Europäische Geschichte* 2 (2001): 249–60; H. Hein-Kircher, "Überlegungen zur Ausprägung und Funktion von Raummythen," in *Deutschlands östliche Nachbarschaften: eine Sammlung von historischen Essays für Hans Henning Hahn*, ed. E. Dmitrów and T. Weger (Frankfurt a.M.: Peter Lang, 2009), 115–18. For contemporary applications of *antemurale* mythology, see Pål Kolstø's contribution and Paul Srodecki's conclusion in this volume.
6. While the concept of nation as an ideology is a specifically modern phenomenon, certain aspects of national awareness and consciousness can be traced back to the late Middle Ages. As an idea of political order, it was enhanced by the work of numerous humanist authors in the fifteenth and sixteenth centuries; see R. Stauber, "Nation," in *Enzyklopädie der Neuzeit*, vol. 8 (Stuttgart: Metzler Verlag, 2008), 1056–82.
7. N. Housley, *Crusading and the Ottoman Threat, 1453–1505* (Oxford: Oxford University Press, 2012), 40.
8. Srodecki, *Antemurale Christianitatis*, 31–39; Krzyżaniakowa, "Polen," 132.
9. For the connection between *timor Tartarorum* and the *antemurale* topos, see Borkowska, "Ideology," 1206; Knoll, "Poland," 385 passim.
10. Paul Srodecki listed many of the early references in his instructive article published in 2012 as well as in his Ph.D. thesis published in 2015. P. Srodecki, "Validissima semper Christianitatis propugnacula. Zur Entstehung der Bollwerksrhetorik in Polen und Ungarn im Spätmittelalter und in der frühen Neuzeit," in *Sarmatismus ver-*

sus Orientalismus in Mitteleuropa, ed. M. Długosz and P.O. Scholz (Berlin: Frank und Timmer, 2012), 133–35; Srodecki, *Antemurale Christianitatis*, 57–104. Some of the sources mentioned that the deal with Poland as a bulwark against non-Christian invasions goes back to the thirteenth century, though not all of them actually refer to one of the abovementioned terms.

11. A. Theiner, ed., *Vetera monumenta historica Hungariam sacram illustrantia*, vol. 2 (Roma: Typis Vaticanis, 1859–1860), 182.
12. Theiner, *Vetera monumenta historica Hungariam sacram illustrantia*, vol. 1, 202.
13. Borkowska, "Ideology," 1208; Srodecki, *Antemurale Christianitatis*, 57–62; Krzyżaniakowa, "Polen," 134.
14. Housley, *Crusading and the Ottoman Threat*, 40 passim; Srodecki, "Validissima semper Christianitatis propugnacula," 140.
15. E. Meuthen, "Der Fall von Konstantinopel und der lateinische Westen," *Historische Zeitschrift* 237 (1983): 1–35. For the capture of Constantinople, see F. Babinger, *Mehmed der Eroberer und seine Zeit. Weltenstürmer einer Zeitenwende* (München: Bruckmann Verlag, 1953; repr. 1987), 67–108.
16. R.-J. Lilie, *Byzanz: Geschichte des oströmischen Reiches 326–1453* (München: C.H. Beck, 2013), 93–106. For the role of 1204 in the Byzantine cultural memory, see A. Külzer, "Die Eroberung von Konstantinopel im Jahre 1204 in der Erinnerung der Byzantiner," in *Quarta Crociata. Venezia—Bisanzio—Impero Latino*, ed. Gherardo Ortalli (Venezia: Istituto Veneto di Scienze, 2006), 619–32.
17. Lilie, *Byzanz*, 26.
18. See J. Helmrath, "Art. Union, kirchliche III. Konzil von Ferrara, Florenz," *Lexikon des Mittelalters* 8 (2002): 1241–42.
19. For the reception of the fall of Constantinople in Europe, see Meuthen, "Der Fall von Konstantinopel"; M. Meserve, *Empires of Islam in Renaissance Historical Thought* (Cambridge, MA: Harvard University Press, 2009), 29–30; D. Mertens, "Europäischer Friede und Türkenkrieg im Spätmittelalter," in *Zwischenstaatliche Friedenswahrung in Mittelalter und Früher Neuzeit*, ed. H. Duchhardt (Köln: Böhlau, 1991), 45–90; J. Helmrath, "Pius II. und die Türken," in *Europa und die Türken in der Renaissance*, ed. B. Guthmüller and W. Kühlmann (Tübingen: Niemeyer, 2000), 89–99.
20. Meuthen, "Der Fall von Konstantinopel," 17 passim. Even though the Popes' claim to organize a crusade against the Turks was criticized due to its lack of effectiveness, it was hardly ever openly rejected; see Housley, *Crusading and the Ottoman Threat*, 50–61.
21. J. Helmrath, "The German 'Reichstage' and the Crusade," in *Crusading in the Fifteenth Century. Message and Impact*, ed. N. Housley (Basingstoke: Palgrave Macmillan, 2004), 53–69; D. Mertens, "'Europa, id est patria, domus propria, sedes nostra'. Zu Funktionen und Überlieferung lateinischer Türkenreden im 15. Jahrhundert," in *Europa und die osmanische Expansion im ausgehenden Mittelalter*, ed. F.-R. Erkens (Berlin: Duncker & Humblot, 1997), 49–52.
22. See "Letter of Piccolomini to Leonardo Benvoglienti" (5 July 1454), in W. Kaemmerer, ed., *Deutsche Reichstagsakten. Ältere Reihe, vol. 19,2: Deutsche Reichstagsakten unter Kaiser Friedrich III.; Abt. 5, part 2. Reichsversammlung zu Frankfurt 1454* (München: Oldenbourg, 2013), 105 (below cit. as RTA 19,2).
23. Housley, *Crusading and the Ottoman Threat*, 27 passim.

24. RTA 19,2, 461; W. Kaemmerer, ed., *Deutsche Reichstagsakten. Ältere Reihe. Abt. 5. vol. 19,1: Deutsche Reichstagsakten unter Kaiser Friedrich III., 1453–1454* (Göttingen: Vandenhoeck & Ruprecht, 1969), 265 (below cit. as RTA 19,1).
25. RTA 19,1, 265; RTA 19,2, 460.
26. Mertens, "Europa, id est patria," 50–51; Helmrath, "German 'Reichstage,'" 53–62.
27. G. di Castiglione, Pollicitus sum, 17 October 1554 Frankfurt, RTA 19,2, Introduction, 565–71; text, 571–84; quotation 576: "*Considerate Ungarie regnum, de cuius laudibus non satis dicere possum, quod tot calamitatibus atque periculis se tociens obiecit pro defensione Christiani status. illius potencia, illius probitas, illius certamina, illius strages pax fuere reliquo orbi.*"
28. RTA 19,2, 576. The speech was written by János Vitéz and performed by Nikolaus Barius (Miklós Bánfalvi), bishop of Erlau, as Vitéz himself could not be present at the Imperial Diet of Regensburg, RTA 19,2, 585 passim.
29. RTA 19,2, 588: "*Obiectu laterum suorum reliquos Christianitatis frontes et pectora tutati sunt . . . ea solicitudo et cura fidei ac fidelium tuendorum prefato serenissimo domino regi hereditario quodam iure a predecessoribus suis relicta est.*"
30. János Vitéz, however, referred to the emperor as the one holding the shield to protect Christianity: "*Gerat ille claves ut pacificus custos, tu* [i.e., imperator] *clipeum ut bellicosus protector,*" in W. Kaemmerer, ed., *Deutsche Reichstagsakten unter Kaiser Friedrich III.; Abt. 5, part 3. Reichsversammlung zu Wiener Neustadt 1455* (München: Oldenbourg, 2013), 451 (below cit. as RTA 19,3).
31. See letter of John Hunyadi to Emperor Frederick III of 10 November, 1454, RTA 19,3, 52–60; letter of John Hunyadi to Emperor Frederick III of 19 December 1454, RTA 19,3, 66–69.
32. RTA 19,3, 68: "*Turci . . . machinantes invadere regnum Hungarie et inde ulterius impetrare Christianitatem.*"
33. RTA 19,2, 522 passim: "*Serpit in dies hoc virus magis ac magis. . . . Hungari . . . hactenus fidei nostre clipeus, nostre religionis murus fuere . . . sive vincitur Hungaria sive coacta iungitur Turcis, neque Italia neque Germania tuta erit neque satis Rhenus Gallos securos reddet.*"
34. Unlike his cospeakers, Piccolomini puts the metaphor of the bulwark repeatedly at the center of his speech. In his opening speech at the Imperial Diet in Wiener Neustadt, for example, he stated, "It is to be feared that this great Kingdom which has been for many centuries the shield of our faith will become part of the dominion of the enemies. If the divine vengeance allows this, there will be nothing in Christianity left secure."
35. The threefold formula of *murus, antemurale,* and *clipeus* (wall, bulwark, and shield) was coined by Piccolomini. RTA 19,2, 495 passim. Piccolomini used this formula in his letters dealing with the Christian defeat at Varna in 1444; see R. Wolkan, ed., *Der Briefwechsel des Eneas Silvius Piccolomini, I. Briefe aus der Laienzeit, 1431–1445,* vol. 1: *Privatbriefe;* vol. 2: *Amtliche Briefe* (Wien: Verlag der Österreichischen Akademie der Wissenschaften, 1909), vol. 1, 548; vol. 2, no. 2, no. 6, and no. 27; RTA 19,3, 456fn 7.
36. RTA 19,3, no. 36, quotation 568: "*Clipeus noster Hungaria est, murusque nostre religionis et antemurale fortissimum. Nisi hanc provinciam tuemur, neque Italia neque Germania quiescit. neque Galliam Rheni fluenta neque Hispaniam Pirenei montes salvare poterunt.*"

37. For the speech "Constantinopolitana clades" and its reception and distribution, see RTA 19,2, 466–72; RTA 19,3, 442.
38. RTA 19,2, 495 passim: *"Neque, si verum fateri volumus, multis ante seculis maiorem ignominiam passa est quam modo Christiana societas. Retroactis namque temporibus in Asia atque in Affrica, hoc est in alienis terris, vulnerati fuimus, nunc vero in Europa, id est patria, in domo propria, in sede nostra percussi cessique sumus."*
39. J. Helmrath, "Enea Silvio Piccolomini (Pius II.). Ein Humanist als Vater des Europagedankens?" in, *Europa und die Europäer: Quellen und Essays zur modernen europäischen Geschichte. Festschrift für Hartmut Kaelble zum 65. Geburtstag*, ed. R. Hohls (Stuttgart: Steiner, 2005), 366.
40. Heidi Hein-Kircher characterizes them as "Raummythen." Hein-Kircher, "Überlegungen," 105–20.
41. J. Osterhammel, "Kulturelle Grenzen in der Expansion Europas," *Saeculum. Jahrbuch für Universalgeschichte* 46 (1995): 108.
42. Pekacz, "Antemurale of Europe," 420.
43. Piccolomini had a major influence on the promotion of the Scythian origin of the Turks; see F. Konrad, "Von der 'Türkengefahr' zu Exotismus und Orientalismus: Der Islam als Antithese Europas (1453–1914)?" in *Europäische Geschichte Online (EGO)*, ed. Institut für Europäische Geschichte (Mainz, 2010), 7, retrieved 15 September 2015 from http://www.ieg-ego.eu/konradf-2010-de; Helmrath, "Pius II. und die Türken," 107–9.
44. RTA 19,2, 515–18; see the Vienna speech, RTA 19,3, 495: *"Neque enim, ut plerique arbitrantur, Asiani sunt ab origine Thurci, quos vocant Theucros, ex quibus est Romanorum origo . . . : Scytharum genus est ex media barbaria profectum . . . gens immunda et ignominiosa, forniocaria in cunctis stuprorum generibus."*
45. RTA 19,2, 470–73.
46. Jürgen Osterhammel described the European perception of the border toward the Ottoman Empire as a "dividing line between imperial, cosmically structured 'civilization' and free roaming, anarchical 'barbarism.'" Osterhammel, "Kulturelle Grenze," 109. There were other perceptions of the Ottoman Empire, such as that of Cardinal Bessarion, who depicted the Ottoman Empire as a highly civilized enemy. See M. Meserve, "Italian Humanists and the Problem of the Crusade," in *Crusading in the Fifteenth Century. Message and Impact*, ed. N. Housley (Basingstoke: Palgrave Macmillan, 2004), 31–38.
47. RTA 19,2, 509: *"Illud horreo, illud abhominor, illud omnino detestor: capta civitate, depositis armis, coniectis in vincula civibus tum maxime sevitum est. Tum filii ante ora parentum occisi, tum viri nobiles velut hostie mactati, tum sacerdotes laniati, tum monchi excarnificati, tum sacre virgines incestate, tum matres ac nurus ludibrio habitate. O miseram urbis faciem! O infelicem populum! O sceleratum Machometum! Quis talia fando temperet lacrimis?"*
48. RTA 19,2, 510 passim: *"Templi dei nostri pseudoprophetae traduntur, divina altaria proteruntur, ossa martyrum et aliorum sanctorum iam cum Christo regnantium aut porcis aut canibus obiciiuntur. franguntur statue, picture delentur; nec matris domini regine celorum, gloriose Marie virginis imagini parcitur. quin et ipsum Christi crucifixi simulacrum cum magno clamore, maiori irrisione, precedentibus tympanis ac tubis in castra defertur, huc atque illuc ludibrio rapitur, conspuitur, luto pro-*

vovitur. o nephas inexpiandum! o ignominiam Christiane gentis! o dedecus nostri nominis sempiternum!"

49. RTA 19,2, 517–18: "*Carnes adhuc equorum vesontium vulturumque comedit, libidini servit, crudelitate succumbit, litteras odit, humanitatis studia persequitur. in cuius manus venisse nunc doctam eloquentemque Greciam, nescio quis satis deflere queat.*" See Piccolomini's emphasis on the ancient literature: RTA 19,2, 518. "*Ac contrita nunc deletaque Grecia, quanta sit facta litterarum iactura, cuncit cognoscitis, qui Latinorum omnem doctrinam ex Grecorum fontibus derivatam non ignoratis.*" RTA 19,2, 520.
50. RTA 19,2, 520: "*An de iustitia belli adversus hec monstra hominum dubitabimus, qui nulla humanitatis studia colunt, qui federa nulla custodiunt, qui sanguinem nostrum sitiunt, qui cedibus saturari non possunt, qui sacra dei nostri omnia pollunt et exterminant?*"
51. For Piccolomini's role of promoting a concept of Europe, see Mertens, "Europa, id est patria"; Konrad, "Türkengefahr," 6–8; Helmrath, "Ein Humanist."
52. RTA 19,2, 495.
53. Ibid., 507.
54. Ibid., 511.
55. Ibid., 529.
56. Ibid., 562.
57. Regarding the repeating of parts of his speeches, see Mertens, "Europa, id est patria," 51 passim.
58. For the following aspects of Piccolomini's career, see V. Reinhardt, *Pius II. Piccolomini. Der Papst, mit dem die Renaissance begann. Eine Biographie* (München: C.H. Beck, 2013).
59. The Imperial Diets can also be characterized as a platform for communication; see RTA 19.2, 32–40.
60. An overview of the audience present at Piccolomini's speech "Constantinopolitana clades" is given in RTA 19,2, 464 passim. According to Dieter Mertens, most intellectuals of the fifteenth century knew Piccolomini's Diet speeches. He proves that famous speeches in the sixteenth century (e.g., by Bessarion and Campano) were based on Piccolomini's speeches; Mertens, "Europa, id est patria," 52.
61. Housley, *Crusading and the Ottoman Threat*, 160.
62. Piccolomini also inserted his Regensburg speech into his history of the Regensburg Imperial Diet as well as in his Commentarii; see R. Wolkan, ed., *Der Briefwechsel des Eneas Silvius Piccolomini. Abt. 3. Briefe als Bischof von Siena*, vol. 1: *Briefe von seiner Erhebung zum Bischof von Siena bis zum Ausgang des Regensburger Reichstages (23. September 1450–1. June 1454)* (Wien: Verlag der Österreichischen Akademie der Wissenschaften, 1918), 538–47.
63. See Piccolomini's letters to Juan de Carvajal and Gregorius Lollius, RTA 19,2, no. 13, 1 and 13, 2. For the distribution of his orations at the Imperial Diet of Wiener Neustadt, see Piccolomini's letters to Nicholas of Cusa (5 May 1455, RTA 19,3, no. 51d) and Cardinal Lodovico Scarampo (29 April 1455, RTA 19,3, no. 27k).
64. See Piccolomini's letter to Nicholas of Cusa (RTA 19,2, no. 13, 6, 31 October 1454).
65. The small number of textual varieties in these copies suggests a fast and synchronic distribution of the text; RTA 19,2, 470–473. With 120 known copies, his Mantua keynote address "Cum bellum hodie," given on 26 September 1459, reached an even broader distribution. Housley, *Crusading and the Ottoman Threat*, 160–61.

66. RTA 19,2, 463.
67. For a better understanding, Piccolomini's speech was immediately translated into German, which furthered its understanding and promotion by the audience. "*Hanc orationem cum verbis latinis pronuntiasset Eneas factumque esset mirum silentium assurgens Ulricus episcopus Gurcensis* [Ulrich Sonnenberger, Bf. Von Gurk] *eandem in sermonem Theutonicum convertit, ne quis ex circumstantibus mentem caesaris ignoraret,*" RTA 19,1, 265. The delegates present at the Imperial Diets cited Piccolomini's speeches in their reports, see, e.g., the reports of the Nuremberg delegates Niklas Muffel and Hans Pirckheimer, RTA 19,3, Nr. 33d, 503–9.
68. The fundamental influence that the development of the printing press had on the dissemination and preservation of texts and on changing public spheres was described in 1979 by Elizabeth Eisenstein in her voluminous book *The Printing Revolution in Early Modern Europe* (Cambridge: Cambridge University Press, 2005).
69. "Constantinopolitana clades" was printed as a single text and as part of a collection of other texts, e.g., as part of Piccolomini's *Epistolae familiars*, printed in Strasbourg in 1478; see RTA 19,3, 442.
70. The practice of annotating humanist orations in general with technical vocabulary is proof that it was used as a style sheet; see RTA 19,3, 447. Johannes Helmrath has repeatedly and perspicuously shown the connection between humanist rhetoric style and the orations against the Turks; see, e.g., Helmrath, "Pius II. und die Türken."
71. Helmrath, "German 'Reichstage,'" 53; Mertens, "Europa, id est patria," 51–52, 56. Piccolomini's speeches were not only adopted because of their content but also because they served as models for an excellent rhetorical style; RTA 19,2, 472.
72. J. Varga, "Europa und 'Die Vormauer des Christentums': Die Entwicklungsgeschichte eines geflügelten Wortes," in *Europa und die Türken in der Renaissance*, ed. B. Guthmüller and W. Kühlmann (Tübingen: Niemeyer, 2000), 60–62.
73. Most prominently is J. Hankins, "Renaissance Crusaders: Humanist Crusade Literature in the Age of Mehmed II," *Dumbarton Oaks Papers* 49 (1995): 111–207; Meserve, "Italian Humanists."
74. Hankins, "Renaissance Crusaders," 123 passim.
75. Quoted in Krzyżaniakowa, "Polen," 138.
76. B. Baldi, *Pio II e le trasformazioni dell'Europa Cristiana, 1457–1464* (Milano: Unicopli, 2006), 173–254.
77. Piccolomini's Diet speeches served as model for papal delegates such as Capistrano and Bessarion; see Mertens, "Europa, id est patria," 52.
78. On Leo X, see K.M. Setton, "Penrose Memorial Lecture. Pope Leo X and the Turkish Peril," *Proceedings of the American Philosophical Society* 113 (1969), 376, 383.
79. Borkowska, "Ideology," 1206; Srodecki, *Antemurale christianitatis*. However, Poland and Hungary were not the only states described as *antemurale* states. Beside various Eastern European territories, the *antemurale* metaphor was also applied to Byzantium, Spain, Venice, and Austria; Borkowska, "Ideology," 1207; Srodecki, *Antemurale christianitatis*, 352–60.
80. Krzyżaniakowa, "Polen," 132 passim. Wictor Weintraub shows that until the second half of the sixteenth century, the most prominent descriptions of Poland as an *antemurale* state were of European rather than Polish origin; Weintraub, "Renaissance Poland," 980. Knoll, too, states that the *antemurale* topos was not yet a national concept in late medieval Poland; Knoll, "Poland."

81. Srodecki, *Antemurale Christianitatis*, 361–68.
82. Borkowska, "Ideology," 1206; Knoll, "Poland," 385–86; Srodecki, *Antemurale Christianitatis*, 57–104.
83. Borkowska, "Ideology," 1208; Srodecki, *Antemurale Christianitatis*, 57–62.
84. See the examples in Borkowska, "Ideology," 1206; Knoll, "Poland," 385 passim; Srodecki, *Antemurale Christianitatis*, 57–104.
85. Srodecki, *Antemurale Christianitatis*, 57–62.
86. Weintraub, "Renaissance Poland"; Krzyżaniakowa, "Polen."
87. In a diplomatic context, and especially in the letters written by the Popes, the attributes of *propugnaculum, antemurale,* and *scutum* became almost inevitable in addressing Hungary; see, e.g., *Vetera monumenta historica Hungariam sacram illustrantia*, vol. 2, 398 (Paul II, 1664); 315 (Callixt III, 1458); 361 (Pius II 1461), 482, (Sixtus IV, 1483); 490 (Sixtus IV, 1484).
88. Weintraub, "Renaissance Poland," 930.
89. For Vitéz's role in promoting the concept of bulwark, see Borkowska, "Ideology."
90. RTA 19,3, 451.
91. The manuscript is preserved in the Praiského Hradu Archives, RTA 19,2, 472.
92. Srodecki, *Antemurale Christianitatis*, 170–216.
93. The development of a national humanist historiography took place in a transnational cultural context. It was mutually connected and reached far beyond the humanist "mainlands" such as Italy. This is proven by the essays collected in J. Helmrath, U. Muhlack, and G. Walther, eds., *Diffusion des Humanismus. Studien zur nationalen Geschichtsschreibung europäischer Humanisten* (Göttingen: Wallstein, 2002) and especially by the introduction of U. Muhlack, "Humanistische Historiographie," 30–34.
94. For the role Callimachus played in the promotion of the *antemurale* concept in Poland, see S. Graciotti, "L'antemurale Pollacco in Italia tra Cinquecento e seicento," in *Il barocchi di un mito. Barocco fra Italia e Polonia*, ed. J. Ślaski (Warszawa: Accademia polacca delle scienze, Comitato degli studi sull'arte, 1977), 304, 322; Srodecki, *Antemurale Christianitatis*, 225–28.
95. Graciotti, "L'antemurale Pollacco in Italia," 304.
96. A. Prezdziecki, ed., *Joannis Długosssi seu longini canonici cracoviensis Historiae Polonicae* (Kraków: Typografia Kirchmayeriana, 1878), vol. 5, 360. See Borkowska, "Ideology," 1207–08; Knoll, "Poland," 921; Krzyżaniakowa, "Polen," 132.
97. RTA 19,2, 495 passim.
98. Srodecki, *Antemurale Christianitatis*, 306.
99. Krzyżaniakowa, "Polen," 140–41. Borkowska, "Ideology of 'antemurale,'" 1210
100. Krzyżaniakowa, "Polen," 140 passim.
101. Weintraub, "Renaissance Poland," 927.
102. Borkowska, "Ideology of 'antemurale,'" 1213.
103. Cit. and transl. Borkowska, "Ideology of 'antemurale,'" 1214.
104. Cit. and transl. ibid., 1214.
105. Ibid., 1208, 1211; Kenneweg, "Antemurale Christianitatis," 76 passim.
106. Jolanta T. Pekacz speaks of "megalomania" and "xenophobia" being closely linked to the *antemurale* reception in Poland; Pekacz, "'Antemurale' of Europe," passim.
107. Krzyżaniakowa, "Polen," 133.
108. Ibid., 140–41; Hein-Kircher, "Überlegungen," 115.

109. Borkowska, "Ideology of 'antemurale,'" 1215 passim; Pekacz, "'Antemurale' of Europe," 421.
110. Helmrath et al., *Diffusion des Humanismus*.

Bibliography

Babinger, F. 1953. *Mehmed der Eroberer und seine Zeit. Weltenstürmer einer Zeitenwende*. München: Bruckmann Verlag (repr. 1987).

Baldi, B. 2006. *Pio II e le trasformazioni dell'Europa Cristiana, 1457–1464*. Milano: Unicopli.

Borkowska, U. 1982. "The Ideology of 'Antemurale' in the Sphere of Slavic Culture (13th–17th Centuries)." In *The Common Christian Roots of the European Nations*, vol. 2., ed. Pontificia Università Lateranense, 1206–1221. Firenze: Le Monnier.

Eisenstein, E. 2005. *The Printing Revolution in Early Modern Europe*. Cambridge: Cambridge University Press.

Graciotti, S. 1977. "L'antemurale Pollacco in Italia tra Cinquecento e seicento." In *Il barocchi di un mito. Barocco fra Italia e Polonia*, ed. J. Ślaski, 302–23. Warszawa: Accademia polacca delle scienze, Comitato degli studi sull'arte.

Hankins, J. 1995. "Renaissance Crusaders: Humanist Crusade Literature in the Age of Mehmed II." *Dumbarton Oaks Papers* 49: 111–207.

Hein-Kircher, H. 2009. "Überlegungen zur Ausprägung und Funktion von Raummythen." In *Deutschlands östliche Nachbarschaften: eine Sammlung von historischen Essays für Hans Henning Hahn*, ed. E. Dmitrów and T. Weger, 105–20. Frankfurt a.M.: Peter Lang.

Helmrath, J. 2000. "Pius II. und die Türken." In *Europa und die Türken in der Renaissance*, ed. Bodo Guthmüller and Wilhelm Kühlmann, 79–137. Tübingen: Niemeyer.

———. 2002. "Art. Union, kirchliche III. Konzil von Ferrara, Florenz." *Lexikon des Mittelalters* 8: 1241–42.

———. 2004. "The German 'Reichstage' and the Crusade." In *Crusading in the Fifteenth Century. Message and Impact*, ed. N. Housley, 53–69. Basingstoke: Palgrave Macmillan.

———. 2005. "Enea Silvio Piccolomini (Pius II.). Ein Humanist als Vater des Europagedankens?" In *Europa und die Europäer: Quellen und Essays zur modernen europäischen Geschichte. Festschrift für Hartmut Kaelble zum 65. Geburtstag*, ed. R. Hohls, 361–69. Stuttgart: Steiner.

Helmrath, J., U. Muhlack, and G. Walther, eds. 2002. *Diffusion des Humanismus. Studien zur nationalen Geschichtsschreibung europäischer Humanisten*. Göttingen: Wallstein.

Housley, N. 2012. *Crusading and the Ottoman Threat, 1453–1505*. Oxford: Oxford University Press,.

Kaemmerer, W., ed. 1969. *Deutsche Reichstagsakten. Ältere Reihe. Abt. 5. vol. 19, 1: Deutsche Reichstagsakten unter Kaiser Friedrich III., 1453—1454*. Göttingen: Vandenhoeck & Ruprecht.

———, ed. 2013. *Deutsche Reichstagsakten. Ältere Reihe, Abt. 5, vol. 19, 2: Deutsche Reichstagsakten unter Kaiser Friedrich III. Reichsversammlung zu Frankfurt 1454*. München: Oldenbourg.

———, ed. 2013. *Deutsche Reichstagsakten unter Kaiser Friedrich III. Abt. 5, Teil 3: Reichsversammlung zu Wiener Neustadt 1455.* München: Oldenbourg.
Kenneweg, A.C. 2012. "Antemurale christianitatis." In *Europäische Erinnerungsorte*, vol. 2: *Das Haus Europa*, ed. P. den Boer, H. Duchhardt, and G. Kreis, 73–81. München: Oldenbourg Verlag.
Knoll, P.W. 1974. "Poland as 'antemurale christianitatis' in the late Middle Ages." *The Catholic Historical Review* 60: 381–401.
Konrad, F. 2010. "Von der 'Türkengefahr' zu Exotismus und Orientalismus: Der Islam als Antithese Europas (1453–1914)?." In *Europäische Geschichte Online (EGO)*, ed. Institut für Europäische Geschichte. Mainz. Retrieved 15 September from http://www.ieg-ego.eu/konradf-2010-de.
Krzyżaniakowa, J. 1996. "Polen als antemurale christianitatis. Zur Vorgeschichte eines Mythos." In *Mythen in Geschichte und Geschichtsschreibung aus polnischer und deutscher Sicht*, ed. A. von Saldern, 132–46. Münster: LIT.
Külzer, A. 2006. "Die Eroberung von Konstantinopel im Jahre 1204 in der Erinnerung der Byzantiner." In *Quarta Crociata. Venezia—Bisanzio—Impero Latino*, ed. G. Ortalli, 619–32. Venezia: Istituto Veneto di Scienze.
Lilie, R.-J. 2013. *Byzanz: Geschichte des oströmischen Reiches 326–1453*. München: C.H. Beck.
Mertens, D. 1991. "Europäischer Friede und Türkenkrieg im Spätmittelalter." In *Zwischenstaatliche Friedenswahrung in Mittelalter und Früher Neuzeit*, ed. H. Duchhardt, 45–90. Köln: Böhlau.
———. 1997. "'Europa, id est patria, domus propria, sedes nostra.' Zu Funktionen und Überlieferung lateinischer Türkenreden im 15. Jahrhundert." In *Europa und die osmanische Expansion im ausgehenden Mittelalter*, ed. F.-R. Erkens, 39–57. Berlin: Duncker & Humblot.
Meserve, M. 2004. "Italian Humanists and the Problem of the Crusade." In *Crusading in the Fifteenth Century. Message and Impact*, ed. N. Housley, 13–38. Basingstoke: Palgrave Macmillan.
———. 2009. *Empires of Islam in Renaissance Historical Thought*. Cambridge, MA: Harvard University Press.
Meuthen, E. 1983. "Der Fall von Konstantinopel und der lateinische Westen." *Historische Zeitschrift* 237: 1–35.
Morawiec, M. 2001. "*Antemurale christianitatis*. Polen als Vormauer des christlichen Europa." *Jahrbuch für Europäische Geschichte* 2: 249–60.
Osterhammel, J. 1995. "Kulturelle Grenzen in der Expansion Europas." *Saeculum. Jahrbuch für Universalgeschichte* 46: 101–38.
Pekacz, J. 1995. "Antemurale of Europe; from the History of National Megalomania in Poland." *History of European Ideas* 20: 419–24.
Prezdziecki, A., ed. 1878. *Joannis Długosssi seu longini canonici cracoviensis Historiae Polonicae*. Kraków: Typogr. Kirchmayeriana.
Reinhardt, V. 2013. *Pius II. Piccolomini. Der Papst, mit dem die Renaissance begann. Eine Biographie*. München: C.H. Beck.
Setton, K.M. 1969. "Penrose Memorial Lecture. Pope Leo X and the Turkish Peril." *Proceedings of the American Philosophical Society* 113: 367–424.
Srodecki, P. 2012. "Validissima semper *christianitatis* propugnacula. Zur Entstehung der Bollwerksrhetorik in Polen und Ungarn im Spätmittelalter und in der frühen

Neuzeit." In *Sarmatismus versus Orientalismus in Mitteleuropa*, ed. M. Długosz and P.O. Scholz, 131–68. Berlin: Frank und Timmer.

———. 2015. *Antemurale christianitatis. Zur Genese der Bollwerksrhetorik im östlichen Mitteleuropa an der Schwelle vom Mittelalter zur Frühen Neuzeit*. Husum: Matthiesen Verlag.

Stauber, R. 2008. "Nation." In *Enzyklopädie der Neuzeit*. Vol. 8, 1056–82. Stuttgart: Metzler Verlag.

Theiner, A., ed. 1859–1860. *Vetera monumenta historica Hungariam sacram illustrantia*. 2 vols. Roma: Typis Vaticanae.

Varga, J. 2000. "Europa und 'Die Vormauer des Christentums.' Die Entwicklungsgeschichte eines geflügelten Wortes." In *Europa und die Türken in der Renaissance*, ed. B. Guthmüller and W. Kühlmann, 55–63. Tübingen: Niemeyer.

Weintraub, W. 1979–1980. "Renaissance Poland and *Antemurale christianitatis*." *Harvard Ukrainian Studies* 3/4: 920–30.

Wolkan, R., ed. 1909. *Der Briefwechsel des Eneas Silvius Piccolomini, I. Briefe aus der Laienzeit, 1431–1445,* vol. 1: *Privatbriefe*. vol. 2: *Amtliche Briefe*. Wien: Verlag der Österreichischen Akademie der Wissenschaften.

———, ed. 1918. *Der Briefwechsel des Eneas Silvius Piccolomini. Abt. 3. Briefe als Bischof von Siena,* vol. 1: *Briefe von seiner Erhebung zum Bischof von Siena bis zum Ausgang des Regensburger Reichstages (23. September 1450–1. June 1454)*. Wien: Verlag der Österreichischen Akademie der Wissenschaften.

PART II

(De-)Sacralizing and Nationalizing Borderlands

CHAPTER 2

Not a Bulwark, but a Part of the Larger Catholic Community
The Romanian Greek Catholic Church in Transylvania (1700–1850)

Ciprian Ghisa

At the beginning of the eighteenth century, all three major regions inhabited by a Romanian majority population were under external occupation: Wallachia and Moldova were under the control of the Turkish Empire, whereas Transylvania was brought into the Habsburg Empire (1691) in the context of the Austrian offensive toward the East after the failed Ottoman siege of Vienna in 1683. If outside of the Carpathians, the Romanian elite focused on the internal situation and tried to find ways to regain internal autonomy and control, in the Principality of Transylvania the situation for the Romanians was very different. A bulwark rhetoric could not be used here, because, as we will see, the "Orthodox danger" was interpreted as coming from inside Romanian society. Instead, the Greek Catholic elites promoted the membership of the larger Catholic community and elaborated the idea of an inner civilizing mission to create an integrating historical link to their "ancestors," the Romans.

Vienna seized control of a Transylvanian principality characterized by multiethnicity and multiconfessionalism. Having deep medieval roots, the political and religious system of Transylvania was based on the existence of three privileged nations (Hungarians, Saxons, Szecklers) and of four officially recognized confessions (Catholicism, Calvinism, Lutheranism, and Unitarianism).[1] The Romanians found themselves outside this system from the political and national perspective as well as from the confessional one, since the Orthodox Church had no official recognition. The Romanians and their religion were only tolerated, and in the seventeenth century were mostly under the strong influence of and pressure from Calvinism, the confession of the Transylvanian princes. The Romanian clergy faced a severe situation, with no social and economic rights, and their priests were assimilated with serfs. Without any theological education, and with many being illiterate, the priests seemingly promoted a cult focused mostly on its ritual elements, filled with numerous superstitions.[2] The Romanians lacked a real intellectual nonclerical elite. The metropolitan from Alba Iulia was their spiritual as well as national and political leader. Their focus was on themselves, and their efforts were constantly directed to the preservation of their own traditions and religiosity.

In the seventeenth century there was no specific, clearly formulated discourse of identity, because the right conditions and persons able to create one did not exist. The Romanians lacked a broader external perspective, except the protection given to them by the Orthodox bishops and princes from Moldova and Wallachia. In a sense, the Romanian population from Transylvania was rather isolated from the key ideological debates of the time. In the absence of a political role and facing so many economic and social difficulties, the most important aspect of their lives was religion. In this sense, the situation in Transylvania resembled the late nineteenth-century position of the Greek Catholic Church in Habsburg Galicia, described by Liliya Berezhnaya in this book.

Supported by the Viennese court, the Jesuits approached the Romanian hierarchy and tried to convince them to accept the union with the Church of Rome, following the model of union offered in the fifteenth century by the Council of Florence. Their initiative was successful and the Union of the Transylvanian Romanians was accomplished in 1697–1700 as a result of three Uniate synods organized in Alba Iulia.[3] The representatives of the clergy, led by the metropolitans Teofil (1692–1697) and Atanasie Anghel (1698–1713), signed three declarations proclaiming the union of the "Romanians' Church in Transylvania" with the "Catholic Church of Rome," accepting "all the elements believed and confessed by this Church" and primarily the four elements of faith discussed at the Council in Florence (papal primacy, filioque, purgatory, and the unleavened bread).

The Eastern rite, their own traditions, liturgical language, calendar, and institutional organization were preserved. At the same time, the Romanians requested the political, social, and economic rights that had been promised by Emperor Leopold I (1640–1705) shortly after the integration of Transylvania in the empire. A proper educated elite started to form step by step after the opening of the first schools, monasteries, and printing house in Blaj in the middle of the eighteenth century. Led by bishops like Inochentie Micu Klein (1732–1745) and Petru Pavel Aron (1751–1764), young men were sent to study abroad in Rome, Vienna, or Hungary. They formed the first intellectual elite of the Romanians from Transylvania and had an immediate impact on education, pastoral activity, and the creation of a specific discourse of identity.

The union led to a confessional separation within the Romanian nation in Transylvania, creating the context for numerous confessional disputes. The newly created Church had to face very difficult challenges, being forced to defend the fundamentals of its doctrine and its loyalty toward the nation. The eighteenth century was mainly the period of confessional disputes between Uniatism and Orthodoxy inside the same national group.

The Orthodox reaction eventually came toward the middle of the eighteenth century. The union was challenged by Orthodoxy, and it paid a very high price for its lack of solidity and organization. The first major action was not taken until 1744, with a second wave in 1759–1761, led by monks supported by the Serbian metropolitan from Karlowitz, who was the only Orthodox hierarch in the territories of the Habsburg monarchy at that time.

The first episode of this inner Romanian confessional confrontation began on 11 March 1744, when the Serbian monk Visarion Sarai (1714–1745) entered Transylvania. As proven at his trial, he had little dogmatic knowledge. But due to his ascetic life and alleged visions of the Virgin Mary, the Romanian population welcomed him as an authentic holy man. His message was direct and had a powerful impact on the people. He denied that he preached against the union, but it is apparent that he portrayed it in gray colors in his sermons, drawing attention to the fact that only those persevering in the faith they were born into could hope for eternal salvation.[4] Likewise, Visarion also contested the validity of the ordinations and baptisms performed by the Uniate Church.[5] In the trial of 27 April 1744, he openly expressed his uncertainty: how was it possible for someone to be saved by belonging to two religions at the same time? This was because, in his opinion, Uniate people professed a religion that was actually a combination of the faith of the Latins and the Orthodox faith,[6] and the Eastern law was lost through union with the Catholics.

The shock was complete, especially as there were several cases in which peasants said that, for the first time, they heard from "a man sent by God" that their priests had accepted the union and that they themselves were considered Uniates. By claiming that the sacraments bestowed by the Uniate priests lacked validity, Visarion actually threatened those who received them with the imminence of hell[7]—a very striking, simple message for people who stated that they had no idea that they were united with the Church of Rome. This led to a violent reaction against the Uniate priests, who were denounced as papists, meaning they belonged to the Latin law, were alien and dangerous, and were "devils from hell."[8] The most surprising fact, though, is that almost fifty years after the celebration of the union, there were still people who had not even heard about it. Without being educated in this sense, without having it explained what being Uniate meant, the believers were left to continue with their old principles.

Under these conditions, we can assert that in 1744, people protected their old Orthodox faith, understood as the sum of the ritual practices inherited from their ancestors. However, we must also take into consideration the fact that this *Romanian*, traditional, Orthodox *law* also contained an ethnic element. The Romanian people identified with it, as it was also their national individuality, differentiating them from the other Transylvanian nations. The historian Inokai Tóth Zoltán (1911–1956) stated, "The essence of the Romanian community was, consequently, Orthodoxy, envisioned in tradition."[9] This is why the Uniate priests were accused of being papists, meaning that they belonged to a different law but also to a different nation. So, in the moment of the first serious confrontation, a real crisis of identity, religious as well as national, exploded.[10]

The union experienced a second blow when the monk Sofronie, again from Karlowitz, came to Transylvania in the second half of 1759. He was much more energetic than Visarion.[11] Sofronie was a virulent opponent of the union. He spoke out against those Uniate priests who had been ordained in Blaj, by the bishop confirmed by the Pope. He openly urged the people to abandon their Uniate clergy and to receive priests who had been ordained according to the Eastern rite, in Karlowitz. The central element of the discourse was connected again to the rite, the law. He took up the idea of Visarion Sarai, according to which the Uniates obeyed two laws so that neither baptism nor the other sacraments performed by the Uniates had any sacramental value.[12]

The Uniates were actually "German-like papist people," so the people feared that if they became Uniates, they would themselves have been transformed into papists.[13] Sofronie directly referred to those elements that had an impact on the people. The historian Ovidiu Ghitta emphasized that the option was expressed as necessarily between, "tradition and innovation; more precisely, between being loyal to a thing very clearly portrayed in their mind at that time (*the old Greek rite*) or to one stigmatized as a carrier of the attribute of the novelty (*the modern union*)."[14]

The effect of these movements was devastating for the Union with Rome. The Uniate Church in Transylvania lost four-fifths of its believers after the events in 1761,[15] and it took it more than thirty years to get back half of them through intensive missionary activity and with the very extensive support of the Austrian Court—including military support, funds, and legislation. A balance between the two Romanian Churches was reached only toward 1850, when approximately 55 percent of the Romanian population of Transylvania was Orthodox and 45 percent was Greek Catholic—

or Uniate. This proportion remained more or less the same until the middle of the twentieth century.

Besides the actions of different monks who came to Transylvania from Serbia or from Wallachia (the last important action of this kind was seen in 1828–1832 in the southern part of Transylvania and was dealt with by the Uniate bishop Ioan Lemeni [1780–1861], who called on the support of the army), the union also had to face the polemic sustained by the non-Uniates through books and manuscripts that contained a strong antiunion message and that had been distributed throughout the Transylvanian parishes (in spite of the many imperial decrees forbidding their introduction and distribution—such as those from 23 November 1746, renewed on 6 June 1768, or those from 1765).

These writings were part of a larger polemic between Catholics and Orthodox that was very energetic in the seventeenth to eighteenth centuries. They were a local reflection, adapted to the specific context of Transylvania, of an increasing tension between the two confessions. The reaction from the wider Orthodox region was sustained and encouraged by Dositheos (1641–1707), the Patriarch of Jerusalem, mostly after 1672, when he spent several years in the Romanian principalities. Many of the Greek books written against Calvinism and Catholicism were printed in Wallachia and Moldavia, where the state authority was a fervent supporter of such activities.[16]

Some of these works were also translated into Romanian. The most important one was the book of Maxim the Peloponnesian, printed in Snagov, near Bucharest, by Antim Ivireanu, the future metropolitan of Wallachia, under the title *Carte sau lumină cu drepte dovediri din dogmele Bisericii Răsăritului asupra dejghinării papistașilor* (Book or Light with True Proofs from the Dogmas of the Eastern Church on the Schism of the Papists, 1699).[17] It was widely distributed in Transylvania, being a pièce de résistance of the antiunion polemic literature. It was structured in chapters, each referring to one of the points from Florence with the purpose of combating them. The main focus was on papal primacy, debated on 164 of the 210 pages of the book.

The Florentine arguments were considered heretical and "novelties," and the Latins were blamed for being responsible for the separation of the Church (*dejghinarea Bisericii*). The message was direct, unambiguous, and blunt. Importantly, these translations of Greek writings do not promote a bulwark myth that could have claimed that Romanian Orthodoxy defended global Orthodoxy in the face of Catholic and Protestant propaganda, as they were meant to address the internal, Romanian situation, with a lot of focus on what was happening in Transylvania after the Union with Rome.

Besides the printed books, various manuscripts also circulated in Transylvania during the eighteenth century. *Întrebări și răspunsuri despre legea a treia ce s-a izvodit adică Uniia în Țara Ardealului* (Questions and Answers on the Third Law that Appeared, Meaning the Union, in the Land of Transylvania) was a text by the hegumen Visarion from the monastery of Upper Sâmbăta (southern Transylvania) from 1746, representing the transcription of a public debate between the Uniate archpriest of Făgăraș, Vasile Baran, and the non-Uniate father Vasile, the future hegumen Visarion, supposedly won by the latter.[18] We may also mention another text, a retort to *Floarea adevărului*, that was published in Blaj in 1750 (see below). It was a manuscript dated between 1750 and 1755, anonymous and brought out in Wallachia, probably in Râmnic, by someone close to Bishop Grigore III (1749–1764) or even by the bishop himself.[19] We could also add different popular texts such as the rhymed chronicle titled *Plângerea sfintei mănăstiri a Silvașului din eparhia Hațegului din Prislop* (The Cry of the Silvaș Monastery from the District of Hațeg from Prislop), which carries a strong antiunion message.[20]

What were the accusations brought by the non-Uniates against the Uniates? First of all, the disagreement on the four doctrinal points brings with it the accusation of heresy. The authors used the arguments that had been frequent in the old disputes between Latins and Greeks, contradicting the principle formulated by the Uniates that only through the union with the Church of Rome had the Romanians finally accepted the entirety of the true faith as an essential condition for redemption. The non-Uniate writers also mentioned the fact that the Church of Rome was guilty of seventy-two heretical doctrines identified by Constantine Panaghiot. This number is given in both aforementioned texts.[21] The 1746 manuscript strongly argued that the idea of entering into possession of the whole arsenal of the true teaching of Christ through the union was in fact a "betrayal" of their own ancestors who had died before 1700. It would have meant that these had suffered eternal damnation. Therefore, the Uniates were the ones that had left the "fatherly law" behind.[22]

These authors also formulated the theory of "the union as the third way." The text from 1746 called the Uniate Church "the Third Church"[23] and addressed believers with the following words: "Uniates, you are not in the law of the Pope and neither in ours."[24] The Uniates were also called "threefold in law, namely Uniates,"[25] whereas the non-Uniates were described as "those who did not accept the third law, namely the non-Uniates."[26] The 1750–1755 text also made a surprising comparison, saying that the Church, "our Mother," was nursing us, "with both her sweet breasts of the old and new laws," whereas the Uniates "devised a new mother with three breasts." The author added, "Of course, a woman with three breasts is impossible to find."[27] He also told the Uniates, "Because as you are right now, you are neither on the side of the Easterners, nor on that of the Westerners, you are neither warm nor cold."[28]

The authors specified that the union was not a real one because it could not reflect the original union between the Church of the East and the Church of the West.[29] The myth of golden origins is traceable in these writings. Obviously, the guilt for the separation belonged to the Westerners, and to the Popes in particular:

> The Church of the East did not separate itself from the Church of Rome; it remained in the state in which the Holy Apostles and the Holy Councils had left it. The Pope separated from it like a putrid limb that was worthy to be thrown away because of his fabrications and impious acts.[30]

Rome was presented as the Great Babylon in these writings, the home of the devils, as predicted in the Book of Revelation 18:2.[31]

These elements lead us to a very important question: what were the main arguments that the Uniates formulated in their discourse? The entire context changed for the union in just fifteen years. The Uniate Church was no longer the Church of all Romanians from Transylvania. At the same time, the position of Orthodoxy was strengthened when an imperial decree from July 1759 acknowledged that the Orthodox population in the province was free to practice its religion. Thus, the Uniate Church ceased to be the single official Church of the Transylvanian Romanians. The change was radical: from majority to minority, from uniqueness to plurality. The response had to come rapidly to consolidate what was left and to be able to counterattack.

The Uniate Church appeared to be a community under siege, and it had to act rapidly to protect its current and future members. In order to achieve these goals, the Uniate discourse focused on the ideas that the Greek Catholic Church was the Church of Christ, its faith was true, and redemption was not linked to the practice of a rigid rite. Step by step, the narrative also approached the topos of the civilizing mission of the Uniate Church for the entire nation, insisting on its membership of the universal community of the Church of Rome, superior in culture and spirit. A bulwark discourse could not be fully promoted, as the "danger" was coming from the inside of the community, and the protective action did not also benefit other communities with the same values and beliefs. Only one element of the bulwark mythology, the topos of the civilizing mission, could be truly elaborated at that time.

The years 1744–1761 proved to be decisive for the union to articulate a clear vision of itself. The Uniate bishops, Petru Pavel Aron (1751–1764), Atanasie Rednic (1764–1772), and Grigore Maior (1772–1782), quickly understood the need for determined action, for real missionary work. The real union could be developed only after the clergy successfully assimilated elements of Catholic dogma and began to present it to the people from their communities.[32] They realized the need to establish an Eastern Catholic identity that was to be completely accepted by the clergy and faithful. The priests had to present the elements of the Catholic faith to the people.

A lot of energy, diplomacy, and determination were needed in order to overcome the limits imposed by people's conservatism. The activity of these bishops meant pastoral visits, district and provincial synods, scholarships for a significant number of future clergymen allowing them to study abroad, the foundation of schools—in the villages, but mainly in Blaj, which became the center of the theological educational system of the Greek Catholics—publication of a large number of books promoting the Union with Rome, and the publication of new liturgical books to replace the Orthodox ones in the parishes. We can notice here a real program of revival, of internal reform of the Greek Catholic Church in the spirit of the post-Tridentine Catholic Reformation.

Thus, in the middle of the eighteenth century, the Greek Catholic hierarchy understood that it was the moment to pursue a major and coherent initiative to form and to strengthen the confessional identity of its own believers. The members of the Greek Catholic elite formulated two types of discourse. The first was meant to convince the faithful of the truthfulness of the Catholic doctrine and of the fact that the union *in fide* did not bring about any changes in the Greek rite.[33] They focused on the presentation of the four Florentine arguments, described not as novelties but as a part of the whole teaching based on the Scripture, confirmed by the Church councils and preached by the Holy Fathers of the Church. The second type of discourse was complementary to the first one. It was constructed as an answer to the accusations brought by the non-Uniates.

This discourse had a defensive and nonunitary character because it only referred to the questions raised by the non-Uniates. This is why we may call it apologetic. The two types of discourses were promoted by a large number of printed books: *Floarea adevărului* (*Flocusculus veritatis*, Blaj, 1750)[34]; *Învăţărură creştinească* (*Doctrina Christiana*, Blaj, four editions between 1755 and 1763); *Dialog ucenicul cu dascălul* (Dialogue between Master and Disciple, 1756); Petru Pavel Aron, *Păstoriceasca datorie* (Duties of Pastoral Life, 1759); Petru Pavel Aron, *Pastoriceasca poslanie* (Pastoral Letter, 1760); Niceta Horvat, *Poslanie* (Letter, Oradea, 1780); Dimitrie Vaida, *Cuvântări* (Orations, Blaj, 1813); Theodor Aron (1803–1867), *Catehetica practică* (Practical Cathechesis, Buda, 1843); Iosif Pop Sălăjean, *Scurtă istorie a credinţei românilor din sfintele cărţi şi adevărate documente dedusă* (Short History of the Faith of the Romanians Blaj, 1845); catechisms; and prayer books.

The central issue of a real union with the Church of Rome, therefore, was faith. The abovementioned books insisted on the idea that this true faith was the Catholic faith, which was believed by the Romanian Uniates.

All necessary elements for redemption are thus included. This faith must be believed and lived in its completeness, as its foundations were Holy Scripture, the Holy Fathers, the Holy Synods, and the books of the Eastern Church.[35] In these territories between Catholicism and Orthodoxy, the Uniate Church became the defender and promoter of the Catholic faith, considered the true religion. From this perspective, the Uniate discourse did not focus on the idea of its uniqueness and specificity but on the inclusion of this Romanian Church into a larger spiritual but also cultural entity, that of the Roman Catholic Church.

This type of discourse led to the creation of a certain level of awareness in the Uniate community of the fact that the Romanian Greek Catholics were the same as the Roman Catholics. In an 1814 sermon by Ioan Lemeni (1780–1861), at that time the archpriest of Cluj, which was published in Hungarian and held at the local academy, one can find a very striking formulation: "we, the Catholic ones."[36] His words are very significant because they do not draw any distinction between the Roman Catholics and the Greek Catholics—all of them belong to the same ecclesiastical community.

Once the Catholic faith was defended and the union *in fide* was proclaimed, the Uniate authors often compared the realities from the time before the union to those from the period after 1700. They described two very contrasting pictures, one completely negative and one absolutely positive. The condition of the Romanian people had been very bad before the union, and this situation supposedly improved significantly afterward.

The first writer to engage with this topic was Dimitrie Vaida (a member of the Blaj chapter) in 1813, who described the situation before the union, stating that the Church of the Romanians was in very poor shape, without books and printing houses, celebrating services in a foreign language, "in Russian," with very poor and uneducated priests. The clergy and the people were enveloped in the "deep darkness of ignorance."[37]

The same idea is revealed in the speech dedicated by Ioan Lemeni to his bishop Ioan Bob (1739–1830) in 1814. The author thanked God for not allowing the Romanian people to remain indefinitely in darkness. He also urged the House of Austria and the leading nations from Transylvania to acknowledge "our nation" as part of the official nations of the country. All progress was possible because the Romanians wanted the restoration of the union of the faith.[38]

The leading intellectual of the 1830 generation of Greek Catholic professors from the Blaj seminary, Timotei Cipariu (1805–1887), stated in the historical introduction to his *Schematismus* from 1842 that the condition of the Romanian clergy from Transylvania changed completely after the union. Certain rights and means for a better material and cultural situation were gained, and this improved condition could be seen after the establishment of the bishop's see in Blaj. The wisdom and the enthusiastic action of the bishops proved how one could obtain great results with few resources.[39]

Iosif Pop Sălăjean wrote in 1845 that the Romanians were unwillingly part of the "nonunion," which caused them deep ignorance, blindness, and even damnation.[40] He also quoted August Treboniu Laurian, one of the leading Romanian fighters for national rights in the years of the 1848 revolution, who once wrote, "The nonunion brought misery to the Romanian people."[41]

So, if this was the situation before the union, what were the benefits supposedly gained by the Romanians after joining it? In a sermon to a rural community who had just accepted the union, Vasile Erdelyi, bishop of Oradea (1794–1862), started his speech with the words of Jesus Christ when entering the house of Zacchaeus: "Today salvation has come to this house" (Luke 19:9).[42] This meant that acceptance of the union ensured the path to redemption. The Greek Catholic bishop specified this idea very clearly: "This village found redemption because you received the holy union."[43] And at the end, he added, "Now you are true Romans, you are sons of our homeland. Now you can be proud because you have the Romans as your ancestors. . . . Now you can hope that your sons will learn and get a better life. So be it."[44]

The myth of origins is apparent in this text. The future bishop of Oradea, Iosif Pop Sălăjean, synthetized these aspects in his book. He recalled the Latin origin of the people, of the language, and of the faith of the Romanians, and then added: "Latin, the mother of our language, is the language of the union of the Church."[45] Therefore, the Romanians had always been united in their hearts with the See of Rome. The chance to restore the effective union arose on the occupation of Transylvania by the House of Austria, who granted the Romanian Uniates privileges and opened the "path for the enlightenment and happiness of the people."[46]

Those rights were given to the clergy. Emperor Charles VI (1685–1740) raised Bishop Inochentie Micu (1692–1768) to the rank of baron and offered other resources to the hierarchs from Blaj. They used these for the welfare of the people: Petru Pavel Aron (1709–1764) founded the printing house, removed the "Russian or the Serbian language" from the divine services, and opened the schools in Blaj and the seminary where famous Romanian writers and thinkers graduated from. Funds were created to improve the state of the clergy. Thus, "The Uniates opened the eyes of the nation."[47] In the end, he concluded, the benefits of the union were the return to Rome; the source of life and truth; a better knowledge of the law and of the faith; superior merits vis-à-vis God; enlightenment, culture, morality, holiness, redemption, unity of the nation, national love, peace, and happiness; better ecclesiastical organization; seminaries; educated clergy; and fame and honor for the nation.[48]

These were the benefits of the union, which opened the paths to redemption, strengthened the awareness of people's Latin origins (an idea that was first formulated by Bishop Inochentie Micu in his memos to the court, trying to prove the noble origins of the humiliated Romanian people), and offered opportunities for education as well as economic, social, and political development.

All these aspects led to the idea that the Uniate Church was the one that protected the nation and awoke and developed the national consciousness of the Romanians. One might note that this type of discourse was formulated early in the nineteenth century. These decades brought another serious challenge for the Romanians from Transylvania: an increasingly intense pressure on the part of Hungarian nationalists, who, especially after 1820–1830, promoted the Hungarian language and the union of Transylvania with Hungary. This was, eventually, the key element in the separation of the Romanians and the Hungarians during the revolution and the civil war from 1848 to 1849. Thus the two Romanian Churches, which in practice provided almost all intellectual leaders of the nation, were distracted from the mere confessional disputes by the need to cooperate for the general good of the nation. The Church hierarchs were the most important leaders of the national movement, following the path opened by Bishop Inochentie Micu Klein (1692–1768) in the decades preceding the middle of the eighteenth century. A relevant example are the memos written in the name of the nation and signed by the bishops, who then promoted them vis-à-vis the state authorities in Transylvania or Vienna.[49]

These moments of cooperation strengthened the idea that the nation had to overcome the confessional separation in order to be able to defend itself in the face of this new external danger—Hungarian nationalism. This was the starting point for several Church reunification projects.

All eighteenth-century Uniate authors spoke about the restoration of the unity of the Christians, willed by God and promoted in the Gospels. However, they did not approach the non-Uniates about reconciliation. As long as they considered the non-Uniates to be heretics and schismatics, reunification was in practice impossible. On the other hand, in 1777, Niceta Horvat from Oradea was a special case, as he had a different aim than the other Uniate writers: the need to find a path for dialogue, a formula that would be acceptable for both sides. Of course, he did not abandon presenting the faith he considered to be true, but he addressed the non-Uniates directly, trying to convince them of the solid grounds for his argument. In the second part of his work, he wrote that the Uniates could not be blamed for anything, but neither could the non-Uniates be blamed for being heretics and schismatics, "especially those who are Romanian." He said that the painful separation of the believers was only in the names of "Uniate" and "non-Uniate."[50] Niceta Horvat called for reconciliation on behalf of the Uniate Church. He did not make any concessions regarding faith but formulated a discourse that was far from the intransigent tone of earlier writings.

A few decades later, in 1838, George Bariț (1812–1893), the founder of the first Romanian journal in Transylvania, also suggested the restoration of the union through the conversion of the Orthodox Romanians to Greek Catholicism.[51] In Oradea, similar proposals were made by the priest Petru Rațiu in 1842 and by the future bishop Iosif Pop Sălăjean in 1845.[52] From this perspective, the unification of the two Churches would have been an assimilation of one by the other, as no side was willing to give up its array of doctrines.[53] Under these conditions, confessional unification was very difficult to accomplish.

But out of the desire to give the nation the unity necessary to make it stronger in its struggle for political, social, and economic emancipation, several proposals were made that tried to ignore the dogmatic aspects. In 1792–1796, Samuil Micu (1745–1806), the leader of the most important generation of Uniate clergymen from the second half of the eighteenth century who studied in Rome, wrote his famous book titled *Scurtă cunoștință a istoriei românilor* (Short Abstract of the History of the Romanians, 1796), in which he stated that the only separation between Romanians was based on the word "Uniate"—which was the same argument as that of Niceta Horvat.

However, he made a step forward, suggesting that the Romanians, regardless of their actual religion, be called *pravoslavnic* (believers of the true faith) in the law of the Eastern Church.[54] Separation was only formal. Micu, along with Aron Budai, the Uniate secretary of the non-Uniate bishop in Sibiu, the non-Uniate vicar Ioan Popovici, and the school inspector Radu Tempea (1768–1824), elaborated the first major reunification project, in 1798, which suggested that all Romanians from Transylvania should unite under the name of "Christians of Greek Orthodox Rite of the Eastern Church, namely Catholics," whereas this united Church was to be called "the Eastern Church of Greek Orthodox Rite, namely Catholic." The Church was to be led by one bishop only. The terminological confusion is obvious, as is the wish of the project's authors to achieve a compromise in order to be able to continue the fight for the national rights of the Romanians.[55]

In the years preceding the 1848 revolution, these ideas were also developed by Bariț. In his article titled "Icoana preotului,"[56] he argued that a good priest does everything to avoid confessional disputes and schisms. He labeled as fanatics all those who maintained the religious separation in the name of complicated elements of doctrine that were actually not understood by the common people.[57]

In a letter to George Bariț from 8 March 1848, August Treboniu Laurian (1810–1881) also argued for one "Romanian Church," for a "national Church," for a "Romanian religion" and for "one Romanian law."[58]

This became an important topic in the context of the revolution. The "National Petition" of 15 May 1848 issued by the National Assembly from Blaj stated in its second point that there should be only one "Romanian Church without any confessional distinction," a formula that is unclear and confusing.[59] Interestingly enough, the petition was signed by the two Romanian bishops who were also the presidents of the National Assembly: the Uniate bishop from Blaj, Ioan Lemeni, and the Orthodox bishop from Sibiu, Andrei Șaguna (1809–1873). There was no specification as to faith or as to ecclesiastical jurisdiction. These issues were left for future discussion. At that moment, the two Churches together were again leading the fight in the defense of the nation against the danger of denationalization.

Conclusions

To sum up, the Romanians were increasingly separated into two confessional groups after 1750–1760, competitive and in opposition, fighting one another for control of believers. In this competition, the two Churches based their actions on the following elements:

- The Uniates relied on the new cultural and educational center built in Blaj, starting under the pastoral rule of Bishop Inochentie Micu Klein; on the newly created ecclesiastical elite trained in the Catholic colleges from Rome, Vienna, Bratislava, and Eger; and on the extensive support of the Austrian Court, whose emperor, also bearing the title of "Roman Emperor," was reminded by the Uniates that the Romanians were a Latin people with roots traceable back to ancient Rome.
- The non-Uniates relied on the support given by the Serbian metropolitan from Karlowitz; the support given from Wallachia, especially from the new bishopric of Râmnic, a center that supported antiunion propaganda around the middle of the eighteenth century; the action of different missionaries coming from outside of Transylvania; and, at least on the level of discourse, the support of the "Great Emperor from Moscow," the Russian tsar. One can see here the echo of the tsars' discourse regarding their role as protectors of Orthodoxy in southeastern Europe, in the Balkans, among the Russophiles in Galicia, or in the Crimea.[60]

As a result, both Romanian Churches developed parallel discourses supporting their respective confessional identities, each one stating that only their own Church was the true Church of Christ, the follower of the Church of the Fathers, the true promoter of the Christian faith of the ecumenical councils, the true preserver of the Greek tradition, and the true Eastern Church. Both Churches felt that the offensive came from the other side and tried to defend their own community of believers. The themes used in the dispute were also used in the larger debate between Catholics and Orthodox. The Uniates saw their integration into the Catholic Church as a distinguishing feature, defending in their books and sermons the Catholic faith as a whole, and did not develop a discourse that would have supported a kind of Greek Catholic specificity.

The major confessional disputes ended after 1780, after the pastoral rule of the Uniate bishop Grigore Maior (1715–1785). The involvement of the state also had a lot of influence in this direction, as the Uniate Church benefited from a lot of direct and indirect support from local or central state authorities. The Orthodox Church was disadvantaged by the authorities in most of the disputes with the Greek Catholics, and it also faced serious material, financial, and organizational shortcomings. A real balance was reached only after 1850.

However, the general political context also changed greatly toward the end of the eighteenth century and at the beginning of the nineteenth century, and the Romanians faced a serious challenge from Hungarian nationalism. This forced the elite of the two Churches to follow their political vocation as well and to lead the Romanian national movement into accepting cooperation and ignoring the doctrinal differences in certain cases and at certain moments.

One can notice that a very specific and clear discourse supporting a bulwark myth was not developed in Transylvania in the eighteenth and early nineteenth centuries. On the one hand, the Romanians did not initially have a proper intellectual elite, and when it was formed in the Uniate Church, its focus was on itself and concerned with protecting the Uniate community in the face of challenges raised by the other Romanian religious community: the Orthodox one. Thus, the "Orthodox danger" was seen as one coming from the inside, not the outside. On the other hand, the Greek Catholic writers developed the idea of this Church's civilizing mission, underpinned by its membership of the large Catholic community, which became synonymous with the idea of progress and cultural superiority. This also allowed a link to be made with the past, with the origins of the nations. It brought the Romanians back into contact with their supposed ancestors, the Romans, with the aim of increasing their national awareness and pride.

NOT A BULWARK, BUT A PART OF THE LARGER CATHOLIC COMMUNITY 75

Ciprian Ghisa is a lecturer at the Faculty of Greek Catholic Theology—Babes-Bolyai University from Cluj-Napoca, Romania. He is a Church historian interested in the interconfessional relations in the Romanian areas in the eighteenth–twentieth centuries; the evolution and elaboration of the discourse of identity of the Romanian Orthodox and Greek Catholic Churches; and the evolution of the ecclesiastical institutions in the eighteenth and nineteenth centuries. He published two books on the Greek Catholic discourse of identity in Transylvania between 1700 and 1850 and the state of the Greek Catholic Church at the mid-nineteenth century.

Notes

1. For the internal political makeup of Transylvania, see M. Bernath, *Habsburgii și începutul formării națiunii române* (Cluj-Napoca: Dacia, 1994), 73–86; L. Periș, *Prezențe catolice în Transilvania, Moldova și Țara Românească 1601–1698* (Blaj: Buna Vestire, 2005), 37–61, 220–29.
2. For the state of the Romanian Transylvanian clergy before the union with Rome, see D. Prodan, *Supplex Libellus Valachorum* (București: Ed. Univ. Victor Babeș, 1948), 136; K. Hitchins, "Înainte de unirea cu Roma," in *300 de ani de la unirea Bisericii românești din Transilvania cu Biserica Romei*, ed. G. Gorun and O. Horea Pop (Cluj-Napoca: Presa Universitară Clujeană, 2000), 51–67.
3. For the context and the decisions of the three Uniate synods from 1697 to 1700, see Bernath, *Habsburgii*, 99–105; Prodan, *Supplex*, 138; Z. Pâclișanu, *Istoria Bisericii Române-Unite, partea Ia 1697–1744* (München: Christliche Stimme, 1995), 30; P. Teodor, "În jurul sinodului mitropolitului Teofil din 1697," in *300 de ani de la unirea Bisericii românești din Transilvania cu Biserica Romei*, ed. G. Gorun and O. Horea Pop (Cluj-Napoca: Presa Universitară Clujeană, 2000), 43–50; G.M. Miron, *Biserica greco-catolică din Transilvania. Cler și enoriași (1697–1782)* (Cluj-Napoca: Presa Universitară Clujeană, 2004), 37–40; N. Dănilă, "Noi considerații privind sinodul din octombrie 1698," in *Spiritualitate transilvană și istorie europeană*, ed. I. Mârza and A. Dumitran (Alba Iulia: Muzeul Național al Unirii, 1998), 286–93.
4. K. Hitchins, "Religia și conștiința națională românească în Transilvania în secolul XVIII," in *Conștiința națională și acțiune politică la românii din Transilvania 1700–1868*, vol. 1, ed. Hitchins (Cluj-Napoca: Dacia, 1987), 45.
5. O. Bârlea, "Biserica Română Unită și ecumenismul Corifeilor renașterii culturale," *Perspective*, nos. 3–4 (January–June, 1983): 70–72.
6. G. Bogdan-Duică, *Călugărul Visarion Sarai. Studui istoric din istoria Transilvaniei* (Caransebeș: Tiparul Tipografiei Diecezane, 1896), 19.
7. Hitchins, "Religia și conștiința națională," 48; M. Săsăujan, *Politica bisericească a Curții din Viena în Transilvania (1740–1761)* (Cluj-Napoca: Presa Universitară Clujeană, 2002), 149–50.
8. Hitchins, "Religia și conștiința națională," 49.
9. I.Z. Tòth, *Primul secol al naționalismului românesc ardelean 1697–1792* (București: Pythagora, 2001), 72.
10. Ibid., 71–72, 143.

11. For further information regarding the activity of Sofronie from Cioara, see also S. Dragomir, *Istoria Desrobirii Religioase a Românilor din Ardeal în secolul XVIII*, vol. 2 (Sibiu: Tipografia arhidiecezană, 1920), 154–93; D. Prodan, *Supplex Libellus Valachorum* (București: Științifică și Enciclopedică, 1984), 205–15; O. Ghitta, *Nașterea unei biserici* (Cluj-Napoca: Presa Universitară Clujeană, 2001), 302–38; Săsăujan, *Politica bisericească*, 230–35; G. Gorun, *Reformismul austriac și violențele sociale din Europa centrală 1750–1800* (Oradea: Muzeului Țării Crișurilor, 1998), 162–79.
12. Dragomir, *Istoria Desrobirii Religioase*, 160; Bârlea, "Biserica Română Unită," 123–24.
13. S. Micu, *Istoria românilor*, vol. 2 (București: Viitorul Românesc, 1995), 339; Dragomir, *Istoria Desrobirii Religioase*, 160.
14. Ghitta, *Nașterea unei biserici*, 307.
15. Bârlea, "Biserica Română Unită," 126–27, 130–31. While in the survey carried out by Bishop Petru Pavel Aron in 1750 there were 550,097 Uniate believers registered in comparison to only 25,065 Orthodox believers, the Austrian general Adolf Buccow counted only 25,164 Uniate families in 1761 compared to 126,652 non-Uniate families. See also Z. Pâclișanu, "Istoria Bisericii Române Unite, 1752–1783, part II" *Perspective*, XIV–XVI, nos. 53–60 (July 1991–June 1993), 38.
16. B. Murgescu, "Confessional Polemics and Political Imperatives in the Romanian Principalities (Late 17th–early 18th Centuries)," in *Church & Society in Central and Eastern Europe*, ed. M. Crăciun and O. Ghitta (Cluj-Napoca: European Studies Foundation Publishing House, 1998), 174–75. For instance, former Jerusalem Patriarch Nectarius's work, "Against the pope's primacy," dedicated to Gheorghe Duca, the prince of Moldavia (1665–1666, 1668–1672, 1678–1683), was printed in Iasi, the capital of Moldova in 1682. In 1683, two fifteenth-century writings were published: "Against the Heresies" by Simeon (archbishop of Thessaloniki, 1381–1429) and "Explanation of the Canons of the Church" by Mark Eugenikos, the Metropolitan of Efes. In 1690, the "Book against the Schism of the Papists" by Maxim from Peloponnese was printed in Bucharest, and so was a book by Meletios Sirigos (1590–1664) against Catholic doctrine and the positions of Patriarch Cyril Lucaris (Patriarch of Constantinople, 1620 and 1638). Between 1692 and 1694, the "Tome of Reconciliation" was printed in Iasi, which contained several texts against Catholicism. In 1694, also in Iasi, the work of John Eugenikos (1394–1454), "Word for Combating the Outlaw and False Decision Composed in Florence at the Synod Held by the Latins" was published. The "Tome of Love against the Latins" was printed in 1698, containing twenty-five writings from different periods against the Latins, followed in 1705, also in Iasi, by the "Tome of Joy," a collection of texts containing, among others, the letter of Photios against Pope Nicolas I (858–867), letters of Ghenadie Scholarios (Patriarch of Constantinople, 1454–1464) against the Florentine Union, texts by Nicolaus Kerameus against papal primacy, and works by Meletios Pegas (Patriarch of Alexandria, 1590–1601) and Dositheos Notaras (Patriarch of Jerusalem, 1669–1707). The book also referred to the situation in Transylvania.
17. M. Păcurariu, *Legăturile Bisericii Ortodoxe din Transilvania cu Tara Românească și Moldova în secolele XVII–XVIII* (Sibiu: Ed. Arhiepiscopia Alba Iulia, 1968), 42; I. Mateiu, "O carte din 1699 contra desbinării religioase," *Revista Teologică* 28, nos. 7–8 (1938): 299–302.
18. The text was published by Ghenadie Enăceanu in the journal *Biserica Orthodoxă Română*. For aspects regarding this text, see G. Enăceanu, "Uniația seu legea a

treia," *Biserica Ortodoxă Română* 7, no. 8 (1883): 496–97; T. Bodogae, *Despre cunoștințele teologice ale preoților români de acum 200 de ani. Semnificația unui manuscris* (Sibiu, 1944), LVIII; Păcurariu, *Legăturile Bisericii Ortodoxe*, 76.

19. The text was published by Teodor Bodogae. About this text, see T. Bodogae, *Despre cunoștințele teologice*, XIII–LXII; Pâclișanu, "Istoria Bisericii Române Unite 1697–1751," 386.
20. For the text, see I. Lupaș, *Cronicari și istorici români din Transilvania. Școala Ardeleană*, vol. 1 (Craiova: Scrisul românesc, f.a.), 58–78.
21. *Întrebări și răspunsuri pentru legea a treia*, 511; Bodogae, *Despre cunoștințele*, 12.
22. *Întrebări și răspunsuri pentru legea a treia*, 503.
23. Ibid., 497.
24. Ibid., 499.
25. Ibid., 501, 504.
26. Ibid., 501, 504.
27. Bodogae, *Despre cunoștințele*, 2–3.
28. Ibid., 12.
29. *Întrebări și răspunsuri pentru legea a treia*, 503.
30. Ibid., 511.
31. Ibid., 504.
32. P. Teodor, "The Confessional Identity of the Transylvanian Greek Catholic Church," in *Confessional Identity in East-Central Europe*, ed. M. Crăciun et al. (Ashgate: Aldershot, 2002), 170.
33. Petru Maior, one of the most important Romanian intellectuals from the end of the eighteenth and beginning of the nineteenth century, asserted: "[Thus], all the Romanians from Transilvania are united with the Church of Rome in faith and not in law, as the Greek law has always been preserved after the Union until today." P. Maior, *Istoria Bisericii românilor*, vol. 1 (București: Viitorul românesc, 1995), 122.
34. The first book was published in the new printing house of Blaj, opened in 1747; it had five chapters, one referring to the idea of the union *in fide* and the others explaining the four points of doctrine from Florence, with a second edition in 1816.
35. *Floarea adevărului*, 23; P.P. Aron, *Păstoriceasca datorie* (Blaj: publ. unknown, 1749), 44, 56; P.P. Aron, *Păstoriceasca poslanie* (Blaj: publ. unknown, 1760), 11, 14.
36. I. Lemeni, *A nagy vátsora* (1814), 20.
37. D. Vaida, *Cuvântări* (Blaj: publ. unknown, 1813), 19–22.
38. I. Lemeni, *Az Istentől küldelett* (1814), 11.
39. T. Cipariu, *Schematismus* (Blaj: Tiparul Tipografiei Diecezane, 1842), XI.
40. I.P. Sălăjean, *Scurtă istorie a credinței românilor din sfintele cărți și adevărate documente dedusă* (Blaj: publ. unknown, 1845), 65.
41. Ibid., 66, 89.
42. See Ms. rom. 271, f. 59–65. This is a copy with some extensions according to an original text registered as Ms. rom. 732, f. 1–4.
43. Ibid., f. 61v.
44. Ibid., f. 64v. The idea of Roman origins was addressed by the bishop in another sermon in which he said: "Rome, from where we, Romanians, have our blood" (Ms. rom. 271, f. 1v.).
45. Sălăjean, *Scurtă istorie*, 64.
46. Ibid., 65–66.

47. Ibid., 66–72, 88.
48. Ibid., 90–91.
49. See the memo titled *Supplex Libellus Valachorum* of Bishop Inochentie Micu Klein in 1744; the memo of the Uniate bishop Ignatie Darabant from Oradea from 1791; the supplex signed by the Uniate bishop Ioan Bob from Blaj and by the Orthodox bishop of Sibiu, Gherasim Adamovici, in 1792; the two supplex memos signed by the Uniate bishop from Blaj, Ioan Lemeni, and by the Orthodox bishop from Sibiu, Vasile Moga, in 1834 and 1842
50. Horvat, *Poslanie*, 1.
51. N. Bocșan, "Națiune și confesiune în Transilvania în secolul al XIX-lea: cazul mitropoliei române," in *Etnie și confesiune în Transilvania: Secolele XIII–XIX* (Oradea: Fundația "Cele Trei Crișuri," 1994), 140–41.
52. Ibid., 140.
53. See also S. Mitu, *Geneza identității naționale la romanii ardeleni* (București: Humanitas, 1997), 371–72.
54. L. Gyemant, *Mișcarea națională a românilor din Transilvania 1790–1848* (București: Editura Științificăși Enciclopedică, 1986), 174.
55. About this project, see Gyemant, *Mișcarea națională*, 175; Mitu, *Geneza identității naționale*, 379; Bocșan, "Națiune și confesiune," 118.
56. G. Bariț, "Icoana preotului," *Foae pentru minte, inimă și literatură*, 10, no. 10 (1847): 77–80, no. 10 supplement: 81–82.
57. Ibid., 79–80.
58. T. Pavel, "Biserica română ca instituție națională în gândirea pașoptistă românească," *AICS* 1 (1994): 71; Bocșan, "Națiune și confesiune," 144.
59. Bocșan, "Națiune și confesiune," 145.
60. See the chapters of Liliya Berezhnaya and Kerstin Jobst in this book.

Bibliography

Aron, P.P. 1749. *Păstoriceasca datorie*. Blaj: publisher unknown.
———. 1760. *Păstoriceasca poslanie*. Blaj: publisher unknown.
Bariț, G. 1847. "Icoana preotului," in *Foae pentru minte, inimă și literature*, no. 10: 77–80; no. 10 supplement: 81–82.
Bârlea, O. 1983. "Biserica Română Unită și ecumenismul Corifeilor renașterii culturale." *Perspective*, nos. 3–4 (January–June): 70–72.
Bernath, M. 1994. *Habsburgii și începutul formării națiunii române*. Cluj-Napoca: Dacia.
Bocșan, N. 1994. "Națiune și confesiune în Transilvania în secolul al XIX-lea: cazul mitropoliei române," in *Etnie și confesiune* în *Transilvania: Secolele XIII–XIX*, 140–41. Oradea: Fundația "Cele Trei Crișuri."
Bodogae, T. 1944. *Despre cunoștințele teologice ale preoților români de acum 200 de ani. Semnificația unui manuscris*. Sibiu: no publisher.
Bogdan-Duică, G. 1896. *Călugărul Visarion Sarai. Studui istoric din istoria Transilvaniei*. Caransebeș: Tiparul Tipografiei Diecezane.
Cipariu, T. 1842. *Schematismus*. Blaj: Tiparul Tipografiei Diecezane.

Dănilă, N. 1998. "Noi considerații privind sinodul din octombrie 1698." In *Spiritualitate transilvană și istorie europeană*, ed. I. Mârza and A. Dumitran, 286–93. Alba Iulia: Muzeul Național al Unirii.

Dragomir, S. 1920. *Istoria Desrobirii Religioase a Românilor din Ardeal în secolul XVIII.* Vol. 2. Sibiu: Tipografia arhidiecezană.

Enăceanu, G. 1883. "Uniația seu legea a treia." *Biserica Orthodoxă Română* 7, no. 8: 496–97.

Floarea adevărului. 1750. Blaj.

Ghitta, O. 2001. *Nașterea unei biserici.* Cluj-Napoca: Presa Universitară Clujeană.

Gorun, G. 1998. *Reformismul austriac și violențele sociale din Europa centrală 1750–1800.* Oradea: Muzeului Țării Crișurilor.

Gyemant, L. 1986. *Mișcarea națională a românilor din Transilvania 1790–1848.* București: Editura Științificăși Enciclopedică.

Hitchins, K. 1987. "Religia și conștiința națională românească în Transilvania în secolul XVIII." In *Conștiința națională și acțiune politică la românii din Transilvania 1700–1868.* Vol. 1, ed. K. Hitchins, 45. Cluj-Napoca: Dacia.

———. 2000. "Clerul român din Transilvania înainte de unirea cu Roma." In *300 de ani de la unirea Bisericii românești din Transilvania cu Biserica Romei*, ed. G. Gorun and O. Horea Pop, 51–67 Cluj-Napoca: Presa Universitară Clujeană.

Horvat, N. 1777. *Poslanie.* Oradea. No publisher.

Lemeni, I. 1814. *A nagy vátsora.* No publisher.

———. 1814. *Az Istentől küldelett.* No publisher.

Lupaș, I. 1933. *Cronicari și istorici români din Transilvania. Școala Ardeleană.* Vol. 1. Craiova: Scrisul românesc.

Maior, P. 1997. *Istoria Bisericii românilor.* Vol. 1. București: Viitorul românesc.

Mateiu, I. 1938. "O carte din 1699 contra desbinării religioase," *Revista Teologică* 28, nos. 7–8: 299–302.

Micu, S. 1995. *Istoria românilor.* Vol. 2. București: Viitorul Românesc.

Miron, G.M. 2004. *Biserica greco-catolică din Transilvania. Cler și enoriași (1697–1782).* Cluj-Napoca: Presa Universitară Clujeană.

Mitu, S. 1997. *Geneza identității naționale la romanii ardeleni.* București: Humanitas.

Murgescu, B. 1998. "Confessional Polemics and Political Imperatives in the Romanian Principalities (Late 17th–early 18th Centuries)." In *Church & Society in Central and Eastern Europe*, ed. M. Crăciun and O. Ghitta, 174–75. Cluj-Napoca: European Studies Foundation Publishing House.

Pâclișanu, Z. 1991–1993. "Istoria Bisericii Române Unite, 1752–1783, part II." *Perspective*, nos. 53–60 (July–June): 38.

———. 1995. *Istoria Bisericii Române-Unite, partea Ia 1697–1744.* München: Christliche Stimme.

Păcurariu, M. 1968. *Legăturile Bisericii Ortodoxe din Transilvania cu Tara Românească și Moldova în secolele XVII– XVIII.* Sibiu: Ed. Arhiepiscopia Alba Iulia.

Pavel, T. 1994. "Biserica română ca instituție națională în gândirea pașoptistă românească." *AICS* 1: 71.

Periș, L. 2005. *Prezențe catolice în Transilvania, Moldova și Țara Românească 1601–1698.* Blaj: Buna Vestire.

Prodan, D. 1984. *Supplex Libellus Valachorum.* București: Științifică și Enciclopedică.

Sălăjean, I.P. 1845. *Scurtă istorie.* Blaj: publisher unknown.
Săsăujan, M. 2002. *Politica bisericească a Curții din Viena în Transilvania (1740–1761).* Cluj-Napoca: Presa Universitară Clujeană.
Teodor, P. 2000. "În jurul sinodului mitropolitului Teofil din 1697." In *300 de ani de la unirea Bisericii românești din Transilvania cu Biserica Romei,* ed. G. Gorun and O. Horea Pop, 43–50. Cluj-Napoca: Presa Universitară Clujeană.
———. 2002. "The Confessional Identity of the Transylvanian Greek Catholic Church." In *Confessional Identity in East-Central Europe,* M. Crăciun et al. Ashgate: Aldershot.
Tòth, I.Z. 2001. *Primul secol al naționalismului românesc ardelean 1697–1792.* București: Pythagora.
Vaida, D. 1813. *Cuvântări.* Blaj: publisher unknown.
Visarion. 1746. *Întrebări și răspunsuri pentru legea a treia ce s-a izvodit adică Uniia în Țara Ardealului.* Sâmbăta de Sus: publisher unknown.

CHAPTER 3

Securitizing the Polish Bulwark

The Mission of Lviv in Polish Travel Guides during the Late Nineteenth and Early Twentieth Centuries

Heidi Hein-Kircher

> Lviv was always faithful! . . . The radiant fire of the Polish culture was the old, dignified town of Lviv, it remained its unshakable shield through centuries. When wild, barbarian incursions of Eastern invasions poured in as a hurricane at the borderlands of Eastern territories, it [Lviv] fulfilled a watchful and strong guard and it brought itself titles through a widely poured stream of blood: [like] "first-rate shield" and "bulwark of Christianity" . . . at the border of two worlds, of European culture and Eastern barbarism, lots of watchtowers arose and descended from the ruins and charred remains, but the huge wave of hostile invasions always broke against the bastion of the city of Lviv.
>
> —A. Medyński, *Lwów*[1]

Assuming that *antemurale christianitatis* is a myth designating a threat scenario, this introductory quotation from a 1937 Polish travel guide gives a typical account of the exemplary way in which Polish travel guides describe the history and significance of Lviv[2]: in heroic words, they ascribe to Lviv (Polish Lwów, Ukrainian L'viv, and Russian Lvov) the mission of a bulwark, the mission to be the eastern fortress and defender of Polishness and of European civilization. As a political myth and by creating a threat scenario, the *antemurale christianitatis* serves to securitize its Polish character by constructing a threat coming from the East and Lviv's role as a bulwark to secure Poland and Europe. It is, therefore, a means to legitimize Polish pretensions about Lviv, to sharpen the Polish identity within and outside the city, to legitimize Polish dominance in the local government as well as in the public sphere before and after 1918 and to legitimize the

Polish claims and the incorporation of Lviv and Eastern Galicia. Because of their specific function, travel guides are a useful source for retracing the narrative construction and spread of the inherent message.

The Polish bulwark mission is one of the most important Polish political myths. In particular, during the second half of the "long" nineteenth century—when Poland as a state vanished from the maps—Polish mental mapping contributed to delimiting the Poles as a national group distinct from others. When the region was partitioned, the myth of the Polish bulwark mission became more and more influential to Polish self-description, self-identification, and historical consciousness because it provided an important myth of space to define Polish territories, and thus to legitimate Polish territorial claims.³

As discussed by Kerstin Weiand in this volume, the notion of *antemurale* evolved from the fifteenth century onward in Polish sources because of the country's geopolitical position at the eastern border of Catholic Christendom and because of its closeness to the Muslim Ottoman Empire. It interpreted Poland as the defender of the Catholic faith, which had been the protector of Christian Europe since the Mongolian invasion in the mid-thirteenth century. At the time, it was used as a religiously motivated argument for international diplomacy. The victory of King Jan III Sobieski (1629–1696) against the Ottomans at the Battle of Kahlenberg near Vienna in 1683 was the last time that the Ottomans truly threatened Europe. It was of special significance for the development of the *antemurale* topos.

First articulated in the fifteenth century, the *antemurale* topos comprised the concept of a confessional and religious border with the Muscovite Orthodox Church and Muslim worlds, on the one hand, and a civilizational and political confine with "Eastern" or "Asiatic barbarism," on the other hand. After the partitions of Poland in the eighteenth century, it changed from a diplomatic argument to a political myth that selectively interpreted the response against attacks coming from the (south)east, and it foregrounded Europe's historical debt to Poland. It was also based on the claim of Polish nationhood that emerged in the period of statelessness during the "long" nineteenth century, but it was also closely tied to the denominational border and conflicts between Western (Catholic) and Eastern (Orthodox) Christendom.

The first step of the general formation of the myth after World War I was the victory against the Red Army near Warsaw in 1920. Because of this *Cud nad Wisłą* (Miracle on the Vistula) that halted the advance of the Red Army, Poland saw itself as the first line of defense against the "Bolshevik threat" in a democratic Western Europe. With this general development, which set the city as the Polish bulwark, Lviv's reputation was sharpened.⁴

The introductory quotation above points directly to the leading questions of this chapter. I discuss the main narrative elements of *antemurale* myth and the steps in its evolution that have been used to characterize the bulwark mission. I focus herewith on a period when the national movements of Poles and Ruthenians became mutually confrontational until the 1930s. My chapter ends at a period when Lviv was the capital of the Voivodship East Galicia in the Polish Second Republic (1918–1939) and Poles asserted their national claims by violently "pacifying" the Ukrainians.[5] I also show how a certain genre of publicity material with a claim to objectivity was used to transmit the myth to a broader public.

This chapter refers to travel guides published in Lviv between the 1870s and the 1930s in Polish and/or by authors stemming mainly from Galicia. I analyze these chronologically in order to provide current desiderata in historical research. Three reasons motivate. First, travel guides have not been systematically analyzed and are seldom used in historical studies. They are not seen in relation to stereotypes and political myths, especially not in relation to Eastern and East Central Europe.[6] Second, while multiethnic Galicia and especially Lviv are *en vogue* as to questions of nationalism and public space, and while there have been some general considerations of the Polish and Lviv's *antemurale* topos since the nineteenth century, there is still a lack of deeper analysis of how the image of Lviv as a bulwark was built up and used as a securitizing mythical narrative.[7] Third, travel literature has not yet been of interest with regard to the analysis of political myths, although it is certainly a genre that functions by transmitting only seemingly objective "neutral" information. By tying these three factors together, I will not only describe the evolution of the myth of Lviv's bulwark mission but also highlight a certain discursive strategy by focusing on the securitizing motives.

My fundamental approach is based on the assumption that in modern societies, referring to security constitutes discursively "a sociocultural value system"[8] and a "gold standard of politics"[9] from which one can deduce perceptions, sense, and orientation that lead to action and that help to reduce social complexity and tackle contingency. Therefore, "securitization" refers to discourses and social interactions regarding the perception, depiction, and production of security (problems),[10] and as a process of communication, "securitization combines the politics of threat design with that of threat management."[11] When "security" is understood as a promise, (re)securitizing processes become important instruments for the symbolic integration of societies and have formative effects on identity building,[12] which may also be inherent in myths. Because of their semantics, bulwark myths, which generally provide orientation and meaning, imply a certain form of "threat design" by focusing on that which should be secured.[13] In this they also contribute to "threat management" within a society and, therefore, gain a securitizing role with regard to the collective group. Thus, a securitizing myth is a form of mythical narration within a society dealing with and explaining an (imagined) threat.

Travel Guides as an Instrument of Mental Mapping

Travel guides provide information about a location before and during visits by claiming to deliver objective information. As a particular genre of purpose-oriented literature, they intend to impart quick information about a foreign space, about sights, and help to orient the traveler within a certain space.[14] They are a specific form of literature published for a particular purpose, that is, they are primarily written for those who visit a given place or as guides to be used as a kind of handbook for those who have been unable to travel to a place or who merely wish to educate themselves about it. What is more, local populations used them quite often as handbooks on local infrastructure facilities and history. Travel guides provide an introduction to the environment, history, demographics, and social conditions. Analyzing their composition it becomes clear that, although they claim to deliver objective information, they are quite subjective. They only mention what is of importance to the author, and so they are related to the author's message.

The guides analyzed for this chapter contain information about urban institutions such as town halls and schools and are thus useful handbooks when no other tourist information is accessible. By highlighting and only describing the (in the authors' eyes) most important sights, they created prior knowledge, expectations, and the desire to visit certain locations; hence there was an element of seduction.[15] Before the start of a journey, they help their readers with the preparation and influence the choice of locations to be visited. More importantly, however, they have an impact on the perception of these locations via the selection of places and objects to be visited and their circumstances. This is aided by the short format and language of presentation and by the selection of illustrations and their captions.

Even if travel guides appear at first glance to be quite descriptive and thus subjective sources of information, the examples used here indicate the contrary: the manner in which travel guides present and label the sights creates a hierarchy of places to visit and forms a kind of catalog of elements in urban space. It is quite obvious that this hierarchy works through inclusion and exclusion—that is, it is also a hierarchy of importance, value, and meaning—which determines which images are used and how they are presented. For example, the analyzed guides mention primarily Polish points of interest and only briefly refer to or even eclipse Jewish or Ruthenian/Ukrainian sights, such as their places of prayer or schools. In this way, they function as a "type of medial optical aid that standardizes and directs the view right from the outset, by emphasizing the foreign in order to strengthen the self. One only sees that which one knows,"[16] and they construct a certain local "topography of memorial culture."[17]

The travel guides operate with deduction and interpretation of the general national master narrative. In contrast, schoolbooks, discussed in this volume by Philipp Hofeneder, comprise the given national master narrative. Travel guides construct their symbolic ascription through their specific mode of presentation that constructs a given and wholly formed image that expresses a specific view and understanding of that society. The cityscape is thus notably pictured and used to contribute to cultural memory[18]; the visitors get a preformed interpretation. As such, the seemingly neutral information is a discursive construction of what is of ideational importance for the author or his principals—in our case, the local government that (co)financed the travel guides. They are a specific form of guided knowledge transfer and dispersion, *der genormte Blick auf das Fremde*[19] (standardized glance at the foreign)[20]—an instrument to appropriate space and to influence the mental mapping of travelers through the only apparent objective composition of texts and descriptions. In our case, the composition of sights and general introductory descriptions implies the message of Lviv being a Polish (and European) rampart against (barbarian) threats from the East.

Descriptions Rendering Lviv as Polish under Galician Autonomy

In the second half of the nineteenth century, Lviv experienced significant development: following the revolution of 1848–1849, the town grew continuously but did not explode as did metropolises in the West. In 1846, Lviv had about 70,000 inhabitants and grew to 103,000 in 1880, 113,000 in 1890, 200,000 in 1900 and about 214,000 people in 1914. The population was ethnically and nationally diverse, as barely half the population was Polish, while approximately 28 percent were Jewish and 20 percent were Ruthenians.[21]

In autumn 1870, Lviv became an autonomous city, with its own statute through which the city could decide on its own cultural and educational politics. Because of Galician political autonomy, political and cultural life was freer than in the other parts of partitioned Poland. As the social borders corresponded more or less with the borders between the nationalities, the legal prescriptions of Lviv's statute influenced the distinctions between the nationalities.[22] Due to these circumstances, Lviv's local government presented the city as a substitute capital (instead of Warsaw) and pursued politics appropriate to this end. For example, the local authorities in Lviv favored their own unencumbered history and rendered the city Polish, for example, through memorials or by naming streets after Polish heroes.

The travel guides, therefore, become a useful instrument to transmit the mission of the Polish local government and to drive perceptions of (Polish) visitors—and, importantly, they were officially commissioned and cofinanced by local authorities (or at least approved by them). Because broader tourism was only slowly emerging by the middle of the nineteenth century, tourism in Lviv was more or less connected to events or visitors coming on official business to the Galician capital.[23] Because of the special conditions that made Galician cultural life relatively free, thousands of visitors (not only the elites) came to visit Jan Matejko's (1838–1893) expositions. In particular, they came to the Galician crown land exposition in 1894, where they could see the famous panorama building of the Kościuszko uprising in 1794 painted by Jan Styka (1858–1925) and Wojciech Kossak (1857–1942).

During the decades leading up to World War I, in particular, the national conflict between Poles and Ruthenians[24]—which had persisted ever since the revolution of 1848—reached its culmination. This became more and more obvious in the public sphere and ultimately led to violent conflicts and demonstrations, with the murder of Governor Andrzej Kazimierz Potocki (1861–1908) in 1908 being the most prominent. The municipality did not rise to the challenge of ascendant national movements and conflicts or to the challenge of violent clashes in public spaces. It made no attempt to reduce the potential for violence. On the contrary, the more it pursued these clearly Polish national attitudes, the more violent conflict ensued. This attitude led to ever more intensive claims about the Polishness of Lviv, wherever and whenever it was possible in verbal or nonverbal communication in Lviv's public sphere and internal politics. The description of Polish topics and the ascribed significance of Lviv for the Polish nation was addressed to Poles living outside the city, too.

During this time, the bulwark myth formed a narrative answer to the "Ruthenian challenge," that is, the Ruthenian national movement that had been gathering momentum since the middle of the nineteenth century and that also laid claim to the possession of Lviv and its role as a Ruthenian national center. As they were not Roman Catholic, the "old" image of a defender of Occidental (Roman) Catholic culture always resonated in the myth, even if only just below the surface. This aspect was not only inherent in the myth but links older interpretations with the contemporary narration of the myth. In general, more or less parallel with the rise of the Ruthenian national movement, an increasing use of the Polish bulwark myth with regard to Lviv could be observed. The evolution of the wording, especially the introductory elements, clearly show the development of this mythical narration and the changing character of the town—hence, it became a kind of counternarration with regard to Ruthenian claims.

A guidebook published in German in 1863 hinted at the latent German character of the town in the period before the enforcement of Polishness,[25] where, for example, one can find traditional or Habsburgian street names. The descriptions are of more or less practical importance, such as those referring to the Christian or Jewish slaughterhouses. This guidebook provides information not for tourists but for Habsburgian civilian and military servants coming to Lviv. Just fifteen years later, and eight years after the implementation of the statute, one still found only "smooth" references to the bulwark mission in a travel book. Emphasizing the Polish character, *Wilda przewodnik po Lwówie* (Wild's Travel Book through Lviv) described Lviv as having always been a Polish town, like a faithful son connected to the fatherland with an unshakable and inexhaustible love. According to the text, it experienced joyful triumphs and painful defeats because no other town had been subjected to so many sieges by the Tatar hordes.[26] Even eight years later, a guidebook on Galician towns[27] still focused on the multiethnic character but already emphasized the achievements of King Jan III Sobieski, presenting him as a symbol of Polish *antemurale*, and hinted at the changing character of Lviv since the 1860s.[28]

In contrast to these more informative passages about Lviv, an 1888 travel guide published on the occasion of the gathering of Polish physicians and natural scientists is more elaborate and descriptive.[29] The historical framing referred to the unsuccessful sieges of the Tatars in 1438 and 1444, which lead to the construction of bastions. It then referred to further unsuccessful sieges by the Tatars and Turks at the end of the century and to subsequent defeats such as the great fire and the Tatar attacks. The text also provided more information about the unsuccessful "aggression" of the Cossack Hetman Bohdan Khmelnytskyi (1595–1657). However, the guidebook asserted, while this was "the most fearful time for Poland, it was the most beautiful for the fame of Lviv."[30] The guide then only briefly described King Jan Sobieski's attendance in town and mentioned the actual plans for the erection of a memorial. These examples of early guidebooks only hint implicitly at the fact that Lviv functioned as a kind of rampart, but they do not refer to its function as a bulwark.

The crown land exposition in 1894—which was intended to showcase Galician achievements for other Austrian citizens, especially the inhabitants of Lviv and Poles from outside Galicia—was the reason for the publication of combined guides on Lviv and the exposition.[31] The German guide was funded and promoted by the local government[32] and was published in Polish and German by the Lviv grammar school professor Albert Zipper (1855–1936), a well-known personage in Galician scientific and cultural life. As the exposition was to demonstrate the achievement of Galician cultural, scientific, and economic life—with thousands of visitors from Galicia, the Russian and Prussian partitions, and other crown lands—the guide was written in a moderate tone and highlighted the achievements of the city.[33]

Another Polish guide, funded by the semiofficial Towarzystwo Upiększenia i Rozwoju Lwowa (Society for the Beautification and Development of Lviv), highlighted Lviv's economic position as a commercial city where Polish life pulsated, a city that was "similar to the Italian commercial republics."[34] In this book, the phrase "bulwark for the whole of Poland"[35] was used with regard to the Khmelnytskyi siege. The *Ilustrowana pamiątka z powszechnej wystawy krajowej* (Illustrated Souvenir of the General Crown Land Exposition),[36] a booklet written for the visiting Polish public, describes Lviv's past as an evolution from its founding by Danilo (1201–1264), prince of Kyiv [Russian: Kiev, Polish: Kijów], to a Polish town since Kazimierz the Great (1310–1370) and following an array of ambushes by Tatars and Turks. However, Lviv "suffered the most"[37] when it was besieged by Cossacks under Bohdan Khmelnytskyi. The guide points out that Lviv had not lost its Polish character when it became Habsburgian. It goes on to mention that following the constitutional reforms of 1860s, Lviv had begun to evolve and take on the "stance of a real capital of the country."[38]

It seems that the crown land exposition, therefore, was a kind of milestone for the development of travel guides about Lviv. The wording in the descriptions of the historical background had not yet become very severe, but one can find the first clear expressions of the bulwark function. An intentional degree of restraint in the official politics of the local government can be observed here because some fifteen years earlier, the town archivist had already stated that Lviv had been for Poland what Poland had been for Europe: *antemurale regni*.[39]

More revealing, for instance, is the elaborate travel guide published on the occasion of the tenth gathering of Polish physicians and natural scientists in Lviv in 1907, which was financially backed by the local government.[40] The foreword made clear that Lviv was the Polish *placówka* (post) that was most directly exposed on the east and that it was the capital of this part of Poland, where freedom of speech and of the national movement was possible and where the life of a free country must pulsate.[41] In contrast to the travel guides mentioned previously, it focused in more detail on Bohdan Khmelnytskyi's siege in 1648, although all sieges by the Tatars and Turks were mentioned.[42] In regard to Khmelnytskyi's siege, the author of the historical introduction, the well-known city archivist Alexander Chołodecki (1865–1944), summed it up as follows:

> Lviv came out of the wave of the Cossack's flood, with honor and glory like never before or after. . . . It saved not only itself, it saved the whole state . . . it became famous as the most faithful and bravest Polish city with the nickname "Poland's bulwark."[43]

The travel guides published in the nineteenth century had to maintain a balance between making claims about Polish character and dominance and not questioning Lviv's belonging to the Habsburg monarchy. In the abovementioned guide book (intended for visitors from all parts of Poland), this issue was solved by mentioning the autonomous status of the city within the monarchy, which opens up a new epoch of Polish life in present times.[44] Mentioning the Cossacks and Hetman Khmelnytskyi is a reference to Ukrainians. Creating the distinction between Lviv and the East implied a threat scenario, from the Tatars, Turks, and so on.

Demonstrating Loyalty and Commitment during World War I

A few weeks after the outbreak of World War I, Lviv was occupied by the Russian army, although it was liberated by the Habsburg army in June 1915. The local self-government that had been established was reversed, but former local authorities headed by Vice-Major Tadeusz Rutowski (1852–1918) had to administer and organize life. It is interesting to note that during World War I, a few German-speaking travel guides were published—not for tourists, but for official and military persons coming to town. Descriptions in these guides evoke associations with war that are not entirely coincidental; one author wrote that since its foundation, the town had been situated at the "pharynx of the Tatars." It had been the "battle-shrouded border bastion on the blood-sodden ground of the endless wrestle and fight of the crude and wilderness of the Orient with the culture of Occident,"[45] but like a "sprouting plant" after each attack of the "wild tribes of Tatars, Vlachs, and Mongols," it rose once again from the "blood-fertilized soil."[46]

A brief account of sieges by Tatars, Cossacks, and Ottomans followed that was intended to explain why Lviv had to play a role as a "proud border and culture fortress" over a period of five centuries. In order to dispel any doubts about Lviv's loyalty to the monarchy, the author explained why the town's inhabitants did not immediately pay homage to the emperor after the Habsburg occupation in 1772. It was because this "platonic protest was the last reflection and echo of the traditional, knightly loyalty to the [Polish] king and patriotism." The author then cautiously criticized the destruction of ramparts that were important for the preservation of cultural heritage. However, he also noted that the town, in connection with its suburbs, formed a "consistent, picturesque townscape."[47] The author went on to explain that after a period of stagnation following the Napoleonic storm, the revolution of 1848, and the glorious development under autonomy:

> [The] terrible and furious tide of the Orient [the Russian invasion] flooded the town and land once more ... the same devastating waves of the Asiatic barbary and savagery surged over the open and peaceful city, an impact to which Lviv and the whole Polish Kingdom have always been exposed. With robbery and murder, with fire and violence, in a manner more terrible and sophisticated than ever before, the wild hordes overpowered town and country. ... For ten months, Lviv endured the ruthlessly hard and tyrannical despotism of the Russians. Following hellish battles and the roar of the most modern weapons and agents of war, on June 22nd the tidal wave of the Orient was rolled back.[48]

This statement links the historical reputation of Lviv with its liberation by the Austrian army, while the rollback is not described in more detail. The drastic and dramatic wording clearly characterizes Russia as barbaric and belligerent, and its rollback is the result of Lviv's historical role. Therefore, the guides deliver not only a sharply formulated rejection of Russian occupation, and with this a kind of manifesto of its loyalty to the Habsburg Empire, but also a manifesto of being Polish.

Emphasizing the Polishness of Lviv after 1918

When the war on Eastern Galicia broke out between the Polish and Ukrainian military the end of World War I, the Polish defense of Lviv became an increasingly important part of the mythical narration of a Polish bulwark. After the victory of the Polish army over the Red Army in 1920, the Polish bulwark myth was adapted to a new political situation: the "Bolshevik threat" and its containment through the Miracle on the Vistula were interpreted in the sense that Poland functioned as a bulwark against the danger emanating (once again) from the East.[49] In this sense, Poland had changed from the "defender of the Catholic faith" to the defender of "democracy" and "Western European culture/civilization" against the "political religion" of Bolshevism. From this, the myth of the "Polish bulwark against Bolshevism" and the myth of Józef Piłsudski (1867–1935) grew into the founding myth of the "Second Polish Republic."

The defense of Lviv became connected with this general Polish myth and took on a local form. Despite the local form of the myth, the mythical status of the city attained overarching, Poland-wide importance exceeding the local motive of narration. *Obrona Lwowa* (the Defense of Lviv) and the role of *orlęta lwowskie* (Lviv's Eaglets) against Ukrainian national troops and then against the Red Army became the legitimizing narrative that justified the incorporation of Lviv and Eastern Galicia into Polish territory. Furthermore, it underpinned Poland's action against the Ukrainians, especially with regard to the "pacification" of Eastern Galicia in 1930 that euphemistically describes the violent operations against the Ukrainian national movement by Polish military.

A corresponding narrative appears in the travel guides for Lviv. An intermediate step can be seen in a guide first published in 1919 for soldiers coming to Lviv that is based on prewar texts by the same author.[50] In the foreword to the guide, he notes that there was not a single "real Polish guide": preceding guides had been printed under Habsburg rule and as such could not be regarded as genuinely Polish. Publishing the guide during the siege of Lviv, the author wanted the soldiers fighting in and for Lviv to experience the city's historical and cultural importance and to thus feel themselves charged with the urgency of its defense. He argued that no other city had ever been such a "rampart [*szaniec*] of the Republic" and "defender against the eastern hordes," upon which the "eyes of the whole nation are looking."[51]

The historical introduction to the war period is interesting, as it extensively explains why the Galician Poles were loyal to the Austrians until 1917 and as, with regard to the defense of Lviv, it refers explicitly to the historical centuries-long mission and its actual role as a *twierdza* (bastion).[52] In the following chapter on Lviv's role as *ognisko Polskiej kultury* (a center of Polish culture), the bulwark motive is depicted in even more detail: "At the borderlands of European culture and Asiatic barbarism, it took on the noble task of a bulwark of civilization ... [and] of the defense of the borderlands [and] of *Rzeczpospolita* (the Republic)" and a "strong leverage of national rebirth."[53]

A small "indispensable vade mecum" for tourists as well as Lviv's citizens and "each social class" was published in 1933 on the occasion of the fifteenth anniversary of "Lviv's homecoming to the fatherland"[54] because of the "new, great period of development,"[55] that is, the founding of Wielki Lwów (Greater Lviv) in 1934. Following the general information on places of interest and institutions, the historical introduction of this guide states that no other Polish town had played a more glorious role throughout the centuries than Lviv,[56] from which it earned the name "bulwark of Poland and Christianity." It is characterized as always "faithful to the fatherland"[57] so that it was the "agency of Polish thoughts and culture for all partitioned lands" in the autonomous era.[58] This role led to the "electrification of the whole of Poland," while the fight against the former partitioning powers and the commitment of Lviv's youth to rescue Poland from the invading Bolshevik hordes[59] were both of special importance in the interwar period.

One particularly interesting source is a guide to the main monument of King Jan III Sobieski, published on the occasion of the 250th anniversary of the victory over the Ottoman Empire in 1683[60] and characterizing Sobieski as a symbol of self-sacrificial dedication to the fatherland. In the foreword, the author says that this should help enforce the Polish spirit and thereby facilitate the conquest of a position of power.[61] This provides only the merest hint of the glorification of Sobieski. During his anniversary celebrations, the myth of the bulwark was virtually omnipresent, although it was connected with the cult of the actual dictator, Józef Piłsudski, who was mythically glorified as the victor over the Bolsheviks.[62] In this guide, the historical importance of Lviv was closely linked with Sobieski, whose glory shined on the historical role of the city.

While this booklet was intended to deliver didactic material for the 250th anniversary of Sobieski, a more comprehensive travel guide to Lviv from 1936 (financed by the City's Department of Public Relations and Tourism)[63] explicitly and quite extensively narrates the self-image of the city, extending earlier accounts and opening and closing the introductory chapter with the Latin *Leopolis semper fidelis*, the heraldic motto of the city.[64]

The text paraphrases the city's rampart functions with regard to the threats' defenses and connects positive references to what Lviv was (and should be) for Poland. So the introduction draws a characteristic outline of the city: the "old fire of Polish culture," "unshakable entrenchment."[65] While "in form of a hurricane, wild barbarian incursions by eastern invaders" endangered the Polish eastern territories (the so-called *kresy*), Lviv functioned as the "forward guard" and always proved worthy of the titles "pride of the kingdom" and "bulwark of [Western] Christianity" and worthy of having received the Virtuti Militari after World War I following its defensive role. Against the "barbarian parades" on the eastern territories, which were like "a never ending chain," there were watchtowers at the very point at which European culture met eastern barbarism. But "particularly rough waves of hostile raids" crashed over the "ever faithful" town. Thus, in repudiating them, Lviv gave "to the altar of the common goods a bloody toll."[66]

The guide recounts the town's role during World War I. Lviv was ascribed the role of witness to the rebirth of Poland because the legions departed from it and because of its national self-sacrifice in fighting the Russian administration's attempts at Russifying the city during the occupation. It goes on to point out that that the city was tested once again when Poland was reborn and when it rose from a bloody vapor, this time resulting in the defense of Lviv against Ukrainian attempts at independence.

Lviv's affiliation with Poland could be described as having been forged with bayonets: *Leopolis semper fidelis*. This invocation of the heraldic motto, bestowed on Lviv by Pope Alexander VII (1599–1667) in 1658, ultimately refers to the city's mission as bulwark and is not only used in this guide but also in other media narrating the *obrona Lwowa:* the defense of Lviv against the Ukrainians.[67]

These exemplary quotations referring to the Polish *antemurale* myth paraphrase the idea that Lviv has always resisted the eastern threat and secured itself as well as Poland. Hence, the narration of the Polish bulwark myth is not only a concept that legitimizes certain claims but also a claim about possessing and defending the city when the affiliation of Galicia and Lviv with the Polish state was contested after 1918 and with regard to disputes in international law. The role of travel guides in this context was to support the argument that Lviv should belong to the Polish state.

The European and Catholic Character of the City

An important and complementary narrative is that of the Europeanness of Lviv. The narration of the bulwark myth not only functions ex negativo by describing that from which one wants to remain distinct and separate but also implies a positive declaration of belonging. This refers to general discourses on Europe because in the nineteenth century, a major discussion focused on the position of the border between Eastern and Western Europe, without questioning whether, in fact, such a border existed at all.[68]

Earlier guides refer extensively to the modern functional buildings, such as the slaughterhouses, the gas and electric plants, and the modern electric tramway that had been in operation since 1894. This demonstrated the great influence of the autonomous local government,[69] which, not coincidentally, financed the urban development guides.[70]

Virtually all travel guides stressed the extensive development and modernization of the city, which took place under the auspices of the autonomous administration, using phrases such as "at first glance modern and international."[71] With this, they strongly linked Lviv with the Polish Galician and local administration, while the "private constructions became unfortunately proletarian ... and had nothing in common with arts and crafts, so that in the twentieth century it had barely obtained its own artistic style."[72]

The guides focused on Renaissance and Baroque buildings, as well as those in the neo-Romantic or Gothic style, and on the modern secessionist architecture from the end of nineteenth century, demonstrating that the city was developing and progressing constantly, always moving forward. Of course, as Renaissance and Baroque styles are connected with Catholicism (particularly the Catholic Counterreformation), these descriptions implicitly show that Lviv was specifically a Catholic Occidental city. In addition to the introductions, which focus on the historical role of the city—especially against the Muslim Ottomans (Turks) and Tatars—these descriptions and related photographs illustrate that Lviv was shaped by an Occidental Catholic culture. However, the guides downplay the aesthetically unremarkable "barracks of banality,"[73] the great residential quarters built since industrialization, which can also be found in other cities (although those in Lviv are smaller). At the same time, they highlight that modernism, which came from Vienna and Berlin, was combined with the Polish influence and that Lviv thus achieved its own unique style.[74]

Such a statement reminds the reader that the styles mentioned are European and have nothing in common with the proletarian style. These modalities link European and Polish influences as modern and confirm the Europeanness and modernity of Polish culture, which was of particular importance before World War I.[75] Implicitly, therefore, all travel guides referred to the general discourse of Galician backwardness and the city's "historiographic imperative,"[76] namely that Lviv as the Galician capital was improving and developing instead of continuing "Galician poverty."[77]

A 1931 guide explicitly stressed that Lviv belonged to the sphere of influence of European civilization. It refers to the French general Ferdinand Foch's (1851–1929) statement with regard to Europe that Lviv, with an intense voice, answered "Poland is here."[78] In reference to the European character, the travel guides described how Lviv was modernized and could catch up with European standards and how it was firm in its Polish character. This connection is crucial: because Lviv is a Polish and a European town, its mission as a bulwark is justified by being the defender of Occidental civilization against oriental barbarism.[79]

Conclusions

These travel guide descriptions, particularly the historical overviews and the specific selection of places to visit that are described in more detail, convey a certain specific narrative construction of Lviv: a very specific Polish perspective and interpretation. They invoke an image of Lviv as a modern city: both Polish and European, both Occidental and Catholic. Travel guides are a specific form of literature that structures and shapes the notions that readers have of the places and regions they describe. The examples presented in this chapter demonstrate that the audience for this literary genre was the Polish nation, and more specifically Poles coming mainly from outside, from the other partitions—Galicia and its capital were a certain replacement for the lost state and capital. Only in the decades before World War I was there another audience addressed by this literature—Habsburgian servants—so that the Polish and the Habsburgian character could generally be noted. During this period, the officially approved and financed guidebooks did not question Lviv's affiliation with the Habsburg Empire, but they highlighted the city's Polish character and its importance for Poland and Europe.

The travel guides described Lviv as *the* Polish town that had been most consistently and severely confronted by the "hordes" coming from the East and that had successfully fulfilled its "divine bulwark mission" for the whole of Poland even if it was destroyed several times. Hence, they transformed the *antemurale* myth into a seemingly objective text form and renarrated it in a specific way. These travel guides highlighted these premises by, for example, describing and illustrating points of interest that represented the master narrative of the Polish national identity. They focused on that which was interpreted to be part of the national achievement and expected to legitimize the Polish dominance in Galicia and claims to it as a possession—inwardly and outwardly. So, they described Lviv as a fortress that was able to defend not only itself and the Polish nation but also (Western) Europe against the "barbarians" whether Turks, Tatars, or the Orthodox and after 1918, the Bolsheviks. Through that interpretation of history, these bulwark myths contributed to the construction of the Polish *kresy* as a conflict region.[80] Clearly, the threat was indicated by the semantics, as the words chosen to refer to the enemies created an emotional demarcation and construction of a menace scenario and by implication Lviv as a "bastion," "shield," "fortress," and "bulwark." The harsh portrayal of the other side as "barbarians" or "hordes" evoked the image of a fortress so that this function was picked up in the presentation of local history and places of interest. The composition of interpreting descriptions explained that only the Poles were able to lead and to prove themselves worthy to rule in the Galician province and, after 1918, to possess it. Hence, the narration of the Polish bulwark mission fulfills these expectations perfectly and thus had a great impact on the Polish mental map formed culturally and religiously as the frontier against the East. Moreover, by being a "shield," Lviv's bulwark mission included a promise to secure Poland because the narration of functioning as a Polish bulwark implied the ability to cope with the eastern threats.

The bulwark mission is a securitizing myth formed through analogies: originally the barbarians threatened Lviv, now it is the Ruthenians/Ukrainians. The securitizing mission of Lviv's bulwark myth had an important impact on Polish mental mapping and self-understanding and hence on Polish nationalism. The securitizing narration of Lviv's mission as a bulwark also explains why the city had to cope with threats provoked by the escalating national conflict between Poles and Ukrainians and why Poles strongly identified with the conflict and fought for it. To this end, travel guides as a genre were used to inform and educate their readers because they picked up the generally accepted interpretation of Poland as a bulwark against the East and sharpened it through the example of Lviv. The local authorities as the (co)sponsors made it their business to ensure Polish national identity and, after 1918, the Polish state. Finally, it was a broad generalized strategy of legitimization. By evoking fears of the "eastern threat," the securitizing bulwark mission in the travel guides helped to legitimize the political claims to the incorporation of *semper fidelis* Polish Lviv and the eastern borderlands. Last but not least, they helped discursively to cope with the perceived threat by promising that Lviv would always function as a bulwark.

Heidi Hein-Kircher earned her M.A. and her Ph.D. in East European history, modern history, political sciences, and Yiddish from Heinrich Heine-University in Düsseldorf. In 2018, she earned her habilitation degree at Philipps University in Marburg. Since 2003, she has been on the research staff of the Herder-Institute for Historical Research in East Central Europe in Marburg, Germany, and since 2009 as the head of department of "academic forum." In her research, she focuses on political and cultural myths in East Central Europe and on urban history of the nineteenth and twentieth centuries in East Central Europe, especially on Lviv in the nineteenth century.

Notes

1. A. Medyński, *Lwów. Przewodnik dla zwiedzających miasta*, 2nd ed. (Lwów: self-publication, 1937), 3–4.
2. The city was officially called "Lemberg" under Habsburg rule until 1918, which is the German form of the Latin Leopolis, while under Polish rule the city was named Lwów. In Russian, the spelling is Lvov, and more recently in Ukrainian, Lviv. I use the English form here. The conceptual work of the collaborative project SFB/TRR 138 "Dynamics of Security" influenced this chapter with regard to "securitizing myths." The SFB/TRR 138 financed the translation from German.
3. H. Hein-Kircher, "Antemurale christianitatis. Grenzsituation als Selbstverständnis," in *Grenzen. Gesellschaftliche Konstitutionen und Transfigurationen*, ed. H. Hecker (Essen: Klartext, 2006), 129–48. A general overview of the roots and development is provided by P. Srodecki, *Antemurale Christianitatis. Zur Genese der Bollwerksrhetorik im östlichen Europa an der Schwelle vom Mittelalter zur Frühen Neuzeit* (Husum: Mathiesen Verlag, 2014).
4. H. Hein-Kircher, "The Idea of Lwów as a Bulwark against the East," in *Imaging the City*, ed. C. Emden, C. Keen, and D.R. Midgley (Frankfurt a.M.: Peter Lang, 2006),

321–38; A.V. Wendland, "'Semper fidelis': Lwów jako mit narodowy Polaków i Ukraińców, 1867–1939," in *Lwów: Miasto-społeczeństwo-kultura*, ed. K. Karolczak and H.W. Żaliński (Kraków: Akademia Pedagogiczna, 2002), 263–73.
5. With regard to the massive conflicts between Poles and Ruthenians, see, C. Mick, *Lemberg, Lwów, L'viv 1914–1947. Violence and Ethnicity in a Contested City* (West Lafayette: Purdue University Press, 2015); T. Amar, *The Paradox of Ukrainian Lviv. A Borderland City between Stalinists, Nazis, and Nationalists* (Ithaca/London: Cornell University Press, 2015).
6. See, P.O. Loew, "Der genormte Blick aufs Fremde. Reiseführer in und über Ostmitteleuropa," *H-Soz-Kult*, retrieved 15 May 2015 from http://www.hsozkult.de/conferencereport/id/tagungsberichte-2473.
7. Some articles dealing with the myths of Lwów do not focus on their function in Polish mental mapping but on "the town of blurred boundaries" (Joseph Roth). See D. Hüchtker, "Der Mythos Galizien. Versuch einer Historisierung," in *Die Nationalisierung von Grenzen. Zur Konstruktion nationaler Identität in sprachlich gemischten Grenzregionen*, ed. M.G. Müller and R. Petri (Marburg: Herder-Institut, 2002), 81–107; K. Jobst, *Der Mythos des Miteinander. Galizien in Literatur und Geschichte* (Hamburg: Deutsche Gesellschaft für Osteuropakunde, 1998); M. Klańska, "Lemberg. Die 'Stadt der verwischten Grenzen,'" *Zeitschrift für Germanistik* 3 (1993): 33–47.
8. E. Conze, "Sicherheit als Kultur. Überlegungen zu einer 'modernen Politikgeschichte' der Bundesrepublik Deutschland," *Vierteljahreshefte für Zeitgeschichte* 53 (2005): 357–80, 362.
9. C. Daase, "Der Wandel der Sicherheitskultur. Ursachen und Folgen eines erweiterten Sicherheitsbegriffs," in *Zivile Sicherheit. Gesellschaftliche Dimensionen gegenwärtiger Sicherheitspolitiken*, ed. P. Zoche, S. Kaufmann, and R. Haverkamp (Bielefeld: Transcript, 2011), 139–60, 139.
10. On critical revision of theories, see T. Balzacq, S. Léonard, and J. Ruzicka, "'Securitization' Revisited: Theory and Cases," *International Relations 2015*, retrieved 16 July 2016 from http://journals.sagepub.com/doi/pdf/10.1177/0047117815596590.
11. Ibid., 3.
12. Conze, "Sicherheit," 363; idem, "Securitization. Gegenwartsdiagnose oder historischer Analyseansatz?" *Geschichte und Gesellschaft* 38 (2012): 453–67, 456.
13. H. Hein-Kircher, "Überlegungen zur Ausprägung und Funktion von Raummythen," in *Deutschlands östliche Nachbarschaften. Eine Sammlung von historischen Essays für Hans Henning Hahn*, ed. E. Dmitrów and T. Weger (Frankfurt a. M.: Peter Lang, 2009), 105–20; idem, "Historische Mythosforschung," in *Digitales Handbuch zur Geschichte und Kultur Russlands und Osteuropa. Themen und Methoden*, retrieved 25 July 2015 from http://epub.ub.uni-muenchen.de/639/1/hein-mythosforschung.pdf. The mutual impact of myths and "security" has not yet been analyzed.
14. P. Kuroczyński, *Die Medialisierung der Stadt. Analoge und digitale Stadtführer zur Stadt Breslau nach 1945* (Bielefeld: Transcript, 2011), 55–56.
15. B. Struck, "Der genormte Blick auf die Fremde. Reisen, Vorwissen und Erwartung. Die Beispiele Italien und Polen im späten 18. Jahrhundert," in *Der genormte Blick aufs Fremde. Reiseführer in und über Ostmitteleuropa*, ed. R. Jaworski, O.P. Loew, and C. Pletzing (Wiesbaden: Harrasowitz, 2011), 11–35, 21.
16. Kuroczyński, *Medialisierung*, 56; T. Weger, "Das jüdische Krakau und das jüdische Prag in deutschsprachigen Reiseführern," in *Nationale Wahrnehmung und ihre Ste-*

reotypsierung. Beiträge zur historischen Stereotypenforschung, ed. H.H. Hahn and E. Mannová (Frankfurt a. M.: Peter Lang, 2007), 191–211, 192.
17. Kuroczyński, *Medialisierung,* 13; H.M. Enzensberger, "Vergebliche Brandung der Ferne. Eine Theorie des Tourismus," *Merkur* 12 (1958): 701–20.
18. Kuroczynski, *Medialisierung,* 13–15.
19. Jaworski et al., *Der genormte Blick aufs Fremde.*
20. Kuroczyński, *Medialisierung,* 56.
21. R.M. Mark, *Galizien unter österreichischer Herrschaft. Verwaltung—Kirche—Bevölkerung* (Marburg: Herder-Institut, 1994), 100–101, 109.
22. The statute especially favored the wealthier (mostly Polish) inhabitants who had the status of citizens. See H. Hein-Kircher, "Jewish Participation in the Lemberg Local Self-Government: The Provisions of the Lemberg Statute of 1870," *Jahrbuch des Simon-Dubnow-Insituts/Simon Dubnow Institute Yearbook* 10 (2011): 237–54.
23. In terms of tourism, Lviv was of lesser importance than Cracow with its medieval buildings and was, according to the German travel guide of 1914, a modern city without individual imprint. M. Orłowicz and R. Kordys, *Illustrierter Führer durch Galizien* (Wien/Leipzig: A. Hartleben, 1914), 38.
24. The East Slavs living in the Habsburg monarchy (especially the Ukrainians, but also smaller ethnic groups like the Hutsuls) were denominated as "Ruthenians" (stemming from Rusyn/Rusin); since the turn of the twentieth century, the denomination "Ukrainians" had become more popular because of diverse political streams within the Ruthenian national movement. With World War I, the denomination largely changed to "Ukrainians." Therefore, "Ruthenian" refers to the later "Ukrainians" in the period before World War I.
25. J. Śleziński, *Neu verbesserter Wegweiser der Koen. Hauptstadt Lemberg oder Uebersicht saemmtlicher Herrn Hauseigenthumer mit Angabe der Hausnnummer, Gassen und Pfarreien* (Lwów: B. Lorje, 1863).
26. S. Kunaszewicz, *Wilda przewodnik po Lwówie* (Lwów: K. Wild, 1878), 52, 85.
27. B. Pawlewski, P. Stwiertnia, and A.S. Świątkowski, *Przewodnik z Krakowa do Lwówa, Podhorzec, Podwołoczysk, Brodów, Słobody Rungurskiej, Czernowiec i po Lwówie* (Lwów: Towarzystwo Politechnicze, 1886).
28. Ibid., 58, 78, 92.
29. *Przewodnik po Lwówie wydany przy wspołudziale Wydziału gospodarczego V. Zjazdu Lekarzy I Pryzrodnikow polskich* (Lwów: Drukarnia Ludowa, 1888).
30. Ibid., 50.
31. A. Zipper, *Führer durch die Allgemeine Landesausstellung sowie durch die Königl. Hauptstadt Lemberg* (Lwów: Ausstellungs-Direktion, 1894).
32. The town council discussed its publication and wished to be informed of its progress. *Gazeta Lwówska,* 20 May 1893.
33. A. Zipper, *Führer; Ilustrowany Przewodnik po Lwowie i Powszechnej Wystawy Krajowej* (Lwów: Towarzystwo Upiększenia i Rozwoju Lwowa, 1894).
34. Ibid., 75.
35. Ibid., 79.
36. W. Rolny, *Ilustrowana pamiątka z powszechnej Wystawy krajowej we Lwówie w roku 1894* (Lwów: Ausstellungs-Direktion, 1894).
37. Ibid., 35.
38. Ibid., 37, 39.
39. State Archives of Lviv Oblast (DALO), fond 3, opis 1, spr. 2804, 9.

40. See remarks on the title page in J. Wiczkowski, *Lwów. Jego rozwoj I stan kulturalny oraz przewodnik po miescie* (Lwów: H. Altenberg, 1907). Because of the intended audience, the focus was on environmental topics, public health, medical institutions, and achievements as well as on higher education, while the cultural institutions were only briefly described.
41. Ibid., V.
42. Similarly "Under the Nose of Tatars" (Sous le nez des Tatars) in *Léopol et ses environs. Petit guide pratique illustré avec plan* (Léopol: Société du Engagement du Tourisme en Galicie, 1910), 51.
43. A. Czołowski, "Pogląd na dzieje Lwowa" [View on the History of Lwów], in Wiczkowski, *Lwów*, 15. A similar tone is found in *Przewodnik po Lwówie oraz najnowszy wykaz ulic, placów, ogrodów itp* (Lwów: Lwowskie Biuro Adrescyjno-Informacyjne, 1910).
44. Wiczkowski, *Lwów*, 23.
45. J. Piotrowski, *Lemberg und Umgebung (Żółkiew, Podhorce, Brzeżany und and.). Handbuch für Kunstliebhaber und Reisende* (Lemberg: H. Altenberg, 1916), 8–9. The publication in German during the war is quite interesting. Because of the lack of references for Lviv, we must resort to Przemyśl as an example. M. Orłowicz, *Illustrierter Führer durch Przemyśl und Umgebung mit besonderer Berücksichtigung der Schlachtfelder und Kriegsgräber 1914–1915* (Przemyśl: Verband der Polnischen Vereine, 1917), 3. The guide was aimed at tourists currently visiting and especially at those who would come after the war. But we can assume that, especially with regard to Lviv, there may have been deeper legitimizing reasons at work.
46. Piotrowski, *Lemberg und Umgebung*, 8–9.
47. All quotations are from Piotrowski, *Lemberg*, 30, 33.
48. Ibid., 36–37.
49. See Paul Srodecki's contribution on the Polish Catholic Right in this volume.
50. M. Orłowicz, *Ilustrowany przewodnik po Lwowie* (Lwów/Warszawa: Książnica-Atlas, 1925; reprint Krosno: Ruthenus, 2005). The first edition was edited as part of the series Uniwersytet żółnierski and was designated for soldiers coming to Lwów (foreword of the second edition, 1925, V); ibid., 58–59. Orłowicz only briefly mentioned the main steps in urban development and the Polonization and rapid development since 1870.
51. See Orłowicz, *Ilustrowany przewodnik*, V, where the foreword of the first edition is reprinted.
52. The explanation is quite long (ibid., 24–35), almost as long as the description of the rest of its history.
53. Ibid., 35, 42.
54. *Ilustrowany przewodnik po Lwowie* (Lwów: Gubrynowicz, 1937), 3.
55. Ibid.
56. A. Czołowski, "Przeszłość Lwowa," in ibid., 68–72, 69–70.
57. Ibid., 70.
58. Ibid., 71.
59. Ibid., 72.
60. Ł. Charewiczowa, *Przewodnik po najważniejszych zabytkach Małopolski Wschodniej związanych z dziejami króla Jana III Sobieskiego* (Lwów: Państwowe Wydawnictwo Książek Szkolnych, 1933).

61. Ibid., 4.
62. Hein-Kircher, *Antemurale*, 138–44.
63. Medyński, *Lwów*.
64. Ibid., 5, 13. See C. von Werdt, "Lemberg [Lviv]," in *Religiöse Erinnerungsorte in Ostmitteleuropa. Konstitution und Konkurrenz im nationen- und epochenübergreifenden Zugriff*, ed. J. Bahlke, S. Rohdewald, and T. Wünsch (Berlin: Akademie Verlag, 2013), 81–90.
65. Medyński, *Lwów*, 1.
66. Ibid., 2.
67. Ibid., 9–10.
68. Generally B. Wöller, *"Europa" als historisches Argument. Nationsbildungsstrategien polnischer und ukrainischer Historiker im habsburgischen Galizien* (Bochum: Winkler, 2014), 93.
69. See *Przewodnik* (1888), 52; *Ilustrowany Przewodnik po Lwowie*, 39.
70. See Jaworski, *Przewodnik po Lwówie*, 30.
71. Orłowicz, *Ilustrowany Przewodnik* (1919), 59.
72. Orłowicz, *Ilustrowany Przewodnik* (1925), 56.
73. Ibid., 59. The lack of individuality, which is at first glance like an "American town," and the few points of interest are the results of a "strange lush and strange heroic past of the town" (Jaworski, *Przewodnik*, 1).
74. Orłowicz, 59–61.
75. The notion is that the slaughterhouse built in 1901 was modeled on foreign slaughterhouses. Wiczkowski, *Lwów*, 60, hints at a "sign of progress" and at an international European level of knowledge. D. Hüchtker, "Der 'Schmutz der Juden' und die 'Unsittlichkeit der Weiber.' Ein Vergleich der Repräsentationen von Armut in Stadt- und Reisebeschreibungen von Galizien und Berlin (Ende des 18./Mitte des 19. Jahrhunderts)," *Zeitschrift für Ostmitteleuropaforschung* 51 (2002): 351–69, 354 shows that in the first half of the nineteenth century, backwardness was a stereotypical description, whereas the increasing modernity of the city has since been focused on as a Polish achievement.
76. Wöller, *"Europa,"* 87.
77. S. Szczepanowski, *Nędza Galicyjska w cyfrach i program energicznego rozwoju gospodarstwa krajowego* (Lwów: Gubrynowicz i Schmidt, 1888).
78. S. Wasylewski, *Lwów* (Poznań: R. Wegner, 1931), 8.
79. Concerning European civilization as an "antinomic distinction," see, Wöller, *"Europa,"* 162–63.
80. The Hessian collaborative research program Conflict Regions in Eastern Europe, in which the author participates, is elaborating a conceptual approach to this multiethnic and imperial shatter zones.

Bibliography

Balzacq, T., S. Léonard, and J. Ruzicka. 2015. "'Securization' Revisited: Theory and Cases." *International Relations*. Retrieved 16 July 2016 from http://journals.sagepub.com/doi/pdf/10.1177/0047117815596590.

Charewiczowa, L. 1938. *Przewodnik po najważniejszych zabytkach Małopolski Wschod-*

niej związanych z dziejami króla Jana III Sobieskiego. Lwów: Państwowe Wydawnictwo Książek Szkolnych.

Conze, E. 2005. "Sicherheit als Kultur. Überlegungen zu einer 'modernen Politikgeschichte' der Bundesrepublik Deutschland." *Vierteljahreshefte für Zeitgeschichte* 53: 357–80.

———. 2012. "Securitization. Gegenwartsdiagnose oder historischer Analyseansatz?" *Geschichte und Gesellschaft* 38: 453–67.

Czołowski, A. 1937. "Przeszłość Lwowa." In *Ilustrowany przewodnik po Lwowie*, 68–72. Lwów: Gubrynowicz.

Daase, C. 2011. "Der Wandel der Sicherheitskultur. Ursachen und Folgen eines erweiterten Sicherheitsbegriffs." In *Zivile Sicherheit. Gesellschaftliche Dimensionen gegenwärtiger Sicherheitspolitiken*, ed. P. Zoche, S. Kaufmann, and R. Haverkamp, 139–60. Bielefeld: Transcript.

Enzensberger, H.M. 1958. "Vergebliche Brandung der Ferne. Eine Theorie des Tourismus." *Merkur* 12: 701–20.

Hein-Kircher, H. 2005. "Historische Kultforschung." *Digitales Handbuch zur Geschichte und Kultur Russlands und Osteuropas*. Retrieved 25 July 2015 from http://epub.ub.uni-muenchen.de/639/1/hein-mythosforschung.pdf.

———. 2006. "Antemurale christianitis. Grenzsituation als Selbstverständnis." In *Grenzen. Gesellschaftliche Konstitutionen und Transfigurationen*, ed. H. Hecker, 129–48. Essen: Klartext.

———. 2006. "The Idea of Lwów as a Bulwark against the East." In *Imagining the City*, ed. C. Emden, C. Keen, and D.R. Midgley, 321–38. Oxford/New York: Peter Lang.

———. 2009. "Überlegungen zur Ausprägung und Funktion von Raummythen." In *Deutschlands östliche Nachbarschaften. Eine Sammlung von historischen Essays für Hans Henning Hahn*, ed. E. Dimitrow and T. Weger, 105–20. Frankfurt a.M.: Peter Lang.

Hüchtker, D. 2002. "Der 'Schmutz der Juden' und die 'Unsittlichkeit der Weiber.' Ein Vergleich der Repräsentationen von Armut in Stadt- und Reisebeschreibungen von Galizien und Berlin (Ende des 18./Mitte des 19. Jahrhunderts)." *Zeitschrift für Ostmitteleuropaforschung* 51: 351–69.

Ilustrowany przewodnik po Lwowie. 1937. Lwów: Gubrynowicz.

Jaworski, F. 1911. *Przewodnik po Lwowie*. Lwów: Połoniecki.

Kunaszewicz, S. 1878. *Wilda przewodnik po Lwowie*. Lwów: K. Wild.

Kuroczynski, P. 2011. *Die Medialisierung der Stadt. Analoge und digitale Stadtführer zur Stadt Breslau nach 1945*. Bielefeld: Transcript.

Loew, P. O. 2009. "Der genormte Blick aufs Fremde. Reiseführer in und über Ostmitteleuropa." Retrieved 15 May 2015 from http://www.hsozkult.de/conferencereport/id/tagungsberichte-2473.

Lwowskie Biuro Adrescyjno-Informacyjne. 1910. *Przewodnik po Lwówie oraz najnowszy wykaz ulic, placów, ogrodów itp*. Lwów: Lwowskie Biuro Adrescyjno-Informacyjne.

Mark, R. 1994. *Galizien unter österreichischer Herrschaft. Verwaltung—Kirche—Bevölkerung*. Marburg: Herder-Institut.

Medyński, A. 1937. *Lwów. Przewodnik dla zwiedzających miasta*. 2nd ed. Lwów: self-publication.

Orłowicz, M. 1917. *Illustrierter Führer durch Przemyśl und Umgebung mit besonderer Berücksichtigung der Schlachtfelder und Kriegsgräber 1914–1915*. Przemyśl: Verband der Polnischen Vereine.

———. 2005. *Ilustrowany przewodnik po Lwowie*. Lwów/Warszawa: Książnica-Atlas 1925; reprint Krosno: Ruthenus.
Orłowicz, M. and R. Kordys. 1914. *Illustrierter Führer durch Galizien*. Wien/Leipzig: A. Hartleben.
Pawlewski, B., P. Stwiertnia, and A.S. Świątkowski. 1886. *Przewodnik z Krakowa do Lwówa, Podhorzec, Podwołoczysk, Brodów, Słobody Rungurskiej, Czernowiec i po Lwówie*. Lwów: Towarzystwo Politechnicze.
Piotrowski, J. 1916. *Lemberg und Umgebung* (Żółkiew, Podhorce, Brzeżany *und and.*). *Handbuch für Kunstliebhaber und Reisende*. Lemberg: H. Altenberg.
Przewodnik po Lwówie wydany przy wspołudziale Wydziału gospodarczego V. Zjazdu Lekarzy I Pryzrodnikow polskich. 1888. Lwów: Drukamia Ludowa.
Rolny, W. 1894. *Ilustrowana pamiątka z powszechnej Wystawy krajowej we Lwówie w roku 1894*. Lwów: Ausstellungs-Direktion.
Śleziński, J. 1863. *Neu verbesserter Wegweise der Koen. Hauptstadt Lemberg oder Uebersicht saemmtlicher Herrn Hauseigenthuemer mit Angabe der Hausnnummer, Gassen und Pfarreien*. Lwów: B. Lorje.
Société du Engagement du Tourisme en Galicie. 1910. *Léopol et ses environs. Petit guide pratique illustré avec plan*. Léopol: Société du Engagement du Tourisme en Galicie.
State Archives of Lwów Oblast (DALO), fond 3 magistrat, opis 1, spr. 2804, 9.
Struck, B. 2011. "Der genormte Blick auf die Fremde. Reisen, Vorwissen und Erwartung. Die Beispiele Italien und Polen im späten 18. Jahrhundert." In *Der genormte Blick aufs Fremde. Reiseführer in und über Osteuropa*, ed. R. Jaworski, P.O. Loew, and C. Pletzing, 11–35. Wiesbaden: Harrasowitz.
Szczepanowski, S. 1888. *Nędza Galicyjska w cyfrach i program energicznego rozwoju gospodarstwa krajowego*. Lwów: Gubrynowicz i Schmidt.
Towarzystwo dla rozwoju i upiększenia miasta Lwowa. 1894. *Ilustrowany Przewodnik po Lwowie i powszechnej Wystawie Krajowej*. Lwów: Towarzystwo dla rozwoju i upiększenia miasta.
von Werdt, C. 2013. "Lemberg [Lviv]." In *Religiöse Erinnerungsorte in Ostmitteleuropa. Konstitution und Konkurrenz im nationen- und epochenübergreifenden Zugriff*, ed. J. Bahlke, S. Rohdewald, and T. Wünsch, 81–90. Berlin/Boston: Akademie Verlag.
Wasylewski, S. 1931. *Lwów*. Poznań: R. Wegner.
Weger, T. 2002. "Das jüdische Krakau und das jüdische Prag in deutschsprachigen Reiseführern." In *Nationale Wahrnehmungen und ihre Stereotypisierung. Beiträge zur historischen Stereotypenforschung*, ed. H. Hahn and E. Mannová, 263–73. Frankfurt a.M.: Peter Hahn.
Wendland, A.V. 2007. "'Semper fidelis': Lwów jako mit narodowy Polaków i Ukraińców, 1867–1939." In *Miasto-społeczeństwo-kultura Lwów*, ed. K. Karolczak and H. Zalinski, 191–211. Kraków: Akademia Pedagogiczna.
Wiczkowski, J. 1907. *Lwów. Jego rozwoj I stan kulturalny oraz przewodnik po miescie*. Lwów: H. Altenberg.
Wöller, B. 2014. *"Europa" als historisches Argument. Nationsbildungsstrategien polnischer und ukrainischer Historiker im habsburgischen Galizien*. Bochum: Winkler.
Zipper, A. 1894. *Führer durch die Allgemeine Landesausstellung sowie durch die Königl. Hauptstadt Lemberg*. Lwów: Ausstellungs-Direktion.

CHAPTER 4

Ghetto as an "Inner *Antemurale*"?

Debates on Exclusion, Integration, and Identity in Galicia in the Nineteenth and Early Twentieth Centuries

Jürgen Heyde

The term "ghetto" was coined at the beginning of the sixteenth century at a time when *antemurale* had become a sort of trademark concept in societies that understood themselves as being the frontier between different cultures. *Antemurale* describes a religiously and politically conceived demarcation through the use of military phrasing; it constructs an opposition that describes the "Other" (beyond the *antemurale*) not just as a political or military enemy, but as an existential threat to the community shielded by the *antemurale*. This demarcation should not only strengthen social cohesion within the "borderland societies" but also appeal to a larger public, namely the European Christian community, linking borderland peripheries with the Christian core of the Holy See.

A quite similar argumentation also applies to the relation with the Jewish population in Europe: the imagination of a religious and cultural Other threatening the Christian society, which was understood as an overarching, transterritorial community. However, the term *antemurale* has not been used with respect to the Jews, as there was no definite borderline that could be used to symbolize the demarcation because the Jews lived among the Christians. But similarly to the political concept of *antemurale*, there had been a demand for separation, for a clear and visible demarcation between Jews and Christians, since the Middle Ages.

The symbol for this demarcation became "ghetto," its walls representing the unequivocal separation of Jews and Christians, as the spatial concept of ghetto reverses and reproduces the *antemurale*. Anne Cornelia Kenneweg distinguishes three spaces constituting the *antemurale:* the inner space that had to be defended, the outer space as the realm of the enemy, and the border envisioned as a wall or bulwark.[1] Ghetto shifts the connotations of the inner and outer space: in ghetto, the hostile realm lies within the walls, which defend the own space on the outside. Just like *antemurale*, the term "ghetto" outlived the early modern constellations in which it was formed and acquired new political importance in the era of nationalism in the nineteenth and twentieth centuries.[2]

In early modern Italy, the word "ghetto" became essentially a synonym for "Jewish quarter," named after the Jewish area of residence in Venice built in 1516 and separated from the city by walls and gates. Voyagers and travelogues made the term known in other European countries, but it appeared as an exclusively Italian phenomenon until the end of the eighteenth century. This changed at the turn from the eighteenth to the nineteenth century, when the early modern ghettos became gradually dismantled and the spatial segregation of the living areas was lifted.

In public discussions, however, the symbolism of ghetto remained important for a long time and became a metaphor for the segregation and exclusion of the Jews by their non-Jewish environment.[3] In Central and Eastern Europe, where emancipation was withheld until the last decades of the nineteenth century, the Jewish debate about ghetto walls forcibly separating Jews and Christians mixed with the Christian myth of *antemurale* shielding Christianity from the infidels.

This chapter discusses the notion of ghetto as a "reversed" or "inner *antemurale*" in various steps from the Middle Ages to the early twentieth century. The first part asks about the ideological fundaments of the debate, the concepts of spatial segregation between Jews and Christians in anti-Jewish polemics since the Middle Ages. The second part compares the remodeling of Jewish areas of residence in Frankfurt, Cracow (Polish: Kraków), and Venice (Italian: Venezia) at the turn from the fifteenth to the sixteenth century. The third part explains how a ghetto memory was constructed and the role it played in the debates about modern Jewish identity between assimilationist and Zionist authors in nineteenth-century Galicia.[4] Both groups saw ghetto as a symbol of drastic separation between the Jewish and Christian populations—the term, therefore, influenced society and politics as well as the cultural and mental realm. Thus the inner-Jewish debates of the nineteenth century reflected the early modern normative narratives.

Still they differed significantly in their assessment of who was to be held responsible for this segregation. Exclusion and marginalization by the Christian authorities were discussed as well as the significance of Jewish existence in the diaspora for the ghetto experience. Another important part of these discussions were the consequences that living under the conditions of the ghetto had for the Jewish population.

The final part of the chapter examines anti-Semitic concepts of ghetto and their relation to the notion of a Christian bulwark against the Jews. Ghetto did not become an important feature in anti-Jewish polemics until the 1920s and 1930s. These authors did not explicitly refer to early modern legislation but appeared well informed about the inner-Jewish debates on ghetto and Jewish identity—of course interpreting them in a way that fit the logic of radical exclusion that was characteristic for the *antemurale* narrative.

Separating Jews and Christians— Ideological Foundations of the Ghetto

The early modern ghetto was as much an ideological construct as it was, in the words of Benjamin Ravid, the leading historian on early modern ghettos, a "geographical reality."[5] Based on studies on early modern Venice and other Italian towns, he defined ghetto as a "compulsory, segregated and enclosed" Jewish quarter.[6] For an analysis of the interrelation between ghetto and *antemurale*, it is necessary to look first at the ideological foundations that led to the installation of such compulsory, segregated, and enclosed quarters. Second, I will briefly compare three Jewish quarters that were established or fundamentally reconstructed by non-Jewish authorities from the late fifteenth to the early sixteenth century: Frankfurt (1463), Cracow (1495), and Venice (1516). In the debates of the nineteenth and twentieth centuries, all three were remembered as ghettos, even though only the Venice Jewish quarter had been called by this name in early modern official documents.

The demand for the spatial segregation of Jewish and Christian living areas was raised for the first time in thirteenth-century church documents, that is in the statutes of the Synod of Wrocław in 1267. The bishops declared that in the province of Gniezno, Jews were not allowed to live intermingled with Christians; in whatever town or village Jews were residing, their homes had to be separated from the Christians' dwellings by a wall or moat.[7] Jewish houses among Christians should be sold or exchanged within a year, or else the bishop would punish those who disobeyed, if necessary by excommunication or interdict. The spatial segregation was part of a wider program of exclusion: the bishops forbade Christians to invite Jews to festivities of any kind or even to eat or dance with them at Jewish weddings or banquets. Neither should they buy meat or any kind of food from Jews. The bishops argued that those restrictions were necessary because Jews regarded Christians as enemies and tried to poison them.[8]

With these arguments, the bishops of the Gniezno archbishopric reacted to several recent developments: on the one hand, the dukes from Austria and Greater Poland and the kings of Bohemia and Hungary had issued privileges encouraging Jews to settle in their territories, and on the other hand, the urban landscape in the region had been fundamentally transformed since the middle of the thirteenth century and by the previous devastations of the Mongol invasion.[9] During the twenty-five years between the Mongolic retreat and the Synod of Wrocław, the most important urban political centers in the Polish lands had been transferred to Magdeburg law and rebuilt in accordance with the new legal framework. The bishops now saw the opportunity to expand the constitutions of the Lateran councils concerning the avoidance of social contact between Jews and Christians and the demand that Jews wear distinguishing marks on their clothing by a new stipulation: the separation of living areas in the newly remodeled cities.

The Catholic clergy could not, however, rely on the monarchs to enforce these postulates, as their policy was aimed at attracting Jews and offering them convenient conditions for settling in these territories. Moreover, the synod stated that Christianity in the Polish lands was endangered by the presence of the Jews, as it still constituted "a young plantlet"—regardless of the fact that the first Polish ruler had adopted Christianity some 300 years before and another had led a European army to defend Christianity from the Mongols at Legnica twenty-five years before the synod. Be that as it may, this young plantlet had to be protected from the Jews by forcing them to live in segregated areas in the cities, separated from the Christians by walls or a moat. The ferocity of the argumentation shows clear parallels to the rhetoric of *antemurale*, with the difference that *antemurale* promised to defend an already (or still) existing separation, whereas the bishops only tried to create one.

The decrees of the Wrocław synod were unique in a double sense: first, no other synod of the time took the anti-Jewish polemics that far and, second, they had no practical consequences at all. During the next decades, there were no attempts to enforce the decreed measures, and none of the following church congregations returned to the matter. Only at the council of Basel in the first half of the fifteenth century was the topic of segregated living quarters discussed again.[10] The clerics again worried about the interaction between Jews and Christians. To lessen the possibility of intensive contact, the council decreed that Jews should be obliged to live in certain quarters, which were separated from the Christians' dwellings and as far away as possible from churches.[11]

This time, however, the question was raised in a different context. The minutes of the council clearly show the aim to underline the supremacy of the Christian faith, but the Jews were no longer described as dangerous enemies to the faith and the faithful. The segregation of Jews and Christians simply appeared as a necessary feature in a well-ordered Christian society.

Segregation and the Restructuring of Jewish Quarters— the Invention of the Ghetto

In the fifteenth century, however, there was political pressure to put the resolutions of the council into practice—and it was the Jews of Frankfurt who were assigned a segregated and walled-up quarter, *Judengasse* (the Lane of the Jews), instead of their old homes around St. Bartholomew's Church.[12] The old Jewish quarter had been situated in the town center. In 1442 and 1458, Emperor Frederick III (1415–1493) had twice demanded that the magistrate expels the Jews from the city. Two years after the second intervention, the magistrate began negotiations with the Jewish community about relocating the Jewish quarter to a new place in the so-called new town, which had been integrated into the city walls in the fourteenth century. When the Frankfurt magistrate debated the establishment of a new segregated quarter there, they provisionally named it *Neu-Ägypten* (New Egypt)—signaling that the transfer constituted a sort of expulsion from the city.[13] The name did not stick; on the contrary, the term *Frankfurter Judengasse* (Frankfurt's Lane of the Jews) underlined the continuing ties to the city.

About three decades later, the Jewish quarter of Cracow was also removed from the town center and relocated to nearby Kazimierz on the other bank of the Vistula River, after the old quarter had burned down in 1494. A contemporary chronicler described the fire and noted that afterward the burghers lobbied for the relocation as if the Jews were to be blamed for the catastrophe. Officially, however, there was an enquiry as to whether the Ottoman delegation was responsible.[14] In this case, the king acted as an intermediary and offered the Jewish community properties he held in Kazimierz; they had been reserved for the university, which was now located in Cracow—where the first Jewish quarter had been. The relocation to Kazimierz was the second in four decades. The Jewish community had sold the area of the oldest Jewish quarter to the university and acquired new grounds a little farther north only a few years before, in 1469. The grounds in Kazimierz offered by the king were not entirely new to the Jews; in 1488, a *circulus Judaeorium* (Jewish market square) was mentioned in the town records in connection with this place.

Miasto żydowskie (the Jewish town), as it was later called, touched the town walls of Kazimierz in the north and east. In the beginning, however, it was open to the Christian neighborhood without a clear demarcation between Jewish and Christian Kazimierz. The Jewish community acted as owner of the plots inhabited by Jews and negotiated an enlargement of the Jewish town with the magistrate three times (1553, 1583, 1608).[15] Christians continued to live in the new Jewish quarter; however, in 1564, the Jewish community received a royal privilege granting the right of first refusal if a Christian sold his property in the Jewish town—mystified later by modern historiography as *privilegium de non tolerandis Christianis* (privilege of not tolerating Christians).[16] A wall between the Jewish and the Christian parts of Kazimierz was mentioned for the first time in the agreement of 1553, but only after the third enlargement was the Jewish quarter separated from the Christian area partially by a wall, partially by a fence. Still much later, after the Austrian occupation of 1796, the new government tried to transform the Jewish town into a segregated, compulsory, and exclusive quarter where all the Jews in the Cracow area must reside—even though they did not call it ghetto but *Revier* (district).[17]

In 1516, the senate of Venice decided to build a compulsory, segregated, and exclusive living quarter for the Jews. The situation was different from Frankfurt and Cracow, as there had been no previous Jewish quarter in the city. Until 1503, Venetian Jews were allowed to reside only in Mestre, on the Terraferma, and not in the city itself. Because of security concerns relating to the war against the league of Cambrai, Jews had been granted permission to stay in Venice proper during the military crisis. As the war was coming to an end, the Venetian authorities were confronted with vociferous demands for an expulsion of the Jews, but they also considered the benefits of a continued Jewish presence in the city.

The senate of Venice decided to build an area of residence for the Jews in an area that had formerly been used as a foundry and therefore had been called "ghetto."[18] This term quickly became generally accepted because it allowed for different interpretations. The senate was able to pretend that it had not created a Jewish quarter in the town, but the edict of 1516 announced that the senate had taken measures to restore the previous situation, when Jews were forbidden to live in the city. The Venetian authorities indeed created a permanent area of residence for the Jews, whose right to stay in the town had always been rigidly limited. So, instead of returning to the status quo ante, the Jews gained a living quarter not exactly in, but very close to, the city.[19]

The document of 1516 thus emphasized at the beginning the aim to reestablish the old order that Jews were not allowed to dwell in the city, which had been circumvented by *perfidia hebraica* as well as by necessity and the extraordinary conditions of the time. In order to end such disorder and inconvenience, "the senate had decreed that the Jews should reside in the court of houses in the ghetto behind the church of San Girolamo."[20]

The rhetoric of restoring a state of separation between Christians and Jews, which had been undermined by "Jewish perfidy," clearly alludes to the *antemurale* narrative. Just like the statute of the Wrocław synod, it evokes the notion of security—to be ensured by the ghetto/separation in general—and thus creates a mythical space of confinement, separating Christians and Jews, order and danger.

Venice and Frankfurt are examples for an "inner *antemurale*," a visible separation and demonstrative exclusion of the Jews who, despite this, ensured their continuous presence as a manifestation of the Other. In Cracow, by contrast, the relocation of the Jewish quarter was effected without any reference to anti-Jewish rhetoric, despite the intensive use of *antemurale* rhetoric in Polish public discourse in the fifteenth century.

In both Frankfurt and Venice, there was political pressure to expel the Jews, not to install permanent residential areas. In Frankfurt, the authorities accepted the established name of *Judengasse*, whereas in Venice, the senate tried not to acknowledge the existence of a Jewish quarter. One of the most important reasons the term "ghetto" became so popular in early modern Italy was that it was open to interpretation from both sides, making it possible to fuse exclusionary rhetoric with inclusionary practice. This ambiguity also becomes evident in the location of many early modern ghettos. While the Jewish area of residence in Venice was placed outside the city center (but decidedly nearer than it had been before 1503), the ghettos in Florence (Italian: Firenze) and Siena that were set up in the sixteenth century were located in the very center of these cities, with gates opening directly to the market square.[21] Thus, while the establishment of Jewish quarters in early modern Italian towns was very often accompanied by the rhetoric of exclusion,[22] David Ruderman has underlined that the institution of the ghetto provided Jews with "a legal and natural residence within the economy of Christian space."[23]

This ambiguity faded during the period of the French Revolution and Napoleon's (1769–1821) conquest of Italy. The revolutionary troops saw the walls of the ghetto as symbols of segregation and inequality—not only separating Jews and Christians but also demarcating social boundaries in general. Therefore, whenever the French army conquered a city, these walls were torn down in an official ceremony and often the street leading to the ghetto was renamed Via libera.[24]

Ghetto and Jewish Identity in Nineteenth-Century Galicia

During the first decades of the nineteenth century, mentions of ghetto appeared sporadically in public debates. They were sometimes used as a metaphor for political oppression, as in the years before the 1848 revolution, when Ludwig Börne (1786–1837) rhetorically asked whether Germany had become "the ghetto of Europe."[25] At other times, ghetto was seen as an equivalent for Jewish quarter, for instance in 1859, when Abraham Gumplowicz (1803–1876) wrote about the first "Germans"—meaning liberal Jews in Western-style clothing—in the streets of the Cracow ghetto.[26] The term became popular in the Jewish assimilationist press in Galicia in the early 1880s mainly for two reasons. The liberal Jewish press could no longer ignore the rise of anti-Semitism in Central Europe. The Jewish press reacted with irritation to the pogroms in the Russian Empire, at first blaming them for "Asian despotism," but could not dismiss the Warsaw incidents around Christmas 1881 in the same way.[27] The rise of anti-Semitism in Hungary, especially the accusation of ritual murder in Tisza-Eszlar, but also the debates on mixed marriages in the Hungarian upper house in 1884, evoked an even stronger reaction.[28] But liberal Jews and their assimilationist agenda found themselves in the crosshairs not only of anti-Semites but also of conservative Jewish circles. Following Maskilic traditions, the assimilationists usually dismissed Rabbinic and Hasidic Judaism as a spent force, a relic of the past, so the liberal Jewish press was enraged in 1882 when the conservatives ensured the ongoing recognition of the cheder schools as part of the Jewish curriculum.[29] The assimilationist camp imagined itself fighting on two frontiers—against anti-Semitism and against traditional or Hasidic Judaism; both were in a way associated with ghetto.

In 1884, the Viennese journalist Isidor Singer (1857–1927) explained the liberal agenda; he pointed out that the Jewish people had been imprisoned in dark, locked ghettos much like cattle for almost 2,000 years, but a few years of freedom brought forth men like Baruch de Spinoza (1632–1677), Felix Mendelssohn Bartholdy (1809–1847), Ferdinand Lassalle (1825–1864), and others. However, the ghetto was not just a part of history overcome by emancipation.[30] Singer mentioned that his remarks represented the liberal Jewish point of view, while there were other fellow Jews who were still "unable to understand the spirit of the time and opt[ed] to stick to all the Talmudic rules, returning to live in the dark gloomy ghettos instead of acknowledging themselves as free citizens of the nineteenth century."[31]

The rift dividing the Jewish population was accentuated even more in an 1883 brochure published in Lviv by Zygmunt Fryling (1854–1931), in which he dealt with the dangers of continuing traditional forms of Jewish education as symbolized by the cheder system.[32] The cheder was, in his words, a symbol of the power that the rabbis and "miracle workers"—that is the Hasidic rebbes—held over the Jewish masses:

> These rabbis rant so fanatically against emancipation because in the old times, when the Jews had been regarded as pariahs and could live in assigned corners only, they were the real kings of the Jews, and nowadays they try to restore the old times in order to reign again in the ghetto.[33]

Leaving the ghetto behind, Fryling and Singer stated, was not about leaving the Mosaic faith and converting to Christianity. For Fryling, the most important feature was to leave all external signs of the ghetto behind: clothes, behavior, customs including the payot (side curls), and—most of all—language, the dreaded jargon, as Yiddish was called by modern Jews at the time.

A decade later, early Zionist authors adopted the notion of ghetto as a sort of prison forced upon the Jews in former times. They also stressed the isolation of the ghetto existence but came to a different conclusion. It was not the road to assimilation that opened up when the walls of the ghetto were torn down, but the possibility for the Jewish people to assert themselves as a nation among others. In one of the first editorials of the newly founded periodical *Przyszłość* (Future), the author proclaimed that the so-called Jewish question was in principle based on the fact that there had been a "foreign element with its strongly formed individualism" among the Christian peoples. When the ghetto walls crumbled, the Jews found themselves in a blatant antagonism to their surroundings that had been masked by the isolation of the ghetto. In the moment of emancipation, the Jews' difference—in customs, character, and way of thinking, in their totally different view of the world—became obvious.[34]

In the following year, Salomon Schiller (1862–1925) compared the ghetto to a prison:

> They locked us up in ghettos, but it was just the fact that they kept us away from themselves with this prison autonomy, which strongly supported the development of independent national and sociocultural characteristics. No less important for our national psyche was the contempt we had for the Arians because that way our consciousness of superiority grew stronger and we were filled with the thought that we are the chosen nation.[35]

He compared the Jewish psyche during the centuries of the ghetto to the mind of a prisoner, whose worldview becomes confined to the prison walls to the point that he starts to hallucinate. The Jews turned to their national heritage, to the voices of the old kings and prophets, awaiting the return of the messiah. Therefore, he concluded, those who accuse Jews of having no fatherland were wrong. The ghetto—and the fact that the Jews survived as a people—was testimony to their "national existence."[36]

Christians imposed the ghetto on the Jews, forcing upon them an existence in isolation and confinement. However, the ghetto enabled the Jews in the diaspora not to become dispersed among the nations but to stick together as a nation. The duality of oppression and preservation was the leading motif in one of the first published sermons of Ozjasz Thon (1870–1936), when he was in Berlin, before he became rabbi at Cracow's temple synagogue.[37] In his sermon, Thon differentiates between the history of the Jews in the ghetto as seen from the outside and from the inside. From the outside, the ghetto represented "a picture of hopelessness, full of hatred and persecution, never a quiet moment for the Jews."[38] The ghetto was the epitome of Jewish suffering in the diaspora. However, one could see an entirely different picture from the inside, for within the walls of the ghetto:

> There lives and works the spirit of the Lord. In the prayer houses hot and heartfelt prayers are directed to the Lord that he may rescue his people. . . . The Jews in the ghetto are singing all the time, and their basic melody is the love of God and his great, chosen nation, Israel.[39]

In a dialectic sense, ghetto became the final part of the Jewish diaspora, the bleakest and darkest point in that period, but exactly that was what heralded the coming of a new era—the return to the land of the fathers and the resurrection of the Jewish nation. Thus ghetto represented, in a way, an entirely Jewish place.

Some of the more secular-minded writers did not share the optimism of Thon and Schiller. An editorial in the Lviv weekly, *Wschód* (East), from 1901 linked ghetto to the proverbial Galician poverty[40] and asked why the Galician Jews seemed unable to adapt to the modern world. It was pointed out that in Galicia:

> The bleak mass of Jewish paupers still lives under medieval conditions. Everything around them is subject to change, but their way of thinking and of making a living still remains archaic. Why is it that Galician Jews have lost their proverbial sense of adaptation and persisted in the narrow confines of the ghetto, in a time when even the eastern Galician peasant adapted to the new conditions and circumstances?[41]

At the beginning of the twentieth century, Zionism became a major force in Galicia, driving the assimilationists to the defensive. The Zionists' main goal, the formation of a Jewish nationality, was directly opposed to the goal of assimilation. After years of deep crisis, when the old assimilationist works in Galicia had ceased to be published, a new weekly under the title *Jedność* (Unity) was formed in Lviv in 1907. The editors and authors frequently referred to ghetto, but they attached a new meaning to the term. Ghetto still embodied isolation but was no longer linked to the past. Instead, it represented a danger for the future, a danger caused by the common machinations of Zionists and anti-Semites who were working to isolate the Jews from their Christian surroundings, destroying the legacy of enlightenment and emancipation.

In 1907, in an editorial in one of the first issues of *Unity*, the author stated that the Jews in Poland had never experienced anything like the chain of persecutions and cruelties the Western European Jews had had to endure. For this reason, he concludes, the centuries-old ties linking the Jewish population to the Polish nation could not be severed by "ad hoc sophisms." For eight centuries, the Jewish people had based their very existence on the fate they shared with the Polish nation, with its history and destiny. The article, which contains not even a passing note of the pogroms of Warsaw in 1881 or in Galicia in 1898, was motivated by an electoral pact between Zionists and Ruthenians during the Galician campaign of 1907—which for the author was a clear sign of treason. Two years later, another editorial proclaimed that the very demand of national autonomy for the Jews was tantamount to a "return to the ghetto."[42] Such a return—from the path of assimilation—whether proposed by Jewish separatists or Polish anti-Semites, could easily be seen as folly by the enlightened parts of Polish society.

The assimilationist press in Galicia at the beginning of the twentieth century fundamentally redefined the ghetto narrative. Their authors no longer focused on ghetto as a historical obstacle to the inclusion of Jews in Polish society. Instead, they envisioned the present society as shared by Poles and Jews but threatened by Zionists and anti-Semites, who were trying to divide the Jewish-Polish symbiosis and move the Polish Jews into a ghetto like the ones that Western European Jews had had to endure for centuries.[43]

The Zionist press paid the assimilationists back in their own coin. For them, ghetto became a derogatory expression for Jews who were trying to ingratiate themselves with anti-Semites or any non-Jewish nationalists, like Rudolf Gall (1873–1939), a Jewish member of the Austrian parliament who voted in favor of honoring the deceased Vienna mayor (and prominent anti-Semite) Karl Lueger (1844–1910) in 1910. His action, the author of an article in *East* deplored, gave testimony to the "crestfallen oppressed psyche of a Jewish ghetto 'Moszko' kissing the whip of his persecutor."[44] At the beginning of the twentieth century, ghetto became more and more detached from historical contexts. Even the link between the connotations oppression/exclusion and isolation/segregation became unclear, while the term "ghetto" itself turned into a sort of negatively loaded emoticon that could be applied to almost random contexts.

The inner-Jewish debates on ghetto mirror many characteristics of the *antemurale* myth, most prominently the notion of violent exclusion. Jewish authors, however, had no interest in upholding the political myth behind it, and thus ghetto slowly eroded into a vaguely negative metaphor before vanishing almost completely from inner-Jewish public discussion in the years before WWI.

Anti-Semitism and the Term "Ghetto"

The term "ghetto" appeared comparatively late in anti-Semitic publications, sporadically just before WWI, though not on a wider scale until the 1920s and 1930s. In Poland, "ghetto" was used in the context of the relation between Polish "hosts" and Jewish "guests" when nationalist writers sought to affirm their position through anti-Semitism after the main goal of the national movement—the resurrection of Polish statehood—had been achieved. The 1920s and 1930s were a time when the *antemurale* motif became popular once again and was directed against mostly communism and the Soviet Union. In Polish nationalist discourse, the *antemurale* motif was used to promote an antagonistic vision of society, a division between Poles and "minorities" through agitation against the latter.[45]

In the case of the Jews, nationalist writers proclaimed that their ideal was to solve the Jewish question through mass emigration of the Jews, but they conceded that such a solution seemed unlikely and impractical because of the great number of Jews living in Poland.[46] National students' organizations as early as the early 1920s lobbied for restrictions against Jewish students in the form of a *numerus nullus,* that is, total exclusion from higher studies, or at least a *numerus clausus.*[47] In 1924, Zbigniew Stypułkowski (1904–1979) elaborated on this demand in the student organ the *Młodzież Wszechpolska* (All-Polish Youth).[48] He postulated an all-encompassing social segregation between Jews and Poles, which meant the elimination of Jews from all fields of Polish state, economic, cultural, ethical, and societal life. He argued that the Jews could achieve a degree of autonomy never realized before, because they would be granted full freedom to set up their ghetto the way they liked. Of course, he added, there had to be several conditions: the Jews were to be totally excluded from the Polish legal and public system and had to organize themselves solely within the confines of Polish statehood. Any contact with world Jewry had to be forbidden in order to avoid any dangers to the Polish state borders.[49] Later, anti-Semitic writers tried to portray the concept of ghettoization as the renewal of an old Jewish tradition, for the Jews had concentrated themselves in Jewish quarters since the Middle Ages and that was, in fact, the origin of the ghetto.[50]

In Germany, concepts of ghettoization did not play an important role even after 1933. Only Peter Heinz Seraphim's (1902–1979) 1937 book

Das Judentum im osteuropäischen Raum (The Jews in the East European Realm) discussed ghetto in relation to Eastern European—meaning mostly Polish—Jews at length. He picked up the Zionist notion of ghetto as a Jewish space and put his own spin on it. He claimed that the medieval ghetto was anything but the bête noir of living space constraints, as had often been said—and "not without purpose." He points to the fact that in medieval towns, artisans of one profession were living in the same street, and he stresses the religious motives for the Jews to favor living in a compact setting because the Talmud forbade them any social interaction with non-Jews.[51]

More important for him, however, was the ghetto's function as the origin of Jewish expansion. In his opinion, the ghetto was the cause of excess population and social misery, which forced the Jews into the non-Jewish branches of the economic and cultural life of the host countries. The ghetto constituted the core of Jewish commercial life and controlled the whole state-wide economic system. Jewish traders, from peddlers and ragmen to middlemen, wholesale merchants, and export merchants lived together in the ghetto. From the ghetto, the Jewish artisan found his way into the factories; in the ghetto the future religious and political leaders were educated; here, the Jewish character in its specific Eastern European form evolved in order to influence its surroundings, the nations where the Jews were living.[52]

Seraphim envisions a fundamental antagonism between the Jewish and non-Jewish populations, but for him the ghetto was not a way to achieve segregation in the sense of the *antemurale* motif. Instead, the ghetto was part of a Jewish conspiracy to undermine and destroy the non-Jewish society. Talking about the early modern ghettos, he does not directly deny any Christian pressure in their evolution but does not elaborate on it—to him, the ghetto was an entirely Jewish institution.[53] In this context, he transforms the Jews from victims to perpetrators whose every action is aimed at harming the non-Jewish societies in which they—being guests—should be assigned a lower status from the very beginning, making their guest privileges revocable at any time.

He wrote his book under the influence of the National Socialist policy that was geared toward isolating and marginalizing the Jews in order to force them into emigration. When the book was published in 1937, the establishment of ghettos was not part of National Socialist politics yet. Seraphim took on the inner-Jewish debates and implicitly argued against the notion of assimilation, which frequently led him to adopt Zionist arguments. In his discussion of Eastern European Jews, he applied German standards, in which assimilation was the rule. He missed the core of the Jewish question in Eastern Europe because he was playing to the expectations of his German public. Thus, while overtly analyzing Eastern European relations, he catered to the anti-Jewish National Socialist policy.

Both Polish and German anti-Semitic writers tried to apply the *antemurale* ratio to the Jews, portraying them as demonic forces threatening the very core of the Polish or German (or even Arian) societies. Their different approaches to ghetto—even though they appeared to be talking about the same Jewish populations—shows that they were in fact talking about very different contexts.

Conclusion

Ghetto and *antemurale* show significant similarities in the way they were conceptualized and in the way they were remembered. Both created an image of the Other as a dangerous enemy that had to be kept at a distance to avoid the destruction of the Christian order. I have analyzed the rhetoric of exclusion and demonization used to justify the need for spatial separation between Christians and Jews in the Middle Ages and shown that the implementation of these demands in the form of segregated Jewish areas of residence could take on many forms in early modern Europe. In early modern practice, more often than not, ghetto implemented the rhetoric of exclusion only superficially; in many ways, it turned out to be a means of integrating Jews into the Christian social order and a way of circumventing more drastic measures of exclusion, such as expulsions.

In modern times, however, when ghettos as compulsory areas of residence had been dismantled, the narrative of exclusion continued to shape the memory of the ghetto. It is striking that this memory was strongest not in those countries where the Jewish quarters had once officially been called ghettos but in those countries where the memory of *antemurale* was kept alive and governments denied Jewish emancipation until the late nineteenth century.

In Jewish memory in Galicia, ghetto as an inverse *antemurale*—where the Jews, although living amid Christians, were separated from them through prisonlike walls—reflected the *antemurale* narrative and told the same story from the victims' point of view. For Eastern European Jews, living in a diaspora dispersed among Christians, ghetto appeared to be the other side of the coin of the Christian exclusionism apparent in the *antemurale* motif. Sensing the impossibility of integration, Zionist writers adopted the underlying idea of a bulwark guarding the culture and conceptualized ghetto as a genuine Jewish space that helped to keep Jewish culture alive in the times of dispersion. Later yet, anti-Semitic authors mixed what they heard about the Jewish ghetto memory with primal concepts of *antemurale* and conceptualized ghetto anew as a means of practical exclusion.

Jürgen Heyde has worked since 2014 as project leader and research associate at the Leibniz Institute for the History and Culture of Eastern Europe (GWZO), University of Leipzig, Germany. He teaches East European History and Jewish History at Martin Luther Universität Halle-Wittenberg, where he was nominated außerplanmäßiger Professor (extracurricular professor) in 2016. He studied Eastern European history, Polish/Slavonic studies, and medieval history from 1987 to 1993 in Giessen, Mainz, Warsaw, and Berlin, and completed his doctorate at the Freie Universität Berlin in 1998.

Notes

1. A.C. Kenneweg, "Antemurale christianitatis," in *Europäische Erinnerungsorte*, vol. 2: *Das Haus Europa*, ed. P.d. Boer, H. Duchhardt, G. Kreis, and W. Schmale (München: Oldenbourg Verlag, 2012), 73.
2. P. Srodecki, *Antemurale christianitatis. Zur Genese der Bollwerksrhetorik im östlichen Mitteleuropa an der Schwelle vom Mittelalter zur Frühen Neuzeit* (Husum: Matthiesen Verlag, 2015).
3. J. Heyde, "Making Sense of 'the Ghetto': Conceptualizing a Jewish Space from Early Modern Times to the Present," in *Jewish and Non-Jewish Spaces in Urban Context*, ed. A. Gromova, F. Heinert, and S. Voigt (Berlin: Neofelis Verlag, 2015), 37–61.
4. The terms "assimilationist" and "Zionist" are used in accordance with their application in contemporary publications. The supporters of assimilation (in today's terms, "integrationists") saw themselves as successors of the Galician Maskilim and the Jewish Enlightenment of the early nineteenth century. They opted for close ties between the Jews and their "host nations" and against messianic dreams of an end to the diasporic existence and a return of the Jewish people to the Holy Land. On the other hand, they vehemently rejected accusations that assimilation would destroy Jewish identity and lead to the extinction of Jewish life. The Galician Zionist (or diaspora nationalist) movement was formed in the 1880s because of the dissatisfaction of younger activists with the lack of progress in the process of emancipation. At the turn of the century, many of them became enthusiastic followers of Theodor Herzl (1860–1904) without believing in emigration as the most important solution to the Jewish question. On the basic characteristics of both movements and their close personal interrelations, see E. Mendelsohn, "Jewish Assimilation in Lvov: The Case of Wilhelm Feldman," *Slavic Review* 28, no. 4 (1969): 577–90, and idem, "From Assimilation to Zionism in Lvov: The Case of Alfred Nossig," *Slavonic and East European Review* 49, no. 117 (1971): 521–34.
5. B. Ravid, "From Geographical Realia to Historiographical Symbol. The Odyssey of the Word 'Ghetto,'" in *Essential Papers on Jewish Culture in Renaissance and Ba-*

roque Italy, ed. D.B. Ruderman, 373–85 (New York: New York University Press, 1992).
6. B. Ravid, "All Ghettos Were Jewish Quarters but Not All Jewish Quarters Were Ghettos," *Jewish Culture and History* 10, nos. 2–3 (2008): 14.
7. I. Zakrzewski and F. Piekosiński, eds., *Kodeks dyplomatyczny Wielkopolski/Codex diplomaticus Poloniae Maioris*, vol. 1 (Poznań: Nakładem Biblioteki Kórnickiej, 1877), 370–75, 423; J. Heil, "Die propagandistische Vorbereitung des Ghettos— Diskussionen um Judenquartiere," in *Frühneuzeitliche Ghettos in Europa im Vergleich*, ed. F. Backhaus, G. Engel, G. Grebner, and R. Liberles, 156–57 (Berlin: Trafo, 2012).
8. "Iudei Christanos, quos hostes reputant, fraudulenta machinatione venenent," in *Kodeks dyplomatyczny Wielkopolski*, 374.
9. Z. Kowalska, "Die großpolnischen und schlesischen Judenschutzbriefe des 13. Jahrhunderts im Verhältnis zu den Privilegien Kaiser Friedrichs II. (1238) und Herzog Friedrichs II. von Österreich (1244)," *Zeitschrift für Ostmitteleuropa-Forschung* 47, no. 1 (1998): 1–20; S. Szczur, *Historia Polski. Średniowiecze* (Kraków: Wydawnictwo Literackie, 2002), 2622–64.
10. G. Alberigo, H. Jedin, J. Wohlmuth, and G. Sunnus, eds., *Dekrete der ökumenischen Konzilien*, vol. 2: *Konzilien des Mittelalters vom ersten Laterankonzil (1123) bis zum fünften Laterankonzil (1512–1517)* (Paderborn: Ferdinand Schöningh, 2000), 483– 84. On debates about *antemurale* at the Council of Basel, see Srodecki, *Antemurale Christianitatis*, 128–42.
11. G. Alberigo et al. *Dekrete der ökumenischen Konzilien*, 483.
12. T. Burger, *Frankfurt am Main als jüdisches Migrationsziel zu Beginn der Frühen Neuzeit. Rechtliche, wirtschaftliche und soziale Bedingungen für das Leben in der Judengasse* (Wiesbaden: Kommission für die Geschichte der Juden in Hessen, 2013), 63–85; F. Backhaus, "Die Einrichtung eines Ghettos für die Frankfurter Juden im Jahre 1462," *Hessisches Jahrbuch für Landesgeschichte* 39 (1989): 59–86.
13. I. Kracauer, *Geschichte der Juden in Frankfurt a.M. (1150-1824)*, vol. 1 (Frankfurt a.M.: Keip, 1987), 205.
14. M. Miechovita, *Chronica Polonorum* (Kraków: Krajowa Agencja Wydawnicza, 1986 [reprint of the edition Cracoviae 1521]), CCCXLIX.
15. M. Piechotka and K. Piechotka, *Oppidum Judaeorum. Żydzi w przestrzeni miejskiej dawnej Rzeczypospolitej* (Warszawa: Krupski i S-ka, 2004), 150–63; B. Krasnowolski, *Ulice i place Krakowskiego Kazimierza. Z dziejów Chrześcijan i Żydów w Polsce* (Kraków: Uniwersytet Jagielloński, 1992); M. Bałaban, *Historja Żydów w Krakowie i na Kazimierzu, 1304–1868*, vol. 1 (Kraków: Nadzieja, 1931), 187–99.
16. J. Heyde, "Raum und Symbol. Das jüdische Viertel in der frühen Neuzeit als 'Ghetto' in den Werken Majer Bałabans," *Kwartalnik Historii Żydów/Jewish History Quarterly* 240, no. 4 (2011): 445–61; J.A. Gierowski, "Die Juden in Polen im 17. und 18. Jahrhundert und ihre Beziehungen zu den deutschen Städten von Leipzig bis Frankfurt a.M.," in *Die wirtschaftlichen und kulturellen Beziehungen zwischen den jüdischen Gemeinden in Polen und Deutschland vom 16. bis zum 20. Jahrhundert*, ed. K.-E. Grözinger (Wiesbaden: Harrassowitz Verlag, 1992), 3–19.
17. M. Bałaban, *Dzieje Żydów w Galicyi i w Rzeczypospolitej Krakowskiej 1772–1868* (Lwów: Księgarnia Polska B. Połonieckiego, 1914), 86–89, 111 passim; E. Bergman, "The *Rewir* or Jewish District and the *Eyruv*," *Studia Judaica* 5, no. 1 (2002): 85–97.

18. B. Ravid, "The Religious, Economic and Social Background of the Establishment of the Ghetti of Venice," in *Gli Ebrei e Venezia*, ed. Gaetano Cozzi (Milano: Edizioni Comunita, 1987), 211–59; idem, "The Venetian Government and the Jews," in *The Jews of Early Modern Venice*, ed. R.C. Davis and B. Ravid (Baltimore: Johns Hopkins University Press, 2001), 3–30.
19. E. Crouzet-Pavan, "Venice between Jerusalem, Byzantium, and Divine Retribution: The Origins of the Ghetto," in *Jews, Christians, and Muslims in the Mediterranean World after 1492*, ed. A. Meyuhas Ginio (London: Frank Cass, 1992), 163–79; R. Finlay, "The Foundation of the Ghetto: Venice, the Jews and the War of the League of Cambrai," *Proceedings of the American Philosophical Society* 126, no. 2 (1982): 140–54.
20. Ravid, "Religious, Economic and Social Background," 248–50.
21. S. Kurth, "Das Florentiner Ghetto. Ein urbanistisches Projekt und seine Ursprünge zwischen Gegenreformation und absolutistischem Herrschaftsanspruch," in *Frühneuzeitliche Ghettos in Europa im Vergleich*, ed. F. Backhaus, G. Engel, G. Grebner, and R. Liberles (Berlin: Trafo, 2012), 173–204.
22. Ravid, "All Ghettos Were Jewish Quarters," 5–24.
23. D.B. Ruderman, "The Cultural Significance of the Ghetto in Jewish History," in *From Ghetto to Emancipation; Historical and Contemporary Reconsiderations of the Jewish Community*, ed. D.N. Myers and W.V. Rowe (Scranton: University of Scranton Press, 1997), 7.
24. P. Mendes-Flohr and J. Reinharz, eds., *The Jew in the Modern World: A Documentary History* (Oxford: Oxford University Press, 1995), 122 (Padova, 28 August 1797); A. Viterbo, "Da Napoleone all'Unità d'Italia," in *Il cammino della speranza: Gli Ebrei e Padova*, vol. 2, ed. C. De Benedetti (Padova: Papergraf, 2000), 1–52.
25. L. Börne, "Menzel der Franzosenfresser," in *Sämtliche Schriften*, vol. 3, ed. I. Rippman and P. Rippmann (Düsseldorf: Melzer, 1964), 889; see R. Erb and W. Bergmann, *Die Nachtseite der Judenemanzipation. Der Widerstand gegen die Integration der Juden in Deutschland 1780–1860* (Berlin: Metropol, 1989), 86–96.
26. A. Gumplowicz, "Jüdische Zustände in Krakau, einst und jetzt," *Jahrbuch für Israeliten* 5 (1858–1859): 178–86, 183. Abraham Gumplowicz was a merchant, a member of the Cracow Chamber of Commerce since 1851, and a member of the Cracow town council since 1853. C. Bąk, "Gumplowicz Abraham (1803–1876)," in *Polski Słownik Biograficzny*, vol. 9 (Warszawa: Polska Akademia Nauk, Instytut Historii, 1960–1961), 148–49; See H. Kozińska-Witt, *Die Krakauer Jüdische Reformgemeinde 1864–1874* (Frankfurt a.M.: Peter Lang, 1999).
27. A. Polonsky, *The Jews in Poland and Russia*, vol. 2: *1881–1914* (Oxford: Littman Library, 2010), 5–17; Y. Bartal, *The Jews of Eastern Europe, 1772–1881* (Philadelphia: University of Pennsylvania Press, 2005), 143–56.
28. R. Patai, *The Jews of Hungary: History, Culture, Psychology* (Detroit: Wayne State University Press, 1996), 347–57; M. Marsovszky, "Antisemitism in Hungary," in *Antisemitism in Eastern Europe. History and Present in Comparison*, ed. H.-C. Petersen and S. Salzborn (Frankfurt a.M.: Peter Lang, 2011), 47–65.
29. T. Gąsowski, *Między gettem a światem. Dylematy ideowe Żydów galicyjskich na przełomie XIX i XX wieku* (Kraków: Instytut Historii UJ, 1996), 55–59.
30. I. Singer, *Sollen die Juden Christen werden? Ein offenes Wort an Freund und Feind*, 2nd ed. (Wien: Verlag Oskar Frank, 1884). Isidor Singer was born in 1859 in Mora-

via; studied in Vienna, where he also worked for the French ambassador; and then emigrated to the United States, where he became coeditor of the *Jewish Encyclopaedia* (12 vols., 1901–1906). He died in New York in 1939. See K. Hödl, "Singer, Isidor (Isidore) (1859–1939)," *Österreichisches Biographisches Lexikon 1815–1950*, vol. 12 (Wien: Österreichische Akademie der Wissenschaften, 2004), 296–97.
31. Singer, *Sollen die Juden Christen werden?*, VI.
32. Z. Fryling, *Klątwa galicyjskich rabinów i cudotwórców* (Lwów: nakł. aut., 1883). Zygmunt Fryling was a writer and publisher. An early member of Agudas Achim in Lviv, he later became editor of *Kurier Lwowski*. R. Manekin, "The Debate over Assimilation in Late Nineteenth-Century Lviv," in *Insiders and Outsiders. Dilemmas of East European Jewry*, ed. R.I. Cohen, J. Frankel, and S. Hoffman (Oxford: Littman Library, 2010), 102–30.
33. Fryling, *Klątwa galicyjskich rabinów*, 11.
34. "Za waszą i naszą wolność," *Przyszłość. Organ narodowej partyi żydowskiej* 13 (5 April 1894), 146 [editorial].
35. S. Schiller, "Nasz byt narodowy (Ciąg dalszy)," *Przyszłość*, 18 (20 June 1896): 139. Salomon Schiller (1862–1925) was born into a Hasidic family. From 1890 onward, he studied in Lviv and later joined the group of editors of *Przyszłość*. He took part in the first Zionist Congress in Basel and emigrated to Jerusalem in 1910. See S. Spitzer, "Schiller, Salomon (1862–1925), Zionist und Hebräist," in *Österreichisches Biographisches Lexikon 1815–1950*, vol. 10 (Wien: Verlag der Österreichischen Akademie der Wissenschaften, 1994), 136.
36. Schiller, "Nasz byt narodowy," 140.
37. Osias (Ozjasz, Jehoshua) Thon, was a rabbi, a leading figure of the Zionist Movement in Galicia, and a politician (a member of the Polish Sejm, 1919–1931). M. Galas, "Ozjasz (Jehoszua) Thon (1870–1936)—Prediger und Rabbiner in Krakau (eine Erinnerung anlässlich seines 75. Todestags)," *Judaica. Beiträge zum Verstehen des Judentums* 67, no. 3 (2011): 311–20; E. Melzer, "Between Politics and Spirituality: The Case of Dr Ozjasz Thon, Reform Rabbi of Krakow," in *Jews in Kraków*, ed. M. Galas and A. Polonsky (Oxford: Littman Library, 2011), 261–68; M. Galas and S. Ronen, eds., *A Romantic Polish-Jew. Rabbi Ozjasz Thon from Various Perspectives* (Kraków: Jagiellonian University Press, 2015).
38. O. Thon, "Ghetto—emancypacja (1895)," in *Kazania 1895–1906*, ed. O.A. Thon, H. Pfeffer, and M. Galas (Kraków/Budapest: Austeria, 2010), 31–32.
39. Ibid., 32; see J. Heyde, "Ghetto and Emancipation. Reflections on Jewish Identity in Early Works of Ozjasz Thon," in *A Romantic Polish-Jew. Rabbi Ozjasz Thon from Various Perspectives*, ed. M. Galas and S. Ronen, 47–59 (Kraków: Jagiellonian University Press, 2015).
40. S. Szczepanowski, *Nędza Galicyi w cyfrach i program energicznego rozwoju gospodarstwa krajowego*, 2nd ed. (Lwów: Gubrynowicz & Schmidt, 1888).
41. *Wschód* 2 (1901), 9 (30.11.1900), 1 [editorial].
42. His "Syon, a . . . 'Dilo,'" *Jedność* 1, no. 7 (19 April 1907): 1–3; see J. Shanes and Y. Petrovsky-Shtern, "An Unlikely Alliance. The 1907 Ukrainian–Jewish Electoral Coalition," *Nations and Nationalism* 15, no. 3 (2010): 483–505.
43. E. Byk, "Rok 1909," *Jedność* 4, no. 1 (1 January 1910): 1–3.
44. [N.N.] "Moralność niewolnicza albo psycha ghettowa. Posłowi Rudolfowi Gallowi do albumu," *Wschód* 11, no. 26 (8 July 1910): 4.

45. See the contribution of Paul Srodecki on the Polish Catholic Right in this volume. Also see H. Hein-Kircher, "Antemurale christianitatis. Grenzsituation als Selbstverständnis," in *Grenzen. Gesellschaftliche Konstitutionen und Transfigurationen*, ed. H. Hecker (Essen: Klartext, 2006), 129–47, esp. 138–44.
46. J. Holzer, "Polish Political Parties and Antisemitism," *Polin. Studies in Polish Jewry* 8 (1994): 194–205.
47. M. Natkowska, *Numerus clausus, getto lawkowe, numerus nullus, "paragraf aryjski." Antysemityzm na uniwersytecie Warszawskim 1931–1939* (Warszawa: Żydowski Instytut Historyczny, 1999); S Rudnicki, "From 'Numerus Clausus' to 'Numerus Nullus,'" *Polin. A Journal of Polish-Jewish Studies* 2 (1987): 246–68.
48. Z. Stypułkowski, "My i Oni," *Wiadomości Akademickie* (10 December 1924): 2–3.
49. Ibid., 2.
50. M. Sobczak, *Stosunek Narodowej Demokracji do kwestii żydowskiej w Polsce w latach 1918–1939* (Wrocław: Akademia ekonomiczna im. Oskara Langego we Wrocławiu, 1998), 116.
51. P.-H. Seraphim, *Das Judentum im osteuropäischen Raum* (Essen: Essener Verlagsanstalt, 1938), 63; see H.-C. Petersen, *Bevölkerungsökonomie, Ostforschung, Politik. Eine biographische Studie zu Peter-Heinz Seraphim (1902–1979)* (Osnabrück: Fibre, 2007).
52. Seraphim, *Das Judentum im osteuropäischen Raum*, 355.
53. Ibid., 356.

Bibliography

Alberigo, G., H. Jedin, J. Wohlmuth, and G. Sunnus, eds., 2000. *Dekrete der ökumenischen Konzilien*, vol. 2: *Konzilien des Mittelalters vom ersten Laterankonzil (1123) bis zum fünften Laterankonzil (1512–1517)*. Paderborn: Ferdinand Schöningh.
Backhaus, F. 1989. "Die Einrichtung eines Ghettos für die Frankfurter Juden im Jahre 1462." *Hessisches Jahrbuch für Landesgeschichte* 39: 59–86.
Bąk, C. 1960–1961. "Gumplowicz Abraham (1803–1876)." In *Polski Słownik Biograficzny*. Vol. 9, 148–49. Warszawa: Polska Akademia Nauk, Instytut Historii.
Bałaban, M. 1914. *Dzieje Żydów w Galicyi i w Rzeczypospolitej Krakowskiej 1772–1868*. Lwów: Księgarnia Polska B. Połonieckiego.
———. 1931. *Historja Żydów w Krakowie i na Kazimierzu, 1304–1868*. Vol. 1. Kraków: Nadzieja.
Bartal, Y. 2005. *The Jews of Eastern Europe, 1772–1881*. Philadelphia: University of Pennsylvania Press.
Bergman, E. 2002. "The *Rewir* or Jewish District and the *Eyruv*." *Studia Judaica* 5, no. 1: 85–97.
Börne, L. 1964. "Menzel der Franzosenfresser." In *Sämtliche Schriften*. Vol. 3, ed. I. Rippmann and P. Rippmann, 871–984. Düsseldorf: Melzer.
Burger, T. 2013. *Frankfurt am Main als jüdisches Migrationsziel zu Beginn der Frühen Neuzeit. Rechtliche, wirtschaftliche und soziale Bedingungen für das Leben in der Judengasse*. Wiesbaden: Kommission für die Geschichte der Juden in Hessen.
Byk, E. 1910. "Rok 1909." *Jedność* 4, no. 1: 1–3.

Crouzet-Pavan, E. 1992. "Venice between Jerusalem, Byzantium, and Divine Retribution: The Origins of the Ghetto." In *Jews, Christians, and Muslims in the Mediterranean World after 1492*, ed. A. Meyuhas Ginio, 163–79. London: Frank Cass.

Erb, R. and W. Bergmann. 1989. *Die Nachtseite der Judenemanzipation. Der Widerstand gegen die Integration der Juden in Deutschland 1780–1860*. Berlin: Metropol.

Finlay, R. 1982. "The Foundation of the Ghetto: Venice, the Jews and the War of the League of Cambrai." *Proceedings of the American Philosophical Society* 126, no. 2: 140–54.

Fryling, Z. 1883. *Klątwa galicyjskich rabinów i cudotwórców*. Lwów: nakł. Aut.

Galas, M. 2011. "Ozjasz (Jehoszua) Thon (1870–1936)—Prediger und Rabbiner in Krakau (eine Erinnerung anlässlich seines 75. Todestags)." *Judaica. Beiträge zum Verstehen des Judentums* 67, no. 3: 311–20.

Gąsowski, T. 1996. *Między gettem a światem. Dylematy ideowe Żydów galicyjskich na przełomie XIX i XX wieku*. Kraków: Instytut Historii UJ.

Gierowski, J.A. 1992. "Die Juden in Polen im 17. und 18. Jahrhundert und ihre Beziehungen zu den deutschen Städten von Leipzig bis Frankfurt a.M." In *Die wirtschaftlichen und kulturellen Beziehungen zwischen den jüdischen Gemeinden in Polen und Deutschland vom 16. bis zum 20. Jahrhundert*, ed. K.-E. Grötzinger, 3–19. Wiesbaden: Harrassowitz Verlag.

Gumplowicz, A. 1858–1859. "Jüdische Zustände in Krakau, einst und jetzt." *Jahrbuch für Israeliten* 5: 178–86.

Heil, J. 2012. "Die propagandistische Vorbereitung des Ghettos—Diskussionen um Judenquartiere." In *Frühneuzeitliche Ghettos in Europa im Vergleich*, ed. F. Backhaus, G. Engel, G. Grebner, and R. Liberles, 156–57. Berlin: Trafo.

Hein-Kircher, H. 2006. "Antemurale christianitatis. Grenzsituation als Selbstverständnis." In *Grenzen. Gesellschaftliche Konstitutionen und Transfigurationen*, ed. H. Hecker, 129–47. Essen: Klartext.

Heyde, J. 2011. "Raum und Symbol. Das jüdische Viertel in der frühen Neuzeit als 'Ghetto' in den Werken Majer Bałabans." *Kwartalnik Historii Żydów/Jewish History Quarterly* 240: 445–61.

———. 2015. "Ghetto and Emancipation. Reflections on Jewish Identity in Early Works of Ozjasz Thon." In *A Romantic Polish-Jew. Rabbi Ozjasz Thon from Various Perspectives*, ed. M. Gałas and S. Ronen, 47–59. Kraków: Wydawnictwo Uniwersytetu Jagiellońskiego.

———. 2015. "Making Sense of 'the Ghetto.' Conceptualizing a Jewish Space from Early Modern Times to the Present." In *Jewish and Non-Jewish Spaces in Urban Context*, ed. A. Gromova, F. Heinert, and S. Voigt, 37–61. Berlin: Neofelis Verlag.

Hödl, K. 2004. "Singer, Isidor (Isidore) (1859–1939)." In *Österreichisches Biographisches Lexikon 1815–1950*. Vol. 12, 296–97. Wien: Österreichische Akademie der Wissenschaften.

Holzer, J. 1994. "Polish Political Parties and Antisemitism." *Polin. Studies in Polish Jewry* 8: 194–205.

Kenneweg, A.C. 2012. "Antemurale christianitatis." In *Europäische Erinnerungsorte*, vol. 2: *Das Haus Europa*, ed. P. den Boer, H. Duchhardt, G. Kreis, and W. Schmale, 73–81. München: Oldenbourg Verlag.

Kowalska, Z. 1998. "Die großpolnischen und schlesischen Judenschutzbriefe des 13. Jahrhunderts im Verhältnis zu den Privilegien Kaiser Friedrichs II. (1238) und Herzog Friedrichs II. von Österreich (1244)." *Zeitschrift für Ostmitteleuropa-Forschung* 47: 1–20.

Kozińska-Witt, H. 1999. *Die Krakauer Jüdische Reformgemeinde 1864–1874.* Frankfurt a.M.: Peter Lang.

Kracauer, I. 1987. *Geschichte der Juden in Frankfurt a.M. (1150–1824).* Vol. 1. Frankfurt a.M.: Keip.

Krasnowolski, B. 1992. *Ulice i place Krakowskiego Kazimierza. Z dziejów Chrześcijan i Żydów w Polsce.* Kraków: Uniwersytet Jagielloński.

Kurth, S. 2012. "Das Florentiner Ghetto. Ein urbanistisches Projekt und seine Ursprünge zwischen Gegenreformation und absolutistischem Herrschaftsanspruch." In *Frühneuzeitliche Ghettos in Europa im Vergleich,* ed. F. Backhaus, G. Engel, G. Grebner, and R. Liberles, 173–204. Berlin: Trafo.

Manekin, R. 2010. "The Debate over Assimilation in Late Nineteenth-Century Lviv." In *Insiders and Outsiders. Dilemmas of East European Jewry,* ed. R.I. Cohen, J. Frankel, and S. Hoffman, 102–30. Oxford/Portland: Littman Library.

Marsovszky, M. 2011. "Antisemitism in Hungary." In *Antisemitism in Eastern Europe. History and Present in Comparison,* ed. H.-Chr. Petersen and S. Salzborn, 47–65. Frankfurt a.M.: Peter Lang.

Melzer, E. 2011. "Between Politics and Spirituality: The Case of Dr Ozjasz Thon, Reform Rabbi of Krakow." In *Jews in Kraków,* ed. M. Galas and A. Polonsky, 261–68. Oxford: Littman Library.

Mendelsohn, E. 1969. "Jewish Assimilation in Lvov: The Case of Wilhelm Feldman." *Slavic Review* 28: 577–90.

Mendes-Flohr, P. and J. Reinharz, eds. 1995. *The Jew in the Modern World. A Documentary History.* New York/Oxford: Oxford University Press.

Miechovita, M. 1986. *Chronica Polonorum.* Kraków: Krajowa Agencja Wydawnicza [reprint of the edition Cracoviae 1521].

Natkowska, M. 1999. *Numerus clausus, getto ławkowe, numerus nullus, "paragraf aryjski". Antysemityzm na uniwersytecie Warszawskim 1931–1939.* Warszawa: Żydowski Instytut Historyczny.

Nossig, A. 1971. "From Assimilation to Zionism in Lvov." *Slavonic and East European Review* 49: 521–34.

Patai, R. 1996. *The Jews of Hungary. History, Culture, Psychology.* Detroit: Wayne State University Press.

Petersen, H.-C. 2007. *Bevölkerungsökonomie, Ostforschung, Politik. Eine biographische Studie zu Peter-Heinz Seraphim (1902–1979).* Osnabrück: Fibre.

Piechotka, M. and K. Piechotka. 2004. *Oppidum Judaeorum. Żydzi w przestrzeni miejskiej dawnej Rzeczypospolitej.* Warszawa: Krupski i S-ka.

Polonsky, A. 2010. *The Jews in Poland and Russia,* vol. 2: *1881–1914.* Oxford: Littman Library.

Ravid, B. 1987. "The Religious, Economic and Social Background of the Establishment of the Ghetti of Venice." In *Gli Ebrei e Venezia,* ed. G. Cozzi, 211–59. Milano: Edizioni Comunita.

———. 1992. "From Geographical Realia to Historiographical Symbol. The Odyssey of the Word 'Ghetto.'" In *Essential Papers on Jewish Culture in Renaissance and Baroque Italy,* ed. D.B. Ruderman, 373–85. New York: New York University Press.

———. 2001. "The Venetian Government and the Jews." In *The Jews of Early Modern Venice*, ed. R.C. Davis and B. Ravid, 3–30. Baltimore: Johns Hopkins University Press.

———. 2008. "All Ghettos Were Jewish Quarters but Not All Jewish Quarters Were Ghettos." *Jewish Culture and History* 10, no. 2–3: 5–24.

Ruderman, D.B. 1997. "The Cultural Significance of the Ghetto in Jewish History." In *From Ghetto to Emancipation; Historical and Contemporary Reconsiderations of the Jewish Community*, ed. D.N. Myers and W.V. Rowe, 7. Scranton: University of Scranton Press.

Rudnicki, S. 1987. "From 'Numerus Clausus' to 'Numerus Nullus.'" *Polin. A Journal of Polish-Jewish Studies* 2: 246–68.

Schiller, S. 1896. "Nasz byt narodowy (Ciąg dalszy)." *Przyszłość* 18 (20 June): 137–40.

Seraphim, P.-H. 1938. *Das Judentum im osteuropäischen Raum*. Essen: Essener Verlagsanstalt.

Shanes, J. and Y. Petrovsky-Shtern. 2010. "An Unlikely Alliance. The 1907 Ukrainian–Jewish Electoral Coalition." *Nations and Nationalism* 15: 483–505.

Singer, I. 1884. *Sollen die Juden Christen werden? Ein offenes Wort an Freund und Feind*. 2nd ed. Wien: Verlag Oskar Frank.

Sobczak, M. 1998. *Stosunek Narodowej Demokracji do kwestii żydowskiej w Polsce w latach 1918–1939*. Wrocław: Wydawnyctwo Akademii ekonomicznej im. Oskara Langego we Wrocławiu.

Spitzer, S. 1994. "Schiller, Salomon (1862–1925), Zionist und Hebräist." In *Österreichisches Biographisches Lexikon 1815–1950*. Vol. 10, 136. Wien: Verlag der Österreichischen Akademie der Wissenschaften.

Stypułkowski, Z. 1924. "My i Oni." *Wiadomości Akademickie* (10 December): 2–3.

Szczepanowski, S. 1888. *Nędza Galicyi w cyfrach i program energicznego rozwoju gospodarstwa krajowego*. 2nd ed. Lwów: Gubrynowicz & Schmidt.

Szczur, S. 2002. *Historia Polski. Średniowiecze*. Kraków: Wydawnictwo Literackie.

Thon, O. 2010. "Ghetto—emancypacja (1895)." In *Kazania 1895–1906*, ed. O.A. Thon, H. Pfeffer, and M. Galas, 31–32. Kraków/Budapest: Austeria.

Viterbo, A. 2000. "Da Napoleone all'Unità d'Italia." In *Il cammino della speranza: Gli Ebrei e Padova*. Vol. 2, ed. C. De Benedetti, 1–52. Padova: Papergraf.

Wschód 2 (1901), 9 (30.11.1900), 11 (1910), 26 (8.7.1910) [editorial].

"Za waszą i naszą wolność," Przyszłość. Organ narodowy partyi żydowskiej, 13 (5.4.1894), 145–48 [editorial].

Zakrzewski, I. and F. Piekosiński, eds. 1877. *Kodeks dyplomatyczny Wielkopolski/Codex diplomaticus Poloniae Maioris*. Vol. 1, 423. Poznań: Nakładem Biblioteki Kórnickiej.

CHAPTER 5

Holy Ground and a Bulwark against "the Other"
The (Re)Construction of an Orthodox Crimea in the Nineteenth-Century Russian Empire

Kerstin S. Jobst

Since March 2014, when Russia annexed the Crimea for the second time after 1783,[1] the impression has arisen that most people in Western Europe discovered a new and until then unknown territory. Maybe older people still remembered the peninsula as a place where politics were made—at the Yalta Conference for instance, convened in the Livadia Palace near Yalta in February 1945, where the heads of the United States, the United Kingdom, and the Soviet Union discussed Europe's postwar reorganization. For enthusiasts of Russian literature, for example, the peninsula on the northern shores of the Black Sea is connected to the names of Alexander Pushkin (1799–1837), Leo Tolstoy (1828–1910), and Anton Chekhov (1860–1904). But for Russians, this area—an exotic (and not only because of its Mediterranean climate), rather un-Russian peninsula at first glance—means much more. For Russians, the peninsula was and is holy ground and a bulwark against the alleged enemies of Orthodoxy and Russianness; that is the central thesis of this chapter.

People who are more or less acquainted with the peculiarities of Russia's emotional bond with the peninsula have tried to explain it with Russia's eternal will to subsume the lands of the Golden Horde; with its imperial legacy, which began with Ivan Grozny (1530–1584) in the sixteenth century[2]; or—more simply—with the notion that the Crimea is for Russia what Mallorca is for the Germans: a beloved tourist destination.[3] Actually it is more complicated. I argue that after Russia's first annexation in 1783, the Crimea underwent a profound transformation in the Russian collective consciousness and in historical memory. In this process, the formerly unknown or at best dangerous territory, home to the long-standing enemy of the Russian soil and Russian Orthodox faith—the Muslim Crimean Tatars—changed into a beloved, familiar, and undoubtedly Russian land, only warmer and more exotic than the northern Russian heartland.[4]

Since the age of nationalism, the place has been highly mythically charged, which helped to transform it into a "real Russian place," where the ethnic, cultural, or religious "Other" was held at a mental and/or actual distance. As a result of this development, the Crimea became (first for the educated elites only, but after decades for their humbler compatriots as well) a real, inalienable Russian place, more central than peripheral. This process of *osvoenie* (appropriation) was constructed via a set of *schemes* or *habits of thinking* worked into the Russian imperial and post-Soviet discourse.

This chapter will not explain this in detail, but as I argued elsewhere, the Crimea became especially dear to the subjects of the tsar—whether they were "white" or "red"—for many reasons.[5] The peninsula had strategic importance in the context of the "Greek Project" (see below) and the Russian policy against the Ottoman Empire,[6] but this colonial acquisition also served as a laboratory for good colonial rule in the decades after its annexation, by which Russia wanted to prove its capacity for the civilizing mission so often connected to bulwark narrations. Moreover, the Crimea was a locus connected with ancient Greece, the classical Tauris, the Scythians, and Mithridates (to name only a few examples), and as such it was precious to the educated upper classes in Europe, whether they were Russians or non-Russians.[7]

Since the last quarter of the nineteenth century, the peninsula developed into an important pleasure periphery for the Russian Empire and especially for the USSR, where millions of Soviet citizens spent their holidays.[8] Apart from the abovementioned importance of the peninsula in literature and the arts,[9] it is deeply embedded in Russian historical and collective memory as an important battleground of the nation due to the Crimean War and World War II. Finally, the Crimea is regarded as the cradle of Christendom and Russian Orthodoxy. In this chapter I will show the importance of this narration of the Crimea in the Russian discourse in connection with bulwark mythology.

The strong emotional bond of the Russians to the Crimea is in fact based on many elements: the idea of the Crimea as a holy ground, a bastion of Orthodoxy, and of Russianness is part of a very close and enmeshed texture.[10] I will argue that Crimea's development into a kind of holy ground since the second half of the nineteenth century was accompanied by a concerted action of concrete political measures by both high clerics and politicians. Since Mara Kozelsky has recently shown the net of political actions in detail[11] and in order to embed the current situation into its historical background, I will concentrate here on the most important elements in the

Russian discourse, which helped to "Christianize" the Crimea and transformed it into holy ground. The inscription of the peninsula as the "Russian Mount Athos"[12] went hand in hand with a series of narrative elements—the mission of the apostle Andrew to the Scythians, St. Constantine's (826–869; Cyril) and St. Methodius's (815–885) mission to the Khazars, and St. Vladimir's (956–1015) baptism in Chersones—constantly told in different contexts and adapted to different circumstances.

I explore the decisive role the Crimea plays simultaneously as a holy ground and (due to the Muslim Tatar element and the Russian-Ottoman history) as a Christian Orthodox bulwark in these Russian debates. This religiously charged image of the Crimea is often connected to the idea that the peninsula had been a Slavic area of settlement for centuries, where community members fought against nonkin. As I will argue, depending on the ideological setting, this holy ground was defined both in religious and sometimes even in secular or national terms—or both at the same time (especially since the 1850s). After a brief look at the relevance of the topic, I will outline and analyze the key elements of the Crimea as a holy ground narrative with its basic topos of a sacralized nation that opposes internal and external enemies.

The Crimea as Holy Ground—Modern References

The conception of the Crimea as holy ground is very timely: in December 2014, in his speech to the Federal Assembly, president Vladimir Putin justified Russia's annexation of Ukraine's autonomous Crimean Peninsula as a matter of justice and redemption. The Crimea, Putin insisted, was as dear to Russians "as the Temple Mount in Jerusalem" is to Jews and Muslims. Its incorporation into Russia in March 2014,

> was an event of special significance for the country and the people, because Crimea is where our people live, and the peninsula is of strategic importance for Russia as the spiritual source of the development of a multifaceted but solid Russian nation and a centralized Russian state. It was in Crimea, in the ancient city of Chersones—or Korsun, as ancient Russian chroniclers called it—that the Grand Prince Vladimir was baptized before bringing Christianity to the Rus.[13]

A majority of the Russian population supports this view because it never accepted the fact that the Crimea was part of independent Ukraine. After the dissolution of the Soviet Union in 1991, many politicians, artists, and intellectuals expressed their uneasiness: the former mayor of Moscow, Iurii Luzhkov, for instance, argued in 1999 that the Crimea was an integral part of Russia, a "Russian Palestine," which unfortunately was under foreign (i.e., Ukrainian) rule.[14] And Alexander Solzhenitsyn (1918–2008), the Nobel Prize winner for literature in 1970, confessed in 1998 that he felt deeply for his compatriots, the Crimean Russians, who were more or less cut off from their *rodina* (motherland), that is from Russia, not from independent Ukraine. "The Crimea," he stated, "is a part of Russia, regardless of her history and her different nations. Once the Crimea was Italian and Tatar, but in the last 200 years, the Crimea was Russian."[15] The Crimea became *nash* (ours) in others' view as well—the centuries before the Russian annexation in 1783 with all its facets, historical layers, and its imprints by different cultures, religions, and ethnicities disappeared in favor of a monolithic Russian perspective.

Russian Crimea? Some Basic Assumptions about the Crimea as Russian and Orthodox in a Historical Perspective

In the course of time, most Russians "forgot" that the Crimea was first and foremost a colonial acquisition; for them, it was (and still is) the most beautiful, the most heroic, and a definitely very Russian part of the fatherland. During this process of mental appropriation, political, Orthodox, academic, and artistic agents had repeatedly attempted to make the peninsula "more Russian" and "more Orthodox" through a set of concrete political measures and discursive strategies.[16] These included, for instance, attempts to increase the Orthodox population and to decrease the numbers of Muslims, and this was an enormously successful strategy. While in the middle of the eighteenth century, Crimea's total population had a Muslim majority of approximately 400,000–500,000 inhabitants, due to wars, invasions, and migrations their number decreased after the annexation to 300,000.[17]

Immediately after the annexation, an estimated 8,000 Muslims left the peninsula, and after the Treaty of Jassy between Russia and the Ottoman Empire in 1791, which secured Russian sovereignty over the Crimea and buried Muslim hopes for a reestablishment of the Sultan's political supremacy, even more Tatars—between 20,000 and 30,000—left the peninsula. In the following decades, their exodus never completely dried out, eventually peaking after the Crimean War. This and the constant influx of settlers—predominantly of Slavic and Orthodox origin—literally made the place less Muslim.[18]

In addition to these practical policies, the stylization of the Crimea as an old Slavic/Russian area of settlement and center of Orthodox Christianity took place—elements that often overlapped. Even Soviet historiography after World War II, which did not emphasize the religious element, supported the thesis of a massive Slavic colonization of the Crimea at least since the Middle Ages.[19] The aim was to underline the link between Russian lands and the Crimea even in ancient times. Such views of the nineteenth century had their tradition: as early as the mid-eighteenth century, the Russian polymath Mikhail Lomonosov (1711–1765) showed himself convinced of the fact that the Sarmatians, who had settled in the Crimea since the fourth century BCE, had actually been Slavs, an idea that he revised only a couple of years later, when he constructed a kinship between the Slavic tribes of the Rus with the Scythians, who for him were of Finnish descent![20] Such interpretations were not undisputed among educated Russians. For the famous Russian historian Vasilii Kliuchevskii (1841–1911), for example, the "presence of Slavs . . . in the midst of these ancient peoples" in the later Russian south had been only marginal in the Middle Ages.[21] But despite such voices, the idea of a Slavic Crimea ever since ancient times had its audible and prominent supporters.

It is undisputed that the Crimea was a site of early Christianity.[22] Due to its peripheral location in the Eastern Roman Empire, it became an important place of exile for clerics who had fallen out of favor.[23] Since the eighteenth century, this early contact with Eastern (not Slavic!) Christianity made the Crimea especially valuable for the Russians because the Tsarist Empire could thus look back on a long tradition of governing a realm of early human civilization. A historically proven connection between East Slavic lands and the peninsula is more recent; it dates back to the tenth century, when Slavic-Norman people from Kyivan Rus appeared on the shores of the Black Sea and on the peninsula. They became another important agent in this area, at times trading peacefully with the Byzantine Empire, the Greek colonies, and the Khazars, "one of the most significant players in the international politics and economy of the Black Sea zone"[24] from the seventh until the tenth century. But sometimes, the people from the north just came to raid.

Although the Crimea and Kyivan Rus had been in a steady process of transfer and communication since then, one cannot speak of a Slavic dominance or majority on the Crimea before the decades after Russian annexation. Since the fifteenth century, when the Muslim Crimean Khanate arose, the Crimea had not even been a predominantly Christian Orthodox territory. This was particularly true for the years immediately prior to the annexation of 1783, when at the behest of Catherine II the descendants of the ancient Pontus Greeks and other Orthodox inhabitants—the so-called *albantsy*—left the peninsula. After the Russian-Ottoman Treaty of Küçük Kaynarca in 1774, the Crimean Khanate became nominally independent but was actually a Russian vassal. With the approval of the Khan, Saint Petersburg had begun again with the settlement of Orthodox colonists of

Slavic and Greek origin. According to Alan Fisher, the latter, the *albantsy*, were no ordinary settlers but pro-Russian military, predominately Greeks,[25] who left the Khanate again only a few years later.

When Catherine II (1729–1796) finally became the ruler of the Crimea, there were barely any Christians, but predominantly Muslims, in the Crimea—it was not Russian soil and therefore there was no reason to label it as a holy ground. Prince Grigorii Potemkin (1739–1791), the conqueror of the peninsula, was aware of this fact. A few months before the annexation, he did not even try to legitimize his plans in terms of a Slavic or Orthodox population on the peninsula, but frankly stressed that the Muslim-ruled Crimea had been annexed for solely strategic and security reasons because its geographical situation was a danger to Russia.[26] Crimea's strategic position was relevant because of Russia's plans for the dissolution of the Ottoman Empire, the so-called Greek Project, something that could not be implemented for many reasons.[27]

Finally, another explanation for Russia's capture of the Khanate was to terminate the "Tatar threat." The Khanate (in alliance with the Ottoman Empire) had been a peril for Russia's open southern borders for centuries. However, it was no longer a real threat to the Russian Empire in the eighteenth century; it was (like the Ottoman Empire) already in a state of decline. In any case, prior to 1783, the acquisition of ancient Slavic Orthodox territory was not a key argument for the annexation, but an anti-Islamic rhetoric was used instead.

The issue is to be found in only a few individual sources written in the years before 1783. In a 1774 report for internal use only, for instance, one Russian emissary mentioned Crimea's significance for Russian Orthodoxy. But the combination of this thesis with a notion of Slavic settlement that has a centuries-old continuity sounds rather unemotional: not far from the "small Greek village Axis Jar [Akhtiiar, later Sevastopol] is located near Cherson[es], the oldest of all Crimean cities. It was founded as early as the time of the Persian monarchy and is famous for the baptism of the Russian Great Prince Vladimir."[28]

The motif of the Crimea as the cradle of Russian Christianity or as an anti-Islamic bulwark, which is typical for the later debates, is reflected a bit more verbosely in the correspondence between Potemkin and Catherine II in 1783. While prior to the annexation, strategic military argumentation weighed most heavily, this time the prince drew his empress's attention to the religious importance of the new acquisition: he was very satisfied that the Taurian Chersones had finally become a part of Russia because it was "the origin of our Christianity and thus also of our humanity." But even here the notion of Vladimir's baptism was combined with other important elements in Russia's justification: the tsarina had defeated the former tyrants of Russia, the Crimean Tatars. Emphasizing the strategic legitimation again, he praised the new borders, which brought peace for the empire, shocked the Ottoman Porte, and aroused the envy of Europe.[29] It is obvious that the correspondence between Catherine II and Prince Potemkin combined a great number of topoi concerning the Crimea that later dominated the Russian debates on the peninsula—among them the Orthodox Crimea. The idea of the Crimea as a place of Russian Christianity became important much later—in the second half of the nineteenth century, especially after the Crimean War, when anti-Islamic and anti-Western discourse elements were frequently combined.

Three Elements of the Narrative of "Crimea as a Holy Ground"

As mentioned above, the "discovery" of the Crimea as a religiously charged *lieu de mémoire* and as the cradle of Christendom and Russian Orthodoxy became relevant for practical politics after the 1850s.[30] This "Orthodox Christian reclamation project"[31] developed into a linear master narrative. It helped to legitimize Russian rule over the peninsula.[32] The years after the Crimean War marked a caesura not only because of the introduction of the Great Reforms but also because of the negotiations about what Russianness meant and who belonged to the nation. As in other parts of Europe, a sacralization of the nation can be observed. Thus in this discourse, the Crimean War developed into a holy war that had been lost against the enemies of Russianness—against Islam, against non-Orthodox Christian powers, against the West, and against Europe.[33] And was the battle for Holy Russia and the holy nation not fought in the Crimea, where the empire had tried to protect the values and the faith of the Slavic community? It is obvious that the locus and the sacralized nation merged into a semantic unity, but how did it work?

First and foremost, the establishment of the Crimea as a holy ground can be traced back to the three already mentioned narratives, containing all the elements that are necessary for this status: first, to grant spiritual importance and dignity; second, to construct the earliest possible link between the Crimea/Russia with Christianity and the Holy Land; third, to claim an early Slavic settlement in the Crimea; and fourth, to transform the peninsula into a theater of a very important event in Russian/East Slavic history. The ancient city of Chersones/Korsun,[34] an important site of archaeological excavations since the nineteenth century and a suburb of Sevastopol today, became the center of these stories because it was an important political and religious outpost of the Byzantine Empire and its bulwark against nomadic tribes from the Eurasian steppes.

None of the narratives was invented in the nineteenth century but had emerged much earlier; however, only then did they become constitutive elements of the discourse. Two of the accounts have a somewhat historical core, but one—as far as we know—belongs to the realm of legends. Taken together, they helped to construct a link between the Crimea and the later Russian heartlands and contributed to the imagined coherence of Slavic Orthodoxy. Since the 1850s, these old stories were depicted again and again, they were repeated, changed, and modified.

A Visitor from the Holy Land in the Crimea: Apostle Andrew

The earliest event is the alleged mission of the apostle Andrew (in Russian: Andrei Pervozvannyi, the First-Called) to the Scythians in 33 CE.[35] Between 600 BCE and 250 CE, the Scythians, an Iranian tribe, had dominated the northern shores of the Black Sea and their hinterland and had symbiotic but not always peaceful relations with Greek cities like Chersones. That Andrew is supposed to have preached in Scythia was first mentioned by Eusebius of Caesarea (265–340) in his Church history. A later apocryphal work called "Legend of the Journey of St. Andrew to Russia" found its way into the *Povest vremennykh let* (Primary Chronicle), the most important source for the reconstruction of the history of the Rus after the fifteenth century.

For the renowned Slavist Adolf Stender-Petersen (1893–1963), the story of apostle Andrew's tour of Russia is "more curious and anecdotal than poetic or profound"[36] but had a long-lasting effect nevertheless. According to the story, the apostle Andrew traveled to the northern shore of the Black Sea and into the lands of the later Kyivan Rus to deliver the word of God.[37] It was told that he came to the area of later Kyiv—the so-called mother of Russian (i.e., East Slavic) cities—where he prophesied the building of the city and erected a cross. On his way from the Holy Land to the north, he also visited—if we follow the account—the Crimea. This event, to which so much importance will be ascribed later, is described quite simply in the Primary Chronicle: "After Andrew had been teaching in Sinope, he came to Korsun [Russian for Chersones], and he saw that from Korsun the mouth of the River Dnieper is in the near distance."[38]

Despite its brevity, this sentence was enough to demonstrate the old connection between the history of the Crimea and Russia, and it was used to legitimize Russian rule. At the time of its adaption in the Russian Orthodox context, during the reign of Tsar Ivan III Vasilevich (1440–1505), its function was to construct a direct link between the East Slavic territories and the Holy Land by omitting the Byzantine parts of the history of Christianizing the Rus.[39]

The Apostles to the Slavs: Constantine (Cyril) and Methodius in the Crimea

The second event is of even greater significance: in 860, the so-called Apostles to the Slavs, Constantine (Cyril) and Methodius conducted their mission to the Khazars,[40] the creators of a powerful polity that dominated the vast area extending from the Volga-Don steppes to the Eastern Crimea and the northern Caucasus from the seventh to the tenth century. Although the Khazar elites could ultimately not be converted by the two missionaries (and adopted a form of the Jewish faith, instead), in retrospect the apostles' presence on the peninsula helped to construct an early connection between the Crimea and the Orthodox Slavic Church. Both apostles are venerated by the Slavs (including the Russians) for many reasons; for example, they are credited with devising the first alphabet for Old Church Slavonic, and they introduced a liturgy that in turn served as a basis for the subsequent spreading of Christianity among the Eastern Slavs.[41]

In Cyril's hagiography, some events are of special importance for the inscription of the Crimea as a holy and Slavic ground. It is related that in 861, while still in Chersones, the brothers found the relics of St. Clement (50–97) of Rome, the third Pope, who was banished from Rome during the reign of Emperor Domitian (51–96) in 94 CE. Clement found his martyrdom there by being thrown from a boat into the sea with an anchor around his neck. Once a year, so it is told, the sea revealed a shrine containing his relics. In the *Zhytie Konstantina Filosofa* (Life of Constantine the Philosopher), we read the following:

> And I heard that the relics of St. Clement still lie in the sea, and I prayed, saying, "I believe in God and I hope for St. Clement that I find his relics and remove them from the sea." And I persuaded the archbishop and the clergy and the pious people to go on a ship, and they sailed to a place where the sea was calm. Having arrived there, they started searching while singing prayers. And a strong scent spread, like from a kind of incense. And then the relics appeared there, and they took them with great honor and glory. And all the priests and the citizens brought them into town.[42]

The brothers took the bones with them when they left the Crimea in 862 and carried them to Rome a few years later.

In the course of the nineteenth century, the "Life of Constantine the Philosopher" became an important source for the Russian Orthodox high clergy for many reasons. It was frequently used to prove that at least some parts of the Crimea were inhabited by a Slavic population at the time of Cyril and Methodius by telling us the following:

And the Philosopher [Cyril] found here a Bible and a Psalter, written in Russian [i.e., *ruskie bukvy*/old Slavonic] characters, and he found a man speaking this language. And he spoke with him and understood the meaning of the language, relating the differences between vowels and consonants with his own language. And praying to God, soon he began to read and speak. Many were amazed and glorified God.[43]

Nineteenth-century authors were enthusiastic about the fact that the apostle Cyril should have found "a scripture that was written in Slavic . . ., here in Korsun, a city in which diverse tribes with their different languages met." It was evidence for them that a Slavic language "had been invented as the common language of the various nations" in the city.[44] This story enjoyed popularity in the Russian Orthodox debates because it seemed suitable to demonstrate once more the presence of Slavic inhabitants on the Crimea in the early Middle Ages and to separate a sacred Crimea (i.e., Christian Slavic) from an unholy peninsula (i.e., non-Christian and non-Slavic). This was also helpful insofar as the annexation of the Crimea in 1783 could be interpreted as a legitimate regaining of an originally Slavic territory—an area that had fallen into false, Muslim hands for centuries. However, new research on this subject concludes that *ruskie bukvy* was just an error and that it was originally *surskie* (Syrian), or it was just an error in copying.[45] In any case, the "Life of Constantine the Philosopher" provides no evidence for a greater number of Slavs in the Crimea as early as the ninth century.

In Tsarist Russia, the apostle Andrew, Pope Clement, St. Cyril, St. Methodius, and others became eloquent witnesses of a Christian Orthodox and/or Slavic Crimea, despite meager historical and archaeological evidence.[46]

The Baptism of the Rus and the Role of the Crimea

Most important for the inscription of the Crimea as holy ground and an Orthodox bulwark is the third event, the alleged baptism of the hitherto pagan Grand Prince of the Rus, Vladimir/Volodymyr (c. 958–1015), mentioned above. This baptism is supposed to have taken place in Chersones in 988 and was followed by the famous mass baptism of Kyiv, which marked the Christianization of the Rus. The circumstances have been a controversial subject of discussion.[47] The presence of Vladimir with his troops in Byzantine Chersones is confirmed by several sources of different origins, not only in the "Primary Chronicle," but also in some Arab sources.[48]

However, several versions exist with regard to the background of Vladimir's baptism and whether this event really took place in Chersones. According to one version, the Byzantine emperors Basil II (958–1025) and

Constantine VIII (960–1028) asked Vladimir for military aid against insurgents. As a reward, they promised him the hand of their sister, Princess Anna (963–1012), in marriage, and Vladimir's baptism was a precondition for that.[49] The "Primary Chronicle" says that Vladimir was a heathen when he arrived in the Crimea and refused to become a Christian right before his marriage to Anna. God's punishment followed promptly and Vladimir went blind! When his future wife, Anna Porphyrogenita (963–1008/1022), convinced him that only through baptism could he restore his eyesight, Vladimir said, "If this proves true, then of a surety is the God of the Christians great," and gave order that he should be baptized. The bishop of Kherson, together with the princess's priests, after announcing the tidings, baptized Vladimir, and as the bishop laid his hand upon him, he straightway received his sight. Upon experiencing this miraculous cure, Vladimir glorified God, saying, "I have now perceived the one true God." When his followers beheld this miracle, many of them were also baptized.[50]

In our context, it is not important whether Vladimir truly became a believer or not. The adoption of Christianity had tactical and political advantages in his time in any case because this step helped Vladimir to stabilize his rule both internally and externally. Irrespective of any other possible and more accurate reconstructions of how the Grand Prince was baptized, it is beyond dispute that the narrative of Vladimir's baptism in Chersones was fundamental to the construction of a very old, very important, and highly symbolic connection between the northern Slavic territories and the Crimea that helped in the age of nationalism to establish the peninsula as holy ground for the Russian nation.

Concluding Remarks

The Crimean War marked a turning point in the Russian discourse on the Crimea regarding the use of a holy ground motif and also in terms of practical politics. The attempts to make the peninsula more Slavic/more Russian became much more concrete: the Crimean Tatars were encouraged to leave for the Ottoman Empire, and they did so in great numbers. Their exodus helped to make the Crimea less Muslim and, because of the immigration of Slavic Orthodox, more Christian, and therefore holy. Before this caesura, often described as the age of nationalism, most members of the Russian elites had often praised more than just one historical layer of Crimea's history and had glorified religious and ethnic diversity alike. One example is Nikolai I. Nadezhdin's (1804–1852) euphoric description of Crimea's historical and cultural variety. A contemporary of Pushkin, he praised the memories of so many centuries and nations, so many events and ideas—from the underground tombs of nameless Scythians in the grave hills of Kerch to the underground shelters of the early Christians in the rocks of Inkerman ... to the place where the blood of martyr Clement poured down to earth ... the Temple of Diana of Tauris, where so many poets drew inspirations, to the church ruins in which Vladimir received the blessing for us![51]

But a parallel development, to create the Russian Athos in the Crimea, can already be observed in this period in the efforts of the archbishops of Cherson and Tauris, Gavriil (Rozanov, 1827–1848) and Innokentii (Borisov, 1848–1857).[52] In the first years, their attempts to implement an Orthodox infrastructure with new churches and monasteries on the peninsula were not yet successful. The Russian administration under its famous governor Mikhail S. Vorontsov (1782–1856) was quite aware of the fact that the peninsula was still a predominantly Muslim ground before the Tatar mass migration after 1856. Therefore, the government limited the Orthodox clergy's zeal.[53] Even when later governors changed their attitudes concerning the creation of a Russian Athos in the Crimea and supported the Orthodox Church more openly, the promise that Catherine II had given, namely no proselytization of Crimea's non-Christian residents, was not broken until the end of the empire. Orthodox mission endeavors were limited to Old Believers, Catholics (such as Polish-born landowners), or Protestants (e.g., German colonists).[54]

In the aftermath of the Crimean War, which was fixed as a kind of religious war within the collective Russian memory, one can observe a fundamental change in the way the Crimea was appropriated into a collective Russian memory: it was no longer the multicolored "Garden of the Empire" Catherine II and her contemporaries praised[55] but was transferred into an Orthodox bulwark and a discursively constructed stronghold of the lawful/true Christian denomination (i.e., *Pravoslavie*). Together with the population exchanges between Russia and the Ottoman Empire, which reached their climax in the 1860s,[56] the Crimea was in fact transformed into a predominantly Orthodox area. And narrative elements such as the alleged mission of the apostle Andrew to the Scythians, Constantine's (Cyril) and Methodius's mission to the Khazars, and Vladimir's baptism in Chersones helped to foster this view.

It has often been discussed that the reign of Alexander III (1881–1896) brought a new quality of Russification and new attitudes toward the religious and ethnic Other. The unity not only between Orthodoxy and the empire but also between Orthodoxy and Eastern Slavs was particularly marked in 1888, during the central celebration in Kyiv of the 900th anniversary of the Christianization of the Rus.[57] In the Crimea, however, this process had started even earlier, under the reign of Alexander II. A telling example is the (re)construction of a cathedral in Byzantine style in Chersones, which started in 1861. It was named after Vladimir and was erected on the spot where the Grand Prince was allegedly baptized. When it was finished fifteen years later, it was one of the largest religious buildings in the Tsarist Empire.[58]

It is important to note that the Crimea has a significant, religiously charged meaning not only for Russians but also for Ukrainians and Crimean Tatars. For the Crimean Tatars, who were deported in 1944 under horrific circumstances and who have been returning from their Central Asian exile in large numbers since the 1990s, the peninsula is *vatan* (home) and the place where the collective trauma of deportation under Joseph Stalin (1878–1953)—the so-called *sürgun*—took place. Since the nineteenth century, it has been a fact for patriotic Ukrainians that Kyivan Rus was not a Russian but a Ukrainian state and that Grand Prince Vladimir was Ukrainian, not Russian. With this attitude, they subscribe to the verdict of their national historian Mykhailo Hrushevskyi (1866–1934), who claimed that Rus and therefore also the Crimea were connected to Ukrainian history.[59] In an internet poll in 2007, Ukrainians chose Chersones to become the fifth major "miracle" of their country.[60]

Both in Ukraine (2008) and in the Russian Federation (2010), the "Day of the Baptism of the Rus" was introduced as an official holiday (although not a day off). The real story of Crimea's Christianization was not as linear as it appeared in nationalistically charged narratives, depicted so often and in so many variations. Nevertheless, every Russian today will subscribe to the following statement about the importance of the Crimea as a holy ground and a bastion against the unholy (foremost the Ukrainians and the Muslim Tatars). It was published in 1910 and could well have been written in 2014: "The history of Christianity in the Crimea is not only very closely related to the history of this place, but to the history of the whole of Russia, and thus for each of us it achieved a special meaning."[61]

Kerstin S. Jobst is a professor of Eastern European history at the University of Wien, Austria. Her fields of research are history of the Crimea and the Black Sea Region, Eastern and Central Eastern Europe, the Caucasus, and the Habsburg monarchy; comparative imperial studies; history of religions and hagiography; cultures of memory; and politics of history. Her list of publications includes *Geschichte der Ukraine* (Stuttgart, 2015), *Die Perle des Imperiums. Der russische Krim-Diskurs im Zarenreich* (Konstanz, 2007), "Where the Orient Ends? Orientalism and Its Function for Imperial Rule in the Russian Empire," in J. Hodkinson et al., *Deploying Oriental-*

ism in Culture and History. From Germany to Central and Eastern Europe (Rochester, 2013), 190–208.

Notes

1. Here I follow the arguments of Otto Luchterhand, an expert of international law, O. Luchterhand, "Die Krim-Krise von 2014. Staats- und völkerrechtliche Aspekte," *Osteuropa* 5–6 (2014): 61–86, who stresses the unlawful character of Russia's policy in 2014.
2. B. Pietrow-Ennker and B. Ennker, "Ein Reich mit Mission: Das Vorgehen Moskaus in der Ukraine-Krise folgt Traditionen und Mustern imperialer Politik, die von russischen Herrschern von Iwan dem Schrecklichen bis zu Stalin vorgezeichnet wurden," *Frankfurter Allgemeine Zeitung*, 12 May 2014, retrieved 9 June 2018 from http://www.faz.net/aktuell/politik/die-gegenwart/russland-ein-reich-mit-mission-12934228.html#void.
3. See the interview with the historian of East European history: Frank Golczewski, "Mallorca der Russen: Der Historiker Frank Golczewski über die Instrumentalisierung von Geschichte in der Krim-Krise und Putins Faible für einen Dissidenten," *Der Spiegel*, 24 March 2014, retrieved 9 September 2015 from http://www.spiegel.de/spiegel/print/d-126149171.html.
4. For the ascription of Crimea as a southern territory, see Kerstin S. Jobst, "Über den russischen Südländer: Zur Funktion der Krim als russischer Süden und des *južanin* (Südländers) im russischen Krim-Diskurs um 1900," in C. Bruns, ed., *Bilder der "eigenen" Geschichte im Spiegel des kolonialen "Anderen": Transnationale Perspektiven um 1900*, special issue, *Comparativ* 19, no. 5 (2009): 34–49.
5. See my book: K.S. Jobst, *Die Perle des Imperiums: Der russische Krim-Diskurs im Zarenreich* (Konstanz: UVK, 2007), where I describe this process of appropriation in detail.
6. Still important is E. Hösch, "Das sogenannte 'griechische Projekt' Katharinas II.: Ideologie und Wirklichkeit der russischen Orientpolitik in der zweiten Hälfte des 18. Jahrhunderts," *Jahrbücher für Geschichte Osteuropas* 12 (1964): 168–206.
7. See A. Zorin, "Krym v istorii russkogo samosoznaniia," *Novoe literaturnoe obozrenie* 31 (1998): 125–43.
8. A. Malgin, *Russkaia Rivera: Kurorty, turizm i otdykh v Krymu v epokhu Imperii (konets XVIII–nachalo XX v.)* (Simferopol: SONAT, 2006). On Soviet tourism in general, see D.P. Koenker, *Club Red: Vacation, Travel, and the Soviet Dream* (Ithaca: Cornell University Press, 2013).
9. See K. Hokanson, "Pushkin's Captive Crimea: Imperialism in The Fountain of Bakhchisarai," in *Russian Subjects: Empire, Nation, and the Culture of the Golden Age*, ed. M. Greenleaf and S. Moeller-Sally (Evanston: Northwestern University Press, 1998), 123–48; S. Karlinsky, "The Amber Beads of Crimea (Pushkin and Mickiewicz)," *California Slavic Studies* 2 (1963): 108–20; M. Cadot, "Exil et poésie: La Crimée de Pouškin et de Mickiewicz," *Revue Études Slaves* 59 (1987): 141–55.
10. In religious and national terms, the Crimea is important for the Crimean Tatars as well, but in this chapter I have to confine myself to the Russian side. For the relevance and the history of the Crimea for Crimean Tatars, see A.W. Fisher, *The Crimean Ta-*

tars (Stanford: Hoover Institute Press, 1978); B.G. Williams, *The Crimean Tatars: The Diaspora Experience and the Forging of a Nation* (Leiden: Brill, 2001).
11. M. Kozelsky, *Christianizing Crimea: Shaping Sacred Space in the Russian Empire and Beyond* (DeKalb: Northern Illinois University Press, 2010).
12. Ibid.
13. V. Putin, "Poslanie Prezidenta Federalnomu Sobraniiu 4 dekabria 2014 goda," retrieved 5 November 2015 from http://www.kremlin.ru/events/president/news/47173.
14. I. Luzhkov, "Russkaia Palestina," *Krymskii Albom 1999* (2000): 5.
15. A.I. Solzhenitsyn, "Ia serdechno, vsei dushoi s krymchanami," *Krymskii Albom 1999* (2000): 130–31.
16. See Jobst, *Die Perle des Imperiums*.
17. P.S. Pallas, *Bemerkungen auf einer Reise in die südlichen Statthalterschaften des Russischen Reiches in den Jahren 1793 und 1794*, vol. 2 (Leipzig: Martini, 1803), 345–47.
18. For a discussion of the reasons for the migrations of Crimean Tatars, see B.G. Williams, "Hijra and Forced Migration from Nineteenth Century Russia to the Ottoman Empire: A Critical Analysis of the Great Crimean Tatar Emigration of 1860–1861," *Cahiers du monde russe* 41 (2000): 79–108 and M. Pinson, "Russian Policy and the Emigration of the Crimean Tatars," *Güney-Doğu Avrupa Araştırmaları Dergisi* 1 (1972): 37–56. For the immigration of other nationalities such as Germans, see, e.g., D. Neutatz, *Die "deutsche Frage" im Schwarzmeergebiet und in Wolhynien: Politik, Wirtschaft, Mentalität und Alltag im Spannungsfeld von Nationalismus und Modernisierung 1856–1914* (Stuttgart: Steiner, 1993); D. Brandes, *Von den Zaren adoptiert: Die deutschen Kolonisten und die Balkansiedler in Neurußland und Bessarabien 1751–1914*, Schriften des Bundesinstituts für ostdeutsche Kultur und Geschichte, 2 (München: Oldenbourg, 1993).
19. See V.P. Diulichev, *Rasskazy po istorii Kryma*, 5th ed. (Simferopol: Biznes-Inform, 2003). Diulichev dates the first appearance of Slavs in Crimea to as early as the "first century of our era" (126). Diulichev was convinced of a Ukrainian colonization of the Crimea from the sixth century. For the Ukrainian variant of this issue, see "Smena narodnostei v Iuzhnoi Rusi. Istoriko-etnograficheskie zametki," *Kievskaia Starina* 2, no. 6 (1883): 399.
20. See Y. Slezkine, "Naturalists versus Nations: Eighteenth-Century Russian Scholars Confront Ethnic Diversity," in *Russia's Orient: Imperial Borderlands and Peoples 1700–1917*, ed. D.R. Brower and E.J. Lazzerini (Bloomington: Indiana University Press, 1997), 50, 57.
21. W. Kliutschewskij (V.O. Kliuchevskii), *Geschichte Rußlands*, vol. 1 (Stuttgart: Deutsche Verlagsanstalt, 1925–1928), 99.
22. See A. Plontke-Lüning, "Christianisierung am Rande des Imperiums: Die Krim," in *Christianisierung Europas: Entstehung, Entwicklung und Konsolidierung im archäologischen Befund; internationale Tagung im Dezember 2010 in Bergisch-Gladbach*, ed. O. Heinrich-Tamáska, N. Krohn, and S. Ristow (Regensburg: Schnell & Steiner, 2012), 343–62.
23. One of them was Pope Martin I, who was abducted by Emperor Constantine II and died at Chersones in 655. He was made a saint and martyr by both the Catholic and the Eastern Orthodox Church, and after his martyrdom his cult developed in Chersones. See Plontke-Lüning, "Christianisierung," 348.

24. C. King, *The Black Sea: A History* (Oxford: Oxford University Press, 2004), 73.
25. A.W. Fisher, *The Russian Annexation of the Crimea 1772–1783* (Cambridge: Cambridge University Press, 1970), 90–91.
26. "Potemkin to Catherine II, 1787 (no date)," in V.S. Lopatin, ed., *Ekaterina II i G.A. Potemkin: Lichnaia perepiska 1769–1791* (Moskva: Nauka, 1997), 155, letter 635.
27. See M.S. Anderson, *The Eastern Question, 1774–1923: A Study in International Relations* (London: Macmillan, 1966); V.N. Vinogradov, "Grecheskii proekt Ekateriny II i Grigoriia Potemkina," 2 October 2015 from http://web.archive.org/web/20091216140052/www.rustrana.ru/article.php?nid=22824.
28. "Podennaia zapiska puteshestviia ego siiatelstva Vasilia Michailovicha Dolgorukova v krymskii poluostrov vo vremia kampanii 1773 goda," *Zapiski Imperatorskogo Odesskogo obshchestva istorii i drevnostei* 29, no. 8 (1872): 186.
29. "Potemkin to Catherine, 5.8.1783," in *Ekaterina II i G.A. Potemkin*, 180–81, letter 674.
30. For details, see Kozelsky, *Christianizing Crimea*, 125–49.
31. P.R. Magocsi, *This Blessed Land: The Crimea and the Crimean Tatars* (Toronto: University of Toronto Press, 2014), 71.
32. See also the contribution of Liliya Berezhnaya and her remarks on the Orthodox Bakhchisarai Holy Dormition Monastery in this volume.
33. See Jobst, *Die Perle des Imperiums*, 380–404. For the Crimean War, see O. Figes, *Crimea: The Last Crusade* (London: Allen Lane, 2010).
34. J.C. Carter, ed., *Crimean Chersonesos: City, Chora, Museum, and Environs* (Austin: University of Texas at Austin, 2003); K.S. Jobst, "Chersones," in *Religiöse Erinnerungsorte in Ostmitteleuropa: Konstitution und Konkurrenz im nationen- und epochenübergreifenden Zugriff*, ed. J. Bahlcke, S. Rhodewald, and Th. Wünsch (Berlin: Akademie-Verlag, 2013), 3–10.
35. L. Müller, *Die Taufe Rußlands: Die Frühgeschichte des russischen Christentums bis zum Jahre 988*. Quellen und Studien zur russischen Geistesgeschichte, 6 (München: Wewel, 1987), 9.
36. A. Stender-Petersen, *Geschichte der russischen Literatur* (München: Beck, 1986), 37, 38: "Die Geschichte fand jedenfalls in Rußland Anklang, sowohl ihres lustigen Inhalts wegen als auch deswegen, weil sie ein direktes Band zwischen dem erstberufenen Jünger Christi und dem Russenlande knüpfte." [The story was in any case well-received in Russia due to its funny content and because it created a direct bond between the first-called disciple of Christ and the land of the Russians.] Stender-Petersen also refers here to the ethnographic content, since Slavic bathing habits are described in a comedic way.
37. See also F. Dvornik, *The Idea of the Apostolicity in Byzantium and the Legend of the Apostle Andrew* (Cambridge, MA: Harvard University Press, 1958); A. Iu. Vinogradov, "Apostol Andrei i Chernoe More," in *Drevneishie gosurdarstva Vostochnoi Evropy*, ed. A.V. Podosinov (Moskva: Vostochnaia Literatura, 1999), 348–68.
38. L. Müller, ed., *Die Nestorchronik: Die altrussische Chronik, zugeschrieben dem Mönch des Kiever Höhlenklosters Nestor, in der Redaktion des Abtes Sil'vestr aus dem Jahre 1116, rekonstruiert nach den Handschriften Lavrent'evskaja, Radzivilovskaja, Akademiceskaja, Troickaja, Ipat'evskaja und Chlebnikovskaja* (München: Fink, 2001), retrieved 18 October 2015 from http://digi20.digitale-sammlungen.de/de/fs1/object/display/bsb00043511_00001.html.

39. X. von Ertzdorff, "Dmitrij Gerasimov and Paolo Giovio: Bericht über Russland 1525," in *Slavica litteraria: Festschrift für Gerhard Giesemann zum 65.Geburtstag*, Opera Slavica, n.s., 43, ed. U. Jekutsch and U. Steltner (Wiesbaden: Harrassowitz, 2002), 249.
40. See J. Bujnoch, ed., *Zwischen Rom und Byzanz. Leben und Wirken der Slavenapostel Kryrillos und Methodios nach den Pannonischen Legenden und der Klemensvita: Bericht von der Taufe Rußlands nach der Laurentiuschronik*, 2nd ed. Slavische Geschichtsschreiber, 1 (Graz: Verlag Styria, 1972), 54–102; F. Dvornik, "The Significance of the Missions of Cyril and Methodius," *Slavic Review* 23, no. 2 (1964): 195–211. Whether Methodius really accompanied his brother Cyril on the mission or whether this variant is a later invention is still under dispute.
41. S.B. Bernshtein, *Konstantin-Filosof i Mefodii: Nachalnye glavy iz istorii slavianskoi pismenosti* (Moskva: Izdatelstvo Moskovskogo Universiteta, 1984).
42. "Zhitie Konstantina-Kirilla: Pamiat i zhitie blazhennogo uchitelia nashego Konstantina Filosofa, pervogo nastavnika slavianskogo naroda," chtenie 3, retrieved 20 October 2015 from http://old-ru.ru/03-42.html.
43. Ibid.
44. V. Jastrebov, "Chersones Tavricheskii," *Kievskaia Starina* 2, no. 5 (1883): 36–37.
45. I thank Prof. Dr. Ludwig Steindorff, University of Kiel, Germany, for this information.
46. For examples, see Kozelsky, *Christianizing Crimea*, 56, 84.
47. Some historians see evidence that he was already baptized before he came to Crimea; see G. Stökl, *Russische Geschichte von den Anfängen bis zur Gegenwart*, 4th ed. (Stuttgart: Kröner, 1983), 59; H. Haumann, *Geschichte Rußlands* (München: Piper, 1996), 45–46.
48. See P. Kawerau, *Arabische Quellen zur Christianisierung Rußlands* (Wiesbaden: Harrassowitz, 1967).
49. For a discussion of the several variants, see Jobst, *Die Perle des Imperiums*, 296–98.
50. S.H. Cross and O.P. Sherbowitz-Wetzor, eds. and trans., *The Russian Primary Chronicle, Laurentian Text* (Cambridge, MA: Mediaeval Academy of America, 1953), 113.
51. "Pismo N.I. Nadezhdina k Iu. N. Bartenevu," *Russkii Arkhiv* 2, no. 12 (1864): 42–47. He was a professor of Moscow University, a friend of Vissarion Belinskii, and the editor of the magazine *Teleskop*, which was banned because of the so-called Chaadaev affair. He was expelled in 1836.
52. See Jobst, *Die Perle des Imperiums*, 292–93; Kozelsky, *Christianizing Crimea*, 53–54.
53. For Vorontsov, see A.L.H. Rhinelander, *Prince Michael Vorontsov: Viceroy to the Tsar* (Montreal: McGill-Queen's University Press, 1990).
54. For details, see Kozelsky, *Christianizing Crimea*, 15–40.
55. A. Schönle, "Garden of the Empire: Catherine's Appropriation of the Crimea," *Slavic Review* 60 (2001): 1–23.
56. Still important is M. Pinson, *Demographic Warfare: Aspects of Ottoman and Russian Policy 1854–1866* (PhD diss., Harvard University, 1970).
57. M. George, "Die 900-Jahr-Feier der Taufe Rußlands im Jahr 1888 und die Kritik Vladimir Sergeevičs Solov'evs am Verhältnis von Staat und Kirche in Rußland," *Jahrbücher für Geschichte Osteuropas* 36 (1988): 15–36.
58. Destroyed during World War II, it was reconstructed after the dissolution of the Soviet Union and consecrated in 2004. It belongs to the Ukrainian Orthodox Church (Moscow Patriarchate).

59. M. Hrushevskyi, "Das übliche Schema der 'russischen' Geschichte und die Frage einer rationellen Gliederung der Geschichte des Ostslaventums," in *Michael Hruschewskyj: Sein Leben und Wirken 1866–1934. Vorträge des Ukrainischen Wissenschaftlichen Institutes anläßlich der Todesfeier an der Friedrich-Wilhelms-Universität zu Berlin* (Berlin: Verlag der Gesellschaft der Freunde des Ukrainischen Wissenschaftlichen Institutes, 1935), 38–48.
60. *Sim chudes Ukrainy*, retrieved 10 October 2015 from http://7chudes.in.ua.
61. A. Berte Delagard, "K istorii khristianstva v Krymu. Mnimoe tysiacheletie," *Zapiski Imperatorskogo Odesskogo obshchestva istorii i drevnostei* 67, no. 28 (1910): 39.

Bibliography

Anderson, M.S. 1966. *The Eastern Question, 1774–1923: A Study in International Relations*. London: Macmillan.

Bernshtein, S.B. 1984. *Konstantin-Filosof i Mefodii: Nachalnye glavy iz istorii slavianskoi pismenosti*. Moskva: Izdatelstvo Moskovskogo Universiteta.

Brandes, D. 1993. *Von den Zaren adoptiert: Die deutschen Kolonisten und die Balkansiedler in Neurußland und Bessarabien 1751–1914*. Schriften des Bundesinstituts für ostdeutsche Kultur und Geschichte, 2. München: Oldenbourg.

Bujnoch, J., ed. 1972. *Zwischen Rom und Byzanz. Leben und Wirken der Slavenapostel Kryrillos und Methodios nach den Pannonischen Legenden und der Klemensvita: Bericht von der Taufe Rußlands nach der Laurentiuschronik*. 2nd ed. Slavische Geschichtsschreiber, 1. Graz: Verlag Styria.

Cadot, M. 1987. "Exil et poésie: la crimée de Pouškin et de Mickiewicz." *Revue Études Slaves* 59: 141–55.

Carter, J.C., ed. 2003. *Crimean Chersonesos: City, Chora, Museum, and Environs*. Austin: University of Texas at Austin.

Cross, S.H. and O.P. Sherbowitz-Wetzor, eds. 1953. *The Russian Primary Chronicle, Laurentian Text*. Cambridge, MA: Mediaeval Academy of America.

Delagard, A.B. 1910. "K istorii khristianstva v Krymu. Mnimoe tysiacheletie," *Zapiski Imperatorskogo Odesskogo obshchestva istorii i drevnostei* 67, no. 28: 39.

Diulichev, V.P. 2003. *Rasskazy po istorii Kryma*. 5th ed. Simferopol: Biznes-Inform.

Dvornik, F. 1958. *The Idea of the Apostolicity in Byzantium and the Legend of the Apostle Andrew*. Cambridge, MA: Harvard University Press.

———. 1964. "The Significance of the Missions of Cyril and Methodius." *Slavic Review* 23, no. 2: 195–211.

Figes, O. 2010. *Crimea: The Last Crusade*. London: Allen Lane.

Fisher, A.W. 1970. *The Russian Annexation of the Crimea 1772–1783*. Cambridge: Cambridge University Press.

———. 1978. *The Crimean Tatars*. Stanford: Hoover Institute Press.

George, M. 1988. "Die 900-Jahr-Feier der Taufe Rußlands im Jahr 1888 und die Kritik Vladimir Sergeevičs Solov'evs am Verhältnis von Staat und Kirche in Rußland." *Jahrbücher für Geschichte Osteuropas* 36: 15–36.

Golczewski, F. 2014. "Mallorca der Russen: Der Historiker Frank Golczewski über die Instrumentalisierung von Geschichte in der Krim-Krise und Putins Faible für einen

Dissidenten." *Der Spiegel*, 24 March. Retrieved 9 September 2015 from http://www.spiegel.de/spiegel/print/d-126149171.html.

Haumann, H. 1996. *Geschichte Rußlands*. München: Piper.

Hokanson, K. 1998. "Pushkin's Captive Crimea: Imperialism in the Fountain of Bakhchisarai." In *Russian Subjects: Empire, Nation, and the Culture of the Golden Age*, ed. M. Greenleaf and S. Moeller-Sally, 123–48. Evanston: Northwestern University Press.

Hösch, E. 1964. "Das sogenannte 'griechische Projekt' Katharinas II.: Ideologie und Wirklichkeit der russischen Orientpolitik in der zweiten Hälfte des 18. Jahrhunderts." *Jahrbücher für Geschichte Osteuropas* 12: 168–206.

Hrushevskyi, M. 1935. "Das übliche Schema der 'russischen' Geschichte und die Frage einer rationellen Gliederung der Geschichte des Ostslaventums." In *Michael Hruschewskyj: Sein Leben und Wirken 1866–1934. Vorträge des Ukrainischen Wissenschaftlichen Institutes anläßlich der Todesfeier an der Friedrich-Wilhelms-Universität zu Berlin*, 38–48. Berlin: Verlag der Gesellschaft der Freunde des Ukrainischen Wissenschaftlichen Institutes.

Jastrebov, V. 1883. "Chersones Tavricheskii." *Kievskaia Starina* 2, no. 5: 36–37.

Jobst, K.S. 2007. *Die Perle des Imperiums: Der russische Krim-Diskurs im Zarenreich*. Konstanz: UVK.

———. 2009. "Über den russischen Südländer: Zur Funktion der Krim als russischer Süden und des *južanin* (Südländers) im russischen Krim-Diskurs um 1900." In C. Bruns, ed. *Bilder der "eigenen" Geschichte im Spiegel des kolonialen "Anderen": Transnationale Perspektiven um 1900*, special issue, *Comparativ* 19, no. 5: 34–49.

———. 2013. "Chersones." In *Religiöse Erinnerungsorte in Ostmitteleuropa: Konstitution und Konkurrenz im nationen- und epochenübergreifenden Zugriff*, ed. J. Bahlcke, S. Rhodewald, and T. Wünsch, 310. Berlin: Akademie-Verlag.

Karlinsky, S. 1963. "The Amber Beads of Crimea (Pushkin and Mickiewicz)." *California Slavic Studies* 2: 108–20.

Kawerau, P. 1967. *Arabische Quellen zur Christianisierung Rußlands*. Wiesbaden: Harrassowitz.

King, C. 2004. *The Black Sea: A History*. Oxford: Oxford University Press.

Kliutschewskij, W. [V.O. Kliuchevskii]. 1925–1928. *Geschichte Rußlands*. Vol. 1. Stuttgart: Deutsche Verlagsanstalt.

Koenker, D.P. 2013. *Club Red: Vacation, Travel, and the Soviet Dream*. Ithaca: Cornell University Press.

Kozelsky, M. 2010. *Christianizing Crimea: Shaping Sacred Space in the Russian Empire and Beyond*. DeKalb: Northern Illinois University Press.

Luchterhand, O. 2014. "Die Krim-Krise von 2014. Staats- und völkerrechtliche Aspekte." *Osteuropa* 5–6: 61–86.

Luzhkov, I. 2000. "Russkaia Palestina." *Krymskii Albom 1999*: 5.

Magocsi, P.R. 2014. *This Blessed Land: The Crimea and the Crimean Tatars*. Toronto: University of Toronto Press.

Malgin, A. 2006. *Russkaia Rivera: Kurorty, turizm i otdykh v Krymu v epokhu Imperii (konets XVIII—nachalo XX v.)*. Simferopol: SONAT.

Müller, L. 1987. *Die Taufe Rußlands: Die Frühgeschichte des russischen Christentums bis zum Jahre 988*. Quellen und Studien zur russischen Geistesgeschichte 6. München: Wewel.

———, ed. 2015. *Die Nestorchronik: Die altrussische Chronik, zugeschrieben dem Mönch des Kiever Höhlenklosters Nestor, in der Redaktion des Abtes Sil'vestr aus dem Jahre 1116, rekonstruiert nach den Handschriften Lavrent'evskaja, Radzivilovskaja, Akademiceskaja, Troickaja, Ipat'evskaja und Chlebnikovskaja*. München: Fink, 2001. Retrieved 18 October 2015 from http://digi20.digitale-sammlungen.de/de/fs1/object/display/bsb00043511_00001.html.

Neutatz, D. 1993. *Die "deutsche Frage" im Schwarzmeergebiet und in Wolhynien: Politik, Wirtschaft, Mentalität und Alltag im Spannungsfeld von Nationalismus und Modernisierung 185–1914*. Stuttgart: Steiner.

Pallas, P.S. 1803. *Bemerkungen auf einer Reise in die südlichen Statthalterschaften des Russischen Reiches in den Jahren 1793 und 1794*. Vol. 2. Leipzig: Martini.

Pietrow-Ennker, B. and B. Ennker. 2014. "Ein Reich mit Mission: Das Vorgehen Moskaus in der Ukraine-Krise folgt Traditionen und Mustern imperialer Politik, die von russischen Herrschern von Iwan dem Schrecklichen bis zu Stalin vorgezeichnet wurden." *Frankfurter Allgemeine Zeitung*. 12 May. Retrieved 9 June 2018 from http://www.faz.net/aktuell/politik/die-gegenwart/russland-ein-reich-mit-mission-12934228.html#void.

Pinson, M. 1970. *Demographic Warfare: Aspects of Ottoman and Russian Policy 1854–1866*. Ph.D. diss., Harvard University.

———. 1972. "Russian Policy and the Emigration of the Crimean Tatars." *Güney-Doğu Avrupa Araştırmaları Dergisi* 1: 37–56.

Pismo, N.I. 1864. "Nadezhdina k Iu.N. Bartenevu." *Russkii Arkhiv* 2, no. 12: 42–47.

Plontke-Lüning, A. 2012. "Christianisierung am Rande des Imperiums: Die Krim." In *Christianisierung Europas: Entstehung, Entwicklung und Konsolidierung im archäologischen Befund; internationale Tagung im Dezember 2010 in Bergisch-Gladbach*, ed. O. Heinrich-Tamáska, N. Krohn, and S. Ristow, 343–62. Regensburg: Schnell & Steiner.

"Podennaia zapiska puteshestviia ego siiatelstva Vasilia Michailovicha Dolgorukova v krymskii poluostrov vo vremia kampanii 1773 goda." 1872. *Zapiski Imperatorskogo Odesskogo obshchestva istorii i drevnostei* 29, no. 8: 186.

Putin, V. 2015. "Poslanie Prezidenta Federalnomu Sobraniiu 4 dekabria 2014 goda." Retrieved 5 November 2015 from http://www.kremlin.ru/events/president/news/47173.

Rhinelander, A.L.H. 1990. *Prince Michael Vorontsov: Viceroy to the Tsar*. Montreal: McGill-Queen's University Press.

Schönle, A. 2001. "Garden of the Empire: Catherine's Appropriation of the Crimea." *Slavic Review* 60: 1–23.

Sim chudes Ukrainy. Retrieved 10 October 2015 from http://7chudes.in.ua.

Slezkine, Y. 1997. "Naturalists versus Nations: Eighteenth-Century Russian Scholars Confront Ethnic Diversity." In *Russia's Orient: Imperial Borderlands and Peoples 1700–1917*, ed. D.R. Brower and E.J. Lazzerini, 27–57. Bloomington: Indiana University Press.

"Smena narodnostei v Iuzhnoi Rusi. Istoriko-etnograficheskie zametki." 1883. *Kievskaia Starina* 2, no. 6: 399.

Solzhenitsyn, A.I. 2000. "Ja serdechno, vsei dushoi s krymchanami." *Krymskii Albom 1999*: 130–31.

Stender-Petersen, A. 1986. *Geschichte der russischen Literatur*. München: Beck.

Stökl, G. 1983. *Russische Geschichte von den Anfängen bis zur Gegenwart.* 4th ed. Stuttgart: Kröner.
Lopatin, V.S., ed. 1997. "Potemkin to Catherine II, 1787 (no date)." In *Ekaterina II i G.A. Potemkin: Lichnaia perepiska 1769–1791,* 155, letter 635. Moskva: Nauka, 1997.
———. 1997. "Potemkin to Catherine II, 5.8.1783." In *Ekaterina II i G.A. Potemkin: Lichnaia perepiska 1769–1791,* 180–81, letter 674. Moskva: Nauka.
Vinogradov, A.I. 1999. "Apostol Andrei i Chernoe More." In *Drevneishie gosurdarstva Vostochnoi Evropy,* ed. A.D. Podosinov, 348–68. Moskva: Vostochnaia Literatura.
Vinogradov, V.N. 2015. "Grecheskii proekt Ekateriny II i Grigoriia Potemkina." Retrieved 2 October 2015 from http://web.archive.org/web/20091216140052/www.rustrana.ru/article.php?nid=22824.
von Ertzdorff, X. 2002. "Dmitrij Gerasimov and Paolo Giovio: Bericht über Russland 1525." In *Slavica litteraria: Festschrift für Gerhard Giesemann zum 65. Geburtstag.* Opera Slavica, Neue Serie 43, ed. U. Jekutsch and U. Steltner, 239–56. Wiesbaden: Harrassowitz.
Williams, B.G. 2000. "Hijra and Forced Migration from Nineteenth-Century Russia to the Ottoman Empire." *Cahiers du monde russe* 41: 79–108.
———. 2001. *The Crimean Tatars: The Diaspora Experience and the Forging of a Nation.* Leiden: Brill.
"Zhitie Konstantina-Kirilla: Pamiat i zhitie blazhennogo uchitelia nashego Konstantina Filosofa, pervogo nastavnika slavianskogo naroda." chtenie 3. Retrieved 20 October 2015 from http://old-ru.ru/03-42.html.
Zorin, A. 1998. "Krym v istorii russkogo samosoznaniia." *Novoe literaturnoe obozrenie* 31: 125–43.

CHAPTER 6
Bastions of Faith in the Oceans of Ambiguities
Monasteries in the East European Borderlands (Late Nineteenth–Beginning of the Twentieth Century)

Liliya Berezhnaya

Ten Commandments for Russia: (1) You have one natural Russian tsar. You shall have no other tsars before the autocratic and Orthodox Tsar. (2) You shall not make yourself a leader from the Jews, Poles, and other foreigners in any of the state offices. You shall not obey or serve them. (3) You shall also treasure the Russian name; you shall not misuse or denigrate it in vain and you shall spread the glory of it all over the world. (4) Remember the Russian nation to keep it illustrious, to provide it with all necessities, and only afterward concern yourself with foreigners. (5) Honor all the foundations on which the Great Russian state is based that your days may be long upon the land. (6) You shall stop murdering the faithful subjects of the Tsar. (7) You shall prohibit the Orthodox to commit adultery, e.g., to marry Jews. (8) You shall prohibit the bureaucratic government to steal from the Russian treasury with the help of foreign loans and inefficient expenses for useless undertakings. (9) You shall not bear false witness against those Russian people who say the truth about foreigners, untalented rulers, thieves, and all your secret and overt enemies. (10) You shall not covet foreign constitutions; you shall not covet Judeo-Masonic teachings, nor the parliamentary waffle, nor anything evil that your neighbors have.[1]

This list of commandments appeared in the daily newssheet *Pochaevskiie izvestiia* (Pochaiv News) in 1908. The Pochaiv Branch of the Union of the Russian People, better known as the Black Hundreds, released these words that glorified monarchy and blamed democracy. The ultra–right-wing monarchist organization found one of its residences in the famous Holy Dormition Lavra of Pochaiv in Volhynia in Western Ukraine. The link between the

Russian Orthodox Church, its monastery, and the radical right movement becomes even more obvious when we consider the leadership of the Union at that time. Local Orthodox priests ran most of the 115 units of the Union. The chair of the Pochaiv Branch, the abbot of the Lavra Vitalii (Maksimenko, 1873–1960), and the archbishop of Volhynia and Zhitomir Antonii (Khrapovitskii, 1863–1936) provided spiritual and ideological guidance.[2]

Such evidence has contributed to the situation in historical scholarship whereby some "Russian liberals, Soviet scholars, and most Western scholars have stereotyped the Church as a whole, and monasteries in particular, as bastions of monarchism and even extreme right-wing parties."[3] Many historians have long assumed that Russian nationalist ideology found ardent support among the Russian Orthodox clergy, particularly after the Revolution of 1905. These generalizations are rather oversimplified and are rightly objected to in recent scholarship.[4] The picture of the political mentality of Orthodox ecclesiastical elites in the twilight of the Romanovs was rather diverse.[5]

Clergy did not speak with a single voice while responding to the challenges of revolutionary unrest and far-reaching social changes. Also, Russian imperial Church policy was neither unified nor always consistent. Indeed, in the second half of the nineteenth century (particularly under the leadership of the chief procurator of the Holy Synod Konstantin Pobedonostsev, 1827–1907), imperial strategy was to safeguard the Church from the influences of modernity.[6] Even then, in multireligious and multiethnic borderland regions, the policy of a "confessional state"[7] was ambiguous, "revealing the tension between the state's attempts to instrumentalize non-Orthodox religions and its apprehensions about the viability of Orthodoxy."[8]

However, in regard to some borderland monastic communities (Pochaiv Lavra is a notorious example), historical assumptions about the high level of right-wing radicalization are definitely true. Several questions emerge in this context. Was Pochaiv Lavra a unique case from the western Russian borders, or did other monastic communities in the region enjoy similar reputations as the "bastions of faith"? Was there any competition among them? If a single case, what made Pochaiv monks so sensitive to nationalist ideologies? Were there any particular historical factors that determined the image of the Pochaiv Lavra as a bastion of Orthodoxy and the Russian imperial idea? Who were the major actors and the audience of such narratives? Finally, are we dealing in such cases with the results of imperial confessional politics or with a kind of process from below that arose as a reaction to the attempts of different actors to nationalize or privatize a multiconfessional borderland?

The answers to these questions lie in the history of monasticism in the border regions between the Habsburg, Russian, and Ottoman Empires. In all these countries, modern times marked the formation of "nationalism aimed at building imperial nations at the heart of empires."[9] These processes were accompanied by the formation of contested nationalisms in border areas that promoted the rise of separatist tendencies and eventually destroyed peaceful coexistence.[10] In the age of nationalism, the "shatterzones of empires"[11] occasionally turned into the battlefields of various national and nationalized imperial ideologies. Churches and religious communities played a crucial role in these contradictions. Monasteries, in particular, were regarded as almost natural bulwarks: they were both popular sanctuaries and historically known military fortresses along the former Christian-Muslin border.[12] In the age of nationalism, different actors tried to privatize historical memory about monasteries' spiritual and military glory. It resulted in the amplification of the role of monasteries in borderland multiconfessional societies as the outposts of "true faith" and "national bastions."

The attempts were not new; they dated back to eighteenth-century confessional regulation, social discipline, and the ideology of enlightened rationalism. In the late nineteenth century, these processes intensified due to the political and cultural dynamics of modernization. In the case of the Russian Orthodox Church, one more factor turned out to be crucial. Despite various secularization attempts, so-called contemplative monasticism enjoyed rising popularity among the lower strata of society.[13] Monasteries all over the Russian Empire, including those on the borderlands, gained in attractiveness as pilgrimage and veneration sites. The idea of a monastery as a religious and political bulwark gained new popularity.

The importance of borderland monasteries in promoting the idea of a national bastion also had to do with the modifications of the *antemurale* myth in modern times. Generally, the idea of a bastion includes several basic components, namely, "the claim of a perennial menace by an 'other' as enemy on a territorial or cultural basis ... ; the claim to defend not only oneself, but also the others ... ; the claim of being chosen to defend a higher or greater entity, which one is a part of."[14] Recent historiography also differentiates between confessional-religious and civilizational-political connotations of the *antemurale* topos.[15] One should, however, specify that the idea of a confessional border within the *antemurale* topos was often perceived as a part of the anti-Ottoman (otherwise interpreted as Saracens, Tatars, pagans, or schismatics) rhetoric as well as of a cultural (civilizational) border. The notion of a cultural frontline manifested itself in the idea of defending Europe against the invasion of Asia and barbarism.[16]

With the rise of modernity, the importance of the anti-Ottoman front receded, whereas the cultural border was brought into the foreground.

Małgorzata Morawiec sees the connection of the decline of the anti-Ottoman rhetoric in eighteenth-century European history writing with the simultaneous transformation of the *antemurale* topos as a political myth.[17] For her, the modern *antemurale* myth bears an omnipotent defense function against all sorts of danger. In this form, it would be much easier to instrumentalize in modern ideologies for various political purposes, in contrast to a purely rhetorical premodern topos of a Christian bastion.

Other historians have paid attention to the "secularization of the *antemurale* myth" in the period of Enlightenment, particularly in Eastern Europe.[18] Some of them specify that the late eighteenth century brought into being a dividing line between the religious and political-civilizational components in *antemurale* ideology. This line was however quite permeable, meaning that "the Christian brand was not totally erased; rather its historical character was more often emphasized."[19] Recently, Andreas Lawaty has argued for the parallel development of the secular and confessional rhetoric of *antemurale* in modern Eastern Europe: "Both forms existed parallel to each other, and could come into use depending on which form would better fit in."[20] In the ideology of romantic nationalism, religious overtones acquired new popularity, culminating in the idea of messianism (e.g., Poland as the Christ of Nations).[21]

It seems that in East European border regions this coexistence sometimes went further, yielding by the end of the long nineteenth century the formation of the sacralized language and imaginary of nationalism.[22] One way or another, religion remained one of the crucial components of the nationalized borderland mythology.[23] It is not, therefore, strange that some borderland monasteries promoted the ideology of a sacralized nation/empire and nationalized religion[24] with one of its important elements—the idea of the *antemurale*.

In what follows, I intend to show by what means these ideas were popularized and what reception they received in their respective audiences. For that I have chosen three monasteries: two Orthodox—the abovementioned Pochaiv Holy Dormition Lavra in Volhynia and the Holy Dormition Monastery in Crimea (close to Bakhchisarai), as well as the Greek Catholic Nativity Monastery in Zhovkva, near Lviv, at that time in Habsburg Galicia. Two of them (Pochaiv and Bakhchisarai) enjoyed a popular fame as Russian Orthodox miraculous sanctuaries, the third one, the Zhovkva Nativity, became an outpost of Greek Catholic mission in the region. All three were popular pilgrimage destinations. Nevertheless, of all three of them only the Pochaiv Lavra remained a miraculous site and an ultraconservative outpost on the western Russian borderlands in cultural memory.

Pochaiv Lavra as a Holy Site

One of the prominent Russian Church historians, Andrei Khoinatskii (1837–1888), wrote at the end of the nineteenth century:

> Pochaiv Dormition Lavra, placed on the border between the Russian Orthodox world and Galicia, serves in this western Russian region as a stronghold and bulwark of Orthodoxy on the western outskirts of Russia, and presents a kind of bridge that brings Greek Orthodoxy forward into Catholic lands. The high Pochaiv bell tower signals with its golden cross toward both sides, East and West, Orthodox and Uniate Galicia Rus, in the hope of imminent unification.[25]

Pochaiv's geographical position determined the prominent role of the monastery in the history of Eastern Christianity. According to legend, the Pochaiv Monastery was founded in 1240 when the monks of the Kyivan Cave's monastery fled from the Mongols and settled in the Pochaiv hills. It is in this very time that the story about the shepherd Ivan Bosyi's vision of the Mother of God is set. The Mother of God stepped on the Pochaiv hill, and the trace that was left of her foot was filled with holy water.[26]

The first written evidence of the Pochaiv Monastery stems from the year 1527, whereas its official founding is connected with the 1597 donation of the Pochaiv landowner, the noblewoman Anna Hojska [Hanna Hoiska]. She donated to the monastery not only land but also a miraculous Theotokos (Mother of God) icon (Byzantine type "Eleusa") that she had received as a present from the Bulgarian metropolitan Neophit.[27]

The Abbot Iov (Zalizo, 1550–1651) played an important role in the history of Pochaiv's monastery and its miraculous icon. He introduced the Studite monastic rule to the monastery and was also successful in gaining the support of other rich Orthodox donors in the region. An important event in the history of Pochaiv is marked by the erection of the Trinity church (1649), where the Theotokos icon was placed for veneration. The formation of the cult of the Pochaiv Monastery and of its icon dates back to the mid-seventeenth century. The epic of the miraculous appearance of the Pochaiv Theotokos during the siege of the monastery by the Turks and Tatars was repeated in various popular songs and copperplates.[28] The story of the heavenly powers' victory over the pagan aggressors strengthened on a symbolic level the bastion role of the Pochaiv Monastery in the Christian history of salvation.[29]

The veneration of St. Iov of Pochaiv developed parallel to the formation of the Pochaiv Theotokos cult. The first vita of the saint was composed by Iov's pupil Dosifei shortly after Iov's canonization in 1659. Importantly, the iconography of Iov from the very beginning was coupled with the depiction of the Pochaiv Theotokos, highlighting the prominent position of the monastery as a holy place.

The Basilian period of the Pochaiv Monastery began in the early eighteenth century. At that time, the monastery came over to the Greek Catholic (Uniate) Church, and in 1739, the Basilian order settled down there.[30] This period witnessed a flourishing of the Pochaiv printing house. In this time, they received abundant financial support from Prince Mikołaj Potocki (1712–1782), who, according to legend, converted from Roman Catholicism to Greek Catholicism under the influence of the miraculous appearance of the Pochaiv Theotokos.[31] After his conversion, the Prince sponsored the construction of the monumental Dormition Cathedral that would further shape Pochaiv's outward image. He also initiated the canonization of St. Iov by the Pope and the coronation of the Pochaiv Theotokos icon according to the Catholic rite.[32] However, only his second request had been fulfilled in 1773. This coronation of the Pochaiv Theotokos icon was a notable event in a series of icon coronations in the eighteenth-century Polish-Lithuanian Commonwealth. A particular competition for Pochaiv in this respect turned out to be the coronation in 1727 of the miraculous Theotokos icon in the nearby Dominican Podkamień monastery.[33]

The coronation of the icon and the construction of the Dormition Cathedral completed the transformation of the Pochaiv Monastery into a sanctuary venerated in both the Orthodox and the Catholic worlds. Generally, until the 1830s, that is, until the end of the Basilian period, conflicts around the monastery's confessional belonging and its miraculous icon were the exception rather than a rule. Notably, this stability remained intact despite all the great geopolitical transformations in the region at the turn of the eighteenth and nineteenth centuries.

Only after the Polish uprising of 1831, in which some of the Pochaiv's Basilians presumably took active part,[34] did it come to political and interconfessional confrontations around Pochaiv. After the uprising, the Russian emperor Nicholas I (1796–1855) ordered the Pochaiv Monastery to be handed back to the Orthodox Church. Two years later, after a proposal made in the Holy Synod, it was decided to grant the monastery the honorable title of a Lavra.[35]

The list of the monastery's donors at that time includes not only the richest noble families of the Russian Empire but also the names of the tsars Nicholas I and Alexander II (1818–1881). The handing over of the Pochaiv Monastery to the jurisdiction of the Russian Orthodox Church contributed to the formation of Russia's mission myth of *protecting* the Orthodox Church against all forms of Catholic proselytism. This idea was made concrete on the level of symbols, rituals, and liturgies. In the 1830s, the period of division between the Russian Orthodox and Greek Catholic cultural memories about the Pochaiv Lavra began. The nationalization of religion and the sacralization of nation/empire brought new political overtones to the Pochaiv's image as a bastion of faith.[36]

The *Antemurale* Image of the Pochaiv Lavra at the Turn of the Nineteenth and Twentieth Centuries

The turn of the nineteenth and twentieth centuries witnessed the formation of two types of memories around the Pochaiv Monastery as a borderland bastion: political (Russian imperial and Ukrainian national) and religious. These narratives in their conflicting and sometimes complementary forms were promoted by clerics and politicians but also by artists, poets, and historians.

The media disseminating the images of Pochaiv as a Russian imperial, an Orthodox, or a Ukrainian national bastion were literary texts, visual artistic forms (church buildings, icons, copperplates), and various performances (religious and political processions).

As far as the Russian imperial image is concerned, it found expression in a revised architectonic form at the beginning of the twentieth century. The archbishop of Volhynia, Antonii (Khrapovitskii), ordered the construction of a new Trinity church in the traditional old Russian style. This was to present a visual contrast to the Baroque Dormition Cathedral, which for the archbishop was "too Catholic" to serve liturgical purposes. The Trinity church was to follow the model of the medieval Trinity Cathedral from the Trinity monastery in Sergiev Posad near Moscow. Like the latter, the Dormition Cathedral and the Trinity church were meant to symbolize the two epochs in the history of the Pochaiv Monastery.

One of the creators of the Russian imperial image of Pochaiv as a borderland bulwark was the monarchical center itself. On the performative level, it found reflection on 13 October 1883 during the solemn celebrations of the fiftieth anniversary of the Pochaiv Lavra's being handed over to the Orthodox Church.[37] Numerous state and Russian Orthodox Church dignitaries took part in these festivities. The Volhynian eparchial press quoted on this occasion the telegram sent to the Pochaiv Monastery in the name of Emperor Nicholas I:

> The Emperor joins his prayers to the celebrations in the ancient Pochaiv Monastery in the memory of its return to the native Orthodox Church. He bequeaths to the Pochaiv Miraculous icon of the Mother of God in his and the Empress's names a precious lamp, which will be delivered shortly afterward. Let its light symbolize the praying unity of the Monarch with his peo-

ple in front of this ancient sanctuary. Let this monastery remain the bastion of Orthodoxy and *russkoi narodnosti* [Russianness] in the Old Russian land.[38]

From this time on, the Pochaiv Lavra gained the image of a stronghold fighting for the liberation and recapture of the Ukrainian territories from Polish rule. Shortly afterward the abovementioned branch of the Union of the Russian People was founded on Pochaiv territory.[39]

The peculiar role of the Pochaiv Lavra in preserving Orthodoxy and Russianness was also expressed in the Russian Orthodox Church press. The official organ of the Volhynian eparchy, *Volynskiie eparchialnyie vedomosti* (Volhynian Eparchial Newspaper, released by the Pochaiv printing press), regularly published articles on the history of the Pochaiv Lavra and its miraculous icon.[40] Notably, some publications were directly reprinted from *Moskovskiie vedomosti* (Moscow Newspaper): The anonymous author of "One of Russia's Borderland Strongholds" (1897) drew parallels between the Pochaiv Lavra as a borderland bastion and other Russian holy sites:

> Moscow, as it is well known, is surrounded along its borders with numerous monasteries.... Moscow in this case presents only the microcosm of Russia. Looking further along our borders, we see the same line of Orthodox strongholds encircling Russia, from the Solovki monastery to the Chersonesos and New Athos monasteries. And we have often seen how, when the state and even national forces were weakened, Holy Russia was safeguarded by its sanctuaries. Even if they lay down in ruins, they remained spiritually uncontested.... So too, like an unshakable bulwark on the far-reaching outskirts of Russian lands, rises the Lavra of Pochaiv.[41]

A couple of years earlier the same periodical had elaborated upon Pochaiv's special pan-Slavic bastion mission: "It might be Divine Providence that on the borders to Prussia that now persecutes Slavic elements, there is a sanctuary in front of which the fraternal union of various Slavic tribes will be joined together."[42] However the most active propagators of the *antemurale* image of the Pochaiv Lavra were the monks themselves. Particularly informative were the newspapers *Pochaiv News* and *Pochaevskii listok* (Pochaiv Leaflet), released on the initiative of the monastery's abbots. The intended audience of both newspapers (*Pochaiv News* as an official voice of the Pochaiv's branch of the Union of the Russian People) was the Orthodox local rural population. The major topics concerned the monastery's religious and political activities and the promotion of ultraright ideas. This included the revival of the *antemurale* rhetoric with its major components—the image of the enemy, the idea of a chosen people, and the concept of belonging to a bigger community.

The image of the enemy propagated in both newspapers was threefold. The harshest criticism fell upon the Jews. The next group were the Polish Catholics. Finally, various political forces in the Russian Empire that endeavored to challenge the institution of the Russian monarchy fell into the category of rebels and state enemies.

The Jews were presented as the "most dangerous and most harmful people for the existence and prosperity of every state, since they undermine all the state's foundations like woodworm."[43] Similar statements were to be found in practically every issue of the *Pochaiv News*. One of the publications reported claims that the local Jews sent an objection to the State Duma against the apparent anti-Jewish propaganda during the liturgies in the Pochaiv Lavra. The preachers had presumably incited the peasants to expel the Jews from the nearby village. The newspaper did not deny these accusations, but it blamed the Jews for the conflict's escalation. According to the article,

> Indeed, the hostile attitude to the Jews among the local peasantry is caused solely by economic reasons. ... The Jews are cheating the peasants and prevent the conduct of trade. ... The Jews have swarmed like worms when someone pours kerosene on them. People, do try it once again, they will disappear then entirely.[44]

Indeed, the appeals to expel the Jews from the region appeared regularly in the right-wing publications of the Pochaiv Lavra. Despite this openly hostile and sometimes brutal rhetoric,[45] such demands were mostly caused by attempts to contest Jews' economic position in the area. The kind of anti-Semitism propagated in the Pochaiv Lavra at that time was "a reaction toward the modern phenomena of industrialization and urbanization, and violent methods."[46] Only in a few cases did the *Pochaiv News* report about the negative role of Jews in Christian history[47]; in most cases, the Jews were depicted as demonic, perfidious, and cunning entrepreneurs and speculators and parasites on peasants' hard lives. They were, according to the Pochaiv's rightists, all guilty for the sufferings and widely spread vices of the Orthodox peasants—drinking and theft.

Scholars of modern Russian Jewish history normally differentiate between anti-Judaism (theological aversion toward the Jewish religion) and anti-Semitism (aversion toward the Jews as ethnic or national group). According to Manfred Hildermeier, the latter should be applied to Russian politics and public opinion from the late nineteenth century on. It was an ideological trend connected with the formation of modern mass society and new political structures.[48] Some scholars pointed out that it was the resurgence of anti-Semitism in Western Europe in the late nineteenth century that found its echo in the Russian capital. Seen from this perspective, anti-Semitism in the Russian Empire was primarily of an anticipatory character.[49] This opinion was objected to by Benjamin Nathans, who affirmed that various forms of discrimination against Jews beginning in the 1880s just "prefigured developments after World War I in right-wing states in Central and Eastern Europe."[50]

The Pochaiv's rightists were in the first ranks to promote anti-Semitic propaganda and criticize Jews' economic position.[51] Even for the imperial center, such appeals seemed to be too radical and might provoke interethnic turmoil and pogroms. As a result, one of the most ardent members of the Pochaiv's Union of the Russian People and the editor of the *Pochaiv News*, hieromonk Iliodor (Trufanov, 1880–1952), was fired in 1907 from his position and sent to Central Russia as an ordinary parish priest.[52] But even afterward the anti-Semitic propaganda in Pochaiv remained very rigid.

In contrast, the Poles were identified exclusively as Catholics who used all possible means to destroy the Orthodox Church and the Russian state. The main line of accusation was constructed along the argument that the Polish Catholic clergy conducted proselytism among the Ukrainian peasants on both sides of the border.[53] The history of Catholic-Orthodox interconfessional conflicts was often used to provide historical parallels and a background to the Polish clergy's ungodly behavior.[54] Besides, the Poles were blamed for conspiracy to demolish Russian imperial structures. A satirical "Polish Catechism" published in the *Pochaiv News* (1908) allegorically explained to readers how such a coup d'état would eventually be realized by peaceful means.[55]

The third group of enemies against which the monks of the Pochaiv Lavra warned its flock were the politicians in favor of reform or even the demolition of the Russian monarchy. A classical opponent in the eyes of the conservative clerics were the leftists who voted for the introduction of constitutional forms of rule. Other hostile political forces were those who opted for more political and religious freedoms. In 1909 the State Duma, in accordance with the Imperial Decree on Religious Tolerance, issued a bill that any adult could change religious adherence without any loss of rights.[56] As a reaction, the *Pochaiv News* printed appeals to anathemize the Duma and to convene the Council of the Russian Orthodox Church to take over parliamentary power: "One should not hesitate! The State Duma has sold our faith!"[57]

Similar appeals to dismiss the activity of the parliament were generally provoked by the threats to Church interests that came from some of the Duma's delegates, such as religious tolerance and control over schools. In the situation of the multiethnic and multiconfessional western borderlands, where the Pochaiv Lavra was situated, such affronts were unambiguously treated as a betrayal of Church and people. Notably, in their fever of blaming the reformists for their godless and shortsighted politics, the Pochaiv monks often referred to the dangers of secularism in Catholic countries. For instance, they described in detail the atrocities of the French Revolution and the sufferings it brought to the Catholic clergy.[58]

Regarding all these dangers, the mission of the Pochaiv Lavra was, according to its press, spiritual guidance, as well as economic and moral support for local peasants on both sides of the border. Remarkably, in the hierarchy of the Church and state enemies (the Jews, the Polish Catholics, and the political reformists) there was no place for the Galician Greek Catholics. These were seen as poor and misguided Russian souls that suffered in the Polish jails. In this tone, the *Pochaiv News* reported about the Galician pilgrims to the Lavra in 1908.[59] They were clearly identified as Russians abroad. Notably, "Russian" in this context was not a description of the Russian nation in ethnic exclusivist terms but rather a collective notion that defined a civic nation. This form of nation included the Great Russians, Little Russians, and White Russians loyal to the emperor and the Orthodox Church. As stated by Argyrios K. Pisiotis, many Russian Orthodox clergymen were concerned with "the erosion of Orthodox confessional unity in late imperial Russia. . . . They wished to use the energy of the rightist movement to defend the Church's privileges, while tempering the rightists' pagan nationalism."[60]

The Pochaiv rightists' loyalty to the Russian monarch could also be seen as a fight for confessional unity to strengthen the Church's positions. The abovementioned archbishop of Volhynia and Zhitomir Antonii (Khrapovitskii) was an ardent supporter of the patriarchate idea. He agitated for the reestablishment of this institution in the Russian Orthodox Church in order to strengthen the Church's position against the state's influences. According to archbishop Antonii, the ideal state form in the Russian Empire should be a government of two principles—that of the tsar and that of the Patriarch.[61]

The promotion of imperial and Orthodox confessional unity lead to further ideological maneuvers in Pochaiv circles. As stated by Klymentii K. Fedevych and Klymentii I. Fedevych, the Ukrainian (otherwise called "Little Russian") monarchists in the late Russian Empire (including the Pochaiv clergy) were active participants in the Ukrainian national discourse contributing to the rise of Ukrainian national consciousness.[62]

It is not therefore strange that Pochaiv Lavra was presented in its press as a stronghold of the Cossack Ukraine that had fought (and was still fighting) for union with the Russian monarchy against the Poles and the Jews.[63] Equally, the modern symbol of the modern Ukrainian independence movement, Taras Shevchenko (1814–1861), was praised there as "the most popular Little Russian poet."[64] The right-wing clergy in this way paid tribute to Shevchenko's anti-Polish and anti-Jewish statements.[65]

The bastion mission of the Pochaiv Lavra had more than just political aspects. Several publications claimed that Pochaiv Lavra belonged to a bigger Orthodox community. Namely, the monks made appeals to improve spiritual life in the western provinces in accordance with the Orthodox traditions of Central Russia. For example, in his "Epistle" from 1911, archbishop Antonii criticized fasting practices before the Holy Communion. He urged the parishioners to resist the unworthy influences of the "local Uniates, imposed by the Catholics, but also of the Calvinists and the Lutherans" and follow the strict traditions "of the Center."[66]

The imperial powers and the monks were not the only ones to popularize the bastion image of the Pochaiv Lavra. At the end of the nineteenth century, several historians discovered Pochaiv Lavra as a subject of their studies. One such monumental work belongs to the Archimandrite Amvrosii (Lototskii), whose *Skazanie istoricheskoie o Pochaevskoi Lavre* (Historical Narration about the Lavra of Pochaiv, 1886) was based on a thorough investigation of the monastery's archive.[67] Later, Andrei Khoinatskii published his *Pochaevskaia Uspenskaja Lavra. Istoricheskoie opisaniie* (The Dormition Lavra of Pochaiv. A Historical Description, 1897), with its emphasis on the image of a "hostile Poland." The successes of the Basilian printing house were silenced; the eighteenth-century architectonic forms were labeled Western influences. Generally, the Greek Catholic period was presented in the monograph as "the lost time."[68]

The popularity of the Pochaiv Lavra's bastion image can be understood only in the context of competing cultures of memory on the lands of the former Polish-Lithuanian Commonwealth in the times of nationalism. It was a continuation of the popular rhetoric of *antemurale* that had existed in these territories since the late Middle Ages. As early as the sixteenth and seventeenth centuries, the borderland Ruthenian (Ukrainian and Belarusian) lands, particularly the Cossack movement, were often presented as a specific Orthodox *antemurale* within the Polish Catholic *antemurale*.[69] In the nineteenth century, this concept was in competition with the emerging bulwark ideology of Polish nationalism. For the latter there was no place for either "Cossack's *antemurale*" or the Orthodox bastions of faith.[70]

The press in Habsburg Galicia at the turn of the nineteenth and twentieth centuries depicted Pochaiv critically as a stronghold of Russian chauvinism, autocracy, and tyranny. One of the cartoons of the Lviv newspaper *Zerkalo* (The Mirror) presented Galician pilgrims (labeled as Russophiles[71]) on their way to the Pochaiv Lavra to pick up salaries. The picture is dominated by the figure of the Russian tsar, who threatens enemies with whips (Figure 6.1).[72]

Furthermore, the Greek Catholic Church in Galicia considered the influence of the Pochaiv Lavra as dangerous. In 1884, the Greek Catholic

Figure 6.1. Cartoon, "Galician Pilgrims Travelling Abroad," *Zerkalo* 15, no. 27 (May 1882): 4. Photo by Liliya Berezhnaya.

consistory in Lviv issued an edict to prohibit pilgrimages to Pochaiv. Some local priests in Galicia even asserted that pilgrims committed a sin because Pochaiv had become a place of hell and schism.[73]

At the beginning of the twentieth century, the Russian bastion image of the Pochaiv Lavra faced challenges not only from the Polish national *antemurale* mythology and Greek Catholic opponents but also from Ukrainian nationalism. During World War I, the Revolution, the Civil War, and the Polish-Ukrainian War, the Lavra was heavily devastated, first by Austrian-Hungarian and then by Russian troops. By the end of the Civil War, the monastery ended up on the territory of the Polish state. It was at that time that the newly established Ukrainian Autocephalous Orthodox Church (UAOC), often presented as a "true Ukrainian Church," delivered its own, nationalized image of the Pochaiv Lavra.

A notorious example of such a nationalization of discourse is the monograph of the Metropolitan of the UAOC, Ilarion (Ivan Ohienko, 1882–1972), *Sviata Pochaivska Lavra* (The Holy Lavra of Pochaiv). The author managed to collect archival documents about the Lavra during the turmoil of the 1917 Revolution and the civil war. The final version of the monograph was published in 1961, in exile. The major idea of the book was to present the history of the Pochaiv Lavra as a Ukrainian national sanctuary. Neither the Russian Orthodox, nor the Greek Catholics, nor even the Polish Catholics had a claim to Pochaiv Lavra's historical past. Neither the Dormition

Cathedral nor the Trinity church represented, according to Ilarion (Ivan Ohienko), the Ukrainian national style.[74] The works of Ukrainian poets and artists, like the lavra's sketches by the abovementioned Taras Shevchenko, were for Ilarion the testimonies of the Lavra's Ukrainianness (*ukrainstvo*). The bastion image of the Pochaiv Lavra is described in the monograph in terms of "the center of Christianisation," "the anti-Uniate fortress," "the bastion of Ukrainianness," and "the all-Volhynian national center."[75]

The idea of the Pochaiv Lavra as the Ukrainian national bastion obviously found resonance among the local population. The slogans popularizing this image were held up during the mass anti-Soviet demonstration near the Pochaiv Lavra in August 1933. In addition, the interwar Polish government promoted the image of the Pochaiv Lavra as a popular sanctuary. In 1929, the Polish president Ignacy Mościcki (1867–1946) visited the Lavra to venerate its miraculous icon.[76]

Amid the "nationalization of discourse" around the Lavra of Pochaiv, constant changes of borders and jurisdictions at the end of the nineteenth century to the beginning of the twentieth century, Pochaiv's sanctuaries continued to be places of veneration and pilgrimage in popular perception. It is difficult to estimate the yearly number of Greek Catholic pilgrims from the Galician territories on the eve of the World War I. *Pochaiv News* reported that there were 20,000 Galician Greek Catholics taking part in the festivities in 1908.[77] Other sources said there were 3,000–5,000 pilgrims.[78] Apparently, these movements across the border were promoted or sometimes hindered by different political forces. Pilgrims to Pochaiv were widely used in this borderland region to realize political aims.[79] Nevertheless, common religious practices indeed bridged the gaps between traditions, political entities, and Church jurisdictions.

Obviously, the recollections of a common past, when the Pochaiv Monastery was not the subject of a divided political memory, persisted for centuries. Even the Russophiles of Galicia, while actively promoting the "Russian imperial image" of Lavra, had to admit this fact. One of their prominent leaders, Fr. Ivan Naumovych (1826–1891),[80] affirmed in 1887 with sorrow, "Just think about it! Here in Pochaiv the Basilian traces are still alive. I would rather have died before witnessing this. The elder people with enthusiasm recall the Basilians."[81]

These recollections were less nostalgic for the lost Basilian jurisdiction and more for the unpoliticized veneration of a holy site. For many Greek Catholic peasants as well as for their Orthodox counterparts, interconfessional contradictions did not mean much. They preserved their "Ruthenian faith," in which the Pochaiv sanctuaries occupied a prominent place. Thus, in the age of nationalism, the Pochaiv Lavra fulfilled the functions of both a bastion and a bridge in the ocean of borderland ambiguities.

Zhovkva Nativity Basilian Monastery— a Ukrainian Bastion in Habsburg Galicia

The image of the Lavra of Pochaiv as the stronghold of ultraright Russian conservatism could flourish only while the monastery continued to be a popular place of religious piety and a political site of memory. Both components contributed to the unique place the Pochaiv Lavra occupied in the East European *antemurale* ideology in the age of nationalism. The Russian imperial image of Pochaiv won out in a symbolic rivalry with other modern national ideologies. No single nearby monastery could challenge the image of Pochaiv as a miraculous pilgrim site.

An alternative challenge also came from the Zhovkva Nativity Basilian Monastery, which, in the interwar period, promoted the *antemurale* idea in its Ukrainian Greek Catholic version. The first mention from the beginning of the seventeenth century relates to the Nativity Church founded by the Polish-Lithuanian Hetman Stanisław Żołkiewski (1547–1620). It was built in the center of the Renaissance city of Zhovkva, which was surrounded by thick walls to protect against Tatar raids. The Church was made into a monastery on the initiative of the bishop of Lviv Iosyf Shumlianskyi (1643–1708),[82] and it suffered a major fire in 1691. Rebuilt with the support of the Polish king Jan III Sobieski (1629–1696), the monastery was given the relics of St. John the New of Suceava, one of the most venerated Orthodox saints, who preached on the territories of modern Moldova and Romania. At that time, the monks of the Uniate Basilian monastic order settled on the territory of the monastery.

The Nativity Church was richly decorated at the end of the seventeenth century due to the efforts of the Zhovkva artistic circle run by iconographer Ivan Rutkovych.[83] Rutkovych himself made paintings of the Nativity Church's iconostasis. In 1783, the monastery had to return St. John's relics. As compensation it received relics of St. Parthenius, venerated both by Catholic and Orthodox churches.

The Nativity monastery acquired stature through the eighteenth century due to the rich donation of the magnate Michał Kazimierz "Rybeńko" Radziwiłł (1702–1762). This bequest elevated the monastery to the level of archimandrite and allowed construction of new buildings. One of these was a huge bell tower built in 1721–1750.[84] The monastery's most important period is, however, connected with the end of the nineteenth to the mid-twentieth centuries, when it was the primary site of the Basilians' publishing activity.

Its development is connected with the changing positions of the Greek Catholic Church toward political national movements in Eastern Galicia. Since the 1860s, the Church hierarchy was torn between Russophile and

Ukrainophile sympathies and priestly vocations. The Russophiles minimized the differences between Little Russians and Great Russians in the Russian Empire and saw all East Slavs as part of a single Russian nationality. The Ukrainophiles maintained that they were the same nationality as the Ukrainians or Little Russians in the Russian Empire.[85] The most considerable response to these tensions was the Dobromyl reform of the Basilian order (1882–1904). The reform emphasized Christian mission and imposed vows of faithfulness to Rome. It also endeavored to renew the missionary work among the Ruthenians in Eastern Galicia by promoting popular piety, catechization at school, and Church scholarship.[86] As stated by John-Paul Himka, "What the order did was to borrow and improve upon the methods of the national movement in order to initiate a religious revival among the spiritually endangered Ruthenian peasantry."[87] One of the initiatives took up the popularization of Christian teaching in the clerical press.[88]

The Zhovkva Nativity Monastery became the center of such activity on the initiative of its hegumen Kyprian Kozlovskyi. In the years to follow, the Zhovkva press printed several valuable contributions to Greek Catholic scholarship, including the series *Analecta Ordinis S. Basilii Magni*.[89] In spring 1887, upon the initiative of Archimadrite Andrei Sheptytskyi (1865–1944), the future Metropolitan of the Greek Catholic Church,[90] the Zhovkva press launched a new monthly journal *Misionar* (Missionary). Very soon, *Missionary* reached a print run of 15,000 copies and became one of the most popular Galician journals.[91]

Like the *Pochaiv News* and the *Pochaiv Leaflet*, the Zhovkva's *Missionary* was a new medium addressing a peasant audience. Extremely cheap and written in simple language, it was primarily aimed at the popularization of Christian teaching. Another aim was the defense of the peasantry against various radical political influences.[92] Like the Pochaiv periodicals, the *Missionary* clearly defined its opponents: materialists, populists, pro-Orthodox periodicals, and political radicals. All of them, except for pro-Orthodox periodicals, were condemned for their connections with the Jews, Poles, and Germans. Radicals in particular were blamed for hidden sympathies with the Jews and Polish socialists:

> You already know that socialism was born from a Jew Marx and a Jew Lassalle, and that it came to us in particular due to the activities of a godless man Drahomanov, who at the beginning was supported by some failed students, like Franko and Pavlyk. . . . This means that the radicals are holding hands with the Polish socialists from Western Galicia, and also with the German socialists, and then in turn with the Jewish socialist generals. Look, my dear brothers, how the devil has gathered together a Jew and the socialist Pavlyk and the radical Ruthenian and has them all lying like Gypsies.[93]

For the authors of the *Missionary*, political radicalism was dangerous for the Galician peasantry because it allegedly propagated anticlericalism and established connections to the local Poles and Jews. Anti-Semitic sentiments on the pages of the *Missionary* were expressed in a less outraged form than in the case of Pochaiv. The Basilians, in contrast to the Pochaiv monks, were more interested in the popularization of anti-Judaic religious prejudices than of national and economic ones. Even so, *Missionary* also supported the boycott of Jewish stores and taverns.[94]

For the Basilians, the popular Galician political movements were dangerous for one more reason. The local Russophiles (otherwise called the Moskvophiles) were often criticized for bringing peasants closer to Russia and the Orthodox Church:

> Not just once has the *Missionary* warned all the Catholic Ruthenians against the false Moskvophile agitation and the Moskvophile periodicals. Why did *Missionary* do so? Was it all about politics? Not at all! And why then? While the Moskvophiles have not only betrayed their folk for Russian rubles, but, more importantly, they started a huge agitation campaign for Orthodoxy, for schism, for separating our Catholic Ruthenians from the Catholic Church.[95]

By fighting the Russophiles, the *Missionary* also challenged the Pochaiv ultraright periodicals that supported the Galician pro-Russian movement. It could not, however, compete with the Pochaiv publications either in popularity or in the radicalism of its statements. Nevertheless, *Missionary* ultimately strengthened the positions of the Russophiles' major opponents—the Ukrainophiles. The Ukrainophiles urged that the development of the Greek Catholic Church be free both from Polish and Russian influences. The *Missionary*'s position generally coincided with the policy of the Greek Catholic Church to become a patron of the Ukrainophile orientation.[96] In this way, the *Missionary* was thought to be a literary bastion against the influences from abroad, both political and religious. At the same time, it highlighted so-called national values and the idea of "our fatherland Ukraine." Particularly intense appeals came during World War I. Notably, the journal did not popularize chauvinistic ideas at that time, instead strongly emphasizing the sufferings of rank-and-file soldiers and the poor fate of Galician peasants. According to the *Missionary*, only the preservation of Christianity, the national character, and love for the Ukrainian fatherland could save the land from devastation:

> In this war we have seen them all. The armies of different nations came through our land. ... These were the Hungarians, the pure Russians, the armies from our Ukrainian lands, the Cherkessians, the Tatars, the Czechs, the Croatians, the German army, and, finally, the Turks. All are different in their fortune.... Each nation has its heart, its fortune. Does our nation also

have it? Yes, it has! ... Oh, our Ukrainian mothers, if you want great children, be yourselves saints and great in your hearts; if you wish our nation all the best, teach your children to live according to the Christian tradition.[97]

The same issue of the *Missionary* sent an encouraging appeal to the readers:

> We have brought immense numbers of sacrifices in this horrible war. We have gladly and courageously brought to the altar of the Fatherland our blood and our property. Did we get something in return? Our Fatherland will rise in its glory and its fame shall spread all over the world. ... The flint stone of peace, the defense for those who suffer, the bastion of justice, the home of a true work, and the sanctuary of high intellectual thought and a selfless spirit will be our Fatherland.[98]

The idea of the Galician Greek Catholic Church as a Ukrainian bastion and a cradle of the "awakened Ukrainian nation" found reflection not only on the pages of the Basilian *Missionary* but also in the painting of Zhovkva Nativity Monastery in the interwar period. The successes of the Zhovkva press allowed the monastery during the 1930s to engage Iulian Butsmaniuk (1885–1967) to paint the interior of the Church of the Sacred Heart of Jesus. This was a part of the restoration project drawn up by Edgar Kováts (1849–1912), a professor holding the Chair of Architecture and Architectural Forms at the Polytechnic School of Lviv to modernize and rebuild the seventeenth-century Nativity Church. The new Church of the Sacred Heart of Jesus had to preserve the major elements of the old Byzantine-style church and to introduce a new side altar dedicated to St. Parthenius, several wall paintings, a four-row iconostasis, and a pulpit.[99] After Kováts' death, the interior paintings were assigned to a young student of the Cracow Fine Arts Academy, Iulian Butsmaniuk.

Again, as it was in the case of the *Missionary*, the paintings were approved and systematically supported by the Metropolitan Andrei Sheptytskyi. The murals were painted in two stages. The first one was painted in 1911–1913, when the monastery's Marian chapel was decorated. The second period began in 1932 after Butsmaniuk had returned home from the World War I internee camps and immigration. By 1939, the major interior paintings in the Church of the Sacred Heart of Jesus were almost finished.[100]

The polychromes of the chapel address Marian iconography. In contrast, the iconography of the Church of the Sacred Heart of Jesus murals includes prophetic and evangelical-apocryphal motifs as well as various hagiographical and historical themes. Butsmaniuk's image of the Lord Almighty demonstrates facial similarities with the Metropolitan Andrei Sheptytskyi.[101] It was the artist's intention to fill the murals with images of contemporaries and historical figures to promote the idea of the continuity and sacrality of Ukrainian history. Among the saints of the Ukrainian

Church, Butsmaniuk also depicted St. Iov of Pochaiv, who was one of the ardent opponents of the union with Rome.[102] The Pochaiv sanctuaries (despite interconfessional contradictions) apparently occupied a significant place in the pantheon of Ukrainian saints.

The artist also painted historical scenes from the recent past that depicted the leaders of the short-lived West Ukrainian National Republic (1918–1919), the fighters of the Sich Riflemen (1917–1919) of the Ukrainian People's Republic (Butsmaniuk was one of them), and a poor kneeling woman with a dead child—a victim of Holodomor, the Soviet Ukrainian famine of 1932–1933.

A huge left-hand mural is devoted to the Union of Brest (1596) that marked the beginning of the Greek Catholic Church in Ukrainian lands. Butsmaniuk painted three groups of some fifty figures. The first one is the Uniate clergy, including St. Iosafat Kuntsevych (c. 1580–1623), one of the most venerated martyrs in the Greek and Roman Catholic churches.[103]

Figure 6.2. Iulian Butsmaniuk, mural in the Church of the Sacred Heart of Jesus in Zhovkva, featuring Bohdan Khmelnytskyi, Ivan Vishenskyi, Ivan Mazepa, Halshka Hulevichyvna, 1932–1939. Wikimedia Commons, public domain.

The second group is the Orthodox clergy and nobility that opposed the union. Finally, the third group are the Cossack hetmans, including Bohdan Khmelnytskyi (1595–1657) and Ivan Mazepa (1639–1709), who were intended to symbolize the Ukrainian fight for independence (Figure 6.2). It seems that for Butsmaniuk (as well as for his patron Andrei Sheptytskyi), Ukrainian unity (despite interconfessional contradictions) was the predominant idea.[104] The vision that Galician Lviv and Soviet Kyiv were once to be in the same state under the aegis of the Greek Catholic Church was symbolically implemented in this mural. It presents all the historical figures in front of the sanctuaries of both cities and the Metropolitan Sheptytskyi between them blessing the Union of Ukraine (Figure 6.3).

On the whole, the murals in the Church of the Sacred Heart of Jesus were meant to exemplify the idea of the Ukrainian bastion in a sacralized form. For the artist and his patrons, this symbolic fortress did not capitulate despite all the defeats of the Ukrainian idea during World War I and its aftermath. Surrounded by foreign powers, the Greek Catholic Church was thought to deliver a particular mission to the believers—the idea of a sacralized and united Ukrainian state. The culmination of Butsmaniuk's version of "nationalized Christianity" in a visual form is the image of the Mother of God with Christ wearing a shirt with Ukrainian national embroidery on one of the church's walls.

Figure 6.3. Iulian Butsmaniuk, mural in the Church of the Sacred Heart of Jesus in Zhovkva, featuring the Brest Union and the heroes of the Cossack Times, 1932–1939. Wikimedia Commons, public domain.

The Orthodox Bakhchisarai Dormition Monastery— a Bastion of Orthodox Christianity in Muslim Surroundings

Moving further southward across the Russian-Austro-Hungarian imperial border, one comes across another of "God's fortresses," the Crimean Orthodox Holy Dormition Monastery in Bakhchisarai. Built into the cliffs, this monastery is situated near Bakhchisarai, the Tatar khan's residence, and Chufut-Kale, the Crimean Karaites' historical fortress and religious center with numerous sacred Jewish gravestones.

The first legends about a miraculous appearance of the Mother of God and the construction of the church in this place presumably date back to the fifteenth century.[105] One relates the story of a poor shepherd who once saw a Theotokos icon with a candle in front of it in the rock cliffs. Although the icon was brought by the local nobleman to his home, it repeatedly returned back to the cliffs. Finally, the local villagers decided to build a Dormition church on this place to remember the date of the icon's first appearance.[106]

The earliest surviving Muscovite records about the Greek Orthodox monastery date back to the late sixteenth–seventeenth centuries.[107] Once the center of Greek Orthodoxy, the Dormition monastery attracted believers as a particularly holy place. Especially on 15 August, the monastery holy day, pilgrims streamed to the Bakhchisarai caves.[108] Moreover, as pointed out by Mara Kozelsky, because the Dormition monastery "was located in the khan's capital, ... it often constituted a contentious contact zone between Tatar and Orthodox populations."[109] Later on, it also became the diocesan seat. From then on, the Metropolitan Ignatius (Gosadino, 1712–1786) called the Christian population in 1778 to move to the Russian territories, to the north coast of the Sea of Azov. As a result of this resettlement, the miraculous Theotokos icon from the Bakhchisarai monastery was transferred to the Dormition Church of Mariupil.[110]

At the beginning of the nineteenth century, the Dormition monastery was practically ruined. Although often visited by travelers, antiquarians, and Russian monarchs,[111] its general condition was very poor. The revival of the monastery is connected with the name of the archbishop of Kherson and Taurida Innokentii (Borisov, 1800–1857).[112] After consecration, the archbishop made a pilgrimage tour around the peninsula to visit the old Christian sanctuaries. This pilgrimage bore a symbolic meaning. Archbishop Innokentii was the initiator of the creation of the "Russian Athos" in Crimea. The idea of restoring the old Christian sanctuaries on the peninsula was connected to the Anthonite movement in the Russian Empire to promote the union between religion and politics during the reign of Nicholas I (1825–1855). It was generally aimed at replacing Mt. Athos, at that time hardly accessible for Russian pilgrims due to the complex political environment and constant Ottoman-Russian conflicts, with the local Russian Orthodox sanctuaries.

Crimea was to occupy a peculiar place in this plan. Archbishop Innokentii claimed that the restored Crimean monasteries were meant not only to borrow their eremitic practices and order from Mt. Athos but also to replace it on the local ground. "Innokentii believed that all Slavs and Orthodox Christians were united by their shared faith, yet like many Russian nationalists, believed that Russia should take the lead."[113] These ideas found reflection in Innokentii's "Notice on the Restoration of the Ancient Holy Sites in the Crimean Rocks" addressed to the Holy Synod in 1849. Innokentii affirmed that this program:

> will sustain the honor of the Christian faith and the Russian government itself in the eyes of the gentiles; the holy sites that deserve the attention of every enlightened person will be preserved from final devastation; the centers of a quiet and salutary influence of the Christian faith upon the Tatar local population—who knows?—could gradually prepare the consolidation of the Crimean Muslims with Christianity; the travelers themselves could enjoy the holy shelters restored and not dead and silent so that their bodies and spirits could repose there.[114]

Generally, the archbishop's plans found positive resonance in St. Petersburg. An objection allegedly came from Prince Mikhail Vorontsov (1782–1856), who believed that strengthening the Orthodox Church's position in Crimea might endanger confessional stability and incite Tatar unrest.[115] However, his voice was not listened to this time. On 15 April 1850, the Holy Synod finally affirmed Innokentii's plan for Crimea. Five holy sites were to be restored in the near future: the Dormition Monastery near Bakhchisarai, the skete of St. Anastasia, the spring of Savlak-Su, the Inkerman Monastery, and the ruins at Chersonesos.[116] The future chief procurator of the Holy Synod, Alexandr Tolstoi (1801–1873), wrote the same year about the political importance of this decision in a letter to archbishop Innokentii:

> I am completely sure that your endeavor will have positive consequences in the near future. In times when the magnificent and ancient building of Christianity was heavily attacked from outside and turned to be unstable inside, the Divine Providence has shown Christianity to our wide and infinite Russia. Who knows what else will happen in the East, and for how long the ancient Mt. Athos will retain? The new one here is necessary, and it is important that it be built on the southern Russian rocks; from here on it will shine for our Eastern and Western coreligionists.[117]

It is unclear whether archbishop Innokentii's intentions to construct the Russian Athos had such far-reaching political perspectives. Most probably, he was interested in the promotion of the Orthodox mission in the Crimean multiconfessional environment and in the endorsement of archaeological scholarship.[118] However, as the letter of Count Tolstoi demonstrates, political implications of the project fostered the revival the old *antemurale* rhetoric in Russian public opinion. The Crimean sanctuaries were regarded as bastions of Christianity to promote links to the Orthodox population in the Black Sea region.

The Dormition monastery was to play a leading role in this project, as was declared in the edict of the Holy Synod. In addition, the official ceremonies on the peninsula were to testify to the particular bastion role of the monastery. Shortly before the monastery reopened its doors, archbishop Innokentii went on another pilgrimage that ended at the Dormition monastery. There he met the Greek Metropolitan Agaphangel to celebrate the Divine Liturgy. The monks of the Kyivan Caves Dormition Lavra donated a Dormition icon to the new monastery.[119] This was intended to amplify the link between Kyivan and Crimean Christians but also to demonstrate continuity with the Kyivan Rus past.

The Russian Athos project in general and the restoration of the Dormition monastery in particular contributed to the Russian Crimea discourse. As demonstrated in Kerstin Jobst's contribution in this volume, since the second half of the nineteenth century, the topos of "Crimea as the cradle of Rus Christianity" dominated these debates, while the period of the Crimean Khanate fell into the category of a selective forgetting.[120] According to Mara Kozelsky, "opening a Christian monument in a city celebrated for its Islamic heritage marked an assertive step forward in a competition between confessional landscapes."[121] By the end of the nineteenth century, Russian imperial and Orthodox readings of Crimean history and landscape had finally won this symbolic competition. The image of Crimea ingrained on the Russian mind was associated with the fashionable holiday resort, Orthodox ancient sanctuaries, and a peaceful and mystical atmosphere.[122] The multiethnic and multiconfessional Crimean past was occasionally presented as a romanticized oriental culture that could not jeopardize the predominantly Russian Orthodox image of Crimea.

The Crimean War (1853–1856), lost by the Russian Empire, contributed significantly to the formation of this narrative. Because other European states fought in this war on the side of the Ottoman Empire, Russian public opinion styled the Russian Empire as the only true Christian power.[123] This bulwark ideology was successfully transferred to some Christian sites in Crimea, with the Dormition monastery as a leading force. The monastery organized communication between the prelates and parish priests during the war; it also served as a waypoint for many refugees.[124] A hospital for wounded Russian soldiers was organized on its territory. After the war, the

Dormition monastery arranged a Russian war cemetery on its territory. In 1875, the St. George Church was erected there for the commemoration of the war victims.[125]

The patriotic war rhetoric contributed greatly to the formation of the Russian Orthodox image of Crimea with almost inevitable references to the *antemurale* topos. Anti-Islamic sentiments and the feeling of a special mission in a fight for the true faith dominated Russian Crimean discourse also after the war's end. Crimea became an important site not only of military but also of religious memory.[126] The Bakhchisarai Dormition Monastery became a visual symbol of the Russian Orthodox *antemurale* idea that was propagated in the official Church press. The local *Tavricheskie eparkhialnyie vedomosti* (Tavria Eparchial News) published several articles emphasizing the Dormition monastery's role in fighting Islam.[127] One of the texts praised the monastery (otherwise called "Panagiia" [All-Holy Protectress Mother of God]): "Its major merit was to support the spirit and energy of the Christians in the fight with the Muslims. It has united the Christians and defended the Holy faith against the wild onslaught of Islam."[128]

The main actors in popularizing the bastion image of the Bakhchisarai Dormition Monastery (skete) were not the Church circles but the Russian secular print media. The St. Petersburg journal *Niva* (Field) wrote in 1870:

> The Bakhchissarai Dormition skete occupies one of the most prominent places among Crimea's many wonders. It represents the deep holiness and uniqueness of this spectacular corner. As a sacred, holy place, the Dormition monastery is a memorial to Christianity in Crimea—erected in terrible years of persecution in the very center of Muslim settlement, it defended Orthodox affairs through the nearly five centuries of struggle with Islam.[129]

In addition, the imperial family's visit to the Dormition monastery in 1860 contributed to the image of a holy site on the Orthodox-Muslim border.[130]

However, in contrast to the case in Pochaiv, the Bakhchisarai monks were little engaged in the construction of this narrative. The monks did not issue any publications, they did not take part in the promotion of offensive nationalistic ideology and Russian rule, and they were not particularly engaged in the conversion activities. The difference between the Pochaiv Lavra and the Bakhchisarai Dormition Monastery was probably determined by their different types of monastic life. The Pochaiv Lavra practiced the so-called cenobitic type of monasticism, which stressed community life, whereas the Bakhchisarai Dormition Monastery followed a blend of eremitic and cenobitic forms.[131] This semieremitic way of life in a monastery allowed monks some more retreat.

Another difference between the *antemurale* image of the Pochaiv Lavra and the Bakhchisarai monastery relates to the nature of imperial borders.

The Pochaiv Lavra founded on the western outskirts of the Russian Empire was seen as the outpost of Eastern Christianity and Russian rule in Catholic and Greek Catholic surroundings. The Orthodox-Catholic-Greek Catholic interconfessional and Polish-Russian national oppositions replaced the old Christian-Muslim antagonisms. The Bakhchisarai Dormition Monastery's bulwark image instead fitted into the centuries-old scheme of the Christian-Muslim struggle, which acquired new overtones during the Crimean War. The rhetorical apparatus was ready and was well elaborated by that time. For that reason, Bakhchisarai Dormition monks could probably let themselves retreat from the Crimean political discourse and devote themselves to prayers.

In addition, archbishop Innokentii's plan to promote Orthodox Christianity among the Tatars opted only for a slow and subtle shift in the confessional balance. Violent means and offensive propaganda were to be avoided where possible. This position fitted into the Tsarist religious policy toward the Crimean Tatars well, particularly before the Crimean War. Afterward, the Russian government officially encouraged the Tatar departure.[132] Still, despite growing suspicion toward the Crimean Tatars in the second half of the nineteenth century, the Crimean Muslim question did not acquire the level of explosiveness of that of the Ukrainian Greek Catholics, Old Believers, Polish Roman Catholics, or even the Jews. The perceived danger on the western borderlands was much higher than on the southern outskirts.[133] This also influenced the modifications of the *antemurale* mythology.

Conclusion

The East European, Eastern rite monasteries were active promoters of national and/or imperial ideologies in the age of nationalism. The transformation of monasteries as holy sites in confessionally and ethnically mixed regions into the "bastions of true faith and nation" was mostly connected with the rise of monastic life and monasticism as a mass phenomenon in the second half of the nineteenth century. The influence of political ideologies on monastic life often resulted in the transformation of the mission idea: many monasteries combined conversion tactics with the promotion of various political ideologies. Many also used modern print media for these purposes. Particularly evident transformation can be traced in the history of two monasteries: the Orthodox Pochaiv Holy Dormition Lavra in Volhynia and the Greek Catholic Nativity monastery in Zhovkva, Eastern Galicia. The former enjoyed the glory of both an interconfessionally venerated miraculous site and a Russian Orthodox imperial bastion. The latter, due to its publication activities and its mural decorations, acquired the image of the Ukrainian national bastion in the Polish Catholic and Russian Orthodox surroundings.

The third type of the monastic bastion imagination includes the Orthodox Bakhchsarai Holy Dormition Monastery in Crimea. The monks of this popularly venerated holy site were not particularly involved in political and ideological struggles. Even so, the monastery's geographical position on the Christian-Muslim border contributed to the formation of its bastion image. It was connected with two focal points of Russian cultural memory and imagination: sacralized anti-Islamic rhetoric and references to the Kyivan Rus past. The Bakhchisarai Dormition Monastery shared the latter reference with the Zhovkva Nativity. But in the Crimean case, the idea of the Russian Athos was supported by Russian public opinion: it juxtaposed Prince Vladimir's baptism with the contemporary presence of Islam on the peninsula. Here, as well as in the Western Russian and Eastern Habsburg borderlands, historical memory was often projected onto the ambiguity of multiconfessional societies.

Liliya Berezhnaya is a research associate at the University of Amsterdam and a visiting professor at KU Leuven in the Faculty of Theology and Religious Studies. She is the author of *Die Militarisierung der Heiligen in Vormoderne und Moderne* (2020), *Iconic Turns: Nation and Religion in Eastern European Cinema Since 1989* (2013; co-edited with Christian Schmitt), and *The World to Come: Ukrainian Images of the Last Judgment* (2015; co-authored with John-Paul Himka).

Notes

1. "10 zapovedei dla Rossii," *Pochaevskiie izvestiia* 548 (1908): 1.
2. D.C. Rawson, *Russian Rightists and the Revolution of 1905* (Cambridge: Cambridge University Press, 1995), 92–95.
3. S.M. Kenworthy, *The Heart of Russia: Trinity-Sergius, Monasticism, and Society after 1825* (Oxford: Oxford University Press, 2010), 262.
4. See, for instance, some recent publications of Argyrios K. Pisiotis, "Between State and Estate: The Political Motivations of the Russian Orthodox Episcopate in the Crisis of Tsarist Monarchy, 1905–1917," *Canadian-American Slavic Studies/Revue canadienne-américaine d'études slaves* 46, no. 3 (2012): 335–63; Pisiotis, "Russian Orthodoxy and the Politics of National Identity in Early Twentieth Century," *Balkan Studies* 43 (2002): 225–43. An appeal to reconsider the position of the Orthodox Church as "handmaiden of the state" in the twilight of the Romanovs was made

by Gregory Freeze in the 1980s. He argued that the Church enjoyed a significant degree of autonomy in the state at that time. Freeze, "Handmaiden of the State? The Church in Imperial Russia Reconsidered," *Journal of Ecclesiastical History* 36, no. 1 (1985): 82–102. See also his "Institutionalizing Piety," 214. On Freeze's argumentation, see S.M. Kenworthy, "Gregory L. Freeze: Historian of the Orthodox Church in Modern Russia," in *Church and Society in Modern Russia. Essays in Honor of Gregory L. Freeze*, ed. M. Hildermeier and E. Kimerling Wirtschafter (Wiesbaden: Harrassowitz Verlag, 2015), 211–29.

5. M. Babkin, *Sviashchenstvo i tsarstvo (Rossiia, nachalo XX v.–1918)* (Moskva: Indrik, 2011).
6. A. Polunov, "Church, Regime, and Society in Russia (1880–1895)," *Russian Studies in History* 39, no. 4 (2001): 33–53, esp. 36–53.
7. Robert Crew coined the term in relation to the Russian imperial tactical alliances with local Muslim elites in his article "Empire and the Confessional State: Islam and Religious Politics in Nineteenth-Century Russia," *American Historical Review* 101, no. 1 (2003): 50–83.
8. P. Werth, "Lived Orthodoxy and Confessional Diversity. The Last Decade on Religion in Modern Russia," *Kritika: Explorations in Russian and Eurasian History* 12, no. 4 (2011): 849–65. Werth refers in his analysis to the recent publications of Mikhail Dolbilov: M. Dolbilov, *Russkii krai, chuzhaia vera. Etnokonfessionalnaia politika imperii v Litvie i Belorusii pri Aleksandre II* (Moskva: Novoe literaturnoe obozrenie, 2010).
9. S. Berger and A. Miller, "Introduction. Building Nations in and with Empires. A Reassessment," in *Nationalizing Empires*, ed. S. Berger and A. Miller (Budapest: Central European University Press, 2014), 4. On the nationalization of the Russian Empire, see, R. Utz, *Rußlands unbrauchbare Vergangenheit. Nationalismus und Außenpolitik im Zarenreich,* Forschungen zur Osteuropäischen Geschichte 73 (Wiesbaden: Harrassowitz Verlag, 2008).
10. Berger and Miller point out that these regionalisms were often promoted by imperial politics. Berger and Miller, "Introduction," 23.
11. O. Bartov and E.D. Weitz, *Shatterzone of Empires. Coexistence and Violence in the German, Habsburg, Russian, and Ottoman Borderlands* (Bloomington: Indiana University Press, 2013).
12. P. Harrison, *Castles of God: Fortified Religious Buildings of the World* (Woodbridge: Boydell Press, 2004).
13. P.N. Zyrianov, *Russkiie monastyri i monashestvo v XIX i nachale XX veka* (Moskva: Verbum-M, 2002).
14. A. Lawaty, "The Figure of 'Antemurale' in the Historiography," in *East and Central European History Writing in Exile 1939–1989,* ed. M. Zadencka, A. Plakans, and A. Lawaty (Leiden: Brill, 2015), 363. See also the contributions of Volodymyr Kravchenko and Pål Kolstø in this volume.
15. H. Hein-Kircher, "Antemurale christianitatis. Grenzsituation als Selbstverständnis," in *Grenzen. Gesellschaftliche Konstitutionen und Transfigureationen,* ed. H. Hecker (Essen: Klartext, 2006), 129–48. Janusz Tazbir argues instead for sacral and geopolitical components. J. Tazbir, "Od antemurale do przedmurza, dzieje terminu," *Odrodzenie i Reformacja w Polsce* 29 (1984): 167–84; Tazbir, *Polskie przedmurze*

chrześcijańskiej Europy: mity a rzeczywistość historyczna (Warszawa: Wydawnictwo Interpress, 1987), 98.
16. See the contribution of Kerstin Weiand in this volume.
17. M. Morawiec, "Vom Topos zum Mythos: Das *antemurale christianitatis* Verständnis bei Europa- Historikern," in *Gebrochene Kontinuitäten: Transnationalität in den Erinnerungskulturen Ostmitteleuropas im 20. Jahrhundert*, ed. A. Gąsior, A.E. Halemba, and S. Troebst (Wien/Köln/Weimar: Böhlau Verlag, 2014), 202, 204.
18. A. Sójka, "Staropolska koncepcja przedmurza w literaturze Oświecenia: zarys problematyki," *Studia Filologiczne* 2 (2001): 115–25; P. Srodecki, *Antemurale Christianitatis. Zur Genese der Bollwerksrhetorik im östlichen Mitteleuropa an der Schwelle vom Mittelalter zur Frühen Neuzeit* (Husum: Matthiesen Verlag, 2015), 339–60.
19. M. Deszczyńska, "Wyobrażenie 'przedmurza' w piśmiennictwie schyłku polskiego oświecenia," *Przegląd Historyczny* 3 (2001): 298. Deszczyńska considers *antemurale* in terms of myth, imaginary, and stereotype, without providing any substantial differentiation.
20. Lawaty, "Figure of 'Antemurale,'" 367. See also Pål Kolstø's contribution in this volume.
21. Hein-Kircher, "Antemurale christianitatis"; B. Wöller, *Europa als historisches Argument. Nationsbildungsstrategien polnischer und ukrainischer Historiker im habsburgischen Galizien* (Bochum: Verlag Dr. Dieter Winkler, 2014), 257–324; A.C. Kenneweg, "Antemurale christianitatis—eine problematische Denkfigur?" in *Gebrochene Kontinuitäten: Transnationalität in den Erinnerungskulturen Ostmitteleuropas im 20. Jahrhundert*, ed. A. Gąsior, A.E. Halemba, and S. Troebst (Wien/Köln/Weimar: Böhlau Verlag, 2014), 217–35.
22. B. Törnquist-Plewa, "Contrasting Ethnic Nationalisms: Eastern Central Europe," in *Language and Nationalism in Europe*, ed. S. Barbour and C. Carmichael (Oxford: Oxford University Press, 2000), 183–220. More specifically on language and nationalism in the East European context, see a very comprehensive study by T. Kamusella, *The Politics of Language and Nationalism in Modern Central Europe* (London: Palgrave Macmillan, 2012).
23. See, for example, the case study of nineteenth-century Silesia in J.E. Bjork, *Neither German nor Pole. Catholicism and National Indifference in a Central European Borderland* (Ann Arbor: University of Michigan Press, 2008).
24. Both terms, "sacralization of the nation" and the "nationalization of religion," describe complementary relations between religion and nation. There are, however, considerable differences between them. While the "sacralization of the nation" refers to the transfer of functions and means of representation from religious systems to the concept of the nation, the "nationalization of religion" implies a complementary process that inscribes nationality into religious frameworks. M. Schulze Wessel, "Einleitung: Die Nationalisierung der Religion und die Sakralisierung der Nation im östlichen Europa," in *Nationalisierung der Religion und Sakralisierung der Nation im östlichen Europa*, ed. M. Schulze Wessel (Stuttgart: Franz Steiner Verlag, 2006), 7; H. Lehmann, "Die Säkularisierung der Religion und die Sakralisierung der Nation im 20. Jahrhundert. Varianten einer komplementären Relation," in *Religion im Nationalstaat zwischen den Weltkriegen 1918–1939*, ed. H.-C. Maner and M. Schulze Wessel (Stuttgart: Franz Steiner Verlag, 2002), 23.

25. A. Khoinatskii, *Pochaevskaia Uspenskaia Lavra. Istoricheskoie opisaniie* (Pochaev: Tipografiia Pochaevskoi Lavry, 1897), 11.
26. P. Rychkov and V. Luts, *Pochaivska Sviato-Uspenska Lavra* (Kyiv: "Tekhnika," 2000), 8 passim.
27. I. Ohienko, *Fortetsia pravoslavia na Volyni. Sviata Pochaivska Lavra* (Kyiv: "Nasha kultura i nauka," 2005), 66 passim.
28. "Oi, zashla zoria vechorovaia," Rychkov and Luts, *Pochaivska Sviato-Uspenska Lavra*, 16 passim.
29. L. Berezhnaya, "'Heilige Gottesmutter von Počajiv, sie wird uns retten!' Die Gottesmutter von Počajiv als Erinnerungsort in der postsowjetischen Ukraine," in *Maria in der Krise. Kultpraxis zwischen Konfession und Politik in Ostmitteleuropa*, Visuelle Geschichtskultur, 10, ed. A. Gąsior (Wien/Köln/Weimar: Böhlau Verlag, 2014), 347–58.
30. The Order of St. Basil the Great (OSBM) was the exclusive form of Greek Catholic monasticism until the end of the nineteenth century. Its origin is connected with the activity of the Metropolitan Iosyf Rutskyi (1574–1637). He envisioned thereby uniting all the monasteries in the Polish-Lithuanian Commonwealth that had accepted the Union of Brest (1596). The Basilians were mostly engaged in educational activity and printing. See D. Galadza, "Greco-Catholic Monasticism in Ukraine: Between Mission and Contemplation," in *Monasticism in Eastern Europe and the Former Soviet Republics*, ed. I.A. Murzaku (New York: Routledge, 2016), 373–74; S. Senyk, "Rutskyj's Reform and Orthodox Monasticism: A Comparison of Eastern Rite Monasticism in the Polish-Lithuanian Commonwealth," *Orientalia Christiana Periodica* 48, no. 2 (1982): 406–30.
31. Khoinatskii, *Pochaevskaia Uspenskaia Lavra*, 99–199.
32. Ohienko, *Fortetsia pravoslavia na Volyni*, 184–93.
33. P. Adelsgruber, L. Cohen, and B. Kuzmany, *Getrennt und doch verbunden. Grenzstädte zwischen Österreich und Russland 1772–1918* (Wien/Köln/Weimar: Böhlau Verlag, 2011), 17–18, footnote 655. See my review of the book: L. Berezhnaya, "The Ambiguity of Imperial Borders; or, How to Write the History of a Borderland City," *H-HistGeog*, July 2014, retrieved 26 May 2018 from http://www.h-net.org/reviews/showrev.php?id=40547.
34. Adelsgruber et al., *Getrennt und doch verbunden*, 181.
35. *Sviato-Uspenskaia Pochaievskaia Lavra. Vzgliad cherez veka. Istoricheskoe povestvovanie v slovach i obrazach* (Pochaev: 2008), 86.
36. L. Berezhnaya, "Kloster Počajiv," in *Religiöse Erinnerungsorte in Ostmitteleuropa. Konstitution und Konkurrenz im nationen- und epochenübergreifenden Zugriff*, ed. S. Rohdewald, J. Bahlcke, and T. Wünsch (Berlin: De Gruyter Verlag, 2013), 74–80.
37. R. Vulpius, *Nationalisierung der Religion. Russifizierungspolitik und ukrainische Nationsbildung 1860–1920* (Wiesbaden: Harrassowitz Verlag, 2005), 201.
38. "Prazdnovaniie (13-go oktiabria) Pochaevskoiu Uspenskoiu Lavroiu petiadisiatiletiia so vremeni vkliucheniia ieia v chislo pravoslavnykh Rossiiskikh Lavr," *Volynskiie eparchialnyie vedomosti. Neofitsialnaia chast* 30 (1883): 904; Adelsgruber et al., *Getrennt und doch verbunden*, 183.
39. Adelsgruber et al., *Getrennt und doch verbunden*, 183–85.
40. For instance, documents related to the Pochaev's history were reprinted in 1895 (nos. 17–19), 1896 (nos. 18–22, 24–26, 29–31, 36), 1898 (nos. 22–23, 27, 29), 1903 (nos. 4, 11–12, 14, 17, 20–23, 25, 29–33, 35), 1904 (1–2, 4, 7, 12). Studies on the

history and miracles of the Pochaiv Theotokos are found in G. Kryzhanosvkii, "Opisaniie ikony Uspeniia Bozhiei Materi," *Volynskiie eparchialnyie vedomosti. Neofitsialnaia chast* 3 (1899): 68–71.
41. "Odna iz pogranichnych sviatyn Rossii," *Volynskiie eparchialnyie vedomosti* 27–28 (1897): 785 (reprint from *Moskovskiie Vedomosti*, no. 247).
42. "Nieskolko slov o znachenii Chentstochovskoi i Pochaevskoi ikon Bozhiei Materi dla nashei zapadno-russkoi okrainy," *Volynskiie eparchialnyie vedomosti. Neofitsialnaia chast* 24 (1890): 786.
43. "Chto govoril o zhidakh nash uchenyi Soloviev," *Pochaevskiie izvestiia* 4 (1908): 2.
44. "Zakoposhilis zhidy," *Pochaevskiie izvestiia* 15 (1908): 2.
45. Some scholars labeled it "(proto-)fascist." H. Rogger, *Jewish Policies and Right-Wing Politics in Imperial Russia* (Los Angeles/Berkeley: University of California Press, 1986), 213, quoted from Pisiotis, "Between State and Estate," 230.
46. Pisiotis, "Between State and Estate," 230.
47. Even the accusation that a local rabbi had introduced special taxes for the Orthodox peasants to support the synagogue had economic overtones. "Ravinskaia kontributsiia," *Pochaevskiie izvestiia* 8 (1908): 3 passim. For an example of religious anti-Judaism as an argument against tolerance, see "Novoie poruganiie i raspiatiie," *Pochaevskiie izvestiia* 80 (1908): 1.
48. M. Hildermeier, "Die jüdische Frage im Zarenreich: zum Problem der unterbliebenen Emanzipation," *Jahrbücher für Geschichte Osteuropas* 32 (1984): 321–57.
49. Rogger, *Jewish Policies and Right-Wing Politics*, 110.
50. B. Nathans, *Beyond the Pale: The Jewish Encounter with Late Imperial Russia* (Berkeley: University of California Press, 2002).
51. The theme of Jewish exploitation was vividly debated in other journals and newspapers of the empire shortly before the pogroms of 1881. According to J.D. Klier, "The longstanding paradigm of 'Jewish exploitation' had already established Jews, in their various guises as inn-keepers, petty tradesmen, and usurers, as the archetypal enemies of peasant prosperity." J.D. Klier, *Imperial Russia's Jewish Question, 1855–1881* (Cambridge: Cambridge University Press, 2005), 454, esp. 300–331.
52. Father M. Khyzhyi, "Istoriia odnogo rasstrigi: ieromonakh Iliodor (Trufanov)," *Alfa i Omega* 2, no. 46 (2006): 96–110.
53. "Liakhi i rusiny," *Pochaevskiie izvestiia* 541 (1908): 1 passim; "Zagovor poliakov," *Pochaevskiie izvestiia* 15 (1908): 2; "Zaboty ksendzov o pravoslavnom dukhovenstve," *Pochaevskiie izvestiia* 123 (1908): 1.
54. "Nashestviie papistov na goru Afonskuiu," *Pochaevskii listok* 23 (1905): 1 passim.
55. "Polskii katekhizis," *Pochaevskiie izvestiia* 86 (1908): 3. See analogous examples in "Zagovor poliakov," *Pochaevskiie izvestiia* 15 (1908): 2 passim; "Zaboty ksiondzov o pravoslavnom dukhovenstve," *Pochaevskiie izvestiia* 123 (1908): 1; "Tainyie knigi poliakov protiv russkikh," *Pochaevskiie izvestiia* 43 (1909): 7 passim; "Mechty liakhov," *Pochaevskiie izvestiia* 138 (1908): 1.
56. Kenworthy, *Heart of Russia*, 264.
57. "Anafema! Prodavshim pravoslavnuiu veru," *Pochaevskiie izvestiia* 792–93 (1909): 2.
58. "O svobodie sovesti," *Pribavleniie k Pochaevskim izvestiiam* 40 (1909): 1.
59. "20 tysiach galichan na bogomolie v Pochaeve na Preobrazheniie," *Pochaevskiie izvestiia* 145 (1908): 2. See also "Medal o prisoiedinenii uniatov," *Pochaevskiie izvestiia* 744 (1909): 3.

60. Pisiotis, "Between State and Estate," 230.
61. Babkin, *Sviashchenstvo i tsarstvo*, 112–18, esp. 116.
62. K.K. Fedevych and K.I. Fedevych, *Za Viru, Tsaria i Kobzaria. Malorossiiski monarkhisty i ukrainskyi nationalnyi rukh (1905–1917 roky)* (Kyiv: Krytyka, 2017), 21.
63. This was the form of the Cossack myth popular among the supporters of the Great Russia idea. On Cossack myth in Russian and Ukrainian history, see S. Plokhy, *The Cossack Myth: History and Nationhood in the Age of Empires* (Cambridge: Cambridge University Press, 2012); J. Bürgers, *Kosakenmythos und Nationsbildung in der postsowjetischen Ukraine*, Konstanzer Schriften zur Sozialwissenschaft, vol. 71 (Konstanz: Hartung-Gorre, 2006).
64. "Portret Shevchenko," *Pochaevskiie izvestiia* 784 (1909): 2.
65. *Pochaiv News* continued to praise Shevchenko even after the publication of his uncensored "Kobzar" in 1907. Fedevych and Fedevych, *Za Viru, Tsaria i Kobzaria* 23: 95–126.
66. "Okruzhnoie poslanie archiepiskopa Antoniia o nedostoinom prichashchenii," *Pochaevskii listok* 7 (1911): 1.
67. A. Lototskii, *Skazaniie istoricheskoie o Pochaevskoi Uspenskoi Lavre* (Pochaev: Tipografiia Pochaevskoi Lavry, 1886).
68. Khoinatskii, *Pochaevskaia Uspenskaia Lavra*.
69. L. Berezhnaya, "Kazackii bastion 17 veka—vygliad iznutri i snaruzhi," in *Religion und Integration im Moskauer Russland. Konzepte und Praktiken, Potentiale und Grenzen. 14.–17. Jahrhundert*, ed. L. Steindorff (Wiesbaden: Harrassowitz Verlag, 2010), 265–96.
70. Wöller, *Europa als historisches Argument*, 257–58, 287–98.
71. On the Russophile movement in Galicia, see A.V. Wendland, *Die Russophilen in Galizien. Ukrainische Konservative zwischen Österreich und Russland 1848–1915* (Wien: Verlag der österreichischen Akademie der Wissenschaften, 2001).
72. The caricature appears in "Podorozh galickich palomnykiv za kordon," *Zerkalo* 15, no. 27 (1882): 4. On Lviv's satirical journal *The Mirror*, see A. Izhevskyi, "Obrazna struktura u grafitsi pochatku 80-kh rokiv XIX st.: satyra chasopysu 'Zerkalo,'" *Narodoznavchi zoshyty* 3–4 (2009): 447–57. On satirical depictions of Russian tsars and Galician Russophiles in Lviv's nineteenth-century political press, see E. Skorupa, *Lwowska satyra polityczna na łamach czasopism humorystyczno-satyrycznych epoki pozytywizmu* (Kraków: Universitas, 1992), 100–117, 137–41.
73. W. Osadczy, "'Na granicy Zachodu i Wschodu.' Monaster Poczajowski w polityce imperialnej Rosji wobec Galicji," *Krakowskie pismo kresowe* 4 (2012): 117.
74. I. Ohienko (Mytropolyt Ilarion), *Sviata Pochaivska Lavra* (Kyiv: Nasha kultura i nauka, 2004), 323 passim, 289–93.
75. Ibid., 379–417.
76. M. Tymoshyk, "Istoriia i siohodennia Sviatoi Pochaivskoi Lavry v konteksti tserkovno-istorychnoi monohrafii mytropolyta Ilariona (Ohienka)," *Trudy Kyivskoi duchovnoi akademii* 2 (2005): 184–97.
77. "20 tysiach galichan na bogomolie v Pochaeve na Preobrazheniie," *Pochaevskiie izvestiia* 145 (1908): 2.
78. Osadczy, "Na granicy Zachodu i Wschodu," 107, 118.
79. Adelsgruber et al., *Getrennt und doch verbunden*, 183–85.

80. Naumovych was a prominent Galician Russophile who was later excommunicated and compelled to move to the Russian Empire, where he served as an Orthodox priest. Galadza, "Greco-Catholic Monasticism in Ukraine," 376.
81. Quoted from Osadczy, "Na granicy Zachodu i Wschodu," 100.
82. On the bishop's activity, see P. Wawrzeniuk, *Confessional Civilizing in Ukraine. The Bishop Iosyf Shumliansky and the Introduction of Reforms in the Diocese of Lviv 1668–1708* (Södertörn: Södertörns Högskola, 2005).
83. V. Sventsytska, *Ivan Rutkovych i stanovlennia realizmu v ukrainskomu maliarstvi XVII st.* (Kyiv: Naukova dumka, 1966).
84. Z. Budzyński, *Kresy południowo-wschodnie w drugiej połowie XVIII wieku. Studia z dziejów społecznych* (Rzeszów: Wydawnictwo Uniwersytetu Rzeszowskiego, 2008), vol. 3, 226.
85. J.-P. Himka, "The Construction of Nationality in Galician Rus: Icarian Flights in Almost All Directions," in R.G. Suny and M.D. Kennedy, *Intellectuals and the Articulation of the Nation* (Ann Arbor: University of Michigan Press, 1999), 124.
86. J.-P. Himka, *Religion and Nationality in Western Ukraine: The Greek Catholic Church and the Ruthenian National Movement in Galicia, 1867–1900* (Montreal/Kingston: McGill-Queen's University Press, 1999), 79–83; M. Vavryk, *Narys rozvytku i stanu Vasylianskoho chyna XVII–XX st. Topohrafichno-statystychna rozvidka* (Roma: PP. Basiliani, 1979), 53–63; Galadza, "Greco-Catholic Monasticism in Ukraine," 377–78; B. Wójtowicz-Huber, "Wielka Reforma Zakonu Ojców Bazylianów w kontekście polsko-ukraińskiej debaty narodowej w Galicji lat osiemdziesiątych XIX wieku," in *Rola monasterów w kształtowaniu kultury ukraińskiej w wiekach XI–XX*, ed. A. Gronek and A. Nowak (Kraków: Szwajpolt Fiol, 2014), 157–66.
87. Himka, *Religion and Nationality*, 161.
88. The Greek Catholic clergy initiated the Ruthenian press in Eastern Galicia in the 1840–1850s. Before World War II, the segment of the clerical press reached some 20 percent of the total press sales. T. Stryjek, "Czasopisma religijne i narodowe w greckokatolickiej diecezji przemyskiej w XIX i XX wieku," in *Polska -Ukraina. 1000 lat sąsiedztwa, Studia z dziejów greckokatolickiej diecezji przemyskiej*, ed. S. Stępień (Przemyśl: Południowo-Wschodni Instytut Naukowy, 1996), vol. 3, 178, 182.
89. M. Lozynskyi, "Religiino-osvitnie knygovydannia v Ukraini: istoriia i suchasnist," *Ukraina: kulturna spadshchyna, natsionalna svidomist, derzhavnist* 19 (2010): 123–24.
90. On Sheptytskyi's life and activity, see P.R. Magosci and A. Krawchuk, eds., *Morality and Reality: The Life and Times of Andrei Sheptyts'kyi* (Edmonton: Canadian Institute of Ukrainian Studies, 1989).
91. H. Binder, "Das ruthenische Pressewesen," in *Die Habsburgermonarchie 1848–1918*, ed. H. Rumpler and P. Urbanitsch (Wien: Verlag der österreichischen Akademie der Wissenschaften, 2006), vol. 8, 2123. Marian Lozynskyi mentions a print run of 20,000 copies. M. Lozynskyi, "Mytropolyt Andrei Sheptytskyi i vasyliianske vydavnytstvo Misionar," *Visnyk Lvivskoho universytetu, Seria zhurnalistyky* 35 (2011): 146–51.
92. Binder, "Das ruthenische Pressewesen," 2123; Himka, *Religion and Nationality*, 161; Stryjek, "Czasopisma religijne i narodowe," 183.

93. "Radikaly-sotsialisty," *Misionar* 10 (1899): 156–57. On the attitudes of the Greek Catholic clergy toward the political activities of Ivan Franko (1856–1916), Mykola Drahomanov (1841–1895), and Mykhailo Pavlyk (1853–1915) in Eastern Galicia in the second half of the nineteenth century, see Himka, *Religion and Nationality*, 149–58.
94. Himka, *Religion and Nationality*, 162, footnote 489.
95. "Ne chytaite bezbozhnykh gazet," *Misionar* 11 (1911): 333–35.
96. This choice was made in accordance with the policy of Rome and Vienna concerning Ruthenian affairs. Both centers considered Ukrainophiles the lesser evil than Russophiles. Himka, "The Construction of Nationality in Galician Rus," 143. See also B. Wójtowicz-Huber, *Duchowieństwo greckokatolickie w ruchu narodowym Rusinów galicyjskich (1867–1918)* (Warszawa: Wydawnictwo Uniwersytetu Warszawskiego, 2008).
97. "Tym ie narid, chym iego materi," *Misionar* 5 (1917): 1 passim.
98. "Voienni zdobutky," *Misionar* 5 (1917): 69.
99. M.I. Orzechowski, "Wall Paintings in the Ukrainian Greek Catholic Church of Christ Lover of Mankind in Zhovkva. History of the Apsidal Scene of *The Ascension of Our Lord* and Its Iconographic Analysis," *Sacrum et Decorum. Materiały i studia z historii sztuki sakralnej* 5 (2012): 44–62.
100. I. Gakh and O. Sydor, eds., *Iulian Butsmaniuk. Stinopys Zhovkivskoi tserkvy Khrysta-Cholovikoliubtsia* (Lviv: Misioner, 2006); M. Chomiak, ed., *Iulian Butsmaniuk. Monohrafichna studiia* (Edmonton: Canadian Institute of Ukrainian Studies, 1992).
101. O. Yakymova, "The Image of Human in the Ukrainian Church Paintings in Eastern Galicia (Halychyna) during the First Third of the 20th Century: The Expression of Inner Changes," *Studia Universitatis Babeş-Bolyai. Historia artium* 1 (2014): 70.
102. Orzechowski, "Wall Paintings," 50, footnote 26.
103. K. Jobst, "Transnational and Trans-Denominational Aspects of the Veneration of Josaphat Kuntsevych," *Journal of Ukrainian Studies (=Religion, Nation, and Secularization in Ukraine)* 37 (2012): 131–53.
104. I. Gakh, "'Bereseiska uniia.' Stinopys Iu. Butsmaniuka u tserkvi Presviatogo Khrystovogo Sertsia u Zhovkvi," in *Beresteiska uniia (1596–1996). Statti i metrialy*, ed. M. Haikovskyi (Lviv: Instytut Istorii Tserkvy Lvivskoi Bohoslovs'koi Akademiï, 1996), 164–66.
105. V. Tur, *Pravoslavnyie monastyri Kryma v XIX-nachle XX vieka* (Kyiv: Stilos, 2006), 117.
106. Dionisii, *Panagiia ili Uspenskii Bakhchisaraiskii v Krymu skit* (Odessa: Tipografia E.I. Fesenko, 1908), 6 passim.
107. Tur, *Pravoslavnyie monastyri*, 117–20.
108. M. Kozelsky, "The Challenges of Church Archaeology in Post-Soviet Crimea," in *Selective Remembrances: Archaeology in the Construction, Commemoration, and Consecration of National Pasts*, ed. P.L. Kohl, M. Kozelsky, and N. Ben-Yehuda (Chicago: Chicago University Press, 2007), 82.
109. Kozelsky, "Challenges of Church Archaeology," 83.
110. Dionisii, *Panagiia*, 11.
111. Ibid., 15; Tur, *Pravoslavnyie monastyri*, 122.

112. N. Barsov, *Materialy dla biografii Innokentiia Borisova, arkhiepiskopa Khersonskogo i Tavricheskogo* (Sankt-Peterburg: Tipografia F. Eleonskogo, 1884); L. Antonova and L. Babinova, "Slovo ob Innokentii—arkhiiepiskope Khersonskom i Tavricheskom," *Krymskii arkhiv* 1 (1994): 101–4.
113. M. Kozelsky, *Christianizing Crimea. Shaping Sacred Space in the Russian Empire and Beyond* (DeKalb: Northern Illinois University Press, 2010), 83.
114. Innokentii, "Zapiska o vosstanovlenii drevnikh sviatykh mest po goram Krymskim," *Khersonskiie eparkhialnyie vedomosti. Pribavleniia* 3 (1861): 178.
115. Kozelsky, *Christianizing Crimea*, 88.
116. Ibid., 85 passim.
117. See V. Kalinovskii, "U istokov vosstanovleniia kolybeli khristianstva na Rusi. Arkhiepiskop Innokentii i Khersonesskaia obitel," *Prostranstvo i vremia* 2 (2014): 209. Kalinovskii examines the restoration activities of the archbishop Innokentii in the context of "Crimean Church studies" and less as part of the processes of Christianization and formation of the political and religious landscape in the region as postulated in Mara Kozelsky's studies. See his latest monograph, V. Kalinovskii, *"Drevnostei—i zamechatelnykh, i interesnykh, i krasivykh—nepochatyi ugolok." Tserkovnoie krymovedenie (1837–1920)* (Kyiv: "Antikva," 2012), 74–75, 102–3.
118. A. Shamanaev, "Russkii Afon arkhiepiskopa Ignatiia: dva vygliada na istoriiu proekta," *Izvestiia Uralskogo federalnogo universiteta. Gumanitarnyie nauki* 124, no. 1 (2014): 280–86.
119. Tur, *Pravoslavnyie monastyri*, 122.
120. See also K. Jobst, *Die Perle des Imperiums. Der russische Krim-Diskurs im Zarenreich* (Konstanz: UVK, 2007), 290–91.
121. Kozelsky, "The Challenges of Church Archaeology," 83.
122. G. Sasse, *The Crimea Question: Identity, Transition, and Conflict* (Cambridge, MA: Harvard University Press, 2007), 56–57.
123. Jobst, *Die Perle des Imperiums*, 295.
124. Kozelsky, *Christianizing Crimea*, 143–44.
125. Tur, *Pravoslavnyie monastyri*, 127, 131.
126. Kozelsky, *Christianizing Crimea*, 151.
127. A. Grozdov, "Svedeniia o Bakhchisaraiskoi Uspenskoi tserkvi, ustroiennoi v kamennoi skale," *Tavricheskiie eparkhialnyie vedomosti* 2–3 (1890): 118–127; A. Nakropin, "Peshchernaia skala Bakhchisaraiskogo Uspenskogo skita. Krymskiie peshchery," *Tavricheskiie eparkhialnyie vedomosti* 2 (1880): 82–90. Grozdov's publication was based on the manuscript study of Father Mikhail (Radionov) that presumably served as the grounding for archbishop Innokentii's "Russian Athos" project. See V. Kalinovskyi, "Monastyri Krymu v studiiakh dukhivnytstva Tavriiskoi eparkhii (XIX—persha chvert XX st.)," *Kraeznavstvo* 1–2 (2010): 143–48.
128. Dionisii, *Panagiia*, 8 passim. Originally published in, *Tavricheskiie eparkhialnyie vedomosti* 6 (1890): 231–56. See also M. Fyofilov, "Istoricheskii ocherk khristianstva v Krymu. Inkermanstkaia kinoviia, Georgiievskii monastyr i Bakhchisaraiskii v Krymu skit," *Tavricheskiie eparkhialnyie vedomosti* 22 (1899): 1464–73; 23 (1899), 1583–93; 5 (1899), 347–58; 9 (1899), 603–15.
129. Quoted from Kozelsky, *Christianizing Crimea*, 172.
130. Ibid., 159.

131. Ibid., 85.
132. Kozelsky, *Christianizing Crimea*, 149.
133. F. Davies, "Confessional Policies toward Jews and Muslims in the Russian Empire and the Case of the Army," in *Jews and Muslims in the Russian Empire and the Soviet Union*, ed. F. Davies, M. Schulze Wessel, and M. Brenner (Göttingen: Vandenhoeck & Ruprecht, 2015), 61; E. Campbell, *The Muslim Question and Russian Imperial Governance* (Bloomington: Indiana University Press, 2014).

Bibliography

"10 zapovedei dla Rossii." 1908. *Pochaevskiie izvestiia* 548: 1.
"20 tysiach galichan na bogomolie v Pochaeve na Preobrazheniie." 1908. *Pochaevskiie izvestiia* 145: 2.
Adelsgruber, P., L. Cohen, and B. Kuzmany. 2011. *Getrennt und doch verbunden. Grenzstädte zwischen Österreich und Russland 1772–1918*. Wien/Köln/Weimar: Böhlau Verlag.
Amvrosii (Lototskii). 1886. *Skazaniie istoricheskoie o Pochaevskoi Uspenskoi Lavre*. Pochaev.
"Anafema! Prodavshim pravoslavnuiu veru." 1909. *Pochaevskiie izvestiia* 2: 792–93.
Antonova, L. and L. Babinova. 1994. "Slovo ob Innokentii—arkhiiepiskope Khersonskom i Tavricheskom." *Krymskii arkhiv* 1: 101–4.
Babkin, M. 2011. *Sviashchenstvo i tsarstvo (Rossiia, nachalo XX v.–1918)*. Moskva: Indrik.
Barsov, N. 1884. *Materialy dla biografii Innokentiia Borisova, arkhiepiskopa Khersonskogo i Tavricheskogo*. Sankt-Peterburg: Tipografia F. Eleonskogo.
Bartov, O. and E.D. Weitz, eds. 2013. *Shatterzone of Empires. Coexistence and Violence in the German, Habsburg, Russian, and Ottoman Borderlands*. Bloomington: Indiana University Press.
Berezhnaya, L. 2010. "Kazackii bastion 17 veka—vygliad iznutri i snaruzhi." In *Religion und Integration im Moskauer Russland. Konzepte und Praktiken, Potentiale und Grenzen. 14.–17. Jahrhundert*, ed. L. Steindorff, 265–96. Wiesbaden: Harrassowitz Verlag.
———. 2013. "Kloster Počajiv." In *Erinnerungsorte in Ostmitteleuropa. Konstitution und Konkurrenz im nationen- und epochenübergreifenden Zugriff Religiöse*, ed. S. Rohdewald, J. Bahlcke, and T. Wünsch, 74–80. Berlin: De Gruyter Verlag.
———. 2014. "The Ambiguity of Imperial Borders; or, How to Write the History of a Borderland City." *H-HistGeog*. July. Retrieved 26 May 2018 from http://www.h-net.org/reviews/showrev.php?id=40547.
———. 2014. "'Heilige Gottesmutter von Počajiv, sie wird uns retten!' Die Gottesmutter von Počajiv als Erinnerungsort in der postsowjetischen Ukraine." In *Maria in der Krise. Kultpraxis zwischen Konfession und Politik in Ostmitteleuropa. Visuelle Geschichtskultur*, 10, ed. A. Gąsior, 347–58. Wien/Köln/Weimar: Böhlau Verlag.
Berger, S. and A. Miller. 2014. "Introduction. Building Nations in and with Empires. A Reassessment." In *Nationalizing Empires*, ed. S. Berger and A. Miller, 1–30. Budapest: Central European University Press.

Binder, H. 2006. "Das ruthenische Pressewesen." In *Die Habsburgermonarchie 1848–1918*, ed. H. Rumpler and P. Urbanitsch, 2091–126. Wien: Verlag der Österreichische Akademie der Wissenschaften.

Bjork, J.E. 2008. *Neither German nor Pole. Catholicism and National Indifference in a Central European Borderland*. Ann Arbor: University of Michigan Press.

Budzyński, Z. 2008. *Kresy południowo-wschodnie w drugiej połowie XVIII wieku. Studia z dziejów społecznych*. Rzeszów: Wydawnyctwo. Uniwersytetu Rzeszowskiego.

Bürgers, J. 2006. *Kosakenmythos und Nationsbildung in der postsowjetischen Ukraine*. Konstanz: Hartung-Gorre.

Campbell, E. 2014. *The Muslim Question and Russian Imperial Governance*. Bloomington: Indiana University Press.

Chomiak, M., ed. 1992. *Iulian Butsmaniuk. Monohrafichna studiia*. Edmonton: Canadian Institute of Ukrainian Studies.

"Chto govoril o zhidakh nash uchenyi Soloviev." 1908. *Pochaevskiie izvestiia* 4: 1–3.

Crew, R. 2003. "Empire and the Confessional State: Islam and Religious Politics in Nineteenth-Century Russia." *American Historical Review* 101, no. 1: 50–83.

Davies, F. 2015. "Confessional Policies toward Jews and Muslims in the Russian Empire and the Case of the Army." In *Jews and Muslims in the Russian Empire and the Soviet Union*, ed. F. Davies, M. Schulze Wessel, and M. Brenner, 47–64. Göttingen: Vandenhoeck & Ruprecht.

Deszczyńska, M. 2001. "Wyobrażenie 'przedmurza' w piśmiennictwie schyłku polskiego oświecenia." *Przegląd Historyczny* 3: 285–300.

Dionisii. 1908. *Panagiia ili Uspenskii Bakhchisaraiskii v Krymu skit*. Odessa: Tipografia E.I. Fesenko.

Dolbilov, M. 2010. *Russkii krai, chuzhaia vera. Etnokonfessionalnaia politika imperii v Litvie i Belorusii pri Aleksandre II*. Moskva: Novoe literaturnoe obozrenie.

Fedevych, K.K. and K.I. Fedevych. 2017. *Za Viru, Tsaria i Kobzaria. Malorossiiski monarkhisty i ukrainskyi natsionalnyi rukh (1905–1917 roky)*. Kyiv: Krytyka.

Fyofilov, M. 1899. "Istoricheskii ocherk khristianstva v Krymu. Inkermanstkaia kinoviia, Georgiievskii monastyr i Bakhchisaraiskii v Krymu skit." *Tavricheskiie eparkhialnyie vedomosti* 22: 1464–73; 23: 1583–93; 5: 347–58; 9: 603–15.

Gakh, I. 1996. "'Bereseiska uniia.' Stinopys Iu. Butsmaniuka u tserkvi Presviatogo Khrystovogo Sertsia u Zhovkvi." In *Beresteiska uniia (1596–1996). Statti i metrialy*, ed. M.Haikovskyi, 164–66. Lviv: Instytut Istorii Tserkvy Lvivskoi Bohoslovs'koi Akademii.

Gakh, I. and O. Sydor, eds. 2006. *Iulian Butsmaniuk. Stinopys Zhovkivskoi tserkvy Khrysta-Cholovikoliubtsia*. Lviv: Misioner.

Galadza, D. 2016. "Greco-Catholic Monasticism in Ukraine: Between Mission and Contemplation." In *Monasticism in Eastern Europe and the Former Soviet Republics*, ed. I.A. Murzaku, 372–96. New York: Routledge.

Grozdov, A. 1890. "Svedeniia o Bakhchisaraiskoi Uspenskoi tserkvi, ustroiennoi v kamennoi skale." *Tavricheskiie eparkhialnyie vedomosti* 2–3: 118–27.

Harrison, P. 2004. *Castles of God: Fortified Religious Buildings of the World*. Woodbridge: Boydell Press.

Hildermeier, M. 1984. "Die jüdische Frage im Zarenreich: zum Problem der unterbliebenen Emanzipation." *Jahrbücher für Geschichte Osteuropas* 32: 321–57.

Himka, J.-P. 1999. "The Construction of Nationality in Galician Rus: Icarian Flights in Almost All Directions." In *Intellectuals and the Articulation of the Nation,* ed. R.G. Suny and M.D. Kenned, 109–69. Ann Arbor: University of Michigan Press.

———. 1999. *Religion and Nationality in Western Ukraine: The Greek Catholic Church and the Ruthenian National Movement in Galicia, 1867–1900.* Montreal/Kingston: McGill-Queen's University Press.

Innokentii. 1861. "Zapiska o vosstanovlenii drevnikh sviatykh mest po goram Krymskim." *Khersonskiie eparkhialnyie vedomosti. Pribavleniia* 3: 177–90.

Izhevskyi, A. 2009. "Obrazna struktura u grafitsi pochatku 80-kh rokiv XIX st.: satyra chasopysu 'Zerkalo.'" *Narodoznavchi zoshyty* 3–4: 447–57.

Jobst, K. 2012. "Transnational and Trans-Denominational Aspects of the Veneration of Josaphat Kuntsevych." *Journal of Ukrainian Studies (=Religion, Nation, and Secularization in Ukraine)* 37: 131–53.

Kalinovskii, V. 2010. "Monastyri Krymu v studiiakh dukhivnytstva Tavriiskoi eparkhii (XIX—persha chvert XX st.)." *Kraeznavstvo* 1–2: 143–48.

———. 2012. *"Drevnostei—i zamechatelnykh, i interesnykh, i krasivykh—nepochatyi ugolok." Tserkovnoie krymovedenie (1837–1920).* Kyiv/Simferopol: "Antikva."

———. 2014. "U istokov vosstanovleniia kolybeli khristianstva na Rusi. Arkhiepiskop Innokentii i Khersonesskaia obitel." *Prostranstvo i vremia* 2: 207–15.

Kamusella, T. 2012. *The Politics of Language and Nationalism in Modern Central Europe.* London: Palgrave Macmillan.

Kenneweg, A.C. 2014. "Antemurale christianitatis—eine problematische Denkfigur?" In *Gebrochene Kontinuitäten: Transnationalität in den Erinnerungskulturen Ostmitteleuropas im 20. Jahrhundert,* ed A. Gąsior, A.E. Halemba, and S. Troebst, 217–35. Wien/Köln/Weimar: Böhlau Verlag.

Kenworthy, S.M. 2010. *The Heart of Russia: Trinity-Sergius, Monasticism, and Society after 1825.* Oxford: Oxford University Press.

———. 2015. "Gregory L. Freeze: Historian of the Orthodox Church in Modern Russia." In *Church and Society in Modern Russia. Essays in Honor of Gregory L. Freeze,* ed. M. Hildermeier and E.K. Wirtschafter, 211–29. Wiesbaden: Harrassowitz Verlag.

Khoinatskii, A. 1897. *Pochaevskaia Uspenskaia Lavra. Istoricheskoie opisaniie.* Pochaev: Tipografiia Pochaevskoi Lavry.

(Khyzhyi), M. 2006. "Istoriia odnogo rasstrigi: ieromonakh Iliodor (Trufanov)." *Alfa i Omega* 2, no 46: 96–110.

Klier, J.D. 2005. *Imperial Russia's Jewish Question, 1855–1881.* Cambridge: Cambridge University Press.

Kozelsky, M. 2007. "The Challenges of Church Archaeology in Post-Soviet Crimea." In *Selective Remembrances: Archaeology in the Construction, Commemoration, and Consecration of National Pasts,* ed. P.L. Kohl, M. Kozelsky, and N. Ben-Yehuda, 71–98. Chicago: Chicago University Press.

———. 2010. *Christianizing Crimea. Shaping Sacred Space in the Russian Empire and Beyond.* DeKalb: Northern Illinois University Press.

Kryzhanosvkii, G. 1899. "Opisaniie ikony Uspeniia Bozhiei Materi." *Volynskiie eparchialnyie vedomosti. Neofitsialnaia chast* 3: 68–71.

Lawaty, A. 2015. "The Figure of 'Antemurale' in the Historiography." In *East and Central European History Writing in Exile 1939–1989,* ed. M. Zadencka, A. Plakans, and A. Lawaty, 360–74. Leiden: Brill.

Lehmann, H. 2002. "Die Säkularisierung der Religion und die Sakralisierung der Nation im 20. Jahrhundert. Varianten einer komplementären Relation." In *Religion im Nationalstaat zwischen den Weltkriegen 1918–1939*, ed. H.-Ch. Maner and M. Schulze Wessel, 13–27. Stuttgart: Franz Steiner Verlag.
"Liakhi i rusiny." 1908. *Pochaevskiie izvestiia* 1–2: 541.
Lototskii, A. 1886. *Skazaniie istoricheskoie o Pochaevskoi Uspenskoi Lavre*, Pochaev: Tipografiia Pochaevskoi Lavry.
Lozynskyi, M. 2010. "Religiino-osvitnie knygovydannia v Ukraini: istoriia i suchasnist." *Ukraina: kulturna spadshchyna, natsionalna svidomist, derzhavnist* 19: 122–28.
———. 2011. "Mytropolyt Andrei Sheptytskyi i vasyliianske vydavnytstvo Misionar." *Visnyk Lvivskoho universytetu, Seria zhurnalistyky* 35: 146–51.
Magosci, P.R. and A. Krawchuk, eds. 1989. *Morality and Reality: The Life and Times of Andrei Sheptyts'kyi*. Edmonton: Canadian Institute of Ukrainian Studies.
"Mechty liakhov." 1908. *Pochaevskiie izvestiia* 1: 138.
Morawiec, M. 2014. "Vom Topos zum Mythos: Das *antemurale christianitatis* Verständnis bei Europa- Historikern." In *Gebrochene Kontinuitäten: Transnationalität in den Erinnerungskulturen Ostmitteleuropas im 20. Jahrhundert*, ed. A. Gąsior, A.E. Halemba, and S. Troebst, 199–216. Wien/Köln/Weimar: Böhlau Verlag.
"Nashestviie papistov na goru Afonskuiu." 1905. *Pochaevskii listok* 23: 1–2.
Nathans, B. 2002. *Beyond the Pale: The Jewish Encounter with Late Imperial Russia*. Berkeley: University of California Press.
"Ne chytaite bezbozhnykh gazet." 1911. *Misionar* 11: 333–35.
"Nieskolko slov o znachenii Chentstochovskoi i Pochaevskoi ikon Bozhiei Materi dla nashei zapadno-russkoi okrainy." 1890. *Volynskiie eparchialnyie vedomosti. Neofitsialnaia chast* 24: 786.
"Novoie poruganiie i raspiatiie." 1908. *Pochaevskiie izvestiia* 80: 1.
"O svobodie sovesti." 1909. *Pribavleniie k Pochaevskim izvestiiam* 40: 1.
"Odna iz pogranichnych sviatyn Rossii." 1897. *Volynskiie eparchialnyie vedomosti* 27–28: 783–85.
Ohienko, I. 2004. *Sviata Pochaivska Lavra*. Kyiv: Nasha kultura i nauka.
———. 2005. *Fortetsia pravoslavia na Volyni. Sviata Pochaivska lavra*. Kyiv: "Nasha kultura i nauka."
"Okruzhnoie poslanie archiepiskopa Antoniia o nedostoinom prichashchenii." 1911. *Pochaevskii listok* 7: 1–2.
Orzechowski, M.I. 2012. "Wall paintings in the Ukrainian Greek Catholic Church of Christ Lover of Mankind in Zhovkva. History of the Apsidal Scene of *The Ascension of Our Lord* and Its Iconographic Analysis." *Sacrum et Decorum. Materiały i studia z historii sztuki sakralnej* 5: 44–62.
Osadczy, W. 2012. "Na granicy Zachodu i Wschodu. Monaster Poczajowski w polityce imperialnej Rosji wobec Galicji." *Krakowskie pismo kresowe* 4: 91–124.
"Peshchernaia skala Bakhchisaraiskogo Uspenskogo skita. Krymskiie peshchery." 1880. *Tavricheskiie eparkhialnyie vedomosti* 2: 82–90.
Pisiotis, A.K. 2002. "Russian Orthodoxy and the Politics of National Identity in Early Twentieth Century." *Balkan Studies* 43: 225–243.
———. 2012. "Between State and Estate: The Political Motivations of the Russian Orthodox Episcopate in the Crisis of Tsarist Monarchy, 1905–1917." *Canadian-American Slavic studies/Revue canadienne-américaine d'études slaves* 46, no. 3: 335–63.

Plokhy, S. 2012. *The Cossack Myth: History and Nationhood in the Age of Empires.* Cambridge: Cambridge University Press.
"Polskii katekhizis." 1908. *Pochaevskiie izvestiia* 86: 3.
Polunov, A. 2001. "Church, Regime, and Society in Russia (1880–1895)." *Russian Studies in History* 39, no. 4: 33–53.
"Portret Shevchenko." 1909. *Pochaevskiie izvestiia* 784: 2.
"Prazdnovaniie (13-go oktiabria) Pochaevskoiu Uspenskoiu Lavroiu petiadisiatiletiia so vremeni vkliucheniia ieia v chislo pravoslavnykh Rossiiskikh Lavr." 1883. *Volynskiie eparchialnyie vedomosti. Neofitsialnaia chast* 30: 898–905.
"Radikaly-sotsialisty." 1899. *Misionar* 10: 156–57.
"Ravinskaia kontributsiia." 1908. *Pochaevskiie izvestiia* 8: 3–4.
Rawson, D.C. 1995. *Russian Rightists and the Revolution of 1905.* Cambridge: Cambridge University Press.
Rogger, H. 1986. *Jewish Policies and Right-Wing Politics in Imperial Russia.* Los Angeles/Berkeley: University of California Press.
Rychkov, P. and V. Luts. 2007. *Pochaivska Sviato-Uspenska Lavra.* Kyiv: "Tekhnika," 2000.
Sasse, G. *The Crimea Question: Identity, Transition, and Conflict.* Cambridge, MA: Harvard University Press.
Schulze Wessel, M. 2006. "Einleitung: Die Nationalisierung der Religion und die Sakralisierung der Nation im östlichen Europa." In *Nationalisierung der Religion und Sakralisierung der Nation im östlichen Europa,* ed. M. Schulze Wessel, 7–14. Stuttgart: Franz Steiner Verlag.
Senyk, S. 1982. "Rutskyj's Reform and Orthodox Monasticism: A Comparison of Eastern Rite Monasticism in the Polish-Lithuanian Commonwealth." *Orientalia Christiana Periodica* 48, no. 2: 406–30.
Shamanaev, A. 2014. "Russkii Afon arkhiepiskopa Ignatiia: dva vygliada na istoriiu proekta." *Izvestiia Uralskogo federalnogo universiteta. Gumanitarnyie nauki* 124, no. 1: 280–86.
Skorupa, E. 1992. *Lwowska satyra polityczna na łamach czasopism humorystyczno-satyrycznych epoki pozytywizmu.* Kraków: Universitas.
Sójka, A. 2001. "Staropolska koncepcja przedmurza w literaturze Oświecenia: zarys problematyki." *Studia Filologiczne* 2: 115–25.
Srodecki, P. 2015. *Antemurale Christianitatis. Zur Genese der Bollwerksrhetorik im östlichen Mitteleuropa an der Schwelle vom Mittelalter zur Frühen Neuzeit.* Husum: Matthiesen Verlag.
Stryjek, T. 1996. "Czasopisma religijne i narodowe w greckokatolickiej diecezji przemyskiej w XIX i XX wieku." In *Polska-Ukraina. 1000 lat sąsiedztwa, Studia z dziejów greckokatolickiej diecezji przemyskiej,* ed. S. Stępień, 177–90. Przemyśl: Południowo-Wschodni Instytut Naukowy.
Sventsytska, V. 1966. *Ivan Rutkovych i stanovlennia realizmu v ukrainskomu maliarstvi XVII st.* Kyiv: Naukova dumka.
Sviato-Uspenskaia Pochaievskaia Lavra. Vzgliad cherez veka. Istoricheskoe povestvovanie v slovach i obrazach. 2008. Pochaev.
"Tainyie knigi poliakov protiv russkikh." 1909. *Pochaevskiie izvestiia* 43: 7–8.
Tazbir, J. 1984. "Od antemurale do przedmurza, dzieje terminu." *Odrodzenie i Reformacja w Polsce* 29: 167–184.

———. 1987. *Polskie przedmurze chrześcijańskiej Europy: mity a rzeczywistość historyczna*. Warszawa: Interpress.
Törnquist-Plewa, B. 2000. "Contrasting Ethnic Nationalisms: Eastern Central Europe." In *Language and Nationalism in Europe*, ed. S. Barbour and C. Carmichael, 183–220. Oxford: Oxford University Press.
Tur, V. 2006. *Pravoslavnyie monastyri Kryma v XIX-nachle XX vieka*. Kyiv: Stilos.
"Tym ie narid, chym iego materi." 1917. *Misionar* 5: 1–2.
Tymoshyk, M. 2005. "Istoriia i siohodennia Sviatoi Pochaivskoi Lavry v konteksti tserkovno-istorychnoi monohrafii mytropolyta Ilariona (Ohienka)." *Trudy Kyivskoi duchovnoi akademii* 2: 184–97.
Utz, R. 2008. *Rußlands unbrauchbare Vergangenheit. Nationalismus und Außenpolitik im Zarenreich*. Forschungen zur Osteuropäischen Geschichte 73. Wiesbaden: Harrassowitz Verlag.
Vavryk, M. 1979. *Narys rozvytku i stanu Vasylianskoho chyna XVII-XX st. Topohrafichno-statystychna*. Roma: PP. Basiliani.
"Voienni zdobutky." 1917. *Misionar* 5: 69.
Vulpius, R. 2005. *Nationalisierung der Religion. Russifizierungspolitik und ukrainische Nationsbildung 1860–1920*. Wiesbaden: Harrassowitz Verlag.
Wawrzeniuk, P. 2005. *Confessional Civilizing in Ukraine. The Bishop Iosyf Shumliansky and the Introduction of Reforms in the Diocese of Lviv 1668–1708*. Södertörn: Södertörns Högskola.
Wendland, A.V. 2001. *Die Russophilen in Galizien. Ukrainische Konservative zwischen Österreich und Russland 1848—1915*. Wien: Verlag der österreichischen Akademie der Wissenschaften.
Werth, P. 2011. "Lived Orthodoxy and Confessional Diversity. The Last Decade on Religion in Modern Russia." *Kritika: Explorations in Russian and Eurasian History* 12, no. 4: 849–65.
Wójtowicz-Huber, B. 2008. *Duchowieństwo greckokatolickie w ruchu narodowym Rusinów galicyjskich (1867–1918)*. Warszawa: Wydawnictwo Uniwersytetu Warszawskiego.
———. 2014. "Wielka Reforma Zakonu Ojców Bazylianów w kontekście polsko-ukraińskiej debaty narodowej w Galicji lat osiemdziesiątych XIX wieku." In *Rola monasterów w kształtowaniu kultury ukraińskiej w wiekach XI–XX*, ed. A. Gronek and A. Nowak, 157–66. Kraków: Szwajpolt Fiol.
Wöller, B. 2014. *Europa als historisches Argument. Nationsbildungsstrategien polnischer und ukrainischer Historiker im habsburgischen Galizien*. Bochum: Verlag Dr. Dieter Winkler.
Yakymova, O. 2014. "The Image of Human in the Ukrainian Church Paintings in Eastern Galicia (Halychyna) during the First Third of the Twentieth Century: The Expression of Inner Changes." *Studia Universitatis Babeş-Bolyai. Historia artium* 1: 67–88.
"Zaboty ksiondzov o pravoslavnom dukhovenstve." 1908. *Pochaevskiie izvestiia* 123: 1.
"Zagovor poliakov." 1908. *Pochaevskiie izvestiia* 15: 2–3.
"Zakoposhilis zhidy." 1908. *Pochaevskiie izvestiia* 15: 2.
Zyrianov, P.N. 2002. *Russkiie monastyri i monashestvo v XIX i nachale XX veka*. Moskva: Verbum-M.

CHAPTER 7
"The Turkish Wall"
*Turkey as an Anti-Communist and
Anti-Russian Bulwark in the Twentieth Century*

Zaur Gasimov

Both the politics and the culture of the Crimean Tatars, Turkestanis, and Azerbaijanis during the past three centuries inside and outside of the Crimean Peninsula, the Caucasus, and Central Asia developed literally in the borderlands of the Slavic and Turkic, Christian, and Muslim worlds as well as on Europe's margins. The Crimean Tatar, Turkestani, and Azerbaijani intellectuals, being as a rule well aware of the Russian and Ottoman cultures and languages, have articulated the interests of their ethnic, religious, and national cause particularly since the Russian conquest at the end of the eighteenth century and throughout the nineteenth century. This chapter examines the contribution of the exiled Turkic[1] politicians and intellectuals Cafer Seydahmet (1889–1960), Muharrem Ergin (1923–1995), and Ahmet Caferoğlu (1899–1975), who were born under tsardom or in Soviet Russia, and their influence on Turkish intellectuals such as Mehmet (Saffet) Arın Engin (1900–1979) and others. It thus also examines the contribution they made to anti-communist thought during their exile in Turkey. The discourses shaped by these intellectuals gave birth to the idea of Turkey as the "last Turkish tower" and of a "Turkish wall."

The aim of the contribution is an attempt to describe the bulwark-related discourses among Muslim intellectuals. The chapter analyzes the anti-communist writings and speeches of the emigrant intellectuals that were published during their lifetimes and posthumously. Their arduous anti-Soviet rhetoric and critique of communism made Istanbul a unique Turkic and Turkish anti-communist bulwark, a certain *antemurale anti-communistatis*. An additional objective of the chapter is to describe the discourse patterns of the Crimean Tatars', Azerbaijanis', and Turkestanis' articulation of their national cause whereby they proclaimed Turkey to be a sort of Turkic bulwark against the Soviets and Russia. The contribution focuses on the specific terms of the Turkic and Turkish notions that in many ways correspond with the European-Christian terminology of bulwark and *antemurale*. It is important to note that neither Turkish nor Turkic intellectuals made use of the notion *antemurale*, the latter appears in the Turkish historiography of Ottoman history and in a few Turkish academic writings devoted to the European perception of the Ottomans.[2]

Turkish–Russian Entanglements: From Cooperation to Confrontation

Just after the proclamation of the Turkish Republic in 1923, after several centuries of devastating wars and deeply rooted geopolitical distortions, Soviet Russia and Turkey were able to achieve a rather high level of bilateral political and economic relations. Bolshevik Russia backed Mustafa Kemal Atatürk (1881–1938) in his war of independence against British, French, Greek and Italian occupation forces, trying to prevent European influence on the Balkans and in the Near East by its direct military assistance to Ankara. During the 1920s and 1930s, Moscow was eager to support the modernization of Kemalist Turkey. Ankara initially forged the strong liaison with Moscow; however, the Turkish government prosecuted the members of the Turkish communist party and condemned communism. A number of Turkish intellectuals were fascinated by the rapid industrialization of the Soviet Union, at the same time rejecting the communist ideological bias. The prominent Turkish writer, public intellectual, and cofounder of an important Ankara-based theoretical journal *Kadro* (Cadre), Yakup Kadri Karaosmanoğlu[3] (1889–1974), wrote in 1932:

> The friendship between us and the Russian revolutionaries on the eve of the war for independence was not a coincidence. In spite of all deep theoretical contradictions between Russian internationalists and Turkish nationalists, the cooperation between the revolutionaries of both sides should not be considered from its very beginning as a political and military necessity.[4]

According to Yakup Kadri, both countries found common ground in the confrontation with "European imperialism"[5] and for some other reasons. Yakup Kadri's vision of the Soviet Union was typical for many post-Ottoman intellectuals, who were fascinated by the rapid modernization process in Soviet Russia but knew little about Soviet reality.

At the same time, Russia embodied a rather ambivalent phenomenon within the Turkish self-narrative of the 1920–1930s. For instance, a school textbook on world history claimed in its chapter "A Glance at Europe," "One could witness a mobilization of Russians around Moscow in the fourteenth century. Having divided the *Altınordu Türk Devleti* (Turkish State of the Golden Horde), Russians started to penetrate into the regions of the Caspian and Azov Sea and the Baltics."[6] The following Russian-Ottoman wars were depicted as a continuity of the Russian-Turkish antagonism, which allegedly took root in the defeat of the Golden Horde.

In the years of World War II, however, Turkey joined the Allies in the final stage of the war. This fact as well as Joseph Stalin's (1878–1953) rethinking of postwar geopolitics damaged Soviet-Turkish relations shortly after the end of World War II. At the end of the 1940s, Moscow launched territorial claims concerning Turkey's eastern provinces bordering on Soviet Armenia and Soviet Georgia.[7] At least since then, Ankara has searched for its national security in the framework of the Western powers' security mosaic and finally joined the North Atlantic Treaty Organization (NATO), becoming an integral part of the anti-Soviet bloc. The aggravation of the Soviet-Turkish relationship gave the numerous exiled Turkic intellectuals a new chance to promote their anti-communist and anti-Soviet ideas in Turkey. Many Azerbaijani, Tatar, and Turkestani political emigrants moved from Europe to Istanbul and Ankara in the late 1940s and early 1950s.

Ethnicity and Religion in the Turkic World

While it was in Europe that the political and cultural concepts of nationalism emerged, it was the Ottoman Empire and tsardom that became important recipients. The metropolis of both empires obtained the ideas of "nation" imported throughout the nineteenth century and underwent a massive nationalist mobilization, particularly in the last quarter of the nineteenth century.[8] Both empires were multiethnic and multiconfessional. A large Turkic population lived both in Ottoman Anatolia and in the regions of the Caucasus of Central Asia as well as on the Crimean Peninsula and along the Volga under tsarist rule. This population's identity was primarily of a religious nature in the first half of the nineteenth century; by considering themselves Muslims, the Turkic societies defined themselves as part of a worldwide Muslim community *ummah* (Turkish *ümmet*). In the second half of the nineteenth century, the expansion of pan-Slavic thought and the rise of Russian nationalism under tsardom caused the emergence of a distinct ethnic identity among the Turkic population on the southwestern and southern borderlands of the Russian Empire.[9]

The Russian Turkic societies, which made up the largest part of the Russian Muslims, started intellectual debates on race, language, and ethnicity.

The intellectuals in Bakhchisarai, Baku, and Kazan discovered their affinities with the Turkic culture outside the tsardom, primarily in the bordering Ottoman Empire as well as in Persia. The journal *Tercüman* (Translator) on the Crimea, founded in 1882, as well as a number of newspapers in Baku, Tbilisi, Kazan, and Ufa that were established at the turn of the century were exemplary for these discourses. These journals became an important medium for the articulation of ethnic identity, group interests, and concerns in the multiethnic imperial context of the late Romanov dynasty. The Turkic intellectuals of the late nineteenth century, such as the Crimean Tatar Ismail Gasprinskii (1851–1914), the Azerbaijani journalist Ali Bey Hüseyinzade (1864–1941), and others became the founders of Turkic nationalism in the Russian Empire. At the same time, they embodied the importation of ethnic nationalism into the Ottoman Empire.

A number of Crimea- and Kazan-born intellectuals, such as Yusuf Akçura(oğlu) (1876–1935) and the abovementioned Ali Bey Hüseyinzade, moved to Ottoman Istanbul and launched publicist and journalistic activities by promoting the idea of pan-Turkic solidarity. Their intellectual writings crucially influenced the emergence of Turkish nationalism in the late Ottoman Empire. In the press circulating between Istanbul, the Crimea, and Baku at the turn of the century and in the first decade of the twentieth century, the Russian Turkic intellectuals began to magnify the Ottoman capital to the status of center of Turkic culture and civilization. For both the Sunni and the Shiite intellectuals from the Russian Caucasus and Central Asia, Istanbul became an embodiment of their ethnic, cultural, and religious affinities and a space ruled by their compatriots.

Istanbul in the Interwar Period

Istanbul and Turkey had a particular significance for the Russian Turkic communities for a number of reasons. First, Istanbul was the capital of a caliphate[10] and of the Ottoman Empire, and later Turkey was perceived as a "Muslim-governed country." Second, the Turkic communities in the Ottoman Empire enjoyed a more privileged position than was the case in the Russian Empire. Third, thousands of Crimean Tatars and Caucasians migrated to Ottoman Anatolia from the Russian Empire, particularly to Istanbul. Therefore, Istanbul, along with other Turkish cities, embodied an important diasporic space for the Russian Turkic societies. Fourth, some of Turkey's most prominent intellectuals, such as writer and essayist Halide Edip Adıvar (1884–1964) and Ziya Gökalp (1876–1924), articulated sympathies toward the Turkic communities in Russia by writing extensively about the imagined space of Turan.[11] Fifth, Istanbul became a place of exile for many former politicians and anti-communist intellectuals of Tatar, Azerbaijani, and other dissidents throughout the twentieth century. Being based at the Bosporus, the emigrants turned the metropole into an important anti-Soviet center by promoting intellectual critiques of communism and Soviet politics and by stylizing Turkey as a unique Turkic bulwark against Russia.

The basis of Turkey's postwar anti-communism and of the idea of a Turkish bulwark against the Soviets and Russia was doubtlessly founded in the interwar period, in spite of the fact that Ankara was eager to maintain good neighborly relations with Moscow. A good example of the interwar debates is the emigrant journal *Odlu Yurt* (Land of Fire).[12] Founded in January 1929 by the Azerbaijani political exile Mahammad Emin Rasulzade (1884–1955), *Land of Fire* became an important medium for the articulation of anti-Russian and anti-communist views.

Land of Fire was a monthly journal in Turkish, based in the center of Istanbul's historic city. Its aim was, among other things, "to inform the Turkic communities about each other and especially to inform readers about reforms in the sole independent republic of the Turkic world—Turkey."[13] Rasulzade's definition of Turkey as "the sole independent republic of the Turkic world" was printed on the cover of every issue of the journal. Rasulzade involved Ahmet Caferoğlu, a young Ph.D. student from the Department of Oriental Studies at Wrocław University (1925–1929) and later exiled academician from the Department of Linguistics at the University of Istanbul, in the editorial work. The Crimean Tatar emigrant Cafer Seydahmet contributed to *Land of Fire* as well.

The editorial of *Land of Fire* of September 1929 was dedicated to the anniversary of Atatürk's successful fight against the allied occupation forces from 26 to 30 August 1922. Having titled the article "The August Victory," the author, obviously the editor-in-chief Rasulzade himself, referred to Atatürk's praise of the Turkish victory over the foreign occupation by claiming, "And indeed the Great Turkish Revolution was born in the enslaved Orient. . . . This sun [the Revolution] influenced by its warmth and light not only Turkey and Anatolia but also the whole Turkish and Islamic Orient."[14] Rasulzade wrote on the significance of Turkish independence for the entire Middle East and particularly for the Turkic communities. The same article was reprinted as the editorial one year later.[15]

In 1930, a new journal was founded by Istanbul-based emigrants of Turkic background. It was called *Bildiriş* (Message), was printed weekly, and had primarily a political agenda. *Land of Fire* promoted the new weekly from the late summer of 1930 onward. The editors claimed in the text announcing *Message* that the weekly was going to inform the audience in Turkey, "the only independent state of the Turkish world and the only republic in the Orient."[16] *Message* itself claimed to represent all of the Turkic communities. However, its editors consisted mostly of Azerbaijani emigrants, and the headquarters of the weekly shared the same address as *Land of Fire*. *Message* was eager to cover a broader geography. Its rhetoric concerning Turkey and its place and pivotal role in the imagined anti-communist alliance were quite similar to those of *Land of Fire*.

The editors of *Message* elucidated the current politics in the Arab world as well as in India and Afghanistan. While *Land of Fire* focused on the Turkic territories of the Soviet Union, *Message* dealt with the Great Middle East and even beyond. Turkey was described not only as the only Turkic state enjoying political independence but also as a pioneer of the republican form of government and self-organization. The emigrants from Russia's Turkic communities who contributed to the journal attempted to elaborate on the pivotal role of Turkey, in the context not only of the ethnic-linguistic proximity but also of the former Ottoman legacy. Both journals were closed down in 1931. Many of the regular contributors to these journals had to leave Turkey for Europe. Ankara still was vitally interested in a close cooperation with Moscow and avoided any eventual aggravation of the bilateral relations.

In 1932, however, the Azerbaijani and Central Asian emigrants in Istanbul and former contributors to *Land of Fire* and *Message* obtained a new chance to articulate their anti-Soviet critique. Ahmet Caferoğlu, the abovementioned Azerbaijani dissident linguist of the University of Istanbul, founded the monthly *Messenger on the Land of Azerbaijan*. Contrary to its forerunners, *Messenger on the Land of Azerbaijan* was a Turkological journal and initially published articles on language policy and the development of linguistics in the Soviet Union as well as contributions on different topics of Oriental and Turkish studies. The articulation of the anti-Soviet critique was much less aggressive, and the editor was primarily interested in topics related to linguistics. Caferoğlu's anti-Russian speech delivered in the context of the International Turkological Congress held in Turkey in the summer of 1934 provoked the downgrading of his academic position at the University of Istanbul. He was heavily criticized in the Soviet Union but also in the Turkish media and condemned by Atatürk's intellectual entourage.[17]

"Türk amacı," 1942–1943

In 1938, on the eve of World War II, Caferoğlu was able to reposition himself at the University of Istanbul and obtained a chair in the Department of the History of the Turkish Language.[18] World War II gave the emigrants new perspectives to speak out on their geopolitical aspirations. In the summer of 1942, Caferoğlu founded the journal *Türk amacı* (Turkish Target). The prominent Turkish historian and politician Fuat Köprülü (1888–1966) was among the authors of the first issue published in July. Other contributors were the Crimean Tatar emigrant Abdullah Zihni Soysal (1905–1983), who was educated in Poland, and the public intellectual of Central Asian background Muharrem Feyzi Togay. In the editorial of the first issue, Caferoğlu argued that the continuity of the *millî Türk fikir heyatı* (national Turkish thought) and of *bundan doğan Türk kültür birliği* (Turkish cultural unity as its result) had always existed. The editor-in-chief did not distinguish between the categories of Turkic and Turkish societies: for him, the only difference between Turkey and the "Turkish lands beyond" was the geography: "[One] of the essential and great duties of the 'Turkish target' is to make the compatriots living in the different places aware of each other."[19]

For "compatriots," he used the term *ırktaş*, which indicates belonging to the same race. By promoting this kind of categorization, a transfer of the racial discourse from Italy and Germany to Turkey is more than evident. In his thematic article on the medieval Central Asian poet Alisher Navoi (1441–1501), Caferoğlu described him as a protagonist of Turkish cultural unity.[20] By doing so, the linguist shaped an imagined intellectual continuity between the Turkic poetry in the Central Asian region, far away from the eastern borders of the Ottoman Empire and contemporary Turkey. Finally, Caferoğlu and his journal also targeted the propaganda of Turkish cultural unity. He applied the same notion of Turkish cultural unity. These parallels were meant to evoke the impression among Turkish readers that the Turkic communities outside of Turkey had an essential importance for Turkish culture and to generate more commitment in Turkish society regarding the loss of the Turkic communities under the Soviet rule.

Cafer Seydahmet's Postwar Writings

Cafer Seydahmet was an important Crimean Tatar politician and Turkish public intellectual. Born on the Crimean Peninsula in 1889, he attended primary and secondary schools in Yalta and in Istanbul. Afterward he studied law at Sorbonne University and then at the University of St. Petersburg. In 1917 and 1918, he was directly involved in politics and in the national movement in Crimea. Seydahmet became the Crimean minister of foreign affairs, but he had to leave the peninsula after the independence experiment was crushed because of the Bolshevik invasion. He spent years in exile in Switzerland and particularly in Turkey. Based in Istanbul, Seydahmet published extensively on the Crimean Tatar cause and was one of the arduous critics of the Soviet regime. Among the large Crimean Tatar emigrant milieu in Turkey and in Europe, Seydahmet was unanimously considered the political leader of the lost Crimean Republic. In this part of the chapter, I focus on several speeches on communism and beyond delivered by Seydahmet in the 1930s and 1940s in different Turkish cities. They were published in 1948 and posthumously in 1965.

Throughout the spring and summer months of 1948, Cafer Seydahmet delivered numerous speeches in Istanbul, Ankara as well as in the industrial cities close to Istanbul, Zonguldak, and Karabük. These speeches were published in a separate booklet in the same year under the title *Rus Tarihinin inkilâba, Bolşevizme ve Cihan inkilâbına sürüklenmesi* (The Way of Russian History toward Revolution, Bolshevism, and World Revolution). Seydahmet intended to show the genesis of Russian imperialism and Soviet politics, and his speeches functioned to warn of the Soviet danger. He mentioned in the preface that he was especially invited to present his speeches to the audience at the Millî Türk Talebe Birliği (National Turkish Student Union) in Istanbul and at the Türk Kültür Derneği (Turkish Cultural Association) in Ankara. Both organizations were nationalistic and state run. Doubtlessly, the serious aggravation of Turkish-Soviet relations was the reason that Seydahmet got involved as a deliverer of clearly anti-Soviet talks. He portrayed the milestones of Russian history since the reign of Ivan the Terrible (1530–1584) and shed light on the development of Russian Communism and tsarist as well as Soviet nationalities' policy.

In this context, Seydahmet depicted the idea of the permanent revolution, initially backed by Vladimir Lenin (1870–1924) and Leo Trotsky (1879–1940). According to him, "Comintern and the present-day Cominform"[21] launched the worldwide revolution project. Seydahmet argued that Great Britain and Turkey were the only countries that acted as a bulwark against the plans of Moscow to initiate the global revolution. Seydahmet's argumentation has plenty of contradictions:

> By its war for independence, Turkey explained to the East how to become free by consolidating the people. Turkey delivered to the East a positive model by its cultural and political development, by promoting peace in its own country, by its national unity and its rejection of the class struggle. Our positive impact on the East embarrassed Red imperialism much more than did the issue of the Bosporus strait.[22]

Seydahmet, along with other emigrant intellectuals, was one of the founders of the idea of Turkey as a protector and enlightener of Asia. Obviously, this approach of criticizing the Soviets was borrowed from Soviet rhetoric itself, which propagated the idea that the October Revolution had a similar role among the peoples of the East.[23] Five years after Seydahmet's death in 1960, the Istanbul-based Crimean Tatar intellectual İbrahim Otar (1913–1986)[24] edited Seydahmet's political speeches and published them in Istanbul. In his introductory chapter, Otar wrote, "He [Seydahmet] was very happy [to witness] the power and strength of Turkey, the only free and independent mother country of Turks all over the world, [he] considered Turkey an orientation pole of the entire Turkishness and the fundament of independence."[25] The terminology used by Otar is quite interesting. Referring to Seydahmet, he described Turkey as *bütün dünya Türklerinin yegâne hür ve müstakil olanı Anatoprak* (the only independent mother country of Turks all over the world) by using *anatoprak* (mother country). Turkey was described literally as the mother country of all Turks worldwide.

The book was published in Turkish in Turkey and was aimed primarily at the Turkish audience. In Turkish, a differentiation between Turkish and Turkic is unusual and has been used only sporadically, in some linguistic and other academic writings. Therefore, Otar used the notion of Turks referring to Russia's Turkic communities. Another phrase, "Kaaba of the entire Turkishness," is also significant. Turkey was described as an orientation pole, something similar to the most important Muslim pilgrimage place (Kaaba) for the entire Turkish community scattered across the globe and for Turkishness. Otar pointed out that "Seydahmet accepted Turks from all over the world, both free and unfree, as a nation."[26] By declaring the Crimean Tatars, Azerbaijanis, and the other Turkic communities of Soviet Central Asia to be "Turks scattered across the globe," Otar intended to forge a stronger emotional liaison between the national and cultural concerns of the Turkic groups in the Soviet Union and the Turks of Turkey, the key recipients of the book's message. By addressing the Turkish audience (called "free Turks"), Otar therefore hoped to increase the affinity and sympathies toward the "captive, unfree Turks."

This way of argumentation corresponded with the public speeches and writings of Cafer Seydahmet. It is worthwhile to analyze the talk delivered to the Millî Türk Talebe Birliği organization in Istanbul in 1954. This talk was titled "The Ideal and the Turkishness" and contained comprehensive information about the Turkic discourses in the late tsardom as well as the Turanist writings of the Diyarbakır-born Turkish intellectual Ziya Gökalp (1876–1924). Seydahmet argued as an arduous adherent of Mustafa Kemal Atatürk and summed up his talk by quoting a quite famous slogan of Atatürk, "How happy I am to say that I am a Turk." The last part of the speech entails the main message of Seydahmet: "Dear brothers, let us honor all heroes who died for the freedom of this sacred land, an eternal fundament of *Türklük* (Turkishness), and all those who served the cultural development of this nation and the Turkish ideal."[27]

Seydahmet mentioned two groups of "heroes" in the same context by using a term with a clear religious connotation, *şehit*, which is usually used when describing Muslim warriors who died in battle against nonbelievers. One group consisted of those who literally died for the independence of the Republic of Turkey as well as of the Turks outside of Turkey, the Turkic communities in the Black Sea region, Central Asia, and even beyond. The second group, according to Seydahmet, were those who served the Turkish ideal and contributed to the establishment of Turkish cultural and civilizational development. His notion of *irfan* partly corresponds to the French *civilization*. Finally, Turkey was proclaimed by Seydahmet to be a "sacred country" and an "eternal base, the fundament of Turkishness."[28] By integrating the activities of Muslim enlightener Ismail Gasprinskii (1851–1914) in Crimea at the turn of the century into his narrative on Turkishness, Seydahmet widened the notion of Turkishness to include the Turkic communities of the former tsardom. By doing so, he intended to evoke the fraternal feelings toward and affinities in Turkish society with the Crimean Tatar cause and other causes.

This integrationist approach, which praised the uniqueness of Turkey as the "only free state of the Turks on earth" and informed readers about the Soviet and other persecutions against the Turkic communities outside of Turkey, was typical not only of Cafer Seydahmet's writings. The Azerbaijani, Central Asian, and other exiled intellectuals in Turkey also used this narrative. They were looking for intellectuals born in Turkey who shared their standpoint.

Arın Engin's Writings

The Turkish intellectual Arın Engin embodied this group of arduous anti-communists and supporters of the idea that Turkey should show more commitment with regard to the Turkic population of the Soviet Union and China. Arın Engin was the pen name of Mehmet Saffet Engin (1897–?), a Turkish educator born in Cyprus. In the early 1920s, Engin studied at Columbia University, and he migrated to Turkey in 1927. He taught at the elite American high school Robert College in Istanbul and then at the Gazi Institute in Ankara. In the 1930s, Saffet Engin became a member of the Türk Tarih Kurumu (Turkish Historical Society), which was a government institution, and became one of the experts of the National Ministry of Education in Ankara. He published extensively on Mustafa Kemal Atatürk, the Turkish Revolution, and a new political ideology for Turkey.

An arduous proponent of Turkey's Western integration and an admirer of European culture and of a large-scale linguistic purification of the Turkish language, Engin authored a monograph *Atatürkçülük savaşımızda Avrupa kültürü nedir ve ne değildir?* (What Is the European Culture in Our Struggle for Atatürkism and What Is It Not?). In this monograph, Engin argued as a staunch advocate of *Türk Bütüncülüğü*, which he himself described as pan-Turkism.[29] According to him, Turkey had to aspire to an integration of all Turkic communities by "giving freedom to compatriots suffering under Bolshevik Moscow colonialism."[30]

Arguing that Ankara should close the "foreign and minorities' primary and secondary schools," Engin wrote that Turkey should pursue pan-Turkist ideas.[31] Engin pointed out that the United States and Great Britain supported anti-Soviet radio station activities in Turkestan. He advocated Turkish involvement in those territories of the Soviet Union and of China that had Turkic populations and saw Turkey's NATO membership as a chance to do so.[32] Engin was in continuous contact with Cafer Seydahmet and other Turkic exiles in Turkey. These exiles, in turn, were in permanent contact with Western diplomats based in Istanbul and Ankara, forging anti-Soviet networks after World War II and cooperating with Radio Free Europe in Munich.[33] In his chapters on the Turkic communities of the Soviet Union, Engin extensively quoted the writings of Azerbaijani and Tatar emigrants such as Ahmet Caferoğlu, Cafer Seydahmet, Zeki Velidi Togan (1809–1970), Abdullah Battal Taymas (1883–1969), and others.[34]

Engin's approach toward NATO corresponded to the opinion of many other Turkish intellectuals, such as Tekin Erer (1921–1997) and A.N. Kırmacı. According to the journalist and politician Tekin Erer,[35] "the NATO alliance is the guarantee of freedom against Red imperialism."[36] It was not the first publication of Erer that promoted the idea of the "Russian danger." In 1966 and 1967, one of Turkey's leading banks published two volumes of his book *Kızıl tehlike* (Red Danger). A.N. Kırmacı devoted one of the chapters of his essay "The Future of Turkey" to the communist activities in Turkey and severely criticized any communist and even socialist activity in Turkey.[37]

Muharrem Ergin between Philology and Politics

Türk Kültürünü Araştırma Enstitüsü (The Institute of Research of Turkish Culture),[38] a government institution based in Ankara, published the monograph of the distinguished Turkish linguist Muharrem Ergin (1923–1995) in 1973. The monograph was titled "The Current Issues of Turkey" and had four reprints until 1988. At that time, Muharrem Ergin (1923–1995) was one of the leading Turkish philologists and an expert in ancient Turkish literature. Ergin was the descendant of an emigrant family from the Ahiska region of Georgia and studied philology at Istanbul University under the exiled Azerbaijani professor Ahmet Caferoğlu.

By publishing this monograph, Ergin addressed topics far removed from classical philology and Turkic linguistics. He delivered a 400-page analysis of a number of aspects of the political, social, and economic as well as cultural life of Turkey by depicting the historical development of Turks and Turkey in the context of the regional history and of international politics. With regard to the broad reception of the monograph, it is interesting how Ergin described Turkish culture and located it in time and space. In the chapter on Turkish culture, Ergin's narrative shaped a cultural continuity of a broad transboundary dimension. He mentioned the names of the Crimea-born Tatar enlightener Gasprinskii and the Turkish nationalist intellectual from Diyarbakır, Ziya Gökalp, the Central Asian medieval poet Alisher Navoi, and the Turkish poet Yahya Kemal (1884–1958).[39] While analyzing the "current situation of the Turkish culture," Ergin wrote:

> Nowadays, there are 200 million people worldwide who share the Turkish culture. Fifty-five million of them live in Turkey, some millions on the Balkans, 160 thousand in Cyprus . . . 70–80 million in the Soviet Union. The only independent state of these Turks nowadays is Turkey. The Turks of Cyprus have been struggling for independence, and they have almost reached their target. Other Turks are under the yoke.[40]

It is clear that Muharrem Ergin used the notion of Turks also for Turkic communities worldwide; the Turkish culture for him was a transboundary phenomenon.

Furthermore, Ergin pointed out the danger for Turkey that was coming from the North. Hinting at Russia, the author stressed that "the danger coming from the North aims at the destruction of Turkishness."[41] In the subchapter on geopolitics, Ergin introduced the notion of *Türk Seddi* (the Turkish wall). According to the author, there has been an eternal confrontation between the industrially highly developed and cold North and the underdeveloped but warm and sunny South. "The South became a playground for the West's exploitation and hunting,"[42] Ergin wrote.

The Western European nations could use the sea routes in order to reach the South, but the Slavs had no access to the sea and had to move toward the South by land. The Slavs, however, were confronted with a major obstacle: "This obstacle is the Turkish wall."[43] Ergin argued that the Turks prevented Russian penetration (as well as that of other Slavs) into Africa, the Middle East, and beyond, and he considered the areas populated by Turkic communities from Anatolia, the Caucasus, Central Asia, and the western provinces of China as parts of the Turkish wall. According to Ergin, Turkey made up the western pole of the Turkish wall. He stressed the importance of Turkey in preventing the spread of Russian-backed communism. A similar argumentation can be found in the essay of Âli Engin published in 1970. Engin wrote: "One can argue that there is no other nation in Asia who gained independence."[44]

The author mentioned that the Bolsheviks mobilized the Muslims of the tsarist empire by promising them autonomy and self-determination. After the fall of tsarism, however, all Turkic states that had emerged from the ruins of the former empire were reconquered by the Red Army shortly afterward. By pointing out the Bolshevik territorial division and its setting up of new administrative borders in former Turkestan, Engin used the notion of "colonization of the Turkish-Islam lands"[45] as well as *türksüzleştirme* (de-Turkization). He wrote, "The policy of this state [of the Soviet Union, Russia] against Turkey is clear: to get Turkey under its control, to seize the straits, to get access to the Mediterranean Sea and to end the hopes of the captive Turkish nations by capturing the last independent Turkish tower."[46]

For Engin, Turkey represented either the only independent Turkish state or a Turkish tower, while the Turkic population of Soviet Azerbaijan and Central Asia was named "captive Turkish nations." According to Engin, Turkey embodied the last hope for those nations under the yoke as well as the bulwark lying in the way of the Soviet expansion toward the Mediterranean.

Ergin belonged to the generation of the emigrant milieu in Istanbul that shared the strong sentiment of laicism, anti-Russian resentments, and fidelity toward Atatürk. In his narrative on Turkishness, Ergin's argumentation regarding religion in general and Islam in particular is of significance. He stressed the importance of laicism for the Turkish society and for Turkey, and he mentioned the Christian Turkic communities such as those of Gagauz in Romania and Moldavia and the Jewish Turkic group of the Karaims in Poland.

At the same time, he pointed out the contribution of the Turks to Islam and argued that "Turkishness and Muslimhood (*müslümanlık*[47]) cannot be separated from each other, cannot be thought of separately."[48] In this context, he criticized with vigor those who promoted the importance of one element of the identity, such as ethnicity (Turkishness, Türklük) over Islamic religiosity and vice versa. For Ergin, the Muslim religion and the linguistic-cultural transboundary identity of Turks should be seen as being in harmony. All Turkish adherents of Kemalism and Turkey-based intellectuals in exile criticized communism and its ideological bias against religion in general and against Islam in particular. The mass closure of the mosques and prohibition of pilgrimage to Mecca were considered a Russification and de-Turkization measure.

Conclusion

According to the Turkish philologist Ahmet B. Ercilasun, "Besides the impact on the development of Turkish nationalism, our intellectuals coming from over there [the Turkic areas of the Soviet Union] contributed to maintaining the public interest in Turkey in the concerns of the Turks outside of Turkey."[49] At the same time, these intellectuals shaped the idea of the Turkish wall and the "only independent and free Turkish state" during the Cold War. This idea of the uniqueness of Turkey, its resistance vis-à-vis the Communist Bloc but also the responsibility it bore for the "Turks outside of Turkey" appeared in the discourses launched by the Crimean and Kazan Tatar as well as exiled Azerbaijani intellectuals in Turkey. These ideas entered the genuine Turkish discourses: the exiles were finally perceived as experts on Russia; their increased authority was doubtlessly caused by the Cold War.

Different from most European projects on *antemurale,* the role of religion (Islam) in the development of the idea of the Turkish wall was secondary. Aware of the Islamic traditions and sharing the principles of moderate Islam, both the exiled intellectuals and their Turkey-born contemporaries were eager to combine laicism with Turkish nationalism. Arguing against the Soviet Union, they tried to vitalize the anti-Russian resentments of the past by praising Turkey as the unique space that could preserve the development of Turkishness. Therefore, the abovementioned Turkish wall was not perceived as a Muslim bulwark against Christianity but as a defender of ethnic, cultural, and linguistic affinity and distinctiveness.

Zaur Gasimov studied international relations, the history of Russia, and the history of the Middle East in Azerbaijan and Germany. In 2009, he graduated from the Ph.D. program at the Catholic University Eichstätt-Ingolstadt and joined the Leibniz-Institute of European History in Mainz, Germany. Since 2013, Gasimov has been a senior research fellow at the German Orient Institute in Istanbul, Turkey. He has published extensively on Russian-Turkish relations and the entangled history of Eastern Europe and the Middle East. His most recent book, *Historical Dictionary of Azerbaijan,* was published by Rowman & Littlefield in 2018.

Notes

1. This notion is primarily of a linguistic nature and defines the communities of Azerbaijanis in the Russian Caucasus and in the northern provinces of Iran, the Crimean, and Kazan Tatars as well as the Turkophone population of Central Asia.

Most Turkic societies are of the Muslim faith, representing both the Sunni and the Shiite (particularly) confessions. The differentiation between "Turkish" and "Turkic" is widespread in international Turkology, corresponding to the Russian terms *tiurkskii* (Turkic) and *turetskii* (Turkish) as well as to the German notions of *turksprachig* (Turkic) and *türkisch* (Turkish).

2. *Birinci Uluslararası İstanbul'un Fethi Sempozyumu* (Istanbul: İstanbul Büyükşehir Belediyesi Kültür İşleri Daire Başkanlığı Yayınları, 1997), 52, 69–70.
3. Yakup Kadri Karaosmanoğlu (1889–1974) was a prominent Turkish writer, literary critic, public intellectual, and politician. In his *Kadro*, he launched a number of contentious articles titled "Ankara, Moscow, Rome." He clearly sympathized with the modernization rhetoric in Mussolini's Italy and in Soviet Moscow during the early 1930s.
4. Yakup Kadri, "Ankara. Moskova. Roma. Bir hatıra," *Kadro. Aylık fikir mecmuası* 7 (1932): 35, cited in Ö. Erdem, ed., *Kadro. Aylık fikir mecmuası. Tıpkı basım (1–18. sayılar) 1932–1933*, vol. 1 (Istanbul: İleri Yayınları, 2011), 349.
5. Ibid.
6. *İlk Mekteplere Mahsus. Yardımcı tarih hulâsası* (Istanbul, 1933), 80.
7. See V.O. Pechatnov, "The Soviet Union and the World, 1944–1953," in *The Cambridge History of the Cold War*, vol. 1: *Origins*, ed. M.P. Leffler and O.A. Westad (Cambridge: Cambridge University Press, 2010), 90–111.
8. See M. Reynolds, *Shattering Empires: The Clash and Collapse of the Ottoman and Russian Empires* (Cambridge: Cambridge University Press, 2011); J.H. Meyer, *Turks across Empires. Marketing Muslim Identity in the Russian-Ottoman Borderlands, 1856–1914* (Oxford: Oxford University Press, 2014). See also the special issue of *European Journal of Turkish Studies* edited by the French expert of the Near East, O. Bouquet, "Transfaires d'empire. Ottomans et Russes, pour une histoire croisée," *EJTS* 22 (2016), retrieved 29 August 2016 from https://ejts.revues.org/5220.
9. For more details on the reciprocal influence of pan-Slavism and pan-Turkism, see Z. Gasimov, "Vom Panslavismus über den Panturkismus zum Eurasismus: die russisch-türkische Ideenzirkulation und Verflechtung der Ordnungsvorstellungen im 20. Jahrhundert," in *Post-Panslavismus: Slavizität, slavische Idee und Antislavismus im 20. und 21. Jahrhundert*, ed. A. Gąsior, L. Karl, and S. Troebst (Göttingen: Wallstein, 2014), 448–72.
10. The rhetoric of the Azerbaijani exiled politician Mahammad Emin Rasulzade, who left for Istanbul in 1922 and published his memoirs on the rise and fall of the Republic of Azerbaijan there, is quite interesting in this context. He defined Turkey as *alem-i islamın ittihad merkezi* (the union center of the Muslim World). The booklet emerged in Ottoman Turkish and was aimed at a Turkish audience. See M.E. Rasulzade, *Azerbaycan Cumhuriyeti. Keyfiyet-i Teşekkülü ve Şimdiki Vaziyeti* (Istanbul: Şehzâdebaşı, 1339–1341), 4.
11. Both intellectuals promoted the idea of Turkish ethnic nationalism and pan-Turkic solidarity as an ideological alternative to the attempts of the late Ottoman elites to launch a supraconfessional and supraethnic identity of Ottomanness (Osmanlı). Halide Edip published a novel, *Yeni Turan* (A New Turan), in 1913, and Gökalp authored a series of writings, "Fundaments of Turkishness," etc. Both intellectuals inspired a radical nationalist essayist, Nihal Atsız (1905–1975), in the 1930–1940s. The most prominent Turkish philosopher, Hilmi Ziya Ülken (1901–1974), popular-

ized the views of Gökalp by devoting a monograph to him in 1942. See H.Z. Ülken, *Ziya Gökalp* (Istanbul: Kanaat kitapevi, 1942), reprinted in 2000 and 2007.

12. *Odlu Yurt. Millî Azerbaycan fikriyatını terviç eden aylık mecmua* (İstanbul: publisher unknown, 1929).
13. Ibid., 45.
14. "Ağustos zaferi münasibetile," *Odlu Yurt* 1 (September 1929), 261.
15. "Ağustos zaferi münasibetile," *Odlu Yurt* 2 (September 1930), 329.
16. "Haftalık gazetemiz!" *Odlu Yurt* 2 (August 1930), 330.
17. Z. Gasimov, "Science Transfer to Turkey. The Life and Work of the Linguist Ahmet Caferoğlu (1899–1975)," *European Journal of Turkish Studies* 22 (2016), retrieved 9 November 2016 from http://ejts.revues.org/5340.
18. For more details on the journal *Türk amacı*, see Z. Gasimov, "Transfer and Asymmetry," *European Journal of Turkish Studies* 24 (2017), retrieved 28 January 2018 from http://journals.openedition.org/ejts/5432.
19. Birkaç söz, *Türk Amacı* 1 (1 July 1942), 1–2.
20. A. Caferoğlu, "Türk Kültür Birliği Hadimlerinden Mir-Ali-Şir Nevaî," *Türk Amacı* 1 (1 July 1942), 6.
21. C.S. Kırımer, *Rus Tarihinin inkılâba, Bolşevizme ve Cihan inkılâbına sürüklenmesi* (Istanbul: Pulhan Matbaası, 1948), 88.
22. Ibid.
23. See the account of the Soviet-Azerbaijani Bolshevik activist N. Narimanov (1870–1925), *Lenin i vostok* (Lenin and the East), cited in http://leninism.su/memory/196-narimanov.html, retrieved 31 January 2016.
24. For more on Seydahmet and his brothers İsmail and İbrahim Otar, see Z. Gasimov, "Krimtatarische Exil-Netzwerke zwischen Osteuropa und dem Nahen Osten," *Österreichische Zeitschrift für Geschichtswissenschaft* 28 (2017): 142–66.
25. İ. Otar, "Cafer Seydahmet Kırımer kimdir?," in Cafer Seydahmet Kırımer: *Mefkûre ve Türkçülük*, ed. I. Otal, vol. 6 (Istanbul: Emel Yayınları, 1965), VI.
26. Ibid., VI.
27. C. Seydahmet, *İdeal ve türklük*, in Otar, "Cafer Seydahmet," 71.
28. Ibid.
29. Â. Engin, *Atatürkçülük savaşımızda Avrupa kültürü nedir ve ne değildir?* (Atatürkkent, Istanbul: Siralar Basimevi, 1960), 146.
30. Ibid.
31. Ibid., 179.
32. Ibid., 180.
33. The memoirs of Cafer Seydahmet as well as his political diary that covered the years between 1954 and 1960 are good examples for the intensive cooperation between the Turkic emigrants and the Western diplomats. See C. Seydahmet, *Bazı hatıralar* (Istanbul: EMEL Türk Kültürünü Araştırma ve Tanıtma Vakfı, 1993).
34. This was also characteristic of other Turkish intellectuals. Âli Engin wrote in his book *Rus-Amerikan yakınlaşması ve Türkiye'nin durumu* that he borrowed parts regarding Russian mythology from the writings of Cafer Seydahmet. Â. Engin, *Rus-Amerikan yakınlaşması ve Türkiye'nin durumu* (Istanbul, 1970), 48.
35. Tekin Erer (1921–1997) was a prominent Turkish journalist, political commentator, and politician. Born in Artvin close to the Turkish-Georgian border, Tekin Erer grew up in Kars. In Istanbul, he forged a brilliant career as a columnist for several dailies.

36. T. Erer, *NATO'nun hür ufukları* (Istanbul: Ak Yayınları, 1969), 9.
37. A.N. Kırmacı, *Türkiye'nin Geleceği* (Istanbul: İstanbul matbaası, 1965), 63–73.
38. *Türk Kültürünü Araştırma Enstitüsü* (TKAE) was founded in November 1961 and it still exists. Since 1964, TKAE has been publishing the periodical *Türk Kültürü Araştırmaları* (Turkish Culture Research, TKA). The first director of TKAE was a professor of Indology from the University of Ankara, Baku-born Abidin İtil (1910–1980). The political emigrants Reşit Rahmeti Arat (1900–1964) and Halil İnalcık (1916–2016) were the first editors-in-chief of the TKA. The institute and its periodical were designed as Sovietological research centers with the main specialization being on history, linguistics, literature, and social changes in the regions of the Caucasus, Central Asia, and the Ural region. The emigrants from the Turkic lands were dominant among the contributors of TKA until the 1990s. For more on the history of TKAE, see B. Gül, ed., *Türk Kültürünü Araştırma Enstitüsü'nün 50. yılına armağan. 50. Yıl sempozyumu bildirileri* (Ankara: Türk Kültürünü Araştırma Enstitüsü, 2012).
39. M. Ergin, *Türkiyenin bugünkü meseleleri*, 4th ed. (Ankara: TAKE Yayıları, 1988), 27.
40. Ibid., 30.
41. Ibid., 55.
42. Ibid., 79.
43. Ibid.
44. Engin, *Rus-Amerikan Yakınlaşması*, 25.
45. Ibid., 26.
46. Ibid., 29.
47. The notions of *müslümanlık* and *Islam* are used synonymously in Turkish.
48. Ergin, *Türkiyenin bugünkü meseleleri*, 202.
49. A.B. Ercilasun, "'Türkiyede' de Türk Dünyası aydılarina genel bir bakış," in Ercilasun, ed., *Türk Dünyası üzerine incelemeler* (Ankara: Akçağ, 2011), 306.

Bibliography

Birkaç söz. 1942. *Türk Amacı* 1 (1 July): 1–2.
Birinci Uluslararası İstanbul'un Fethi Sempozyumu. 1997. Istanbul: İstanbul Büyükşehir Belediyesi Kültür İşleri Daire Başkanlığı Yayınları.
Bouquet, O. 2016. "Transfaires d'empire. Ottomans et Russes, pour une histoire croisée." *European Journal of Turkish Studies* 22. Retrieved 29 August 2016 from https://ejts.revues.org/5220.
Caferoğlu, A. 1942. "Türk Kültür Birliği Hadimlerinden Mir-Ali-Şir Nevaî." *Türk Amacı* 1 (1 July), 6.
Engin, Â. 1960. *Atatürkçülük savaşımızda Avrupa kültürü nedir ve ne değildir?* Atatürkkent, Istanbul: Siralar Basimevi.
———. 1970. *Rus-Amerikan yakınlaşması ve Türkiye'nin durumu*. Istanbul: Sebilürreşad Neşriyat Bürosu.
Ercilasun, A.B. 2011. "Türkiyede'de Türk Dünyası aydılarina genel bir bakış." In *Türk Dünyası üzerine incelemeler*, ed. A.B. Ercilasun, 306. Ankara: Akçağ.
Erdem, Ö., ed. 2011. *Kadro. Aylık fikir mecmuası. Tıpkı basım (1–18. sayılar) 1932–1933*. Vol. 1. Istanbul: İleri Yayınları.

Erer, T. 1969. *NATO'nun hür ufukları*. Istanbul: Ak Yayınları.
Ergin, M. 1988. *Türkiyenin bugünkü meseleleri*, 4th ed. Ankara: TAKE Yayıları.
Gasimov, Z. 2014. "Vom Panslavismus über den Panturkismus zum Eurasismus: die russisch-türkische Ideenzirkulation und Verflechtung der Ordnungsvorstellungen im 20. Jahrhundert." In *Post-Panslavismus: Slavizität, slavische Idee und Antislavismus im 20. und 21. Jahrhundert*, ed. A. Gąsior, L. Karl, S. Troebst, and W. Helm, 448–72. Göttingen: Wallstein.
———. 2016. "Science Transfer to Turkey. The Life and Work of the Linguist Ahmet Caferoğlu (1899–1975)." *European Journal of Turkish Studies* 22. Retrieved 9 November from http://ejts.revues.org/5340.
———. 2017. "Krimtatarische Exil-Netzwerke zwischen Osteuropa und dem Nahen Osten." *Österreichische Zeitschrift für Geschichtswissenschaft* 28: 142–66.
———. 2017. "Transfer and Asymmetry." *European Journal of Turkish Studies* 24 (2017). Retrieved 28 January 2018 from http://journals.openedition.org/ejts/5432.
Gül, B., ed., 2012. *Türk Kültürünü Araştırma Enstitüsü'nün 50. yılına armağan. 50. Yıl sempozyumu bildirileri*. Ankara: Türk Kültürünü Araştırma Enstitüsü.
Ilk Mekteplere Mahsus. Yardımcı tarih hulâsası. 1933. Istanbul: Akşam kitaphanesi.
Kırımer, C.S. 1948. *Rus Tarihinin inkilâba, Bolşevizme ve Cihan inkilâbına sürüklenmesi*. Istanbul: Pulhan Matbaası.
———. 1993. *Bazı hatıralar*. Istanbul: EMEL Türk Kültürünü Araştırma ve Tanıtma Vakfı.
Kırmacı, A.N. 1965. *Türkiye'nin Geleceği*. Istanbul: İstanbul matbaası, 63–73.
Meyer, J.H. 2014. *Turks across Empires. Marketing Muslim Identity in the Russian-Ottoman Borderlands, 1856–1914*. Oxford: Oxford University Press.
Narimanov, N. 2016. *Lenin i vostok*. Retrieved 31 January 2016 from http://leninism.su/memory/196-narimanov.html.
Odlu Yurt. Millî Azerbaycan fikriyatını terviç eden aylık mecmua. 1929. Istanbul: publisher unknown.
Otar, İ. 1965. "Cafer Seydahmet Kırımer kimdir?" In *Cafer Seydahmet Kırımer: Mefkûre ve Türkçülük*, ed. I. Otar. Vol. 6. Istanbul: Emel Yayınları, 71.
Pechatnov, V.O. 2010. "The Soviet Union and the World, 1944–1953." In *The Cambridge History of the Cold War*, vol. 1: *Origins*, ed. M.P. Leffler and O.A. Westad, 90–111. Cambridge: Cambridge University Press.
Rasulzade, M.E. 1339–1341. *Azerbaycan Cumhuriyeti. Keyfiyet-I Teşekkülü ve Şimdiki Vaziyeti*. Istanbul: Şehzâdebaşı.
Reynolds, M. 2011. *Shattering Empires: The Clash and Collapse of the Ottoman and Russian Empires*. Cambridge: Cambridge University Press.
Seydahmet, C. 1993. *Bazı hatıralar*. Istanbul: EMEL Türk Kültürünü Araştırma ve Tanıtma Vakfı.
Ülken, H.Z. 1942. *Ziya Gökalp*. Istanbul: Kanaat kitapevi (reprinted 2000 and 2007).

Part III

Promoting *Antemurale* Discourses

CHAPTER 8

Why Didn't the *Antemurale* Historical Mythology Develop in Early Nineteenth-Century Ukraine?

Volodymyr Kravchenko

The second half of the eighteenth and first half of the nineteenth century is one of those "invisible" periods in the history of Ukraine, when it disappears from a political map but continues to exist as a social reality, represented in intellectual discourses. This period is important for understanding, first, the specifics of modern Ukrainian nation building and, second, the formation of national myths and stereotypes, which maintain their mobilization potential even today. However, the very meaning of "Ukraine" in the Russian Empire remains ambiguous and what was considered "Ukrainian" at a time when Ukrainian society was deprived of its sovereignty as well as of administrative, territorial, social, and national integrity remains open to different interpretations.

The Ukrainian nation-building process in the Russian Empire does not always fit into classical concepts and paradigms. There are many controversies surrounding our current understanding and interpretations of the relationship between different stages and components of this process as well as between controversial and usually hybrid forms of collective identity, including Little Russian, Ukrainian, Russian, and others.[1]

The concept of Ukrainian national space presents another aspect of the modern nation-building process.[2] Ukraine's elusive external borders easily turned into internal boundaries and vice versa, following the ever-changing political situation in the eastern part of Europe. Different regions of what is now Ukraine were involved in the divisions and subdivisions of this territory between various imperial and national states and discourses. Understanding the specifics of Ukrainian history during this stateless era is not possible without taking into consideration the broader geopolitical, geocultural, and imperial contexts. Roman Szporluk defined Ukrainian national space as being "the peripheries of several nations, which themselves were civilizational peripheries of the West."[3] I have found this formula quite applicable for the purposes of this chapter.

Whether from the Western or the Russian perspective, Ukrainian lands played an important role in the process of permanent remapping and reidentification both of the Eastern European and Russian boundaries and their respective identities.[4] As Serhiy Bilenky puts it, "The inclusion or exclusion of Ukrainian lands was a decisive factor in the struggle for the symbolic dominance over Eastern Europe and for the geopolitical rearrangement of the region."[5] All of the Eurasian empires and peoples were challenged by the identity issue and tried to find a proper balance between imperial, regional, social, and national categories. Historical mythologies have been the most important components of any regional, imperial, or national political program and processes. Mythically loaded historical narratives were used to legitimize a nation by shaping its identity and territory. Externally, these narratives help to separate nations from their enemies: "Domestically, they [the narratives] rely upon a politically fabricated pool of myths and symbols . . ., which includes deliberate forgetting and historical error as crucial elements for successful nation building."[6]

Mythology was crucial for the community to overcome the challenge of losing coherence, to weather a crisis of meanings, and to function as therapy for collective historical memory.[7] It is no wonder that mythology plays a prominent role in the Ukrainian modern nation-state building process.[8]

Any historical mythologies, as a rule, included certain variations on the theme of *antemurale*.[9] In the late eighteenth century, an emerging *civilizational geopolitics* prompted conceptual reinterpretation of the *antemurale* mythology in terms of a geopolitical and secular civilizational mission.[10] According to Stefan Berger, "Historians constructed transnational missions—either European or imperial—for their respective nations, either centered around the idea of protecting Europe from the infidel or in the form of a civilizing mission of the imperial center vis-à-vis its peripheries."[11] The *antemurale* mythology, which "is in fact a *major driving force* behind the formation of historical group myths," "functions as a boundary-defining mechanism that distinguishes various communities from each other."[12] This mechanism works not only in space but also in time.

It can be argued that the very name "Ukraine," which means "borderland," as well as the geopolitical status of the Ukrainian border regions and the presence of a special borderline population—the Cossacks—all suggest that the Ukrainian soil should be favorable for the creation and development of a historical and political mythology of *antemurale*, which is inherent in other peoples and nations in the regions of Central and Eastern Europe. Ukrainian history reveals many *antemurale* possibilities: in its connections with the nomads and the Muslim world, the Polish-Lithuanian Commonwealth, and the Muscovite autocracy. Surprisingly, the *antemurale* mythology has been poorly represented in both the Ukrainian historical narrative and the (geo)political imagination.[13]

Below, I will try to trace the elements of the *antemurale* mythology in the Ukrainian historical writings of the late eighteenth century until the 1840s, that is, the Little Russian era of national history. For this purpose, I will concentrate on the national and geopolitical discourses in Ukrainian-related historical narratives produced by Ukrainian, Russian, and European authors. In terms of representation, the historically shaped idioms of *kozatstvo/ kozachestvo* (Cossackdom), Malorossiia (the Little Russia), and the Ukraine seem to be the most recognizable markers of Ukrainian history and geography at the turn of the nineteenth century. In this chapter, they are used as social constructs, the meanings of which were subject to continuous debate and reinterpretation in the course of their nationalization in modern Ukrainian and Russian historical narratives.[14]

The problem of representativeness in the name "Ukraine" is complicated by contradictory terminology.[15] Names of Ukrainian territories and ethnos changed depending on the context—and sometimes the same names were even endowed with different meanings. Moreover, the language and terminology used to describe Ukrainian lands were never uniform, being borrowed from a variety of literary traditions. The literary Russian language, which served as an imperial lingua franca at that time, was still in the process of secularization under Western influence while the Ukrainian language was just starting its long journey from the spoken vernacular to a fully fledged language of high culture.

In this chapter, the definition of "Little Russian" and its derivatives will be used to characterize the historical period of Ukrainian history from the end of the eighteenth up to the middle of the nineteenth century, which was labeled by Ivan Lysiak-Rudnytskyi (1919–1984) as "a sort of prolonged epilogue to the Cossack era," during which "the nobility of Cossack origin continued to be the leading class of society."[16] Accordingly, Little Russian collective identity as well as the designation of its imagined space are devoid of negative and political connotations.[17] After the dissolution of the autonomous Cossack system, Little Russian identity gradually acquired an ethnocultural dimension and extended beyond the regional and administrative boundaries of the Little Russian governorate of the Russian Empire.

The adjective "Ukrainian" stands, depending on the context, as a synonym for "Little Russia"; in the modern sense, the word is also used to define the contemporary period of Ukrainian national development beginning approximately in the 1840s as well as its respective identity. I see no gap between the Little Russian and Ukrainian stages of the modern nation-building process. The Ukrainian identity did not merely replace the Little Russian one; the two have created a kind of symbiosis, within which they give in to each other's initiative in the course of nation building, depending on (geo)political circumstances in the region to the east of Europe. However, they are different in terms of their respective social bases as well their attitudes toward Russia and Russian-speaking culture.

Finally, "Russia" and its derivatives are used in this chapter in two ways: in the broad sense, as a synonym for the Russian Empire and in the narrower sense, as a synonym for the descriptor *velikorusskii* (Great Russian), which refers to Russia proper as one of the components of the imagined Rus World, along with Little Russia, Velikorossiia (Great Russia) as well as White, Red, and Black Russias.[18] The "Rus World" idea, based on the historical legacy of Kyiv, was articulated by Ukrainian and Belarusian Orthodox intellectuals in the second half of the seventeenth century and was adopted by the Russian elites for the purpose of imperial nation building. In the early nineteenth century, the concept of "Russia" was still relatively new and not fully developed in terms of modern cultural nationalism.[19] Ukrainians for a long time supplied the Russian imperial elites with the ideas of early modern and even modern nationalism, elaborated during their struggle with Polonism.[20]

Ukraine as a Cossackdom

The Cossack descriptor served as the main symbolical designation of the Ukrainian borderlands from the era of the Renaissance.[21] It is commonly believed that the Cossack identity of the land was semantically connected to the name *ukraina*—which meant "frontier, borderland" in Ukrainian as well as in Polish and Russian. Historians came to agree that, since the middle of the seventeenth century, the Cossack state had been transformed into the early modern nation of Cossack Little Russia, which was largely patterned on the Polish *szlachta* model and possessed its own, estate-bound political consciousness as well as a collective identity.[22] However, until the middle of the nineteenth century, Ukrainian Cossackdom remained a highly debatable phenomenon, inspiring diametrically opposed opinions and contradictory interpretations in various historical-national discourses. Numerous historians continued to discuss whether Cossacks were a social class, a separate ethnos, or a "motley collection of peoples," and they also debated how the Cossack units located along the borders of the Russian Empire differed from each other.

There were several Cossack units based on their respective *ukraines:* the Zaporozhian Sich, Little Russia (the Hetmanate), and Sloboda Ukraine. The Zaporozhian Cossack mythology is considered the oldest among them. The Sich attitude and policy toward the Little Russian Cossack state (the Hetmanate) was rather particular. Depending on the balance of power on the Eastern European border, the Zaporozhian host could easily slip across the symbolic line separating Orthodoxy from Catholicism and Christendom from Islam—thus demonstrating the conditionality of the symbolic realm's linear characteristics as well as the articulated and mutually exclusive identities in this region.

Most often, the Zaporozhian Cossacks identified themselves with a bastion mythology that was first created in sixteenth–seventeenth-century Orthodox Church circles and was later popularized in the so-called Cossack chronicles.[23] The idea of the "Cossack bastion" in these sources relied not so much on a specific border territory as on the social identity and serving ethos of the military community.[24] The Enlightenment historical discourse of the Zaporozhian Cossacks had been full of controversies. Voltaire compared them to filibusters and doubted their commitment to Christianity.[25] His younger contemporaries felt more favorably toward the Zaporozhian Cossacks, comparing them to the knights of Malta. "Similarly to the Maltese cavaliers, they considered their community's main obligation to be the waging of incessant war against unbelievers," asserted Gerhard Friedrich Miller (1705–1783), a German historian in Russian imperial service.[26]

Similar analogies can be found in many other historical texts from the second half of the eighteenth century.[27] Comparing the Cossacks to the medieval Catholic knights was complemented by analogies from antiquity. The republic of Rome and Sparta of Greece were popular symbols used to explain and understand the phenomenon of the Zaporozhian Cossack's stronghold, the Sich.[28]

However, the Zaporozhian Cossacks were slightly at odds with the *antemurale* civilizational discourse. Russia's decision to liquidate the Zaporozhian Sich in 1775 was motivated by both geopolitical and civilizational reasons. The imperial manifest issued in this regard in 1776 (drafted by the abovementioned G.F. Miller) was generally based on a secular Enlightenment paradigm. Accordingly, the Zaporozhian Cossacks were relegated, along with the seminomadic Crimean Tatars, to the far side of the symbolic line dividing barbarism from civilization. After the Sich was liquidated in 1775, almost all historical and geographical studies published in Russia demonstrated an openly hostile attitude to the Zaporozhians. Clearly, this made the image of the Zaporozhian Christian *antemurale* debatable, to put it mildly.

A new imperial civilizational project of Novorossiia (New Russia) dismissed the Sich in its role of a military bastion of Christianity. Accordingly, the Zaporozhian Sich religious *antemurale* mythology was replaced by the New Russia civilizational mythology of enlightenment and prosperity.[29] The city of Odessa became its most recognizable symbol, comparable only to St. Petersburg. Remarkably, however, the New Russia civilizational project was unable to displace the Zaporozhian Cossack legacy of the regions completely. Plans of the Polish pro-Napoleon officers to reanimate the Sich to its former military glory in order to create an anti-Russian Cossack buffer state only confirm this statement, no matter how far from reality these plans appeared to be.[30]

Slobidska (Sloboda) Ukraine (a historical-geographical region in northeastern Ukraine) was another Cossack military region designed originally to protect Russia against the Crimean Tatars.[31] The territory of the Cossack regiments along the Russian-ruled frontier was alternatively called "Muscovite/Moscow's Ukraine/Ukraina/*ukraina.*" Its relationships with both the Zaporozhian Sich and the Hetmanate were controversial. This region became a basis for a local, Cossack-defended version of the Russian *antemurale.*

Illia Kvitka (1745–1817) and Hryhorii Kvitka (1778–1843), both members of the provincial Cossack elite, considered Sloboda Ukraine to be a veritable *barrier,* protecting Russia simultaneously from the Crimean Tatars and from the "fickle and traitorous" Little Russian Cossacks.[32] However, the Sloboda Ukraine *antemurale* discourse remained underdeveloped—overtaken and overshadowed by the dynamic Novorossiia. Sloboda Ukraine's image was transformed from a bulwark into an intermediary region between Russia proper and Novorossiia—a crossroads or transitional region lacking clear, linear, symbolic boundaries.[33] Besides, the image of a Sloboda Ukraine loyal only to Russia was very soon supplanted by the ethnic Little Russia: Russian travelers perceived Sloboda Ukraine to be Little Russia as early as the beginning of the nineteenth century.[34]

Finally, the Little Russian Cossack state, or Hetmanate, had also been perceived for a long time as just another Cossack border region. The geopolitical ambitions of the Hetmanate, which for decades circled through the enchanted geopolitical quadrate of the neighboring, empowering rival empires of the Romanovs, the Ottomans, Sweden, and the Polish-Lithuanian Commonwealth, are well known. Hetman Ivan Mazepa (1639–1709), the last Ukrainian Cossack leader who clearly expressed his geopolitical ambitions, became the most recognizable and the most controversial symbol of Ukrainian sovereignty and Western-oriented policy.[35] Contrary to him, Hetman Bohdan Khmelnytskyi (1595–1657), the founding father of the Cossack state, became a symbol of pro-Russian and anti-Polish Ukrainian geopolitical orientation.[36]

The dramatic geopolitical changes that engulfed the Ukrainian lands during the era of Enlightenment attracted the attention of many European historians.[37] However, even the most famous of them were sometimes confused, first, by the Cossacks' constant changing allegiances during the numerous wars and, second, by the contradictory Russian and Polish interpretations of these events. In the writings of Voltaire (1694–1778) is perhaps the most vivid example of how Ukrainian history could be depicted from the opposing perspectives. In the *Histoire de Charles XII* (History of Charles XII) the French philosopher presented Ukraine as a freedom-seeking country that struggled for its independence.[38] Later on, in his *Histoire de l'Empire de Russie sous Pierre Le Grand* (History of the Russian Empire under Peter the Great), the author expressed a diametrically opposed view about Hetman Mazepa and his deeds in the spirit of the official Russian narrative.[39]

In order to understand these contradictions, one should take into account that the Russian Empire, led by Catherine II (1729–1796) and later by Alexander I (1777–1825), was favorably presented by the European enlightened narrative as a promising, albeit backward, model of enlightened centralism. When the Russian Empire replaced the Polish-Lithuanian Commonwealth as master of the region, the perceived border between Europe and Asia on the mental map of European Enlightenment moved correspondingly eastward.[40] Thus, as stated by Janusz Tazbir (1927–2016), "The Polish bulwark changed into a useless fiction."[41] When Voltaire pointed out that Ukraine was compelled by its precarious geopolitical situation to seek foreign protection,[42] he was quite certain that Russia seemed to be the best choice for the Ukrainians. Many of his European followers shared this opinion.

The French-German historian Jean-Benoît Schérer (1741–1824), in his two-volume *Annales de la Petite-Russie; ou Histoire des Cosaques-Saporogues et des Cosaques de l'Ukraine* (Annals of Little Russia or the History of the Zaporozhian Cossacks and the Ukrainian or Little Russian Cossacks), combined some elements of the European religious and the civilizational discourses from *antemurale* mythology.[43] He points out that the Ukrainian Cossacks defended Poland from "Turks, Russians, and Tatars" and the Mediterranean provinces of Europe from unidentified "Eastern barbarians."[44] At the same time, he presents the Cossacks as free citizens, fighting for freedom and against religious and social enslavement: "Trained like the Spartans, always armed like the Romans; unlike these two, however, the citizens of this republic have not conquered foreign lands, only defended their altars and domestic hearths bravely and constantly, preferring the rough nomadic life to the relaxations of bondage."[45]

The Austrian historian Johann Christian von Engel (1770–1814) also presents Ukraine as a civilizational wall between Europe and Asia.[46] He emphasized Ukraine's geopolitical importance and avows that the relations between Poland, Sweden, Russia, and Transylvania are impossible to understand without considering the Ukrainian factor. Moreover, Engel contemplates an alternative course of events in this region had the Cossack wars in the late seventeenth and early eighteenth centuries been successful. In his words, if circumstances had been different, then "today, we might possibly have a Ukrainian Highness from the Mazepa dynasty, a Grand Duchy of Sweden in the North, and no Aleksandr Suvorov (1730–1800) occupying Warsaw in 1795."[47] Although Engel perceived Ukraine as an integral national entity, separate from Russia, he considered the alliance between Great Russia and Little Russia to be natural and the differences between them to be insignificant.

The image of Ukraine as a freedom-seeking nation that might eventually renew its independent status never disappeared from the intellectual horizon of European authors. It is therefore not surprising that, in this context, the imagined Ukraine and its regions from time to time gained geopolitical significance in the course of various moves to divide the Russian Empire and create buffer states on its southern and western borders. Polish historical thought, with its Cossack mythology, played an especially active role in this respect.[48] However, it had no chances to gain political support from the Little Russian elite, whose historical narrative remained fundamentally anti-Polish and pro-Russian.

Ukraine as Little Russia

After the elimination of Cossack autonomy in Russia, the Ukrainian landed gentry came to replace the Cossack officers as the main representative class of Ukrainian society. Changes in the social status of the local elites prompted changes in the collective identity of the Little Russian nobility, which was now distinguished not so much by social rights and privileges as by a common history, territory, and a relatively new concept of ethnicity. Thus, the supposed "epilogue to the Cossack era" can be alternatively described as an era of further consolidation of the Little Russian identity, which has been updated in the process of the development of Ukrainian studies as well as in both Russian language and vernacular fiction.

As the role of Cossackdom gradually decreased, the role of the Cossack marker in the collective identity of the local elites declined concomitantly. The Cossack-based Hetmanate became an object of severe criticism from both the Russian and the Ukrainian sides.[49] For many educated Ukrainians, the system of Cossack autonomy failed to stand the test of time. Practically all Cossack hetmans were accused of abuses of power, violating the rights and freedoms of other classes, particularly the nobility and the municipalities, and of an inability to carry out the reform of the Cossack army, and so on.[50] Interestingly, for Opanas Shafonskyi (1740—1811), one of the many Ukrainians in Russian imperial service, even Bohdan Khmelnytskyi did not look like a hero and founding father of Cossack freedom, but a rebel, a leader of *chern* (rabble), similar to Stepan Razin (1630–1671) and Iemelian Pugachev (1742–1775).[51]

The liquidation of the Hetmanate and of Cossack autonomy did not spark resistance similar to the uprisings of the Polish gentry. On the contrary, the Ukrainian intellectuals of the age of the Enlightenment resembled their Scottish contemporaries who justified the union of Scotland with England as progress for their country.[52] The pro-Russian orientation at that time was characteristic not only of Ukrainians but also of other local elites in Eastern Europe, including a part of the Polish gentry that considered incorporation of their homeland into the Russian Empire to be quite natural and inevitable.[53] That is why Ukrainians became "among the most enthusiastic builders of an imperial Russian national identity—as a way to become European."[54]

The Cossack historical mythology can be considered one of the most vivid examples of what George Schöpflin identifies as *"myths of military valour."*[55] Historical records of the Ukrainian Cossacks recount dozens of battles fought in different places under various banners. Some of them, for example, the Battle of Khotyn (1621), the Battle of Konotop (1659), and the Battle of Poltava (1709), contained undeniable myth-making potential. However, none of these battles could be accepted without reservation as a symbol of national solidarity as was the highly mythologized Battle of Kulikovo (1380) in the Russian historical narrative, the Battle of Kosovo (1389) in Serbian historiography, and the Battle of Grunewald (1410) in Polish historical writings. The Little Russian patriots simply had to reconsider the Cossack phenomenon and its role in the national historical narrative.

Historians tend to separate Cossackdom and Little Russia in the process of symbolic territorialization and ethnicization of the latter.[56] The Cossack military-historical mythology has been gradually replaced with the mythology of Little Russian statehood based on the principle of historical legitimism. Little Russian historians—from Semen Divovych (1730s–after 1763) to the anonymous author of the *Istoriia Rusov* (History of the Rus),[57] Olexii Martos (1790–1842), and Mykola Markevych (1804–1860)—are eager to remind their Russians counterparts that, when it voluntarily came under the protection of the tsars, Little Russia contributed enormously to Russia's rise to greatness on account of its densely populated lands, effective army, and enlightened clergy. Thus, the historical Cossack Little Russia was endowed by its patriots with the characteristics of a fully developed, true, normal modern state, along with all the necessary institutions, symbols, and policy. In other words, Little Russia now appeared not as a Cossack Zaporozhian army, always ready to fight with any enemy, but in the form of a sovereign nation, that is, a state, with an appropriate territory.

"The Cossack is a national Little Russian warrior," asserts *Novy slovotolkovatel, raspolozhennyi po alfavitu* (A New Dictionary Organized in Alphabetical Order), a dictionary of foreign words compiled by Mykola Ianovskyi and published in St. Petersburg in 1803–1804.[58] This brief formula seems to symbolize the dawn of a new stage in Ukrainian historical thought, in which the Cossack identity is transformed from an object of diverse etymological and ethnographic exercises into an important, albeit not the main, attribute of modern national statehood. In the *History of the Rus*, all of the humiliating defeats for the Cossacks turned into brilliant victories in order to confirm that they were dictated by the national interests. Cossack military glory remains an important symbol of the Little Russian state discourse, but not the main one.

Cossack battles were assigned another important function by the author of the *History of the Rus*. As Anthony Smith (1939–2016) put it, "The wanderings, battles and exploits in which 'our people' and their leaders participated took place in a particular landscape, and the features of that landscape are part of those experiences and the collective memories to which they give rise."[59] Thus, the numerous Cossack battles depicted in the *History of the Rus*, with all their geographic details, functioned as markers of Little Russian territory and its borders. The author also emphasizes the motive of subordinating all the Cossack military units to the Little Russian hetman and attributing their respective regions to the historical and political territory of Little Russia.[60]

Above all, this concerned the Zaporozhian Sich: although Little Russian historians demonstrate a negative attitude toward the Sich, labeling it an "uncivilized" "rabble" of "bandits" who made no difference between attacking Tatars and their fellow countrymen,[61] it is more important for them to emphasize the Cossack's subordination to the hetman than to destroy their entire reputation as defenders of Christianity. The author of the *History of the Rus* tries to convince his readers that the Zaporozhian Cossacks were merely border guards recruited from the Little Russian Cossacks and completely subordinated to the hetman. By doing so, the Little Russian patriots located the Sich in the symbolic space of Little Russia, not in the Cossackdom. For that reason, the Little Russian elite publicly protested against the inclusion of the former Sich lands into the newly established Novorossiia province.[62]

The above applies to Sloboda Ukraine. The attitude of the Little Russian elites to their Sloboda Ukrainian counterparts was mocking and lenient rather than hostile. The Little Russians made fun of their eastern neighbors, mocking their claim to noble status, and even rejecting their right to call themselves Cossacks.[63] The author of the *History of the Rus* considered the special status of Sloboda Ukraine Cossacks illegitimate, the result of local selfishness and Russian corruption.[64] Obviously, such an interpretation rejected any independent political ambitions and claims of the Sloboda Ukrainian Cossacks.

Based on an analysis of Little Russian historical texts, we can conclude that, despite numerous administrative perturbations, terminological chaos, and endless debates between historians and philologists, the imagined spatial parameters of Little Russia have remained stable: it included not only the adjacent Cossack regions of the former Zaporozhian and Sloboda Ukrainian Cossack units but also the right bank of the Dnipro River[65] and even the western lands of Galicia.[66] In regard to the latter, the Cossack marker of Little Russian territory was supplemented with observations on the ethnicity of the local population.[67] Thus, there is no need to conclude that Little Russia was limited to left-bank Ukraine only or that Ukraine displaced Little Russia in the form of a broader national space "from the Carpathian Mountains to the Don River." In the majority of historical and geographical texts dating from the latter half of the eighteenth century and the early nineteenth century, the names "Ukraine" and "Little Russia" are not in opposition, but act as synonyms.

The geographic terms "Little Russia" and "Ukraine" continued to be used in parallel, although perhaps in a certain hierarchy. It is worth noting that "Ukraine" is often used to emphasize the marginal, peripheral status of Little Russia or some of its regions; the term retains a semantic connection with the Cossacks and the Polish historiographical tradition to limit Ukraine to the right bank of the Dnipro River only. There could be several local *ukraines* but only one Little Russia. This implies a tendency toward restructuring the symbolic space of Little Russia and transforming its southern, eastern, and western lands into the borderlands of the Little Russian heartland. However, this tendency did not develop, for reasons that will be discussed below.

Fatal Geography

As the Hetmanate gradually lost its geopolitical significance, the *antemurale* Cossack mythology, in both its religious and geopolitical versions, was gradually replaced with the images of a "fatal geography" or a "land-in-between."⁶⁸ This trend had a longstanding tradition in the definition of Ukraine's geopolitical identity and was also associated with Hetman Mazepa.⁶⁹ However, it fully manifested itself only one hundred years after his death in the *History of the Rus*. The author of this work, who remains anonymous, gives us a most elaborate retrospective picture of the Ukrainian geopolitical situation.

In the *History of the Rus*, Cossack Ukraine is depicted as a fully legitimate player on the international stage, equal to any other country, and completely independent since 1649, when the Zboriv Treaty was signed between the Polish-Lithuanian Commonwealth and the newly proclaimed Cossack state of Bohdan Khmelnytskyi. However, the author concludes that Ukraine was not able to keep its independence because of its "fatal geography," lack of "natural borders," and unfriendly neighbors. He paints a vivid picture of a suffering country:

> as if it was created for, or condemned to, ruin from the frequent invasions of foreigners [*inoplemennikov*] and even more frequent raids and battles from neighboring peoples. The Ukraine ultimately underwent all kinds of destruction and conflagrations due to incessant internal warfare and carnage and is literally stained and drenched with the blood of man and covered with ashes.⁷⁰

Surrounded by hostile "virtually irreconcilable peoples," Ukraine, according to the author of the *History of the Rus*, could remain neither an independent nor a neutral country. He attributes to Bohdan Khmelnytskyi, the most popular Ukrainian hetman, the axiom that foreign protection would be "not only useful but almost inevitable to us, and a sensible person, or a perfect politician, will notice at first glance that the very position of our land, open from all sides and awkward to defend, renders us a playground of unknown destiny and random chance."⁷¹ Conversely, the Little Russian historical narrative in general did not accept Hetman Mazepa as a symbol of Ukrainian independence and freedom.⁷²

The image of Ukraine's fatal geography was promoted also by Mykola Markevych in his *Istoriia Malorossii* (History of Little Russia, 1840–1844).⁷³ This treatise aimed to justify the historical futility of the idea of Ukrainian independence and the necessity of Russian protection:

> We were surrounded by Warsaw, Constantinople, and Moscow. Our borders were not reinforced with any natural barriers; we had neither gold for money nor copper for cannons, nor iron for weapons and harness, not even salt for bread. Just a broad steppe with plentiful grain and hay, but the more of them, the less of money. We were fated to live either pastorally, if our grain exports were banned, or as brigands, which our neighbors would not allow/ countenance. In this situation, what choice did we have . . . ? Poland would

badger Little Russia from the west, Moscow from the east and the north, and Turkey and Crimea from the south. We would have not a single peaceful day in our separate life.⁷⁴

This thesis that the absence of natural borders proved independent existence to be impossible was considered an axiom of geopolitical thinking of that time; it helps, for example, to justify the need for Poland to be part of the Russian Empire.⁷⁵ Instead, the idea of Russia as less evil for Ukraine had a much more solid foundation in the form of realpolitik and a common religion. The Great Russians—no matter how cruel, corrupted, or ridiculous they were depicted as being by the author of the *History of the Rus*—are never considered the main Other: this place is always reserved for the Poles.

The author of the *History* does not spare emotional arguments and vivid descriptions in order to prove the ethical and moral superiority of his compatriots over the Poles. The latter appear to truly personify the worst of human qualities. The author describes them as the very definition of "barbarism" and compares them to the "fierce Japanese," who in this case symbolize Asia, thus placing historical Poland outside the European symbolic space. If historical materials compel the author to recognize the presence of bad hetmans in Ukraine's past, he attributes a Polish ethnic origin to them. The anti-Polonism of the *History of the Rus* goes hand in hand with anti-Semitism, which presumably is a reaction to the incorporation of a part of the Polish-Lithuanian Commonwealth, with its large Jewish population, into the Russian Empire.

Cradle of Rus

The new historical narrative defines the central place of Little Russia within the symbolic space of the "Rus World" (not to be confused with the "Russian World"). Little Russia claims superiority over all other Russias, including Great Russia.

"I know that you are Russia and that is my name too," Little Russia replies to Great Russia in Semen Divovych's famous historical-political dialogue of 1762.⁷⁶ Hryhorii Poletyka (1725–1784), the distinguished champion of the Ukrainian *szlachta*'s political rights, called his fatherland "Russia,"⁷⁷ as did his contemporary and fellow historian Petro Symonovskyi (Petr Simonovskii, c. 1717–1809).⁷⁸ Andrian Chepa (1760s–c. 1820), a Little Russian patriot and collector of Cossack historical documents, proudly called the history of his people "a glorious branch of *rossiiskoi* [Rossian] history."⁷⁹ The author of the *History of the Rus* argues that Little Russia is, in fact, the true Russia and therefore can be considered an "older sister" in relation to

Great Russia. Little Russian historical discourse, based on the mythology of the "Cradle of Rus," supports the claims of the Little Russian elites "to prove that 'we got here first.'"[80]

The image of the "Little Russian gem" in the crown of the Russian Empire or "Ukraine-*pysanka*,"[81] elaborated in the early nineteenth century, aimed to buttress the Cradle of Rus mythology. The cliché of Ukraine as the "land of Canaan," flowing with milk and honey and rich in landscapes and plentiful resources, had been known since the Renaissance. The Enlightenment era historiography slightly modified this image with analogues from antiquity; Johann Gottfried Herder (1744–1803) recorded his prediction about Ukraine as a future "New Hellas."[82] Citing Linnaeus (1707–1778), Schérer described it as the protoancestor of practically all European "tribes and nations," simultaneously perpetuating the stereotype of it being "one of the most beautiful, although least cultivated, regions of Europe."[83]

It took no time at all for this image of the Little Russian gem, so far removed from the image of the Cossack military formation, to be adopted by the Ukrainian as well as Russian historical-literary traditions.[84] It was also accompanied by comparisons of Little Russia to Italy, which, according to Serhiy Bilenky, contributed to a feminization of the former in the Russian literary discourse.[85] The ethnically informed image of the "Ukraine-*pysanka* (a Ukrainian Easter egg)" would for some time balance the Enlightenment era criticism of the Hetmanate as a neglected civilizational periphery, deprived of good governance.

The Cradle of Rus mythology, as well as the Ukraine-*pysanka* image, facilitated the transfer of Little Russia from the periphery to the center of the Rus World. The fact that Kyiv— the spiritual symbol of the Rus World—was located on the Ukrainian-Polish borderland only encouraged the imperial center to reconquer the right bank of the Dnipro River from the Polish cultural "yoke." The Kyiv local authorities continued to view the Little Russian/Ukrainian cultural activities favorably. The Western, anti-Polish geocultural vector remained the chief orientation of the symbolic expansion of the territory of Little Russia during the long nineteenth century.

Further expansion of the symbolic borders of the Rus World to the West activated a relatively new component of the Russian-Polish borderland— the *haidamaky* (eighteenth-century Orthodox Cossack-peasant insurgents against the Polish *szlachta*).[86] Unsurprisingly, the *haidamaky* underwent a postmortem historical metamorphosis similar to that of the Zaporozhian Cossacks. The Kharkiv Romantics virtually conflated the Zaporozhian Cossacks and the *haidamaky* as noble warriors against Polish persecution.[87] Mykhailo Maksymovych (1804–1873) and Mykola Markevych legitimized the topic of the 1768 Koliivshchyna rebellion by including it in the Little Russian narrative.

During the era of Romanticism, the new generation of Romantic "populists" "no longer possessed the specifically 'political' consciousness of the previous generations of the noble patriots."[88] The mythology of the fully fledged Little Russian state was replaced with the cult of the Zaporozhian Sich; the latter underwent yet another metamorphosis from the border guards to a symbol of the Rus World. In Nikolai Gogol's (1809–1852) novel *Taras Bulba* (Taras Bulba, 1842), the Zaporozhian Cossacks do not simply fulfill the function of defending the Rus World Orthodoxy against the Catholic West; they are fully fledged, ideal representatives of the Slavic-Orthodox brotherhood, according to the Cradle of Rus mythology.[89] In the early work of Maksymovych, the image of the Little Russian state was replaced with the image of the Cossack "comet," which absorbed the "Asian-invasive" influences of the East and whose explosive dynamics brought many troubles for neighboring peoples.[90]

The Romantics also transformed the symbolic space of Ukrainian history into a kind of Eurasian interface—a place where European cultural elements intertwined with those of Asia. In contemplating the historical identity of Little Russia, Mykhailo Maksymovych wrote that its population

> comprised not only Slavic tribes but also European ones and, it seems, even more Asian ones.... Bravery in raids, exuberant abandon in celebration, and carefree indolence in peacetime—these are features of the wild Asian peoples of the Caucasus, whom today we involuntarily recall when looking at the Little Russian in his suit and with his habits.[91]

Gogol considered Little Russia/Ukraine to be "the most liminal of spaces, and therefore the most boundless, as a Russian meeting ground of east and west, Tatar and Pole, a space which is aptly expressed in the figure of the Cossack."[92]

This image was complemented with Panteleimon Kulish's (1819– 1897) observation on the Little Russians who "lie with their head in Europe, but their feet in Asia."[93] As a result, the Ukrainian national space acquired a distinct cultural profile but lost its historical-political boundaries, which in turn led to the erosion of the mythology of the Little Russian statehood. It would take at least two generations of nationally minded intellectuals to restore the principle of historical legitimacy and the principle of a national state with clearly defined political borders.

Little Russia and Russia

Little Russia was able to operate autonomously in the loosely defined realm of the Rus World as long as its existence did not undermine the imperial dynasty and religious pillars of the Russian Empire. The hierarchy of the historical regions and their borders, and the periphery and center of Rus/Russia, remained an open question, inasmuch as none of the criteria for defining the Russian heartland were used consistently enough to give the historic nucleus of the Russian Empire the appearance of wholeness.[94] As Alexei Miller put it, "The ruling dynasty had resisted 'nationalization' longer than in the majority of the European states. . . . The 'nation' did not rule and had no system of political representation."[95] In light of this, it seems like the difference between empire and nation in the case of Russia did exist.[96] This difference deepened with the further secularization and nationalization of the Rus World by the Russian elites.

The Little Russian national narrative still had an impact on the lagging Russian nation-building process, especially in the context of growing Polish nationalism. It explains to some degree the phenomenon of the short-term fashionability of all things Little Russian within educated Russian society (*Ukrainofilia*) in the 1830s. It started with Dmitrii Bantysh-Kamenskii's (1788–1850) *Istoriia Maloi Rossii* (History of Little Russia) in 1822 and continued with the collection of the *Malorossiiskie pesni* (Little Russian Songs) published in 1827 by Mykhailo Maksymovych (1804–1873). Both of these works became sources of inspiration for many Russian writers, including Alexander Pushkin (1799–1837) and Faddei Bulgarin (1789–1859), as well as composers and other artists. Russian imperial culture also absorbed the latest intellectual innovations of Little Russian studies along with their myths and images, including Ukraine-*pysanka*, the Ukrainian space, and, of course, the Romantic cult of the Zaporozhian Cossacks.

Official Russian historiography no longer tolerated the enlightened criticism of the Cossacks that was articulated by Little Russian patriots themselves in the early nineteenth century. In the new Russian historical narrative, the Zaporozhian Cossacks were transformed from marauding bands that were "peculiar and contrary to the very intentions of the Creator" to a symbol of Russian military glory and defense of Orthodoxy and autocracy.[97] The paradigm shift was facilitated by the Turkish and Napoleonic wars as well as the Polish Uprising of 1830, which occasionally prompted Cossack recruitment/conscription projects or even plans to reinstate the Cossacks as a military entity.[98]

In the context of the above, the Zhytomyr-born, Vilnius-educated, and Odessa-based amateur historian Apollon Skalkovskyi (1808–1899) deserves special attention. He completely revised the negative image of the Zaporozhian Sich in the Russian historical narrative.[99] He revived the image of the Zaporozhian *antemurale* as Christendom's stronghold against Muslim aggression. This image also returns the Zaporozhians to the civilizational discourse from which they had previously been excluded by the imperial New Russia project.¹⁰⁰ Skalkovskyi, who at first had been harshly negative about the Koliivshchyna rebellion, later reconsidered his perception of the *haidamaky* and attributed to them the mission of defending the Orthodox religion.¹⁰¹ It is worth noting that Ukrainian/Little Russian intellectuals expressed sharp criticism of this author, probably because of his Polish connections. However, mutual relations within the Ukrainian-Polish-Russian symbolical triangle were changing to the detriment of the former. The polemics that exploded around Mykola Markevych's *History of Little Russia*, published at the beginning of 1840s, demonstrates it eloquently.¹⁰² The author of the book—a politically loyal Ukrainian landowner and proud Little Russian patriot—argued against Ukrainian independence and did his best to justify its full incorporation into the Russian Empire. However, he did present the Ukrainian past in terms of a fully fledged nation-state history, in the spirit of the *History of the Rus*, which became his main source of inspiration.

It was precisely the nation-state paradigm of Little Russian history that provoked prominent Russian intellectuals of different political orientations to unleash their hostility toward Markevych's narrative. A popular Russian writer and journalist of Polish descent, Osip Senkovskyi (Józef Sękowski, 1800–1858) scorned the very idea of a normal Ukrainian historical process. According to him, the Cossacks, being the main representatives of Ukrainian history, acted as a devastating force, alien to culture and civilization, that plagued the adjacent states of Russia and the Polish-Lithuanian Commonwealth with senseless rebellions and sheer anarchy.

The Little Russian gentry felt insulted and attempted to present Senkovskyi's critique as a "Polish intrigue" against the "true Russians" and submitted an official complaint to the Russian authorities, but they encountered a wall of misunderstanding. Russian censors actually came to the defense of Senkovskyi and accused the Little Russians of provincial narrow-mindedness and bias.¹⁰³ They identified the Zaporozhian Sich with the Hetmanate in their role of anti–state military formations created by uncontrollable Cossacks. In fact, the imperial officials made it clear that there were certain limits for Little Russian patriotism and its anti-Polish discourse. It should be noted that they began to express concern about excessive Little Russian patriotism even before the Cyril and Methodius Brotherhood (Ukrainian secret society) was discovered by the imperial authorities.

Characteristically enough, the views of the Russian imperial loyalists are fully supported by the Russian opposition critic Vissarion Belinsky (1811–1848), who went much further in criticizing the Little Russian state historical narrative. Commenting on Markevych's *History of Little Russia*, the Russian critic noted that Little Russia had never been a state and, consequently, had no history, in the strict sense of the word; according to him,

Little Russians had always been a tribe and not a nation, and the so-called Hetmanate and Zaporozhian Sich were some kind of strange communities "in the Asian style," and so on.[104] The main paradox of this critique is that both ultraloyal Ukrainian Markevych and opposition-minded Russian Belinsky actually argued for the same thing: they saw a need for Little Russia to be fully merged with the Russian Empire and were convinced of the impossibility of its independent existence. However, Belinsky denied not just the future but also the whole history of Ukraine, which had been dismissed from the civilization discourse altogether.

What was more troubling for the Little Russian patriots is that at least some of the Russian intellectuals started signaling their overt skepticism about the Cradle of Rus mythology. Nikolai Polevoi (1796–1846) was perhaps the first among them—he denied the Little Russians the right to be called "Russian" altogether. In his opinion, the Little Russians were completely different from ethnic Russians in their language, culture, and history.[105] The views of Polevoi appeared to be too radical and too innovative to be shared by Russian enthusiasts who favored the idea of the Rus World. However, some of the Russian "Slavophiles" who were more sensitive to the ethnocultural aspects of Russian national identity were already moving in the direction indicated by Polevoi. The influential Russian historian Mikhail Pogodin (1800–1875), for example, dismissed the Ukrainian exclusive claim to the Kyivan inheritance in an attempt to establish the Great Russian priority over Kyivan Rus.[106]

All these factors mean that, given the Russian Empire's gradual nationalization of the Rus World, it did not need Little Russia as a national heartland or even as a separate entity in its struggle against Polonism. Obviously, Russian intellectuals already had their own image of the Rus historical heartland, associated with the Great Moscow Principality rather than with Little Russia disguised as Kyivan Rus.[107] The Little Russian narrative created by the local patriots had neither a future nor even a past. Only a radical reorientation could offer a way out of this existential crisis. That is when new Ukraine came to the rescue of old Little Russia.

Conclusions

The answer to the question posed by the title of this chapter may be short or long. The short answer is that neither Ukraine in its modern form and space nor the developed mythology of its separate national and geopolitical identity existed at the time described in this chapter. There were some elements of an *antemurale* mythology presented in the Cossack-oriented historical narratives, but they were not properly articulated and did not develop into a holistic national narrative in order to occupy the same place in the Little Russian collective identity, as shown by the example of neighboring Poland.

The long answer is based on the thesis of heterogeneity, ambiguity, and a variety of identities and competing mythologies—not just for Ukraine, but also for the whole space of Europe and Russia, on which Ukraine directly depended. The discourses of fatal geography, the land in-between, definitely overcame the boundary-making mythology and prevented the structuring of Ukrainian national space into the categories of center and periphery. The Little Russian mythology of the Cradle of Rus was intended to alleviate the boundary status of Little Russia in the vast space of the Rus World. However, gradual secularization and nationalization of the latter tended to marginalize Little Russia in the permanently expanding space of the Russian Empire.

From the perspective of the Russian imperial center, Ukrainian lands could have appeared as a Russian imperial bulwark to the south and the west. However, both of them—the southern and the western borders of the Russian Empire alike—appeared not so much in the form of a bulwark, as a moving frontier, aimed at the reunion of the former lands of Rus. Historical Little Russia played an important but only temporary and limited role in this process. The imperial center was not interested in creating an alternate wall between the historical Little Russia and Poland; its aim was to integrate both of them into the imperial system and to maintain the balance of interests between ethnic and religious communities in the politically sensitive region.

A fully fledged *antemurale* mythology could be developed only on the basis of those representative symbols that were marginalized in the Little Russian historical narrative, namely, Ukraine and Cossacks. The new Ukrainian historical narrative had to rearrange the symbols already accumulated by the Little Russian narrative. Within this narrative, the mythology of national statehood gave way to the mythology of the Cossacks, which turned into a symbol of social equality,[108] while the social, democratic dimension of the narrative distinguished the Ukrainian version of the Cossacks from the Little Russian one. Historical Little Russia entered the very center of the Rus World just for a while, and very soon was forced to return to its border, represented by the Zaporozhian Sich. Being reimagined as a bastion of freedom, the latter became the social heartland of modern Ukraine, no matter how real or utopian this image appeared at the beginning of the twentieth century.

It was only at the turn of the twentieth century that modern Ukraine began to construct its own symbolic national space, beyond the boundaries of the Rus World. It was made possible by two major events: first, a conceptual revolution brought about by Mykhailo Hrushevskyi's (1866–1934) seminal multivolume *Istoriia Ukrainy-Rusi* (History of Ukraine-Rus),[109] which established the foundation for Ukraine's own secular *antemurale* ideology as the eastern frontier of Europe, and, second, the geopolitical upheaval of 1914–1918 and the subsequent integration of the western regions into the Ukrainian nation-state building process. However, it took another hundred years for the *antemurale* mythology to gain a political dimension, and limited support, in Ukrainian society. Given the historical experience and geopolitical position of Ukraine, few will be able to predict the political future and place of this mythology in the national and geopolitical discourse. It seems like the latter will be dictated by the strategy of survival in one of the most turbulent territories of Eastern Europe. In addition, the Ukrainian geopolitical wall can easily be turned into a gate, open in either direction.

Volodymyr Kravchenko is a professor in the Department of History and Classics and the director of the Contemporary Ukraine Studies Programs of the Canadian Institute of Ukrainian Studies at the University of Alberta, Edmonton. He is the author of about 170 articles, book chapters, and monographs on Ukrainian historiography (since the end of the eighteenth to the twenty-first century), historical legacy, and Kharkiv (city and region). Fields of interest include also East European, Soviet, and Russian studies in general.

Notes

1. See reviews and historiographical summaries of the issue of Ukrainian modern nation building in T. Hen-Konarski, "No Longer Just Peasants and Priests: The Most Recent Studies on Nation Building in Nineteenth-Century Ukraine," *European History Quarterly* 45, no. 4 (2015): 713–37; S. Bilenky, "The Ukrainian National Movement in the Nineteenth Century: Context, Timing, Issues," in *Fashioning Modern Ukraine: Selected Writings of Mykola Kostomarov, Volodymyr Antonovych, and Mykhailo Drahomanov*, ed. S. Bilenky (Edmonton-Toronto: CIUS Press, 2013), XIII–XLVI; A. Kappeler, "Hromadianska chy etnichna natsia? Zauvahy z teorii ta istoriohrafii," in *Ukraina: Protsesy natsiotvorennia*, ed. A. Kappeler (Kyiv: K.I.C., 2011), 13–30; I. Hrytsak, *Strasti za natsionalismom. Stara istoria na novyi lad: Esei* (Kyiv: Krytyka, 2011); G. Kasianov and Ph. Ther, eds., *Laboratory of Transnational History* (Budapest: CEU Press, 2009).
2. See K. Halushko, *Rus-Malorosia-Ukraina: nazva i terytoria* (Kyiv: Likbez, 2017); Halushko, *Ukraina na karti Evropy: Ukraina ta ukraintsi u kartohrafii vid Antychnosti do XX stolittia* (Kyiv: Kyivskii Universytet, 2013); B. Hal, "Geocontsept 'Malorosia' na mentalnykh mapakh XVIII—pershoi polovyny XIX st.," *Eidos* 7 (2013): 93–109; S. Bilenky, *Romantic Nationalism in Eastern Europe: Russian, Polish, and Ukrainian Political Imaginations* (Stanford: Stanford University Press, 2012); A.

Kotenko, "Construction of Ukrainian National Space by the Intellectuals of Russian Ukraine, 1860–70s," in *Mapping Eastern Europe*, ed. J. Happel and Ch. Werdt (Münster: LIT Verlag, 2010), 37–60; Z.E. Kohut, "Mazepa's Ukraine: Understanding Cossack Territorial Vistas," *Harvard Ukrainian Studies* 31 (2009–2010): 1–28.
3. R. Szporluk, "Ukraine: From an Imperial Periphery to a Sovereign State," *Daedalus* 126, no. 3 (1997): 86.
4. T. Zarycki, *Ideologies of Eastness in Central and Eastern Europe* (London: Routledge, 2014); L. Wolff, *The Idea of Galicia: History and Fantasy in Habsburg Political Culture* (Stanford: Stanford University Press, 2010); Wolff, *Inventing Eastern Europe. The Map of Civilization on the Mind of the Enlightenment* (Stanford: Stanford University Press, 1994); I. Neumann, *Uses of the Other. "The East" in European Identity Formation* (Minneapolis: University of Minnesota Press, 1999).
5. S. Bilenky, *Eastern Europe in Search of a Nation: Romantic Nationalism and Imagined Communities in Ukraine, Poland, and Russia, 1830s–1840s* (Toronto: University of Toronto Press, 2007), 15.
6. H. Wydra, "Introduction. Democracy in Eastern Europe—Myth and Reality" in *Democracy and Myth in Russia and Eastern Europe*, ed. A. Wöll and H. Wydra (London/New York: Routledge, 2008), 7.
7. G. Schöpflin, "The Functions of Myth and a Taxonomy of Myths," in *Myths and Nationhood*, ed. G. Schopflin and G. Hosking (New York: Routledge, 1997), 19–24.
8. S. Plokhy, *The Cossack Myth: History and Nationhood in the Age of Empires* (Cambridge: Cambridge University Press, 2012); H. Hrabowych, *Do istorii ukrainskoi literatury* (Kyiv: Krytyka, 1997); A. Wilson, "Myths on National History in Belarus and Ukraine," in *Myths and Nationhood*, ed. G. Hosking and G. Schöpflin (London, 1997), 182–97; J.A. Armstrong, "Myth and History in the Evolution of Ukrainian Consciousness" in *Ukraine and Russia in Their Historical Encounter*, ed. P.J. Potichnyj et al. (Edmonton: CIUS Press, 1992), 125–39; N. Iakovenko, "Kilka sposterezhen nad modyfikatsiamy ukrainskoho natsionalnoho mifu v istoriohrafii," *Dukh i Litera* 3–4 (2001), last retrieved 18 March 2018 from http://www.ukrhistory.narod.ru/texts/yakovenko–5.htm.
9. A. Lawaty, "The Figure of Antemurale in the Historiography," in *East and Central European History Writing in Exile 1939–1989*, ed. M. Zadencka et al. (Leiden: Brill, 2015), 360–74; P. Kolstø, "Assessing the Role of Historical Myths in Modern Society," in *Myths and Boundaries in South-Eastern Europe*, ed. P. Kolstø (London: Hurst, 2005), 1–34.
10. M. Deszczyńska, "Wyobrażenie przedmurza w piśmiennictwie schyłku polskiego oświęcenia," *Przegląd Historyczny* 92, no. 3 (2001): 289; J.A. Agnew, *Geopolitics: Revisioning World Politics* (London/New York: Routledge, 1998), 87.
11. S. Berger, "History Writing and Constructions of National Space: The Long Dominance of the National in Modern European Historiographies," in *Palgrave Handbook of Research in Historical Culture and Education*, ed. M. Carretero et al. (Basingstoke: Palgrave Macmillan UK, 2017), 44.
12. Kolstø, "Assessing the Role of Historical Myths," 3, 13–14. See also Pål Kolstø's contribution in this volume.
13. H.-M. Tychka, "Idea peredmuria Evropy v ukrainsko-polskomu protystoianni za Skhidnu Halychynu pid chas Paryzkoi myrnoi konferentsii," *Viiskovo-naukovyi*

visnyk 25 (2016): 182–97; A. Woldan, "The Notion of *Antemurale Christianitatis* in Connection with the City of Lemberg/Lwów/Lviv," *Studi Slavistici* 9, no. 1 (2012): 53–69.

14. S. Bilenky, *Romantic Nationalism;* Z.E. Kohut, "The Development of a Ukrainian National Historiography in Imperial Russia" in *Historiography of Imperial Russia. The Profession and Writing History in a Multinational State,* ed. T. Sanders (Armonk: M.E. Sharpe, 1999), 453–77; S. Velychenko, *National History as Cultural Process: A Survey of the Interpretations of Ukraine's Past in Polish, Russian, and Ukrainian Historical Writing from the Earliest Times to 1914* (Edmonton: CIUS Press, 1992).

15. A.L. Kotenko, O.V. Martynuk, and A.I. Miller, "'Maloross': evoliutsia poniatia do Pervoi mirovoi voiny," *Novoe Literaturnoe Obozrenie* 108 (2010): 9–27; V. Masliichuk, "'Vid Ukrainy do Malorosii': Regionalni nazvy ta natsionalna istoria," in *Ukraina: Protsesy natsiotvorennia,* ed. A. Kappeler (Kyiv: K.I.C., 2011), 229–45; N. Iakovenko, "Choice of Name versus Choice of Path: The Names of Ukrainian Territories from the Late Sixteenth to the Late Seventeenth Century" in *Laboratory of Transnational History,* 117–48; A. Miller, *The Ukrainian Question: The Russian Empire and Nationalism in the Nineteenth Century* (Budapest: CEU Press, 2003), 25–27.

16. I.L. Rudnytsky, *Essays in Modern Ukrainian History* (Edmonton: CIUS Press, 1987), 11–36; 37–48; 123–42.

17. B. Hal, "Heocontsept 'Malorosia' na mentalnykh mapakh XVIII—pershoi polovyny XIX st.," *Eidos* 7 (2013): 93–109; A. Tolochko, *Kievskaia Rus i Malorossia v XIX veke* (Kyiv: Laurus, 2012); Z. Kohut, "The Development of a Little Russian Identity and Ukrainian Nation-Building," *Harvard Ukrainian Studies* 10, nos. 3–4 (1986): 559–76.

18. F. Polunin and G. Miller, *Geograficheskii leksikon Rossiiskogo gosudarstva* (Moskva: Izdatelstvo Moskovskogo Universiteta, 2012), 276. See also S. Plokhy, *The Origins of the Slavic Nations: Premodern Identities in Russia, Ukraine, and Belarus* (Cambridge: Cambridge University Press, 2006); A. Malashevych, "Borotba za 'ruske pervorodstvo (z istorii naukovoi dyskusii 'iuzhan' i 'severian' u vysvitlenni chasopysu 'Vestnik Evropy')," *Problemy istorii Ukrainy XIX– pochatku XX st.* 6 (2003): 383–94.

19. I. Orlai, "O Iugo-Zapadnoi Rusii (pismo iz Nezhyna k sekretariu Obshchesna)," *Trudy i Zapiski Obshchesnva Istorii i Drevnostei Rossiiskikh* 3, no. 1 (1826): 227; Z.E. Kohut, "Origins of the Unity Paradigm: Ukraine and the Construction of Russian National History (1620–1860)," *Eighteenth-Century Studies* 35, no. 1 (2001): 70.

20. F. Sysyn, "Spodivani ukraintsi," *Krytyka: Retsenzii, esei, ohliady* 5 (2002): 17–21; D. Saunders, *The Ukrainian Impact on Russian Culture: 1750–1850* (Edmonton: CIUS Press, 1985).

21. D. Vyrskyi, *Richpospolytska istoriohrafia Ukrainy (XV—seredyna XVII st.),* 2 vols. (Kyiv, 2008); F. Sysyn, "The Reemergence of the Ukrainian Nation and Cossack Mythology," *Social Research* 58, no. 4 (1991): 845–64; O.W. Gerus, "Manifestations of the Cossack Idea in Modern Ukrainian History: The Cossack Legacy and Its Impact," *Ukrainskyi Istoryk* 1–2 (1986): 22–39.

22. F. Sysyn, "Concepts of Nationhood in Ukrainian History Writing, 1620–1690," *Har-*

vard *Ukrainian Studies* 10, nos. 3–4 (1986): 393–423; Z. Kohut, "Kordony Ukrainy: terytorialni vizii kozakiv vid hetmana B.Khmelnytskoho do hetmana I.Samoilovycha," *Ukrainskyi istorychnyi zhurnal* 3 (2011): 50–73; Z. Kohut, "Mazepa's Ukraine: Understanding Cossack Territorial Vistas," *Harvard Ukrainian Studies* 31, nos. 1/4 (2009): 1–28; S. Bahro, "Uiavlennia pro kozatsku vitchyznu v suchasnii istoriohrafii," *Naukovi Zapusky NaUKMA. Istorychni nauky* 143 (2013): 48–54.

23. L. Berezhnaya, "'Kazacki bastion' 17 veka—vzgliad snaruzhi i iznutri," in *Religion und Integration im Moskauer Russland. Konzepte und Praktiken, Potentiale und Grenzen. 14.–17. Jahrhundert,* ed. L. Steindorff (Wiesbaden: Harassowitz Verlag, 2010), 269–97.

24. R. Lindheim and G.S.N. Luckyj, eds., *Towards an Intellectual History of Ukraine: An Anthology of Ukrainian Thought from 1710 to 1995* (Toronto: University of Toronto Press, 1996), 69–71; *Ukrainska literatura XVIII stolittia: Poetychni tvory, dramatychni tvory, prozovi tvory* (Kyiv: Dnipro, 1984).

25. V. Adadurov, "Ukrainske kozatstvo v uiavi frantsuzkoho uriadu doby Napoleona," *Ukraina v Tsentralno-Skhidnii Evropi (z naidavnishykh chasiv do kintsia XVIII st.)* 6 (2006): 398.

26. *Noveyshii i polnyii geograficheskii slovar,* part 2 (Moskva, 1788), 260; *Sochinenia i perevody, k polze iuveseleniiu sluzhashchie* (May etc., 1760).

27. D. Nalyvaiko, *Ochyma Zakhodu: retseptsia Ukrainy v Zakhidnii Evropi XI–XVIII st.* (Kyiv: Osnovy, 1998), 419, 430–31.

28. J.J. Müller, "Istorychna dysertacia pro kozakiv, jaku predstavleno u prymishchenni filosofskoho fakultetu na publichnyj rozhliad pid holovuvanniam messiar Hotfrida Weifa z Toruni u Prusii," *Kyivska Starovyna* nos. 4–5 (1996): 74.

29. A. Zorin, *Kormia dvuglavogo orla. Literatura i gosudarstvennaia ideologia v Rossii v poslednei treti XVIII–pervoi treti XIX veka* (Moskva: Novoe literaturnoe obozrenie, 2001), 115.

30. V. Adadurov, *"Napoleonida" na Skhodi Evropy: Uiavlennia, proekty ta diialnist uriadu Frantsii shchodo pivdenno-zakhidnykh okrain Rosiiskoi imperii na pochatku XIX st.* (Lviv: Vydavnytstvo UKU, 2007).

31. V. Masliichuk, *Provintsia na perekhresti kultur. Doslidzhennia z istorii Slobidskoi Ukrainy XVII—XIX st.* (Kharkiv: Pryvatnyi Muzei Miskoi Sadyby, 2007); Masliichuk, *Kozatska starshyna slobidskykh polkiv druhoi polovyny XVII—pershoi tretyny XVIII st.* (Kharkiv : Pryvatnyi Muzei Miskoi Sadyby, 2009).

32. In a letter to the Russian publisher Andrei Kraevskii dated 28 December 1841, Hryhorii Kvitka (Osnovianenko) asserted: "We in Sloboda Ukraine are not part of Little Russia. While they, the Little Russians, consulted and discussed how to split off from the wicked Poles, and to whom it would be convenient to attach, well, our forefathers were more decisive; they took themselves off to our kinsman the Russian tsar, settled in *slobodas* along the frontier (*ukraina*) . . . and have since fended off the Tatars and been a bulwark for Russia." See H. Kvitka-Osnovianenko, *Zibrannia tvoriv u semy tomakh,* vol. 7: *Istorychni, etnohrafichni, literaturno-publitsystychni statti, lysty* (Kyiv, 1981), 337, see also 143–44.

33. D.I. Bagalei and D.P. Miller, *Istoria goroda Kharkova za 250 let iego sushchestvovaniia,* vol. 2 (Kharkov: Zilberberg & Sons, 1912), 973; V. Karazin, *Sochineniia, pisma i bumagi* (Kharkov: Izdatelstvo Kharkovskago Universiteta, 1910), 485.

34. V.V. Kravchenko, *Kharkiv/Kharkov: stolitsia pogranichia* (Vilnius: EHU Press, 2010).
35. T. Prymak, "The Cossack Hetman: Ivan Mazepa in History and Legend from Peter to Pushkin," *The Historian* 76, no. 2 (2014): 237–77; T. Grob, "Mazepa as a Symbolic Figure of Ukrainian Autonomy," in *Democracy and Myth in Russia and Easter Europe*, ed. A. Wöll and H. Wydra (London/New York: Routledge, 2008), 79–97.
36. A.M. Glaser, ed., *Stories of Khmelnytsky: Competing Literary Legacies of the 1648 Ukrainian Cossack Uprising* (Stanford: Stanford University Press, 2016).
37. Nalyvaiko, *Ochyma Zakhodu*.
38. D. Nalyvaiko, "Nimetsko-ukrainski vzaiemyny XVIII st.: retseptsia Ukrainy v Nimechyni, ii etapy i tendentsii," *Magisterium, Literaturoznavchi studii* 8 (2002): 95.
39. V.V. Kravchenko, "Ivan Mazepa v ukrainskii istorychnii literaturi XVIII ta pershoi chverti XIX st.," in V.V. Kravchenko, *Ukraina, imperia, Rossia. Vybrani statti z modernoi istorii ta istoriohrafii* (Kyiv: Krytyka, 2011), 277–98.
40. M. Bassin, "Russia between Europe and Asia," *Slavic Review* 50, no. 1 (1991): 4.
41. J. Tazbir, "The Bulwark Myth," *Acta Poloniae Historica* 91 (2005): 78.
42. Adadurov, "Ukrainske kozatstvo v uiavi frantsuzkoho uriadu," 409.
43. J.-B. Schérer, *Annales de la Petite-Russie; ou Histoire des Cosaques-Saporogues et des Cosaques de l'Ukraine, ou de la Petite-Russie, depuis leur origine jusqu'à nos jours; suivie d'un abrégé de l'histoire des hettmans des Cosaques, & des pièces justificatives* (Paris: Cachet, 1788). I used the Ukrainian edition: J.-B. Schérer, *Litopys Malorosii abo Istoria kozakiv-Zaporozhtsiv ta kozakiv Ukrainy, abo Malorosii* (Kyiv: Ukrainskyi pysmennyk, 1994).
44. Schérer, *Litopys Malorosii*, 7.
45. Ibid., 7.
46. J.C. Engel, *Geschichte der Ukraine und der ukrainischen Cosaken, wie auch der Königreiche Halitsch und Wladimir* (Halle: Johann Jacob Gebauer, 1796). I used the Ukrainian edition: J.C. Engel, *Istoriia Ukrainy ta ukrainskykh kozakiv* (Kharkiv: Fakt, 2014).
47. Engel, *Istoriia Ukrainy*, 382.
48. V. Adadurov, "Dosvid istrorychnoho uiavlennia: uriad Napoleona i pro ukrainski zemli Rosiiskoi imperii," *Eidos* 2 (2006): 405–28; Bilenky, *Eastern Europe in Search of a Nation*, 85–86, 121–22.
49. *Zamechania, do Maloi Rossii prinadlezhashchie* (Moskva: Universitetskaia tipografia, 1848); V.V. Kravchenko, "Do problemy otsinky reform v ukrainskii istorychnii dumtsi druhoi polovyny XVIII st." in *Poklykannia, Zbirnyk prats na poshanu profesora, o. Iuria Mytsyka*, ed. P. Sokhan, A. Boiko and V. Brekhunenko, (Kyiv: Kyiv: Instytut Ukrainskoi arkheohrafii ta dzhereloznavstva, 2009), 372–82.
50. V.V. Kravchenko, "Do problemy otsinky"; A. Shafonskii, *Chernihovskoho namestnichestva topohraficheskoe opisanie* (Kiev: Izdatelstvo Kievskogo Universiteta, 1851), 65–66; M. Berlinskii, "Neskolko glav iz sochinenia 'Istoricheskoe obozrenie Malorossii i goroda Kieva,'" *Molodyk na 1844 god* (Sankt Peterburg, 1844), 188.
51. Shafonskii, *Chernihovskoho namestnichestva*.
52. Berger, "History Writing and Constructions," 40–41.
53. Deszczyńska, "Wyobrażenie przedmurza," 298.
54. R. Szporluk, "The Western Dimension of the Making of Modern Ukraine," in *Contemporary Ukraine on the Cultural Map of Europe*, ed. L.M.L. Zaleska-Onyshkevych and M. Revakovych (Armonk: M.E. Sharpe, 2009), 9.

55. G. Hosking and G. Schöpflin, eds., *Myths and Nationhood* (London: Hurst, 1997), 25.
56. B. Hal, "Geotsoncept 'Malorosia' na mentalnykh mapakh," 99.
57. *Istoria Rusov ili Maloi Rossii* (Moskva: Chtenia v obshchestve istorii i drevnostei rossiiskikh, 1846).
58. Kravchenko, *Ukraina, imperia, Rossia*, 339–54.
59. A.D. Smith, *Myths and Memories of the Nation* (Oxford: Oxford University Press, 1999), 150.
60. The Cossack marker appeared to be useful for the same purposes in post-Soviet Ukraine. See S. Plokhy, "Historical Debates and Territorial Claims: Cossack Mythology in the Russian-Ukrainian Border Dispute," in *The Legacy of History in Russia and the New States of Eurasia*, ed. S.F. Starr (Armonk/London, 1994), 147–70.
61. Shafonskii, *Chernihovskoho namestnichestva*, 51; V.T. Narezhnyi, *Bursak* (Moskva: Khudozhestvennaia Literatura, 1822).
62. See Z. Kohut, *Russian Centralism and Ukrainian Autonomy: Imperial Absorption of the Hetmanate, 1760's–1830's* (Cambridge, MA: Harvard University Press, 1988), 94; B. Hal, "'Ne ustupat ni na odin shag zemli!': Do istorii rozmezhuvannia malorosiiskykh namisnytstv i Novorosiiskoi hubernii (1782–1783 rr.)," *Istoriia i kultura Prydniprovia: Nevidomi ta malovidomi storinky: Naukovyi shchorichnyk* 5 (2008): 99–129. On the geopolitical significance of *Novorossia* for Ukrainian nation building, see R. Szporluk, "Ukraine: From an Imperial Periphery to a Sovereign State," *Daedalus* 126, no. 3 (1997): 107. Regarding Ukraine's representation in the Russian geographical narrative, see L. Gorizontov, "Podneprovie i Severnoie Prichernomorie v mnogotomnykh opisaniakh Rossiiskoi Imperii rubezha XIX–XX vekov: terminologicheskie aspekty," *Slavianovedenie* 3 (2016): 72–77.
63. "Otvet malorossiiskikh kozakov ukrainskim slobozhanam (naidennyi v Glukhovskom arkhive)," *Kievskaia starina* 10 (1884): 550–52. This work was published in *Ukrainska literatura XVIII st.*, 215–16, under the title *Satyra na Slobozhan* (A Satire against the Residents of Sloboda Ukraine).
64. *Istoria Rusov*, 109.
65. In my opinion, the author of *The History of Rus* was, in fact, not hostile to the term "Ukraine" in principle. He did not show his negative attitude to the most obvious use of this term in the name of the "Sloboda-Ukrainian province." His critique was directed against those historians who used the name "Ukraine" in order to prove the historical affiliation of the right bank of the Dnipro River with Poland. For a different interpretation of the corresponding fragment of the text, see S. Plokhy, "Ukraine or Little Russia? Revisiting an Early Nineteenth-Century Debate," *Canadian Slavonic Papers* 48, nos. 3–4 (2006): 348, 351.
66. N. Markevich, *Istoriia Malorossii*, vol. 1 (Moskva: August Semen, 1842–1843), 134–35, 186, 300, 382.
67. R. Szporluk, "Mapping Ukraine: From Identity Space to Decision Space," *Journal of Ukrainian Studies* (Summer 2008–Winter 2009): 441–52.
68. N. Iakovenko, "Ukraina mizh Skhodom i Zakhodom: proekcia odniei idei," in *Paralelnyi svit: doslidzhennia z istorii uiavlen ta idei v Ukraini XVI–XVII st.* (Kyiv: Krytyka, 2002), 333–65.
69. *Istoria Rusov*, 202.

70. Ibid., II.
71. Ibid., 98.
72. Kravchenko, "Ivan Mazepa," 277–98.
73. V.V. Kravchenko, *Narysy z ukrainskoi istoriohrafii epokhy natsionalnoho Vidrodzhennia (druha polovyna XVIII—seredyna XIX st.)* (Kharkiv: Osnova, 1996); O. Ias, "Doslidnytskyi instrumentarii ta intelektualni zasady 'Istorii Malorossii' Mykoly Markevycha," *Ukrainskyi istorychnyi zhurnal* 1 (2006): 27–42.
74. Markevich, *Istoria Malorossii*, vol. 2, 65–66.
75. Bilenky, *Eastern Europe in Search of a Nation*, 56.
76. *Ukrainska literatura XVIII st.: Poetychni tvory, dramatychni tvory, prozovi tvory* (Kyiv: Dnipro, 1983), 394.
77. "Vozrazhenie deputata Grigoriia Poletiki na Nastavlenie Malorossiiskoi kollegii gospodinu zh deputatu Dmitriiu Natalinu," *Chteniia v Obshchestve istorii i drevnostei rossiiskikh* 3 (1858): 98.
78. P. Simonovskii [Symonovskyi], *Kratkoe opisanie o kazatskom malorossiiskom narode i o ego voennykh delakh* ... (Moskva: Moskovskoe obshchestvo istorii i drevnostei rossiiskih, 1847), 2–3.
79. V. Gorlenko [Horlenko], "Iz istorii iuzhno-russkogo obshchestva nachala XIX veka (Pisma V.I. Chernysha, A.I. Chepy, V.G. Poletiki i zapiski k nim)," *Kievskaia starina* 1 (1893): 53.
80. Kolstø, "Assessing the Role of Historical Myths," 21–22.
81. The Ukrainian word *pysanka* literally means "Easter egg"; in a figurative sense, a comparison with *pysanka* is used to depict something beautiful (country, village, person, etc.).
82. Nalyvaiko, *Ochyma Zakhodu*.
83. Schérer, *Annales de la Petite-Russie*, 132.
84. I. Markovich, *Zapiski o Malorossii, ee zhiteliakh i proizvedeniakh*, vol. 1 (Sankt Peterburg: Gubernia, 1798).
85. Bilenky, *Eastern Europe*, 141–43.
86. B. Skinner, "Borderlands of Faith: Reconsidering the Origins of a Ukrainian Tragedy," *Slavic Review* 64, no. 1 (2005): 88–116; Z. Kohut, "Myths Old and New: The Haidamak Movement and the Koliivshchyna (1768) in Recent Historiography," *Harvard Ukrainian Studies* 1, no. 3 (1977), 359–78.
87. Kravchenko, *Narysy*.
88. Bilenky, "Ukrainian National Movement," xxx.
89. S. Yoon, "Transformation of a Ukrainian Cossack into a Russian Warrior: Gogols 1842 'Taras Bulba,'" *Slavic and East European Journal* 49, no. 3 (2005): 430–44; E. Bojanowska, *Nikolai Gogol between Ukrainian and Russian Nationalism* (Cambridge, MA: Harvard University Press, 2007).
90. M.A. Maksimovich, *Sobranie sochinenii*, vol. 2 (Kiev: M.P. Fritz, 1877), 440–41.
91. Ibid., 440.
92. M. Frazier, "Space and Genre in Gogols Arabeski Source," *Slavic and East European Journal* 43, no. 3 (1999): 452–70. Interesting observations on the Zaporozhian Sich symbolic space can be found in S. Nevolnichenko, "Mir i antimir v povesti N.V. Gogolia 'Taras Bulba,'" *Voprosy Literatury* 4 (2008): 241–63.
93. J. Remy, *Brothers or Enemies. The Ukrainian National Movement and Russia, from*

the 1840s to the 1870s (Toronto/Buffalo/London: University of Toronto Press, 2016), 58.
94. J. Burbank and M. von Hagen, "Coming into the Territory: Uncertainty and Empire," in *Russian Empire: Space, People, Power, 1700–1930*, ed. J. Burbank, M. von Hagen, and A.V. Remnev (Bloomington: Indiana University Press, 2007), 5.
95. A. Miller, *The Romanov Empire and Nationalism: Essays in the Methodology of Historical Research* (Budapest: CEU Press, 2008), 164.
96. For the opposite view, see J. Østbø, *The New Third Rome. Readings of a Russian Nationalist Myth* (Stuttgart: Ibidem-Verlag, 2016), 12.
97. A. Kovalchuk, *Narrating the National Future: The Cossacks in Ukrainian and Russian Romantic Literature* (Ph.D. diss., University of Oregon, 2017); Yoon, "Transformation of a Ukrainian Cossack"; J. Kornblatt, *The Cossack Hero in Russian Literature* (Madison: University of Wisconsin Press, 1992).
98. See, for example, Ievgenii (Bolkhovitinov), *Opisanie Kievosofiiskogo sobora i Kievskoi eparkhii* (Kiev: Tipografiia Kievo-Pecherskoi Lavry, 1825), 116; *Russkii Vestnik*, part 16 (12) (1) (4) (1811), 14–18; A.B. Roginskii, *Russkie istoricheskie povesti pervoi poloviny XIX veka* (Moskva: Khudozhestvennaia literatura, 1986), 174.
99. Kravchenko, *Narysy*; L. Novikova, *"Istoriohraf" Pivdennoi Ukrainy Apollon Skalkovskyi: intelektualna apolohia imperskoi polityky ta regionalnoi samobutnosti* (Odesa: Vydavnytstvo Odeskoho Universytetu, 2012).
100. Russian imperial historians continued to be divided in their attitude toward the role of the Cossacks in Russian history: one can compare, for example, the views of Mykola (Nikolai) Kostomarov and Sergei Soloviov.
101. J. Jurecki, "Uwagi nad dziełem: 'Najazdy Hajdamaków na Zachodnia Ukraine w XVIII wieku,'" *Tygodnik Peterzsburski* 45 (15–27 czerwca 1845): 289–92.
102. Kravchenko, *Narysy*; P. Bushkovitch, "The Ukraine in Russian Culture 1790–1860: The Evidence of the Journals," *Jahrbücher für Geschichte Osteuropas, Neue Folge* 39, no. 3 (1991): 339–63.
103. Rossiiskii Gosudarstvennyi Istoricheskii Arkhiv, B. 772. op. I., d. 1670, ll. 40–44.
104. V. Belinskii, *Sobranie sochinenii v 9 tomakh*, vol. 5: *Statti, recenzii i zametki, aprel 1842–noiabr 1843* (Moskva: Khudozhestvennaia Literatura, 1979).
105. V.V. Kravchenko, "Nikolai Polevoi i zvychaina skhema ruskoi istorii," in *Ukraina, imperia, Rossia* (Kyiv: Krytyka), 355–68.
106. N. Barsukov, *Zhizn i trudy M. P. Pogodina*, vol. 1 (St. Petersburg, 1888), 153–54; V. Lytvyn, ed., *Ukraina i Rosiia v istorychnii retrospektyvi* (Kyiv, 2004), 1, 343.
107. L. Gorizontov, "The 'Great Circle' of Interior Russia: Representations of the Imperial Center in the Nineteenth and Early Twentieth Centuries," in *Russian Empire. Space, People, Power, 1700–1930*, ed. J. Burbank, M. von Hagen, and A. Remnev (Bloomington: Indiana University Press, 2007), 67–93; M.V. Loskoutova, "A Motherland with a Radius of 300 Miles: Regional Identity in Russian Secondary and Post-Elementary Education from the Early Nineteenth Century to the War and Revolution," *European Review of History* 91 (2002), 7–22.
108. *Kyrylo-Mefodiivske Tovarystvo*, vol. 1 (Kyiv: Naukova Dumka, 1990), 152–69.
109. Z. Kohut, "The Development of a Ukrainian National Historiography in Imperial Russia," in *Historiography of Imperial Russia: The Profession and Writing of History in a Multinational State*, ed. T. Sanders (Armonk: M.E. Sharpe, 1999), 468.

Bibliography

Adadurov, V. 2006. "Dosvid istrorychnoho uiavlennia: uriad Napoleona i pro ukrainski zemli Rosiiskoi imperii." *Eidos* 2: 405–28.

———. 2006. "Ukrainske kozatstvo v uiavi frantsuzkoho uriadu doby Napoleona." *Ukraina v Tsentralno-Skhidnii Evropi (z naidavnishykh chasiv do kintsia XVIII st.)* 6: 398, 409.

———. 2007. *"Napoleonida" na Skhodi Evropy: Uiavlennia, proekty ta diialnist uriadu Frantsii shchodo pivdenno-zakhidnykh okrain Rosiiskoi imperii na pochatku XIX st.* Lviv: Vydavnytstvo UKU.

Agnew, J.A. 1998. *Geopolitics: Re-visioning World Politics*. London/New York: Routledge.

Anonymous. 1848. *Zamechania, do Maloi Rossii prinadlezhashchie*. Moskva: Chteniia v Obshchestve istorii i drevnostei rossiiskikh.

———. 1983. "Satyra na Slobozhan." In *Ukrainska literatura XVIII stolittia: Poetychni tvory, dramatychni tvory, prozovi tvory*, 215–16. Kyiv: Dnipro.

Armstrong, J.A. 1992. "Myth and History in the Evolution of Ukrainian Consciousness." In *Ukraine and Russia in Their Historical Encounter*, ed. P.J. Potichnyj, J. Pelenski, M. Raeff, and G.N. Zekulin, 125–39. Edmonton: CIUS Press.

Bagalei, D.I. and D.P. Miller. 1912. *Istoria goroda Kharkova za 250 let iego sushchestvovaniia, Istoricheskaia monografia*. Vols. 1–2. Kharkov: Zilberberg & Sons.

Bahro, S. 2013. "Uiavlennia pro kozatsku vitchyznu v suchasnii istoriohrafii." *Naukovi Zapusky NaUKMA. Istorychni nauky* 143: 48–54.

Barsukov, N. 1888. *Zhizn i trudy M. P. Pogodina, v 22 tomakh*. Vol. 1. St. Petersburg: Stasiulevich.

Bassin, M. 1991. "Russia between Europe and Asia." *Slavic Review* 50, no. 1: 4.

Belinskii, V. 1979. *Sobranie sochinenii v 9 tomakh*, vol. 5: *Statti, recenzii i zametki, aprel 1842–noiabr 1843*. Moskva: Khudozhestvennaia Literatura.

Berezhnaya, L. 2010. "'Kazacki bastion' 17 veka—vzgliad snaruzhi i iznutri." In *Religion und Integration im Moskauer Russland. Konzepte und Praktiken, Potentiale und Grenzen. 14.–17. Jahrhundert*, ed. L. Steindorff, 269–97. Wiesbaden: Harassowitz Verlag.

Berger, S. 2017. "History Writing and Constructions of National Space: The Long Dominance of the National in Modern European Historiographies." In *Palgrave Handbook of Research in Historical Culture and Education*, ed. M. Carretero, S. Berger, and M. Grever, 44. Basingstoke: Palgrave Macmillan UK.

Berlinskii, M. 1844. "Neskolko glav iz sochinenia 'Istoricheskoe obozrenie Malorossii i goroda Kieva.'" In *Molodyk na 1844 god*, 188. Sankt Peterburg: Ukrainskii literaturnyi sbornik.

Bilenky, S. 2007. *Eastern Europe in Search of a Nation: Romantic Nationalism and Imagined Communities in Ukraine, Poland, and Russia, 1830s–1840s*. Toronto: University of Toronto Press.

———. 2012. *Romantic Nationalism in Eastern Europe: Russian, Polish, and Ukrainian Political Imaginations*. Stanford: Stanford University Press.

———. 2013. "The Ukrainian National Movement in the Nineteenth Century: Context, Timing, Issues." In *Fashioning Modern Ukraine: Selected Writings of Mykola Kostomarov, Volodymyr Antonovych, and Mykhailo Drahomanov*, ed. S. Bilenky, XIII–XLVI. Edmonton: CIUS Press.

Bojanowska, E. 2007. *Nikolai Gogol between Ukrainian and Russian Nationalism*. Cambridge, MA: Harvard University Press.
Burbank, J. and M. von Hagen. 2007. "Coming into the Territory: Uncertainty and Empire." In *Russian Empire: Space, People, Power, 1700–1930*, ed. J. Burbank, M. von Hagen, and A.V. Remnev, 1–32. Bloomington: Indiana University Press.
Bushkovitch, P. 1991. "The Ukraine in Russian Culture 1790–1860: The Evidence of the Journals." *Jahrbücher für Geschichte Osteuropas, Neue Folge* 39, no. 3: 339–63.
"Delo kancelarii Ministerstva narodnogo prosveshchenia po Glavnomu upravleniu tcenzury po pis'mu g. Kievskogo voennogo i Volynskogo general-gubernatora." *Rossiiskii Gosudarstvennyi Istoricheskii Arkhiv*, B.772. op. I.,d. 1670, ll. 40–44.
Deszczyńska, M. 2001. "Wyobrażenie przedmurza w piśmiennictwie schyłku polskiego oświęcenia." *Przegląd Historyczny* 92, no. 3: 289.
Engel, J. Ch. 1796. *Geschichte der Ukraine und der ukrainischen Cosaken, wie auch der Königreiche Halitsch und Wladimir*. Halle: Johann Jacob Gebauer.
———. 2014. *Istoriia Ukrainy ta ukrainskykh kozakiv*. Kharkiv: Fakt.
Evgenii (Bolkhovitinov), I. 1825. *Opisanie Kievosofiiskogo sobora i Kievskoi eparkhii*. Kiev: Tipografiia Kievo-Pecherskoi Lavry.
Frazier, M. 1999. "Space and Genre in Gogol's Arabeski Source." *Slavic and East European Journal* 43, no. 3: 452–70.
Gerus, O.W. 1986. "Manifestations of the Cossack Idea in Modern Ukrainian History: The Cossack Legacy and Its Impact." *Ukrainskyi Istoryk* 1–2: 22–39.
Glaser, A.M. 2016. *Stories of Khmelnytsky: Competing Literary Legacies of the 1648 Ukrainian Cossack Uprising*. Stanford: Stanford University Press.
Gorizontov, L. 2007. "The 'Great Circle' of Interior Russia: Representations of the Imperial Center in the Nineteenth and Early Twentieth Centuries." In *Russian Empire. Space, People, Power, 1700–1930*, ed. J. Burbank, M. von Hagen, and A. Remnev, 67–93. Bloomington: Indiana University Press.
———. 2016. "Podneprovie i Severnoie Prichernomorie v mnogotomnykh opisaniakh Rossiiskoi Imperii rubezha XIX–XX vekov: terminologicheskie aspekty." *Slavianovedenie* 3: 72–77.
Gorlenko [Horlenko], V. 1893. "Iz istorii iuzhno-russkogo obshchestva nachala XIX veka (Pisma V. I. Chernysha, A. I. Chepy, V. G. Poletiki i zapiski k nim)." *Kievskaia starina* 1: 53.
Grob, T. 2008. "Mazepa as a Symbolic Figure of Ukrainian Autonomy." In *Democracy and Myth in Russia and Eastern Europe*, ed. A. Wöll and H. Wydra, 79–97. London/New York: Routledge.
Hal, B. 2008. "'Ne ustupat ni na odin shag zemli!': Do istorii rozmezhuvannia malorosiiskykh namisnytstv i Novorosiiskoi hubernii (1782–1783 rr.)." *Istoriia i kultura Prydniprovia: Nevidomi ta malovidomi storinky: Naukovyi shchorichnyk* 5: 99–129.
———. 2013. "Geocontsept 'Malorosia' na mentalnykh mapakh XVIII—pershoi polovyny XIX st." *Eidos* 7: 93–109.
Halushko, K. 2013. *Ukraina na karti Evropy: Ukraina ta ukraintsi u kartohrafii vid Antychnosti do XX stolittia*. Kyiv: Kyivskyi Universytet.
———. 2017. *Rus-Malorosia-Ukraina: nazva i terytoria*. Kyiv: Likbez.
Hen-Konarski, T. 2015. "No Longer Just Peasants and Priests: The Most Recent Studies on Nation Building in Nineteenth-Century Ukraine." *European History Quarterly* 45, no. 4: 713–37.

Hrabowych, H. 1997. *Do istorii ukrainskoi literatury.* Kyiv: Krytyka.
Hrytsak, I. 2011. *Strasti za natsionalismom. Stara istoria na novyi lad: Esei.* Kyiv: Krytyka.
Iakovenko, N. 2001. "Kilka sposterezhen nad modyfikatsiamy ukrainskoho natsionalnoho mifu v istoriohrafii." *Dukh i Litera* 3–4. Retrieved 18 March 2018 from http://www.ukrhistory.narod.ru/texts/yakovenko-5.htm.
———. 2002. "Ukraina mizh Skhodom i Zakhodom: proekcia odniei idei." In *Paralelnyi svit: doslidzhennia z istorii uiavlen ta idei v Ukraini XVI–XVII st.*, ed. N. Iakovenko, 333–65. Kyiv: Krytyka.
———. 2009. "Choice of Name versus Choice of Path: The Names of Ukrainian Territories from the Late Sixteenth to the Late Seventeenth Century." In *Laboratory of Transnational History*, ed. G. Kasianov and P. Ther, 117–48. Budapest: CEU Press.
Ias, O. 2006. "Doslidnytskyi instrumentarii ta intelektualni zasady 'Istorii Malorossii' Mykoly Markevycha." *Ukrainskyi istorychnyi zhurnal* 1: 27–42.
Istoria Rusov ili Maloi Rossii. 1846. Moskva: Chtenia v obshchestve istorii i drevnosti rossiiskikh.
Jurecki, J. 1845. "Uwagi nad dziełem: 'Najazdy Hajdamaków na Zachodnia Ukraine w XVIII wieku.'" *Tygodnik Peterzsburski* 45: 289–92.
Kappeler, A. 2011. "Hromadianska chy etnichna natsia? Zauvahy z teorii ta istoriohrafii." In *Ukraina: Protsesy natsiotvorennia*, ed. A. Kappeler, 13–30. Kyiv: K.I.C.
Karazin, V. 1910. *Sochineniia, pisma i bumagi.* Kharkov: Izdatelstvo Kharkovskago Universiteta.
Kasianov, G. and P. Ther, eds. 2009. *Laboratory of Transnational History.* Budapest: CEU Press.
Kohut, Z.E. 1977. "Myths Old and New: The Haidamak Movement and the Koliivshchyna (1768) in Recent Historiography." *Harvard Ukrainian Studies* 1, no. 3: 359–38.
———. 1986. "The Development of a Little Russian Identity and Ukrainian Nation-Building." *Harvard Ukrainian Studies* 10, nos. 3–4: 559–76.
———. 1988. *Russian Centralism and Ukrainian Autonomy: Imperial Absorption of the Hetmanate, 1760's–1830's.* Cambridge, MA: Harvard University Press.
———. 1999. "The Development of a Ukrainian National Historiography in Imperial Russia." In *Historiography of Imperial Russia. The Profession and Writing History in a Multinational State*, ed. T. Sanders, 453–77. Armonk: M.E. Sharpe.
———. 2001. "Origins of the Unity Paradigm: Ukraine and the Construction of Russian National History (1620–1860)." *Eighteenth-Century Studies* 35, no. 1: 70–76.
———. 2009–2010. "Mazepa's Ukraine: Understanding Cossack Territorial Vistas." *Harvard Ukrainian Studies* 31: 1–28.
———. 2011. "Kordony Ukrainy: terytorialni vizii kozakiv vid hetmana B. Khmelnytskoho do hetmana I. Samoilovycha." *Ukrainskyi istorychnyi zhurnal* 3: 50–73.
Kolstø, P. 2005. "Assessing the Role of Historical Myths in Modern Society." In *Myths and Boundaries in South-Eastern Europe*, ed. P. Kolstø, 1–34. London: Hurst.
Kornblatt, J. 1992. *The Cossack Hero in Russian Literature.* Madison: University of Wisconsin Press.
Kotenko, A.L. 2010. "Construction of Ukrainian National Space by the Intellectuals of Russian Ukraine, 1860–70s." In *Mapping Eastern Europe*, ed. J. Happel and C. Werdt, 37–60. Münster: LIT Verlag.

Kotenko, A.L., O.V. Martynuk, and A.I. Miller. 2010. "'Maloross': evoliutsia poniatia do Pervoi mirovoi voiny." *Novoe Literaturnoe Obozrenie* 108: 9–27.

Kovalchuk, A. 2017. *Narrating the National Future: The Cossacks in Ukrainian and Russian Romantic Literature.* Ph.D. diss., University of Oregon.

Kravchenko, V.V. 1996. *Narysy z ukrainskoi istoriohrafii epokhy natsionalnoho Vidrodzhennia (druha polovyna XVIII—seredyna XIX st.).* Kharkiv: Osnova.

———. 2009. "Do problemy otsinky reform v ukrainskii istorychnii dumtsi druhoi polovyny XVIII st." In *Poklykannia, Zbirnyk prats na poshanu profesora, o. Iuria Mytsyka*, ed. P. Sokhan, A. Boiko, and V. Brekhunenko, 372–82. Kyiv: Instytut Ukrainskoi arkheohrafii ta dzhereloznavstva.

———. 2010. *Kharkiv/Kharkov: stolitsa pogranichia.* Vilnius: EHU Press.

———. 2011. "Ivan Mazepa v ukrainskii istorychnii literaturi XVIII ta pershoi chverti XIX st." In *Ukraina, imperia, Rossia. Vybrani statti z modernoi istorii ta istoriohrafii*, 277–98. Kyiv: Krytyka.

———. 2011. "Nikolai Polevoi i zvychaina skhema ruskoi istorii." In *Ukraina, imperia, Rossia. Vybrani statti z modernoi istorii ta istoriohrafii*, 355–68. Kyiv: Krytyka.

Kvitka-Osnovianenko, H. 1981. *Zibrannia tvoriv u semy tomakh*, vol. 7: *Istorychni, etnohrafichni, literaturno-publitsystychni statti, lysty.* Kyiv: Naukova dumka.

Lawaty, A. 2015. "The Figure of Antemurale in the Historiography." In *East and Central European History Writing in Exile 1939–1989*, ed. M. Zadencka, A. Plakans, and A. Lawaty, 360–74. Leiden: Brill.

Lindheim, R. and G.S.N. Luckyi, eds. 1996. *Towards an Intellectual History of Ukraine: An Anthology of Ukrainian Thought from 1710 to 1995.* Toronto: University of Toronto Press.

Loskoutova, M.V. 2002. "A Motherland with a Radius of 300 Miles: Regional Identity in Russian Secondary and Post-Elementary Education from the Early Nineteenth Century to the War and Revolution." *European Review of History* 91: 7–22.

Lytvyn, V. and V. Smolii, eds. 2004. *Ukraina i Rosiia v istorychnii retrospektyvi: Narysy v 3-kh tomakh*, vol. 1: *Ukrainski proekty v Rosiiskii imperii.* Kyiv: Naukova dumka.

Maksimovich, M.A. 1877. *Sobranie sochinenii.* 2 vols. Kiev: M.P. Fritz.

Malashevych, A. 2003. "Borotba za 'ruske pervorodstvo (z istorii naukovoi dyskusii 'iuzhan' i 'severian' u vysvitlenni chasopysu 'Vestnik Evropy')." *Problemy istorii Ukrainy XIX– pochatku XX st.* 6: 383–94.

Markevich, N. 1842–1843. *Istoriia Malorossii.* 5 vols. Moskva: August Semen.

Markovich, I. 1798. *Zapiski o Malorossii, ee zhiteliakh i proizvedeniakh.* Part 1. Sankt Peterburg: Gubernia.

Masliichuk, V. 2007. *Provintsia na perekhresti kultur. Doslidzhennia z istorii Slobidskoi Ukrainy XVII—XIX st.* Kharkiv: Pryvatnyi Muzei Miskoi Sadyby.

———. 2009. *Kozatska starshyna slobidskykh polkiv druhoi polovyny XVII—pershoi tretyny XVIII st.* Kharkiv: Pryvatnyi Muzei Miskoi Sadyby.

———. 2011. "'Vid Ukrainy do Malorosii': Regionalni nazvy ta natsionalna istoria." In *Ukraina: Protsesy natsiotvorennia*, ed. A. Kappeler, 229–45. Kyiv: K.I.C.

Miller, A. 2003. *The Ukrainian Question: The Russian Empire and Nationalism in the Nineteenth Century.* Budapest: CEU Press.

———. 2008. *The Romanov Empire and Nationalism: Essays in the Methodology of Historical Research.* Budapest: CEU Press.

Müller, J.J. 1996. "Istorychna dysertacia pro kozakiv, jaku predstavleno u prymishchenni filosofs'koho fakul'tetu na publichnyj rozhliad pid holovuvanniam messiar Hotfrida Weifa z Toruni u Prusii." *Kyivska Starovyna* 4–5: 67–81.
Nalyvaiko, D. 1998. *Ochyma Zakhodu: retseptsia Ukrainy v Zakhidnii Evropi XI–XVIII st.* Kyiv: Osnovy.
———. 2002. "Nimetsko-ukrainski vzaiemyny XVIII st.: retseptsia Ukrainy v Nimechyni, ii etapy i tendentsii." *Magisterium, Literaturoznavchi studii* 8: 95.
Narezhnyi, V.T. 1983. *Sobranie sochinenii v 2 tomakh*, vol. 2: *Bursak*. Moskva: Khudozhestvennaia Literatura.
Neumann, I. 1999. *Uses of the Other. "The East" in European Identity Formation.* Minneapolis: University of Minnesota Press.
Nevolnichenko, S. 2008. "Mir i antimir v povesti N.V. Gogolia 'Taras Bulba.'" *Voprosy Literatury* 4: 241–63.
Noveyshii i polnyii geograficheskii slovar. Part 2. Moskva, 1788.
Novikova, L. 2012. *"Istoriohraf" Pivdennoi Ukrainy Apollon Skalkovskyi: intelektualna apolohia imperskoi polityky ta regionalnoi samobutnosti.* Odesa: Vydavnytstvo Odeskoho Universytetu.
Orlai, I. 1826. "O Iugo-Zapadnoi Rusii (pismo iz Nezhyna k sekretariu Obshchesna)." *Trudy i Zapiski Obshchesnva Istorii i Drevnostei Rossiiskikh* 3, no. 1: 227.
Østbø, J. 2016. *The New Third Rome. Readings of a Russian Nationalist Myth.* Stuttgart: Verlag.
Plokhy, S. 1994. "Historical Debates and Territorial Claims: Cossack Mythology in the Russian-Ukrainian Border Dispute." In *The Legacy of History in Russia and the New States of Eurasia*, ed. S.F. Starr, 147–70. Armonk: M.E. Sharpe.
———. 2006. *The Origins of the Slavic Nations: Premodern Identities in Russia, Ukraine, and Belarus.* Cambridge: Cambridge University Press.
———. 2006. "Ukraine or Little Russia? Revisiting an Early Nineteenth-Century Debate." *Canadian Slavonic Papers* 48, no. 34: 348, 351.
———. 2012. *The Cossack Myth: History and Nationhood in the Age of Empires.* Cambridge: Cambridge University Press.
Poletika, G. 1858. "Vozrazhenie deputata Grigoriia Poletiki na Nastavlenie Malorossiiskoi kollegii gospodinu zh deputatu Dmitriiu Natalinu." *Chteniia v Obshchestve istorii i drevnostei rossiiskikh* 3: 1–102.
Polunin, F. and G. Miller. 1773. *Geograficheskii leksikon Rossiiskogo gosudarstva.* Moskva: Izdatelstvo Moskovskogo Universiteta.
Prymak, T. 2014. "The Cossack Hetman: Ivan Mazepa in History and Legend from Peter to Pushkin." *The Historian* 76, no. 2: 237–77.
Remy, J. 2016. *Brothers or Enemies. The Ukrainian National Movement and Russia, from the 1840s to the 1870s.* Toronto: University of Toronto Press.
Roginskii, A.B. 1986. *Russkie istoricheskie povesti pervoi poloviny XIX veka.* Moskva: Khudozhestvennaia literatura.
Rudnytsky, I.L. 1987. *Essays in Modern Ukrainian History.* Edmonton: CIUS Press.
Saunders, D. 1985. *The Ukrainian Impact on Russian Culture: 1750–1850.* Edmonton: CIUS Press.
Schérer, J.-B. 1788. *Annales de la Petite-Russie; ou Histoire des Cosaques-Saporogues et des Cosaques de l'Ukraine, ou de la Petite-Russie, depuis leur origine jusqu'à nos*

jours; suivie d'un abrégé de l'histoire des hettmans des Cosaques, & des pièces justificatives. Paris: Cachet.

———. 1994. *Litopys Malorosii abo Istoria kozakiv-zaporozhtsiv ta kozakiv Ukrainy, abo Malorosii.* Kyiv: Ukrainskyi pysmennyk.

Schöpflin, G. 1997. "The Functions of Myth and a Taxonomy of Myths." In *Myths and Nationhood*, ed. G. Schopflin and G. Hosking, 19–24. London/New York: Routledge.

Schöpflin, G. and G. Hosking, eds. 1997. *Myths and Nationhood.* London: Hurst.

Shafonskii, A. 1851. *Chernihovskoho namestnichestva topohraficheskoe opisanie.* Kiev: Izdatelstvo Kievskogo Universiteta.

Simonovskii [Symonovskyi], P. 1847. *Kratkoe opisanie o kazatskom malorossiiskom narode i o ego voennykh delakh.* Moskva: Moskovskoe obshchestvo istorii i drevnostei rossiiskih.

Skinner, B. 2005. "Borderlands of Faith: Reconsidering the Origins of a Ukrainian Tragedy." *Slavic Review* 64, no. 1: 88–116.

Smith, A.D. 1999. *Myths and Memories of the Nation.* Oxford: Oxford University Press.

Sochinenia i perevody, k polze iuveseleniiu sluzhashchie. May etc., 1760.

Sokhan, P.S. 1990. *Kyrylo-Mefodiivs'ke Tovarystvo.* Vol. 1. Kyiv: Naukova Dumka.

Sysyn, F. 1986. "Concepts of Nationhood in Ukrainian History Writing, 1620–1690." *Harvard Ukrainian Studies* 10, nos. 3–4: 393–423.

———. 1991. "The Reemergence of the Ukrainian Nation and Cossack Mythology." *Social Research* 58, no. 4: 845–64.

———. 2002. "Spodivani ukraintsi." *Krytyka: Retsenzii, esei, ohliady* 5: 17–21.

Szporluk, R. 1997. "Ukraine: From an Imperial Periphery to a Sovereign State." *Daedalus* 126, no. 3: 85–120.

———. 2008–2009. "Mapping Ukraine: From Identity Space to Decision Space." *Journal of Ukrainian Studies* 33–34: 441–52.

———. 2009. "The Western Dimension of the Making of Modern Ukraine." In *Contemporary Ukraine on the Cultural Map of Europe*, ed. L.M.L. Zaleska-Onyshkevych and M. Revakovych, 3–17. Armonk: M.E. Sharpe.

Tazbir, J. 2005. "The Bulwark Myth." *Acta Poloniae Historica* 91: 73–97.

Tolochko, A. 2012. *Kievskaia Rus i Malorossia v XIX veke.* Kyiv: Laurus.

Tychka, H.-M. 2016. "Idea peredmuria Evropy v ukrainsko-polskomu protystoianni za Skhidnu Halychynu pid chas Paryzkoi myrnoi konferentsii." *Viiskovo-naukovyi visnyk* 25: 182–97.

Ukrainska literatura XVIII stolittia: Poetychni tvory, dramatychni tvory, prozovi tvory. 1983. Kyiv: Dnipro.

Velychenko, S. 1992. *National History as Cultural Process: A Survey of the Interpretations of Ukraine's Past in Polish, Russian, and Ukrainian Historical Writing from the Earliest Times to 1914.* Edmonton: CIUS Press.

Vyrskyi, D. 2008. *Richpospolytska istoriohrafia Ukrainy (XV—seredyna XVII st.).* 2 vols. Kyiv: Instytut Istorii Ukrainy.

Wilson, A. 1997. "Myths on National History in Belarus and Ukraine." In *Myths and Nationhood*, ed. G. Schöpflin and G.G. Hosking, 182–97. New York: Routledge in association with the School of Slavonic and East European Studies, University of London.

Woldan, A. 2012. "The Notion of *Antemurale Christianitatis* in Connection with the City of Lemberg/Lwów/Lviv." *Studi Slavistici* 9, no. 1: 53–69.

Wolff, L. 1994. *Inventing Eastern Europe. The Map of Civilization on the Mind of the Enlightenment.* Stanford: Stanford University Press.

———. 2010. *The Idea of Galicia: History and Fantasy in Habsburg Political Culture.* Stanford: Stanford University Press.

Wydra, H. 2008. "Introduction. Democracy in Eastern Europe—Myth and Reality." In *Democracy and Myth in Russia and Eastern Europe*, ed. A. Wöll and H. Wydra, 1–24. London/New York: Routledge.

Yoon, S. 2005. "Transformation of a Ukrainian Cossack into a Russian Warrior: Gogols 1842 'Taras Bulba.'" *Slavic and East European Journal* 49, no. 3: 430–44.

Wöll, A. and H. Wydra, eds. 2008. *Democracy and Myth in Russia and Eastern Europe.* London/New York: Routledge.

Zarycki, T. 2014. *Ideologies of Eastness in Central and Eastern Europe.* London: Routledge.

Zorin, A. 2001. *Kormia dvuglavogo orla. Literatura i gosudarstvennaia ideologia v Rossii v poslednei treti XVIII-pervoi treti XIX veka.* Moskva: Novoe literaturnoe obozrenie.

CHAPTER 9

Translating the Border(s) in a Multilingual and Multiethnic Society
Antemurale *Myths in Polish and Ukrainian Schoolbooks of the Habsburg Monarchy*

Philipp Hofeneder

Myths are an important part not only of creating one's own worldview but also of creating borders with respect to alleged differing religions, cultures, and political entities.[1] A classic example in this respect is the concept of *antemurale christianitatis*. This mythic narrative on bulwarks, which was born in the fifteenth century and reached its peak in the sixteenth and seventeenth centuries, established a huge religious demarcation line. Myths connected to the bulwark trope seem to be clearly situated and contain two more or less opposing positions encompassing two relatively independent and differing cultural or religious communities. While politically unifying against an external enemy, these myths clearly also functioned as an internal mobilizer. In many cases they consisted of repeated elements, such as an alleged historical beginning and unique characteristics.[2]

The situation changed fundamentally with the emergence of nation-states beginning at the end of the eighteenth century. From then on, myths consisted not of one general myth but of a whole bundle of myths, which might also create a bundle of borders. This even holds true for societies (not to mention nations) that were characterized by differing ethnic groups. Therefore, myths connected to the concept of *antemurale christianitatis* subsequently changed in the course of history, from a cultural and/or religious myth concerning two strictly disconnected cultural or political entities, to a discourse conducted by representatives from differing but also neighboring cultures and even agents of the same society.[3]

In the course of this chapter, I will highlight some core problems of these modern national bulwark myths in a traditional multilingual and multiethnic society. Although there is little or no doubt among researchers about what these nationalized *antemurale* myths looked like,[4] I will take a closer look at how these new myths developed, how they were communicated, and how they interacted with other myths.[5] My focus lies not on the consistency of these myths but on the channels through which they were communicated. This is in line with recent developments in research, which place stronger focus on the agents of cultural exchange.[6] Who formulated these myths? How did they take root in society? Were they altered in the course of their spread? Are there any differences between the original formulation and the popular forms? Questions about their verbal dissemination and the possible ways of societal dissemination come to the fore.

While, originally, bulwark myths united several cultures and were religiously motivated, they were increasingly integrated into the emerging national movements in the nineteenth century.[7] It therefore seems to be important to examine how existing myths were prepared so that they fitted into regional and/or (emerging) national cultures. While examining written and published documents, such as primers and other schoolbooks, we have to be aware that they can be treated only as a point of departure. Subsequently, it was the teachers who reformulated the content with respect to their own political beliefs.

The starting point of my considerations will be the educational system of the Habsburg monarchy, with special reference to the crownland Galicia after 1848. Concentrating on two big ethnic groups, the Poles and the Ukrainians, I would like to show how myths were shaped through mutual interaction. It will then be possible to demonstrate that in the course of the 1860s a modern set of ideas connected to the *antemurale* myths was already emerging, which was closely connected to the birth of a Ukrainian political party that spread the belief that Ukrainian culture is independent from Russian culture.[8]

Schoolbooks are a useful source in this respect for several reasons. Immediately after 1848, when several languages were implemented in the educational system (*landesübliche Sprachen*), a huge number of schoolbooks, primers, anthologies, and grammars were published. All too often, they were initially written in German and only afterward translated into one of the nine other officially recognized languages. In some cases, we know there were secondhand translations, when schoolbooks originally written in German were translated into Polish and only afterward unofficially translated into Ukrainian.

Communication of History

The educational system in the Habsburg monarchy played an important role in the spreading of political and historical myths. Closely connected to this question is book production in general. What did the production of books in these languages look like? Were there enough printing houses? How did censorship work?[9]

With respect to the Ukrainians in the Habsburg monarchy, most of the abovementioned factors changed dramatically after 1848. First, after the revolution of 1848, instruction in Galician schools was conducted in Ukrainian for the first time in all relevant subjects. Up to 1848, this had taken place only in the subjects of Ukrainian (or "Ruthenian" as it was called then) and religion. Of course, it took some years to implement this legal requirement. As a result of the absence of Ukrainian schoolbooks and of trained teachers and the fact that the Ukrainian language itself had to develop with respect to terminology, German (and to a lesser extent Polish) still dominated in Galicia in the first years after 1848.[10]

Regarding the overall distribution of books, the situation in the 1850s still needed to be improved. From 1848 to 1860, a total of 864 books, brochures, newspapers, and the like were published in Ukrainian in the Habsburg monarchy.[11] More than 60 percent of the production was concentrated in Lviv. Another issue was the omnipresent censorship, which, as I will argue later, was double-sided in the Ukrainian case. But even books that were not censored and could be printed (even in comparatively high circulations) often did not sell. From Iakiv Holovatskyi's well-known 1848 Ukrainian grammar with a print run of 10,000 copies, only 600 were sold due to problems within the distribution network.[12] In this respect, schoolbooks are of central relevance.

The Significance of Schoolbooks for the Spreading of Myths

First, schoolbooks are part of everyday culture, which gives us an immediate impression of how a society is structured.[13] In comparison to other publications, schoolbooks often had an impressive circulation even at the time: 5,000, 10,000, and even as many as 20,000 copies of one Ukrainian schoolbook were not uncommon.[14] They were distributed all over Galicia, as they were compulsory reading at schools. As early as the 1850s, almost 10 percent of all book production consisted of schoolbooks, which made them an important contribution to the overall production numbers.[15] Like every other official publication, schoolbooks had to undergo multistage censorship. Depending on the type of schoolbook, they received the imprimatur from the ministry of education in Vienna or the Galician education board, which Poles had dominated since at least 1867. Once the newer books were approved for schools, the older, previously approved books had to be discontinued. Thus we can be sure that current schoolbooks were used in classes, although we know of several cases in which teachers received a warning for using older or even unapproved books.[16]

Authors of schoolbooks were all too often prominent figures of the national revivals. Oleksandr Barvinskyi (1847–1926), Iakiv Holovastkyi (1844–1888), Vasyl Kovalskyi (1826–1911), Omelian Ohonovskyi (1833–1894), Omelian Partytskyi (1840–1895), Markiian Shashkevych (1811–1843), and Ivan Verchratskyi (1818–1891), just to name a few, were better known for their political work and/or their achievements in science. In fact, we do not know of any women authors of Galician schoolbooks.

Holovatskyi was the first to become a professor of Ukrainian language and literature in 1849; he also became the principal of the University of Lviv. He was a member of the state-sponsored commission that was responsible for the translation of laws into Ukrainian as well as for the compilation of a legal dictionary.[17] Vasyl Kovalskyi was a well-known lawyer and deputy to the Galician parliament as well as to the Austrian parliament. The other authors listed above also worked in important and influential positions in addition to writing books.

More than 500 schoolbooks in Ukrainian were approved between 1848 and 1918.[18] It is worth noting that the content of schoolbooks often changed only superficially. That is why a lot of text appears in different schoolbooks over a long period, being adjusted only to the political views of the editor(s). Authors could normally be connected with a certain political party. Nevertheless, authors of a new generation preferred to republish these texts and adjust them to their own political views rather than write them completely anew. This and the fact that particularly anthologies for the subject "Ukrainian" gathered texts that were initially published in completely different contexts—such as newspapers, fictional literature, or publications from Russian-dominated Ukraine—allow us to treat schoolbooks as a kind of panopticon of Ukrainian literature. That is why within a Ukrainian context, schoolbooks fulfill a rather unique position. At least during the first years after 1848, they had been one of the most important forms for the distribution of myths in a written form.

For the present study, I take history schoolbooks and the anthologies mentioned above as an important point of reference. Immediately after 1848, there were only two kinds of history schoolbooks. First, books that contained so-called world history and dealt with history beyond the Habsburg monarchy. This includes works such as Antonín Gindely's *Lehrbuch der allgemeinen Geschichte für Ober-Gymnasien* (General History Textbook for Upper Schools) and Wilhelm Pütz's *Grundriss der Geographie und Geschichte der alten, mittlern und neuern Zeit* (An Overview of Geography and Ancient, Medieval, and Modern History).[19] Second were history schoolbooks that dealt exclusively with Habsburg history from an imperial position, so that these almost solely contained the Austrian parts of the monarchy (*Kernlande*). To a minor extent, they were also translated or rewritten in the officially acknowledged languages. Examples are Iulian Vyslobotskyi's (1819–1871) *Korotkyi ocherk istorii Avstriiskoi derzhavy* (Short Outline of the History of the Austrian State, 1855). In these first years after 1848, books with a national—that is, Ukrainian—point of view were not published.

Myths as a Part of Everyday Education

That is why Ukrainian history schoolbooks were uncommon immediately after 1848. Ukrainian myths spread in other books such as anthologies. These books, called *chytanky*, were a compilation of different texts for almost all school subjects. Although they were intended for Ukrainian language classes, they were undoubtedly also used in other classes.[20] The following passage is taken from Omelian Partytskyi's *Ruska chytanka dlia nyzhshych klias serednych shkil* (Ukrainian Primer for Lower Grades of Secondary Schools, 1871), which was part of a broader publication activity of the so-called *narodovci* (Populists).[21]

> By that the frontier guard of Rus was established, which from the very beginning had a holy task: to defend the borders of Rus against predacious attacks from Asiatic savages like the Mongols, Tatars, and any other Muslims, who nomadized and raided at the south-eastern borders of the Minor Rus.[22]

This fragment, titled *Pochatky kozachchyny* (The Origins of Cossackdom), reveals several typical approaches to the communication of historical myths at that time. First, Bohdan Didytskyi (1827–1909), the author of the text, was an exponent of the Russophiles and therefore stood in political and cultural opposition to Partytskyi, the editor of the anthology. This is also the reason why the text is signed with his initials only (B.D.). The fragment was presumably taken from his famous *Narodnaia Istoriia Rusi ot nachala do noveishych vremen* (National History of Rus from the Beginning to Recent Times), which was published as a book in 1870.[23] Partytskyi revised the text so that the populists could publish it. Removing the all too Russophile wording, a bundle of myths was left that could be seen as entirely Ukrainian. In this respect, the Cossacks worked solely as a bulwark toward the nonbelievers, wild Asiatic tribes that constantly attacked them. Irrespective of the revision of the text, several phrases remind us of the original idea of the author. It is sufficient to mention the use of Malaia Rus (the Little Russia), which indicates its Russophile origin. Beyond that, pupils aged ten to fourteen were confronted with the idea of the Cossacks as *pohranichna storozha* (a frontier guard) of the whole Rus. This statement had an obvious religious dimension, putting the Cossacks on the front line in the fight for civilization against barbarism. The exact wording of *kochuvaly* (nomadize) and *rozbiinychyly* (highwayman, predator) corresponds to similar myths in Western Europe.

The abovementioned fragment was based on myths that encompassed positions of the Russophiles as well as the populists. If we look at a history schoolbook published later, we see a very different approach. The following fragment is taken from the *Ruska chytanka dlia shkil vydilovych* (Ukrainian Primer for Secondary Schools), which was published anonymously in 1904 and was compiled for Polish and Ukrainian classes. The entire book was written in Ukrainian but was enlarged by dozens of footnotes, explaining words and phrases incomprehensible to Polish-speaking pupils.[24] Obviously, the author supported the populist movement, which was true of all authors of officially approved schoolbooks at that time.

> The famous Sich was a frontier guard which defended the freedom and faith of the Ukrainian people against the Tatars and Turks. . . . The Sich was a free society of knights. Everyone who valued his own faith was accepted, faithfully and earnestly served society and the elder Atamans and defended their faith and freedom. . . . They were of Greek faith: they saw the Mother of God as their patron and protector of the freedom and faith of the Zaporozhian Sich.[25]

While the overall orientation did not change, we see several revisions from Bohdan Didytskyi's 1871 version. As time went by, national myths could be expressed in more detail. We are dealing here with a typical bulwark myth adapted to the needs of the time. In the 1871 publication, the Cossacks function as a frontier guard for all of Rus; in the 1904 version, they defended only the Ukrainian people against the invaders. The Cossacks epitomized the frontier guard and were thus part of a bigger civilization in the former version. In the latter version, the conflicts were presented as a fight between the Sich and the raiding nonbelievers. From this point of view, the Cossacks were emancipated from being mere frontier guards to being nationalized guards of an independent and autonomous country. In this respect, Cossacks were seen as heroic and brave knights (*rycar* in the western Ukrainian form) who defended their faith and freedoms.

This comparison shows that in the course of the second half of the nineteenth century, bulwark myths did not change dramatically but were increasingly more detailed and were thus exploited by national movements. In 1904, it was not sufficient to draw a visible line between religious and cultural differences. Different cultural and political elements had to be included.

Nevertheless, bulwark myths were omnipresent in schoolbooks at that time, whether they were imperial ones written by German-speaking authors, Ukrainian, or, as the following example will show, Polish ones. Now I detail the extent to which they had to interact with already existing myths and how they were adapted to the needs of the relevant public.

Polish Myths as a Starting Point for Ukrainian Self-Conception

With the Austro-Hungarian Compromise of 1867, educational policy was transferred from the imperial capital to the crownland of Galicia. Only overall control stayed in Vienna. From this time on, questions concerning the foundation of schools, the language of instruction, and other important issues were under the supervision of the Galician educational board (German: *Landesschulrat*; Polish: *rada szkolna krajowa*).[26] This gave Polish authorities the opportunity to control important issues concerning education in Galicia. One of these issues was the approval of schoolbooks. Beyond that, they could support their own projects with financial contributions through the Galician parliament.

In this situation, Polish and Ukrainian educational issues were closely tied together. One interesting example with regard to the bulwark topic is a history schoolbook written by the famous Polish historian Anatol Lewicki (1841–1899). He was the son of a Greek Catholic priest and a Polish mother who studied at the University of Lviv. Afterward, he was engaged in pedagogical issues and worked at the regional department of the educational board. In 1883, he became professor of Austrian history at the Jagiellonian University in Cracow and full professor in 1887. From 1894 to 1895, he was dean of the philological department. Besides several book-length works, Lewicki was also the author of one of the most popular history schoolbooks at that time.

First published in 1884, his *Zarys historyi Polski i krajów ruskich z nią połączonych* (Outline of the History of Poland and Ruthenian Lands Connected to It) was republished several times and was used at Polish schools in Galicia even in the interwar period. This book deals with Polish history in its broadest sense from the very beginning to the end of the eighteenth century. A second edition was already published in 1888. Five years later, Lewicki published an abridged version, which I shall discuss later in detail.

After 1897, the book was again published in a revised and enlarged version that also encompassed the history after the partitioning of Poland.[27]

Lewicki's book was by no means the only history schoolbook, but it was a very important one for several reasons.[28] It was translated into Ukrainian and published as *Istoriia kraiu rodynnoho* (History of the Home Country, 1895). While prior to 1895 books for other subjects were already either officially translated from Polish into Ukrainian or via other languages,[29] Lewicki's book was the first history schoolbook translated directly from Polish. In what follows, I shall discuss why the book was translated into Ukrainian. Based on some fragments, I will show how the translator was able to transform the overall orientation so that this schoolbook could function as a Ukrainian history book.

As was common in the Habsburg monarchy at that time, history schoolbooks covered history and geography together. Pupils were thus confronted with historical events and geographical descriptions. As we can assume from the title itself, Lewicki's intention was to write a history of Poland in its broadest sense, encompassing the old Jagiellonian idea of a Polish state. A closer look at the table of contents seems to confirm our assumption. After a short geographical introduction titled *Przegląd geograficzny ziem dawnej Polski* (Geographical Survey of the Former Polish Lands) and two other short chapters about the Slavs' roots and their interdependence, *Początki Słowian* (Slavic Origins) and *Słowianie w stosunkach ze sąsiadami* (The Slavs in Their Relationship to Their Neighbors), the pupils learned about the formation of the Polish state.

While his overall historiographical approach is oriented toward the history of ruling dynasties, every chapter is expanded by several social, economic, and cultural aspects. In this respect, Lewicki aimed to write Polish history from a multilayered point of view, including different ethnic and social groups.

While there is no doubt that this history has to be understood as Polish, the author strongly criticizes major parts of Polish history.[30] One of the main reasons Poland lost its independence was not because of the aggression of neighboring states (which would have been difficult to express in an officially approved history schoolbook) but owing to the Polish gentry and several Polish kings and queens. In the passage about the liberum veto, we read that it was the higher nobility, the gentry, and even the ruling dynasties who damaged the Polish state. However, deputies from foreign countries played the most destructive role. For Lewicki, the liberum veto was an expression of the overall decline of Polish society.

As time went by, the situation in Poland became worse. In a rather open-minded way, Lewicki describes the ongoing decline of morality and patriotism. Further, the spreading of religious intolerance and the overall decline of public life were for Lewicki the main reasons for Poland's deterioration. The ongoing expansion toward the east, which was seen as the expansion of civilization, resulted in social and political troubles neglected by the state.

Translating Polish Cultural Borders

As we have seen, Anatol Lewicki presented Polish history in a critical way. We can assume that this was one of the major reasons it was later translated into Ukrainian. Another reason was the fact that Lewicki's edition of 1884 was revised and shortened. The second edition of 1893, which was the basis of the translation into Ukrainian, displays a new set of ideas. While the first edition put Polish history in the center and gathered the history of other nations or ethnic groups around it, in the second edition the reader was confronted with a Galician approach. Originally, Lewicki described history from the point of view of the ruling Polish dynasties such as the Piasts, the Jagiellonians, and the elective monarchy. Non-Polish elements were always presented only afterward. Now Polish and Ukrainian history were contrasted with one another and seen as two important parts. The overall wording hardly changed; nevertheless, Ukrainian history was now presented more as an integral part of Polish history, while Polish views and Polish kings and queens still took the leading role.

This Galician history schoolbook concentrated, therefore, on Polish and Ukrainian matters. In 1895, it was translated into Ukrainian under the title *Istoriia kraiu rodynnoho* (History of the Home Country), officially approved as a schoolbook and funded by the regional educational board. Ivan Matiiv (1859–1925), member of the board and school inspector for Galicia, functioned as a translator. In 1907, a Ukrainian version of the book was published in Kyiv.[31]

This suggests that the translation not only underwent the normal censorship practices but was generated under the direct survey of Polish censorship. Two different kinds of translations are known. Normally, German schoolbooks, published in Vienna, were translated into all or some of the officially acknowledged languages. Immediately after 1848, books for almost all subjects were translated, whereas new books were compiled only for the subjects Ukrainian and religion. The more the educational system was developed, the fewer books were translated. That is why Polish schoolbooks were often written by Polish authors instead of being translated.[32]

While books in Ukrainian were often translated from German due to the absence of original books, sometimes they were also translated directly from Polish. It even happened that a Ukrainian author had written a book in Polish prior to 1848 and only afterward translated it into Ukrainian.[33]

The third reason Lewicki's book was translated is that it could serve as the first history schoolbook without a solely imperial approach. As mentioned above, history schoolbooks were of the utmost importance and therefore were supposed to represent only the official history of the Habsburg monarchy, without considering regional or even national accounts. Therefore, there was no history schoolbook up to the 1890s that showed a clear Ukrainian perspective. Iulian Vyslobotskyi's book *Korotkyj ocherk istorii Avstriiskoi derzhavy* (A Short Outline of the History of Austrian State, 1855) mentioned above was predominantly about the Habsburg family. Only some minor passages had been added about Ukrainian history. Only the big anthologies from the Russophiles and populists reveal several texts with historical topics. Dmytro Vyntskovskyi's *Narys istorii avstriisko-uhorskoi monarchii* (Survey of the History of the Austro-Hungarian Monarchy, 1881) shows a similar approach. It was intended as a schoolbook for teachers. Other books, such as Omelian Barvinskyi's *Istoriia Rusi* (History of Rus, 1880) and *Iliustrovana Istoriia Rusi vid naidavniishych do nyniishnych chasiv* (Illustrated History of Rus from the Earliest to Recent Times, 1890), did not get approved. The first history schoolbook originally written in Ukrainian with a Ukrainian approach was Bohdan Barvinskyi's *Opovidannia z ridnoi istorii* (Tales from the Home Country), which was not published until 1911.[34]

The different titles of the individual books already show a clearly political motivation. While Polish books indicate the topic in their title (i.e., Polish history), Ukrainian schoolbook titles were normally limited to mere allusions. That is why pupils were not confronted with Ukrainian history but merely with the history of their home country or even with mere tales, as the title of Bohdan Barvinskyi's book suggests.

Nevertheless, Matiiv's translation showed several significant modifications and can therefore be seen as an attempt to rewrite Polish history as it was described by Lewicki. Some typical shifts occurred in the introductory chapter. The original *Przegląd geograficzny ziem dawnej Polski* (Geographical Survey of the Ancient Polish Lands) became *Ohliad geografichnyi zemel ruskych, polskych i lytovskych* (Geographical Survey of the Ukrainian, Polish, and Lithuanian Lands). "Ancient Poland" was now divided into three different parts, the Ruthenian, Polish, and Lithuanian lands. Subsequently, the whole book was rearranged. After some geographical and prehistorical introduction, the book started with the *Istoriia Rusi* (History of Rus) and not, as it had before, with Polish history and the founder of the first Polish state, Mieszko I. The translation started with Rurik and Oleh/Oleg and described eastern Slavic history up to the year 1387. Only then were pupils confronted with the *Istoriia Polshchy* (History of Poland) for the first time. The first seventy-five pages were exclusively dedicated to the history of Rus.

After some forty pages about Mieszko I, the second chapter of the book dealt with the formation of *derzhava lytovsko-rusko-polska* (the Lithuanian-Ukrainian-Polish state), as Matiiv then called *Rzeczpospolita Polska*.³⁵

A critical point, which was debated in several chapters of the book, concerns the heritage of Rus. Who becomes the legitimate successor of the first East Slavic state? Lewicki wrote about it extensively and concluded that only the principality of Galicia represented the legal heritage, while later developments, like the rise of Muscovy, were discounted as non-Slavic evolutions. In the original, we read:

> At the same time, explicit differences between the eastern and the western half of the state emerged, which then was called Rus. In the eastern half, non-Slavic people have always settled alongside Slavic people, who, after they were together with the Slavs subordinated by the eastern Slavic Varangians, took over from the Slavs not only their name, but also their language and had, under the same ruler, a common history with the Slavs. But the differences which existed between these and the native Slavs from Rus remained and later led to a political partition.³⁶

The most important myths with regard to the heavily intertwined history are collected in this short passage. For Lewicki, Rus was inhabited by Slavic and non-Slavic tribes. Rus broke up with the decline of Kyiv in the thirteenth century. For him, only the western part was the legitimate successor of the former Rus, which later became the Galician principality. The eastern part later became the principality of Muscovy, which lost its contacts with the civilized world.

Matiiv could easily build on Lewicki's historical construction. While Lewicki only afterward incorporated Ukrainian lands into Polish history (the relevant chapter came after the Polish ones), Matiiv achieved a huge effect by drawing this part to the front. At the same time, the actual wording almost stayed the same. Only some minor amendments occurred. The reference to the eastern, non-Slavic parts of Rus was underlined by adding that they were Finns and Chudes. Only in the translation was the Galician principality called *korinna Rus* (the indigenous Rus); this was to underline its importance in contrast to the former political and cultural center of Kyiv. Interestingly, Matiiv informed the reader that even after the decline of Kyiv, faith still unified the former parts of Rus, to establish another border toward the Polish culture. We read the following line in the translation: "But the difference between them existed at all times, and now, where the state of the Rurik dynasty is disintegrated, this difference has led to a complete division of these two parts so that only faith is still connecting them."³⁷ Matiiv adds a subordinate clause at the end of the sentence that is missing in the original. By that, the former Rus is described as culturally divided but still unified by religion, which makes it an important point of reference regarding Catholic Poland.

Matiiv broadened Lewicki's approach, which was his only possible way to alter the original. On the one hand, he took over those myths that would fit the Ukrainian point of view. On the other hand, he added some other myths, which were absent earlier. Of course, Matiiv could not express these new myths directly or in an elaborate style. He had to restrict himself to adding some words or phrases so that an attentive teacher could elaborate this position in class.[38] One such amendment that needed later clarification was the reference to faith, which still united the former parts of Rus— against Poland and Catholicism—which was not explicitly mentioned.

In this introductory chapter, Matiiv already tried to connect medieval history with the national approach of the nineteenth century. While it was not important for Lewicki whether the Varangians were of Slavic or non-Slavic origin, the translator uses this situation to put a sharp division between Russian and Ukrainian history. Again, it was sufficient to add a few words or phrases to convey his idea. Only in the Matiiv version did the Varangians come to Kyiv and separately also to the region around the Dnieper River, which was regarded no later than the nineteenth century as the cradle of the Ukrainian national revival.[39] These Varangians, we read next, were completely disconnected from Rurik. Such amendments occurred throughout the entire book. Sviatoslav, the honorable prince, was described in detail by Lewicki. Matiiv added to this description that he was wearing the typical haircut of the Cossacks.[40] Again, this passage is missing in the original.

Up to now we can see that Matiiv took over several existing myths. By adding some phrases, he presented another point of view. The overall censorship and the Polish-dominated education board, which had the book translated and financed, prevented him from going into more detail. Nevertheless, we can clearly see that Matiiv was not interested in adopting all the myths. Especially in the chapters concerning the Cossacks, which encompassed different texts in different chapters, he added a lot of new information. In these cases, we can trace at least three major transformations.

Matiiv tried to represent the Cossacks as well as the whole of Ukraine as an independent ethnic group and the Ukraine as an autonomous country, although it was dominated by foreign states. Lewicki characterized the Cossacks as a mere social phenomenon by writing, "The rebelling Cossacks did not revolt against the king or the Polish state, but against the upper nobility and the gentry."[41] Matiiv just added the information that the Cossacks also fought against the Catholic faith at the end of the sentence. All at once the Cossacks were transformed into an ethnic group distinguished by religion. Although the Cossacks were meant to be presented as a transethnic group, unifying people of different ethnic, religious, and social backgrounds, this picture underwent an important chance in the course of the book. The first Cossack upheavals in the sixteenth century "had no religious or national character, but were solely a social movement,"[42] which is missing in both of the Polish versions. Matiiv writes that "the whole population of Ukraine was willing to fight for their personal freedom and did not want to go back to serfdom."[43] Again, this passage is completely missing in the Polish version. As mentioned before, these revisions can be seen as singular amendments or minor revisions scattered throughout the entire text.

Generally, Matiiv tried to convey the most positive picture of the Cossacks, at the same time avoiding any negative characterization. The description of the Cossack Hetman Bohdan Khmelnytskyi is twice as long in Ukrainian as it is in the Polish version. He now turned into an educated man of his time who spoke Polish, Latin, and Turkish fluently.[44] Further, the revenge for the taking of his estates and his wife became the main reasons for the rebellion under his leadership. His collaboration with Muscovy was not approved of by the higher Ukrainian clergy in the Ukrainian version. In the original Polish version, Khmelnytskyi was characterized in a completely different manner. He was shown as a person who collaborated with the Russian tsar and even betrayed the Turkish sultan. The only reason for his insurrection was personal revenge.

Overall, the Cossacks, and with them Ukraine in general, were presented as a compact group standing in total opposition to Poland to the one side and Russia to the other. By now, we can trace two different approaches to bulwark myths in the translation of Matiiv. First, Matiiv took over existing myths because they fit into his own approach to create the Cossack *antemurale* myth. Concerning "noncivilized Asian tribes," he saw the Ukrainians and Cossacks as legal successors to the Poles. Modifications took place only when they were useful for the Ukrainian point of view. Second, we observe myths that conflicted with Ukrainian approaches and therefore had to be changed more radically. This holds true for the description of the Cossacks, which were a mere social phenomenon for Lewicki. In Matiiv's version, the Cossacks were an open social category consisting of different ethnic groups.[45]

Conclusion

Antemurale myths began to transform in the nineteenth century into what was known as national myths. While the mere content of these myths is rather well known, in this short case study I took a closer look at how these myths were spread in society and how they were communicated.

Schoolbooks have been relatively neglected up to now in this respect. Several features make them an interesting research subject. At least within the Ukrainian context, schoolbooks in the nineteenth century had a relatively large circulation. In addition, their obligatory use at schools makes them an important feature in the communication of information, but also of myths. More often than not, schoolbook authors were leading representatives of national movements, their authorship being just one aspect of their activity. Beyond that, schoolbooks by their very form prove to be suitable for the communication of myths. Due to their limited content and the relationship between information and emotions, schoolbooks were very appropriate for presenting simplified myths with national contents.

There is now the question of how these existing myths could be spread within society. We took a close look at the production and spreading of written texts. The production of books written in Ukrainian after 1848 started from a very low level and experienced several problems in the course of the following years: lack of printing houses, financial troubles, and, not to forget, censorship, which in Galicia came from two sides. Especially after 1867, a lot of educational issues were transferred to the crownland, which was then dominated by the Poles. The approval of schoolbooks, the appointment and/or transfer of teachers, and the funding of books were totally or partly effected by the Polish-dominated school education board. In this situation, the development and communication of Ukrainian myths, whether they concerned religious or cultural questions, could only emerge within a Polish context.

One such example is Lewicki's attempt, which is very interesting for two reasons: on the one hand, it represented a survey of the "old Poland" from its very beginning under Mieszko I up to the partitions of Poland. There is no doubt that Lewicki presented Polish history from the point of view of a former political and cultural Great Power. On the other hand, however, he heavily criticized key elements of this history. That is why it could be published in Polish but also why it was later translated into Ukrainian. Matiiv's Ukrainian translation became the first officially approved Ukrainian history schoolbook with an at least partly Ukrainian approach. Subsequently, the translation had to be supervised by the Polish-dominated Galician education board.

The ongoing national confrontation in Galicia, which began in the nineteenth century, exploited these myths and added new mythologies. While classical *antemurale* myths can be seen as a border between two sides, the new national (Polish and Ukrainian) myths established imagined borders regarding several social, ethnic, and religious groups. Ethnic, cultural, and later also political independence and uniqueness are what became most important within this historiographical approach. It is this kind of interpretation that made it possible to translate this schoolbook into Ukrainian without having to adopt a clear Polish point of view. While Poland was the uniting factor against barbarous tribes from Asia and non-Slavic inhabitants from the Russian Empire in the Polish original, in the Ukrainian version it was the Cossacks who guaranteed this. In this respect, Lewicki's own critical historical approach, combined with only minor amendments and alterations in the Ukrainian translation, supplied the foundation for creating national myths in a Ukrainian translation of a Polish history schoolbook.

Philipp Hofeneder is a postdoctoral researcher at the Karl-Franzens-University in Graz, Austria. He specializes in multilingual and multiethnic empires, such as the Habsburg monarchy, the Russian Empire, and the Soviet Union, and conducts research on translation culture. His recent publications include *Die mehrsprachige Ukraine. Übersetzungspolitik in der Sowjetunion von 1917 bis 1991* (2013); "Der lange 'Schatten' imperialer Historiografie. Karamzins 'Geschichte des russischen Reiches' in Übersetzungen," *Zeitschrift für Ostmitteleuropa-Forschung* 65, no. 4 (2016): 508–30; "Das Übersetzungswesen im kommunistischen Polen zwischen Dominanz und Vielfalt (1944–91)," *Babel* 62, no. 2 (2016): 233–52; "Sowjetische Translationskultur. Das Übersetzungswesen als ein Instrument der Heterogenisierung," in *Going East: Discovering New and Alternative Traditions in Translation Studies*, ed. L. Schippel and C. Zwischenberger (2017), 339–63.

Notes

1. Research on this topic is extensive. See, for instance, H. Hein-Kircher, "Überlegungen zu einer Typologisierung von politischen Mythen aus historiographischer Sicht—ein Versuch," in *Politische Mythen im 19. und 20. Jahrhundert in Mittel- und Osteuropa*, ed. H. Hein-Kircher and H.H. Hahn (Marburg: Verlag Herder Institut, 2006), 407–24; H.H. Hahn and R. Traba, eds., *Deutsch-Polnische Erinnerungsorte*, 5 vols. (Paderborn: Schöningh, 2012–2015).
2. See the chapter by Pål Kolstø in this volume.
3. This leads, as mentioned in the introduction to this volume, to a secularization of religious myths. For more characteristics see P. Kolstø, ed., *Myths and Boundaries in South-Eastern Europe* (London: Hurst, 2005); for a case study with respect to Ukraine, see R. Vulpius, *Nationalisierung der Religion: Russifizierungspolitik und ukrainische Nationsbildung 1860–1920* (Wiesbaden: Harassowitz Verlag, 2005).
4. In the case of Polish and Ukrainian, see J.R. Hodkinson and J. Walker, eds., *Deploying Orientalism in Culture and History: From Germany to Central and Eastern Europe* (Rochester: Camden House, 2013), and, in particular J. Heiss and J. Feich-

tinger, "Distant Neighbors: Uses of Orientalism in the Late Nineteenth-Century Austro-Hungarian Empire," 148–65 in this volume. See also R. Born and S. Lemmen, eds., *Orientalismen in Ostmitteleuropa: Diskurse, Akteure und Disziplinen vom 19. Jahrhundert bis zum Zweiten Weltkrieg* (Bielefeld: Transcript, 2014), 148–65; J. Tazbir, *Polska przedmurzem Europy* (Warszawa: Twój styl, 2004).

5. As shown elsewhere, translations played an important role in that respect; see P. Hofeneder and B. Wöller, "Übersetzung als Geschichtskonstruktionen. Die Bedeutung der Ruska istoryčna biblioteka in ukrainischen Identitätsbildungsprozessen" *Lebende Sprachen* 57, no. 2 (2012): 288–313.

6. Ph. Ther, "The Transnational Paradigm of Historiography and its Potential for Ukrainian History," in *A Laboratory of Transnational History*, ed. G. Kasianov and Ph. Ther (Budapest: Central European University Press, 2009), 81–116; A.V. Wendland, "Jenseits der Imperien: Mychajlo Drahomanov und die Anfänge einer Verflechtungsgeschichte der Ukraine," in *Imperienvergleich. Festschrift für Andreas Kappeler*, G. Hausmann and A. Rustemeyer (Wiesbaden: Harrassowitz Verlag, 2008), 221–46.

7. M. Aust, *Polen und Russland im Streit um die Ukraine: konkurrierende Erinnerungen an die Kriege des 17. Jahrhunderts in den Jahren 1934 bis 2006* (Wiesbaden: Harrassowitz Verlag, 2009); M. Aust, K. Ruchniewicz, and S. Troebst, eds., *Verflochtene Erinnerungen: Polen und seine Nachbarn im 19. und 20. Jahrhundert* (Köln/Weimar/Wien: Böhlau Verlag, 2009).

8. About the so-called *narodovci*, the Ukrainian popular movement starting in the 1860s, see in particular O. Sereda, "'Whom Shall We Be?' Public Debates over the National Identity of Galician Ruthenians in the 1860s," *Jahrbücher für Geschichte Osteuropas* 49, no. 2 (2001): 200–212.

9. For more about these developments, see S. Pacholkiv's work *Emanzipation durch Bildung. Entwicklung und gesellschaftliche Rolle der ukrainischen Intelligenz im habsburgischen Galizien (1890–1914)* (Wien: Verlag für Geschichte und Politik, 2002), which was translated and heavily expanded into Ukrainian under the title *Ukrainska intelihentsiia u Habsburzkii Halychyni: Osvichena verstva i emansypatsiia natsii*, retrieved 7 November 2016 from http://uamoderna.com/images/novi_publikacii/Svyatoslav-Paholkiv/Pacholkiv_Ukr_inteligentcia.pdf.

10. Official sources confirm this. In a decree from 1848, we read the following lines: "Da sich die ruthenische Sprache dermal noch nicht in jenem Zustande der Ausbildung befindet, der sie zum Vortrage in allen wissenschaftlichen Fächern eignet, dass es ferner theils an den fähigen Lehrkräften und an den erforderlichen Lehrbüchern fehlt, um eine gleichmäßige Betheiligung der ruthenischen Sprache in dem öffentlichen Unterrichte in den ruthenischen Theilen Galiziens, wie selbe die polnische und deutsche Sprache unter gleichen Verhältnissen bereits genießen, sogleich im vollen Maße eintreten zu lassen." A. Fischel, *Das österreichische Sprachenrecht. Eine Quellensammlung* (Brünn, 1910), 84.

11. I. Levytskyi, *Halytsko-ruskaia bybliohrafiia XIX-ho stolitiia z uvzhliadneniem ruskych izdanii poiavyvshychsia v Uhorshchyni y Bukovyni (1801–1886)*, vol. 1 (Lviv, 1888), X.

12. A.V. Wendland, *Die Russophilen in Galizien. Ukrainische Konservative zwischen Österreich und Russland 1848–1915* (Wien: Verlag der österreichischen Akademie der Wissenschaften, 2001), 67–68.

13. For an overview of relevant literature, see E. Fuchs, I. Niehaus, and A. Stoletzki, *Das Schulbuch in der Forschung. Analysen und Empfehlungen für die Bildungspraxis* (Göttingen: Vandenhoeck & Ruprecht, 2014), 21–40; R. Bernhard, S. Grindel et al., eds., *Mythen in deutschsprachigen Geschichtsschulbüchern. Von Marathon bis zum Élysée-Vertrag* (Göttingen: Vandenhoeck & Ruprecht, 2017).
14. For detailed figures, see O. Sedliar, "Vydavnycha diialnist tovarystva 'Halytsko-ruska matytsia' (1848–1870)," *Visnyk Lvivskoho universytetu. Seria knyhoznavstvo* 3 (2008): 76–115; M. Vozniak, *Halytski hramatyky ukrainskoi movy pershoi polovyny XIX st.* (Lviv, 1911), 172ff.
15. I. Levytskyi, *Halytsko-ruskaia bybliohrafiia XIX-ho stolitiia dopolnennaia russkymy izdaniiamy vyshedshymy v Venhrii y Bukovyni (1801–1886)*, vol. 2 (Lviv, 1895), XXI.
16. "Es ist eine durch die eigene Wahrnehmung des Ministeriums, sowie durch vielseitige Klagen bestätigte Thatsache, dass an den Volksschulen und Bürgerschulen die gesetzlichen Vorschriften, welche die Wahl der Lehrbücher und sonstigen Lehrmitteln regeln, vielfach unbeachtet bleiben, dass Lehrmittel, welche die Zulässigkeitserklärung des Ministeriums nicht erlangt haben, im Gebrauche belassen und dass nicht selten die Schüler sogar verhalten werden, außer den eingeführten Lehrtexten noch andere Bücher anzukaufen, die ihnen von den Lehrern unbefugterweise als Hilfsbücher bezeichnet werden." *Volksschulgesetze. Die Reichs- und Landesgesetze mit den einschlägigen Ministerial=Verordnungen und Erlässen erläutert durch die Entscheidungen des k.k. Verwaltungsgerichtshofes und des k.k. Reichsgerichtes*, 4 vols. (Wien, 1888), 15.
17. The dictionary was published in 1851 under the title *Juridisch-politische Terminologie für die slavischen Sprachen Oesterreichs. Von der Commission für slavische juridisch-politische Terminologie. Deutsch-ruthenische Separat-Ausgabe* (Wien, 1851).
18. For an overview, see the bibliography by Levytskyi as well as L. Ilnytska and L. Kruzhelnytska, eds., *Repertuar ukrainskoi knyhy 1798–1916. Materialy do bibliohrafii*, 9 vols. (Lviv, 1995–2005).
19. It is worth noting that Pütz, who was born in Germany, had his book translated not only into the officially acknowledged languages of the monarchy but also into several others such as English (with a second version for America), Finnish and even Russian. I would like to thank Dr. Jan Surman for this information.
20. The first *chytanka*, which remained the only one for a long time, was V. Kovalskyi's *Ruska chytanka dlia nyzhshoi hymnazii* (Wien, 1852).
21. While Partytskyi's books were for lower grades, Oleksandr Barvinskyi published two volumes for upper grades, titled *Ruska chytanka dlia vysshoi hymnasii* (Lviv, 1870). Together, these three volumes comprise more than 700 pages and encompass texts for every relevant subject.
22. O. Partytskyi, *Ruska chytanka dlia nyzhshych klias serednych shkil* (Lviv: Nakladom tovarystva "Prosvita," 1871), 393.
23. Originally, Didytskyi's work was published in the periodical *Halychanyn* (The Galician) in 1869.
24. Interestingly, these footnotes only dealt with words used in those parts of Ukraine that were under Russian rule and, therefore, often showed no congruence with Polish.
25. *Ruska chytanka dlia shkil vydilovych* (Lviv: Nakladom tovarystva k. vydavnytstva shkilnych knyzhok, 1904), 110.

26. A. Sirka's work *The Nationality Question in Austria Education. The Case of Ukrainians in Galicia 1867–1914* (Frankfurt a.M.: Peter Lang, 1980) takes a closer look at this issue.
27. The title of the enlarged version was *Zarys historyi Polskiej aż do najnowszych czasów* (Outline of Polish History up to Recent Times).
28. Besides state-ordered translations of official schoolbooks such as A. Gindely's translation into Polish, *Dzieje powszechne dla wyższych klas szkół średnich. Według czwartego wydania przełożył M. Markiewicz*, 3 vols (Rzeszów, 1878–1879) or A. Popliński, *Dzieje powszechne skrócone, przełożył na język polski Z. Sawczyński*, 3 vols (Kraków, 1865). See also B. Zawadzki, *Illustrowana historya najnowszych czasów* (Wien, 1897).
29. As a juxtaposition of several editions demonstrates, translations from German into Ukrainian were sometimes undertaken via Polish. Beside pragmatic reasons, these secondhand translations were obviously used to prevent Ukrainian terminology and overall style being explicitly influenced by Polish.
30. The so-called Cracovian History School, of which Lewicki was a member, was famous for its critical approach of some elements of Polish history.
31. A. Lewicki, *Istoriia kraiu rodynnoho. Uchebnyk dlia vysshych klias shkil serednych* (Lviv, 1895). I could not find out whether this version is a mere reedition of the 1895 edition or a completely new translation of the Polish original.
32. Schoolbooks in Galicia were sometimes written in Polish and had to be used in Polish and Ukrainian classes, such as L. Olewiński, *Czytanka stenografii polskiej i ruskiej szkoły* (Lviv, 1864).
33. This holds true for Vasyl Ilnitskyi, the director of the academic gymnasium in Lviv. He was also the author of several schoolbooks. His book *Logika przerobiona podług Becka dla użytku szkół gimnazjalnych* (Lwów, 1873), written in Polish, was translated into Ukrainian in 1880. Again, this book goes back to J. v. Beck's *Grundriß der empirischen Psychologie und Logik* (Stuttgart: Verlag der J.B. Metzler'schen Buchhandlung, 1841).
34. A detailed list of schoolbooks used at Galician schools at that time is missing up to now. The existing bibliographies contain no exhaustive collection (see, e.g., the abovementioned Levytskyi). The annual reports, which had to be published compulsorily at every Galician school starting in the 1850s, are a good point of departure for such a list, as they normally encompass all the schoolbooks used at that school.
35. Indeed, Lewicki already uses the expression *państwo litewsko-ruskopolskie* in the original.
36. A. Lewicki, *Zarys historyi Polski i krajów ruskich z nią połączonych. Podręcznik szkolny aprobowany przez wysoką c.k. radę szkolną krajową. Wydanie skrócone* (Kraków: Nakładem autora, 1893), 47.
37. Lewicki, *Istoriia kraiu rodynnoho*, 144.
38. As mentioned earlier, through the approbation of new schoolbooks older ones went out of use and were therefore prohibited. We must not forget that other documents that initially were not part of compulsory schoolbooks were also used at school.
39. The original formulation was *v okolyci naddniprianski*, which refers to the Dnieper Ukraine on either side of the middle course of the Dnieper River.
40. In the original the Ukrainian word for this haircut, an *oseledets* is mentioned.

41. Lewicki, *Zarys historyi Polski*, 140.
42. Lewicki, *Istoriia kraiu rodynnoho*, 191.
43. Ibid., 206.
44. See the original formulation: "I buv na svii chas cholovikom obrazovanym, bo hovoryv plavno po polsky, latynsky i turetsky." Lewicki, *Istoriia kraiu rodynnoho*, 203.
45. Similar approaches are known from Russophile authors, such as Bohdan Didytskyi mentioned above. While describing Cossacks in his books, he consistently points to the fact that there were Ukrainian as well as Russian Cossacks.

Bibliography

Aust, M. 2009. *Polen und Russland im Streit um die Ukraine: konkurrierende Erinnerungen an die Kriege des 17. Jahrhunderts in den Jahren 1934 bis 2006*. Wiesbaden: Harrassowitz Verlag.

Aust, M., K. Ruchniewicz, and S. Troebst, eds. 2009. *Verflochtene Erinnerungen: Polen und seine Nachbarn im 19. und 20. Jahrhundert*. Köln/Weimar/Wien: Böhlau Verlag.

Barvinskyi, O. 1870. *Ruska chytanka dlia vysshoi hymnasii*. Lviv.

Beck, J. 1841. *Grundriß der empirischen Psychologie und Logik*. Stuttgart: Verlag der J.B. Metzler'schen Buchhandlung.

Bernhard, R. and S. Grindel et al., eds. 2017. *Mythen in deutschsprachigen Geschichtsschulbüchern. Von Marathon bis zum Élysée-Vertrag*. Göttingen: Vandenhoeck & Ruprecht.

Born, R. and S. Lemmen, eds. 2014. *Orientalismen in Ostmitteleuropa: Diskurse, Akteure und Disziplinen vom 19. Jahrhundert bis zum Zweiten Weltkrieg*. Bielefeld: Transcript.

Burckhard, M. 1888. *Volksschulgesetze. Die Reichs- und Landesgesetze mit den einschlägigen Ministerial=Verordnungen und Erlässen erläutert durch die Entscheidungen des k.k. Verwaltungsgerichtshofes und des k.k. Reichsgerichtes*. 4 vols. Wien: Manz.

Commission für slawische juridisch-politische Terminologie. 1851. *Juridisch-politische Terminologie für die slavischen Sprachen Oesterreichs. Deutsch-ruthenische Separat-Ausgabe*. Wien: Kaiserlich-Königliche Hof- und Staatsdruckerei.

Fischel, A. 1910. *Das österreichische Sprachenrecht. Eine Quellensammlung*. Brünn: F. Irrgang.

Fuchs, E., I. Niehaus, and A. Stoletzki. 2014. *Das Schulbuch in der Forschung. Analysen und Empfehlungen für die Bildungspraxis*. Göttingen: Vandenhoeck & Ruprecht.

Gindely, A. 1878–1879. *Dzieje powszechne dla wyższych klas szkół średnich. Według czwartego wydania przełożył M. Markiewicz*. 3 vols. Rzeszów.

Hein-Kircher, H. 2006. "Überlegungen zu einer Typologisierung von politischen Mythen aus historiographischer Sicht—ein Versuch." In *Politische Mythen im 19. und 20. Jahrhundert in Mittel- und Osteuropa*, ed. H. Hein-Kircher and H. Henning Hahn, 407–24. Marburg: Verlag Herder Institut.

Heiss, J. and J. Feichtinger. 2014. "Distant Neighbors: Uses of Orientalism in the Late Nineteenth-Century Austro-Hungarian Empire." In *Orientalismen in Ostmitteleuropa: Diskurse, Akteure und Disziplinen vom 19. Jahrhundert bis zum Zweiten Weltkrieg*, ed. R. Born and S. Lemmen, 148–65. Bielefeld: Transcript.

Henning Hahn, H. and R. Traba, eds. 2012–2015. *Deutsch-Polnische Erinnerungsorte*. 5 vols. Paderborn: Schöningh.
Hodkinson, J.R., and J. Walker, eds. 2013. *Deploying Orientalism in Culture and History: From Germany to Central and Eastern Europe*. Rochester: Camden House.
Hofeneder, P. and B. Wöller. 2012. "Übersetzung als Geschichtskonstruktionen. Die Bedeutung der Ruska istoryčna biblioteka in ukrainischen Identitätsbildungsprozessen." *Lebende Sprachen* 57, no. 2: 288–313.
Ilnitskyi, V. 1873. *Logika przerobiona podług Becka dla użytku szkół gimnazjalnych*. Lwów.
Ilnytska L. and L. Kruzhelnytska, eds. 1995–2005. *Repertuar ukrainskoi knyhy 1798–1916. Materialy do bibliohrafii*. 9 vols. Lviv.
Kolstø, P., ed. 2005. *Myths and Boundaries in South-Eastern Europe*. London: Hurst.
Kovalskyi, V. 1852. *Ruska chytanka dlia nyzhshoi hymnazii*. Wien.
Levytskyi, I. 1888. *Halytsko-ruskaia bybliohrafiia XIX-ho stolitiia z uvzhliadneniem ruskych izdanii poiavyvshychsia v Uhorshchyni y Bukovyni (1801–1886)*. Vol. 1. Lviv.
———. 1895. *Halytsko-ruskaia bybliohrafiia XIX-ho stolitiia dopolnennaia russkymy izdaniiamy vyshedshymy v Venhrii y Bukovyni (1801–1886)*. Vol. 2. Lviv.
Lewicki, A. 1893. *Zarys historyi Polski i krajów ruskich z nią połączonych. Podręcznik szkolny aprobowany przez wysoką c.k. radę szkolną krajową. Wydanie skrócone*. Kraków: Nakładem autora.
———. 1895. *Istoriia kraiu rodynnoho. Uchebnyk dlia vysshych klias shkil serednych*. Lviv.
Olewiński, L. 1864. *Czytanka stenografii polskiej i ruskiej szkoły*. Lviv.
Pacholkiv, S. 2002. *Emanzipation durch Bildung. Entwicklung und gesellschaftliche Rolle der ukrainischen Intelligenz im habsburgischen Galizien (1890–1914)*. Wien: Verlag für Geschichte und Politik.
Partytskyi, B. 1871. *Ruska chytanka dlia nyzhshych klias serednych shkil*. Lviv: Nakladom tovarystva "Prosvita."
Popliński, A. 1865. *Dzieje powszechne skrócone, przełożył na język polski Z. Sawczyński*. 3 vols. Kraków.
Ruska chytanka dlia shkil vydilovych. 1904. Lviv: Nakladom tovarystva k. vydavnytstva shkilnych knyzhok.
Sedliar, O. 2008. "Vydavnycha diialnist tovarystva 'Halytsko-ruska matytsia' (1848–1870)." *Visnyk Lvivskoho universytetu. Seria knyhoznavstvo* 3: 76–115.
Sereda, O. 2001. "'Whom Shall We Be?' Public Debates over the National Identity of Galician Ruthenians in the 1860s." *Jahrbücher für Geschichte Osteuropas* 49, no. 2: 200–212.
Sirka, A. 1980. *The Nationality Question in Austria Education. The Case of Ukrainians in Galicia 1867–1914*. Frankfurt a.M.: Peter Lang.
Tazbir, J. 2004. *Polska przedmurzem Europy*. Warszawa: Twój styl.
Ther, Ph. 2009. "The Transnational Paradigm of Historiography and Its Potential for Ukrainian History." In *A Laboratory of Transnational History*, ed. G. Kasianov and Ph. Ther, 81–116. Budapest: Central European University Press.
Vozniak, M. 1911. *Halytski hramatyky ukrainskoi movy pershoi polovyny XIX st.* Lviv.
Vulpius, R. 2005. *Nationalisierung der Religion: Russifizierungspolitik und ukrainische Nationsbildung 1860–1920*. Wiesbaden: Harassowitz Verlag.

Wendland, A.V. 2001. *Die Russophilen in Galizien. Ukrainische Konservative zwischen Österreich und Russland 1848–1915.* Wien: Verlag der österreichischen Akademie der Wissenschaften.

———. 2009. "Jenseits der Imperien: Mychajlo Drahomanov und die Anfänge einer Verflechtungsgeschichte der Ukraine." In *Imperienvergleich. Festschrift für Andreas Kappeler,* ed. G. Hausmann and A. Rustemeyer, 221–46. Wiesbaden: Harrassowitz Verlag.

Zawadzki, B. 1897. *Illustrowana historya najnowszych czasów.* Wien.

CHAPTER 10

Mediating the *Antemurale* Myth in East Central Europe
Religion and Politics in Modern Geographers' Entangled Lives and Maps

Steven Seegel

Maps are tools of literacy that reflect Europe's confessional and identity politics, its development of mass media, its exceptionalisms and unstated prejudices, and its recurrence of national-territorial conflicts. The 1883 *Mapa Polski za Panowania Krola Jana Sobieskiego wydana w dwochsetną rocznicę odzieczy Wiednia* ("Map of Poland during the Reign of King Jan Sobieski, published on the 200th Anniversary of the Defense of Vienna"), to take one example, was widely disseminated in its day. It was inspired by the romantic national works of the émigré historian Joachim Lelewel (1786–1861) and Maria Regina Nałęcz Korzeniowska (1793–1874), the aunt of Joseph Conrad (1857–1924). It commemorated Poland as integral to European civilization and a representation of the *antemurale*, or bulwark, in eastern zones of influence. It offered an icon and a weapon for Poland in an ordered historical and territorial way and where the country's geobody had persisted after its partitions despite being wiped off the map of Europe.

Printed in Vienna and Poznań and distributed in Cracow, the 1883 map supposed Poland's defense of Christian unity according to official and heraldic seals, like golden rings in a chain, with a portrait of King Jan III Sobieski (1629–1696) and the Latin epitaph *Non spoliator sum sed liberator* (I am not a destroyer but a liberator).[1] It suggested the depths of a national *antemurale* in the contested spaces of imperial borderlands. Following this, I argue that the emotional, and often religious, intensity of such myths and their mediators, which lay just beneath the surface of political discourses in East Central Europe, demonstrates the hidden anxieties in transformations of map purveyors' transnational lives into nationalizing European bourgeois professionals, the identities of which were anything but settled. Maps

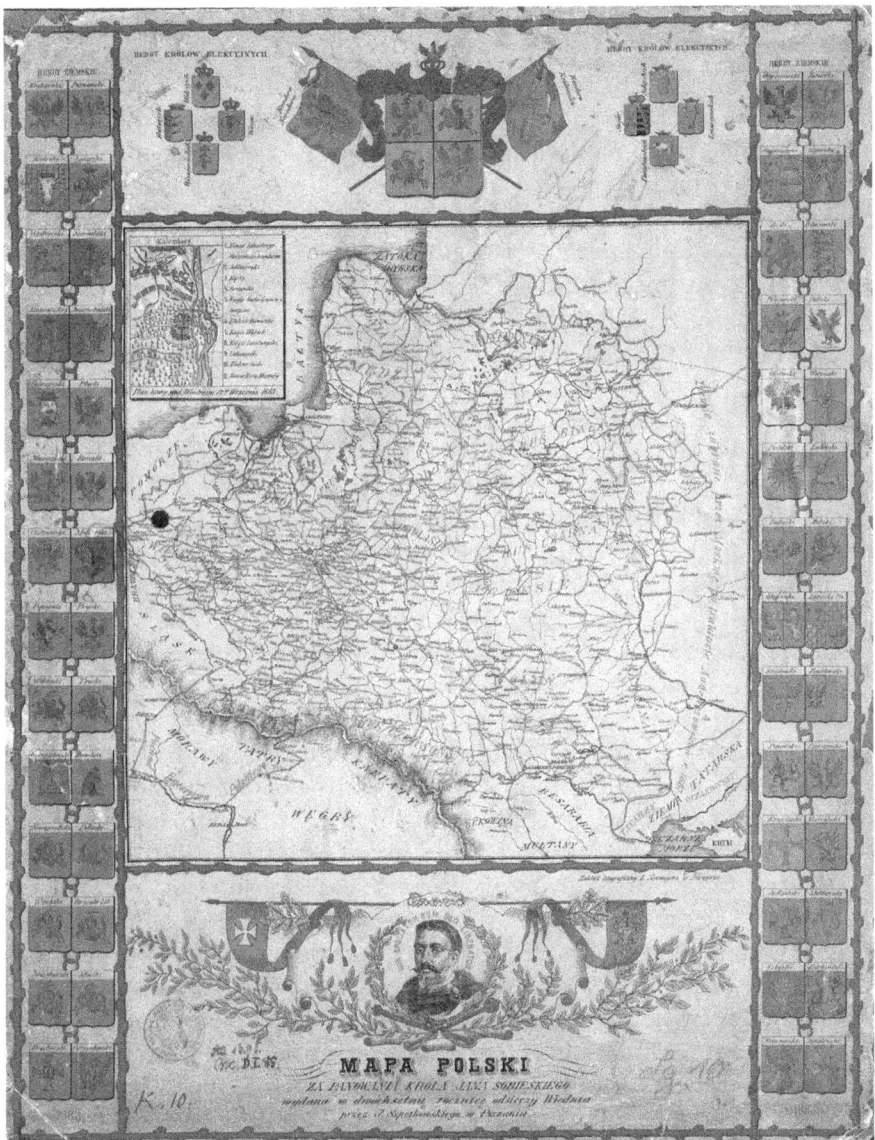

Map 10.1. Map of Poland during the reign of King Jan Sobieski, published on the 200th anniversary of the Defense of Vienna, 1883. Map by J. Szpetkowski. Wikimedia Commons, public domain.

were integral to projects of and by Europe's civilizing men, who instrumentally entangled history with cartography and geography with geopolitics in the late nineteenth and early twentieth centuries.

Lives and Maps: Broadening Contexts for *Antemurale*

Because geographers assumed the roles of expert academics and leaders of national schools, often to tragic ends in East Central Europe, the chapter's key question for its modern historical period is one of time, space, and motivation—how, when, why, and where the geographers produced their many historical, ethnographic, and political maps as visual tools, texts, and objects. By the *antemurale* myth in this setting, I mean the basic tendency of nationalizing professionals to generate selective, if not exclusionary, discursive uses of history and geography by the color- and line-drawing purposes of territorialization. The *antemurale* myth is commonly held as a Christian one, but that is only one aspect of it.

The transnational lives, contacts, and careers of the geographers discussed here—Albrecht Penck (1858–1945) of Germany, Eugeniusz Romer (1871–1954) of Poland, Stepan Rudnytskyi (1877–1937) of Ukraine, and Count Pál Teleki (1879–1941) of Hungary—offered scientific exceptionalist visions of borderland spaces. I selected the transnational approach here rather than one of recalibrated mutually exclusive nationalities in East Central Europe—for example, in the Polish-German case—principally because all of the geographers spoke and could be considered German, both in the regions from which they emerged and in their personal and professional lives.

These individuals are therefore not reduced to comparative imperiology or studies of nationality on exclusive trajectories, for geographers transferred and copied maps to appeal to the *antemurale* myth and frame political exceptionalism after 1914. This was in conjunction with the legacies of nineteenth-century romantic nationalism and positivism and Europe's colonial era notions about priorities of settlement, progress, unity, privilege, and kin-state power. The geographers tended to suppress religious backgrounds and complex kinship origins for political reasons and in the name of objectivity. They also marginalized complex premodern legacies of toleration, borderland fluidity, confessional transfer, and intermarriage in their lives, particularly in the multicultural zones of the Habsburg Empire, the Russian Empire (including the Pale of Settlement), Poland-Lithuania, and the Cossack Hetmanate.[2]

In the four brief case studies that follow, geographers' spatial politics as friends and enemies were aggravated by the two world wars. Those discourses persisted during the period of "high modernity," as described by the Harvard historian Charles Maier from roughly the 1830s to 1970s, in reference to the habit of postdynastic governments to obsess over state governmentality and the rational management of their lands, populations, and resources.[3] Geographers pledged expertise for national causes, deploying maps in Europe's high era of colonial occupation and biological notions of race, class, gender, and sexual difference.[4] *Antemurale* myths of a *mission civilisatrice* sort,[5] as in the 1883 Polish map, were thus promoted by geographers as actors through the medium of cartography when they perceived that their status was threatened by rival powers, or during and after World War I by the end of "heroic" (customarily white and male) colonial dreams of conquest, unity, and the subjugation of nature.

Late nineteenth- and early twentieth-century century promoters of (geo)political maps in East Central Europe regarded themselves as public servants and engaged scientific experts, not usually as people of privilege. Bourgeois academics in geography, by custom and habitus, saw themselves not as limited but universally as enlightened men—in short, establishment scientists who operated stateside as experts in Europe. They saw themselves as organically connected with nature, and at the same time empowered over lands and peoples whom they mapped, quantified, classified, and surveyed.[6] If expansion and unification for empires and nationalities were dominant projects of the era, then the line-drawing, grid-like ethnoschematization of Europe's populations was a powerful communicative medium.

Mappers of modern East Central Europe thus advanced trends of nation and state building, specialization, and professionalization in this manner, being among the era's most prominent media and historical actors. By studying *antemurale* structures and discourses in maps, we may better consider the spatial turn, as well as the vast and growing scholarship in feminist geography, critical geography and cartography, the digital humanities, and GIS studies.[7] Szpetkowski's 1883 bulwark map was part of a modernizing era of mental maps in which geographers created new tools and linked themselves further to developing subdisciplines (anthropology, ethnography, geology, hydrography, oceanography, chorography, climatology, historical geography) for mapmaking.[8] Positivist traditions and notions of progress in geography, however useful as tools, did not eradicate earlier imperialisms or romantic national iconographies in the Vienna Congress system. For geographers in German-dominated East Central European academe, professionalization was a double-edged sword because the formation of national schools could pose a threat to empires, and after the 1848–1849 revolutions, the intensification of nationalizing discourses in geography was often a result of oppressive imperial policies. In places like Habsburg Galicia, it became difficult if not impossible to map out fully on racial/ethnic lines (if that was desirable) the identities of Jews, Eastern Orthodox peoples, Ruthenians/Ukrainians, hybrid peoples, or else polylingual populations having complex mixed origins and biographies of plural or indeterminable nationality.

More concretely, patterns of the *antemurale* included visions and transformations of local geography into grander visions of East and West, in the form of shared myths that were interpersonal and intensely biographical.[9] Political visions became part of the nationalizing process of professional geography, in which maps were dressed in authoritative garb. This could be seen by the aesthetics of color on true military-topographical maps, which were hardly neutral. No single code existed, but one can suggest certain cultural similarities. Red represented what was warm, vital, dangerous, or powerful; blue was for water, or something cool, pure, serene, and deep; green was the forest or vegetation, something organic, natural, and peaceful; brown was earthy, also signifying natural borders or landforms such as hills and mountains.

Lines were important, too. In political maps, the thick or bold line was a fixed boundary or territorial divide; the dotted line was an open frontier, the mark of permeability or an invading other; the absent or silent line, like white spots on a colonial map, symbolized providential areas for expansion or conquest. In the first two cases, when entangled geographers gazed to Europe's East or West in the profound hope of unity and belonging, their inclusive visions were narrow and often of a discriminatory sort.

Albrecht Penck's Central Europe

In their entangled lives and careers, Albrecht Penck in Vienna and Berlin and Eugeniusz Romer (1871–1954) in Lviv were promoters of maps, but they had opposing views of the Mitteleuropa (Central Europe) idea as it had been advanced by Friedrich Naumann (1860–1919). By the early twentieth century, Romer in his political geography notably considered Poland to be outside of a German economic and political zone, instead preferring to situate it in Western Europe.[10] Penck, born in 1858, was baptized in a Lutheran church and educated in Leipzig and Munich. He found a deeper purpose in the study of geology and geography.[11] He entered Leipzig University in 1875 at the age of seventeen, specializing in the natural sciences. In 1877, he published his first paper on glacial deposits. He worked on the geological survey of Saxony and prepared scientific maps of Central Europe as a whole or in part, including the *Geologische Spezialkarte des Königreich Sachsen* ("Geological and Special Map of the Kingdom of Saxony"), in 1878.[12] Penck's approach to geography supplemented the Eurocentric geographical and morphological sciences of nineteenth-century giants such as Alexander von Humboldt (1769–1859), Johann Wilhelm Ritter (1776–1810), and Ferdinand von Richthofen (1833–1905).

In the early 1890s, Penck's maps were relatively unknown, and he was not too adept as a cartographer. Nevertheless, he became an empirical re-

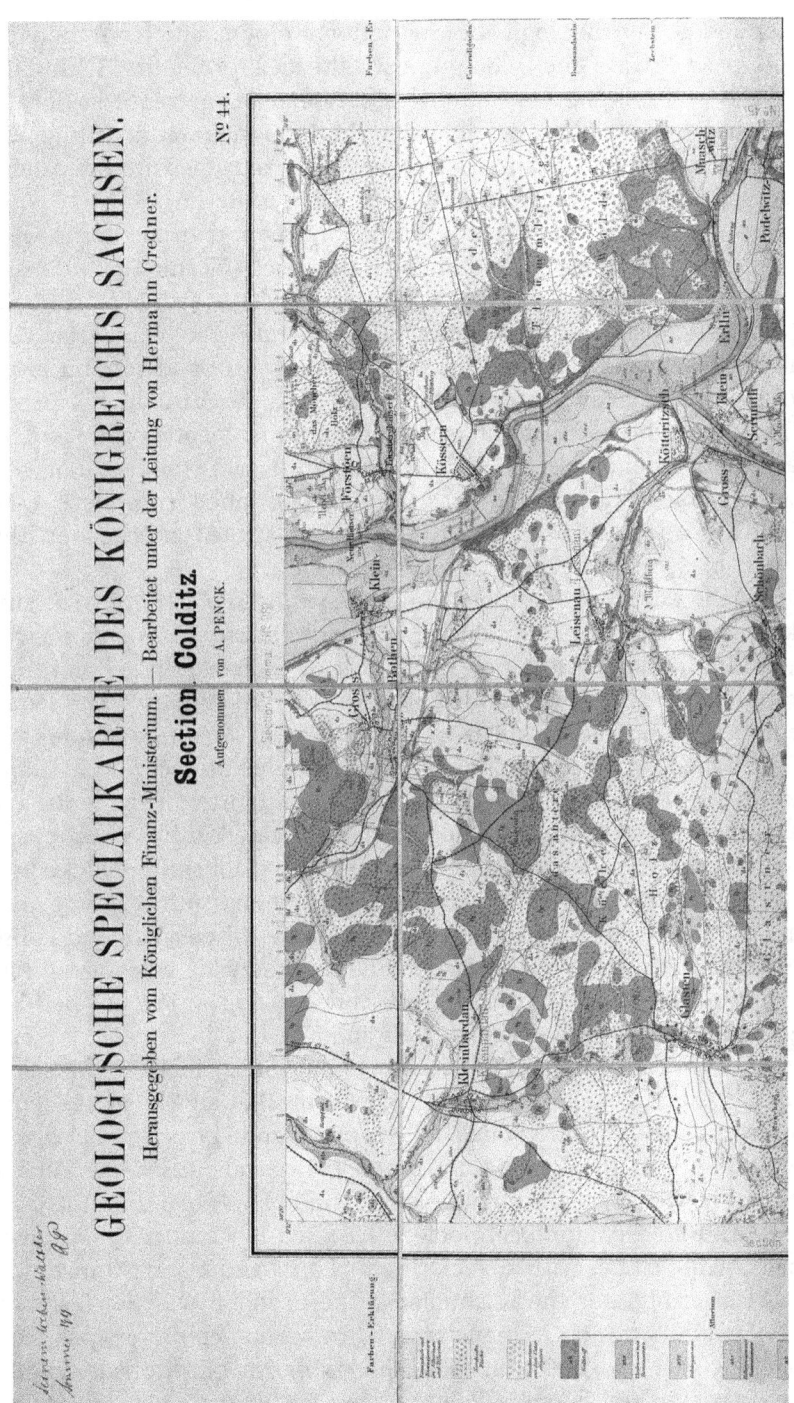

Map 10.2. Geological and special map of the Kingdom of Saxony, 1878. Map by Albrecht Penck. Reprinted from Albrecht Penck, *Geologische Spezialkarte des Königreich Sachsen* (Leipzig: Giesecke & Devrient, 1878).

searcher and geomorphologist of international repute, and from there his interests grew. It was Penck who proposed the idea for the first 1:1 million map of the world, at an international geographers' conference in Bern in 1891. He lectured at Harvard and Yale in the 1900s. He was a visiting professor in 1908–1909 at Columbia University, on exchange with the American geographer William Morris Davis, who went to Berlin.

During World War I, especially in his involvement with the Berlin Geographical Society, having insisted on the Kaiserreich (German Empire) as a great power and absolving Germany for any role whatsoever in starting the war, he fell into disfavor in the United States, Great Britain, and France. In the fall of 1914, he was detained and questioned by Scotland Yard on suspicion of espionage.[13] Penck ordered the arrest of Romer in 1916, his former Polish student, who had just published his monumental atlas of Poland for the cause of independence. In 1917–1918, Penck became the rector of what is now Humboldt University in Berlin, and he continued from there, as he had done as the former director of the Kaiser's Institute for Oceanography, to support projects of German colonial expansion.

During the Paris negotiations from January to June 1919, a frustrated Penck moved much more ominously into *Revisionspolitik* (revision policy). This led him away from the pre-1914 spirit of exchange in geomorphology, for which he had been known abroad.[14] On 9 February 1919, Penck wrote an article in *Deutsche Allgemeine Zeitung* in which he announced, in Romer's shadow, the start of a major cartographic project for Germany. Penck's maps of February–March 1919 in their coloration, symbols, and content were intended to raise the German educated public's awareness. He included a small-scale map to challenge Polish claims. But Penck's map had unclear frontiers, a perennial problem of nineteenth-century German maps, and it was inconsistent in its grouping of German and Polish settlements. The vaguely *völkisch* racial/ethnic/linguistic category of *rein deutsch* (pure German) in the legend was coded to appear Polish—perhaps exaggerating a Polish, and Slavic, demographic threat.

As Guntram Herb pointed out in his seminal study in 1996 *Under the Map of Germany*, Penck created the impression that all the areas identified by cross-hatching were Polish. His maps expanded from earlier black-and-white work in the Leipzig-illustrated periodical *Illustrierte Zeitung* (Illustrated Newspaper) and a color version on Polen (Poland) in the journal of the Berlin Geographical Society. He used black dots to designate Germans, white circles with a black rim for Poles, and black-rimmed dots with a black center for the Kashubians. The problem was that symbols for the Kashubians and Germans seemed to merge; color versions were needed. And so it was: in the one published in Berlin, blue dots designated the Germans and red dots the Poles, while Kashubians were represented by blue-gray dots, which unfortunately could not be easily distinguished from Germans.[15] Penck had stumbled upon a major problem for the German Question since 1848 and in the high era of Europe's expansion: that an expansive, dispersed, bourgeois German civilization could neither be bounded nor represented on flattened grids in Central Europe.[16]

Hence the main problem with any German *antemurale* in the modern era, as opposed to the Polish ones that had derived from Galicia: by the early to mid-1920s, Albrecht Penck was openly advocating *völkisch* revision, as an objective scientist. He helped to institutionalize anti-Polish, anti-Slavic, and antidemocratic *Ostforschung* (Eastern studies) among experts in interwar Germany's burgeoning geographical profession. Arguing against Versailles and Polish gains in Silesia, Pomerania, and the Danzig corridor, Penck produced his famous *Volks-und-Kulturboden* map and text in 1925, a concept that had earlier antecedents in Europe's geosophical discourses and *Siedlung* (German colonial settlement). Germans of Bohemia, Moravia, and Silesia, Penck reasoned by loosely associating *Volk*, *Kultur*, and *Boden* (nation, culture, and land), would reap the benefits of German culture, language, and agriculture. Revisionist maps thus represented an

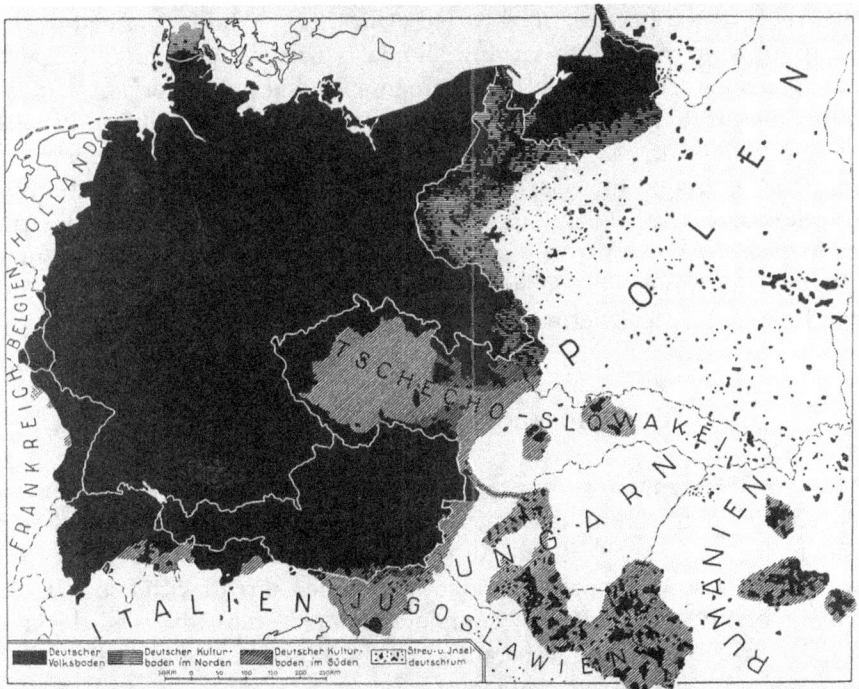

Map 10.3. German ethnic and cultural lands, 1925. Map by Albrecht Penck. Courtesy Cornell University, PJ Mode Collection of Persuasive Cartography.

aestheticization of Poland as German colonial space in the East, a quasi-religious and quasiscientific continuation of the *antemurale* as Eurocentric defense—and for the intellectual, spiritual, cultural, economic, and geospatial penetration of open frontiers.[17]

Penck's infamous map illustrated the convergence after 1918–1919 of three main trends in German geographical discourses: *Geopolitik* or *Weltpolitik* as an alchemic language of power; the *völkisch* tradition as a romantic desideratum for unity, harmony, and totality in a premodern past; and anti-Slavic *Ostforschung* against the threats of other guilds of experts. Penck's map was drawn by the artist Arnold Hillen Ziegfeld, and it appeared in Leipzig in the *Deutscher Schutzbund* (DSB, League for the Protection of Germans). It was prepared for a *völkisch* compilation of essays, *Volk unter Völkern* (Nation under Nations), published in German in Wrocław in 1925.[18]

Looking eastward to Romer's Poland, where he had gained prestige as a geographer in the Second Republic, Penck's graphology of *Volks- und Kulturboden* saw Germans as unified even when they were not, as they furthered Europe's settlements by cultivation of their ethnicity and land cultivation.[19] There was more to it, for Penck's work was also a self-portrait that represented his dreams directed at Romer's Poland—the end of the status for which he, a state-serving colonial bourgeois academic, an expert, a religious person, and a dutiful German-speaking public servant, had labored his entire life.[20] Younger German *Ostforscher* often followed Penck's model in objecting to Soviet communism as well as Slavic democratic rule on the pretext that Germans were under an unlawful occupation by Czechoslovakia and Poland. In this sense, the *antemurale* myth was instrumentalized by experts who spoke *colonially* as well as postimperially after 1918, as they forged ethnocentric narratives in their maps of frontier gains and losses, historical victimhood, and territorial revision.[21]

Eugeniusz Romer's Modern Poland

Meanwhile Eugeniusz Romer, born in Lviv in 1871, had origins in a mixed Polish aristocratic family dating back at least to the fifteenth century. Being able to write and speak fluent German, the Galician's contact with Penck was significant. As a graduate student, he studied abroad with Penck in the Vienna of 1895–1896. Romer completed his research, advanced through the Austro-Hungarian-Polish ranks, and in 1911 was appointed chair of geography at the University of Lviv.

Romer supported linguistic and cultural Polonization, against the use of Ukrainian in schools, throughout Galicia. He quickly realized that the science he had learned in Germany and Austria could be of great service to the Polish political cause, and in an international context. Referring to a synthesis of physical geography, climatology, and statistics, Romer in 1912 defined what he called the "bridge position" in which he favored the renewal of Polish political independence as a strong state stretching from the Baltic to the Black Sea. At the International Geographical Congress in Paris in 1913, Romer was dismayed by Penck's imagined Mitteleuropa spheres in Polish historical lands and worked on revising the maps and atlases of Poland's natural borders. Romer's World War I geography was thus a fierce publicity campaign, which required the exceptionalist idea that Poland was inseparable from European civilization.

Romer's maps during World War I significantly showed an adaptation and integration of the *antemurale* myth as objective knowledge, or at least the aspects of it that suited Poland's exceptionalist place in Europe. His

Map 10.4. Military-political map of Poland, 1916. Map by Eugeniusz Romer. Courtesy Library of Congress. Retrieved 14 June 2018 from https://blogs.loc.gov/loc/files/2017/01/Figure-1.jpeg.

1916 *Geograficzno-statystyczny atlas Polski* (Geographical-Statistical Atlas of Poland) was printed in Vienna, Warsaw, and Cracow with text in Polish, French, and German and an astounding sixty-five maps and thirty-two tables. Information dealt with hypsometry, geology, climate, vegetation, history, and economics. Romer paid attention to borders, population density, and demographics, and he offered separate tables for Poles, Roman Catholics, Jews, Poles in the borderlands, Poles in Lithuania and Rus, and churches. He compiled the data from the Central Statistical Committee in Vienna, the House of Trade and Industry, the University of Vienna, libraries including the Jagiellonian library in Cracow, and private collections of professors, ministers, priests, and antiquarians.[22]

Romer's separate 1916 *Wojenno-polityczna mapa Polski* (Military-Political Map of Poland) was published in brochure form in Vienna and Lviv on the occasion of the Two Emperors' Declaration of 5 November 1916.[23] Disseminated by Polish papers and geography newsletters, Romer included maps indicating Polish historical and (quantifiable) linguistic boundaries. He applied categories of nationality in listing "Polish Ethnographic Area with Greater Than 50 Percent Poles," "Sphere I and Sphere II of Polish Interests," and "The Polish Crownlands under German and Austrian Occupation," with indications of military fronts. Romer's maps became standard scientific sources and were imitated as models at the many diplomatic congresses and peace negotiations after the war.[24]

Under the surface rationality of maps as (geo)political discourses lay deeply interpersonal and subjective notions of place and space—emotion, cognition, and perception—of which the bulwark myth of religious exceptionalism was significant in East Central Europe. The mapping of Penck's Germany and Romer's Poland may seem like opposite political cases, one in support of monarchy and the other a republic, but it is plausible that the local confessional and identity politics of the *antemurale* concept in East Central Europe undergirded their geospatial visions as scientific geographers. Beyond their growing obsession with population politics in heartlands and on frontiers and evident politicization of census data and statistical demography in contested German-Polish borderlands, the self-definition of both scientific men significantly derived from Europe's religious traditions.

Penck's evangelical Lutheran underpinnings had given him a start for early schooling in Munich and his first trip abroad, to Scandinavia. The trip was financed by an affluent Protestant donor of scholarships in Leipzig, August de Wilde (1881–1950), who made confessional identity a precondition of eligibility.[25] Protestant Saxony for the geographer therefore was symbolic as a place for Penck's identity, integral to the opportunities he enjoyed in Bismarck's era of German unification.[26] He married a fellow Lutheran, Ida von Ganghofer (1863–1944), the daughter of August von Ganghofer (1827–1900), who was a powerful ministerial councilor of Bavaria. Ida was also the sister of Ludwig von Ganghofer (1855–1920), the popular mid-nineteenth-century writer in the *Heimat* genre.

Romer, despite what he viewed as his Germanized father's disinclination toward religion, was baptized in the Catholic Church and exposed to such traditions in Habsburg Poland. His family had been involved in the two failed Polish uprisings of 1830–1831 and 1863–1864. He was educated after 1867 in a Galicia under Habsburg rule that was becoming autonomous and was swiftly Polonized by the local administration. He studied geography in Lviv and abroad in Berlin and Vienna, and in 1899, he married Jadwiga Rossknecht, who spoke German and had been raised as a Polish Catholic in Cracow, but also came from a mixed family.[27] In their memoirs written during the 1940s, Penck and Romer often reflected back to their Protestant (coded as German) and Catholic (coded as Polish) religious identities, underscoring national difference in their Europe that had been destroyed.

Stepan Rudnytskyi's Cross-Border Ukraine

Stepan Rudnytskyi, born in Peremyshl in 1877, also had been a student of Penck in Central Europe. A Ruthenian (in the Habsburg designation) but not of noble origin, his plebeian branch of the Rudnytskyi family in the Habsburg lands had come from the village of Avhustov, not far from Ternopil. Denys, his grandfather, was a Greek Catholic priest. Lev, his father, was educated in the German language as well as history and geography, and he worked as the director of classical gymnasia throughout Galicia. Emilia Taborska, his mother, was of Armenian background and also came from a family of priests in Ruthenia.[28] In his formative years of education in prewar Galicia, Rudnytskyi gained his credentials, by German standards, as an academic geographer, sent by the geographer Antoni Rehman (1840–1917) in Lviv, who also trained Romer, to study with Penck in Vienna and then under Karl Uhlig (1872–1938) in Tübingen and Penck's colleague Eduard Brückner (1862–1927) in Berlin.

Rudnytskyi, in effect, chose modern Ukraine as a professional and a nationalizing person: he mastered a good deal of advanced work in geomorphology, physical geography, anthropogeography, climatology, and astrogeography. He became well versed in geographers' scientific writings in German, French, Polish, Ukrainian, and Russian. During the course of World War I, Rudnytskyi earned the acclaim of German geographers. He was heralded, ahead of Romer, as Ukraine's most talented geographer.

Rudnytskyi's local Galician frames of 1914 were therefore not Polish but of an educated and highly academically oriented Ukrainian bourgeoisie: he had been a follower of the historian Mykhailo Hrushevskyi (1866–1934) and became a vocal advocate of Ukrainian independence. Involved with the Shevchenko Scientific Society before 1914, during the war Rudnytskyi joined the international Union for the Liberation of Ukraine.[29]

In 1914, Rudnytskyi published works in support of Ukraine, initially with the backing of the Central Powers from Berlin and Vienna, but he favored the world of empires less than the creation of a future independent federal Ukrainian republic. When he fled Lviv for Vienna at the start of the war, together with many influential Ukrainian scholars, writers, scientists, and activists, Rudnytskyi took part in the Union for the Liberation of Ukraine, publishing works under the name "Levenko."

In the Habsburg wartime capital he translated his major work, the "Short Geography of Ukraine," from Ukrainian to German for use in and beyond the Central Powers' territories. Working for the government in exile of the West Ukrainian National Republic, the "Short Geography of Ukraine" was rendered *Ukraina: Land und Volk* in Berlin in 1915 and 1916. The substantial 416-page work, which featured forty illustrated tables and six maps, secured his scientific reputation in Berlin and Vienna. It elevated his status as an expert on the East, especially in the eyes of Penck. Rudnytskyi's generally German-inspired, Ukrainocentric map with open frontiers for Ukrainian dispersal (in pink) to a colonial east, the *Ethnographische Übersichtkarte von Osteuropa* (Ethnographic Survey Map of Eastern Europe) was appended to the 1916 edition of *Ukraina: Land und Volk* and published in Vienna. The book itself emphasized Ukraine's cross-border unity along the Zbruch and eastward across the Eurasian steppes. At this key juncture for modern Ukraine, Rudnytskyi's ethnocentric geography of Ukraine was printed in English, French, German, Italian, Hungarian, Czech, and Russian. Notably, it was never translated into Polish.

In terms of the *antemurale* concept, Rudnytskyi's position was indeed transnational, never in a one-to-one postcolonial dialectic with a single nationality. While his application of the idea was surely about territory, nationality, and closed lines around borders in a modern conventional sense, he also followed German and European colonial frontier logic by showing the maximum number of Ukrainian speakers. Thus the *antemurale* became an idée fixe in conational unity with this caveat: what to other powers seemed like Ukrainian complicity with foreign powers, or the invention of a Ukrainian nation by Germans or Austrians or others, from his Ukrainocentric standpoint in modern Europe would geopolitically *prevent* a fratricidal war in the Habsburg-Russian zones of 1914–1915, and thus the dissolution of old Europe, between Ruthenians and Little Russians in their towns, cities, and settlements on opposite sides of the Zbruch River.[30] But to place Ukraine on Europe's map, Rudnytskyi from East Galicia conceived of Ukrainians much as Romer from Lviv had nationally drawn Poles and Poland, as a dispersed yet ordered group sharing a common history, culture, language, and territorial frontiers for open settlement.

His black-and-white map, *Das Wohngebiet der Ukrainer in Europa*, with his own English title *The Ukrainian Territory in Europe*, appeared in the original German-language editions in Vienna in 1914 and Berlin in 1915 of *Ukraina und der Ukrainer* (Ukraine and the Ukrainians).[31] In addition, in his 1915 pamphlet "Chomu my khochemo samoistinoi Ukrainy?" (Why Do We Want an Independent Ukraine?), reprinted in Vienna, Berlin, Lviv, and Stockholm, he again mixed science and propaganda to argue for the rights of Ukrainians.[32] In the 1916 article, "Ukrainska sprava zi stanovyshcha politychnoi heohrafii" (The Ukrainian Question from the Standpoint of Political Geography), which appeared in the Ukrainian daily *Dilo* (Deed) and was printed in Lviv, he advanced the idea of national-geographic unity on frontiers. In 1917, he followed the model of Romer's atlas of 1916 by preparing separate maps for a historical atlas of Ukraine. These were never published as a single folio.

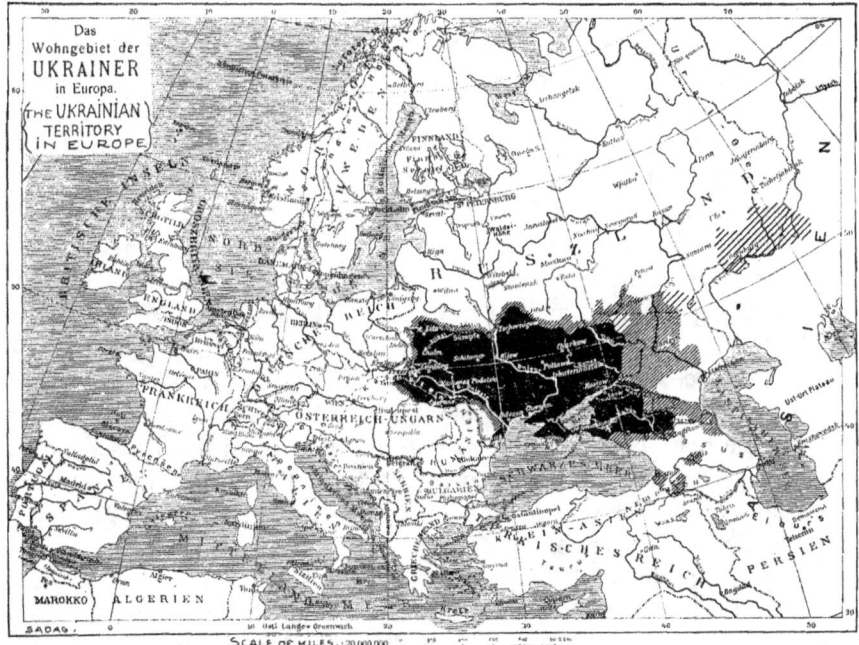

Map 10.5. The Ukrainian territory in Europe, 1914. Map by Stepan Rudnytskyi. Reprinted from Stepan Rudnyts'kyi, *Ukraina und die Ukrainer* (Berlin, 1915).

These were among Rudnytskyi's seminal works during World War I, which also included his scientific maps as mediated objects. As Ihor Stebelsky has noted, Rudnytskyi's prominent tricolor map *Ohladova karta ukrainskykh zemel* (A Survey Map of Ukrainian Lands) appeared at the end of the popular land and people volume of 1914–1919 in many languages. It highlighted distribution of Ukrainians in pink, the favorite subliminal color of British imperial maps, and showed a slowing natural terrain in brown, with outlines of rivers, settlements, and Ukrainophone place-names in a prominent black.[33]

From 1917–1918 onward, Rudnytskyi continued to make and reprint additional, visually attractive thematic maps in color. There was the *Map of Ukraine* and *Stinna fizychna karta Ukrainy* (Physical Wall Map of Ukraine), both in Vienna in 1918. Also printed was the French-language *L'Ukraine, un aperçu sur son territoire, son people, ses conditions culturelles, ethnographiques, politiques et économiques* (Ukraine: An Overview of Its History, Its People, and Its Cultural, Ethnographic, Political, and Economic Conditions), in Bern in 1919, and the bilingual German-Ukrainian *Ukraina u svoikh etnohrafichnykh mezhakh/Die Ukraina in ihren ethnographischen Grenzen* (Ukraine in Its Ethnographic Borders), coauthored with Heorg von Hasenko (1894–1933), or Heorhii Hasenko, in Vienna and Kyiv in 1920.[34] These were clearly intended as both science and propaganda for the interwar promotion in Central Europe and beyond of Ukraine, Ukrainians, and interdisciplinary Ukrainian studies.

In the early 1920s, Rudnytskyi wrote two seminal works from exile on Ukraine's political geography, the 1921 *Ohliad terytorii Ukrainy* (Survey of the Territory of Ukraine) and the 1923 *Osnovy zemleznannia Ukrainy* (Foundations of Ukrainian Geography). He drew from his German training in physical and human geography, down to the components of scale, color, and lines in the mapping of nationality by culture and language, to argue for European unity and the integrity of Ukraine's territorial lands and peoples.[35]

In this sense, Rudnytskyi's maps of Ukraine during World War I were the product of Europe's colonial, national, and high imperial age, but they also may be read as an attempt in Europe's East to *avoid* further violent cross-border conflict for Ukrainians (e.g., Ruthenians, Little Russians, and Ukrainians) across Habsburg-Romanov imperial lines before 1914 at the imagined natural marker of the Zbruch River.[36] Rudnytskyi was profoundly shaped by the nationalizing violence of World War I and his experience of exile from Galicia, and after the fall of empires, he became a marginalized figure in Central Europe. During the Polish-Ukrainian War of 1918–1919, he lost his position as a lecturer at the University of Lviv. Rudnytskyi, as a

MEDIATING THE *ANTEMURALE* MYTH IN EAST CENTRAL EUROPE 277

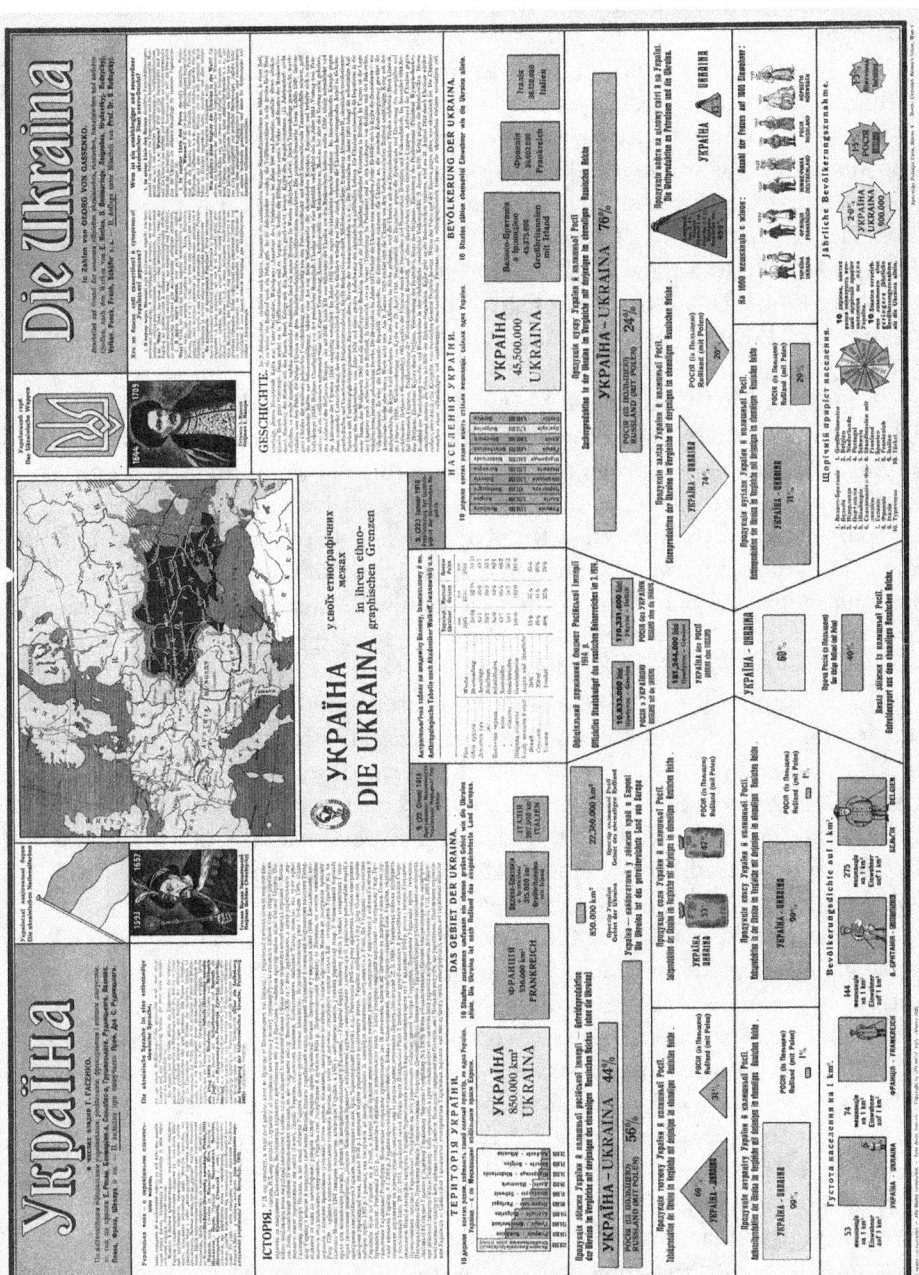

Map 10.6. Ukraine in its ethnographic borders, 1920. Map by Stepan Rudnytskyi and Heorg von Hasenko. Courtesy Harvard Map Collection, Harvard Library.

Germanophone academic geographer, went into Central European exile in Prague and Vienna, along with other members of the Galician Ukrainian intelligentsia.

The U.S. geographer Isaiah Bowman relied almost exclusively on Romer, rather than Penck or Rudnytskyi's maps and data. Bowman denied any chance for Ukrainian national self-determination, the position Rudnytskyi and his idol Hrushevskyi had supported; he, too, imagined Poland's religious foundations against Soviet power and as the easternmost bastion of Western civilization. Rudnytskyi had to remain in exile in postwar Central Europe, unable to appeal to the victorious Allies after World War I or to return to Polish Lviv after the Polish-Ukrainian War of 1918–1919 to teach at interwar Poland's newly named, claimed, and restored Jan Kazimierz (1609–1672) University.

In turns toward a European West as *the* civilization and *the* successor to Christendom, and by excluding the Orthodox or Muslim East from the map of Europe, such geographers were actors who used maps and *antemurale* myths very selectively as a modern tool to sacralize and instrumentalize the past. We can thus reassess Rudnytskyi's key scientific role, relative to the other geographers' subjective maps, in the shaping of Ukraine's transnational geography, and as an imagined bulwark against Polish imperial and Soviet revolutionary power in the East, in late nineteenth- and early twentieth-century transnational spaces.[37]

The Ukrainian Rudnytskyi as an expatriate shared with his friends and adversaries the professional ethos of East Central European geography and a desire to expand the growing discipline into other scientific fields and nationalizing walks of life. Each geographer's national school and disciples believed in the modern cult of the academic expert that emerged out of the heroic explorer tradition of nineteenth-century geographical societies and that became prized by interwar states.

As Rudnytskyi finally and fatefully decided to quit Central Europe and repatriate to Kharkiv in 1925–1926, it was to manage and direct state institutions in the New Economic Policy (NEP) era for the bourgeois future of a Ukrainian national geography. He worked as an expert in Soviet Ukrainian scientific institutions, but these were taken over during the Stalinist revolution. When Rudnytskyi was arrested in 1933, he was charged with fascism and counterrevolutionary activity, and he was executed along with many other prominent activists in the Ukrainian intelligentsia at Solovets Islands near the White Sea in 1937. Among Europe's modern geographers who used maps fluently, he was part of the pre-1914 era's episteme of nineteenth-century progress, nature, exploration, and open frontier space. Integral to the geographers' identities was the discursive (ab)use of the *antemurale* myth to Europe's invented East in which they held fast not only to geographic science but also to the maps of a providential, often religious, and Eurocentric geosophy.

Count Pál Teleki's Carte Rouge of Hungary

The fourth and final example of the use and abuse of the *antemurale* myth is Count Pál Teleki (1879–1941). He came from an aristocratic political family in Transylvania, whose origins date back to the fourteenth century. Specifically in early modern Transylvanian borderlands, the *antemurale* myth for Hungary was grounded in the count's own political memory and kinship relations. Born in Budapest on 1 November 1879, a subject like the Polish Romer of the Austro-Hungarian dual monarchy, Pál János Ede Teleki de Szék was shaped by his family's long history in Transylvania. He belonged to a multigenerational clan of landholders who were Calvinists or Roman Catholics, varying in their piety in Transylvania. Mihály II Teleki (1634–1690), the clan's most famous ruler, supported Poland and cooperated with King Jan Sobieski; he worked closely with Prince György II Rákóczi (1593–1648; r. 1648–1660) and later Mihály II Apafi (1632–1690; r. 1662–1690). Mihály II Teleki negotiated skillfully for Transylvania's autonomy, and in 1685 he received the title of count from the Habsburgs, after Sobieski's 1683 defeat of Ottoman forces at the battle for Vienna.[38]

The *antemurale* myth became a deep structural aspect of Teleki's early transnational life, education, and marriage. Baptized Roman Catholic, according to his father's wishes, Pál learned German well before he attended his first school, a Lutheran elementary school. In his young dream of becoming a geographer-scientist in the mold of Alexander von Humboldt or David Livingstone (1813–1873), Teleki earned repute in the late 1900s as a traveler to the Sudan and historian of Europe's early modern cartography of Japan. He served briefly in World War I, but his main function was as a geography expert.

With Baron Nopsca von Felső-Szilvás (1877–1933), a specialist on Albania who had also mapped out the Balkans in the older colonial manner, Teleki assisted in producing the Carte Rouge of 1918–1919, in its full title the *Magyarország néprajzi térképe a népsűrűség alapján* (Ethnographical Map of Hungary, Based on the Density of Population), drawing from a 1903 Hungarian ethnographic map and Austro-Hungarian census statistics, up to and including the 1910 imperial survey.[39] It served as a Magyar rebuke to the French delegation's leading expert, the geographer Emmanuel de Martonne (1873–1955), who favored a broader Romanian statehood and used a similar technique for showing population density in his maps of Transylvania.[40] Teleki insisted on the science of geography in historic Hungary—the crown lands of St. Stephen (969–1038)—and further followed the uncertain logic of modernization theory: that the density of middle-class assimilated Magyars increased as nonurban peasants moved and settled, like migrating colonists, into their natural enclaves in cities.[41]

Teleki therefore proved that all nationalities could be measured by density and in the same way. As if he were mapping the frontiers of the U.S. West for a white, European conquering power, he and Nopsca left deserted or uninhabited the uplands, marshes, plains, mountainous areas, lowlands, and frontiers having few inhabitants. Magyars became the ethnocentric norm in bright red. Based on 1910 Austro-Hungarian census data, entire districts were shown as bereft of populations that were actually there.[42] This geography dominated Teleki's universal scheme while representing colonial nineteenth-century Europe's science, progress, and civilization.[43]

In his unyielding efforts to revise the Trianon Treaty of 1920, which reduced Hungary's population from 20.9 million to 7.6 million and its territory by over two-thirds, leaving the country landlocked in Europe, Teleki did not stop with maps.[44] The count stressed Hungary's Christian origins, raising the issue of land reform and recounting the benevolent rule of conservative-liberal aristocrats who once distanced the country from German (i.e., Reformation) influence. Though not very pious in his early life despite his education by the Piarists, after 1918–1919 he recast Transylvania as a religious and cultural space that was integral to Hungary. In the Danubian Basin, he viewed Budapest as the locus for the Magyar bourgeoisie and as essential to patterns of European urbanization and settlement. Only if and when non-Magyars of the East—that is Orthodox Romanians, East European Jews arriving in Hungary, Slavic peoples in Ukraine and Russia, and various other nonurban minorities—assimilated to his nineteenth-century romantic national ideals of Magyar high culture and language, would they become European. White areas in the Carte Rouge depicted low population densities for rural and mountainous non-Magyar nationalities, signifying a Europe that was not yet.

Teleki's spatial turn toward maps and the bulwark concept as a signal for perceived external threats was therefore conspicuously conservative: in interwar Hungary, he favored a Magyar bourgeoisie and European counterrevolution that tended to be anticommunist and anti-Semitic, as he himself was.[45] He supported Hungary's restored power and unity as a professor of economic geography at Budapest University and a known internationalist advocate of Trianon revision throughout the 1920s and 1930s.[46] His mental map of Hungary was illiberal, especially when he served as prime minister first from July 1920 to April 1921 and then again from February 1939 to April 1941.

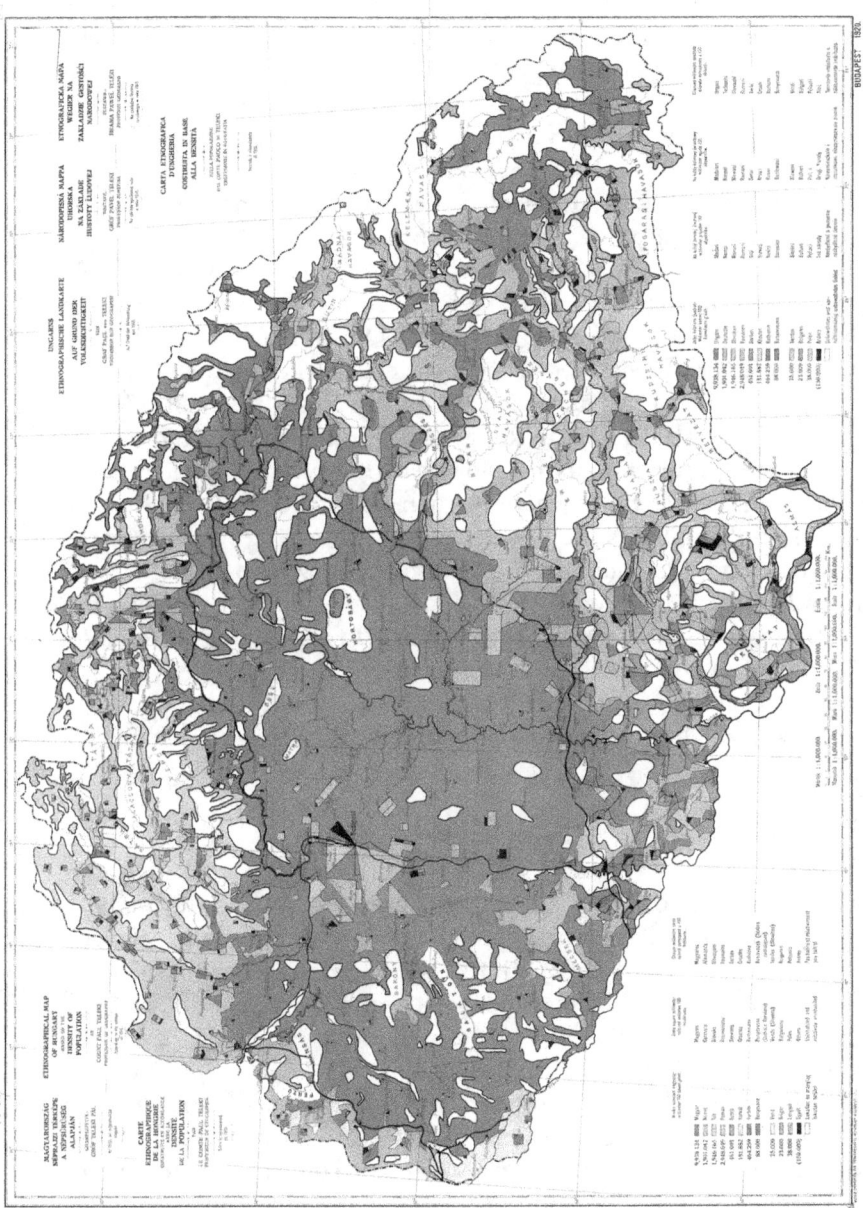

Map 10.7. Ethnographical map of Hungary, based on population density, 1919. Map by Count Pál Teleki. Reprinted from Count Pál Teleki, *Magyarország néprajzi térképe a népsűrűség alapján* (Budapest: Magyar Földrajzi Intézet, 1919).

With the First Vienna Award of 2 November 1938, Hitler granted Hungary the historic St. Stephen lands in Southern Slovakia and Carpathian Rus.[47] In March 1939, Teleki's new government under Horthy's regency took advantage of Nazi gains by laying Hungary's claims to territorial Ukraine, in the mountainous Carpatho-Ukraine region. The prime minister's calculations were perfectly in tune with the *antemurale* myth—a historic Polish-Hungarian fraternity as a Christian bulwark for Europe, for the Polish-Hungarian border in 1939 was imagined as a Western moral frontier space. Friendship with Poland reflected both the persistence of romantic nationalism and Europe as a Christian civilization.

Sensing conflict with the Third Reich over Hungary's borders, Teleki was a product of his pre-1914 past: he believed in Europe as a Christian ideal in the 1930s, but he watched in horror as Poland's fate was sealed by blueprints for a Nazi-Soviet two-front invasion. Teleki's mythic appeal in 1939 to the idea of Polish-Hungarian friendship was his way of infusing the legacy of the post-1918 Carte Rouge and Europe's geographic science with nineteenth-century romantic nationalism. It was also the legacy of the premodern *antemurale* myth, which by then was a cliché, an idea tracing back at least to King Louis the Great (1326–1382) of the Anjou dynasty, born and baptized a Catholic in Visegrád in 1326, who became in 1342 the king of Hungary and Croatia and the king of Poland.[48] The geographer worked to salvage his lost maps and grand plans: to regain losses at Trianon in 1920, to continue the myth of timeless national fraternity between Poland and Hungary, and to support the restoration of a Christian Hungary in Europe, emotionally and preeminently based on the *antemurale* myth.

Conclusion

Through the medium of maps, geographers used history and the *antemurale* concept discursively as fantasy, an effective way to make grand revisionist claims. Maps were windows into a geocoded world, as John Pickles has noted, a subrational language among geographers of an imperialist and nationalist sort.[49] This lasting and powerful allure of the bulwark myth is evident in the continued emotional and cognitive uses of maps. It can be illustrated by the cartographic fantasies and frustrations of Europe's map men—the civilizing, explorer-type colonial experts who, before 1914, operated within objective ethnocentric science and discursive practices of East Central European modern politics.[50] The *antemurale* had incredible staying power in Europe's borderlands well through the high age of modern territoriality from the 1830s to the 1970s, as scientific geographers went in search of early modern to modern continuity, constructed discourses about exceptionalism in the era of modern nationalism, and aimed to place their homelands of Germany, Poland, Ukraine, and Hungary on the map of Europe.

Maps were graphic media, tools, and texts deployed by geographers as historical actors, who presupposed Europe's uniqueness on nation building, or nationalizing, terms. Seeking to define nationality and to put people in their place, they were fond of modern territorial notions of nation-states and statecraft: that three-dimensional people of local, mixed, or nationally indifferent origins had to be sorted in an orderly manner and that such people as populations were legible, measurable, quantifiable, and therefore mappable. If persons were mere objects of mobilization, then following such logic they surely could be made literate and politically conscious by maps, choose to mobilize by religion and nationality, and identify with one's correct group.

For the purpose of the maps discussed in this chapter, this can be seen in four specific and selective ways related to the structures, discourses, and broader effects of the *antemurale* myth. First, the maps tapped into the premodern bulwark idea of a Christian Europe, thus instrumentalizing both religion and nationalism for late nineteenth- and early twentieth-century territorial and geopolitical causes. Second, the maps supposed not only that people were part of cultural and political units in a place called Europe but also that they should embrace by religion and culture their rooted homeland and adopt a patriotic pride of place, according to gendered notions of fixed settlement, kin-state affiliation, and belonging. Third, such maps articulated literacy in a nineteenth-century graphic way as linear progress in regard to geographies of a stateless nation's distant past and uncertain future, as well as the historic future of nations in a unified Europe and the world. Fourth and most significantly, by the aesthetic minutiae of lines (bold for closed borders, suggesting unlawful containment or occupation, or dotted or absent for open frontiers, signifying a natural need for the geobody to expand), place-names (in native and mutually exclusive tongues), and colors (the signaling of danger or importance, propaganda-style, with pink or vibrant red), maps offered a spatial grammar for *antemurale*-inspired geographers as past and present agents of Europe's imagined unity.

Steven Seegel is a professor of history at the University of Northern Colorado. He is the author of *Mapping Europe's Borderlands: Russian Cartography in the Age of Empire* (University of Chicago Press, 2012), *Ukraine under Western Eyes* (Harvard University Press, 2013), and *Map Men: Transnational Lives and Deaths of Geographers in the Making of East Central Europe* (University of Chicago Press, 2018). He has also translated over 300 entries for the U.S. Holocaust Memorial Museum's multivolume *Encyclopedia of Camps and Ghettos, 1933–1945*, ed. Geoffrey P. Megargee (Indiana University Press, 2009–present).

Notes

1. J. Szpetkowski, *Mapa Polski za Panowania Krola Jana Sobieskiego wydana w dwochsetną rocznicę odzieczy Wiednia* (Wien/Poznań: L. Neumeyer, 1883). The map was reprinted in Cracow and soon spread to atlases, posters, and local religious calendars in autonomous Galicia. Its design depicted Poland's battle against the Ottoman Turks as a struggle for Europe. See my *Mapping Europe's Borderlands: Russian Cartography in the Age of Empire* (Chicago: University of Chicago Press, 2012), 180–85.
2. P. Srodecki, "Antemurale Christianitatis," in *Religiöse Erinnerungsorte in Ostmitteleuropa: Konstitution und Konkurrenz im nationen- und epochenübergreifenden Zugrif*, ed. J. Bahlcke, S. Rohdewald, and T. Wünsch (Berlin: Akademie-Verlag, 2013), 804–22.
3. C.S. Maier, "Transformations of Territoriality, 1600–2000," in *Transnationale Geschichte: Themen, Tendenzen und Theorien*, ed. G. Budde, S. Conrad, and O. Janz (Göttingen: Vandenhoeck & Ruprecht, 2010), 32–55.
4. For recent historiography and criticism of colonial/postcolonial binarism in East Central Europe, see the introduction by R. Healy and E. Dal Lago, eds., *The Shadow of Colonialism on Europe's Modern Past* (New York: Palgrave Macmillan, 2014), 3–22; K. Kaps and J. Surman, "Postcolonial or Post-Colonial? Post(-)colonial Perspectives on Habsburg Galicia," *Historyka: Studia metodologiczne* 42 (2012): 7–35.
5. On the concept of *mission civilisatrice* as part of *antemurale* mythology see the introduction to this book.
6. M.G. Hannah, *Governmentality and the Mastery of Territory in Nineteenth-Century America* (Cambridge: Cambridge University Press, 2000); G. Bederman, *Manliness and Civilization: A Cultural History of Gender and Race in the United States, 1880–1917* (Chicago: University of Chicago Press, 1995); M. Kimmel, J. Hearn, and R. Connell, eds., *Handbook of Studies on Men and Masculinities* (Thousand Oaks: Sage, 2005).
7. See, for instance, P. Hubbard and R. Kitchin, eds., *Key Thinkers on Space and Place* (London: Sage, 2010); L. Nelson and J. Seager, eds., *A Companion to Feminist Geography* (London: Blackwell, 2005); and L. McDowell, *Gender, Identity, and Place: Understanding Feminist Geographies* (Minneapolis: University of Minnesota Press, 1999).
8. P. Haslinger and V. Oswalt, eds., *Kampf der Karten: Propaganda- und Geschichtskarten als politische Instrumente und Identitätstexte* (Marburg: Herder-Institut, 2012); P.R. Gould, *On Mental Maps* (Ann Arbor: University of Michigan, 1966); F. Benjamin Schenk, "Mental Maps: Die kognitive Kartierung des Kontinents als Forschungsgegenstand der europäischen Geschichte," Europäische Geschichte Online. 2013, retrieved 16 September 2014 from http://ieg-ego.eu/de/threads/theorien-und-methoden/mental-maps/frithjof-benjamin-schenk-mental-maps-die-kognitive-kartierung-des-kontinents-als-forschungsgegenstand-der-europaeischen-geschichte;

"Mental Maps: Die Konstruktion von geographischen Räumen in Europa seit der Aufklärung," *Geschichte und Gesellschaft* 28 (2002): 493–514; S. Damir-Geilsdorf, A. Hartmann, and B. Hendrich, eds., *Mental Maps—Raum—Erinnerung: Kulturwissenschaftliche Zugänge zum Verhältnis vom Raum und Erinnerung* (Münster: LIT Verlag, 2005).

9. V. G. Liulevicius, *The German Myth of the East: 1800 to the Present* (Oxford: Oxford University Press, 2009) and G. Lilevicius, ed., *War Land on the Eastern Front: Culture, National Identity and German Occupation in World War I* (Cambridge: Cambridge University Press, 2000); G. Thum, "Megalomania and Angst: The Nineteenth-Century Mythicization of Germany's Eastern Borderlands," in *Shatterzone of Empires: Coexistence and Violence in the German, Habsburg, Russian, and Ottoman Borderlands*, ed. O. Bartov and E.D. Weitz (Bloomington: Indiana University Press, 2013), 42–60; G. Thum, ed., *Traumland Osten: Deutsche Bilder vom östlichen Europa im 20. Jahrhundert* (Göttingen: Vandenhoeck & Ruprecht, 2006).

10. M. Heffernan, *The Meaning of Europe: Geography and Geopolitics* (London: Routledge, 2000), 71–76.

11. K. Raj, *Relocating Modern Science: Circulation and the Construction of Knowledge in South Asia and Europe, 1650–1900* (New York: Palgrave Macmillan, 2007), 223–34.

12. A. Penck, *Geologische Spezialkarte des Königreich Sachsen* (Leipzig: Giesecke & Devrient, 1878).

13. A. Penck, "Professoren als Spione. Abwehr von Prof. Dr. Albrecht Penck, Direktor des geographischen Instituts der Berliner Universität" (1917), Albrecht Penck Papers (Archive of the Institut für Länderkunde in Leipzig), Kasten 877, Signatur 36/4; on the British-German geopolitics of the matter in the early stages of World War I, M. Heffernan, "Professor Penck's Bluff: Geography, Espionage and Hysteria in World War I," *Scottish Geographical Journal* 116, no. 4 (2000): 267–82.

14. A. Mehmel, "Deutsche Revisionspolitik in der Geographie nach dem ersten Weltkrieg," *Geographische Rundschau* 47 (1995): 498–505.

15. For textual analysis, see G.H. Herb, *Under the Map of Germany: Nationalism and Propaganda 1918–1945* (London/New York: Routledge, 1997), 124–29. Without Polish-language sources, however, Herb only noted the quarrels as they appeared in public and in German print or maps. See also K. Kopp, *Germany's Wild East: Constructing Poland as Colonial Space* (Ann Arbor: University of Michigan Press, 2012); A. Schweiger, *Polens Zukunft liegt im Osten: Polnische Ostkonzepte der späten Teilungszeit, 1890–1918* (Marburg: Verlag Herder-Institut, 2014); and G. Briesewitz, *Raum und Nation in der polnischen Westforschung: Wissenschaftsdiskurse, Raumdeutungen und geopolitische Visionen im Kontext der deutsch-polnischen Beziehungsgeschichte, 1918–1948* (Osnabrück: Fibre, 2014).

16. E.A. Drummond, "From 'verloren gehen' to 'verloren bleiben': Changing German Discourses on Nation and Nationalism in Poznania," in *The Germans and the East*, ed. Ch. W. Ingrao and F.A.J. Szabo (Lafayette: Purdue University Press, 2009), 226–40; D. Blackbourn and R.J. Evans, eds., *The German Bourgeoisie: Essays on the Social History of the German Middle Class from the Late Eighteenth to the Early Twentieth Century* (London: Routledge, 1993).

17. M. Fahlbuch, "Volks- und Kulturbodenforschung in der Weimarer Republik: Der 'Grenzfall' Böhmen und Mähren," in *Kontinuität und Diskontinuität der deutschen*

Geographie in Umbruchphasen: Studien zur Geschichte der Geographie, ed. U. Wardenga and I. Hönsch (Münster: Institut für Geographie der Westfälischen Wilhelms-Universität, 1995), 100–12.

18. A. Penck, "Deutscher Volks- und Kulturboden," in *Volk unter Völkern: Bücher des Deutschtums*, vol. 1: *Für den Deutschen Schutzbund*, ed. K.C. von Loesch (Breslau: Ferdinand Hirt, 1925), 62–73.
19. I. Haar, "German Ostforschung and Anti-semitism," in *German Scholars and Ethnic Cleansing, 1919–1945*, ed. I. Haar and M. Fahlbusch (New York: Berghahn Books, 2005), 21.
20. Ibid., 30–31.
21. J. Piskorski and J. Hackmann, "Polish myśl zachodnia and German Ostforschung: An Attempt at Comparison," in *German Scholars and Ethnic Cleansing, 1919–1945*, ed. I. Haar and M. Fahlbusch (New York: Berghahn Books, 2005), 260–71; J.M. Piskorski, J. Hackmann, and R. Jaworski, eds., *Deutsche Ostforschung und polnische Westforschung im Spannungsfeld von Wissenschaft und Politik: Disziplinen im Vergleich* (Osnabrück/Poznań: Poznańskie Towarzystwo Przyjaciół Nauk, 2002).
22. E. Romer, *Geograficzno-statystyczny atlas Polski* (Warszawa/Kraków, 1916).
23. E. Romer, *Wojenno-polityczna mapa Polski (Z powodu Manifestu z 5 listopada 1916 r.)* (Lwów: Książnica Polska Towarzystwa Nauczycieli Szkół Wyższych, 1916).
24. On Romer and problematic issues of mapping "historical" borders, see Schweiger, *Polens Zukunft liegt im Osten*, 110–11; P. Eberhardt, *Polska i jej granice: Z historii polskiej geografii politycznej* (Lublin: Wydawnictwo Uniwersytetu Marii Curie-Skłodowskiej, 2004), 88–90.
25. *Erinnerungen von Albrecht Penck*, K. 871, S. 3, 70, Albrecht Penck Papers, Archive of the Institut für Länderkunde in Leipzig.
26. Ibid., 71.
27. On Romer's background, see M. Mroczko, *Eugeniusz Romer (1871–1954) Biografia polityczna* (Słupsk: Wydawnictwo Naukowe Akademii Pomorskiej w Słupsku, 2008); J. Babicz, "Eugeniusz Romer, 1871–1954," in *Geographers: Biobibliographical Studies*, vol. 1, ed. T.W. Freeman et al. (Salem: Mansell, 1977), 89–96; S.M. Brzozowski, "Eugeniusz Mikołaj Romer," in *Polski słownik biograficzny*, vol. 31/4, ed. E. Rostworowski (Wrocław: Polska Akademia Umiejętności, 1989), 636–45; J. Ostrowski, J. Pasławski, and L. Szaniawska, eds., *Eugeniusz Romer geograf i kartograf trzech epok* (Warszawa: Biblioteka Narodowa, 2004); and Seegel, *Mapping Europe's Borderlands*, 243–53.
28. G. Hausmann, "Das Territorium der Ukraine: Stepan Rudnyckyjs Beitrag zur Geschichte räumlich-territorialen Denkens über die Ukraine," in *Die Ukraine: Prozesse der Nationsbildung*, ed. A. Kappeler (Köln: Böhlau, 2011), 145–57; I. Stebelsky, *Placing Ukraine on the Map: Stepan Rudnyts'kyi's Nation-Building Geography* (self-published by the author, 2014), 20–25; Stebelsky, "Putting Ukraine on the Map: The Contribution of Stepan Rudnyts'kyi to Ukrainian Nation-Building," *Nationalities Papers* 39, no. 4 (2011): 587–613; for detailed, but more conventional, struggle for the nation studies, see P. Shtoiko, *Stepan Rudnytskyi, 1887–1937: Zhyttepysno-bibliohrafichnyi narys* (Lviv: NTSh, 1997); O. Shablii, *Akademik Stepan Rudnytskyi: fundator ukrainskoi heohrafii* (Lviv: Lvivskyi Natsionalnyi Universytet im. Ivana Franka, 1993).

29. V. Kubijovyč, "Rudnytsky, Stepan," in *Encyclopedia of Ukraine*, vol. 4, ed. D. Husak Struk (Toronto: University of Toronto Press, 1993), 428.
30. For a political-geographical analysis of Rudnytskyi's practices, see G. Hausmann, "Das Territorium der Ukraine"; G. Hausmann, "Die Kultur der Niederlage: Der Erste Weltkrieg in der ukrainischen Erinnerung," *Osteuropa* 64, no. 2–4 (2014): 127–40; Stebelsky, *Placing Ukraine on the Map*, 20–25.
31. S. Rudnytskyi, *Das Wohngebiet der Ukrainer in Europa at the end of Ukraina und die Ukrainer* (Wien: Verlag des Allgemeinen Ukrainischen Nationalrates, 1915 [1914]), reprinted Berlin.
32. Sh. Levenko [pseud. Stepan Rudnytskyi], *Chomu my khochemo samoistinoi Ukrainy* (Wien: no publisher, 1915), reprinted as *Chomu my khochemo samoistinoi Ukrainy*, ed. Oleh Shablii. Lviv: Svit, 1994.
33. Stebelsky, *Placing Ukraine on the Map*, 18–19; and on the importance of Rudnytskyi's geographical works and Ukraine maps, see A. Veronika Wendland, "Ikonografen des Raumbilds Ukraine: eine europäische Wissenstransfergeschichte," in *Kampf der Karten: Propaganda- und Geschichtskarten als politische Instrumente und Identitätstexte*, ed. P. Haslinger and V. Oswalt (Marburg: Verlag Herder-Institut, 2012), 101–3; G. Hausmann, "Maps of the Borderlands: Russia and Ukraine," in *The Shadow of Colonialism on Europe's Modern Past*, ed. R. Healy and E. Dal Lago (New York: Palgrave, 2014), 204–6.
34. S. Rudnytskyi and H. von Hasenko, *Ukraina u svoikh etnohrafichnykh mezhakh/ Die Ukraina in ihren ethnographischen Grenzen* (Wien/Kyiv: Christopher Reisser's Söhne, 1920).
35. S. Rudnytskyi, *Ohliad terytorii Ukrainy* (Wien: Franko & Son, 1921); *Osnovy zemleznannia Ukrainy* (Prague: Vydavnytstvo Ukrainskoho universitetu v Prazi, 1923; reprinted in Lviv, 1924, and Uzhhorod, 1926). On country descriptions of this era, see T. Lam, *A Passion for Facts: Social Surveys and the Construction of the Chinese Nation-State, 1900–1949* (Berkeley: University of California Press, 2011).
36. On the towns and cities on both sides of this border, see P. Adelsgruber, L. Cohen, and B. Kuzmany, eds., *Getrennt und doch Verbunden: Grenzstädte zwischen Österreich und Russland, 1772–1918* (Wien: Böhlau Verlag, 2013).
37. P. Ther, "The Transnational Paradigm of Historiography and Its Potential for Ukrainian History," in *A Laboratory of Transnational History: Ukraine and Recent Ukrainian Historiography*, ed. G. Kasianov and P. Ther (Budapest: Central European University Press, 2008), 81–114.
38. B. Ablonczy, *Teleki Pál* (Budapest: Osiris, 2005), trans. T.J. DeKornfield and Helen D. DeKornfield as *Pál Teleki, The Life of a Controversial Hungarian Politician (1874–1941)* (Boulder: Social Science Monographs, 2006); Ablonczy, ed., *Teleki Pál: Válogatott politikai írások és beszédek* (Budapest: Osiris, 2000); Ablonczy, *A visszatért érdély, 1940–1944* (Budapest: Jaffa Kiadó, 2011); Ablonczy, ed., *Teleki Pál: Válogatott politikai írások és beszédek* (Budapest: Osiris, 2000).
39. P. Teleki, *Magyarország néprajzi térképe a népsűrűség alapján* (Budapest: Magyar Földrajzi Intézet, 1919).
40. H. Case, "Revisionism in Regional Perspective," in *Territorial Revisionism and the Allies of Germany in the Second World War: Goals, Expectations, Practices*, ed. M. Cattaruzza, S. Dyroff, and D. Langewiesche (New York: Berghahn Books, 2012),

72–91; on revisionism as ideology in interwar Hungary, see M. Zeidler, *A revíziós gondolat* (Pozsony: Kalligram, 2009).
41. Á. Papp-Váry, *Magyarorszag története térképeken* (Budapest: Kossuth Kiadó-Cartographia, 2002), 56–57.
42. Ibid., 252–253. Papp-Vary praises the "novelty and objectivity" of the Carte Rouge as "fully credible from a scientific point of view." For a more careful analysis of Hungary's policies toward its Romanian and Jewish minorities, see H. Case, *Between States: The Transylvanian Question and the European Idea during World War II* (Stanford: Stanford University Press, 2009), 39–48.
43. M.H. Edney, "The Irony of Imperial Mapping," in *The Imperial Map: Cartography and the Mastery of Empire*, ed. J.K. Akerman (Chicago: University of Chicago Press, 2009), 11–45; M.H. Edney, "Cartography without 'Progress': Reinterpreting the Nature and Historical Development of Mapmaking," *Cartographica* 30, nos. 2–3 (1993): 54–68.
44. I. Romsics, *The Dismantling of Historic Hungary: The Peace Treaty of Trianon, 1920* (Boulder: East European Monographs, 2002).
45. P.A. Hanebrink, *In Defense of Christian Hungary: Religion, Nationalism, and Anti-semitism, 1890–1944* (Ithaca: Cornell University Press, 2006); B.R. Berglund and B. Porter-Szűcs, eds., *Christianity and Modernity in Eastern Europe* (Budapest: Central European University Press, 2010); B. Porter-Szűcs, *Faith and Fatherland: Catholicism, Modernity, and Poland* (Oxford: Oxford University Press, 2011).
46. P. Teleki, *The Evolution of Hungary and Its Place in European History* (New York: Macmillan, 1923) was an early collection of his lectures and essays that reflected his revisionist position. A collection of his essays later appeared as *Európáról és Magyarországról* (Budapest: Athenaeum, 1934).
47. Case, *Between States*, 9–66.
48. So went the proverbial sayings that emerged around the first partition of Poland: *Polak, Węgier—dwa bratanki/i do szabli, i do szklanki,/oba zuchy, oba żwawi,/ niech im Pan Bóg błogosławi* (Two cousins—Pole and Hungarian/right for the sabre and the party glass/both are courageous, both are lively/may God bless them) and *Lengyel, magyar—két jó barát,/együtt harcol s issza borát* (Two good mates—Pole and Hungarian/battle together and drink their wine). On the uses and abuses of the stereotype, see M. Mitrovits, *Lengyel, magyar—"két jó barát": A magyar-lengyel kapcsolatok dokumentumai, 1957–1987* (Budapest: Napvilág Kiadó, 2014).
49. John Pickles develops this key concept in *A History of Spaces: Cartographic Reason, Mapping, and the Geo-coded World* (London: Routledge, 2004) in the growing field of critical cartography studies.
50. H. Hein-Kircher and H.-H. Hahn, eds., *Politische Mythen im 19. und 20. Jahrhundert im Mittel- und Ostmitteleuropa* (Marburg: Herder-Institut, 2006).

Bibliography

Ablonczy, B. 2006. *Teleki Pál*. Budapest: Osiris, 2005, translated by T.J. DeKornfield and Helen D. DeKornfield as *Pál Teleki, The Life of a Controversial Hungarian Politician (1874–1941)*. Boulder: Social Science Monographs.

———. 2011. *A visszatért érdély, 1940–1944*. Budapest: Jaffa Kiadó.

———, ed. 2000. *Teleki Pál: Válogatott politikai írások és beszédek*. Budapest: Osiris.
Adelsgruber, P., L. Cohen, and B. Kuzmany, eds. 2013. *Getrennt und doch Verbunden: Grenzstädte zwischen Österreich und Russland, 1772–1918*. Wien: Böhlau Verlag.
Babicz, J. 1977. "Eugeniusz Romer, 1871–1954." In *Geographers: Biobibliographical Studies*. Vol. 1, ed. T.W. Freeman et al. Salem: Mansell, 89–96.
Bederman, G. 1995. *Manliness and Civilization: A Cultural History of Gender and Race in the United States, 1880–1917*. Chicago: University of Chicago Press.
Berglund, B.R. and B. Porter-Szűcs, eds. 2010. *Christianity and Modernity in Eastern Europe*. Budapest: Central European University Press.
Blackbourn, D. and R.J. Evans, eds. 1993. *The German Bourgeoisie: Essays on the Social History of the German Middle Class from the Late Eighteenth to the Early Twentieth Century*. London: Routledge.
Briesewitz, G. 2014. *Raum und Nation in der polnischen Westforschung: Wissenschaftsdiskurse, Raumdeutungen und geopolitische Visionen im Kontext der deutsch-polnischen Beziehungsgeschichte, 1918–1948*. Osnabrück: Fibre.
Brzozowski, S.M. 1989. "Eugeniusz Mikołaj Romer." In *Polski słownik biograficzny*. Vol. 31/4, 636–45. Wrocław: Polska Akademia Umiejętności.
Case, H. 2009. *Between States: The Transylvanian Question and the European Idea during World War II*. Stanford: Stanford University Press.
———. 2012. "Revisionism in Regional Perspective." In *Territorial Revisionism and the Allies of Germany in the Second World War: Goals, Expectations, Practices*, ed. M. Cattaruzza, S. Dyroff, and D. Langewiesche, 72–91. New York: Berghahn Books.
Damir-Geilsdorf, S., A. Hartmann, and B. Hendrich, eds. 2005. *Mental Maps—Raum—Erinnerung: Kulturwissenschaftliche Zugänge zum Verhältnis vom Raum und Erinnerung*. Münster: LIT Verlag.
Drummond, E.A. 2009. "From 'verloren gehen' to 'verloren bleiben': Changing German Discourses on Nation and Nationalism in Poznania." In *The Germans and the East*, ed. Ch. W. Ingrao and F.A.J. Szabo, 226–40. Lafayette: Purdue University Press.
Eberhardt, P. 2004. *Polska i jej granice: Z historii polskiej geografii politycznej*. Lublin: Wydawnictwo Uniwersytetu Marii Curie-Skłodowskiej.
Edney, M.H. 1993. "Cartography without 'Progress': Reinterpreting the Nature and Historical Development of Mapmaking." *Cartographica* 30, no. 2–3: 54–68.
———. 2009. "The Irony of Imperial Mapping." In *The Imperial Map: Cartography and the Mastery of Empire*, ed. J.K. Akerman, 11–45. Chicago: University of Chicago Press.
Erinnerungen von Albrecht Penck, K. 871. 1943–1945. Albrecht Penck Papers, Archive of the Institut für Länderkunde in Leipzig.
Fahlbuch, M. 1995. "Volks- und Kulturbodenforschung in der Weimarer Republik: Der 'Grenzfall' Böhmen und Mähren." In *Kontinuität und Diskontinuität der deutschen Geographie in Umbruchphasen: Studien zur Geschichte der Geographie*, ed. U. Wardenga and I. Hönsch, 100–112. Münster: Institut für Geographie der Westfälischen Wilhelms-Universität.
Gould, P.R. 1966. *On Mental Maps*. Ann Arbor: University of Michigan.
Haar, I. 2005. "German Ostforschung and Anti-semitism." In *German Scholars and Ethnic Cleansing, 1919–1945*, ed. I. Haar and M. Fahlbusch, 1–27. New York: Berghahn Books.
Hanebrink, P.A. 2006. *In Defense of Christian Hungary: Religion, Nationalism, and Antisemitism, 1890–1944*. Ithaca: Cornell University Press.

Hannah, M.G. 2000. *Governmentality and the Mastery of Territory in Nineteenth-Century America.* Cambridge: Cambridge University Press.
Haslinger, P. and V. Oswalt, eds. 2012. *Kampf der Karten: Propaganda- und Geschichtskarten als politische Instrumente und Identitätstexte.* Marburg: Herder-Institut.
Hausmann, G. 2011. "Das Territorium der Ukraine: Stepan Rudnyckyjs Beitrag zur Geschichte räumlich-territorialen Denkens über die Ukraine." In *Die Ukraine: Prozesse der Nationsbildung,* ed. A. Kappeler, 145–57. Köln: Böhlau.
———. 2014. "Die Kultur der Niederlage: Der Erste Weltkrieg in der ukrainischen Erinnerung." *Osteuropa* 64, nos. 2–4: 127–40.
———. 2014. "Maps of the Borderlands: Russia and Ukraine." In *The Shadow of Colonialism on Europe's Modern Past,* ed. R. Healy and E. Dal Lago, 194–210. New York: Palgrave.
Healy R. and E. Dal Lago, eds. 2014. *The Shadow of Colonialism on Europe's Modern Past.* New York: Palgrave Macmillan.
Heffernan, M. 2000. "Professor Penck's Bluff: Geography, Espionage and Hysteria in World War I." *Scottish Geographical Journal* 116, no. 4: 267–82.
———. 2000. *The Meaning of Europe: Geography and Geopolitics.* London: Routledge.
Hein-Kircher H. and H.-H. Hahn, eds. 2006. *Politische Mythen im 19. und 20. Jahrhundert im Mittel- und Ostmitteleuropa.* Marburg: Herder-Institut.
Herb, G.H. 1997. *Under the Map of Germany: Nationalism and Propaganda 1918–1945.* London/New York: Routledge.
Hubbard, P. and R. Kitchin, eds. 2010. *Key Thinkers on Space and Place.* London: Sage.
Kaps K. and J. Surman. 2012. "Postcolonial or Post-Colonial? Post(-)colonial Perspectives on Habsburg Galicia." *Historyka: Studia metodologiczne* 42: 7–35.
Kimmel, M., J. Hearn, and R. Connell, eds. 2005. *Handbook of Studies on Men and Masculinities.* Thousand Oaks: Sage.
Kopp, K. 2012. *Germany's Wild East: Constructing Poland as Colonial Space.* Ann Arbor: University of Michigan Press.
Kubijovyč, V. 1993. "Rudnytsky, Stepan." In *Encyclopedia of Ukraine.* Vol. 4, ed. D. Husak Struk, 428. Toronto: University of Toronto Press.
Lam, T. 2011. *A Passion for Facts: Social Surveys and the Construction of the Chinese Nation-State, 1900–1949.* Berkeley: University of California Press.
Levenko, Sh. [pseud. S. Rudnytskyi]. 1915. *Chomu my khochemo samoistinoi Ukrainy.* Wien: no publisher. Reprinted as *Chomu my khochemo samoistinoi Ukrainy,* ed. Oleh Shablii. Lviv: Svit, 1994.
Liulevicius, V.G. 2000. *War Land on the Eastern Front: Culture, National identity and German Occupation in World War I.* Cambridge: Cambridge University Press.
———. 2009. *The German Myth of the East: 1800 to the Present.* Oxford: Oxford University Press.
Maier, C.S. 2010. "Transformations of Territoriality, 1600–2000." In *Transnationale Geschichte: Themen, Tendenzen und Theorien,* ed. G. Budde, S. Conrad, and O. Janz, 32–55. Göttingen: Vandenhoeck & Ruprecht.
McDowell, L. 1999. *Gender, Identity, and Place: Understanding Feminist Geographies.* Minneapolis: University of Minnesota Press.
Mehmel, A. 1995. "Deutsche Revisionspolitik in der Geographie nach dem ersten Weltkrieg." *Geographische Rundschau* 47: 498–505.

Mitrovits, M. 2014. *Lengyel, magyar—"két jó barát": A magyar-lengyel kapcsolatok dokumentumai, 1957–1987.* Budapest: Napvilág Kiadó.
Mroczko, M. 2008. *Eugeniusz Romer (1871–1954) Biografia polityczna.* Słupsk: Wydawnictwo Naukowe Akademii Pomorskiej w Słupsku.
Nelson, L. and J. Seager, eds. 2005. *A Companion to Feminist Geography.* London: Blackwell.
Ostrowski, J., J. Pasławski, and L. Szaniawska, eds. 2004. *Eugeniusz Romer geograf i kartograf trzech epok.* Warszawa: Biblioteka Narodowa.
Papp-Váry, Á. 2002. *Magyarorszag története térképeken.* Budapest: Kossuth Kiadó-Cartographia.
Penck, A. 1878. *Geologische Spezialkarte des Königreich Sachsen.* Leipzig: Giesecke & Devrient.
———. 1917. "Professoren als Spione. Abwehr von Prof. Dr. Albrecht Penck, Direktor des geographischen Instituts der Berliner Universität." Albrecht Penck Papers (Archive of the Institut für Länderkunde in Leipzig), Kasten 877, Signatur 36/4.
———. 1925. "Deutscher Volks- und Kulturboden." In *Volk unter Völkern: Bücher des Deutschtums*, vol. 1: *Für den Deutschen Schutzbund*, ed. L. von Broecker, E. Frobenius, K. Christian von Loesch, and A.H. Ziegfeld, 62–73. Breslau: Ferdinand Hirt.
Pickles, J. 2004. *A History of Spaces: Cartographic Reason, Mapping, and the Geo-coded World.* London: Routledge.
Piskorski, J.M. and J. Hackmann. 2005. "Polish myśl zachodnia and German Ostforschung: An Attempt at Comparison." In *German Scholars and Ethnic Cleansing, 1919– 1945*, ed. I. Haar and M. Fahlbusch, 260–71. New York: Berghahn Books.
Piskorski, J.M., J. Hackmann, and R. Jaworski, eds. 2002. *Deutsche Ostforschung und polnische Westforschung im Spannungsfeld von Wissenschaft und Politik: Disziplinen im Vergleich.* Osnabrück/Poznań: Poznańskie Towarzystwo Przyjaciół Nauk.
Porter-Szűcs, B. 2011. *Faith and Fatherland: Catholicism, Modernity, and Poland.* Oxford: Oxford University Press.
Raj, K. 2007. *Relocating Modern Science: Circulation and the Construction of Knowledge in South Asia and Europe, 1650–1900.* New York: Palgrave Macmillan.
Romer, E. 1916. *Geograficzno-statystyczny atlas Polski.* Warszawa/Kraków.
———. 1916. *Wojenno-polityczna mapa Polski (Z powodu Manifestu z 5 listopada 1916 r.).* Lwów: Książnica Polska Towarzystwa Nauczycieli Szkół Wyższych.
Romsics, I. 2002. *The Dismantling of Historic Hungary: The Peace Treaty of Trianon, 1920.* Boulder: East European Monographs.
Rudnytskyi, S. 1915 [1914]. "Das Wohngebiet der Ukrainer in Europa." *Ukraina und die Ukrainer.* Wien: Verlag des Allgemeinen Ukrainischen Nationalrates. Reprinted Berlin.
———. 1921. *Ohliad terytorii Ukrainy.* Wien: Franko & Son.
———. 1923. *Osnovy zemleznannia Ukrainy.* Prague: Vydavnytstvo Ukrainskoho universitetu v Prazi, reprinted in Lviv, 1924, and Uzhhorod, 1926.
Rudnytskyi, S. and H. von Hasenko. 1920. *Ukraina u svoikh etnohrafichnykh mezhakh/ Die Ukraina in ihren ethnographischen Grenzen.* Wien/Kyiv: Christopher Reisser's Söhne.
Schenk, F.B. 2002. "Mental Maps: Die Konstruktion von geographischen Räumen in Europa seit der Aufklärung." *Geschichte und Gesellschaft* 28: 493–514.

———. 2014. "Mental Maps: Die kognitive Kartierung des Kontinents als Forschungsgegenstand der europäischen Geschichte." Europäische Geschichte Online. Retrieved 16 September 2014 from http://ieg-ego.eu/de/threads/theorien-und-methoden/mental-maps/frithjof-benjamin-schenk-mental-maps-die-kognitive-kartierung-des-kontinents-als-forschungsgegenstand-der-europaeischen-geschichte.

Schweiger, A. 2014. *Polens Zukunft liegt im Osten: Polnische Ostkonzepte der späten Teilungszeit, 1890–1918.* Marburg: Verlag Herder-Institut.

Seegel, S. 2012. *Mapping Europe's Borderlands: Russian Cartography in the Age of Empire.* Chicago: University of Chicago Press.

Shablii, O. 1993. *Akademik Stepan Rudnytskyi: fundator ukrainskoi heohrafii.* Lviv: Lvivskyi Natsionalnyi Universytet im. Ivana Franka.

Shtoiko, P. 1997. *Stepan Rudnytskyi, 1887–1937: Zhyttepysno-bibliohrafichnyi narys.* Lviv: NTSh.

Srodecki, P. 2013. "Antemurale Christianitatis." In *Religiöse Erinnerungsorte in Ostmitteleuropa: Konstitution und Konkurrenz im nationen- und epochenübergreifenden Zugriff*, ed. J. Bahlcke, S. Rohdewald, and T. Wünsch, 804–22. Berlin: Akademie-Verlag.

Stebelsky, I. 2011. "Putting Ukraine on the Map: The Contribution of Stepan Rudnyts'kyi to Ukrainian Nation-Building." *Nationalities Papers* 39, no. 4: 587–613.

———. 2014. *Placing Ukraine on the Map: Stepan Rudnyts'kyi's Nation-Building Geography.* Self-published by the author.

Szpetkowski, J. 1883. *Mapa Polski za Panowania Krola Jana Sobieskiego wydana w dwochsetną rocznicę odzieczy Wiednia.* Wien/Poznań: L. Neumeyer.

Teleki, P. 1919. *Magyarország néprajzi térképe a népsűrűség alapján.* Budapest: Magyar Földrajzi Intézet.

———. 1923. *The Evolution of Hungary and Its Place in European History.* New York: Macmillan.

———. 1934. *Európáról és Magyarországról.* Budapest: Athenaeum.

Ther, P. 2008. "The Transnational Paradigm of Historiography and Its Potential for Ukrainian History." In *A Laboratory of Transnational History: Ukraine and Recent Ukrainian Historiography*, ed. G. Kasianov and P. Ther, 81–114. Budapest: Central European University Press.

Thum, G. 2013. "Megalomania and Angst: The Nineteenth-Century Mythicization of Germany's Eastern Borderlands." In *Shatterzone of Empires: Coexistence and Violence in the German, Habsburg, Russian, and Ottoman Borderlands*, ed. O. Bartov and E.D. Weitz, 42–60. Bloomington: Indiana University Press.

Thum, G., ed. 2006. *Traumland Osten: Deutsche Bilder vom östlichen Europa im 20. Jahrhundert.* Göttingen: Vandenhoeck & Ruprecht.

Wendland, A.V. 2012. "Ikonografen des Raumbilds Ukraine: eine europäische Wissenstransfergeschichte." In *Kampf der Karten: Propaganda- und Geschichtskarten als politische Instrumente und Identitätstexte*, ed. P. Haslinger and V. Oswalt, 85–120. Marburg: Verlag Herder-Institut.

Zeidler, M. 2009. *A revíziós gondolat.* Pozsony: Kalligram.

CHAPTER 11

Bulwarks of Anti-Bolshevism
Russophobic Polemic of the Christian Right in Poland and Hungary in the Interwar Years and Their Roots in the Nineteenth Century

Paul Srodecki

Both Hungary and Poland considered themselves the most important bulwarks of European freedom and civilization against the Bolshevik danger in the East. Alongside historical fears, two events were responsible for the widespread anticommunism in both countries. In Poland, this was the invasion of the Red Army in the Polish-Soviet War of 1919–1920 and the so-called *Cud nad Wisłą* (Miracle on the Vistula): the victory of the Polish army under József Piłsudski (1867–1935) over Soviet troops in the Battle of Warsaw in August 1920. In Hungary, the anti-Bolshevik stance had its roots in the short-lived Hungarian Soviet Republic (March to August 1919) and the so-called *vörösterror* (Red Terror), a series of politically motivated atrocities aimed at crushing political rivals during the four-month regime of the Hungarian communists.

In both the Polish and the Hungarian case, the anti-Bolshevik propaganda of the interwar period drew heavily upon the long-standing rhetoric, dating back to the Middle Ages, that positioned these two countries as the *avant poste* of Latin Christianity. The Roman Catholic Church contributed to a considerable extent to the consolidation of these two nations' understanding of themselves as walls against the barbaric, non-Christian (and in this case Bolshevik) East.

Poland

The roots of the Polish bulwark propaganda targeted at Russia and the Soviet Union can be found in the late fifteenth and sixteenth centuries.[1] Beginning with Jan Ostroróg's (1565–1622) *Monumentum pro reipubli-*

cae ordinatione, in which the voivode of Poznań described the Kingdom of Poland as "the outermost picket of all Christian kingdoms" in its fight against Ottomans, Tatars, Vlachs, and Muscovites,[2] Muscovy arose as the number one enemy of the Polish-Lithuanian Commonwealth. In various propagandistic poems, memoranda, books, and diplomatic letters of the sixteenth and seventeenth centuries, Poland was styled as the "perpetual bulwark of [Latin] Christianity against Moscow's schismatics." The Muscovite state as well as the Orthodox Church at large were denounced as "gens barbara, gens incompta" (barbaric nation, rude nation) or "pestis Moscovitica" (Muscovite pest).[3]

Muscovy did not belong to Europe in the worldview of the European humanists. Situated in *Sarmatia asiatica*,[4] the Muscovites were seen as descendants of the Mongols and, therefore, as thoroughly Asiatic—as "Moscos Asiaticos" (Asian Muscovites) as Erasmus (1466–1536) of Rotterdam wrote in 1535.[5] The ideological foundations of this pejorative explanatory pattern originated in the late ancient/early medieval *plaga orientalis* tradition, which itself drew its inspiration from biblical tales of the fierce and cruel nomadic peoples of the eastern steppes. Thus, Eurasian intruders such as the Huns, Alans, Khazars, Magyars, Mongols, and Tatars and also (in some sources) Islamic invaders such as the Arabs and Ottomans were identified by the Christian Occident as the biblical Gog and Magog.[6] Besides Jan Ostroróg, Polish dignitaries, scholars, and clergymen, including Maciej Miechowita (1457–1523), Piotr Tomicki (1464–1535), Jan Łaski the Elder (1456–1531), Stanisław Orzechowski (1513–1566), Erazm Ciołek (1474–1522), and Krzysztof Warszewicki (1543–1603) were mainly responsible for the negative image of Muscovy and later Russia.[7]

Added to this alienating equation of the Muscovites with Eurasian nomads was the dichotomy between Latin and Greek Christianity, described by Wolfgang Geier as an "inner *antemurale*."[8] From the High Middle Ages onward, these two constructions of alterity were consciously compiled and transferred to the East Slavs, as, perhaps best, summed up by Pope Gregory X (1210–1276) in 1273, "Rutheni sunt scismatici et Tartarorum nichilominus servitores."[9]

These two topoi—that of Muscovites or Russians as cruel and Asiatic-barbaric *inimici Europae* and that of Poland as the sole bulwark against these "schismatic Russian hordes"—were eagerly reactivated by the Polish elites in the nineteenth century, when Romantic and nationalistic writers and publicists such as Stanisław Staszic (1755–1826), Juliusz Słowacki (1809–1849), Kazimierz Kelles-Krauz (1872–1905), Józef Ignacy Kraszewski (1812–1887), and Henryk Sienkiewicz (1846–1916) reminded their public of the role Poland had once played for Europe against the Tatars, the Ottomans, and, most of all, the Russians. Compared to the late Middle Ages and the early modern period, priority was now given to the defense not only of Latin Christianity but also of European culture, the European system of values and the civilizing achievements of the West in general.

A free Polish state was to be a strong bulwark of European freedom and a barrier against Russian enslavement and bondage. This topos gained in popularity in the late nineteenth and early twentieth centuries in particular. Polish historians, writers, theologians, and political publicists such as Adam Pajgert (1829–1872), Adam Szelągowski (1873–1961), Stanisław Zakrzewski (1873–1936), Oskar Halecki (1891–1973), Kazimierz Konarski (1886–1972), and Nikodem Cieszyński (1886–1942) canvassed the rest of Europe for a free Poland, this natural *antemurale* against Russia, and warned the West against Russian imperialism and its political system which was presented as built intrinsically upon slavery.[10]

When it became clear at the end of World War I that a Polish state would reappear on the European map—whether as a puppet state of the Central Powers or as a free state following the victory of the Entente—publicists such as the Roman Catholic priest Nikodem Cieszyński and the historian Kazimierz Konarski published several articles about the role of Poland as a bulwark against the East, that is, against Russia and, after 1917, against the "new" revolutionary threat from the Bolsheviks.[11] As early as 1915, Władysław Smoleński (1851–1926) wrote in his essay *Naród polski w walce o byt* (The Polish Nation in Its Struggle for Survival) that Poland, in fighting innumerable wars against the Asiatic-barbaric Moscow, had defended the culture and civilization of the West from the cruel East.[12]

The National Catholic Right, after regaining sovereignty in 1918, revived this established pattern. Especially against the backdrop of the Paris Peace Conference of 1919 (which eventually resulted in the Treaty of Versailles), countless pamphlets and articles appeared that underlined Poland's right to exist while pointing out its importance as a bulwark against mighty Germany and fierce Russia. One of the most widespread works of this kind was Jan Tarnowski's *La Pologne rempart de la civilisation*, in which the Polish publicist demanded a Poland extending from the Baltic to the Black Sea. He saw this as the only way to fulfill Poland's duties as a stronghold of the West against the Russian and German threats.[13]

Inspired by the collapse of the partitioning powers, the historian Władysław Konopczyński (1880–1952), for instance, questioned the bulwark status of other countries, such as Austria, Hungary, Ukraine, and Venice. Referring to several events in Polish history, he enumerated all the battles fought against the "infidels," such as those at Legnica 1241, Varna 1444, Ţuţora 1620, Khotyn 1621 and 1673, and Vienna 1683, and concluded that the historical mission of the Rzeczpospolita had always been to be a bulwark of Western culture.[14] This was especially the case after the victory in the Polish-Soviet War from 1919 to 1921, when numerous right-wing publicists reiterated the role of Poland as a defender of Europe against Bolshevism.[15] In 1922, for example, Wincent Lutosławski (1863–1954) wrote:

> Europe needs for its social progress and its security from Asia a country that could separate it from Asia. Moscow cannot be this country, for it is itself Asian. This Europe-guarding country has always been Poland and should remain Poland. . . . Europe needs a vivid wall, a free Rzeczpospolita, that can defend it from the East. This is Poland's raison d'être—its mission.[16]

The historian and philosopher Feliks Koneczny (1862–1949) was even more radical and, in his much cited work *Polskie Logos a Ethos. Roztrząsania o znaczeniu i celu Polski* (The Polish Logos and Ethos. Reflections on the Importance and Goal of Poland), he demanded a complete distinction between the Western and the Eastern worlds, which he considered to be inferior to the Latin civilization of the West. Any attempts to mix both cultural circles would lead to a catastrophe for the more developed side, that is, the European. Thus, according to Koneczny, one of the biggest mistakes in Polish history was the Union of Brest of 1596 and the attempts of the Roman Catholic Church in Poland to accept compromises with the Orthodox world,

> If there were no Union of Brest, if there were not this unfortunate striving for a synthesis of the West with the East in the Church, the Roman Catholic hierarchy would already have reached to the Urals in the eighteenth century, and Western civilization would be victorious in Russia.[17]

Similar to Wincent Lutosławski, Koneczny saw Poland's reason for existence as being a vivid beacon of Western civilization and, at the same time, an invincible bulwark against the savage East:

> Our historic relation to Europe has long since been described with the epithet of a "forewall." We have a serious duty as guards in defense of Western civilization. . . . Our fight against Russia was, remains, and always will be an unchanging struggle for civilization, a fight for the defense of Latin civilization. . . . Even at its most difficult times, Poland has always been a forewall for Europe against Eastern barbarity.[18]

Remarkably, in contrast to other Polish historians, publicists, and theologians of that time, Koneczny did not share the messianic concepts of Poland's religious mission in the East. According to him, no nation has a genuine destiny by necessity. Moreover, political and cultural goals have their source in rational decisions and in attempts to survive as a nation, "The goal of a nation cannot be a priori. . . . Every nation determines for itself its own goal. This can vary in different periods."[19] Koneczny concluded that the best path for Poland would not only be to remain within Western civilization but also to defend it and, at the same time, spread it to the East.

It was especially the right-wing sector around the Roman Catholic Church in Poland that represented the most important promoter of the bulwark rhetoric against Soviet Russia and, after 1922, the Soviet Union.[20] In a memorandum published in the journal *Przewodnik Katolicki* (Catholic Guide) in 1920, the priest Stanisław Ciążyński (1889–1942) declared that defending Latin Christianity from the schismatic and pagan East had been Poland's duty and calling from the Middle Ages until modern times. Now that Europe was facing an even greater threat from the East, that is, the "Bolshevik nonbelievers," he argued, Poland's destiny as Europe's levee against the East was more relevant:

> And so today, Poland—hardly risen from its grave—is immediately faced by its historical task, as if the Lord would like to show us that we must go the way of our ancestors, the defenders of the faith and freedom. What actually is our fight against Bolshevism? It is a fight in defense of Christianity and Western civilization, as it was centuries ago when we repulsed the pagan ferocity of the East. Like then, we also have to deal today with a barbarity that is devastating our country, burning down, robbing, hijacking, enlisting men to the Red Army, maltreating women. These are the same savages as the Tatars of the past centuries, only more dangerous because they are equipped with the newest means of technology and worse because they consciously aim to overthrow the civilization established on the Christian foundation. . . . This wave of barbarity hits the Polish rampart, which must stand firm, must endure the blows, for Poland today is, as it was centuries ago, the bulwark of Europe, the bulwark of Christianity.[21]

Referring to the domino effect theory, Ciążyński underlined Poland's importance for Europe and sketched a picture of the imminent downfall of Western civilization should the Polish outpost fail:

> Today, too, the eyes of the whole world are turned to us, will Poland show enough resistance, will it not be overcome? French writings remind us of our dignity as a forewall of Christianity and take note that we have never deserved this name more than now, for the fate of the West today depends on our endurance. There is no exaggeration in this. If the Polish dam were to break and the Bolsheviks were to unite with the Germans who conspire criminal plans, not only Poland would perish, but also the liberty of all Europe.[22]

The Roman Catholic Church in Poland willingly drew parallels between Polish victories in the past and the triumph over Soviet Russia in 1920, pointing out that "throwing the enemy out of the frontiers of the fatherland . . . brought a new shine to the Polish arms" and affirmed "the old tradition that Poland is the rampart of Christianity and the defense of Western culture."[23] Additionally, Poland's National Catholic Right felt vindicated and encouraged in their anti-Bolshevik position by the Holy See, which—in contrast to its strict neutrality in World War I—now openly showed sympathy for the Polish fight against the Red Army. Thus, the Polish episcopate wrote a letter to Pope Benedict XV (1854–1922) on July 7, 1920, calling on him for spiritual as well as diplomatic support in their conflict with Soviet Russia. The letter was subscribed inter alia by cardinal and primate of Poland Edmund Dalbor (1869–1926), cardinal and archbishop of Warsaw Aleksander Kakowski (1862–1938), archbishop of Cracow Adam Stefan Sapieha (1867–1951), and the Armenian Catholic archbishop of Lviv, Józef Teodorowicz (1864–1938). The clergymen referred to Poland's historical position as the main rampart of Christianity:

> Holy Father! Our fatherland has been fighting with the enemy of the Christian Cross, the Bolsheviks, for two years now. The resurrected Poland, which is exhausted by the four-year struggles of adjacent states on its soil, which is devastated by the current war, is making its final effort. If Poland surrenders to the Bolshevik assault, the whole world will be threatened with defeat, a new flood will swamp it, a flood of murder, hatred, conflagration, desecration of the Cross. Holy Father, in this difficult moment we ask you to pray for our fatherland. Pray that we will not be defeated and—with God's help—[that we will] protect with our own torsos like a wall the world from the menacing danger.[24]

The appeal of the Polish clergy resonated with and was taken up by Benedict XV in a very similar epideictic way. He remembered the close historical relations between the Holy See and Poland. One month later, for instance, on 5 August, the Pope wrote to the Cardinal Vicar Basilio Pompilj (1858–1931):

> When all civilized nations shrouded themselves in silence from the superiority of power over right, only the Holy See protested against the lawless partition of Poland and against the no less iniquitous oppression of the Polish people. Currently, there are much more serious things at stake, currently, not only is the national existence of Poland in danger, but the whole of Europe is also threatened by the cruelties of a new war. Therefore, not only love for Poland, but also love for the whole of Europe commands us to desire the uniting of all believers with us in begging the Almighty that, through the intercessions of the Most Holy Virgin Patroness of Poland, He will be willing to save the Polish nation from this final defeat and that He will wish to divert this new plague from Europe, which is drained by bloodshed.[25]

After the defeat of the Red Army in the so-called Battle of Warsaw in August 1920, Benedict XV expressed his congratulations to the Polish episcopate and once again underlined the importance of the Polish victory over the Bolsheviks, who followed a "heinous doctrine." With regard to the domino effect theory, the Pope underlined that the Soviet Russian attack on Poland, that *baluardo dell'Europa*, aimed not only to destroy the latter but also to annihilate the whole Christian world.[26]

The Catholic Church in Poland saw itself as the moral guardian of "Polishness" (as it in fact still does!), as the only constant in Polish history and thus as mainly responsible for creating Polish culture throughout the centuries. In their eyes, being Polish meant being Catholic. The clearest expression of this attitude can perhaps be found in an article from the journal *Wiadomości Archidyecezyalne Warszawskie* (News of the Archdiocese Warsaw), which discusses the resolutions made by the Catholic Convention in Poznań in 1920. The symbiotic relationship between the Church and the state is described as follows,

> All the speakers [at the assembly in Poznań] consistently underlined the necessity of united action of the whole nation and also reiterated that, especially in the hard days of bondage, the Catholic Church was the cement that bound the nation. The Church has led the nation throughout all its previous existence. Currently, following the lack of liberty and on the edge of some sort of new life, indeed, the nation should continue to follow her example.[27]

During the Polish-Soviet War, numerous propaganda posters were published in both Poland and Soviet Russia to mobilize the people and garner their support. The Soviets eagerly drew the picture of the bourgeois "Polish lords/masters," who were illustrated as bad and dangerous for the Russian peasantry, just like the tsarists and their White movement.[28] In Poland, anti-Bolshevik propaganda posters were readily combined with the bulwark topos.[29] Using memorable allegories, Poland was portrayed as a defensive shield and a strong wall against the Soviet threat.[30] While openly referring to the old *antemurale christianitatis* image, Polish propaganda posters of the early 1920s often equated the fight against the Bolsheviks with a divinely legitimized defense of the Christian faith.[31]

In this religious context, Soviet Russia appeared as a multiple-headed mythological Hydra or rather—with a clear reference to the Apocalypse from the Book of Revelation—the biblical dragon and thus the symbolical embodiment of pure evil and the Antichrist. Poland, conversely, was depicted as the dragon slayer par excellence, continuing the tradition of Christian narratives about Michael the Archangel and Saint George.[32] The presentation of the Bolshevik danger was also mixed with the stereotype of a greedy, scheming, and plotting Jew, collaborating with the Soviets and threatening Christianity. Moreover, Jews were portrayed as the personification of the Bolshevik and were made solely responsible for communism.[33]

Figure 11.1. Polish recruitment poster dated 1920. The text reads: "To Arms! Save the Fatherland! Remember well our fate." Wikimedia Commons, public domain.

Against this background, it is hardly surprising that the Polish bulwark topoi of the interwar period distinguished themselves—as in the centuries before—by significant flexibility. Anti-Russian and anticommunist slogans were often paired with anti-Semitism. The Catholic priest Marian Wiśniewski, for instance, expressed understanding for the harsh measures of Hitler's Germany against Jews in the 1930s and linked them to the defense of German as well as Western culture. In his eyes, the anti-Jewish policy of the National Socialists was a kind of "vigorous self-defense against the Jewish pest." Acting against the Eastern "Judeo-Bolshevism" meant to Wiśniewski defending European Christianity—something that "does not deserve condemnation by Christians," as he wrote in the Marist newspaper *Pro Christo* in July 1934.[34] Furthermore, in Poland the *antemurale* motif was used not only to distance its own cultural circle from the East but also to underline the Polishness of the *Kresy Wschodnie* (The Eastern Borderlands). Poland's role as a bulwark was always connected to its civilizing mission on the eastern border of European culture, as Władysław Tomkiewicz (1899–1982) emphasized in the *Przegląd Powszechny* (General Review) in 1933:

> In the second half of the seventeenth century, the Ruthenian language loses its place at the peak of the social ladder in Red Ruthenia, Volhynia, and, especially, in Podolia, limiting itself to the small courts of the minor nobility, within monastic walls and inside commoners' chambers. The territorial differences disappear slowly, and everyone who works has a voice and decides—the population integrates itself into Polish and Latin culture. Only the Ukraine, and in particular Kyiv, put up strong resistance against the Polish and Catholic influences.[35]

Adam Romer (1892–1965), a politician of the nationalist Stronnictwo Prawicy Narodowej (National Right-Wing Party), demanded a cultural conquest of the eastern borderlands, that is, a Polonization of the Belarusian and Ukrainian minorities in eastern Poland. He argued that this was essential for the survival of Poland, this fierce *avant poste* of the West and for the whole of Europe.[36] Oskar Halecki (1891–1973), another influential representative of the idea of a Polish cultural mission in the East, who nota bene never denied his proximity to the Roman Catholic Church, always underlined that only a strong Poland could keep the Bolsheviks out of Europe.[37] But once again, the strongest anti-Bolshevik propaganda connected with the *antemurale* topos came from the Roman Catholic clergy itself. "Being a bulwark" also remained Poland's main task in the twentieth century, as Jan Urban, a Catholic priest and executive editor of the Jesuit *General Review*, stated in 1927:

> With its back to the Western frontier, Poland's face should be directed to the East.... We consider "the great idea" of Poland today the same way in which it was considered some centuries before the partitions, as being the forewall of Christianity. Before the partitions, Poland was aware of this vocation and it fulfilled these tasks in different ways.... However, the religious and cultural mission of Poland in the East is not over yet.... First of all, we have to create from our breasts, and much more from our souls, from our beliefs and principles a wall through which the pestilence of Bolshevism cannot cross further to the West. We are called upon to be the forewall of Christianity and the Christian culture, even when the Bolshevik power is broken.[38]

Unlike Feliks Koneczny, Urban did not connect Poland's raison d'être to nationalistic or cultural/civilizational approaches. In his eyes, the Polish bulwark was founded solely on theology. Poland had a religious mission to fulfill, according to the priest, "The vocation of a nation ... is not what a nation thinks of itself in time, but what God thinks of them in eternity." Thus, "the big idea of Poland, as by the way of any other nation, can only be a religious idea, an idea for realizing God's kingdom."[39] And in contrast to Koneczny, Jan Urban saw in the Union of Brest with the Ruthenian Church of Rus, the Metropolia of Kyiv-Halych and all Rus a valuable example of integration worthy of being applied. The Orthodox Eastern Slavs should be integrated into the Roman Catholic Church and should preserve a certain degree of autonomy. Only then could the Christian world confront the Bolshevik danger:

> From Poland's first task in the East—i.e., continuing to be the rampart of Christianity and Christian civilization—arises the second task, Poland must pursue domestic policies that are truly Slavic. All concepts of an enforced Polonization of our *Kresy*, which would only be an inner Polonization, should be deliberately and definitely abandoned for both national as well as ethical and religious reasons.[40]

Similar statements can be found in the journal *Mały Dziennik* (Little Journal), published by the Franciscans from 1935 onward. Maksymilian Kolbe (1894–1941), who was canonized postmortem by the Roman Catholic Church, was its chief editor and a notable contributor writing several anti-Bolshevik essays filled with bulwark allegories.[41]

In 1937, the Roman Catholic Church in Poland organized a congress in Poznań, I Kongres Chrystusa Króla (First Congress of Christ the King), which was dedicated solely to the fight against Bolshevism. The patron of this event was Pope Pius XI (1857–1939) himself, who, in his letter to the participants dated 3 May 1937, showed great satisfaction with the fact that the congress was being "held in a country which rightly is called and always has been the rampart of Christianity." Similar to the Polish clergymen and publicists, Pius XI compared past *defensio fidei* events from Polish history to the contemporary situation in the East, "Although Polish soil was attacked and invaded countless times in the past by heretics and schismatics, the Poles retained their Catholic faith." Nowadays, he continued, Poland was facing an even greater and more evil threat, "the godless communistic precepts and conspiracies." According to the Pope, the congress should prepare mentally "God's knights" in Poland for an eventual victory of Christianity over Bolshevism.[42]

Pius' explanations were based mainly on his anticommunist encyclical *Divini Redemptoris*, published only three months earlier, in which he had set out to "expose once more in a brief synthesis the principles of atheistic Communism as they are manifested chiefly in Bolshevism."[43]

One year later, during the ceremonies marking the canonization of the Jesuit Andrzej Bobola (1591–1657), the Polish clergy reminded the Polish faithful of the "cruelty" of the East. The fact that Bobola was murdered by schismatic Ukrainian Cossacks and that his mortal remains were desecrated by Bolshevik troops and moved as a curiosity to the Museum of Hygiene of the People's Commissioners of Health in Moscow was more than "proof" of innate Russian barbarity. In this context, with regard to the inhumanity of the Muscovites, who always were more Asiatic than European and who became even more perfidious following the foundation of the Soviet Union and the establishment of communism, the priest Szczepan Sobalkowski (1901–1958) wrote that Poland must now, more than ever, be a firm "bulwark of Christianity" against evil wickedness.[44] This outpost must remain Catholic or it would cease to exist, concluded Sobalkowski in his memorandum *Krew, która woła* (Blood, Which Is Calling).[45]

Hungary

One can find a very similar anti-Bolshevik bulwark rhetoric in interwar Hungary. However, unlike the Polish example, Hungarian anti-Bolshevik propaganda did not have its roots in the late Middle Ages and the early modern period. At that time, Hungary was primarily seen as a *propugnaculum christianitatis* against the Ottomans and, to a lesser extent, the schismatic Vlachs and Moldovans and the heretic Hussites. Anti-Russian elements in the Hungarian *antemurale* topos first appeared in the middle of the nineteenth century. Following the crushing of the Hungarian Revolution of 1848/1849 by Austrian and especially Russian auxiliary troops, Hungarian publicists and freedom fighters styled Hungary as a bulwark of freedom and liberty. It was Lajos Kossuth (1802–1894) in particular who propagated this picture of Hungary in Western Europe as well as in the United States. After the Crimean War, anti-Russian propaganda was in vogue in the West.

According to Kossuth, a liberated Hungarian state would be "destined to become once again the vanguard of civilization, and of the religious liberty of the whole of the European continent against the encroachments of Russian despotism, as it has already been the barrier of Christianity against Islamism."[46] In Kossuth's eyes, the good of Hungary was closely linked to a unified and strong Germany, which would allow the Hungarians entrance into the Western Christian community. Here again, Kossuth referred to the former *antemurale* status of his homeland, which—according to him—the Hungarians owed solely to the Germans. Furthermore, Kossuth suggested a return to previous German-Hungarian relations, outlining the importance of a powerful Germany and its function as a superior bulwark for European freedom:

> Now, by the God who led my people from the prairies of far Asia to the banks of the Danube—of the Danube, whose waves have brought religion, science, and civilization from Germany to us, and in whose waves the tears of Germany and Hungary are mingled; by the God who led us, when on the soil watered by our blood we were the bulwark of Christendom. ... The peace of Europe cannot be secured without a strong Germany, and that Germany cannot be strong without freedom. A free Germany is a bulwark against the encroachments of France and the arrogance of Russia. Germany enslaved is either the prey of the former or the tool of the other.[47]

On the other hand, Kossuth, who—as one of the main leaders of the Hungarian Revolution of 1848—had fled from the Habsburg regime to the West, accused Austria of abusing the "Hungarian bulwark" and defamed the Habsburg monarchy as a furtive outpost of the Russians, who had helped the Austrians to suppress the Hungarian revolutionary army:

> In consequence of the geographical situation of her dominions, and being also sovereigns of Hungary, it was chiefly the house of Austria which was considered to be and cherished as the great bulwark against Russia. ... Austria, who was to have balanced Russia, is thrown into her scale, instead of being a barrier, she is her vanguard, and her tool—her high road to Constantinople, her auxiliary army to flank it.[48]

Only an independent Hungary, therefore, freed from the devious Habsburgs, could again be a barrier against Eastern despotism and hinder Russia, the biggest threat to European culture, from penetrating further into the West:

> The power of Hungary, thus established, is a basis indispensable to the freedom of Europe. ... The enemy of European freedom is Russia. Now, can Hungary be a barrier to secure Europe against this power of Russia? I answer, yes. ... Hungary is a nation of fifteen million, and can muster at least one million brave citizen soldiers. I hope this may be regarded, then, as positive proof of what I say about the ability of Hungary to resist the power of despotism, and defend Europe against Russian encroachments. ... With Hungary once free, Russia would never dare to threaten European liberty again.[49]

Hungarian nationalists also pilloried the rising pan-Slavism of the nineteenth century, as they feared an awakening of various national movements in areas like Slovakia, Croatia, and northern Serbia. All of these were areas that were seen as traditionally Hungarian or were situated in the Kingdom of Hungary. Miklós Wesselényi (1796–1850) wrote as early as 1843 to the German public, "This (Pan-)Slavism, which is spreading throughout Europe and undermining so many countries, is that which is threatening our fatherland and our nation, more than any other, with its downfall."[50] Furthermore, using the old bulwark allegory, Lajos Kossuth cautioned the French public in the late 1850s, "The truth is that the national life, strength and liberty of Hungary are certainly Europe's avenues against Pan-Slavism."[51] The Hungarian publicist Dániel Irányi (1822–1892) and the French historian Charles-Louis Chassin (1831–1901) went one step further in their joint work *Histoire politique de la révolution de Hongrie 1847–1849* when they claimed:

> In empowering itself, Hungary would have provided Europe with an enormous service, particularly in the current circumstances. . . . The bulwark of Christianity and civilization against the Turks since the Middle Ages, it must remain the insurmountable barrier for civilization and the French Revolution, which has since become universal, against the Russians, those conquerors of the modern world.[52]

Throughout the second half of the nineteenth century and up until the end of Habsburg dominion in Hungary in 1918, Russophobic rhetoric remained a significant constant in the discourse of Hungarian nationalists. The increasing anti-Russian elements in the Hungarian bulwark topos were actually given an additional boost with the end of World War I as well as the failure of the short-lived Hungarian Soviet Republic (March to August 1919) and the so-called Red Terror, a series of politically motivated atrocities aimed at crushing political rivals during the four-month regime of the Hungarian communists. Hungary, like the newly founded Polish state, was now seen both in Hungary itself and in the rest of Europe as an invincible wall against "the terrible wave of Bolshevism."[53]

As in other European countries where communists tried to establish a Soviet Republic in the aftermath of World War I, the Red Terror was followed by the counterrevolutionary *fehérterror* (White Terror), which aimed to crush the Hungarian Communist movement. The bulwark topos was used once again, this time as a powerful rhetorical tool to justify the repressive violence of the right-wing against communists, leftists, and Jews. The ideological foundations of the counterrevolutionaries were built upon the so-called *A szegedi gondolat* (Szeged Idea), which promoted a radical protofascist ideology with irredentist claims to former Hungarian territories. One of the leading thinkers of this movement was the later prime minister of Hungary, Gyula Gömbös (1886–1936), who was a major force in the purge of communists from Hungarian society after the collapse of the short-lived Hungarian Republic of Councils under Béla Kun (1886–1938). Moreover, as was common in other European ultranationalist movements in the early twentieth century, one of the main elements of the Szeged Idea was the theory of the existence of a Judeo-Bolshevik conspiracy in the Hungarian state, seeking to demolish Hungary from within.[54]

In the following years, similar to their counterparts in Poland, the Hungarian nationalists endeavored to build Hungarian identity upon the *an-*

temurale topos and thus to locate Hungary clearly within the Western world. The Christian Right saw Hungary's historic mission as a bulwark of Europe once again resuscitated. Serving as a new *antemurale* against the Bolshevik threat served the political elites as a powerful legitimization for counterrevolutionary actions. At the same time, the bulwark topos was instrumentalized by the national Catholic extremists to appeal against the Treaty of Trianon (1920) and therefore to support the policy of border revisions, so popular among the public in interwar Hungary. Only a strong Hungary in its old borders could guarantee Europe its freedom and wealth and protect it from the despotic system of the Soviets.[55]

It was above all Gyula Szekfű who played a leading role in this interwar reactivation of the Hungarian bulwark topos. In several essays published in the 1920s and 1930s, Szekfű styled Hungary as the most important rampart of Christian Western Europe against the Bolshevik threat from the Soviet Union. According to Szekfű, the fragmentation of Hungary after Trianon was a major mistake on the part of the victorious powers France and Great Britain, since a great and strong Hungarian state could have stopped a Bolshevik invasion, whereas a patchwork of small independent states would be no hurdle for the Russian communists in the case of a Soviet attack. On the other hand, Szekfű also exploited the *antemurale* topos to promote confessional unity. Hungary was strong and it was the shield of Christianity when it was homogenously Catholic, Szekfű argued. Beyond this ultimate Hungarian outpost of Western civilization there was nothing but barbarity and undeveloped savagery:

> Indeed now, as the waves of Reformation and Counterreformation flooded medieval Hungary one after the other, these waves again stopped at the eastern borders, again Hungary was Europe's furthermost border region.... The religious movement thus again proved that Hungary was a territory of Europe, even more its outermost region beyond which there was no more European culture nor European development.[56]

Another interesting similarity to the Polish anti-Bolshevik interwar bulwark propaganda was the emphasis placed on the crushing of the Hungarian Soviet Republic. The chief administrative judge Aladár Székács, for example, attributed global historical importance to the victory of the Hungarian nationalists over the Communists in 1919, in his opinion, the suppression of the short-lived Hungarian Soviet Republic reminded the rest of Europe of the ancient vocation of the Hungarian people to face and stop all dangers and threats emanating from the East.[57]

The national Catholic movement also used the bulwark allegory to support any revanchist territorial claims. A special delegation consisting of members of the Hungarian clergy and politicians was sent to Rome in the early 1930s to make clear to the Holy See the need to return Upper Hungary, that is Slovakia, back to the Hungarian motherland, since only a unified Carpathian "wall" under Hungarian rule could save the free European cultural circle from Bolshevik enslavement.[58] Pál Teleki (1879–1941), who was called "the architect and father of the Hungarian revision," did not, in the crushing of the Hungarian Soviet Republic, see the end of Hungary's fight against communism. Rather, the world was warned to expect an upcoming ideological war in which Hungary, as the first European country of a solely "Christian (Roman Catholic) and nationalistic orientation," would again arise as the fiercest rampart and barrier of the Western World.[59]

The anti-Bolshevik *antemurale* motif formed an essential part of intra-Hungarian nationalistic discourses until the collapse of the Hungarian state at the end of World War II and the proclamation of the Hungarian People's Republic, a satellite state of the Soviet Union.[60] Against the backdrop of an unhesitating "fascisization" of the state apparatus and political and public life, Russophobic rhetoric, mixed with anti-Semitic stereotypes, increased substantially in the 1930s and especially during the first half of the 1940s. During the Spanish Civil War (1936–1939)—similar to other rightist European countries—various anticommunist articles, pamphlets, and speeches combined with the Catholic historical *antemurale* narratives appeared in Hungary. The Jesuit Béla Bangha (1880–1940), for instance, appealed for Christian unity within the whole of Europe and Hungary in particular, since it was important to resist the Communist movement "in the middle of a world turned toward Bolshevism, at the height of social hatred and destructive anarchy."[61]

However, emphasizing Hungary's status as a bastion against a Jewish-Communist world conspiracy was linked in particular to the Hungarian fascist dictator Ferenc Szálasi (1897–1946), Nemzetvezető (the Leader of the Nation), and his infamous Arrow Cross regime during World War II. The *antemurale* motif was an important part of the anti-Semitic and anticommunist propaganda of Szálasi and the Hungarian fascist movement, especially in the last years of World War II.[62] Interestingly, however, this was not only a Hungarian (or, in the prewar years, also Polish) phenomenon, for similar bulwark images can be found in other European fascist countries, most notably in Nazi Germany (1933–1945).[63]

The Messianic Mission of the Bulwark States

In both cases, the Polish and the Hungarian bulwark topoi were also mixed with messianic ideas and self-images. In Poland, the most significant occurrence of this interdependence was the very popular slogan *Polska Chrys-*

tusem narodów (Poland, the Christ of Nations), which—according to some Polish scholars—originated in the so-called Sarmatian ideology of the early modern Rzeczpospolita, whose most famous propagator was the Romantic poet Adam Mickiewicz (1798–1855).[64]

A further development of this concept in Poland in the nineteenth century was *Winkelriedyzm* (Winkelriedism), which was built upon the hero cult of the mythical Swiss freedom fighter Arnold Winkelried (died 1303) who fought the Habsburgs in the Late Middle Ages. Polish writers such as Juliusz Słowacki and Zygmunt Krasiński (1812–1859) drew parallels between Winkelried, who had sacrificed himself, and the Polish nation. Słowacki coined the phrase, well-known in Poland, *Polska Winkelriedem narodów!* (Poland, Winkelried of nations!). Unlike Polish messianism, which accepted Poland's role as a martyr as God-given, the "Winkelriedists" of the nineteenth century propagated an active involvement in the resistance movement against the partitioning powers and repeatedly called for military opposition.[65] The Catholic Right in Poland incorporated these images into their own ideas of the Polish *antemurale.* In their eyes, Poland was an altruistic bulwark that fought for Christian values and the liberty of Europe against the despotism and barbarity of the Russian East without any help from the West.

In Hungary, there was a very similar topos mixed with bulwark images in that of the *querela Hungariae* (Hungary's complaint). It can be found in the Hungarian national anthem as well as other things.[66] Originally connected to the Ottoman conquest and Hungary's sacrificial role in holding back the Turks from the rest of Europe, this motif, together with the Hungarian *propugnaculum* concept, has been used since the nineteenth century to describe Hungary's difficult but heroic geographical and political situation at the front of European civilization.[67] Like the supporters of Polish messianism, Hungarian historians, publicists, and politicians underlined Hungary's sacrificial mission, claiming that it had always protected Europe from the barbarity of the East but that it had never received any significant help from the West in return. Quite the contrary, in the past, Europe had allowed the land to perish under the Muslim hordes of the Ottomans, and—a very common motif in the interwar period—it would again stand idly by and watch while Hungary was left alone against the Bolshevik threat.[68]

Paul Srodecki is a research assistant at the Christian-Albrechts-Universität zu Kiel in Germany. He is also a vice-project leader of the EU-funded research project Collective Identity in Social Networks in East Central Europe at the University of Ostrava, Czech Republic. His areas of research include history of East Central Europe from the Middle Ages to modern times; identity, alterity, and alienity constructions; history of the crusades; and history of political thoughts. He is the author of the monograph *Antemurale Christianitatis. Zur Genese der Bollwerksrhetorik im östlichen Mitteleuropa an der Schwelle vom Mittelalter zur Frühen Neuzeit* (Matthiesen Verlag, 2015).

Notes

1. For the *antemurale christianitatis* concept under the Jagiellonians, see P. Srodecki, "Universe christiane reipublice validissima propugnacula—Jagiellonian Europe in Bulwark Descriptions around 1500" in *The Jagiellonians in Europe. Dynastic Diplomacy and Foreign Relations*, ed. A. Bárány (Debrecen: Lendület Hungary in Medieval Europe Research Group, 2016), 57–74.
2. J. Ostroróg, "Monumentum pro reipublicae ordinatione," in *Jana Ostroroga żywot i pismo "O naprawie Rzeczypospolitej." Studyum z literatury polityczněj XV wieku*, ed. A. Pawiński (Warszawa: Drukarnia S. Olgebranda, 1884), 136. See J. Krzyżaniakowa, "Polen als antemurale christianitatis. Zur Vorgeschichte eines Mythos," in *Mythen in Geschichte und Geschichtsschreibung aus polnischer und deutscher Sicht*, ed. A. von Saldern (Münster: Lit, 1996), 139.
3. E.S. Piccolomini, "Cosmographia seu Rerum ubique gestarum historia locorumque description," in *Opera geographica et historica*, ed. J. Melchior (Helmstadii: pub. unknown, 1699), 278. See E. Klug, "Das 'asiatische' Russland. Über die Entstehung eines europäischen Vorurteils," *Historische Zeitschrift* 245, no. 2 (1987): 271.
4. Klug, "Das 'asiatische' Russland," 273.
5. Letter of 24 May 1535 in E. von Rotterdam, *Opvs epistolarvm*, vol. 11, ed. S.P. S. Allen et al. (Oxonii: Clarendon, 1947), no. 3020, 135. See Klug, "Das 'asiatische" Russland," 281.
6. S.D. Westram, "Against Gog and Magog," in *Text and Territory: Geographical Imagination in the European Middle Ages*, ed. S. Tomasch and S. Gilles (Philadelphia: University of Pennsylvania Press, 1998), 56–57; E.J. van Donzel and A.B. Schmidt, *Gog and Magog in Early Eastern Christian and Islamic Sources. Sallam's Quest for Alexander's Wall* (Leiden/Boston: Brill, 2010); Srodecki, *Antemurale Christianitatis*, 49–52.
7. Ibid., 292–303.
8. W. Geier, *Südosteuropa-Wahrnehmungen. Reiseberichte, Studien und biographische Skizzen vom 16. bis zum 20. Jahrhundert* (Wiesbaden: Harrassowitz, 2006), XIII.
9. "The Ruthenians are schismatics and nonetheless servants of the Tatars." "Letter of December 15, 1273," in *Preußisches Urkundenbuch*, vol. 1.2, ed. R. Philippi (Königsberg: Hartung, 1909), no. 315, 215. See P. Srodecki, "Die Angst vor dem Osten. Europa und die religiöse motivierten Identitäts-, Alteritäts- und Alienitätskonstruktionen im Mittelalter und der Frühen Neuzeit," in *Identitätsentwürfe im östlichen Europa – im Spannungsfeld von Selbst- und Fremdwahrnehmung*, ed. H.-J. Bömelburg, M. Kirchner, M. Koller, and M. Wingender (Wiesbaden: Harrassowitz, 2018), 11–34; ibid., "Antemurale-based frontier identities in East Central Europe and their ideological roots in medieval/early modern alterity and alienity dis-

courses," in *Collective Identity in the Context of Medieval Studies*, ed. M. Antonín Malaníková and R. Antonín (Ostrava: Filozofická fakulta OU, 2016), 97–120.
10. Srodecki, *Antemurale Christianitatis*, 341ff.
11. J. Tazbir, *Polska przedmurzem Europy* (Warszawa: Twój Styl, 2004), 170f.
12. Ibid., 171.
13. J. Tarnowski, *La Pologne rempart de la civilisation* (s.l., 1919), 1.
14. W. Konopczyński, "Obrona kultury zachodniej," in *Polska w kulturze powszechnej*, vol. 1, ed. F. Koneczny (Kraków: Krakowska Ekspozytura Biura dla Społek oszczęd. i pożyczek, 1918), 36–48.
15. See B. Korzeniewski, "Wróg nadchodzi polska propaganda polityczna w obliczu bitwy warszawskiej," *Przegląd Historyczny* 95 (2004): 467–84.
16. W. Lutosławski, *Praca narodowa. Program polityki polskiej* (Vilnius: Księgarnia Stowarzyszenia Nauczycielstwa Polskiego, 1922), 189–90. See W. Jaworski, *Eleuteryzm i mesjanizm. U źródeł filozofii społecznej Wincentego Lutosławskiego* (Kraków: Abrys, 1994); J.J. Jadacki, "Wincenty Lutosławski. Rozdział z dziejów myśli polskiej," in *Lutosławscy w kulturze polskiej*, ed. B. Klukowski (Drozdowo: Towarzystwo Przyjaciół Muzeum Przyrody w Drozdowie, 1998), 54–87; G. Łukomski, "Stereotyp najeźdźcy w czasie wojny polsko-bolszewickiej 1918–1920," in *Swoi i obcy*, vol. 1, ed. M. Kosman (Poznań: Wydawnictwo Naukowe Instytutu Nauk Politycznych i Dziennikarstwa Uniwersytetu Im. Adama Mickiewicza, 2004), 161–73; Tazbir, *Polska przedmurzem Europy*, 179.
17. Feliks Koneczny, *Polskie Logos a Ethos. Rozstrząsania o znaczeniu i celu Polski*, vol. 2 (Poznań/Warszawa: Księgarnia Św. Wojciecha, 1921), 23.
18. Ibid., 82, 85.
19. Ibid., 22.
20. W. Mysłek, *Przedmurze. Szkice z dziejów Kościoła katolickiego w II Rzeczypospolitej* (Warszawa: Wydawnictwo Spółdzielcze, 1987); U. Caumanns, *Die polnischen Jesuiten, der Przegląd powszechny und der politische Katholizismus in der Zweiten Republik. Ein Beitrag zur Geschichte der katholischen Presse Polens zwischen den Weltkriegen (1918–1939)* (Dortmund: Forschungsstelle Ostmitteleuropa, 1996); idem, "Soviet Russia vs. Nazi-Germany. Poland's Big Neighbours from the Viewpoint of the Polish Jesuits (1918–1939)," in *Churches in the Century of the Totalitarian Systems*, ed. J. Kłoczowski, W. Lenarczyk, and S. Łukasiewicz (Lublin: Instytut Europy Środkowo-Wschodniej, 2001), 83–90.
21. S. Ciążyński, "Przedmurze Chrześcijaństwa," *Przewodnik Katolicki* 26, no. 35 (1920): 357.
22. Ibid.
23. Citation from *Wiadomości Archidyecezyalne Warszawskie* 10, no. 12 (1920): 250.
24. Citation from W.J. Wysocki, "Kościół Polski wobec najazdu bolszewickiego w 1920 roku," in *W nieustannej trosce o polską diasporę. Tom studiów historycznych i politologicznych dedykowany Księdzu Arcybiskupowi Szczepanowi Wesołemu*, ed. R. Nir, M. Szczerbiński, K. Wasilewski, and C. Bugdalski (Gorzów Wielkopolski: Stowarzyszenie Naukowe "Polska w Świecie," 2012), 82.
25. Benedict XV, "Con vivo compiacimento," retrieved 27 October 2018 from https://w2.vatican.va/content/benedict-xv/it/letters/1920/documents/hf_ben-xv_let_19200805_vivo-compiacimento.html. See *Wiadomości Archidyecezyalne Warszawskie* 10, nos. 9–10 (1920): 185.

26. Letter of 8 September 1920, Benedict XV, "Cum de Poloniae," retrieved 27 October 2018 from https://w2.vatican.va/content/benedict-xv/it/letters/1920/documents/hf_ben-xv_let_19200908_cum-poloniae.html. See *Wiadomości Diecezjalne Podlaskie* 2, nos. 11–12 (1920): 222–23.
27. *Wiadomości Archidyecezyalne Warszawskie* 10, no. 12 (1920): 249.
28. A.J. Leinwand, "Bolszewicki plakat propagandowy w okresie wojny polsko-bolszewickiej 1920 roku," *Studia z dziejów Rosji i Europy Środkowo-Wschodniej* 27 (1993): 75–87.
29. S. Szczotka, "Wizerunek bolszewika w polskich plakatach propagandowych z wojny polsko-rosyjskiej 1919–1920 ze zbiorów Muzeum Niepodległości w Warszawie," *Niepodległość i Pamięć* 19, nos. 1–4 (2012): 205–13; K. Paduszek, *Działalność propagandowa służb informacyjno-wywiadowczych Wojska Polskiego w czasie wojny polsko-bolszewickiej 1919–1921. Organizacje, metody, treści* (Toruń: Adam Marszałek, 2004).
30. Manon [pseudonym of an anonymous poster illustrator], *Do broni. ratujmy ojczyznę! pamiętajmy dobrze o naszym przyszłym losie* (Lwów: Zakład Artystyczno-Litograficzny Adolfa Hegedüsa, 1920); E. Bartłomiejczyk, *Na pomoc! wszystko dla frontu! wszyscy na front!* (Warszawa: Lit. Art. W. Główczewski, 1920). See A. Gąsiorowska and M. Lewnau, eds., *Poland First to Fight. Katalog polskiego plakatu wojskowego* (Warszawa: Andrzej Zasieczny, 2002), 47, 55.
31. Anonymous, *Kto w Boga wierzy—w obronie Ostrobramskiej, pod sztandar Orła i Pogoni!* (s.l., after 1920), Muzeum Niepodległości w Warszawie, Nr. inw. MN-Pl.2014. See Gąsiorowska and Lewnau, *Poland First to Fight*, 41.
32. J.P., *Do broni. wstępujcie do armji ochotniczej!* (s.l., 1920), Muzeum Niepodległości w Warszawie, Nr. inw. MN-Pl.2042. See Gąsiorowska, *Poland First to Fight*, 38.
33. Anonymous, *Znowu łapy żydowskie? Nie, przenigdy!* (s.l., 1919), Muzeum Niepodległości w Warszawie, Nr. inw. MN-Pl.2011.
34. M. Wiśniewski, "Z rozmyślań czerwcowych," *Pro Christo* 7 (1934): 490. See F. Adamski, "The Jewish Question in Polish Religious Periodicals in the Second Republic: The Case of the Przegląd katolicki," *Polin: Studies in Polish Jewry* 8 (2004): 129–45; A. Landau-Czajka, "The Image of the Jew in the Catholic Press during the Second Republic," *Polin: Studies in Polish Jewry* 8 (2004): 146–75; idem, "Polish Press Reporting about the Nazi Germans' Anti-Jewish Policy, 1933–1939," in *Why Didn't The Press Shout? American & International Journalism during the Holocaust*, ed. R.M. Shapiro (New York: Yeshiva University Press, 2003), 411–28.
35. W. Tomkiewicz, "Zasięg kolonizacji polskiej na ziemiach ruskich," *Przegląd Powszechny* 197 (1933): 32–57, 48f.
36. Tazbir, *Polska przedmurzem Europy*, 185.
37. Ibid., 172.
38. J. Urban, "O ideę dla Polski," *Przegląd Powszechny* 176 (1927): 11–12. See Caumanns, *Die polnischen Jesuiten*, 113; V. Pollmann, *Untermieter im christlichen Haus. Die Kirche und die "jüdische Frage" in Polen anhand der Bistumspresse der Metropolie Krakau 1926–1939* (Wiesbaden: Harrassowitz, 2001), 161; Tazbir, *Polska przedmurzem Europy*, 184f.; H. Hein-Kircher, "Antemurale christianitatis—Grenzsitutation als Selbstverständnis," in *Grenzen. Gesellschaftliche Konstitutionen und Transfigurationen*, ed. H. Hecker (Essen: Klartext, 2006), 139.
39. Urban, "O ideę dla Polski," 8, 11.

40. Ibid., 14.
41. Tazbir, *Polska przedmurzem Europy*, 185.
42. Letter published in *Miesięcznik Kościelny* 52, no. 6 (1937): 193–96; Tazbir, *Polska przedmurzem Europy*, 185.
43. A copy of the encyclical can be accessed at http://w2.vatican.va/content/pius-xi/en/encyclicals/documents/hf_p-xi_enc_19031937_divini-redemptoris.html, retrieved 13 September 2018.
44. Tazbir, *Polska przedmurzem Europy*, 185.
45. S. Sobalkowski, *"Krew, która woła..." 6 przemówień na temat znaczenia kanonizacji św. Andrzeja Boboli dla Polski i każdego z nas z dołaczeniem triduum ku jego czci* (Kielce: self-published, 1938).
46. "Speech of December 18, 1852, held in New York (NY)," L. Kossuth, *Select Speeches*, ed. Francis W. Newman (New York: C.S. Francis, 1854), 105f.
47. "Speech of June 22, 1852, held in New York (NY)," in Kossuth, *Select Speeches*, 400–402.
48. "Speech of June 4, 1852, held in Syracuse (NY)," in Kossuth, *Select Speeches*, 388–89.
49. "Speech of December 16, 1852, held in New York (NY)," in Kossuth, *Select Speeches*, 98f.
50. M. Wesselényi, *Eine Stimme über die ungarische und slawische Nationalität* (Leipzig: W. Vogel, 1844), 69.
51. L. Kossuth, *L'Europe, l'Autriche et la Hongrie* (Bruxelles: Fr. van Meenen et comp., 1859), 23: "La vérité est que la vie nationale, la force et la liberté de la Hongrie, sont certainement les boulevards de l'Europe contre le Panslavisme." See L. Terbe, "Egy európai szálloige életraiza (Magyarország a kereszténység védőbástyája)," *Egyetemes Philológiai Közlöny* 60 (1936): 328; S. Őze and N. Spannenberger, "Hungaria vulgo appelatur propugnaculum Christianitatis. Zur politischen Instrumentalisierung eines Topos in Ungarn," in *Beruf und Berufung. Geschichtswissenschaft und Nationsbildung in Ostmittel- und Südosteuropa im 19. und 20. Jahrhundert*, ed. M. Krzoska and H.-Chr. Maner (Münster: Lit, 2005), 32.
52. See Terbe, "Egy európai szálloige életraiza," 328; D. Irányi and C.-L. Chassin, *Histoire politique de la révolution de Hongrie 1847–1849*, vol. 1: *Avant la guerre* (Paris: Pagnerre, 1859), 64.
53. M.A.L. Gomèz, *Qu'adviendra-t-il de la Hongrie?* (Genève: pub. unknown, 1919), 6.
54. P.A. Hanebrink, *In Defense of Christian Hungary. Religion, Nationalism, and Antisemitism, 1890–1944* (Ithaca/London: Cornell University Press, 2006), 47–107. See R.L. Braham, "Hungarian Press, 1938–1945," in *Why Didn't the Press Shout. American & International Journalism during the Holocaust*, ed. R.M. Shapiro (Hoboken: Yeshiva University Press, 2003), 371–88.
55. M. Schmidt, "Der ungarische Revisionismus," in *1939, an der Schwelle zum Weltkrieg. Die Entfesselung des Zweiten Weltkrieges und das internationale System*, ed. K. Hildebrand, J. Schmädeke, R. Süßmuth, and K. Zernack (Berlin/New York: W. de Gruyter, 1990), 135–40; A. Kovács-Bertrand, *Der ungarische Revisionismus nach dem Ersten Weltkrieg. Der publizistische Kampf gegen den Friedensvertrag von Trianon (1918–1931)* (München: Oldenbourg, 1997); Á. von Klimó, *Nation, Konfession, Geschichte. Zur nationalen Geschichtskultur Ungarns im europäischen Kontext (1860–1948)* (München: Oldenbourg, 2003), 244–88.
56. G. Szekfű and B. Hóman, *Magyar Történet*, vol. 4 (Budapest: Királyi magyar egye-

temi nyomda, 1928–1934), 232. See Hanebrink, *In Defense of Christian Hungary,* 122.
57. See Klimó, *Nation, Konfession, Geschichte,* 214.
58. E. Hrabovec, "Die Slowakei, der Heilige Stuhl und die Großmächte 1939–1945," in *Nation, Nationalitäten und Nationalismus im östlichen Europa. Festschrift für Arnold Suppan zum 65. Geburtstag,* ed. A. Suppan, M. Wakounig, W. Mueller, M. Portmann, A. Biricz, A. Rathberger, and D. Schriffl (Wien/Berlin/Münster: Lit, 2010), 541.
59. See Őze and Spannenberger, "Hungaria vulgo appelatur propugnaculum *Christianitatis,*" 32–33.
60. See R. Paksa, *Magyar nemzetiszocialisták. Az 1930-as évek szélsőjobboldali mozgalma, pártjai, politikusai, sajtója* (Budapest: Osiris, 2013).
61. B. Bangha, "Mit várhatunk az Eucharisztikus Világkongresszustól?" *Magyar Kultúra* 24, no. 5 (1937): 131–33. See Hanebrink, *In Defense of Christian Hungary,* 145.
62. See R. Paksa, *Szálasi Ferenc és a hungarizmus* (Budapest: Jaffa Kiadó, 2013); M. Rady, "Ferenc Szálasi, 'Hungarism' and the Arrow Cross," in *In the Shadow of Hitler. Personalities of the Right in Central and Eastern Europe,* ed. R. Haynes and M. Rady (London: I.B. Tauris, 2011), 261–77; P. de Vago, *Ferenc Szalasi and the Arrow Cross Movement* (Canterbury: Steven Books, 2007); R.L. Braham, "The Hungarian Press, 1938–1945," in *Why Didn't the Press Shout? American & International Journalism during the Holocaust,* ed. R.M. Shapiro (New York: Yeshiva University Press, 2003), 371–88; M. Szöllösi-Janze, *Die Pfeilkreuzlerbewegung in Ungarn. Historischer Kontext, Entwicklung und Herrschaft* (München: Oldenbourg, 1989).
63. Srodecki, *Antemurale Christianitatis,* 349–52.
64. K. Obremski, "Sarmacki mesjanizm," *Ogród* 7 (1994): 119–30; J. Garewicz, "Sarmatyzm i mesjanizm. Tezy do dyskusji," in *August Cieszkowski (1814–1894). W setną rocznicę śmierci,* ed. B. Markiewicz and S. Pieróg (Warszawa: Polskie Towarzystwo Filozoficzne, 1996), 11–15; E. Pluskiewicz, "Mesjanizm w myśli polskiej pierwszej połowy XIX wieku," *Zeszyty Naukowe Politechniki Śląskiej* 748 (1983): 105–15; J. Salamon, "Mesjanizm polski XIX wieku na tle historycznych uwarunkowań," *Zeszyty Naukowe Uniwersytetu Jagiellońskiego. Studia Religiologica* 23 (1990): 49–69; B. Dopart, "Polska—Chrystusem narodów?" in *"Dziady" Adama Mickiewicza. Poemat, adaptacje, tradycje,* ed. B. Dopart (Kraków: Towarzystwo Autorów i Wydawców Prac Naukowych Universitas, 1999), 70–92; A. Landgrebe, *"Wenn es Polen nicht gäbe, dann müsste es erfunden werden." Die Entwicklung des polnischen Nationalbewusstseins im europäischen Kontext von 1830 bis in die 1880er Jahre* (Wiesbaden: Harrassowitz, 2003), 74–85, 166–77; M. Prussak, *"Po ogniu szum wiatru cichego." Wyspiański i mesjanizm* (Warszawa: IBL, 1993); W. Jaworski, *Eleuteryzm i mesjanizm. U źródeł filozofii społecznej Wincentego Lutosławskiego* (Kraków: Abrys, 1994); J. Krasicki, *Eschatologia i mesjanizm. Studium światopoglądu Mariana Zdziechowskiego* (Wrocław: Wiedza o Kulturze, 1994).
65. M. Inglot, *"Kordian" Juliusza Słowackiego* (Warszawa: Wydawnictwa Szkolne i Pedagogiczne, 1993), 20, 25f., 31, 48; S. Makowski, *Juliusz Słowacki* (Warszawa: Wydawnictwa Szkolne i Pedagogiczne, 1980), 248–53.
66. See P. Ötvös, "Klage und Hoffnung. Vom Fremd- und Eigenbild der Ungarischen Nation," *Das achtzehnte Jahrhundert und Österreich. Jahrbuch der Österreichischen Gesellschaft zur Erforschung des achtzehnten Jahrhunderts* 12 (1997): 103–8.

67. See M. Imre, "Der Topos 'Querela Hungariae' in der Literatur des 16. Jahrhunderts. Paulus Rubigallus—Ursinus Velius," in *Iter Germanicum. Deutschland und die Reformierte Kirche in Ungarn im 16.–17. Jahrhundert*, ed. A. Szabó (Budapest: Kálvin K., 1999), 39–117; I. Bitskey, "A nemzetsors toposzai a 17. Századi magyar irodalomban" in *Nemzet—identitás—irodalom. A nemzetfogalom változatai és a közösségi identifikáció kérdései a régi és a klasszikus magyar irodalomban*, ed. P. Bényei and M. Gönczy (Debrecen: Kossuth Egyetemi Kiadó, 2005), 13–33.
68. N. Spannenberger, *Die katholische Kirche in Ungarn 1918–1939* (Stuttgart: 2006), 122–24; S. Öze and N. Spannenberger, "Zur Interpretation der mittelalterlichen Staatsgründung in der ungarischen Geschichtsschreibung des 19. und 20. Jahrhunderts," *Jahrbücher für Geschichte und Kultur Südosteuropas* 2 (2000): 63–64.

Bibliography

Adamski, F. 2004. "The Jewish Question in Polish Religious Periodicals in the Second Republic: The Case of the Przeglad katolicki." *Polin: Studies in Polish Jewry* 8: 129–45.
Anonymous. 1919. *Znowu łapy żydowskie? Nie, przenigdy!* (s.l., 1919), Muzeum Niepodległości w Warszawie, Nr. inw. MN-Pl.2011.
Anonymous. 1920. *Kto w Boga wierzy—w obronie Ostrobramskiej, pod sztandar Orła i Pogoni!* (s.l., after 1920), Muzeum Niepodległości w Warszawie, Nr. inw. MN-Pl.2014.
Bangha, B. 1937. "Mit várhatunk az Eucharisztikus Világkongresszustól?" *Magyar Kultúra* 24, no. 5: 131–33.
Benedict XV. "Cum de Poloniae." Retrieved 30 April 2018 from https://w2.vatican.va/content/benedict-xv/it/letters/1920/documents/hf_ben-xv_let_19200908_cum-poloniae.html.
———. 2015. "Con vivo compiacimento." 13 October. Retrieved 14 March 2018 from https://w2.vatican.va/content/benedict-xv/it/letters/1920/documents/hf_ben-xv_let_19200805_vivo-compiacimento.html.
Bitskey, I. 2005. "A nemzetsors toposzai a 17. Századi magyar irodalomban." In *Nemzet—identitás—irodalom. A nemzetfogalom változatai és a közösségi identifikáció kérdései a régi és a klasszikus magyar irodalomban*, ed. P. Bényei and M. Gönczy, 13–33. Debrecen: Kossuth Egyetemi Kiadó.
Braham, R.L. 2003. "The Hungarian Press, 1938–1945." In *Why Didn't the Press Shout. American & International Journalism during the Holocaust*, ed. R.M. Shapiro, 371–88. New York: Yeshiva University Press.
Caumanns, U. 1996. *Die polnischen Jesuiten, der Przegląd powszechny und der politische Katholizismus in der Zweiten Republik. Ein Beitrag zur Geschichte der katholischen Presse Polens zwischen den Weltkriegen (1918–1939)*. Dortmund: Forschungsstelle Ostmitteleuropa.
———. 2001. "Soviet Russia vs. Nazi-Germany. Poland's Big Neighbours from the Viewpoint of the Polish Jesuits (1918–1939)." In *Churches in the Century of the Totalitarian Systems*, ed. J. Kłoczowski, W. Lenarczyk, and S. Łukasiewicz, 83–90. Lublin: Instytut Europy Środkowo-Wschodniej.
Ciążyński, S. 1920. "Przedmurze Chrześcijaństwa." *Przewodnik Katolicki* 26, no. 35: 357.

de Vago, P. 2007. *Ferenc Szalasi and the Arrow Cross Movement.* Canterbury: Steven Books.
Dopart, B. 1999. "Polska—Chrystusem narodów?" In *"Dziady" Adama Mickiewicza. Poemat, adaptacje, tradycje,* ed. B. Dopart, 70–92. Kraków: Towarzystwo Autorów i Wydawców Prac Naukowych Universitas.
Garewicz, J. 1996. "Sarmatyzm i mesjanizm. Tezy do dyskusji." In *August Cieszkowski (1814–1894). W setną rocznicę śmierci,* ed. B. Markiewicz and S. Pieróg, 11–15. Warszawa: Polskie Towarzystwo Filozoficzne.
Gąsiorowska, A., and H. Lewnau, eds. 2002. *Poland First to Fight. Katalog polskiego plakatu wojskowego.* Warszawa: Andrzej Zasieczny.
Geier, W. 2006. *Südosteuropa-Wahrnehmungen. Reiseberichte, Studien und biographische Skizzen vom 16. bis zum 20. Jahrhundert.* Wiesbaden: Harrassowitz Verlag.
Gomèz, M.A.L. 1919. *Qu'adviendra-t-il de la Hongrie?* Genève: pub. unknown.
Hanebrink, P.A. 2006. *In Defense of Christian Hungary. Religion, Nationalism, and Antisemitism, 1890–1944.* Ithaca/London: Cornell University Press.
Hein-Kircher, H. 2006. "Antemurale christianitatis—Grenzsitutation als Selbstverständnis." In *Grenzen. Gesellschaftliche Konstitutionen und Transfigurationen,* ed. H. Hecker, 129–47. Essen: Klartext.
Hrabovec, E. 2010. "Die Slowakei, der Heilige Stuhl und die Großmächte 1939–1945." In *Nation, Nationalitäten und Nationalismus im östlichen Europa. Festschrift für Arnold Suppan zum 65. Geburtstag,* ed. M. Wakounig, A. Suppan, M. Wakounig, W. Mueller, M. Portmann, A. Biricz, A. Rathberger, and D. Schriffl, 539–60. Wien: Lit.
Imre, M. 1999. "Der Topos 'Querela Hungariae' in der Literatur des 16. Jahrhunderts. Paulus Rubigallus—Ursinus Velius." In *Iter Germanicum. Deutschland und die Reformierte Kirche in Ungarn im 16.–17. Jahrhundert,* ed. A. Szabó, 39–117. Budapest: Kálvin K.
Inglot, M. 1993. *"Kordian" Juliusza Słowackiego.* Warszawa: Wydawnictwa Szkolne i Pedagogiczne.
Irányi, D. and C.-L. Chassin. 1859. *Histoire politique de la révolution de Hongrie 1847–1849,* vol. 1: *Avant la guerre.* Paris: Pagnerre.
J.P. 1920. *Do broni. Wstępujcie do armji ochotniczej!* (s.l.), Muzeum Niepodległości w Warszawie, Nr. inw. MN-Pl.2042.
Jadacki, J.J. 1998. "Wincenty Lutosławski. Rozdział z dziejów myśli polskiej." In *Lutosławscy w kulturze polskiej,* ed. B. Klukowski, 54–87. Drozdowo: Towarzystwo Przyjaciół Muzeum Przyrody w Drozdowie.
Jaworski, W. 1994. *Eleuteryzm i mesjanizm. U źródeł filozofii społecznej Wincentego Lutosławskiego.* Kraków: Abrys.
Klug, E. 1987. "Das 'asiatische' Russland. Über die Entstehung eines europäischen Vorurteils," *Historische Zeitschrift* 245: 265–89.
Koneczny, F. 1921. *Polskie Logos a Ethos. Rozstrząsania o znaczeniu i celu Polski.* Vol. 2. Poznań/Warszawa: Księgarnia Św. Wojciecha.
Konopczyński, W. 1918. "Obrona kultury zachodniej." In *Polska w kulturze powszechnej.* Vol. 1, ed. F. Koneczny, 36–48. Kraków: Krakowska Ekspozytura Biura dla Spółek oszczęd. i pożyczek.
Korzeniewski, B. 2004. "Wróg nadchodzi polska propaganda polityczna w obliczu bitwy warszawskiej." *Przegląd Historyczny* 95: 467–84.
Kossuth, L. 1854. *Select Speeches,* ed. Francis W. Newman. New York: C.S. Francis.

———. 1859. *L'Europe, l'Autriche et la Hongrie.* Bruxelles: Fr. van Meenen et comp.
Kovács-Bertrand, A. 1997. *Der ungarische Revisionismus nach dem Ersten Weltkrieg. Der publizistische Kampf gegen den Friedensvertrag von Trianon (1918–1931).* München: Oldenbourg.
Krasicki, J. 1994. *Eschatologia i mesjanizm. Studium światopoglądu Mariana Zdziechowskiego.* Wrocław: Wiedza o Kulturze.
Krzyżaniakowa, J. 1996. "Polen als antemurale christianitatis. Zur Vorgeschichte eines Mythos." In *Mythen in Geschichte und Geschichtsschreibung aus polnischer und deutscher Sicht,* ed. A. von Saldern, 132–46. A. Münster: Lit.
———. 2003. "Polish Press Reporting about the Nazi Germans' Anti-Jewish Policy, 1933–1939." In *Why Didn't the Press Shout? American & International Journalism during the Holocaust,* ed. R.M. Shapiro, 411–28. New York: Yeshiva University Press.
Landau-Czajka, A. 2004. "The Image of the Jew in the Catholic Press during the Second Republic." *Polin: Studies in Polish Jewry* 8: 146–75.
Landgrebe, A. 2003. *"Wenn es Polen nicht gäbe, dann müsste es erfunden werden." Die Entwicklung des polnischen Nationalbewusstseins im europäischen Kontext von 1830 bis in die 1880er Jahre.* Wiesbaden: Harrassowitz.
Leinwand, A.J. 1993. "Bolszewicki plakat propagandowy w okresie wojny polsko-bolszewickiej 1920 roku." *Studia z dziejów Rosji i Europy Środkowo-Wschodniej* 27: 75–87.
Łukomski, G. 2004. "Stereotyp najeźdźcy w czasie wojny polsko-bolszewickiej 1918–1920." In *Swoi i obcy.* Vol. 1, ed. M. Kosman, 161–73. Poznań: Wydawnictwo Naukowe Instytutu Nauk Politycznych i Dziennikarstwa Uniwersytetu Im. Adama Mickiewicza.
Lutosławski, W. 1922. *Praca narodowa. Program polityki polskiej.* Vilnius: Księgarnia Stowarzyszenia Nauczycielstwa Polskiego.
Makowski, S. 1980. *Juliusz Słowacki.* Warszawa: Wydawnictwa Szkolne i Pedagogiczne.
Manon [pseudonym of an anonymous poster illustrator]. 1920. *Do Broni. Ratujmy ojczyznę! pamiętajmy dobrze o naszym przyszłym losie.* Lwów: Zakład Artystyczno-Litograficzny Adolfa Hegedüsa.
Miesięcznik Kościelny. 1937. 52: 6.
Mysłek, W. 1987. *Przedmurze. Szkice z dziejów Kościoła katolickiego w II Rzeczypospolitej.* Warszawa: Wydawnictwo Spółdzielcze.
Obremski, K. 1994. "Sarmacki mesjanizm." *Ogród* 7: 119–30.
Ostroróg, J. 1884. "Monumentum pro reipublicae ordinatione." In *Jana Ostroroga żywot i pismo "O naprawie Rzeczypospolitej." Studyum z literatury politycznéj XV wieku,* ed. A. Pawiński, 136. Warszawa: Drukarnia S. Olgebranda.
Ötvös, P. 1997. "Klage und Hoffnung. Vom Fremd- und Eigenbild der Ungarischen Nation." *Das achtzehnte Jahrhundert und Österreich. Jahrbuch der Österreichischen Gesellschaft zur Erforschung des achtzehnten Jahrhunderts* 12: 103–8.
Őze, S. and N. Spannenberger. 2000. "Zur Interpretation der mittelalterlichen Staatsgründung in der ungarischen Geschichtsschreibung des 19. und 20. Jahrhunderts." *Jahrbücher für Geschichte und Kultur Südosteuropas* 2: 61–77.
———. 2005. "Hungaria vulgo appelatur propugnaculum Christianitatis. Zur politischen Instrumentalisierung eines Topos in Ungarn." In *Beruf und Berufung. Geschichtswissenschaft und Nationsbildung in Ostmittel- und Südosteuropa im 19. und 20. Jahrhundert,* ed. M. Krzoska and H.-C. Maner, 19–39. Münster: Lit.

Paduszek, K. 2004. *Działalność propagandowa służb informacyjno-wywiadowczych Wojska Polskiego w czasie wojny polsko-bolszewickiej 1919–1921. Organizacje, metody, treści.* Toruń: Adam Marszałek.
Paksa, R. 2013. *Magyar nemzetiszocialisták. Az 1930-as évek szélsőjobboldali mozgalma, pártjai, politikusai, sajtója.* Budapest: Osiris.
———. 2013. *Szálasi Ferenc és a hungarizmus.* Budapest: Jaffa Kiadó.
Philippi, R., ed. *Preußisches Urkundenbuch.* Vols. 1 and 2. Königsberg: Hartung, 1909.
Piccolomini, E.S. 1699. "Cosmographia seu Rerum ubique gestarum historia locorumque description." In *Opera geographica et historica*, ed. J.M. Sustermann, 278. Helmstadii: pub. unknown.
Pluskiewicz, E. 1983. "Mesjanizm w myśli polskiej pierwszej połowy XIX wieku." *Zeszyty Naukowe Politechniki Śląskiej* 748: 105–15.
Pollmann, V. 2001. *Untermieter im christlichen Haus. Die Kirche und die "jüdische Frage" in Polen anhand der Bistumspresse der Metropolie Krakau 1926–1939.* Wiesbaden: Harrassowitz.
Prussak, M. 1993. *"Po ogniu szum wiatru cichego." Wyspiański i mesjanizm.* Warszawa: IBL.
Rady, M. 2011. "Ferenc Szálasi, 'Hungarism' and the Arrow Cross." In *In the Shadow of Hitler. Personalities of the Right in Central and Eastern Europe*, ed. R. Haynes and M. Rady, 261–77. London: I.B. Tauris.
Salamon, J. "Mesjanizm polski XIX wieku na tle historycznych uwarunkowań." *Zeszyty Naukowe Uniwersytetu Jagiellońskiego. Studia Religiologica* 23: 49–69.
Schmidt, M. 1990. "Der ungarische Revisionismus." In *1939, an der Schwelle zum Weltkrieg. Die Entfesselung des Zweiten Weltkrieges und das internationale System*, ed. K. Hildebrand, J. Schmädeke, R. Süßmuth, and K. Zernack, 135–40. Berlin/New York: de Gruyter.
Sobalkowski, S. 1938. *"Krew, która woła . . ." 6 przemówień na temat znaczenia kanonizacji św. Andrzeja Boboli dla Polski i każdego z nas z dołączeniem triduum ku jego czci.* Kielce: self-published.
Spannenberger, N. 2006. *Die katholische Kirche in Ungarn 1918–1939.* Stuttgart: Franz Steiner.
Srodecki, P. 2015. *Antemurale Christianitatis. Zur Genese der Bollwerksrhetorik im östlichen Mitteleuropa an der Schwelle vom Mittelalter zur Frühen Neuzeit.* Husum: Matthiesen Verlag.
———. 2016. "Antemurale-Based Frontier Identities in East Central Europe and Their Ideological Roots in Medieval/Early Modern Alterity and Alienity Discourses." In *Collective Identity in the Context of Medieval Studies*, ed. M. Antonín Malaníková and R. Antonín, 97–120. Ostrava: Filozofická fakulta OU, 2016.
———. 2016. "Universe christiane reipublice validissima propugnacula—Jagiellonian Europe in Bulwark Descriptions around 1500." In *The Jagiellonians in Europe. Dynastic Diplomacy and Foreign Relations*, ed. A. Bárány, 57–74. Debrecen: Lendület Hungary in Medieval Europe Research Group.
———. 2018. "Die Angst vor dem Osten. Europa und die religiöse motivierten Identitäts-, Alteritäts- und Alienitätskonstruktionen im Mittelalter und der Frühen Neuzeit." In *Identitätsentwürfe im östlichen Europa – im Spannungsfeld von Selbst- und Fremdwahrnehmung*, ed. H.-J. Bömelburg, M. Kirchner, M. Koller, and M. Wingender, 11–34. Wiesbaden: Harrassowitz Verlag.

Szczotka, S. 2012. "Wizerunek bolszewika w polskich plakatach propagandowych z wojny polsko-rosyjskiej 1919–1920 ze zbiorów Muzeum Niepodległości w Warszawie." *Niepodległość i Pamięć* 19: 205–13.
Szekfű, G. and B. Hóman. 1928–1934. *Magyar Történet*. 4 vols. Budapest: Királyi magyar egyetemi nyomda.
Szöllösi-Janze, M. 1989. *Die Pfeilkreuzlerbewegung in Ungarn. Historischer Kontext, Entwicklung und Herrschaft*. München: Oldenbourg.
Tarnowski, J. 1919. *La Pologne rempart de la civilisation*. s.l.
Tazbir, J. 2004. *Polska przedmurzem Europy*. Warszawa: Twój Styl.
Terbe, L. 1936. "Egy európai szálloige életraiza (Magyarország a kereszténység védőbástyája)." *Egyetemes Philológiai Közlöny* 60: 297–349.
Tomkiewicz, W. 1933. "Zasięg kolonizacji polskiej na ziemiach ruskich." *Przeglad Powszechny* 197: 32–57.
Urban, J. 1927. "O ideę dla Polski." *Przegląd Powszechny* 176: 3–17.
van Donzel, E.J. and A.B. Schmidt. 2010. *Gog and Magog in Early Eastern Christian and Islamic Sources. Sallam's Quest for Alexander's Wall*. Leiden/Boston: Brill.
von Klimó, A. 2003. *Nation, Konfession, Geschichte. Zur nationalen Geschichtskultur Ungarns im europäischen Kontext (1860–1948)*. München: Oldenbourg.
von Rotterdam, E. 1947. *Opvs epistolarvm*. Vol. 11, ed. P. Stafford Allen et al. Oxonii: Clarendon.
Wesselényi, M. 1844. *Eine Stimme über die ungarische und slawische Nationalität*. Leipzig: W. Vogel.
Westrem, S.D. 1998. "Against Gog and Magog." In *Text and Territory: Geographical Imagination in the European Middle Ages*, ed. S. Tomasch and S. Gilles, 54–76. Philadelphia: University of Pennsylvania Press.
Wiadomości Archidyecezyalne Warszawskie. 1920. 10, no. 12.
Wiadomości Diecezjalne Podlaskie. 1920. 2, nos. 11–12.
Wiśniewski, M. 1934. "Z rozmyślań czerwcowych." *Pro Christo* 7: 490.
Wysocki, W.J. 2012. "Kościół Polski wobec najazdu bolszewickiego w 1920 roku." In *W nieustannej trosce o polską diasporę. Tom studiów historycznych i politologicznych dedykowany Księdzu Arcybiskupowi Szczepanowi Wesołemu*, ed. R. Nir, M. Szczerbiński, K. Wasilewski, and C. Bugdalski, 81–105. Gorzów Wielkopolski: Stowarzyszenie Naukowe "Polska w Świecie."

CHAPTER 12

Defenders of the Russian Land
Viktor Vasnetsov's Warriors and Russia's Bulwark Myth

Stephen M. Norris

> Only the sick and poor man does not remember and appreciate his childhood and youth . . . it is worse when the *narod* (people) do not remember, value, and love their history!
> —Viktor Vasnetsov to Vladimir Stasov[1]

> The question to ask of pictures . . . is not just what they mean or do but what they *want*—what claim they make upon us, and how we are to respond?
> —W.J.T. Mitchell, *What Do Pictures Want?*

Viktor Vasnetsov (1848–1926) worked on and off for nearly twenty years on his painting *Bogatyri* (Warriors). When he finished in 1898, it was almost universally hailed as a masterpiece. Vladimir Stasov, the preeminent cultural critic of the era, compared it to Ilia Repin's (1844–1930) *Burlaki na Volge* ("Barge Haulers on the Volga," 1870–1873) as one of two paintings that perfectly captured the spirit of Russia. "In both paintings," Stasov wrote, "one sees all the strength and might of the Russian people." Stasov also claimed that Repin's painting contained *bogatyri* but that it depicted Russian strength as "oppressed and downtrodden." By contrast, Stasov said, Vasnetsov's *Warriors* possesses a strength that is "triumphant, calm, imposing, fearing no one and carrying out by its own will what it pleases and what it deems necessary for everyone, for the people."[2]

Here, then, is a famous painting being declared famous by a famous critic; this opening vignette tells us much about how Vasnetsov's canvas became hailed as one that expressed some sort of Russianness. In her incisive short article about Vasnetsov's painting, Helena Goscilo writes, "As a redoubtable protector of national borders and Orthodox Christianity, the Russian *bogatyr* looms large in multiple cultural genres throughout the ages."[3] Vasnetsov's warriors are the most famous of their kind; Goscilo explains, "Known to all Russians irrespective of their geographical roots, intellectual training, political affiliation, or attitude toward art, these figuratively executed images reflect Vasnetsov's retrospective preoccupation with heroic legends and legendary heroism."[4] Eventually, Goscilo concludes, they became "sedimented in the nation's collective unconscious and, under Soviet rule, reinforced by a uniform educational system dedicated to the selective preservation of national history, Vasnetsov's *bogatyri* are Russia's heroic border guards of the empire, functioning as a reassuring emblem of indomitable strength and invincibility."[5]

Stasov's anointing of *Warriors* is therefore part of a larger story about this piece of art, which I trace below. Before the painting could be declared a canvas that embodied "the strength and might of the Russian people," before it could become "sedimented in the nation's unconsciousness," it had to be imagined, painted, and then interpreted. Less than twenty years after Stasov's declaration, revolutions and political change brought the Bolsheviks to power. They preached a rejection of most of the old ways of life, including religion and nationalism, in favor of implementing entirely new ways to create a society and its inhabitants. Yet *Warriors* survived this turmoil and eventually served as an embodiment of Russian nationhood and, with it, a symbolic bulwark.

The Warriors represents a particular form of a bulwark myth. As the editors note in their introduction to this volume, these myths contain certain components, among them the claim of a perennial menace outside the border, the claim to defend oneself and others within a given territory, and the claim of a civilizing mission as part of this defense. A bulwark myth attempts to mobilize people, to unite the community contained within the bulwark. It also serves as a form of political myth, one that provides a story about the origins of a given community and that often features heroes.

Vasnetsov's painting brings these mythic components into being by creating a visual shorthand for a Russian bulwark myth, capturing heroes but also heroic models on canvas. While other chapters in this volume explore the more familiar *antemurale* myths developed in the region with Russia and Russians as "Others" against whom the community needed to defend itself, Russians also narrated versions of the bulwark myth and located it on the same borderlands. In this version, the Ukrainian borderlands could be made "Russian" and serve as the location for the necessity of Russian imperial defense (in a roughly similar way that monasteries in the same region became bulwarks of Russianness, as Liliya Berezhnaya discusses in her chapter).

What follows is the tale of a painting told across half a century. Two episodes in this story stand out. First, the reception *Warriors* and its creator received from late nineteenth-century Russian critics. For people such as Stasov, the painting was a masterpiece of Russian nationalist art that was not tied to Vasnetsov's religiosity. Others, by placing Vasnetsov's work at the St. Vladimir Cathedral in Kyiv alongside the *bogatyri*, believed that the warriors personified a sort of Orthodox patriotism.[6] What they agreed upon was that the borderland on which the three stood was Russian and that it should be guarded against Russia's enemies. Vasnetsov's religiosity was also an issue Soviet critics had to wrestle with, the second episode in the story traced below. In the late 1930s, the warriors reappeared in Stalinist culture. Soviet writers interpreted Vasnetsov's painting as a nationalist one that could inspire citizens to defend their socialist motherland. By placing this interpretation on the three warriors, they ignored whatever traces of religiosity the canvas might contain.

In both episodes, Vasnetsov's warriors became understood as timeless soldiers willing to defend a Russian and then Soviet landscape whenever called to do so. *Warriors* therefore became an important element in the creation of a Russian bulwark myth, one that stressed how the steppe needed to be defended against all invaders. The painting, in other words, provided a call for mobilization, a crucial component of bulwark myths. Through the stories told about the *bogatyri* in Vasnetsov's canvas, we can begin to trace how the painting served as an embodiment of an always-evolving Russianness and how first Russian and then Soviet critics made claims upon the painting, mobilizing the canvas and the warriors within it. In both episodes recounted below, Russian and Soviet critics transformed the three warriors on horseback into living, breathing contemporaries and the land around them into a real landscape that even gave off a smell. This canvas bulwark thus speaks to how odor is not just a biological or psychological phenomenon but a historical and cultural one as well.[7] The painting, as more than one viewer commented, "smelled like Old Rus," therefore providing the canvas with the emotional, intimate appeal that called on viewers to act as the warriors did and to defend the Russian soil.

A Whiff of the Past: Making History, Painting Canvas Bulwarks

Before turning to what Viktor Vasnetsov wrote about his work and what others had to say about it, we should look at the painting itself.

Across an enormous canvas, three warriors rest on horseback (Figure 12.1).[8] The figure on the far left of the painting is stern and bearded and draws his sword from a scabbard. Next to him, in the middle of the scene, the biggest of the three warriors shields his eyes from the sun as he gazes

Figure 12.1. Viktor Vasnetsov, *Bogatyri*, 1898. Photograph by anagoria. Wikimedia Commons, public domain.

out in the distance. A mace is slung around his right arm while he clutches a *rogatina*, a spearlike weapon preferred by ancient Slavs, in his left hand. The last warrior, and the only one without a beard, also focuses his eyes in the same direction, clutching his bow, ready to let loose an arrow if need be. The three warriors, as virtually everyone who gazed at the painting knew, were the three most famous medieval *bogatyri* from Russian legends: Dobrynya Nikitich, Ilia Muromets, and Alyosha Popovich. Nikitich was known in the legends that had circulated over the centuries for his courage, Muromets for his physical and spiritual strength, Popovich for his cleverness. They also symbolized three social estates: Popovich the priests (the popular stories about him state he is the crafty son of a priest), Nikitich the nobility (the *byliny* tell of his close connections to the Kyivan Rus princes), and Muromets the peasantry (in the legends, he was the son of a peasant from the village of Murom).⁹

They stand on a borderland, the steppe region just as it gives way to woodlands in the southwesternmost regions of the Russian Empire, the hooves of the horses firmly planted on Russian soil. They sit in a defensive position, ever ready to drive enemies off the soil. This painting, then, reclaims the myth of the "lands of the Rus," which Geoffrey Hosking has characterized as "the master image" that princes and chroniclers used from the eleventh to the fifteenth centuries to "conjure up the idea of what they were fighting to unite and to defend."[10] Vasnetsov has transferred this medieval concept to the nineteenth century, transforming the borderlands of Old Rus into Russian national territory.

The painting also transfers the notions of unity and defense present in the medieval "master image" into a more modern setting. Vasnetsov himself participated in this retrofitting: according to the legend the artist liked to tell, his warriors emerged out the Russian soil itself. When he was working at the artistic community at Abramtsevo, an estate near Moscow owned by the industrialist Savva Mamontov (1841–1918) and by the 1870s and 1880s ground zero for artistic attempts to invent Russianness, Vasnetsov gazed at the land around him and saw medieval warriors lurking beneath the bark of local trees. Later, after he had finished his painting, the painter declared that the Abramtsevo forest was nothing less than "our mother Russia." "Like those oaks," he declared, timeless warriors and a timeless patriotic-religious spirit also grew, for Russia (or its trees, or its defenders) is "not something you can catch with your bare hands." "She," Vasnetsov claimed, "is not afraid of snow storms or hurricanes, or the passing centuries."[11] From the get-go, therefore, or at least from the moment he had finished *Warriors* and it had been sanctified as Russian national art, Vasnetsov imagined his art to be a patriotic landmark.

Vasnetsov, the son of a priest and grandson of an icon painter, grew up in a village within the Viatka district. He always claimed that he developed an interest in the tales, legends, and faith of Russia's *narod*. One of the favorite subjects of these stories, and one that matters for the painting he later completed, was Ilia Muromets, who had long been a popular persona in the *byliny* and *lubki*. At the time Vasnetsov was contemplating the trees at Abramtsevo, Russian ethnographers were also recording and transcribing some of the epics. In 1871, for example, Aleksandr Fedorovich Gilferding (1831–1872) translated a version of "Ilia Muromets and Nightingale the Robber" in the Olonets province. In it, Muromets is characterized as a "famous Holy Russian *bogatyr*," with an unerring sense of rightness and devoutness.[12]

Muromets often quarrels with Prince Vladimir and other aristocrats, as many songs illustrate, but he is always ready to defend his land (usually the city of Kyiv) and his faith. Here, too, a certain historical retrofitting is taking place: these nineteenth-century versions of Russian folktales lay claim to the heritage of Kyivan Rus for the Russian Empire. The soil that Muromets traverses—made up in the tales of swamps, streams, birches, grasses, meadows, dark woods, and hills—is Russian, the very same soil on which Vasnetsov spotted his warriors.[13]

This sort of characterization appealed to the budding artist. By 1858, when he was ten, Vasnetsov had already begun to develop a talent for painting. He started formal training at a seminary, working with an icon painter in Viatka. His work gained him acceptance to the Imperial Academy of Arts in 1867, just four years after a group of painters had declared their secession from that institution and launched the Association of Traveling Art Exhibits. Thus, Vasnetsov went to Petersburg at a time when the realist artistic revolution was under way in Russia, but it was a movement that young Vasnetsov only took part in later, after the association had adopted its name, *Peredvizhniki* ("Wanderers" or "Itinerants"), in 1870. Championed by the critic Vladimir Stasov (1824–1906) and by the Moscow prince-industrialist Pavel Tretiakov (1832–1898), the wanderers laid the foundations of a national artistic culture in Russia, one promoted by the critic and made permanent by the industrialist's building of a museum bearing his name to house Russian art.

Vasnetsov's journey from potential icon painter to national painter reflected broader artistic and historical trends in the region. By the late nineteenth century, an increasing number of painters working across imperial borders in Central and Eastern Europe also saw their canvases as sites to articulate national traditions. These history painters have not been well explored by scholars,[14] yet their works in many ways furthered the ongoing constructions of nationhoods in important ways. A host of artists began to capture national traits in their canvases, helping in the process to build artistic bulwarks. Jan Matejko (1838–1893), Ilia Repin (1844–1930), Vasily Surikov (1848–1916), Vasnetsov (1848–1926), Mykola Pimonenko (1862–1912), Alphonse Mucha (1860–1939): this is a list of fairly well-known painters in Eastern Europe, yet their works, particularly the "national" canvases they painted in the late nineteenth and early twentieth centuries have not been studied as important sites of memory, nationhood, and historical interpretations.

Warriors emerged out of these regional, transnational, and transimperial concerns. In many ways, the history painters who created canvas bulwarks evolved out of the discussions in the 1830s and 1840s in Central and Eastern Europe, when romantic nationalism took hold in the region. As Serhiy Bilenky argued in his recent book, East European intellectuals in those decades imagined the "representation of nation-ness" in the region, or "a vision and division of geographic, symbolic, and social space, which eventually resulted in the unmaking of some national projects and the making of others (or, to use Alexei Miller's terms, how nationalists in the region superimposed 'ideal fatherlands' on each other)."[15]

His book is explicitly comparative in approach and charts the process of how romantic ideas of nationality entered these lands by the 1830s and 1840s as well as how intellectuals fused language, religion, history, and institutions to envision separate nations that often overlapped with each other. Central to these discourses, as Bilenky discusses, is how Orthodoxy and Catholicism functioned within them—Orthodoxy could refer to Russians and/or Ukrainians; but Catholicism was Polish. The result was a series of "nation-centered idioms" created by different groups, some overlapping, others competing, even within a single national imagining (Ukrainianness, for example). Bilenky's focus is on intellectuals and writers, but the national imaginings they conjured up were ones that artists reworked later in the century, transferring ideas of ideal fatherlands onto canvases.

Paintings such as Vasnetsov's depiction of medieval warriors, Ilia Repin's *Zaporozhtsy pishut pismo turetskomu sultanu* ("Reply of the Zaporozhian Cossacks to Sultan Mehmed IV of the Ottoman Empire," 1891), Jan Matejko's *Bitwa pod Grunwaldem* ("The Battle of Grunwald," 1878), and his *Jan Sobieski pod Wiedniem* ("Jan III Sobieski in the Battle of Vienna," 1883) functioned as canvas bulwarks, for they provided important visual representations of *antemurale* myths. Although the Polish *antemurale christianitatis* version is the most well known,[16] Russia also developed its own bulwark myth. Vasnetsov's painting provided four key features of an *antemurale* myth: demarcation, defense, protection, and commitment.[17] The warriors on horseback stood on a clearly demarcated steppe, they were ready to defend it and protect others who lived on it, and they were committed to this defense as long as needed. Vasnetsov's painting served as a "boundary-defining mechanism," or rather a "boundary-reclaiming mechanism," as Pål Kolsto discusses in his contribution.

In order for *Warriors* to function as a canvas bulwark, however, viewers, critics, and state officials had to talk about the three, talk to them, and convince them and others that they were needed to defend the Russian soil.[18] Vasnetsov's canvas, in other words, had to come to life and be embraced as a living entity, containing warriors who would inspire viewers to defend their motherland.

When the painting first debuted, it was discussed within the contexts of Vasnetsov's other works, particularly his recently completed religious frescoes in Kyiv, and as part of ongoing debates about Russian national art. Vasnetsov befriended Wanderers such as Ivan Kramskoi (1837–1887) and Ilia Repin, and communicated with them for years, but his work represented another path in the journey to Russian national art. In the traces he has left (letters, biographical accounts), Vasnetsov emerges as an artist who married his interest in Russian folklore and Russian national traditions to his sense of himself as a Russian, Orthodox believer.[19]

In a sense, though, this fairly consistent worldview created two Vasnetsovs in the 1870s and 1880s, at least among the critics and other artists who began to interpret his work. One was the younger *peredvizhnik*, an artist who created national works such as *Chaepitie v traktire* ("Tea Drinking at a Tavern," 1874) and *Vitiaz na rasputie* ("The Knight at the Crossroads," 1878). The other Vasnetsov was the deeply religious painter who agreed in 1884 to spend five years in Kyiv working on the frescoes for a new cathedral, St. Vladimir's, that told the history of the conversion to Orthodoxy in 988. Of course, these two Vasnetsovs were one and the same person—he consistently joined his interest in Old Russia, in its traditions and its faith, to his work, regardless of where he found himself. His Kyiv commission helped to testify to that city's status as Russian, in a sense prefiguring his canvas containing the three warriors: both projects imagined Kyivan Rus as a Russian national heritage and by extension, viewers as "children of Rus."[20]

The problem in making Vasnetsov and his canvases into subjects came with how that art became public in the late nineteenth century, as Katia Dianina has recently argued. Art, she writes, became a familiar marker of national belonging in the decades after 1860s, in part because of the explosion of newspaper culture and in part because of the public exhibitions that the itinerants pioneered. At the same time, Russian national art provoked heated debates: few agreed about the details, but the conversation itself mattered a great deal in establishing artistic culture as Russian and an important aspect of belonging.[21]

Vasnetsov's bifurcation occurred in these intense debates: for some, particularly Stasov, he was a national painter and his warriors defended Russian land; for others, he was a Russian Orthodox painter, whose frescoes helped to create a new, national, religious art and whose warriors defended a sacred realm. David Jackson has noted how Vasnetsov's "divergence from mainstream realism exercised not only his contemporaries but later taxed Soviet art historians." In a paradoxical sense, Jackson argues, his work is "not dissimilar to the paradigm of Soviet Realism in that it encompasses mass aspiration through the medium of popular culture and seeks to image romantically what should be, rather than what is, a form of 'true lies.'" Vasnetsov, though, looked backward, to "what might have been" based on "traditional religious values," ones he expressed in his other works and at St. Vladimir's Cathedral in Kyiv.[22] Ultimately, Jackson sees Vasnetsov as an artistic outgrowth of the mid to late nineteenth-century "Slavic revival" and a painter who possessed "more of a religious than national temperament, but the two were deeply intertwined."[23]

Vasnetsov himself viewed his painting as a living thing that could inspire others. While at Abramtsevo, he wrote that he was thinking of the "good, strong" *bogatyri*.[24] In an October 1897 letter to Mamontov, Vasnetsov declared that he "has only one motherland . . . Rus," which he gladly gave his heart to.[25] He later recalled that the image was "not a painting" but something constantly present, like life itself.[26] His art and faith were linked: as he wrote in a letter from 1891, "Praise be to God, we share a love for and solace in art."²⁷ Stasov, however, tended to interpret Vasnetsov as an artist for "the people" and one who dramatically captured "ancient Rus" in meaningful ways.²⁸

In these readings, "Rus" and its borderlands become imagined as a Russian bulwark in need of defense. At the same time, the critic did not mention Vasnetsov's work on St. Vladimir's and the religious component to his painting. Instead, Stasov declared in 1899 that Vasnetsov's works, now prominently displayed at the Tretiakov Gallery, had already entered "into our souls and hearts," making them religious-like in their effect.²⁹ They captured the *mudrost narodnaia* (people's wisdom), none better than *Warriors*, which Stasov was already declaring to be one of the best paintings "in the history of Russian art."³⁰ Muromets, in Stasov's viewing, stands ever ready to strike the enemy, while Dobrynya also wields his Slavic sword, ready to defend against the enemy. Alyosha, the youngest, is less serious but no less ready to fight. In the way he describes the warriors and even their horses (Alyosha's is said to be concentrating, not on heroic deeds of the past but on the here and now of the land beneath him); Stasov transforms the three into contemporaries.³¹ This imagining, in other words, became the first attempt to mobilize Vasnetsov's canvas bulwark: the warriors were not just from the past, they could guard the Russian land in the present. Other spectators wrote similarly about Vasnetsov's canvas.³²

Stasov, in his book, enshrined Vasnetsov and his canvases as the best examples of "real" Russian history: in these paintings and in *Warriors* particularly, authentic Russian national history resided, for they captured traditions not borrowed from elsewhere.³³ The *bogatyri*, in other words, were made to fit within the influential critic's view that Russian art should liberate itself from Western conventions and that true national art would portray the people's lives and teach them how to live.³⁴

The same year *Warriors* appeared, however, the painter was celebrated in one of the first full-length books dedicated to his work. The work celebrated in it was not his famous painting but the images he had completed for St. Vladimir's Cathedral in Kyiv (Figure 12.2).³⁵ A. Sobolev referred to Vasnetsov's work as a "powerful example of our national saying: the news is delivered from heart to heart." He concluded that Vasnetsov's work was both an example of Russian religious painting and a work that inspires authentic feelings in Russian Orthodox Christians.³⁶ When he was at work in Kyiv, the artist wrote friends and colleagues, including Mamontov, letters filled with his sense that he was doing "God's work," at various times even sending Easter greetings.³⁷ In an 1891 *Novoe vremia* (New Times) article about St. Vladimir's, M.M. Ivanov (1859–1935) wrote that the artists who worked on it helped to establish "examples of a new religious style of painting," singling out Vasnetsov in this regard and for his ability to capture "our

Figure 12.2. Viktor Vasnetsov, *Kreshcheniie Rusi*, 1896. Special stamp to commemorate the 1,025th anniversary of the Christianization of Rus by the Russian Post, Publishing and Trade Centre "Marka," 2013. Design of the souvenir sheet by A. Moscovets. Scanned by Dmitry Ivanov. Wikimedia Commons, public domain.

national outlook, through our stories, through the way we were, through our regions, where the smells of Rus and the Russian soul are."[38]

The cathedral now contains "a new, national trend," one that is not located only in Kyiv but is "for all Russia," for it captures the religious aspect of national art.[39] This sort of characterization continued: writing in the religious journal *Mir Bozhii* (God's World/Peace), S. Makovskii mused in 1898 that Vasnetsov, who had mostly become known for his art based on folklore, had managed at St. Vladimir's to capture a spirit of *narodnost* that also included religious themes.⁴⁰

Vasnetsov connected his work on *Warriors* to his faith, writing to V.T. Georgievskii in March 1898, "I am now busy finishing *Warriors*, and by Easter, if God grants it, they will be completely done."⁴¹ He also wrote Stasov in May 1898 and stated that while the work was about Old Rus, it was also religious in orientation because "I am a true Orthodox, Russian believer" and "We are all born into the Orthodox Church, live with an Orthodox God, and will die with Him."⁴² Later that year, Vasnetsov again wrote to his critical patron, saying that the biography Stasov had written about him was only partly true, in that while he did indeed love epic tales and considered himself to be a painter of *narodnost*, he also inherited "religious and philosophical ideas" from his father and transferred this inheritance to his canvas.⁴³

When *Warriors* appeared, Stasov was not the only one to anoint it as a national epic. *Petersburgskaia gazeta* (Petersburg Newspaper) declared it to be "one of the most significant works of art" in Russia and one where "in it, one can sense the power of the *russkii narod* (Russian people)."⁴⁴ Writing again in *God's World/Peace,* S. Makovskii connected the painting to the artist's work in Kyiv, asserting, "Currently, everyone's attention is devoted to his huge canvas, *Bogatyri."* Although Makovskii praised that work and others with medieval themes, he noted, "Along with the good in the exhibit comes the bad" and cited some of the artist's portraits: "No, Vasnetsov is not a portraitist!"⁴⁵ In the end, though, Makovskii concluded that Vasnetsov's work on historical themes also made him *svoi khudozhnik* (our artist).⁴⁶

What this inclusion meant, of course, depended on the way you viewed Vasnetsov and what, at least by 1900, was his most famous canvas. Regardless of which Vasnetsov you gravitated toward, by the turn of the twentieth century it was clear that Viktor Vasnetsov had captured the spirit of Old Rus and its warriors on canvas: his *Warriors,* in short, functioned as a canvas bulwark that was redolent of Old Rus and that asked onlookers to consider its warriors as contemporaries ready to rise to the defense of the motherland. The painting captured what Molly Brunson has argued (in reference to Repin's 1885 *Ivan Groznyi i syn iego Ivan 16 noiabria 1581 goda,* "Ivan the Terrible and His Son Ivan") is "the unique potential of the painterly medium to represent history, to lift it into the present and into the human."⁴⁷ Russian critics helped to identify the warriors as living, breathing people and the landscape around them as a living space, one that even gave off an odor. Artist and critics alike helped to transfer the ancient soil of the Kyivan Rus borderland into the more modern soil of Russia, providing the origin story so vital to political myths. The *bogatyri* spoke to viewers, inspired them, and provided them with the spirit necessary to defend the present-day motherland.

Smelling Rus: Mobilizing the Russian Spirit in the Soviet Century

In November 1938, Vasnetsov's *bogatyri* made an appearance in *Pravda* (The Truth). On the back page of the newspaper, an article announced the opening of an exhibition of Russian historical works at the Tretiakov Gallery. More than 600 paintings filled thirteen rooms at the museum, including a number singled out by *Pravda*. Among them was *The Warriors*. The laconic description simply noted that the exhibit had opened, that visitors could now see historical themes and historical canvases on display, and that they would witness a monumental assembly of art from the eighteenth, nineteenth, and twentieth centuries assembled from across the USSR.[48]

Despite the dry tone, *Pravda's* article spoke of an important event and an important process underway in Joseph Stalin's (1878–1953) Soviet Union. The event was the exhibition itself, which was nothing less than a reintroduction—and perhaps better explained as a reincorporation—of tsarist national art into Soviet culture. *Literaturnaia gazeta* (Literary Newspaper) announced that the rationale for the show was "the workers' enormous interest in history, particularly the heroic past of the Russian people."[49]

Vasnetsov's *Warriors* appeared along with Repin's *Ivan the Terrible and His Son Ivan, 16 November 1581,* Vasilii Surikov's *Pokoreniie Sibiri Iermakom Timofeevichem* (The Conquest of Siberia by Iermak, 1895), *Utro streletskoi kazni* (The Morning of the Streltsy Execution, 1881), Pavel Vereshchagin's (1842–1904) 1812 canvases, and many others. The show, as correspondence and comments in the official visitors' book indicate, helped visitors, in the words of one, "to reinforce our grasp over the history of our state's development."[50] This revival, as David Brandenberger notes, came at a time in Stalinist culture when martial themes dominated and when, as a guidebook to a Hermitage show dedicated to the subject declared, "in the past, much like today, the Russian people have had to wage just wars against foreign invaders who try to shatter the unity and inviolability of our motherland."[51]

The process is what Kevin M.F. Platt and Brandenberger have usefully labeled "epic revisionism"—that is, how heroes from the Russian national past came to figure prominently in Stalinist public culture to a degree in the late 1930s that they even overshadowed the heroes of the Russian Revolution and civil war.[52] Platt and Brandenberger (and their fellow authors) focus on writers and historical figures within this process (i.e., Leo Tolstoy [1828–1920], Mikhail Lermontov [1814–1841], Aleksandr Nevskii [1220–

1263]), but we might extend it to include works of art that represented both cultural and historical figures. The 1938 Tretiakov exhibit, in short, reinstated both Vasnetsov and his *Warriors* as national heroes, while taking any association with Russian Orthodoxy away from them. Just as Vasnetsov reclaimed these ancient warriors for a nineteenth-century Russian nationalist narrative, so too did this twentieth-century exhibit reclaim Vasnetsov for a new narrative: Ilia Muromets and his fellow warriors still guarded Kyivan Rus, but they now guarded a *Soviet* motherland.

In the official book printed for the exhibition, M. Aptekar situated the work on display within a very particular, and typically teleological, historical framework. The historical paintings represented a perfect point where factual-based history met legendary stories in a format easily accessible to the masses. Previously, Aptekar wrote, "the people" consumed myths, legends, and stories. This "history" gave way to history as a science, one based on facts, but many of these works were not available to the masses. What was needed, he declared, was a format in which people could *vdokhnut vozdukh proshlogo* (inhale the air of the past)."[53] The history painters accomplished this feat, and it was still meaningful to "the people of the great Soviet Union," for they can see in the works *tak bylo—tak budet* (so it was, so it will be).[54] Knowing the past, Aptekar declared (paraphrasing Karl Marx [1818–1883]), was a way to achieve the radiant future of communism. Russian historical painting, because it was realistic and accessible to all, represented a path to this future.

Within this framework, Vasnetsov initially received short shrift. Aptekar does not mention him or any of his works by name in his catalog. Instead, Repin and his fellow "wanderers" Surikov and Vereshchagin received the most attention. In their historical works, particularly those that deal with Peter I, one can see "the foundation of the great Stalinist communist democracy," which was tied to the history of "our great motherland."[55] Vasnetsov, although included, was still too problematic, too religious, his works perhaps smelling too ancient.

Yet *Warriors* emerged from the exhibition to stand guard again. The same year the exhibit opened, Alexander Gerasimov (1881–1963) finished his canvas *Stalin i Voroshilov na progulke v Kremle. Dva vozhdia posle dozhdia* (I.V. Stalin and Klimentii Voroshilov in the Kremlin after the Rain, 1938). The painter claimed he drew inspiration from Vasnetsov's famous canvas: "I admit that this picture was constantly before my eyes; there are three warriors there, and here stand two warriors—our Soviet ones."[56] Reviewing the Tretiakov exhibit, N. Morgunov, writing in *Krasnaia zvezda* (Red Star), declared that *Warriors* embodied "all the distinctive, immemorial characteristics of the great Russian people," traits that included strength, invincibility, nobility, great folk wisdom, a hatred of enemies, and selfless bravery. Morgunov concluded that these characteristics are present in all of Vasnetsov's works as well as the best works in the exhibition, which marked a great "political-educational event," for it captured the heart of the Russian people.[57]

In a sense, these words became a template for evaluating Vasnetsov's canvas thereafter. They also served as the first attempts to use *Warriors* for the repurposing of the nineteenth-century Russian bulwark myth into a Soviet bulwark myth. Gerasimov and Morgunov claimed the Soviet people needed to unite, to be inspired by these canvas warriors, to breathe in their spirit. In writing these words, they were updating the version of the bulwark myth that Vasnetsov and his critics articulated a few decades earlier. Morgunov authored a full-length study of Vasnetsov in 1940 that resuscitated the historical painters and their works of the late nineteenth century, declaring Vasnetsov to be an exemplary practitioner of national art. Morgunov devoted six of forty-five pages to *Warriors*. He traced its origins to the early 1880s, seeing the canvas as the result of a long process and therefore the culmination of Vasnetsov's career. *Warriors* emerged in this retelling as an attempt to find, capture, and then render Russianness itself. Vasnetsov's painting depicted defense of the motherland as a timeless quality all viewers should embrace: the warriors stood on the soil of ancient Rus, but the very same soil now formed the Soviet motherland.

The long quest to realize this masterpiece, which took twenty years, allowed Morgunov to ignore the artist's work on St. Vladimir Cathedral in Kyiv, a project that gets only one paragraph. Instead, throughout the 1880s and 1890s Vasnetsov painted subjects close to that of the *bogatyri*—*Ivan Tsarevich na serom volke* (Ivan Tsarevich Riding the Gray Wolf, 1889), for example—while his real work was in making his *Warriors* come alive. The result, at least in this Soviet retelling, was that this painting came to symbolize his entire life's work and that even contemporaries viewed it as a national one. Morgunov quotes Repin, who stated that the *bogatyri* represent "all the strength and might of the Russian people."[58]

By 1940, in other words, Vasnetsov had come to be seen in the USSR as a supreme realist artist who captured the essence of Russianness, and his *Warriors* now became his most famous work, the result of heroic labor across two decades. It is Repin's characterization, as Morgunov concludes, that makes the painting "understood and close to the workers of the USSR" as well as to "all good people in our socialist motherland."[59] Vasnetsov, the biography notes, died in 1926, but his life after 1898 was finished in two pages—his real significance, the book indicates, ended in 1898.

The warriors guarding the Soviet-Russian motherland in 1938 and 1940 were mobilized for a real war in 1941. Vasnetsov's heroes became emblems of the military might and strength of the Russian people.[60] One writer declared that Vasnetsov's painting, despite being completed in "an age of reaction," should be understood as one in which the artist "saw the slumbering gigantic strength of the Russian people and believed that in the not too distant future it would awaken and display itself in all its *bogatyri*-like power."[61] Another report written after the war had ended suggested that the Red Army had fought "for peace in the world" and vigilantly guarded "the borders of our Motherland." These warriors of the present "especially cherish these images of the defenders of the Russian land, just keepers of the people's peace."[62] Vasnetsov's warriors still demarcated an important border (in 1941, between the socialist world and the fascist one), they still defended national soil, they still protected an Orthodox population (now citizens of the "socialist paradise"), and they were still committed to their duties. Even in the Soviet Union, *Warriors* functioned as a canvas bulwark.

In fall 1946, the very same 1938 Hermitage exhibition, which was called the "Martial History of the Russian People," reopened. Similar shows appeared in Moscow too—*Vecherniaia Moskva* (Evening Moscow) ran an August 1947 piece with a picture of visitors in front of Vasnetsov's *Warriors*.[63] One visitor wrote in the Tretiakov's guest book that "just a glimpse of the historic jewel paintings of the great artists awakens in you a sense of internal strength in an instance," concluding that "here is the Russian spirit; here is the smell of Rus."[64] By 1946, in yet another publication devoted to the artist, A.K. Lebedev could open with the words "who does not know his *Warriors* who so carefully guarded 'our earth,'"[65] noting that the painting emerged out of the 1870s' and 1880s' interest "in Russian national stories, in *bogatyri* epics, in Russian national songs, and in national history."[66] Once again Vasnetsov's Kyiv work is relegated to secondary status (a page and a half) to get to the end of *Warriors*, which is declared to "symbolize the greatness, bravery, beauty, and strength of the Russian people."[67] In this biography, the artist, having completed this monumental, timeless work dies twenty-eight years later in the very next paragraph.

For the centennial of Vasnetsov's birth, *Pravda* featured an article celebrating his Russianness, noting how his art captured *narodnyi* (the national), and once again declaring *Warriors* to be his most monumental work, which captured "*okhrana zemli russkoi* (the guardians of the Russian land)."[68] V. Zhuravlev, the author of the article, praised Vasnetsov's historical works and declared *The Warriors* to be timeless figures, calm, assured, and still guarding "our motherland." By the time of his centenary, therefore, Vasnetsov and his most famous painting could already be slotted into familiar scripts, even if they had not existed a decade before.

In a book published to celebrate the birthday, M.Z. Kholodovskaia quoted Stasov at the outset to frame the study in terms of Vasnetsov's connection to the Russian people before moving on to a potted biography of the artist's life. This retelling had some new elements sprinkled in—early on he quotes the artist's belief that he "always and only lived in Rus"[69]—but mostly the story is familiar, including how Vasnetsov connected factual history to canvas. Once again, his work in Kyiv is relegated to minor status, still holding steady at one paragraph and without a single illustration devoted to it. Once again pride of place is given to *Warriors*, the germ of which was planted in the early 1880s and evolved over "nearly 20 years."[70] Vasnetsov's "patriotic" canvases include Old Rus, they are dear to the hearts of the masses, but they still do not smell of the Orthodox faith.

This retrofitting continued during the Nikita Khrushchev (1894–1971) era, representing one small example of how the culture of Stalinist nationalism survived the dictator's death. In a 1959 book devoted to the painter's life and works, Nataliia Morgunova-Rudnitskaia stuck to the parameters established twenty years earlier. Vasnetsov is declared to be "one of the most famous and well-loved names among Russian artists," because his works perfectly captured Russian history and contained the elements of *moguchii i velikii narod* (the mighty and great people) (echoing Ivan Turgenev's [1818–1883] famous idea of the "great, mighty Russian language").[71]

In this retelling of previous retellings, Morgunova-Rudnitskaia situates the birth of *The Warriors* in the early 1870s, when Vasnetsov began to paint folkloristic and historical themes that culminated in his best-known work, *Warriors* (and she asks the rhetorical question "Who does not know *Bogatyri*, ... and his other pictures on historical and legendary themes!").[72] The 1959 story culminates with his 1898 painting (his work in Kyiv gets one parenthetical statement), which the author argues is "the synthesis of Vasnetsov's ideas about the lofty qualities of the Russian people and the expression of his deep love for them." The three warriors were "the result of his profound understanding of and deep knowledge of the oral traditions, history, and everyday life of the people."[73] These combinations make the *bogatyri* timeless, ever ready "to protect the borders of the Russian land and look carefully into the distance."[74]

These articles—from Zhuravlev's to Morgunova-Rudnitskaia's—illustrate that for bulwark myths to be long lasting, they need to be continuously invoked. Vasnetsov's canvas functioned as an expression of a Russian bulwark myth precisely because so many people constantly wrote about it using similar terms and using it as a means to call for unity, to ask others to be inspired to defend the motherland. Just twenty years after *The Warriors* made a triumphant reentry, this time into Soviet culture, the stories about them and their creator became fixed.

The ancient *bogatyri* were timeless, ready to guard the motherland whenever she called. Their creator was always searching to find the trio of guardians, worked hard to capture their lofty qualities, and painted a masterpiece that spoke to his love for the Russian people. His earlier canvas bulwark had now become a Soviet bulwark myth: if Vasnetsov and his contemporaries had to envision the Ukrainian borderlands as Russian by seeing the warriors as timeless "children of Rus," now the trio guarded Soviet land and protected the Soviet border. By the 1950s, Vasnetsov's warriors also guarded postage stamps, cigarette cases, postcards, and other objects. That the very same painter spent years living and working in Kyiv to paint frescoes in a church and that his warriors may have been Orthodox believers did not feature in this biographical refashioning in the life of a painting. This is the view of the three warriors that dominated the rest of the Soviet era: once the heroes of *byliny*, the *bogatyri* appeared on late Soviet ephemera and even starred in Aleksandr Ptushko's (1900–1973) film *Ilia Muromets* (1956).[75]

Conclusion

Pravda also celebrated Vasnetsov's 150th birthday in 1998. Fifty years after the communist newspaper helped to ignite the public process of turning the artist's warriors into a Soviet bulwark myth, the same paper again highlighted "the warrior of the Russian brush (the title of the article)." "Today," wrote Larisa Iagunkova, "when the Russian man is standing at a crossroads," the canvas could yet again rally the "defenders and saviors of Rus."[76] No other painting or work of Vasnetsov's is mentioned in the birthday article. Of course, Vasnetsov's 150th birthday was in 1998, nearly seven years after the USSR's collapse and a time when *Pravda* was operating on life support and no longer appearing daily. By that time, Vasnetsov and his most famous work had been reinterpreted yet again by late Soviet critics, who helped to restore the artist's religiosity to the interpretations of his paintings.[77]

Iagunkova's article was not celebratory, but a lament. By 1998, Vasnetsov's *bogatyri* had become commercial icons, guarding the labels of beer, cigarettes, candies, and other items for sale in the new Russia. The *Pravda* piece in a sense lamented this seemingly sad state of the once-mighty warriors and the loss of their Soviet era status as patriotic defenders of a socialist motherland. The piece, however much it might be seen as a relic of old times, also indicates just how powerful the Soviet era imagery of the *bogatyri* was and just how persistent the use of the canvas to articulate a bulwark myth could be.

Ten years later, in 2008 the St. Petersburg publisher Aurora put out a glossy, expensive coffee table–style book about Vasnetsov. Titled *Viktor Vasnetsov i religiozno-natsionalnoie napravlenie v russkoi zhivopisi kontsa XIX—nachala XX veka* (Viktor Vasnetsov and the Religious-National Turn in Russian Painting at the End of the Nineteenth and Beginning of the Twentieth Centuries), the book perfectly captured the dominant trend in understanding Vasnetsov since the end of communism. The biography of the painter and his most famous creation are reversed (or perhaps they come full circle). The introduction starts not with the *Wanderers* or the sociopolitical significance of the Russian realism they advocated but with the emergence of a particularly Russian version of national-religious art that had deeper roots but that became even more significant in the mid-nineteenth century. Vasnetsov was still born into a world of peasants and folktales, but now the author writes that in his work, "Vasnetsov sang the glory of the Russian land—the guardian of Orthodoxy."[78]

The first work reproduced in this retelling is *The Warriors*, which is described along with his other paintings on Rus and on Russian folklore themes as religious in nature. The bulk of the chapter, however, is devoted to Vasnetsov's work at St. Vladimir's, which is described in great detail. The author concludes this biographical sketch by declaring that Vasnetsov ultimately presented Russia with the images of its "heroic (*bogatyrskaia*) history and its unique culture, illuminated by the true faith."[79]

Yet *The Warriors* still could be mobilized as part of a revitalized *antemurale* myth. By the time the 2008 book appeared, the St. Petersburg-based animation studio Melnitsa had made three movies starring the three warriors in Vasnetsov's painting (they have subsequently made three more films starring the trio).[80] In them, and in the 2008 book cited above, the trio made famous in Vasnetsov's painting could again defend a revitalized Russian motherland and protect a renewed Russian border: in these reinventions of the bulwark myth, the setting in Kyivan Rus spoke to the contested nature of Russian-Ukrainian relations after the collapse of the USSR. Muromets and his comrades could again be cast as "children of Rus" guarding Russian soil. Vasnetsov's canvas was also mobilized in other ways. In 2012, the school systems in Zheleznogorsk, in the Krasnoiarsk region, developed a curriculum unit titled *Bogatyri zemli russkoi* (Heroes of the Russian Land). Young students are asked to pretend they are in an art museum and see Vasnetsov's most famous painting (along with some other works).[81]

The curriculum guide for teachers envisions having the teacher act as a tour guide who elicits responses that situate the three warriors as timeless defenders of the Russian land. The overall aims, however, are twofold: to reinforce knowledge about Russian epics and heroes of wars and to introduce ideal images of masculinity to boys. At the end of the guide, the boys are asked to draw an image on the theme "I am a future defender," while the girls are asked to complete a drawing on "what we want to see our boys become when they grow up."

Vasnetsov's *Warriors* has a story worth telling. The painting's role in fixing an important image of border guards ever ready to protect their land took time to develop and required some creative interpretations, particularly during the Soviet era, when Vasnetsov's religiosity (and that of his canvases) caused consternation. Yet the *bogatyri* have remained as an important symbol of Russianness. They can be mobilized to defend the steppe borderland however it is imagined, ever ready to defend changing Russian values. The three can also be imagined as defenders of a more sacred, Orthodox landscape, as the recent coffee table book illustrates. And finally, the curricular use of the three warriors attests to how the *bogatyri* have helped to construct a particular form of Russian masculinity across more than a century.[82] The painting has proved malleable yet vital to the articulation of a specific Russian bulwark myth.

In a sense, Vasnetsov's canvas bulwark proved to be so successful because it functioned as a national image that allowed critics to "see" the nation as a "vivid, palpable, and tangible" thing. One important aspect of this role was the way that critics in both the Russian Empire and the Soviet Union used *Warriors* to identified the steppe as Russian soil, to articulate the notion that this landscape needed to be defended, and to argue that the three warriors on it embodied the masculine, patriotic essence needed to inspire viewers to defend the borderlands. No doubt they will continue to be called on to defend the Russian soil and act as a canvas bulwark again and again.

Stephen M. Norris is Walter E. Havighurst Professor of Russian History and director of the Havighurst Center for Russian and Post-Soviet Studies at Miami University (OH). He is the author or editor of seven books, including *A War of Images: Russian Popular Prints, Wartime Culture, and National Identity, 1812–1945* and *Blockbuster History in the New Russia: Movies, Memory, Patriotism*. He is currently writing a biography of the Soviet political caricaturist Boris Efimov titled *Communism's Cartoonist: Boris Efimov and the Soviet Century*.

Notes

1. L. Korotkina, ed., *Viktor Vasnetsov: pisma, novye materialy* (Sankt Peterburg: ARS, 2004), 12. I want to thank Liliya Berezhnaya for inviting me to write about this subject. I also thank my colleagues Karen Dawisha, Ted Holland, Neringa Klumbyte, Dan Scarborough, and Ben Sutcliffe for their suggestions.
2. Cited in L. Hughes, "Monuments of Identity," in *National Identity in Russian Culture: An Introduction*, ed. S. Franklin and E. Widdis (Cambridge: Cambridge University Press, 2004), 181–82. The cover of the book features Vasnetsov's painting.

3. H. Goscilo, "Viktor Vasnetsov's *Bogatyrs:* Mythic Heroes and Sacrosanct Borders Go to Market," in *Picturing Russia: Explorations in Visual Culture,* ed. V. Kivelson and J. Neuberger (New Haven: Yale University Press, 2008), 248.
4. Ibid.
5. Ibid., 249.
6. John Strickland has studied how the last decades of the nineteenth century and early decades of the twentieth saw a rise in the tradition he calls "Orthodox patriotism." This notion "claimed that Russia possessed a national character rooted in the Orthodox Christian faith, which was her destiny to preserve and disseminate." See his *The Making of Holy Russia: The Orthodox Church and Russian Nationalism before the Revolution* (Jordanville: Holy Trinity Publications, 2013), location 64 of the Kindle edition. I thank Dan Scarborough for bringing this book to my attention.
7. C. Classen, D. Howes, and A. Synnott, *Aroma: The Cultural History of Smell* (London/New York: Routledge, 1994), 3.
8. V. Vasnetsov, *Bogatyri,* 1898. From M. Aptekar, *Russkaia istoricheskaia zhivopis* (Moskva: Iskusstvo, 1939). The painting is 116 x 175 inches (295 x 446 cm).
9. I thank Dan Scarborough for making this connection.
10. G. Hosking, "The Russian National Myth Repudiated," in *Myths and Nationhood,* ed. G. Hosking and G. Schöpflin (London/New York: Routledge, 1997), 200.
11. Cited in Hughes, "Monuments and Identity," 181.
12. The tale is included in J. Bailey and T. Ivanova, ed. and trans., *An Anthology of Russian Folk Epics* (Armonk: M.E. Sharpe, 1998), 28–36. The cover features Vasnetsov's painting.
13. In this fashion, these folktales and Vasnetsov's painting help to answer the question posed by Volodymyr Kravchenko in his chapter. An *antemurale* myth did not develop in nineteenth-century Ukraine because the Ukrainian lands were imagined to be Russian, part of the larger national narrative developed in that century that viewed the Russian imperial state to be the heir to Kyivan Rus.
14. The tendency in Russian art history has been to focus on the realist art of the 1860s and 1870s that emerged out of the famous 1863 revolt in the Petersburg Art Academy. The so-called *peredvizhniki* focused on realism as a means to depict social issues and the natural, national landscapes of Russia. Their revolt and their works have been the subject of numerous publications, including English-language ones. Vasnetsov and later historical painters, however, have factored as minor characters at best in this scholarship because their works looked backward and often employed religious elements. In her pioneering work, for example, Elizabeth Valkenier only has Vasnetsov as a minor figure—she established *The Wanderers* as mostly critical realists, their art as political. She also opens by declaring that the movement was "born of protest in 1863 and died of senility in 1923," only for it to be resurrected ten years later to become the basis for Socialist realism. See E. Valkenier, *Russian Realist Art* (Ann Arbor: Ardis, 1977), xi. In his *Between History and Myth: Stories of Harald "Fairhair" and the Founding of the State* (Chicago: University of Chicago Press, 2014), Bruce Lincoln mentioned Vasnetsov only three times; Orlando Figes, in his *Natasha's Dance: A Cultural History of Russia* (New York: Metropolitan Books, 2003) did so only seven times.
15. S. Bilenky, *Romantic Nationalism in Eastern Europe: Russian, Polish, and Ukrainian Political Imaginations* (Palo Alto: Stanford University Press, 2012), vii.
16. See N. Davies, "Polish National Mythologies," in *Myths and Nationhood,* ed. G.

Hosking and G. Schöpflin (London/New York: Routledge, 1997), 141–57; W. Weintraub, "Renaissance Poland and *Antemurale Christianitatis*," *Harvard Ukrainian Studies*, nos. 3/4 (1979–1980): 920–30; J. Pekacz, "Antemurale of Europe: From the History of National Megalomania of Poland," *History of European Ideas* 20, no. 1–3 (1995): 419–24.

17. Heidi Hein-Kircher charts these characteristics of an *antemurale* myth in her article "The Idea of Lviv as a Bulwark against the East," in *Imagining the City*, vol. 2, ed. Ch. Emden, C. Keen, and D. Midgley (Frankfurt a.M.: Peter Lang, 2006), 321–38.
18. Here I draw on W.J.T. Mitchell's insistence that images are alive, have needs, and evolve. See W.J.T. Mitchell, *What Do Pictures Want? The Lives and Loves of Images* (Chicago: Chicago University Press, 2006).
19. See Korotkina, *Viktor Vasnetsov*.
20. Vasnetsov's work in Kyiv came at a time when Russian nationalists living in and around that city developed a powerful nationalist narrative. The southwest borderlands, which had long been contested and multiethnic, became imagined as a bastion of Russianness. See F. Hillis, *Children of Rus': Right-Bank Ukraine and the Invention of a Russian Nation* (Ithaca: Cornell University Press, 2013).
21. K. Dianina, *When Art Makes News: Writing Culture and Identity in Imperial Russia* (DeKalb: Northern Illinois University Press, 2013).
22. D. Jackson, *The Wanderers and Critical Realism in Nineteenth Century Russian Painting* (Manchester: Manchester University Press, 2011), 143–44.
23. Ibid., 146.
24. V. Vasnetsov, *Pisma, dnevniki, vospominaniia, suzhdeniia sovremennikov* (Moskva: Iskusstvo, 1987), 24–25.
25. Ibid., 22.
26. Ibid., 25.
27. Ibid., 31.
28. Ibid., 322–29.
29. Ibid., 326.
30. Ibid., 327.
31. Ibid., 327–28.
32. See ibid., 332–33.
33. V. Stasov, *Iskusstvo XIX veka* (Sankt Peterburg: Niva, 1901), retrieved 15 March 2018 from http://az.lib.ru/s/stasow_w_w/text_1901_iskusstvo_19_veka.shtml.
34. Figes, *Natasha's Dance*, 178.
35. V. Vasnetsov, *Kreshcheniie Rusi* (1896). WikiArt.
36. A. Sobolev, *Zhivopis V. M. Vasnetsova v Kievskom Sobore* (Moskva: Universitetskaia tipografiia, 1898), 5.
37. Korotkina, *Viktor Vasnetsov*, 89–96.
38. Ibid., 147–49.
39. Ibid.
40. Ibid., 161–64.
41. Ibid., 114.
42. Ibid., 115.
43. Ibid., 119.
44. Ibid., 165.
45. Ibid., 170–71.
46. Ibid., 172.

47. M. Brunson, "Painting History, Realistically: Murder at the Tretiakov," in *From Realism to the Silver Age: New Studies in Russian Artistic Culture*, ed. R.P. Blakesley and M. Samu (DeKalb: Northern Illinois University Press, 2014), 96.
48. "Vystavka russkoi istoricheskoi zhivopisi," *Pravda* 11 (November 1938), 6.
49. Cited in D. Brandenberger, *National Bolshevism: Stalinist Mass Culture and the Formation of Modern Russian National Identity, 1931–1956* (Cambridge: Harvard University Press, 2003), 89–90.
50. Cited in ibid., 105.
51. Ibid., 90–91.
52. K.M.F. Platt and D. Brandenberger, eds., *Epic Revisionism: Russian History and Literature as Stalinist Propaganda* (Madison: University of Wisconsin Press, 2006).
53. M. Aptekar, *Russkaia istoricheskaia zhivopis* (Moskva: Iskusstvo, 1939), 3.
54. Ibid., 4.
55. Ibid., 15–16.
56. Cited in J. Plamper, *The Stalin Cult: A Study in the Alchemy of Power* (New Haven: Yale University Press, 2012), 105.
57. N. Morgunov, "Vystavka russkoi istoricheskoi zhivopisi," *Krasnaia zvezda* 46, 26 February 1939, 4.
58. N. Morgunov, *Viktor Vasnetsov: Sokrovishcha mirovogo iskusstva* (Moskva: Iskusstvo, 1940), 42.
59. Ibid., 42.
60. See N.M. Shchekotov, *Bogatyri: kartina Viktora Vasnetsova* (Moskva: Iskusstvo, 1943). Repin's Cossacks were also mobilized for the fight: Stalin himself loved the painting and a 1943 pamphlet declared the work to be "truly national" and one that could inspire present-day defenders of Moscow. See Hughes, "Monuments and Identity," 185.
61. Cited in Hughes, "Monuments and Identity," 186
62. Cited in Hughes, "Monuments and Identity," 186.
63. The photo appeared in a feature on Moscow's 800th birthday in *Vecherniaia Moskva*, 28 August 1947.
64. Cited in Brandenberger, *National Bolshevism*, 223.
65. A.K. Lebedev, *Viktor Mikhailovich Vasnetsov, 1848–1926* (Moskva: Iskusstvo, 1946), 3.
66. Ibid., 15–16.
67. Ibid., 41.
68. "Vydaiushchiisia russkii khudozhnik," *Pravda*, 16 May 1948, 3.
69. M.Z. Kholodovskaia, *V. Vasnetsov* (Moskva: Izdatelstvo izobrazitelnykh istkusstv imeni A.S. Pushkina, 1949), 6.
70. Ibid., 23.
71. N. Morgunova-Rudnitskaia, *Viktor Mikhailovich Vasnetsov* (Moskva: Iskusstvo, 1959), 3. I thank Ben Sutcliffe for the Turgenev connection.
72. Ibid.
73. Ibid., 8.
74. Ibid.
75. The movie poster featured the three actors playing the famous three bogatyrs in a pose resembling Vasnetsov's painting. The reviews of the film, however, mostly focused on the fact that it was the first Soviet movie made in CinemaScope, which

critics declared to be a sign that domestic movies were catching up and overtaking the West. The plot of the film adheres to the epic stories with the exception of religion. Most of the reviews also noted that the film captured beautiful shots of the Russian landscape and the essence of ancient Rus, echoing some of the language used to describe Vasnetsov's painting. See M. Beliavskii, "Tekhnicheskie novinki i mysl khudozhnika," *Iskusstvo kino* 8 (1960), 108–9; A. Golovnia, "Neskolko nabliudenii," *Iskusstvo kino* 3, March 1957, 104–9; and N. Zelichenko and L. Tamashin, "Opyt ekranizatsii byliny," *Iskusstvo kino* 2, 1957, 78–82. The Soviet critics did not mention Vasnetsov in these articles, but viewers, including contemporary ones, did: a post from August 2009 on the kinopoisk.ru site devoted to Ptushko's film declares that the director "revitalized all the famous paintings by Vasnetsov ... and the epic heroes spoke, began to move around, and opened up the world of Holy Rus, retrieved 16 April 2014 from http://www.kinopoisk.ru/film/42586/.

76. L. Iagunkova, "Bogatyr russkoi kisti," *Pravda*, 19 May 1998, 4.
77. Nadezhda Shanina, in *Victor Vasnetsov* (Leningrad: Aurora Art Publishers, 1979), declared that his "historical-religious compositions were a means toward the enlightenment of the people, and consequently he [Vasnetsov] regarded his work on the cathedral [St. Vladimir's] as a high moral responsibility (98)." *Warriors* still represented a "patriotic mission" (110) that "will never cease to stir in us our most sacred and intimate feelings—love of our country and its people (120)." Liliia Kudriavtseva, in *Bogatyri zemli russkoi: o kartinakh V. M. Vasnetsova* (Moskva: Malysh, 1981), which was primarily aimed at schoolchildren, would continue to identify the three as warriors defending the frontier. Lidia Iovleva, in *V. Vasnetsov: iz sobraniia gosudarstvennoi Tretiakovskoi Galerei. Albom* (Moskva: Iskusstvo, 1984), would highlight Vasnetsov's religious upbringing as the son of a country priest and acknowledged his work at St. Vladimir's. She argued that the frescoes in Kyiv "not only expressed religious dogmas, but also became a monument to Kyivan Rus, the cradle of the Russian state, and the Russian nation" (24, 28). Finally, Vladislav Bakhrevskii's *Viktor Vasnetsov* (Moskva: Molodaia gvardiia, 1989), which appeared in the "Lives of Remarkable People" series, restored Vasnetsov's Orthodox faith as an important component of his patriotism and his artistic works.
78. V.O. Gusakova, *Viktor Vasnetsov i religiozno-natsionalnoe napravlenie v russkoi zhivopisi kontsa XIX—nachala XX veka* (Sankt Peterburg: Aurora, 2008), 27.
79. Ibid., 79. The rest of the book then traces Vasnetsov's other contemporaries, focusing not on the "Wanderers" but on Mikhail Nesterov, Mikhail Vrubel, Nikolai Kharlamov, Foma Railian, and Valerian Otmar.
80. Details can be found on the studio's official website, retrieved 15 March 2018 from http://www.melnitsa.com.
81. "Lokalnaia programma: 'malchiki i devochki—dva raznykh mira,'" Zheleznogorsk-Ilimskii, 2012.
82. See B.E. Clements, "Introduction," in *Russian Masculinities in History and Culture*, eds. E. Clements, R. Friedman, and D. Healey (Basingstoke: Palgrave Macmillan, 2002), 1–14. In her survey of the volume's theme, Evans Clements begins with the mythic Russian *bogatyr* as an idealized form of Russian masculinity. Vasnetsov's warriors serve as an excellent example of the heroism and valor Russian soldiers were supposed to embody, the subject of Karen Petrone's essay in the *Russian Masculinities* volume.

Bibliography

Aptekar, M. 1939. *Russkaia istoricheskaia zhivopis*. Moskva: Iskusstvo.
Bailey, J. and T. Ivanova, ed. and trans. 1998. *An Anthology of Russian Folk Epics*. Armonk: M.E. Sharpe.
Bakhrevskii, V. 1989. *Viktor Vasnetsov*. Moskva: Molodaia gvardiia.
Beliavskii, M. 1960. "Tekhnicheskie novinki i mysl khudozhnika." *Iskusstvo kino* 8: 108–9.
Bilenky, S. 2012. *Romantic Nationalism in Eastern Europe: Russian, Polish, and Ukrainian Political Imaginations*. Palo Alto: Stanford University Press.
Brandenberger, D. 2003. *National Bolshevism: Stalinist Mass Culture and the Formation of Modern Russian National Identity, 1931–1956*. Cambridge: Harvard University Press.
Brunson, M. 2014. "Painting History, Realistically: Murder at the Tretiakov." In *From Realism to the Silver Age: New Studies in Russian Artistic Culture*, ed. R.P. Blakesley and M. Samu, 94–110. DeKalb: Northern Illinois University Press.
Classen, C., D. Howes, and A. Synnott. 1994. *Aroma: The Cultural History of Smell*. London: Routledge.
Clements, B.E. 2002. "Introduction." In *Russian Masculinities in History and Culture*, ed. E. Clements, R. Friedman, and D. Healey, 1–14. Basingstoke: Palgrave Macmillan.
Davies, N. 1997. "Polish National Mythologies." In *Myths and Nationhood*, ed. G. Hosking and G. Schöpflin, 141–57. London: Routledge.
Dianina, K. 2013. *When Art Makes News: Writing Culture and Identity in Imperial Russia*. DeKalb: Northern Illinois University Press.
Figes, O. 2003. *Natasha's Dance: A Cultural History of Russia*. New York: Metropolitan Books.
Golovnia, A. 1957. "Neskolko nabliudenii." *Iskusstvo kino* 3 (March): 104–9.
Goscilo, H. 2008. "Viktor Vasnetsov's *Bogatyrs*: Mythic Heroes and Sacrosanct Borders Go to Market." In *Picturing Russia: Explorations in Visual Culture*, ed. V. Kivelson and J. Neuberger, 248–53. New Haven: Yale University Press.
Gusakova, V.O. 2008. *Viktor Vasnetsov i religiozno-natsionalnoe napravlenie v russkoi zhivopisi kontsa XIX—nachala XX veka*. Sankt Peterburg: Aurora.
Hein-Kircher, H. 2006. "The Idea of Lviv as a Bulwark against the East." In *Imagining the City*. Vol. 2, ed. Ch. Emden, C. Keen, and D. Midgley, 321–38. Frankfurt a.M.: Peter Lang.
Hillis, F. 2013. *Children of Rus': Right-Bank Ukraine and the Invention of a Russian Nation*. Ithaca: Cornell University Press.
Hosking, G. 1997. "The Russian National Myth Repudiated." In *Myths and Nationhood*, ed. G. Hosking and G. Schöpflin, 198–210. New York: Routledge.
Hughes, L. 2004. "Monuments of Identity." In *National Identity in Russian Culture: An Introduction*, ed. S. Franklin and E. Widdis, 171–96. Cambridge: Cambridge University Press.
Iagunkova, L. 1998. "Bogatyr russkoi kisti." *Pravda*, 19 May, 4.
Iovleva, L. 1984. *V. Vasnetsov: iz sobraniia gosudarstvennoi Tretiakovskoi Galerei. Albom*. Moskva: Iskusstvo.
Jackson, D. 2011. *The Wanderers and Critical Realism in Nineteenth Century Russian Painting*. Manchester: Manchester University Press.

Kholodovskaia, M.Z. 1949. *V. Vasnetsov.* Moskva: Izdatelstvo izobrazitelnykh istkusstv imeni A.S. Pushkina.
Korotkina, L., ed. 2004. *Viktor Vasnetsov: pisma, novye materialy.* Sankt Peterburg: ARS.
Kudriavtseva, L. 1981. *Bogatyri zemli russkoi: o kartinakh V.M. Vasnetsova.* Moskva: Malysh.
Lebedev, A.K. 1946. *Viktor Mikhailovich Vasnetsov, 1848–1926.* Moskva: Iskusstvo.
Lincoln, B. 2014. *Between History and Myth: Stories of Harald "Fairhair" and the Founding of the State.* Chicago: University of Chicago Press.
"Lokalnaia programma: 'malchiki i devochki—dva raznykh mira.'" Zheleznogorsk-Ilimskii, 2012.
Melnitsa official website: http://www.melnitsa.com.
Mitchell, W.J.T. 2006. *What Do Pictures Want? The Lives and Loves of Images.* Chicago: University of Chicago Press.
Morgunov, N. 1939. "Vystavka russkoi istoricheskoi zhivopisi." *Krasnaia zvezda* 46, 26 February, 4.
———. 1940. *Viktor Vasnetsov: Sokrovishcha mirovogo iskusstva.* Moskva: Iskusstvo.
Morgunova-Rudnitskaia, N. 1959. *Viktor Mikhailovich Vasnetsov.* Moskva: Iskusstvo.
Pekacz, J. 1995. "Antemurale of Europe: From the History of National Megalomania of Poland." *History of European Ideas* 20, nos. 1–3: 419–24.
Plamper, J. 2012. *The Stalin Cult: A Study in the Alchemy of Power.* New Haven: Yale University Press.
Platt K.M.F. and D. Brandenberger, eds. 2006. *Epic Revisionism: Russian History and Literature as Stalinist Propaganda.* Madison: University of Wisconsin Press.
Shanina, N. 1979. *Victor Vasnetsov.* Leningrad: Aurora Art Publishers.
Shchekotov, N.M. 1943. *Bogatyri: kartina Viktora Vasnetsova.* Moskva: Iskusstvo.
Sobolev, A. 1898. *Zhivopis V.M. Vasnetsova v Kievskom Sobore.* Moskva: Universitetskaia tipografiia.
Stasov, V. 1901. *Iskusstvo XIX veka.* Sankt Peterburg: Niva. Retrieved 15 March 2018 from http://az.lib.ru/s/stasow_w_w/text_1901_iskusstvo_19_veka.shtml.
Strickland, J. 2013. *The Making of Holy Russia: The Orthodox Church and Russian Nationalism before the Revolution.* Jordanville: Holy Trinity Publications.
Valkenier, E. 1977. *Russian Realist Art.* Ann Arbor: Ardis.
Vasnetsov, V. 1896. *Kreshcheniie Rusi.* WikiArt. Retrieved 27 October 2018 from https://www.wikiart.org/en/viktor-vasnetsov/the-baptism-of-russia-1896.
———. 1939. "*Bogatyri*, 1898." In *Russkaia istoricheskaia zhivopis*, ed. M. Aptekar. Moskva: Iskusstvo.
———. 1987. *Pisma, dnevniki, vospominaniia, suzhdeniia sovremennikov.* Moskva: Iskusstvo.
Vecherniaia Moskva. 28 August 1947.
Viewers on the *kinopoisk.ru* site: http://www.kinopoisk.ru/film/42586/.
"Vydaiushchiisia russkii khudozhnik." 1948. *Pravda*, 16 May, 3.
"Vystavka russkoi istoricheskoi zhivopisi." 1938. *Pravda*, 11 November, 6.
Weintraub, W. 1979–1980. "Renaissance Poland and *Antemurale Christianitatis*." *Harvard Ukrainian Studies* 3/4: 920–30.
Zelichenko, N. and L. Tamashin. 1957. "Opyt ekranizatsii byliny." *Iskusstvo kino* 2: 78–82.

PART IV

Reflections on the Bulwark Myths Today

CHAPTER 13

Antemurale Thinking as Historical Myth and Ethnic Boundary Mechanism

Pål Kolstø

In 1969, the Norwegian anthropologist Fredrik Barth (1928–2016) wrote an article that fundamentally changed our understanding of how ethnic groups and social identities are constituted.[1] The traditional view had been that groups are held together by the "cultural stuff" they have in common, but this proved problematic for various reasons. The common culture approach implicitly ignored cultural differences within groups, made it difficult to explain cultural change, and did not sufficiently allow for cultural overlap and continuity between and among groups. Barth saw the boundary between groups as the locus of identity formation and differentiation. As a social anthropologist, he focused on the role of boundary markers—or *diacritica*—in relations between ethnic groups. Later researchers have expanded this approach to include the study of nationalism,[2] macroregions,[3] and social groups in general.[4]

As with all pioneer works, Barth's new approach has been readjusted and refined by later scholars. He had focused primarily on material and visible objects as boundary markers; however, boundaries of the kind we are discussing here are not something "out there" but are located in "the minds of the beholders."[5] Almost all features of culture may become the substance of a boundary if they distinguish one's own group from surrounding groups. This was emphasized by one of Barth's earliest disciples, the U.S. political scientist John Armstrong (1922–2010), who saw various kinds of symbols and myths as equally important for the drawing of ethnic and other cultural boundaries as the material *diacritica* that Barth had focused on.[6] Armstrong did not develop his ideas on the construction of ethnic myths in any great detail, but ten years ago I made an attempt to flesh them out in a rudimentary typology of boundary-constituting myths. I identified four different historical myths:[7]

1. the myth of *antiquitatis* (being those who arrived first in a particular territory and therefore had a particularly strong claim to it);
2. the myth of being *sui generis* (being in possession of a unique culture not shared by anyone else);
3. the myth of *martyrium* (having been chronically victimized throughout the ages and thereby able to claim the moral high ground); and
4. the myth of being *antemurale* (being the defenders of a larger civilization faced with outside assailants).

The list is not exhaustive; other myths can no doubt be identified. Moreover, these four are not mutually exclusive: members of a group may draw on several myths simultaneously, even when that might seem logically impossible. In particular, the two last myths—*martyrium* and *antemurale*—often go hand in hand. Nor is this surprising: the valiant guardians defending a larger civilization against the enemy at the gates—or the frontline defenders of civilization as such against barbarism—will naturally incur suffering and death in the course of their battles.

This chapter further develops my concept of the *antemurale* myth as a boundary-defining mechanism. I argue that the understanding of the world as being populated by antagonistic civilizations—most famously associated with U.S. political scientist Samuel Huntington (1927–2008)—easily lends itself to *antemurale* thinking. However, whereas Huntington saw religions as the main ingredients of the world civilizations, I contend that no "objective" religious difference is necessary in order to construct an *antemurale* boundary. Indeed, political and cultural activists may employ *antemurale* arguments to distinguish their group or their country from a neighboring group or country that traditionally adheres to the same religion. This is not to say that *antemurale* boundary drawing is totally haphazard or that all kinds of mental maps and identification structures are equally probable. Certain patterns can be discerned, but they seem to be influenced more by power differentials between groups than by religious or other cultural differences.

While my observations are too few to allow me to offer any "sociological laws" or regularities, I venture a hypothesis: that weaker groups (smaller groups, groups with few material resources, and groups with unclear or weak collective identity) are likely to employ *antemurale* arguments to distinguish themselves from stronger, overweening neighbors; whereas stronger groups (larger groups, groups with more material resources, and groups with a robust self-awareness) will tend to de-emphasize their identity distance from culturally similar neighboring groups and subsume them under their own instead.

The Myth of Being *Antemurale*

Historically, the *antemurale* concept derives from the designation of certain Central and Eastern European countries in the late Middle Ages and early modern era, such as the Habsburg monarchy, Venice and Poland, as *antemurale christianitatis,* as amply documented in other chapters in this book. The first to use this concept were Popes who wanted to rally support for a concerted Christian mobilization against the Ottomans in order to evict the Muslims from Europe. The *antemurale* message addressed the frontline countries bordering on Muslim areas that would inevitably be heavily involved in this battle. Often, however, the religion to be defended was more narrowly defined as Western Christianity, or Roman Catholicism, rather than Christianity as such. The Poles, therefore, also defended their country and the civilization it represented against another Christian nation, the Orthodox Muscovites.[8] Similarly, the Croats often viewed the position of the Orthodox Serbs as highly suspect. In many cases they were placed "beyond the pale" or "outside the gates."[9]

As we shall see, in contemporary usages of the *antemurale* myth, the imaginary wall may similarly be drawn in such a way that an Orthodox population ends up on the outside. At the same time, we can note that *antemurale* self-legitimation has also been used within Western Christendom, as when Protestants have vilified—even demonized—Catholic Christians. After the Reformation, England and Holland saw themselves as the bulwarks of Protestant liberty against Catholic despotism.[10]

One might think that in today's secularized Europe the very concept of *antemurale* countries would be anachronistic: however, while most Western Europeans may not profess any strong religious identity, the *antemurale* mental frame is flexible enough to be adapted to new historical circumstances. For instance, in the twentieth century many anti-Communist Poles updated the anti-Russian *antemurale* myth to be directed against Soviet atheists. In most contemporary incarnations, the concept of being "European" has been retained but is now more related to secular values—individualism, entrepreneurial spirit, respect for human rights, and so on. In this incarnation of the myth, being "European" and being "*Western* European" are also conflated.

Typologically, the myth of *antemurale* differs greatly from the myth of being *sui generis.* Rather than insisting on the uniqueness of the group, as the *sui generis* mythomoteurs[11] do, the group is now included in some larger and allegedly superior cultural identity that enhances its status vis-à-vis the other groups that do not belong. Rather than drawing a border around the group, equally strong on all sides, the differences that distinguish the group from one specific neighbor are magnified out of all proportion, while boundaries in other directions are de-emphasized.

The *murus*, or the Wall, is the ultimate boundary metaphor, the final line of defense of the cosmos or order against the forces of chaos and disorder. The *antemurale* myth stresses not only that "our" group is an integral part of "the true civilization" but also that it represents *its very outpost*. Throughout history, the Wall has again and again been assailed by the dark forces of the other side, and the group has been chosen by Divine Providence to sacrifice itself in order to save the civilization of which it is a part. The *antemurale* myth often acquires messianic overtones: the group—in the modern era increasingly identified as "the nation"—is seen as a collective Christ that gives its life for others. The main characteristics of an *antemurale* nation, then, can be summarized as a perception of belonging to a superior civilization; a geographically peripheral position within that civilization, directly confronting an allegedly inferior civilization; a hypertrophic understanding of the differences between these civilizations; and a messianic obligation to defend, and if necessary die for, the larger civilization to which one belongs.[12]

Antemurale myths may be symmetrical or asymmetrical. We can find instances in which both opposing groups agree that a civilizational wall separates them but at the same time hold diametrically opposed views as to just who represents the forces of cosmos and of chaos. At other times one group may de-emphasize—perhaps even deny—the cultural difference between themselves and a neighboring group, while this neighbor will do its utmost to erect an identity barrier between them, even going to ludicrous lengths to prove the insuperable differences. While asymmetrical myths are probably more common, Europe versus the Islamic world in the Middle Ages was an example of a symmetrical *antemurale* myth. The Muslim Arabs and Ottomans were, no less than the Christian Europeans, convinced that they represented a superior civilization, the only true one: they were defending the "true faith" against the barbarians of the North. As Bernard Lewis explains,

> In this holy war, Europe was a frontier to which the Ottomans, and indeed many other Muslims, looked in much the same way as Europeans were to view the Americas from the sixteenth to the eighteenth century. Beyond the northern and western frontier lay rich and barbarous lands to which it was their sacred mission to bring religion and civilization, order and peace.[13]

In most instances, *antemurale* mythmaking is obviously an instrument of politics—as are, indeed, all historical myths—designed to strengthen the in-group in question vis-à-vis other groups that are seen as threatening. To call it a political device is to emphasize the element of power and power relations. *Antemurale* myths are normally invoked by smaller and vulnerable groups in order to enhance their relative power in one direction by latching on to a larger, powerful group in another direction. They try to enlist the support of stronger groups by claiming that they share with them not only a common identity/culture/history but also *a common enemy*. This is often a crucial method of recruiting allies. If the frontline states are the ones that will have to bear the brunt of the battle and suffer more human loss as the defenders of the gate, reasons of equity and "burden sharing" dictate that nations safely located to the rear, far removed from the danger and the Wall, must contribute more otherwise. Power politics is by no means a matter of counting cannons, manpower, and economic strength only: it also includes strategies of legitimization.[14]

The task of constructing, interpreting, and manipulating worldviews normally falls on intellectuals. They are the ones who provide the vocabulary and the arguments for particular ideologies. However, as Karl Mannheim (1893–1947) has pointed out,[15] intellectuals are often *freischwebende* (free floating) and may pursue their own agendas, which do not necessarily coincide with the interests of the state as the current state leaders define them, or even with the perceptions of the average member of the public. State leaders may draw on the services of the mythmaking intelligentsia whenever they feel this may be useful and then discard them as a nuisance when the intellectuals come up with utopian or crackpot ideas that cannot be harnessed to power politics. If and when intellectual *antemurale* ideas fail to resonate in the corridors of power as well as among the population at large, the mythmakers consign themselves to cultural isolation even in their own countries, as "voices crying in the wilderness."

Contemporary Usages of the *Antemurale* Myth: Milan Kundera and Samuel Huntington

Some of the most striking examples of *antemurale* mythmaking today may be found in Eastern Europe, and, remarkably, the tropes and categories employed are often quite similar to the medieval prototype. The Wall is frequently invoked by using religious language, even if the setting has become thoroughly secular. An example of this is the article "The Tragedy of Central Europe" that Czech novelist Milan Kundera published in the *New York Review of Books* in 1984, when the Cold War was at its coldest. As "Central," Kundera defined the parts of Europe that belonged culturally to "the West" but that after World War II had ended up politically in "the East." Kundera has often been interpreted as making a plea for the acceptance of "Central Europe" as an old and well-established but little recognized geographical subunit of Europe. Some of his remarks do allow such an interpretation, but that was not his main message. Instead of a tripartite Europe consisting of West, Central, and East, Kundera's vision of the continent was bifurcated. There are only two Europes—West and East:

> "Geographic Europe" (extending from the Atlantic to the Ural Mountains) was always divided into two halves that evolved separately: one tied to ancient Rome and the Catholic Church, the other anchored in Byzantium and the Orthodox Church. After 1945, the border between the two Europes shifted several hundred kilometers to the West, and several nations that had always considered themselves to be Western woke up to discover that they were now in the East.[16]

The fact that, at the time when Kundera was writing, there were *three* Europes was considered a historical aberration and the result of a political crime. Europe had been divided twice over: by a centuries-old cultural fault and now by a new political "iron curtain." In Kundera's ideal world, one of them—the political (and physical) wall—could and should be done away with; the cultural divide would remain.

According to Kundera, this cultural divide of Europe follows religious lines: the 1054 Great Schism between Orthodoxy and Catholicism established an insurmountable barrier. Only the Catholic and Protestant parts of the Communist Bloc would qualify for inclusion in his category of "Central Europe." In his essay Kundera was exclusively occupied with Russia as Central Europe's "constituting Other"[17] and brushed aside the fact that the traditional faith in many parts of the region that ended up to the east of the Iron Curtain after 1945 has long been Orthodox Christianity. This was the case with Romania and Bulgaria, while Yugoslavia (according to Kundera's religious criterion) would be cut in two parts: the northern regions adhere to Roman Catholicism; further south and east, Orthodoxy predominates, along with Islam. Southeastern Europe was conspicuously absent from Kundera's mental map; this region did not fit into his dichotomous model and was simply ignored.[18]

In 1989 Kundera's dream was realized: the Berlin Wall came tumbling down, and with it the entire political bifurcation of Europe. Certain half-hearted attempts were made to create new Central European regional collaboration structures, but with few results. Instead, the Catholic countries of "the new Europe" (U.S. defense secretary Donald Rumsfeld's phrase) all strove to be included in Western political structures—NATO (North Atlantic Treaty Organization) and the EU—as rapidly as possible, and they eventually succeeded. With their newly acquired Westernness, their centralness could be tossed aside as a stepping stone. After the EU accession of Poland, Hungary, Slovakia, and the Czech Republic, Central Europe lost its raison d'être as a political program.[19] The concept continued to be used as a loose geographical designation but was infrequently evoked in political discourse.

In 1993, another famous article, this time by the U.S. political scientist Samuel Huntington (1927–2008), made waves by employing analytical frames remarkably similar to those of Kundera.[20] Huntington, who had earlier written a euphoric book on the unstoppable march of democracy throughout the world,[21] had turned pessimist and no longer expected "the West" to be able to export its societal model to other continents. Using a geological metaphor, he now divided the world into cultural "tectonic plates," each of which represented one of the world's great civilizations. World civilizations were doomed to collide at the edges: metaphorical volcanoes and earthquakes erupted, producing dangerous and volatile conflict zones. Huntington predicted that the deadliest violent conflicts worldwide would explode precisely along the "fault lines"—another geological metaphor—between civilizations.

Historically, as pointed out above, civilizations have been defined mainly through religion, and this is also how Huntington saw them.[22] Most of his categories had religious designations—Islamic, Hindu, and Buddhist. However, some macroregions did not fit readily into this pattern, so the civilizational categories of "Latin America" and "Africa" were defined along other lines, or not defined at all.[23] And, oddly, Huntington split Christendom up into two subgroups, "Western" and "Orthodox." It was not immediately apparent why this division should be more fundamental than, for instance, the distinction between Shia and Sunni in Islam; nor was the fact that Protestantism and Catholicism should be lumped together in one category, while Eastern Orthodoxy—which in many theological and ethical questions has more in common with Catholicism than has mainstream Protestantism—was separated.

A remarkable consequence of Huntington's model was that Eastern Christians were presented as having more in common with Muslims than with their Western coreligionists. His civilizational map of Europe features a thick line running between "Western Christianity circa 1500," to the West, and "Orthodox Christianity and Islam," to the East.[24] This line, which follows precisely the line that Kundera one decade earlier had drawn between East and West, represents the "Eastern boundary of Western civilization," according to Huntington. Even more than Kundera's idea of a captured Western Europe, Huntington's conception illustrates how old religious categories can be manipulated to fit contemporary political needs.

Not surprisingly, Huntington's model was enthusiastically embraced by politicians and intellectuals in the frontline states (as he defined them)—

Estonia, Latvia, Lithuania, Poland, Slovakia, Hungary, and Croatia.[25] All of them ended up on the western side of the civilizational fault line. The fact that on his map they also became *antemurale* states was an important bonus. Their exposed position as outposts bordering on alien civilizations to the east could be exploited for all it was worth to lobby for economic support from the stronger and richer nations that belonged to the same civilization: the West.

For the political leaders in Ukraine, Belarus, and Romania, however, the situation was more problematic. During the Counter-Reformation, "Uniate" churches—that is, churches that recognize the authority of the Roman Pope but have an Orthodox liturgy and rituals—had been created in the Western parts of all of them, and so the civilizational fault line on Huntington's map ran straight through these countries. He chose to ignore—or was ignorant of the fact—that the Uniate churches in Ukraine and Belarus today cover only a minuscule part of the population. Even so, Huntington insisted that, not only historically but even today, "Ukraine. . . . is a cleft country with two distinct cultures. The civilizational fault line between the West and Orthodoxy runs through its heart and has done so for centuries."[26] Apparently contradicting himself, however, two pages down he declared, "If civilization is what counts, . . . violence between Ukrainians and Russians is unlikely. These are two Slavic, primarily Orthodox people who have had close relationships for centuries and between whom intermarriage is common." For many Ukrainians this analysis was hardly reassuring: it left them in limbo as neither East nor West.

Moving the Wall further East: *Antemurale* Thinking in Orthodox Countries toward an Orthodox Neighbor

Huntington had offered his model not as a blueprint for aggression but, on the contrary, as an invitation to Russia to "live and let live." Indeed, the very concept of *antemurale* presents the frontline population as *defenders* of the religion/civilization, not as attackers. The logic behind both the Great Wall of China and the Berlin Wall—and behind the entire Iron Curtain—was to leave the Outsiders alone as long as they left the people on the Inside in peace. Typically, Huntington was highly critical to NATO expansion too far eastward; only those parts of Europe that rightfully belonged to the West by dint of historical religion ought to be invited in:

> NATO expansion limited to countries historically part of Western Christendom. . . guarantees to Russia that it would exclude Serbia, Bulgaria, Romania, Moldova, Belarus, and Ukraine as long as Ukraine remained united.

NATO expansion limited to Western states would also underline Russia's role as the core state of a separate, Orthodox, civilization, and hence a country that should be responsible for order within and along the boundaries of Orthodoxy.[27]

The losers in this "spheres of interest" thinking were those Serbians, Bulgarians, and others who identified themselves with Europe (or simply wanted to take part in the higher standard of living in the West) and sought to be let in. For them, this kind of civilizational thinking was simply a sellout, especially if they also saw Russia as an overhanging threat to both their security and their national identity. Precisely because they shared a common historical religion with Russia—and often also spoke similar Slavic languages—many Russians tended to regard them simply as "little brothers." The looming shadow of Russia was particularly ominous where there was a common border with Russia and where the territories that now made up their nation-states had historically been part of the Russian Empire. This was the case with three nations: Belarusians, Ukrainians, and Georgians.

The Georgians could take some comfort in the fact that they speak a non-Slavic language; they could thus be more secure in their self-identity and in their cultural distance from Russia and all things Russian. The Belarusians and Ukrainians, however, were keenly aware that many Russians denied the existence of separate Belarusian and Ukrainian identities altogether. In the prerevolutionary Russian Empire, the people whom we today call "Russians" were referred to as *Velikorossy* (Great Russians). The concept of "Russians" was also used, but as a collective noun that comprised three branches—the Belarusians and the Ukrainians, in addition to the Great Russians.[28] The same triune way of thinking is reflected in much contemporary Russian political rhetoric, as when in one and the same speech it can be claimed that "Ukrainians and Russians are brotherly people" but also that "Ukrainians and Russians are *one* people" (see below).

Confronted with the threat of being gobbled up by their overwhelming eastern neighbor, some Belarusian, Ukrainian, and Georgian intellectuals and politicians in different periods of nation building have sought refuge in *antemurale* mythologization. They insist that a massive civilizational chasm separates them from the Russians. This boundary cannot be defined by religion—Eastern Orthodox on both sides—so it must be demarcated by something else. Typically, that is a rather vague notion of "Europeanness" to which they claim to belong. However, this identity will separate them from the Russians only if the Russians can be firmly excluded from this same European civilization—a corollary they are normally prepared to draw.

Exactly which civilization Russian culture is held to belong to may differ in these narratives. Sometimes Russia is said to be a continent unto itself, a separate entity between East and West—a notion that many Russian intellectuals have toyed with throughout the ages.²⁹ At other times, Russia is said to belong to a Eurasian civilization, benefiting from its intermediary location between Europe and Asia and drawing impulses from both of them. This is a position shared by some Russian intellectuals, first developed by the Eurasianists in European exile in the 1920s and picked up again by Russian neo-Eurasianists, such as Alexander Dugin, today.³⁰ And finally, Russian culture can be depicted as being primarily or essentially Asian/Oriental, behind a deceptive European mask. This viewpoint does not find any supporters in the Russian identity debate but is occasionally set forth by anti-Russian *antemurale* thinkers in the neighboring states.

I now turn to some *antemurale* ideas presented in the identity debates in the three Orthodox countries that flank Russia to the West and South—Belarus, Ukraine, and Georgia. No claim is made that they represent a dominant narrative in their respective countries; quite the contrary, a strong case can be made that in Belarus, in particular, such perspectives are marginal.³¹ In Ukraine and Georgia they are more widespread, but here also these ideologemes have fluctuated, reflecting the ups and downs of political relations with Russia and, not least, the military confrontations between these countries and Russia since 2008. No doubt, the connection between action and discourse is dialectical: antagonistic discourse and demonizing narratives about the Other may precipitate violent actions, but, conversely, warfare leading to suffering and death will inevitably be reflected in perceptions of the enemy, whoever that may be.

Belarusian *Antemurale* Thinking

Belarusian national identity is generally regarded as quite vague and insecure, the country being squeezed in between two nations with a long cultural history and robust self-confidence—Poland and Russia.³² Any attempt the Belarusians might make to distance themselves from the Poles would risk throwing them into the embrace of the Russians, and vice versa. Therefore, the dominant tendency in Belarusian identity building has focused on the *sui generis* myth: to carve out an identity that differs from both the eastern and western neighbor, focused on the Belarusian language and the Uniate Belarusian Church.³³

Historically, Polishness has probably exerted a stronger pull on Belarusian intellectuals than has Russian culture; in 1863–1864, for instance, many of them made common cause with the insurrectionaries in the second Polish rebellion. All this changed, however, in the second half of the twentieth century, when Belarus was rebuilt after the devastations of World War II and brought back onto its feet in a Sovietized Russian mold. An increasing number of Belarusians in general and intellectuals in particular traded in their Belarusian language in favor of Russian, and in the secularized Soviet society the religious tradition of uniatism could no longer function as a bulwark against Russian influence. Perestroika, however, saw the emergence of a fledgling Belarusian nationalist movement, modeled on similar movements in the Baltics and in Ukraine, and attempts were again made to construct a unique Belarusian national identity. Spearheaded by Belaruskii Narodnyi Front ("The Belarusian Popular Front," BPF), these attempts yielded meager results. The BPF rhetoric then grew increasingly shriller and relied on stark *antemurale* tropes.

A typical exponent of the strident and uncompromising BPF language was Genad Saganovich, who in April 1993 wrote an article in the Belarusian newspaper *Narodnaia gazeta* (Popular Newspaper).[34] Under the title "The Russian Question from the Viewpoint of a Belarusian," he argued that the Russians had never managed to formulate a national idea or to develop a national consciousness. The medieval doctrine of "Moscow as the third Rome" had rapidly been transformed into an imperial ideology; being God's "chosen people" became a Russian national idea. Under Soviet rule this imperial consciousness was strengthened even further.

If someone living in Russia previously saw himself first and foremost as a subject of the tsar, then under the new conditions he identified himself with the state powers and its organs—the army, the police, and other oppressive structures. This had dire consequences for Russia's relationship with Belarus. As Saganovich saw it, for two entire centuries, war had defined the relationship between the two neighboring peoples. Anticipating Huntington's article by a few months, Saganovich proffered an analysis quite in line with the "clash-of-civilizations" thesis:

> Whenever I look to the past, each time I become convinced that at least from the beginning of the thirteenth century and until the annexation of the Belarusian region, each century drove us further apart.... So, yes, I dare to say that these were two different worlds, two different societies. The defining quality of the former was democracy and freedom, of the latter, totalitarianism and despotic rule.[35]

Similar ideas were also propounded by BPF leader Zianon Pazniak, who in 1993 participated in a roundtable discussion organized by the Belarusian journal *Neman*.[36] Pozniak's main message was that "a national state is the highest cultural and social value achievable," and "without a national consciousness no independent, free, and strong state is possible." This should be the ultimate aim of all Belarusians, he maintained. Pazniak saw Belarus as occupying an important geopolitical position between East and West, but he rejected as dangerous nonsense any talk about a national mission as "a bridge between Europe and Asia."

> Belarus is not a "bridge," but a country of the eastern part of Europe with a European people with a specifically European history and culture. It was torn from the structures of European civilization by force and experienced horrible destruction, but now we again stand before the possibility of resurrecting as a nation and returning to the fold of its historically, traditional cultural-national life. Belarus is Europe.[37]

Pazniak's reasoning here echoed Kundera's 1984 article—with the important difference that he had moved the civilizational wall through Europe considerably eastward.

Russia was decidedly *not* part of Europe, but it was not exactly Asia either, Pazniak maintained. In his view, "If only what we had found to the east of Belarus had been Asia, I think things might have been easier for us. The difficulty consists precisely in this that we are confronted with a peculiar country and a peculiar phenomenon—*Aziachina* (Asianness) dressed up in European clothing." This made it more difficult to detect the true nature of Russia and created an extremely sinister situation. In the view of the BPF leader, the border between Belarus and Russia represented a classical civilizational boundary: Belarus was a prototypical frontline state, an *antemurale* nation.

The next year Pazniak repeated many of the same points in an article in *Popular Newspaper*, this time with rather transparently racist overtones.[38] Explaining why Russia represented a deadly threat to Belarus, he resorted to historical determinism. An imperial state with an imperial public consciousness, an imperialist expansive policy, and a multinational structure, he argued, can never become democratic:

> Democracy and imperialism are incompatible. They are antipodes. The existence of the Russian state is dramatic for the Russian society itself primarily because as a result of its imperial content no *polnotsennaia* (full-fledged) European Russian nation has been formed. This is *loskutnyi* (a scrappy) people with no clearly delineated national territory, interspersed with Finno-Ugric, Turkic, Mongolian and other enclaves.[39]

This article brought a flurry of irate rebuttals and may well have administered the coup de grace to BPF-type nationalism.[40] The Belarusian population at large was not receptive to BPF's ideas—as indirectly acknowledged by Pazniak himself. For instance, he pointed out that since independence was achieved in 1991, the publication of books in the Belarusian language had been severely curtailed but "hardly anybody seems to notice." Belarusians clearly preferred to read books in Russian. So much for that massive civilizational gap between Belarusness and Russianness!

Ukraine as an *Antemurale* Country

Volodymyr Kravchenko points out in this volume that even though Ukraine for centuries represented the border region between the Catholic, Orthodox, and Muslim worlds, *antemurale* historical mythology did not develop in eighteenth-century or early nineteenth-century Ukraine, primarily because Ukraine was subsumed under the larger *russkii mir* (Russian world) concept. *Antimurale* crept into Ukrainian historiography only with the writings of Mykhailo Hrushevskyi (1866–1934) in the early twentieth century. For Hrushevskyi, the important identity wall was not against the Crimean Tatars, Ottomans, or other Muslim groups but against another Orthodox people and fellow Slavs, the Russians. Since then, *antemurale* perceptions have permeated Ukrainian nationalism, and always with the sharpest edge against the Russians.

Andrew Wilson has described Ukrainian nationalism as "a minority faith."[41] Even so, nationalism in Ukraine is clearly a stronger societal force with deeper historical roots than anything we can find in Belarus. In the interwar period, some right-wing Ukrainian intellectuals propounded an illiberal variety of nationalism that is often referred to as "integral nationalism."[42] One of the most influential and prolific of these writers was Dmytro Dontsov (1883–1973), who later exerted considerable influence on several Ukrainian nationalist parties and movements, particularly in western regions.[43]

Dontsov expounded his ideas in various books, the most important of which was *Pidstavy nashoi polityky* (The Foundations of Our Politics, 1921).[44] Here, he presented Ukraine as squeezed in between two fundamentally different mental worlds—Europe and Russia. To say that this was a clash between two "civilizations" would be inaccurate, since Russia, in his view, did not represent any kind of civilization but the opposite—barbarism. Even worse, Russia was obsessed by a messianic mission to impose its barbarous culture upon the outside world: in earlier times through the idea of "Moscow as the third Rome" and, later, through the Third International. The formidable task placed upon the Ukrainian nation was to be at the forefront in the battle to stem the advances of Russia:

> This our eternal struggle against the chaos from the East, in defense of the entire culture of the West—through our own statehood and culture—precisely this defines the Ukrainian national idea, and this must be the foundation of our entire political program. And truly, which of the two principles on

this continent that will be victorious—the European or the Muscovite—will depend upon the part Ukraine will play in this battle.⁴⁵

Dmytro Dontsov belonged to the extreme right, but *antemurale* thinking in Ukraine is not restricted to integral nationalists. The political elite across the board agrees that in order to build a Ukrainian nation-state, Ukraine needs a unique and separate national culture and identity, and this can be created only by emphasizing the cultural distance from Russian culture and language. That is the main reason virtually all Ukrainian politicians at the national level—even those from the Russian-speaking East—have rejected all demands to elevate Russian as a second state language as soon as they achieve positions of power in Kyiv.⁴⁶ The best example is perhaps Leonid Kuchma from the eastern city of Dnipropetrovsk, who, during the presidential elections in 1994, campaigned on a ticket to elevate the status of Russian, a pledge that made him popular among voters in the eastern parts of the country. However, when he was installed in office in Kyiv this promise was soon forgotten.⁴⁷ Precisely because the cultural distance between Ukraine and Russia is so short, it seems vitally important for Ukrainian state leaders and intellectuals to exaggerate it out of all proportion.

These attempts at cultural disentanglement may become rather ludicrous, as when certain linguistic differences between the two languages are adduced as evidence that "there exists no European nation more different from the Ukrainian than the Russian."⁴⁸ But serious scholarly publications, like *Politychna Dumka* (Political Thought), have also published articles aimed at underpinning an understanding of Ukrainian culture as significantly more European than the Russian. Discussing "Ukraine and Russia in the context of European values," an article in that journal in 1993 claimed that the basic Russian ideas were "primitive collectivism and equality, as well as illusions of social equality and justice, and hatred toward the rich." The Ukrainian people, by contrast, had luckily avoided the influence of the peasant community—the *mir*—and had instead developed concepts of the free life derived from the Cossack philosophy and free spirit as well as from the Magdeburg laws found in earlier times in some West Ukrainian cities. Therefore, "it is Ukraine (more than Russia) that is the carrier of the European mentality, which has been forming for centuries on the foundation of Ukraine's history, traditions, systems of values and of everything else that reflects the spirit of a nation."⁴⁹

The same kind of rhetoric can be found today. For Ukrainian politicians, the war in Eastern Ukraine—which they with good reason see as a Russian proxy war—has further accentuated the urgent need to distance themselves from all things Russian. Thus, in spring 2015 President Petro Poroshenko claimed on several occasions that Ukraine is a *forpost* ("outpost" or "advance post") of European civilization in the struggle for freedom and democracy.[50] "Outpost" is a military metaphor, and this is pure and undiluted *antemurale* rhetoric. Exactly in which direction the frontline between European Ukraine and its un-European enemy was running was not quite clear in Poroshenko's statements. On one occasion, he referred simultaneously to Ukraine's participation in World War II, when the enemy was Nazi Germany, and to the war in Eastern Ukraine. With its heroism and its sacrifices in the struggle for the liberation of Europe, Poroshenko declared, the Ukrainian people had made an invaluable contribution to the victory over Nazism in 1939–1945, adding, "and today Ukraine is also an outpost of European civilization in the struggle for freedom, democracy, and European values." Ukrainian sacrifices in World War II—when Ukrainians were fighting in the ranks of the Soviet Army—and in the most recent war on Ukrainian territory were presented as two sides of the same coin. "Ukraine is defending not only its own country but also the Eastern world *rubezh* (frontier) of democracy and freedom. Ukraine today is a genuine outpost of Europe. Therefore, we selflessly uphold our right to be an inalienable part of European civilization." Poroshenko's choice of words here makes sense only if we assume that he is excluding Russia from European civilization.[51]

Georgia

In Georgia we can find two discourses on Georgian-Russian relations, one focusing on the similarities between the two countries, the other underlining differences. The emphasis on dissociation dominates, while voices stressing the common features of Russian and Georgian cultures represent a self-critical opposition.[52] Former president Mikheil Saakashvili is among those who on occasion have handed out sweeping characterizations of the entire Russian people in commenting on the actions of the Russian state. For instance, at a joint press conference with U.S. Secretary of State Condoleezza Rice after the August War in 2008, Saakashvili called the Russian troops "coldblooded murderers and barbarians."[53]

> The Russians behave as if they lived in the eighteenth or nineteenth century. The only difference is that in the past there were no stock exchanges or live television. But their habits, expressions, and passion for alcohol remain the same. In the past, no one took pictures of their robbery while today the TV footage shows how they load toilets onto their tanks. One might think that they are barbarians from a bygone century.[54]

While it is not difficult to understand why negative portrayals of Russians and Russia would proliferate after the August War, it is worth noting that they can also be found in Saakashvili's earlier utterances. Thus, for instance, in 2006 many Russians became upset when it was reported that Saakashvili, at the Sixteenth Economic Forum in Poland, had compared the Russians to the nomadic Huns, who invaded Europe from Asia in the fourth century.[55]

At other times, however, Saakashvili has emphasized Russia's strong cultural traditions. In an interview with Belarusian television in 2010, he remarked, "I am perhaps the last, or penultimate, Georgian president who can quote Pushkin, Lermontov, Brodsky, and Esenin."[56]

Negative characteristics of Russians dominate in the Georgian media discourse. For instance, under the headline "Russia—the Belly of Evil," the writer and academician Nodar Koberidze quoted novelist Grigol Robakidze (1882–1962), who had once warned, "The Russian is a Scythian with Mongolian eyes, a horrible, wicked race, hateful toward all that is human." This hatred toward humanity, Koberidze claimed, stems from the inferiority complex that the Russians cannot rid themselves of. "When they came out of the woods, they realized that they were not up to such things as administering a state, and called in the Scandinavians, the so-called Varangians [to do it for them]."[57] In October 2008, some two months after the August War, the Georgian movie director Otar Ioseliani told the Ukrainian newspaper *Ezhenedelnik 2000* (Weekly 2000):

> Russia has never psychologically grown out of serfdom even after it was abolished. First and foremost Russia represses its own people, who continue to live in slavery.... We will never have peace with Russia! If previously we felt contempt for them, now a feeling of hatred has appeared.[58]

At the same time, it has been important for most Georgian intellectuals to emphasize that Georgia, in contrast to Russia, is a *European* country through and through. In April 1999, the Georgian prime minster Zurab Zhvania (1963–2005) declared from the rostrum of the Council of Europe: "I am a Georgian, consequently I am a European."[59]

In 2006 Saakashvili maintained that the Georgians have been Europeans ever since Prometheus was chained to a rock in Georgia and since the Argonauts came to this country in search of the Golden Fleece.[60] Saakashvili has often pointed to Georgia's Christian identification, stressing how Georgia had received the Gospel long before most contemporary West European nations: "We are not the new Europe or the old Europe; we are the ancient Europe."[61] Avto Dzhokhadze, executive director of the Caucasus Institute for Peace, Democracy and Development, points out that in the Georgian self-perception, its geographical position makes the country a "forward boundary of Christian Europe," a kind of *antemurale christianitatis*.[62]

While concepts of Georgia as a European country have dominated the political discourse in Tbilisi since independence, alternative views exist as well. Some scholars and analysts argue that Georgia lies at a crossroads of civilizations, straddling the border between East and West. For instance, Gigi Tevzadze, rector of Ilia Chavchavadze State University, has stressed the importance of the idea of a crossroads of cultures in Georgian cultural and intellectual self-identification.[63] Similarly, historian Nino Chikovani of the Department of Cultural Studies at Tbilisi State University has argued, "Georgia has always been a contact zone, a crossroads of Western and Eastern civilizations."[64] In the 1990s, the idea of a crossroads was promulgated by President Eduard Shevardnadze (1928–2014): the history of Georgia was formed by the Silk Road, he explained, while another type of East-West connection, the pipelines, symbolizes Georgia's future.[65]

Russian Attitudes toward Their Orthodox Neighbors

Identity formation is not only relational; it is also reciprocal. How Russia's nearest Orthodox neighbors perceive Russia is strongly influenced by how Russia views them.

As in Georgia, we can find in Russia two discourses, one emphasizing dissociation while the other highlights shared features of Russian and Georgian cultures. However, whereas the former discourse dominates in Georgia, Russians tend to stress commonality. In Russia the message that Russia and Georgia are closely related, fraternal peoples—*bratskie narody*— has been officially endorsed by both Dmitry Medvedev and Vladimir Putin. The 2008 August War is presented as a regrettable but temporary aberration from what has been and should remain a fraternal relationship between the two countries. However, no one in Russia has any doubts about who is the older and who is the younger of these two "brothers."

As early as his first statement after the start of the August War, Putin declared, "In Russia we have always had an enormous respect for Georgia. The Georgian people we regard as fraternal." Prime Minister Putin expressed the conviction that this positive attitude would survive "in spite of the criminal policy of the current leadership in this country."[66]

This conciliatory message was soon repeated by other Russian officials,[67] becoming a standard ingredient in political statements. In a meeting between Russian civil society activists on 19 September 2008, then President Medvedev stated:

> To us it is axiomatic that the Georgian people are of course not to be blamed for the aggression and the genocide [of the South Ossetian people]. This is the guilt of the criminal and irresponsible regime that unleashed this war.... For centuries relations between our peoples have been fraternal.[68]

The *bratskie narody* metaphor is a cliché from the Soviet terminological repertoire, but it should be recognized as more than a knee-jerk reaction inherited from the Communist past. It also reflects the inequality in the relationship between Russians and Georgians, which should sensitize us to the importance of power relations in the study of reciprocal identity formations. Russian leaders employ the same kind of fraternal terminology toward the Ukrainians as toward the Georgians, but they go one step further, denying any difference between the two peoples. In his landmark speech on 18 March 2014 in the Kremlin, celebrating the incorporation of the Crimean oblast into the Russian Federation, President Putin employed the brotherly peoples metaphor.[69]

However, he also made another claim, apparently very similar but in fact radically different: Russians and Ukrainians, he maintained, are "*one people.*" It is not clear how this is to be interpreted, but it sounds very much like a throwback to the prerevolutionary concept of the tripartite Russian nation, consisting of a Great Russian, a *Malorusskii*, or "Little Russian," and a Belarusian branch—with no doubt as to which group naturally takes the lead in this trinity. By subsuming the Ukrainians under a common national identity umbrella, Putin effectively wiped the separate Ukrainian nation out of existence. Interestingly, this element in his rhetoric predates the 2014/2015 Ukrainian crisis. As early as September 2013, Putin made the same claim: "We [Russians and Ukrainians] are *odin narod* (one people)."[70] It is against this background that the Ukrainians' insistence on an identity wall separating them from their mighty northern neighbor must be understood.

Conclusions

Identities are always relational. You define who you are through a contrast with the Other. *The boundary* is the locus of identity formation—with individuals as well as with collectives, including ethnic groups and nations. Furthermore, as Iver B. Neumann has pointed out, in these processes the neighbors you want to dissociate yourself from are more important than the ones you want to emulate.[71] Therefore, *antemurale* theories tell us not only something about how a nation or ethnic group perceives one of its neighbors but also something about their self-perception.

Identity relations, like other relations, involve power. Russia is a much larger, stronger, and more populous state than its Orthodox neighbors and has to a considerable degree influenced their history, while they have generally played far more limited roles in Russian history.

In conflict situations involving two culturally related nations, the larger and more powerful nation will tend to underscore similarities and downplay differences, whereas the smaller and weaker one will insist that the boundary between the two is strong and real. The larger group has an interest in subsuming its neighbors under some common identity since this may legitimize continued hegemony, while the weaker part may fall back on a combination of two different strategies.[72] It may claim to be unique, *sui generis*, one of a kind. But those who stand alone in the world are vulnerable and exposed, so a *sui generis* identity is often supplemented with the claim that "our nation" is indeed a member of a larger community—but that is a *different* community from the one dominated by the (former) hegemon. For some politicians and intellectuals in Georgia, Ukraine, and Belarus this alternative community is Europe. Their political leaders have gone out of their way to stress that their countries belong to European civilization and that they have an important contribution to offer to this value community. They should be recognized as outposts of European civilization toward the East, defenders of the gate, or, as it was called in medieval and early modern Europe, nations *antemurale*.[73]

If the *sui generis* myth is a strategy of dissociation, *antemurale* thinking represents a new association. Of course, membership in the new community cannot shield the country from the former hegemon if the hegemon also belongs to it. With Georgia, Ukraine, and Belarus, *antemurale* thinkers in these countries must convince their fellow Europeans—and themselves—that Russians are *not* Europeans and do not belong inside the gates.

The myth of being *antemurale* is a boundary marker created to emphasize the cultural distance between groups. It maximizes the effect of this boundary by claiming that it represents a civilizational divide. The evidence mustered is cultural: historical, religious, linguistic, and so on. As I see it, however, it is not these cultural differences per se that drive the mythogenesis but concerns about power and power relations. Whatever else the *antemurale* myth has been in the history of European nations, it is primarily a weapon in the hands of weak nations confronted by what they perceive as strong and aggressive neighbors.

Pål Kolstø is a professor of Russian and post-Soviet studies at the University of Oslo, specializing in nationalism, nation building, ethnic relations, and unrecognized states in the former Soviet Union. He is the author or editor of ten books on these topics, most recently *Russia before and after Crimea* (Edinburgh University Press, 2018) and *The New Russian National-*

ism: *Imperialism, Ethnicity and Authoritarianism, 2000–2015* (Edinburgh University Press, 2016; both edited with Helge Blakkisrud).

Notes

1. F. Barth, "Introduction," in *Ethnic Groups and Boundaries. The Social Organization of Culture Difference*, ed. F. Barth (Bergen: Universitetsforlaget, 1969), 9–37. Sinisa Malesevic sees Barth's article as "a Copernican revolution." S. Malešević, *The Sociology of Ethnicity* (London: Sage, 2004), 2. See also A. Wimmer, *Ethnic Boundary Making. Institutions, Power, Networks* (Oxford: Oxford University Press, 2013); A. Cohen, ed., *Signifying Identities: Anthropological Perspectives on Boundaries and Contested Values* (London: Routledge, 2000); H. Vermeulen and C. Govers, eds., *The Anthropology of Ethnicity: Beyond "Ethnic Groups and Boundaries"* (Amsterdam: Het Spinhuis, 1994); P. Kolstø, ed., *Myths and Boundaries in South-Eastern Europe* (London: Hurst, 2005).
2. Th. H. Eriksen, *Ethnicity & Nationalism: Anthropological Perspectives* (London: Pluto Press, 1993); D. Conversi, "Reassessing Current Theories of Nationalism: Nationalism as Boundary Maintenance and Creation," *Nationalism and Ethnic Politics* 1 (1995): 73–85.
3. I.B. Neumann, *Uses of the Other: "The East" in European Identity Formation* (Minneapolis: University of Minnesota Press, 1999).
4. R. Jenkins, *Social Identities* (London: Routledge, 1996).
5. A. Cohen, *The Symbolic Construction of Community* (London: Routledge, 2008), 12; see also M. Guibernau, *Belonging: Solidarity and Division in Modern Societies* (Cambridge: Polity Press, 2013), 37.
6. J.A. Armstrong, *Nations before Nationalism* (Chapel Hill: University of North Carolina Press, 1982), 8–9; Z. Mach, *Symbols, Conflict, and Identity: Essays in Political Anthropology* (New York: State University of New York Press, 1993), 57; Kolstø, *Myths*, 16–34.
7. Kolstø, *Myths*, 16–34.
8. Mach, *Symbols*, 185; A. Lawaty, "The Figure of 'Antemurale' in the Historiography at Home and in Exile," in *East and Central European History Writing in Exile 1939–1989*, ed. M. Zadencka, A. Plakans, and A. Lawaty (Leiden and Boston: Brill, 2015), 360–74.
9. See, e.g., I. Zanic, "The Symbolic Identity of Croatia in the Triangle Crossroads–Bulwark–Bridge," in Kolstø, *Myths*, 35–76.
10. J. Hutchinson, *Nations as Zones of Conflict* (London: Sage, 2005), 19. To be sure, Catholics often retaliated in kind.
11. "Mythomoteurs" is the term John Armstrong and Anthony Smith use to denote myths as historical "movers." It combines the French words for "myth" and "engine." See P. Kolstø, "John Armstrong: Typologies and Grand Narratives," *Nations and Nationalism* 21 (2015), 177–81.
12. Lawaty, "The Figure of 'Antemurale,'" 360–74. For the main components of the *antemurale* mythology, see also the introductory chapter in this book.
13. B. Lewis, *The Muslim Discovery of Europe* (New York: Norton, 1982), 29.

14. R.S. Barker, *Legitimating Identities: The Self-presentation of Rulers and Subjects* (Cambridge: Cambridge University Press, 2001).
15. K. Mannheim, *Ideology and Utopia* (London: K. Paul, Trench, Trubner, 1936).
16. M. Kundera, "The Tragedy of Central Europe," *New York Review of Books* 31, no. 7 (1984): 33–38.
17. I.B. Neumann, "Russia as Central Europe's Constituting Other," *East European Politics and Societies* 7 (1993): 349–69.
18. P. Kolstø, "'Western Balkans' as the New Balkans: Regional Names as Tools for Stigmatization and Exclusion," *Europe-Asia Studies* 68, no. 7 (2016): 1–19.
19. J. Le Rider, "Mitteleuropa, Zentraleuropa, Mittelosteuropa: A Mental Map of Central Europe," *European Journal of Social Theory* 11, no. 2 (2008): 155–69; M. Todorova, *Imagining the Balkans* (Oxford: Oxford University Press, 2009), 190.
20. S. Huntington, "The Clash of Civilizations?" *Foreign Affairs* 72 (1993): 22–49.
21. S. Huntington, *The Third Wave: Democratization in the Late Twentieth Century* (Norman: University of Oklahoma Press, 1991).
22. S. Huntington, *The Clash of Civilizations and the Remaking of World Order* (London: Free Press, 1996), 28.
23. J.J. Kirkpatrick, "The Modernizing Imperative: Tradition and Change," in *Foreign Affairs. The Clash of Civilizations? The Debate*, 20th anniversary ed. (New York: Foreign Affairs, 2013), 51–54.
24. Huntington, *Clash of Civilizations*, 159.
25. For instance, Huntington's book was translated into Estonian in 1999 with a foreword by the then-minister of foreign affairs Toomas Ilves (S. Huntington, *Tsivilisatsioonide kokkupõrge ja maailmakorra ümberkujundamine* [Tartu: Fontes, 1999]). A leading Estonian intellectual, sociologist Marju Lauristin, references Huntington to underpin her assertion that ethnic nationalism was not the most decisive factor in the dissolution of the Soviet Union. Instead, she claims, it was "precisely the civilizational conflict between the Russian-Soviet Empire, the 'New Byzantium' of the twentieth century, and the Baltic and other East-European nations, representing the Western traditions of individual autonomy and civil society." M. Lauristin and P. Vihalemm, eds., *Return to the Western World, Cultural and Political Perspectives on the Estonian Post-Communist Transition* (Tartu: Tartu University Press, 1997), 29. By contrast, in Russia Huntington's ideas were received with a strong dose of skepticism. See, e.g., V.V. Afanasev, "Konseptsiia tsivilizatsii Samuela Khantingtona," in *Rossiia i Evropa. Natsii v epokhu globalizatsii*, ed. V.V. Afanasev (Moskva: MGU, 2009), 146–56; and K. Govorun, "Interpretiruia 'russkii mir': Slozhnoe obshchestvo," *Russkii zhurnal* 6 (October 2015), retrieved 13 March 2018 from http://www.russ.ru/Mirovaya-povestka/Interpretiruya-russkij-mir.
26. Huntington, *Clash of Civilizations*, 165.
27. Ibid., 162.
28. Th. Shanin, *Russia as a "Developing Society"* (London: Macmillan, 1985), 58. In official Russian statistics, the Ukrainians were referred to as *Malorossy*, or "Little Russians."
29. See N. Riazanovsky, *Russia and the West in the Teaching of the Slavophiles* (Gloucester: Peter Smith, 1952).
30. See, for instance, M. Laruelle, *Russian Eurasianism: An Ideology of Empire* (Baltimore: Johns Hopkins University Press, 2008).

31. In 2000, 42.6 percent of the respondents in a survey in Belarus agreed with the statement "The Belarusians are a part of a triune Russian people." See N. Bekus, *Struggle over Identity: The Official and the Alternative "Belarusianness"* (Budapest: Central European University Press, 2010).
32. N. Vakar, *Belorussia: The Making of a Nation: A Case Study* (Cambridge, MA: Harvard University Press, 1956); D.R. Marples, *Belarus: A Denationalized Nation* (Amsterdam: Harwood Academic Publishers, 1999). But see also Bekus, *Struggle over Identity*.
33. See J. Zaprudnik, *Belarus: At a Crossroads in History* (Boulder: Westview, 1993).
34. G. Saganovich, "Russkii vopros s tochki zreniia Belarusa," *Narodnaia gazeta* (30 April 1993), 7, 14.
35. Saganovich, "Russkii vopros."
36. Z. Pozniak [Pazniak], "Natsionalnoe gosudarstvo est naivysshaia kulturnaia i obshchestvennaia tsennost Belorusskii shliakh 'Kruglyi stol v redaktsii zhurnala,'" *Neman* (1993): 3–43.
37. Ibid.
38. Z. Pozniak [Pazniak], "O russkom imperializme i ego opasnosti," *Narodnaia gazeta* (1994): 15–17.
39. Ibid.
40. In P. Kolstø, *Political Construction Sites: Nationbuilding in Russia and the Post-Soviet States* (Boulder: Westview, 2000), 163–67, I argued that the demise of BPF was caused by "self-inflicted wounds" rather than by "murder."
41. A. Wilson, *Ukrainian Nationalism as a Minority Faith* (Cambridge: Cambridge University Press, 1997).
42. J. Armstrong, *Ukrainian Nationalism 1939–1945* (New York: Columbia University Press, 1955); A.J. Motyl, *The Turn to the Right: The Ideological Origins and Development of Ukrainian Nationalism, 1919–1929* (New York: Columbia University Press, 1980); M. Shkandrij, *Ukrainian Nationalism: Politics, Ideology, and Literature, 1929–1956* (New Haven: Yale University Press, 2015). "Integral nationalism" (*nationalisme intégral*) was first developed in France in the late nineteenth and early twentieth centuries by intellectuals such as Charles Maurras. Among its defining characteristics were statism, militarism, and anti-individualism. It is often regarded as protofascist.
43. See, e.g., P.A. Rudling, "The Return of the Ukrainian Far Right. The Case of VO Svoboda," in *Analyzing Fascist Discourse: European Fascism in Talk and Text*, ed. R. Wodak and J.E. Richardson (London: Routledge, 2013), 228–55.
44. D. Dontsov, *Pidstavy nashoi polityky* (New York, 1957 [1921]).
45. Dontsov, *Pidstavy*, 87.
46. I argue this point in *Political Construction Sites*, 168–93.
47. "Leonid Kuchma prinial prisiagu narodu Ukrainy i pristupil k ispolneniiu svoikh obiazannostei." *Rabochaia gazeta Ukrainy*, 21 July 1994, 1.
48. Author's interview at the headquarters of the Ukrainian Popular front RUKH in Kyiv, September 1994. For instance, while the most common Ukrainian word for "leader" is *holova*, meaning "head," a typically Russian term for the same is *predsedatel*, derived from the Russian word for "to sit." According to my Ukrainian informant, this proved which part of the body was more important for Ukrainian and Russian leaders, respectively!

49. V. Polokhalo et al., "Ukraine and Russia in the Context of European Values," *Politychna dumka* 1 (1993), 139–41, esp. 140.
50. "Ukraina iavliaetsia forpostom evropeiskoi tsivilizatsii v borbe za svobodu i demokratiiu—Poroshenko," UNIAN, retrieved 8 November 2016 from http://www.unian.net/politics/1073218-ukraina-yavlyaetsya-forpostom-evropeyskoy-tsiviliza tsii-v-borbe-za-svobodu-i-demokratiyu-poroshenko.html; "Ukraina seichas nastoiashchii forpost Evropy—Poroshenko," retrieved 8 November 2016 from http://www.segodnya.ua/ukraine/ukraina-seychas-nastoyashchiy-forpost-evropy-porosh enko-548608.html.
51. For the wider ramifications of the war in Donbass on the Ukrainian identity debate, see Tatiana Zhurzhenko, "From Borderlands to Bloodlands," *Transit: Europäische Revue 45 (Ukraine—the Unexpected Revolution)*, retrieved 13 March 2018 from http://www.iwm.at/read-listen-watch/transit-online/borderlands-bloodlands.
52. This section builds on my coauthored article (with Aleksandr Rusetskii), "Power Differentials and Identity Formation: Images of Self and Other on the Russian–Georgian Boundary," *National Identities* 14, no. 2 (2012): 139–55.
53. "Russkie voiska manevriruiut bliz Tbilisi," 2008, retrieved 13 March 2018 from http://kavkazcenter.com/russ/content/2008/08/16/60293.shtml.
54. P. Smolar, "Saakashvili: 'Rossiia nastolko uiazvima!'" 2008, retrieved 8 November 2016 from http://inosmi.ru/world/20080921/244130.html.
55. A. Bonner, "Georgian Losses and Russia's Gain," *Middle East Policy Council* 15, no. 4 (2008), retrieved 5 November 2018 from http://mepc.org/georgian-losses-and-russias-gain. See also Kolstø and Rusetskii, "Power Differentials," 148.
56. A. Petrov, "Batka otvetil Putinu, vypustiv v efir Saakhashvili," *Svobodnaia pressa* (16 July 2010), retrieved 8 November 2016 from http://svpressa.ru/society/article/27841/?go=popul.
57. N. Koberidze, "Ruseti—sashoi borotebisa [Russia—the womb of evil]," *Saerto Gazeti* (August 2008), retrieved 13 March 2018 from http://kardu.wordpress.com.
58. Quoted from A. Rutkovskii, "Do i posle Ioseliani," *Ezhenedelnik*, no. 43 (2000), retrieved 8 November 2016 from http://sir-michael.ru/zakkurapiya/postsovetskoe-prostranstvo/gruziya/do-i-posle-ioseliani/.
59. Á.P. Scholtbach and G. Nodia, *The Political Landscape of Georgia. Political Parties: Achievements, Challenges, and Prospects* (Delft: Eburon Caucasus Institute for Peace, Democracy and Development, 2006).
60. "Saakashvili ustanovil svoe rodstvo s Prometeem" (14 November 2006), retrieved 8 November 2008 from lenta.ru/news/2006/11/14/prometeus/.
61. Cited in S. Tarasov and D. Ermolaev, "Osennee obostrenie ili geopoliticheskie tezisy Mishiko Saakashvili," *Rossiiskie vesti* (8–15 October 2008), retrieved 8 November 2008 from http://rosvesty.ru/1931/interes/?id=1000000230.
62. A. Dzhokhadze, "Rossiia glazami gruzina" (19 April 2007), retrieved 8 November 2008 from http://www.apsny.ge/society/1177005060.php.
63. G. Tevzadze, "Speech at Symposium on 'Georgia at the Crossroads of European and Asian Cultures," *Harriman Institute* (4 May 2009), retrieved 8 November 2016 from http://harriman.columbia.edu/files/harriman/01397.pdf.
64. N. Chikovani, "Georgia on the Crossroad of Civilizations" (n.d.), retrieved 8 November 2016 from http://www.nplg.gov.ge/caucasia/messenger/eng/n3/summary/27.htm.

65. Tevzadze, "Speech."
66. V. Putin, "Gruziia nanesla smertel'nyi udar po svoei gosudarstvennosti," *Komsomolskaia Pravda* (9 August 2008), retrieved 8 November 2016 from http://www.kp.ru/daily/24143/361219.
67. See, e.g., the statement by the Russian ambassador to Estonia: Nikolai Uspenskii, "Nikolai Uspenskii: gruziny—bratskii narod." Retrieved 8 November 2016 from http://rus.delfi.ee/daily/politics/article.php?id=19558690.
68. "Stenograficheskii otchet o vstreche s prestaviteliami obshchestvennykh organizatsii" (19 September 2008), retrieved 8 November 2016 from http://news.kremlin.ru/transcripts/8209.
69. V. Putin, "Obrashchenie Prezidenta Rossiiskoi Federatsii" (18 March 2014), retrieved 8 November 2016 from www.kremlin.ru/news/20603. See also the analysis of this speech in Kerstin Jobst's contribution in this volume.
70. V. Putin, "Interviu Pervomu kanalu i agentstvu Associated Press" (3 September 2013), retrieved 3 November 2016 from http://kremlin.ru/events/president/news/19143.
71. Neumann, *Uses of the Other.*
72. Kolstø, *Myths,* 19–20.
73. Ibid., 24–25.

Bibliography

Afanasev, V.V. 2009. "Konsteptsiia tsivilizatsii Samuela Khantingtona." In *Rossiia i Evropa. Natsii v epokhu globalizatsii,* ed. V.V. Afanasev, 146–56. Moskva: MGU.

Armstrong, J. 1955. *Ukrainian Nationalism 1939–1945.* New York: Columbia University Press.

———. 1982. *Nations before Nationalism.* Chapel Hill: University of North Carolina Press.

Barker, R.S. 2001. *Legitimating Identities: The Self-Presentation of Rulers and Subjects.* Cambridge: Cambridge University Press.

Barth, F. 1969. "Introduction." In *Ethnic Groups and Boundaries. The Social Organization of Culture Difference,* 9–37. Bergen: Universitetsforlaget.

Bekus, N. 2010. *Struggle over Identity: The Official and the Alternative "Belarusianness."* Budapest: Central European University Press.

Bonner, A. 2008. "Georgian Losses and Russia's Gain," *Middle East Policy Council,* vol. 15, no. 4. Retrieved 5 November 2018 from http://mepc.org/georgian-losses-and-russias-gain.

Chikovani, N. n.d. "Georgia on the Crossroad of Civilizations." Retrieved 13 November 2016 from http://www.nplg.gov.ge/caucasia/messenger/eng/n3/summary/27.htm.

Cohen, A. 2008. *The Symbolic Construction of Community.* London: Routledge.

Cohen, A., ed. 2000. *Signifying Identities: Anthropological Perspectives on Boundaries and Contested Values.* London: Routledge.

Conversi, D. 1995. "Reassessing Current Theories of Nationalism: Nationalism as Boundary Maintenance and Creation." *Nationalism and Ethnic Politics* 1: 73–85.

Dontsov, D. 1995 [1921]. *Pidstavy nashoi polityky.* New York: no publisher.

Dzhokhadze, A. "Rossiia glazami gruzina." 19 April 2007. Retrieved 13 November 2008 from http://www.apsny.ge/society/1177005060.php.
Eriksen, T.H. 1993. *Ethnicity & Nationalism: Anthropological Perspectives*. London: Pluto Press.
Govorun, K. 2015. "Interpretiruia 'russkii mir': Slozhnoe obshchestvo." *Russkii zhurnal*. 6 October. Retrieved 13 March 2018 from http://www.russ.ru/Mirovaya-povestka/Interpretiruya-russkij-mir.
Guibernau, M. 2013. *Belonging: Solidarity and Division in Modern Societies*. Cambridge: Polity Press.
Huntington, S. 1991. *The Third Wave: Democratization in the Late Twentieth Century*. Norman: University of Oklahoma Press.
———. 1993. "The Clash of Civilizations?" *Foreign Affairs* 72: 22–49.
———. 1996. *The Clash of Civilizations and the Remaking of World Order*. London: Free Press.
———. 1999. *Tsivilisatsioonide kokkupõrge ja maailmakorra ümberkujundamine*. Tartu: Fontes.
Hutchinson, J. 2005. *Nations as Zones of Conflict*. London: Sage.
Jenkins, R. 1996. *Social Identities*. London: Routledge.
Kirkpatrick, J.J. 2013. "The Modernizing Imperative: Tradition and Change." In *Foreign Affairs. The Clash of Civilizations? The Debate*, 20th anniversary ed., 51–54, 159. New York: Foreign Affairs.
Koberidze, N. 2008. "Ruseti—sashoi borotebisa. [Russia—the womb of evil]." *Saerto Gazeti*. 8 August. Retrieved 13 March 2018 from http://kardu.wordpress.com.
Kolstø, P. 2000. *Political Construction Sites: Nationbuilding in Russia and the Post-Soviet States*. Boulder: Westview.
———, ed. 2005. *Myths and Boundaries in South-Eastern Europe*. London: Hurst.
———. 2015. "John Armstrong: Typologies and Grand Narratives." *Nations and Nationalism* 21: 177–81.
———. 2016. "'Western Balkans' as the New Balkans: Regional Names as Tools for Stigmatization and Exclusion." *Europe-Asia Studies* 68, no. 7: 1–19.
Kolstø, P. and A. Rusetskii. 2012 "Power Differentials and Identity Formation: Images of Self and Other on the Russian–Georgian Boundary." *National Identities* 14, no. 2: 139–55.
Kundera, M. 1984. "The Tragedy of Central Europe." *New York Review of Books* 31, no. 7, 33–38.
Laruelle, M. 2008. *Russian Eurasianism: An Ideology of Empire*. Baltimore: Johns Hopkins University Press.
Lauristin, M. and P. Vihalemm, eds. 1997. *Return to the Western World, Cultural and Political Perspectives on the Estonian Post-Communist Transition*. Tartu: Tartu University Press.
Lawaty, A. 2015. "The Figure of 'Antemurale' in the Historiography at Home and in Exile." In *East and Central European History Writing in Exile 1939–1989*, ed. M. Zadencka, A. Plakans, and A. Lawaty, 360–74. Leiden and Boston: Brill.
"Leonid Kuchma prinial prisiagu narodu Ukrainy i pristupil k ispolneniiu svoikh obiazannostei." 1994. *Rabochaia gazeta Ukrainy*, 21 July, 1.
Le Rider, J. 2008. "Mitteleuropa, Zentraleuropa, Mittelosteuropa: A Mental Map of Central Europe." *European Journal of Social Theory* 11, no. 2: 155–69.

Lewis, B. 1982. *The Muslim Discovery of Europe.* New York: Norton.
Mach, Z. 1993. *Symbols, Conflict, and Identity: Essays in Political Anthropology.* New York: State University of New York Press.
Maleševic, S. 2004. *The Sociology of Ethnicity.* London: Sage.
Mannheim, K. 1936. *Ideology and Utopia.* London: K. Paul, Trench, Trubner.
Marples, D.R. 1999. *Belarus: A Denationalized Nation.* Amsterdam: Harwood Academic.
Motyl, A.J. 1980. *The Turn to the Right: The Ideological Origins and Development of Ukrainian Nationalism, 1919–1929.* New York: Columbia University Press.
Neumann, I.B. 1993. "Russia as Central Europe's Constituting Other." *East European Politics and Societies* 7: 349–69.
———. 1999. *Uses of the Other: "The East" in European Identity Formation.* Minneapolis: University of Minnesota Press.
Petrov, A. 2010. "Batka otvetil Putinu, vypustiv v efir Saakhashvili." *Svobodnaia pressa.* 16 July. Retrieved 13 November 2016 from http://svpressa.ru/society/article/27841/?go=popul.
Polokhalo, V. et al. 1993. "Ukraine and Russia in the Context of European Values." *Politychna dumka* 1: 139–41.
Pozniak [Pazniak], Z. 1993. "Natsionalnoe gosudarstvo est naivysshaia kulturnaia i obshchestvennaia tsennost. Belorusskii shliakh: 'Kruglyi stol v redaktsii zhurnala.'" *Neman*, 3–43.
———. 1994. "O russkom imperializme i ego opasnosti." *Narodnaia gazeta*, 15–17.
Putin, V. 2008. "Gruziia nanesla smertel'nyi udar po svoei gosudarstvennosti." *Komsomolskaia Pravda.* August 9. Retrieved 13 November 2016 from http://www.kp.ru/daily/24143/361219.
———. 2013. "Interviu Pervomu kanalu i agentstvu Associated Press." 3 September. Retrieved 3 November 2016 from http://kremlin.ru/events/president/news/19143.
———. 2014. "Obrashchenie Prezidenta Rossiiskoi Federatsii" March 18. Retrieved 13 November 2016 from www.kremlin.ru/news/20603.
Riazanovsky, N. 1952. *Russia and the West in the Teaching of the Slavophiles.* Gloucester, MA: Peter Smith.
Rudling, P.A. 2013. "The Return of the Ukrainian Far Right. The Case of VO Svoboda." In *Analyzing Fascist Discourse: European Fascism in Talk and Text*, ed. R. Wodal and J.E. Richardson, 228–55. London: Routledge.
"Russkie voiska manevriruiut bliz Tbilisi." 2008. Retrieved 13 March 2018 from http://kavkazcenter.com/russ/content/2008/08/16/60293.shtml.
Rutkovskii, A. 2008. "Do i posle Ioseliani." *Ezhenedelnik 2000*, 43. 24–29 October. Retrieved 13 November 2016 from http://sir-michael.ru/zakkurapiya/postsovetskoe-prostranstvo/gruziya/do-i-posle-ioseliani/.
"Saakashvili ustanovil svoe rodstvo s Prometeem." 14 November 2006. Retrieved 13 November 2008 from https://lenta.ru/news/2006/11/14/prometeus/.
Saganovich, G. 1993. "'Russkii vopros' s tochki zreniia Belarusa." *Narodnaia gazeta*, 30 April, 7, 14.
Scholtbach, A.P. and G. Nodia. 2006. *The Political Landscape of Georgia. Political Parties: Achievements, Challenges, and Prospects.* Delft: Eburon Caucasus Institute for Peace, Democracy and Development.
Shanin, T. 1985. *Russia as a "Developing Society."* London: Macmillan.

Shkandrij, M. 2015. *Ukrainian Nationalism: Politics, Ideology, and Literature, 1929–1956*. New Haven: Yale University Press.
Smolar, P. 2008. "Saakashvili: 'Rossiia nastolko uiazmima!'" Retrieved 13 November 2016 from http://inosmi.ru/world/20080921/244130.html.
"Stenograficheskii otchet o vstreche s prestaviteliami obshchestvennykh organizatsii." 19 September 2008. Retrieved 13 November 2016 from http://news.kremlin.ru/transcripts/8209.
Tarasov, S. and D. Ermolaev. 2008. "Osennee obostrenie ili geopoliticheskie tezisy Mishiko Saakashvili." *Rossiiskie vesti*. 8–15 October. Retrieved 13 November 2008 from http://rosvesty.ru/1931/interes/?id=1000000230.
Tevzadze, G. 2009 "Speech at Symposium on 'Georgia at the Crossroads of European and Asian Cultures.'" *Harriman Institute*. 4 May. Retrieved 13 November 2016 from http://harriman.columbia.edu/files/harriman/01397.pdf.
Todorova, M. 2009. *Imagining the Balkans*. Oxford: Oxford University Press.
"Ukraina seichas nastoiashchii forpost Evropy—Poroshenko." 2014. Retrieved 13 November 2016 from http://www.segodnya.ua/ukraine/ukraina-seychas-nastoyashchiy-forpost-evropy-poroshenko-548608.html.
"Ukraina iavliaetsia forpostom evropeiskoi tsivilizatsii v borbe za svobodu i demokratiiu—Poroshenko." 2015. UNIAN. Retrieved 13 November 2016 from http://www.unian.net/politics/1073218-ukraina-yavlyaetsya-forpostom-evropeyskoy-tsivilizatsii-v-borbe-za-svobodu-i-demokratiyu-poroshenko.html.
Uspenskii, N. 2008. "Nikolai Uspenskii: gruziny—bratskii narod." Retrieved 13 November 2016 from http://rus.delfi.ee/daily/politics/article.php?id=19558690.
Vakar, N. 1956. *Belorussia: The Making of a Nation: A Case Study*. Cambridge, MA: Harvard University Press.
Vermeulen, H. and C. Govers, eds. 1994. *The Anthropology of Ethnicity: Beyond "Ethnic Groups and Boundaries."* Amsterdam: Het Spinhuis.
Wilson, A. 1997. *Ukrainian Nationalism as a Minority Faith*. Cambridge: Cambridge University Press.
Wimmer, A. 2013. *Ethnic Boundary Making. Institutions, Power, Networks*. Oxford: Oxford University Press.
Zanic, I. 2005. "The Symbolic Identity of Croatia in the Triangle Crossroads–Bulwark–Bridge." In *Myths and Boundaries in South-Eastern Europe*, ed. P. Kolstø, 35–76. London: Hurst.
Zaprudnik, J. 1993. *Belarus: At a Crossroads in History*. Boulder: Westview.
Zhurzhenko, T. 2018. "From Borderlands to Bloodlands." *Transit: Europäische Revue* 45 *Ukraine—the Unexpected Revolution*. Retrieved 13 March 2018 from http://www.iwm.at/read-listen-watch/transit-online/borderlands-bloodlands.

CHAPTER 14

Concluding Thoughts on Central and Eastern European Bulwark Rhetoric in the Twenty-First Century

Paul Srodecki

Being a forewall of the European hinterland that lies farther to the West has been one of the most popular topoi within the national discourses all over Central and Eastern Europe at the latest since the late Middle Ages and remained a main autostereotype in these regions during the nineteenth and twentieth centuries. The Russian Revolution of 1917 and the founding of the Soviet Union in 1922 even led (especially in Poland) to an increase in the use of the bulwark rhetoric in the interwar period. And even if the popularity of the *antemurale* myths somehow suffered after 1945, when the entirety of Eastern and a large part of Central Europe fell into the Soviet sphere and Communist-led regimes were established (being a bulwark now meant defending the "free" Communist East against the "unfree," imperialistic and capitalistic West). All over this region the old *antemurale* topoi continued to serve as useful propagandistic tools of the anti-Communist underground and had an obvious revival after the breakdown of the Soviet Union and its satellite states in 1989–1991. Deeply engraved in national historical consciousnesses and collective memories, we can find legacies and modifications of the *antemurale* topoi all over the abovementioned regions today.

The enlargement of the European Union in 2004 did not only increase its population considerably. With the admission of the ten new accession countries, the borders of the now 25-member Union, which, following the accessions of Romania, Bulgaria, and more recently Croatia, now consists (before Brexit) of twenty-eight states, were advanced far to the East. From the very beginning, a lively security debate accompanied the expansion of the EU, combined with old ideas of Europe as a stronghold. Even before the actual enlargement, however, the new EU eastern border was often understood by politicians, journalists, and scientists as an economic and cultural demarcation line and was stylized as a bulwark protecting "fortress Europe."[1]

Poland's eastern border was of particular interest to the Western public: *1,200 Kilometers Bulwark of the West. A Journey Along the New Eastern Border of the EU* was the title of a documentary on the eastern Polish border with Ukraine, Belarus, and the Russian exclave of Kaliningrad shot by director Christoph-Michael Adam in spring 2003 and shown on the German public television channel Phoenix.[2] The following example shows that this idea also resonated outside of Europe: as early as August 2000, Steven Erlanger titled his *New York Times* article "Poland Finds Itself the Border of West Europe" and stated dryly, "This is the border where Europe ends."[3]

At the same time, the enlargement in 2004 also opened doors for further states to join the EU, for example Ukraine. Ukraine's geostrategic significance was also described with *antemurale* topoi. In October 2000 Markus Wehner predicted in the *Frankfurter Allgemeine Zeitung* that Ukraine would become an important partner in European security policy soon after Poland's accession to the EU, and thus be a bulwark against illegal migration, drug smuggling, and illicit arms trafficking.[4] However, the EU's tightened border policy after the turn of the millennium also caused sharp criticism, especially in the left-leaning political camp. For example, the World Socialist Web Site, the online information center of the Trotskyist International Committee of the Fourth International (ICFI), alleged that the EU had turned its "external borders into a veritable bulwark against . . . refugees for whom it has become impossible to enter legally."[5]

Around the turn of the millennium, however, this bulwark discourse could mainly be found in Poland itself. It was charged with a lot of pathos and openly linked to older national self-portraits. The conservative daily newspaper *Rzeczpospolita* (Commonwealth or Republic) described the impending relocation of the EU's external border to Bug River in September 1998 as *przedmurze gospodarcze* (an economic forewall), adding with some pride, "Polish customs officers will protect the entire European Union."[6] In this context, traditional national topoi of the forewall of Christendom were reactivated by Polish journalists, as summarized in an article by the journalist and satirist Józef Burniewicz:

> In the Middle Ages, Poland was the pinnacle of the Papal empire against its eastern neighbors. . . . Today, our country, turned historically into the right direction, has taken over the role of the forerunner of EU interests. And true to the Sarmatian tradition, they guard these interests even at the expense of their own, that is our interests.[7]

Hence, we can find some interesting parallels as well as slight differences between *antemurale* thinking of the past and present. As Liliya Berezhnaya and Kerstin Jobst demonstrate in their chapters, at the turn of the nineteenth and twentieth centuries the denominational aspect still played a crucial role in the popularization of the *antemurale* topoi.

In Poland and Hungary, however, the secular momentum within the bulwark rhetoric has been more and more important since the very beginning of the nineteenth century. Defending Europe now also meant defending its secular values and the achievements of the Enlightenment against a despotic and barbarian East (i.e., Russia). As in the past, today it is paramount with regard to the "Othering" of Islamic societies and Russia (as demonstrated in Pål Kolstø's contribution). In fact, what has remained very significant for *antemurale* rhetoric since the early modern period is its alienating use to exclude political or religious dissidents within one's own country. And even if the question of inner societal walls, as shown by Jürgen Heyde and Ciprian Ghisa in the earlier examples, is today less articulated in some parts of Central and Eastern Europe, being a bulwark against inner enemies still plays a major (if not the main) role in the political discourse, especially of today's Poland and Hungary.

The Ukrainian Conflict and the European Refugee Crisis

The fact that the bulwark discourses analyzed in this book have not lost their relevance is shown by the recent events in Ukraine. Against the backdrop of the developments on the so-called Euromaidan between November 2013 and February 2014, as well as the subsequent tensions between Kyiv and Moscow over the Crimea and the status of the Russian minority in eastern and southern Ukraine, the bulwark argument was or is still used as a propaganda tool by the respective parties of the conflict, although it does not have such a long tradition in Ukraine as it does in other national traditions, as shown by Volodymyr Kravchenko in this volume. For the pro-Western Euromaidan movement as well as the West per se, Ukraine is considered as a "bulwark against Russian imperialism,"[8] while the Crimea itself has served, as Kerstin Jobst points out, as a bulwark due to Othering of the non-Orthodox societies. The project to build a 2,295-kilometer-long and heavily fortified defensive belt on the Ukrainian-Russian border was characteristically named *Stina* (wall) and was presented to the world public in autumn 2014 as a "European bulwark" against a genuinely "aggressive Russia" by the Ukrainian prime minister Arsenii Iatseniuk.[9]

Since the outbreak of the Ukrainian crisis, on the other hand, Moscow and the pro-Russian separatists in eastern and southern Ukraine have never tired of referring to the outpost role of Russia and the Russian-speaking regions in Ukraine against the west Ukrainians, who have since been denounced as neofascist puppets of the "imperialistic" United States and the EU.[10]

In turn, the crisis in Ukraine in 2014 brought vast parts of Central and Eastern Europe into the center of the West's attention, as the British publicist Nile Gardiner summarized in early June 2014, "By its sheer size alone, as the largest post-communist nation in the European Union, Poland carries significant weight. [It is] really the frontline of the NATO alliance, and, together with the Baltic states, a bulwark against Russia."[11]

Remarkably, this mixture of bulwark and messianic topoi is currently also experiencing a renaissance of interest in public debates in Poland and Hungary. Against the backdrop of the Ukrainian crisis and the current refugee issues, there is a growing body of populist opinion from the right, very strong in both countries, polemicizing against the "new threats" from the East and reactivating old *antemurale* images.[12]

However, whereas in the run-up to the EU accession of both countries in 2004, as shown before, the focus in the bastion rhetoric was more on the inclusion and the emphasis on belonging to a community (in this case, Europe or the European Union), the weight has clearly shifted to an excluding momentum: the defense of one's own country in particular or of one's own culture in general (i.e., Europe or the "Christian Occident") against several out-groups who are considered genuinely hostile is now in the foreground. The Hungarian state, for instance, once again sees itself as a bulwark of Western civilization against the "wicked" Muslim world—a bulwark, according to messianic ideas, abandoned by the rest of Europe, as recently described by Hungary's foreign minister Peter Szijarto: "What happened [the refugee problem] is the consequence of the failed migration policy of the European Union and the irresponsible statements made by European politicians."[13]

Similar Islamophobic slogans, filled with bulwark metaphors, can also be heard from the Polish Right. In September 2016, Elżbieta Witek, for instance, at that time press officer for the ruling Prawo i Sprawiedliwość ("Law and Justice," PiS) party, equated Poland's negative attitude on the refugee issue with the country's perseverance in the days of the early modern anti-Turkish and anti-Muscovite wars. It was the Poles who had once protected Europe from external enemies, and it is Poland again that is saving Europe from the new "flood of Islam." The merits of Poland have long been forgotten and repressed by Europe. According to Witek, all proposals from Brussels or Berlin regarding the division of refugees within the EU were not a sign of solidarity but rather a reckless dictation. In the past, Poland repeatedly risked its own welfare for the freedom of Europe:

The Poles have shown for centuries that freedom is a fundamental thing for them. Poles fought for the freedom of the United States, they were the most loyal soldiers of Napoleon, they co-liberated Belgium and the Netherlands [from National Socialist Germany], they took part in the Battle of Monte Cassino. We stopped the Turks [before Vienna 1683] as well as the onslaught of the Bolsheviks in 1920.[14]

Here Witek played on the numerous Polish-Turkish wars of the late Middle Ages and early modern times with the Battle of Vienna in 1683 as its culmination as well as the Miracle on the Vistula in Warsaw's Polish culture of remembrance in the wake of the Polish-Soviet war of 1919–1921.

Against the backdrop of this anti-Islamic mood in many parts of the population as well as in politics, it is not surprising that in Poland and Hungary, the Pegida (Patriotische Europäer gegen die Islamisierung des Abendlandes, "Patriotic Europeans against the Islamization of the Occident") movement, which originated in Germany, quickly found many imitators. In winter 2015–2016, for example, several major demonstrations Przeciw islamizacji Europy (Against the Islamization of Europe) took place in the largest Polish cities.[15] Unlike in Germany, however, the high attendance at such questionable events was not limited to a specific part of the country. While west of the Oder-Neisse border the Pegida demonstrations were mostly in the four-digit area in the new federal states, and the number of right-leaning so-called patriots were limited to a few hundred in West Germany, in Poland the demonstrations were quite large-scale events in all parts of the country. Unlike in Germany, the left-wing counterdemonstrations were also usually limited, even counting the counterdemonstrations, to just a few dozen persons, in comparison to the rest of Poland.

In Warsaw, for instance, Robert Winnicki, the leader of the far-right nationalistic party Ruch Narodowy (National Movement), declared that the goal of all such rallies held in Poland was to defend or repress the "immigrant raid" on Europe. In the eyes of the Polish new right-wing movement, Poland is now serving as a shining example for the whole of Central Europe and has taken on the leading role in this region as a defender of European culture and values. According to Winnicki,

> Central Europe is in a moderately good situation, because we do not have millions of Muslims at home, just like Germans do. The Germans envy us that we are a country so homogeneous—religiously homogeneous. Very good, we want to take care of it. We do not want Islamic districts in Poland.[16]

The marches of the Polish branch of the Pegida movement, which attracted several thousand visitors, were financially supported by the Młodzież Wszechpolska (All-Polish Youth), various ultras movements from the football milieu and right-wing populist, Euroskeptic and open-right parties such as the aforementioned National Movement, Kukiz'15, KORWiN (renamed Wolność, which means "Liberty," in October 2016) and Kongres Nowej Prawicy (Congress of the New Right). According to Winnicki, the demonstrations in Poland are only one part of a larger anti-Islamic movement in Europe.

Poland in particular—and here Winnicki refers to older bulwark pictures—would, as in previous centuries, play one of the most important roles in it and help "to build Europe into a fortress"[17] and to defend it against external enemies: "We want Poland to stay Poland; that there would be no Islamic neighborhoods here. That, by Western-European model, there were no robbers, rapes or even murders. We simply want to stop the wave of invasion of people from foreign cultural circles."[18] Representative of the Islamophobic attitude of the demonstrators was also the statement of the member of the Sejm (Polish Parliament) Adam Andruszkiewicz said, "We as the Polish people have the right to say whether we want Islamic immigrants or not. We say we do not want them. Period!"[19]

Bulwarks against Western Decadence: Central European Euroskepticism

Andruszkiewicz, who is a member of the newfound nationalistic party Wolni i Solidarni (Free and Solidary), originally got his parliamentary seat as a candidate on the list of the right-wing populist movement Kukiz'15. The latter won 8.8 percent of the votes in the 2015 parliamentary elections, making it the third strongest faction behind PiS and Platforma Obywatelska ("Civic Platform," PO). In another statement made on the public news channel TVP Info in early January 2018, Andruszkiewicz emphasized the tight relations between the nationalistic movements in Poland and Hungary and outlined the picture of both countries as defenders and supporters of the "real" European cause while simultaneously fighting the Islamic threat from the East and the decadent and corrupt (because mainly leftwing) West:

> The mad policy of France and Germany can lead to the breakdown of the project of a united Europe. It is not Poland and Hungary who want to destroy the idea for Europe, but we want a Europe of the fatherlands, not a Europe of Tusk, Juncker, and Timmermans, a Europe under the sign of the crescent. It is Poland and Hungary that are becoming the real Europe, and the rest of Europe is becoming a place where you can even die on New Year's Eve.[20]

This picture is also shared by Jarosław Kaczyński, the leader of the governing national-conservative PiS, who called the refugee crisis the biggest threat for Europe in decades. Simultaneously, he repeatedly spoke of "fortress Poland" and "fortress Europe" in his speeches—cleverly using these terms rhetorically as synonyms.[21]

The parliamentary elections in October 2016 also turned it into a vote on the country's immigration policy. With this rhetoric, the party chairman of the PiS joined the long line of right-wing populist Western and Central European parties, such as the French Rassemblement National (National Rally)—better known as the Front National (National Front)—led by Marine Le Pen, the UK Independence Party led by Nigel Farage, the Hungarian Orbán-led party Fidesz—Magyar Polgári Szövetség (Hungarian Civic Alliance, Fidesz)—the Austrian Freiheitliche Partei Österreichs ("Freedom Party of Austria," FPÖ), the Dutch Partij voor de Vrijheid ("Party for Freedom," PVV) with its openly anti-Islamic leader Geert Wilders, and not least the German Alternative für Deutschland ("Alternative for Germany," AfD). The repeated slogan that one should not make decisions for the people against their will proved to be a skilful move by the former prime minister Kaczyński. This statement implied that the previous, quite open-minded policy toward receiving refugees of the liberal-conservative PO, which was in power previously, was against the interests and desires of its own people and was therefore illegitimate.

Equating fortress Poland with fortress Europe should also give supporters as well as undecided voters an inclusive sense of belonging to something greater. The Euroskeptic PiS thus instrumentalized Europe for the courtship of its own voters and suggested that, in their anti-Islamic attitude, they wanted only the best for the rest of the continent, while the ruling PO, Brussels, as well as other left-wing EU states, including Angela Merkel's Germany, acted against Europe. On the other hand, Kaczyński endeavored to highlight the threat scenarios that had repeatedly been propagated as an appendage to the bulwark in the centuries before, which had warned against the flooding of Christian Europe by an essentially hostile and aggressive-expansionist Islamic world. Poland as a "land of freedom" will continue to defend the "freedom of Europe" from the unfree world of Islam in the future, Kaczyński said.[22]

Ironically, despite all the anti-Islamic, anti-immigrant, homophobic, and Euroskeptic positions he and his party took all those years, Kaczyński calls the Poland under the rule of PiS an "island of tolerance," as he stated in September 2017 at one of the monthly marches to mark the 2010 Polish Air Force Tu-154 crash in which inter alia his twin brother died:

> And be sure that we will have such a Poland. Nobody will impose on us from the outside. Even if in certain matters we remain alone in Europe, we will remain and we will be this island of freedom, tolerance, all that was so pres-

ent in our history. I repeat: the victory is close, we must simply continue patiently, with a full determination to move forward. As in these processions.[23]

Interestingly, Kaczyński's statements are similar to those of other right-wing politicians all over Europe. Meanwhile, anti-Islamic slogans are socially acceptable in large parts of the population in Germany, France, the United Kingdom, the Netherlands, Belgium, Switzerland, Denmark, Norway, Sweden, Italy, and other countries. Along with Poland, they played a major role in election campaigns in Austria, the Czech Republic, Slovakia, and Croatia. Most recently, the Euroskeptic right-wing Slovenska demokratska stranka ("Slovenian Democratic Party," SDS) rallying around its leader Janez Janša, who mainly built his campaign on anti-immigrant rhetoric, won the run for Slovenian parliament in June 2018—although a center-left coalition was finally formed around the second largest party, the List of Marjan Šarec, as the country's first minority government and, thus, the SDS had to go into opposition.

But it is Viktor Orbán, Janša's personal long-time ally from Hungary, who—in a similar fashion as Kaczyński and all the other right-wing politicians in Poland—in the last years mostly took advantage of the anti-Muslim atmosphere among his own population. Thus, it is not surprising that the Islamophobic statements of Orbán as well as of other Hungarian politicians from Fidesz or (even more alienating) the ultraradical nationalist Jobbik Magyarországért Mozgalom ("The Movement for a Better Hungary," Jobbik) resemble the slogans of the Polish right-wing mentioned above: Islam must be banned and Muslims generally driven out of Hungary and Europe. These and similar slogans have been recited time and time again by representatives of Fidesz and Jobbik over the past three years.

At the end of 2015, Orbán, an avowed Euroskeptic who opposes any further EU integration, compared his tough stance on the refugee issue with the perseverance of the medieval Kingdom of Hungary against the Ottoman threat, citing the status of the country as one of Europe's first "strongholds." The Hungarian prime minister compared the barrier fence built against illegal migrants along Hungary's borders with Serbia and Croatia in 2015 with a new bulwark against Islam.[24] Stopping illegal migrants was Orbán's core policy during his election campaign for a third straight term in winter and spring 2018: "Migration is like rust that slowly but surely would consume Hungary," the prime minister said at his final rally in April 2018.[25]

A popular motif in this revived bulwark rhetoric is the merging of old ideas in Poland and Hungary, according to which both countries would defend Europe from the East, on the one hand, and their own countries from the aggressive and dominant West, on the other. Both contemporary

Poland and Hungary would stand here as firm bulwarks of Christian Europe against Russia and the Islamic world, and, on the other hand, they also would fight against the supposedly socialist and thus politically diseased secular EU often denounced as a *Euro-kolkhoz*. Here again, as in the case of Ukraine, Georgia, and Russia as scrutinized by Pål Kolstø in this book, old resentments associated with the negative experiences of the communist era were refreshed and connected with the bulwark topos and spread to Brussels. Józef Burniewicz sarcastically summarized these bidirectional bulwark stereotypes in his abovementioned article:

> It turns out that the weather-beaten idea that Poland must be a firewall of something in this part of Europe because only then it will mean something, is still up to date. . . . The brave soldier Švejk would say with certainty that a country that, at the expense of its citizens, protects the EU's interests from its eastern neighbors and the Roman Curia's interests against its Western neighbors, suffers from schizophrenia.[26]

Healing Europe from external as well as internal threats became the core rhetoric of the national right in Poland and Hungary. Just recently, against the background of the Polish Independence Day commemorations in November 2017, Kaczyński underlined Poland's past and present role as a defender of Latin Christianity. In a sense, the leader of the PiS referred to older bulwark topoi when describing the Poles (meaning, of course, only the Catholic majority) as the only European people who finally and successfully will heal what is, in his eyes, a diseased Europe. He sees Europe as overrun by mostly Muslim immigrants and totally paralyzed and imprisoned by Brussels' bureaucracy: "Being a Pole . . . means being somebody who matters. Moreover, it means being someone who points the way for today's sick Europe toward recovery, the way toward fundamental values. The way back toward true liberty, the way toward victory and strengthening of our civilization based on Christianity."[27]

This rhetoric, built upon deeply Euroskeptic ideas of the Polish branch of Eurorealism,[28] however, was nothing new for Jarosław Kaczyński. It was found as early as the 2005 political program. While running for the Polish presidency, Kaczyński's brother Lech specified the main targets of the PiS in the foreword of the strategic paper "Polska katolicka w chrześcijańskiej Europie" (Catholic Poland in Christian Europe):

> For the decisive majority of us, the politicians, the activists and the members of PiS, the Catholic faith is simply the truth that gives us direction for our life and activity. For all of us, it is a value that has to be respected and defended. The content of this compendious work . . . is the commitment of PiS in the service of Christian values. It primarily covers our activities in the

national field, in all dimensions—from the material and tax laws of the family to the systemic foundations of the moral order. However, it goes further—it also shows the work of the members of PiS in the Strasbourg Parliament for Christian Europe. For we are aware that, as Julian Klaczko wrote, an independent Poland will not survive in Europe that is hostile to our values.[29]

These views are eagerly supported by the Catholic Church in Hungary and Poland, which is another parallel to the interwar period. Bishop László Kiss-Rigó of Szeged-Csanád gave the clearest expression to this new *antemurale* scenario, built upon fear, when he stated, "This is an invasion. They come here crying 'Allahu Akbar.' They want to take over."[30] Thus it is hardly surprising that the newly built 175-kilometer (109-mile) long and four-meter (13-foot) high fence along the southern border to Serbia is described exaltedly by the Hungarian Right as a new bulwark of Christianity.[31]

Interestingly, Polish and Hungarian Euroskepticism is not limited to these countries. It is a phenomenon very well known in other European countries. And as in Poland and Hungary, it is very often mixed with *antemurale* pictures. In Germany, for instance, the new right-wing involved in the Pegida movement sees itself as the new bulwark against a hostile non-European world, that is, the Islamic countries as well as "degenerate" enemies within as leftists, liberals, or other political activists who do not share their worldviews. Interestingly, in doing so they take up the bulwark rhetoric of the national-socialists from the 1920s, 1930s, and 1940s, who stylized Germany and (in the end days of World War II) Europe as a bulwark against savage Eastern Judeo-Bolshevism.[32]

The bulwark topos is even more popular these days in Austria, which—like Poland and Hungary—can look back on a long tradition of using this rhetoric. Similar to both countries, the so-called *Türkenkriege*—the early modern wars against the Ottoman Empire—as well as the two sieges of Vienna in 1529 and in particular 1683 play a major role in the Austrian collective memory and self-consciousness. This "frontier orientalism," as pointedly described by Andre Gingrich, has been one of the main recurring topics within Austrian nationalist discourse in the past few decades.[33]

And as in Polish and Hungarian right-wing parties, in Austria, anti-Islamic views have noticeably increased in the past several years in the political scene. A leading role here plays the nationalist conservative and populist party FPÖ, which gained 26 percent of the vote in nationwide 2017 legislative snap elections and entered government as the junior partner of the winner, the Euroskeptic Österreichische Volkspartei ("Austrian People's Party," ÖVP), with its chancellor Sebastian Kurz. Rejecting Islam from Europe is one of the major pillars of the FPÖ, as stated by one of its leaders, Johann Gudenus: "Islam has nothing to do with Europe. Islam is not part of

Europe; it is not part of it. The misconception that there could be a European Islam has long been refuted."[34]

Vienna and its history as a city, which resisted Ottoman armies in the early modern period twice, especially make the Austrian capital a sought-after goal for a lot of contemporary right-wing activists from all over Europe. Thus, it should not be surprising that Geert Wilders, the founder and current leader of the Dutch Euroskeptic and populist PVV, openly referred in his speech held in Vienna in March 2015, which was cited by many right-wing magazines, internet blogs, and forums, to the Austrian capital's role as Europe's forewall against Islam:

> Vienna is a worldwide symbol of resistance to Islam. In Vienna, the Islamic invasion of the West was stopped in 1683. Islam was defeated at the gates of Vienna. All of you and I are inside these gates. In the city that Islam could not defeat. And we have a clear message for Islam—the same message that king Jan Sobieski had when he hurried to Vienna in 1683 to defend the city from the Turks: They will not defeat Vienna! The clear message we have is that we will defeat Islam![35]

While referring to Sobieski and picking up the Polish momentum in the Austrian *antemurale* topoi, Wilders very finely showed in his speech the flexibility of the Central and Eastern European bulwark rhetoric, which—as it used to be in early modern times—returned to be a more and more transnational phenomenon. Wilders's speech also demonstrates the pan-European popularity of the bulwark myth. The strong affinity for the Central and Eastern European anti-Islamic and Euroskeptic governments and political parties can be found everywhere else among right-wing activists all over Europe. For them, these regions are portrayed as "the last barrier between Christianity and Islam" and the old and new self-declared bulwark status serves somehow as a holy grail. The Italian journalist Giulio Meotti summarizes it like this: "Like it or not, the last chance to save Europe's roots might well come from the former communist members of the EU—those who defeated the Ottomans in 1699 and now feel culturally threatened by their heirs."[36]

The Modern Bulwark Myth and the "Politics of Eternity"

As clearly demonstrated in other chapters of this book, the modern bulwark motives in these regions are a sort of what Timothy Snyder recently described as "politics of eternity."[37] Although Snyder used this metaphor to describe Russian politics, especially under the rule of Vladimir Putin, the term suits states in which the bulwark idea counts as one of the essential self-describing national myths very well. Snyder's "politics of eternity" places "one nation at the center of a cyclical story of victimhood," in our case the messianic victimhood of a country (Poland, Hungary, Austria, Croatia, Ukraine, Georgia, etc.) that is situated at the frontier of a cultural circle (Christian Europe) and that has, for centuries, eagerly and self-sacrificingly defended the hinterland from the supposedly barbarian and uncivilized out-groups (Muslims, schismatics, heretics, Muscovites, Bolsheviks, Asians, Africans, etc.).

Such constructions of alterities and alienities are constitutive for the bulwark topoi of frontier societies.[38] In this kind of alienating rhetoric, the periphery experiences an appreciation in importance, since it takes on important strategic functions as the defender of the cultural center lying farther inland. Whereas one hundred years ago *antemurale* topoi were mainly brought to the wider public via newspapers, propaganda posters, schoolbooks, maps, or paintings, as presented in this volume by Philipp Hofeneder, Stephen Norris, and Steven Seegel, today mass media such as television, radio, and, last but not least, the internet play the most important role in disseminating the picture of the aforementioned countries as bulwarks of the European hinterland and underlining their messianic mission.

It is not surprising that the bulwark topos was willingly instrumentalized by the national movements of the nineteenth and twentieth centuries in Central and Eastern Europe. The outpost rhetoric was used to reinforce and legitimize concepts of national or imperial identities and—as in the case of the Second Polish Republic in the interwar period—the resurgent striving for regional supremacy.

To this day, as shown in many chapters of this book, the image of a "forewall" or "bulwark" has remained an important, integrative anchor of identity and collective memory in Central and Eastern Europe. Interestingly, on the one hand, this bulwark rhetoric serves in the countries of the former mentioned region—Poland, Hungary, Croatia, Germany (in particular the new federal states), Austria, and so on—to demarcate from Eastern Europe and Asia (or even Africa), which are defamed as barbarous and backward, as well as from the "decadent" and "degenerated" West with the EU and Brussels as the representative aims of criticism of the new right-wing movements. Thus, it is not surprising that the idea of Central or of East Central Europe as in-between regions arose in these countries—beginning with the German idiom *Zwischeneuropa* concept from Oskar Halecki's "Jagiellonian Europe," who called the Eastern part of Central Europe "the borderlands of Western civilization."[39] For the latter, the *antemurale* topoi that occurred in Poland, Hungary, Croatia, and Austria in the Middle Ages and were strengthened in the early modern times were mirroring like nothing else the frontier self-attribution of these countries.

Drawing a significant line to delimit this part of Europe from a supposedly "backward" and often disavowed as "semi-Asian" Eastern Europe still plays a major role in the current national self-consciousnesses of Poland, Hungary, Croatia, and other East Central European countries.[40] Interestingly, on the other hand, the bulwark topoi were also successfully adapted by some Eastern European and Caucasian countries—for example, Ukraine, the Baltic states, and Georgia—to differentiate from the regions that lie more in the East (especially Russia and the Islamic world) and to underline their own allegiance to the European culture and value community by simultaneously denying their belonging to Eastern Europe or Asia.

However, this is nothing new to the bulwark rhetoric, for it has served—as demonstrated by Kerstin Weiand, Pål Kolstø, Heidi Hein-Kircher, and my own contribution on the Christian Right in interwar Poland and Hungary—as a principle for orientation since the late Middle Ages, attributing several countries with a sense of their own "Europeanness," that is, the affiliation to a Christian Occident or, in secular discourses, to Europe and the West. What is more, as far as domestic policy is concerned, it also forms the foundation for a rhetoric that promotes the exclusion of political opponents and dissidents. In this sense, twentieth-century Turkish nationalists in Zaur Gasimov's contribution have much in common with the contemporary national right policies of the Kaczyńskis or Orbáns. Being against such policies means undermining the Polish, Hungarian, Russian, Ukrainian, and other countries' bulwarks set against external and (what seems even more important nowadays in these societies) internal enemies, so the argumentation that is often leveled goes. Then again, in the self-conceptions of the right-wing parties, undermining the *antemuralia* means doing harm to their own nation as a whole and, supposedly as a consequence, to the European hinterland in particular.

The aforementioned examples from the past two decades show that the autostereotype of being a rampart nation is as present today in Central and Eastern Europe as it was in the nineteenth and twentieth centuries. To conclude, the bulwark topoi have been reloaded under the auspices of current resurgent nationalisms and populisms. And as in the past, they have definitely reinforced these movements. Their still valid flexibility is mirrored in their wide use within the modern mass media, especially in the various political portals, blogs, vlogs, forums, and such on the internet. Now the bulwark argument serves as a useful tool of the political Right that helps to exclude and alienate the presumed outer and inner enemies.

Paul Srodecki is a research assistant at the Christian-Albrechts-Universität zu Kiel in Germany. He is also the vice–project leader of the EU-funded research project "Collective Identity in Social Networks in East Central Europe" at the University of Ostrava, Czech Republic. His areas of research include the history of East Central Europe from the Middle Ages to modern times; identity, alterity, and alienity constructions; the history of the Crusades; and the history of political thought. He is the author of the monograph *Antemurale Christianitatis. Zur Genese der Bollwerksrhetorik im östlichen Mitteleuropa an der Schwelle vom Mittelalter zur Frühen Neuzeit* (Matthiesen Verlag, 2015).

Notes

1. B. Zandonella, *Pocket Europa. EU-Begriffe und Länderdaten* (Bonn: Bundeszentrale für politische Bildung, 2006), 48. See also J. Krause, *Die Grenzen Europas. Von der Geburt des Territorialstaats zum Europäischen Grenzregime* (Frankfurt a. M.: Peter Lang, 2009); D. Bingen and K. Wóycicki, eds., *Deutschland—Polen—Osteuropa. Deutsche und polnische Vorüberlegungen zu einer gemeinsamen Ostpolitik der erweiterten Europäischen Union* (Wiesbaden: Harrassowitz, 2002).
2. P. Srodecki, *Antemurale Christianitatis. Zur Genese der Bollwerksrhetorik im östlichen Mitteleuropa an der Schwelle vom Mittelalter zur Frühen Neuzeit* (Husum: Matthiesen Verlag, 2015), 11.
3. S. Erlanger, "Poland Finds Itself the Border Cop of West Europe," *New York Times*, 28 August 2000, retrieved 26 May 2018 from http://www.nytimes.com/2000/08/28/world/poland-finds-itself-the-border-cop-of-west-europe.html.
4. M. Wehner, "Die Ukraine will nicht aus Europa ausgeschlossen werden. Die Ostgrenze aus östlicher Sicht," *Frankfurter Allgemeine Zeitung*, 11 October 2000, 3. See R. Lindner, "Die Ukraine und Deutschland im neuen Europa," in *Die neue Ukraine. Gesellschaft—Wirtschaft—Politik (1991–2001)*, ed. G. Simon (Köln, Weimar, and Wien: Böhlau, 2002), 302 passim.
5. B. Fehlau, "EU-Osterweiterung und die Grenzen," *World Socialist Web Site*, 26 April 2001, retrieved 26 May 2018 from http://www.wsws.org/de/articles/2001/04/pole-a26.html.
6. J.B. "Polscy celnicy będą chronić całą Unię Europejską," *Rzeczpospolita*, 24 September 1998, retrieved 26 May 2018 from http://archiwum.rp.pl/artykul/194367-Przed murze-gospodarcze.html.
7. J. Burniewicz, "Szwejk stawia Polsce diagnozę," *Polytikier*, 12 April 2013, retrieved from http://politykier.pl/kat,126154,wid,15490577,wiadomosc.html?ticaid=610d4b (file is not accessible).
8. Z. Brzezinski, "Zbigniew Brzezinski Offers Support for Ukraine's EuroMaidan (VIDEO)," *Kyiv Post. Ukraine's Global Voice*, 15 January 2014, retrieved 26 May 2018 from http://www.kyivpost.com/opinion/op-ed/brzezinski-offers-support-for-ukraines-euromaidan-video-334984.html. See also "Bollwerk gegen Putin. Ukraine flirtet mit den Oligarchen," *ntv*, 25 March 2014, retrieved 26 May 2018 from http://www.n-tv.de/politik/Ukraine-flirtet-mit-den-Oligarchen-article12533111.html; P. Sonne, "Rivals Clash on Crimea's Fate," *The Wall Street Journal*, 26 February 2014, retrieved 26 May 2018 from https://www.wsj.com/articles/protests-

stoke-fears-over-crimean-separatism-1393415227; S. Jenkins, "Crimea: All This Virile Cold War Talk Won't Force Vladimir Putin to Slink Back," *The Guardian*, 25 March 2014, retrieved 26 May 2018 from http://www.theguardian.com/commentisfree/2014/mar/25/crimea-cold-war-vladimir-putin-russia.
9. V. Noskov, "Ukraine Builds a 'European Bulwark' to Separate Itself from Aggressive Russia," *Euromaidan Press. News and Views from Ukraine*, 15 October 2014, retrieved 26 May 2018 from http://euromaidanpress.com/2014/10/15/ukraine-builds-a-european-bulwark-to-separate-itself-from-aggressive-russia/.
10. T. Bancroft-Hinchey, "The Incoherence of Western Foreign Policy," *PRAVDA.Ru*, 6 June 2014, retrieved 26 May 2018 from http://english.pravda.ru/opinion/columnists/06-06-2014/127751-western_incoherence-0/; "Eastern Ukrainian City of Donetsk Rallies in Favor of Independence Referendum," *Russia Today*, 5 April 2014, retrieved 26 May 2018 from http://rt.com/news/ukraine-donetsk-rally-referendum-601.
11. M. Snowiss, "Poland 'Frontline' in US Effort on Ukraine," *Voice of America News*, 3 June 2014, retrieved 26 May 2018 from https://www.voanews.com/a/poland-frontline-in-us-effort-on-ukraine/1928449.html.
12. See also Pål Kolstø's contribution to this volume.
13. T. Piatak, "The New Bulwark of Christendom," *Chronicles. A Magazine of American Culture*, 9 September 2015, retrieved 9 November 2016 from https://www.chroniclesmagazine.org/the-new-bulwark-of-christendom/.
14. "PiS: To Polska obroniła Europę przed Turkami i bolszewią. O tym trzeba pamiętać!," *Fronda—Portal poświęcony*, 10 September 2015, retrieved from http://www.fronda.pl/a/pis-to-polska-obronila-europe-przed-turkami-i-bolszewia-o-tym-trzeba-pamietac,56666.html 2605.2018.
15. "By Polska pozostała Polską. Protest przeciw islamskim migrantom z udziałem szefowej niemieckiej PEGIDY," *TVP Info*, 2 February 2016, retrieved 26 May 2018 from https://www.tvp.info/23917179/by-polska-pozostala-polska-protest-przeciw-islamskim-migrantom-z-udzialem-szefowej-niemieckiej-pegidy.
16. "Manifestacje przeciwko imigrantom. W Warszawie pod hasłem 'przeciw islamizacji' Europy," *Polsatnews*, 6 February 2016, retrieved 3 June 2018 from http://www.polsatnews.pl/wiadomosc/2016-02-06/manifestacje-przeciwko-imigrantom-w-warszawie-pod-haslem-przeciw-islamizacji-europy/.
17. "W Warszawie odbyła się manifestacja 'Przeciw islamizacji Europy,'" *Parlamentarny*, 6 February 2016, retrieved 26 May 2018 from http://www.parlamentarny.pl/wydarzenia/w-warszawie-odbyla-sie-manifestacja-przeciw-islamizacji-europy,5218.html.
18. "By Polska pozostała Polską."
19. "Przeciwnicy przyjmowania nielegalnych imigrantów manifestowali w Warszawie," in *Polityka.pl*, 6 February 2016, retrieved 26 May 2018 from https://wpolityce.pl/spoleczenstwo/280814-przeciwnicy-przyjmowania-nielegalnych-imigrantow-manifestowali-w-warszawie.
20. "UE zmierza ku przepaści? Andruszkiewicz: 'My chcemy Europy Ojczyzn, a nie Europy Tuska, Junckera i Timmermansa, pod znakiem półksiężyca," *Polityka.pl*, 2 January 2018, retrieved 26 May 2018 from https://wpolityce.pl/polityka/374605-ue-zmierza-ku-przepasci-andruszkiewicz-my-chcemy-europy-ojczyzn-a-nie-europy-tuska-junckera-i-timmermansa-pod-znakiem-polksiezyca.

21. See esp. Jarosław Kaczyński's speech in the Polish Sejm in September 2015: "Mocne przemówienie! Jarosław Kaczyński w Sejmie o imigrantach," in *Portal wPolityce.pl*, 15 September 2015, retrieved 26 May 2018 from https://www.youtube.com/watch?v=fYcVL_CLxRU.
22. Ibid.
23. "Jarosław Kaczyński na miesięcznicy: będziemy wyspą wolności i tolerancji w Europie," *Niezależna.pl*, 10 September 2017, retrieved 26 May 2018 from http://niezalezna.pl/202885-jaroslaw-kaczynski-na-miesiecznicy-bedziemy-wyspa-wolnosci-i-tolerancji-w-europie-wideo.
24. "The Guardian View on Hungary and the Refugee Crisis: Orbán the Awful," *The Guardian*, 6 September 2015, retrieved 4 May 2018 from http://www.theguardian.com/commentisfree/2015/sep/06/the-guardian-view-on-hungaryand-the-refugee-crisis-orban-the-awful.
25. "Hungary Election. Victor Orban's Fidesz Party Hopes for Third Straight Term," 8 April 2018, retrieved 2 May 2018 from http://www.bbc.com/news/world-europe-43687870.
26. Burniewicz, "Szwejk."
27. J. Kaczyński's speech held 10 November 2017 at the Piłsudski Square in Warsaw: "Jarosław Kaczyński."
28. See W. Paruch, "W obronie interesów narodowych i tożsamości politycznej Europy Środkowo-Wschodniej. Eurorealizm w myśli politycznej Prawa i Sprawiedliwości," in *Rodzinna Europa. Europejska myśl polityczno-prawna u progu XXI wieku*, ed. P. Fiktus, H. Malewski, and M. Marszał (Wrocław: Uniwersytet Wrocławski, 2015), 413–24; G. Załęski, *Eurosceptycyzm* (Rzeszów: Uniwersytet Rzeszowki, 2013); K. Zuba, *Polski eurosceptycyzm i eurorealizm* (Opole: Wydawnictwo Uniwersytetu Opolskiego, 2006).
29. L. Kaczyński, "Wstęp," in *Polska katolicka w chrześcijańskiej Europie*, ed. Komitet Wyborczy Prawo i Sprawiedliwość (Warszawa: Komitet Wyborczy Prawo i Sprawiedliwość, 2005), 7.
30. Piatak, "New Bulwark."
31. T. Stark, "Európa és a kereszténység védőbástyája?," *HVG*, 22 September 2015, retrieved 9 November 2016 from http://hvg.hu/velemeny/20150922_Europa_es_a_keresztenyseg_vedobastyaja); T. Várkonyi, "A kereszténység védőbástyája," *NSZ. Népszava online*, 20 October 2015, retrieved 9 November 2016 from http://nepszava.hu/cikk/1073668-a-keresztenyseg-vedobastyaja/.
32. See F. Finkbeiner, "Pegida: Wieder mal die Rettung des Abendlandes," *Blickpunkt WiSo*, 4 March 2015, retrieved 3 June 2018 from https://www.blickpunkt-wiso.de/post/1492/print/; R. Hank, "Abendland war stets ein Kampfbegriff," *Frankfurter Allgemeine Zeitung*, 22 December 2014, retrieved 3 June 2018 from http://www.faz.net/aktuell/wirtschaft/wirtschaftspolitik/pegida-abendland-war-stets-ein-kampfbegriff-13333220.html; V. Plichta, "Reich—Europa—Abendland. Zur Pluralität deutscher Europaideen im 20. Jahrhundert," *Vorgänge. Zeitschrift für Bürgerrechte und Gesellschaftspolitik* 154 (2001): 60–69.
33. A. Gingrich, "Blame It on the Turks: Language Regimes and the Culture of Frontier Orientalism in Eastern Austria," in *Diskurs—Politik –Identität. Festschrift für Ruth Wodak*, ed. R. Wodak and R. de Cillia (Tübingen: Stauffenburg Verlag, 2010), 71–81; Gingrich, "Frontier Myths of Orientalism: The Muslim World in Public and

Popular Cultures of Central Europe," *MESS. Mediterranean Ethnological Summer School* 2 (1998): 99–127; Gingrich, "The Nearby Frontier: Structural Analyses of Myths of Orientalism," *Diogenes* 60, no. 2 (2015): 60–66. See F. Hafez, *Islamophober Populimus. Moschee- und Minarettbauverbote österreichischer Parlamentsparteien* (Wiesbaden: Verlag für Sozialwissenschaften, 2010).

34. R. Eisenreich and M. Krupa, "Sie wollen nicht beißen, nur rauchen. Seit Kurzem regiert in Österreich die rechte FPÖ—und gibt sich ungewohnt handzahm. Hat sich die Partei geändert?" *DIE ZEIT* 53 (2017), retrieved 3 June 2018 from https://www.zeit.de/2017/53/fpoe-oesterreich-heinz-christian-strache-partei-ziele/seite-2.
35. "Wilders in Wien: Johann Sobieski lebt in uns!" *PI-NEWS (Politically Incorrect)*, 27 March 2015, retrieved 3 June 2018 from http://www.pi-news.net/2015/03/wilders-in-wien-johann-sobieski-lebt-in-uns/.
36. G. Meotti, "Eastern Europe. The Last Barrier between Christianity and Islam," *Gatestone Institute. International Policy Council*, 20 September 2016, retrieved 3 June 2018 from https://www.gatestoneinstitute.org/8972/eastern-europe-christianity-islam.
37. T. Snyder, *The Road to Unfreedom: Russia, Europe, America* (New York: Tim Duggan Books, 2018).
38. P. Srodecki, "Die Angst vor dem Osten. Europa und die religiöse motivierten Identitäts-, Alteritäts- und Alienitätskonstruktionen im Mittelalter und der Frühen Neuzeit," in *Identitätsentwürfe im östlichen Europa – im Spannungsfeld von Selbst- und Fremdwahrnehmung*, ed. H.-J. Bömelburg, M. Kirchner, M. Koller, and M. Wingender (Wiesbaden: Harrassowitz, 2018), 11–34; P. Srodecki, "Antemurale-Based Frontier Identities in East Central Europe and Their Ideological Roots in Medieval/Early Modern Alterity And Alienity Discourses," in *Collective Identity in the Context of Medieval Studies*, ed. M. Antonín Malaníková and R. Antonín (Ostrava: Filozofická fakulta OU, 2016), 97–120.
39. O. Halecki, *The Limits and Divisions of European History* (London and New York: Sheed & Ward, 1950); O. Halecki, *Borderlands of Western Civilization: A History of East Central Europe* (New York: Ronald Press, 1952); O. Halecki, "Idea jagiellońska," *Kwartalnik Historyczny* 51, nos. 1–2 (1937): 486–510; G. Wirsing, *Zwischeneuropa und die deutsche Zukunft* (Jena: Diederichs, 1932). See H. Konrad and M. Stromberger, "Der kurze Traum von Selbstständigkeit. Zwischeneuropa," in *Globalgeschichte. Die Welt 1000–2000*, vol. 7: *Die Welt im 20. Jahrhundert nach 1945*, ed. W.L. Bernecker (Wien: Mandelbaum-Verlag, 2010), 54–79; H.-J. Bömelburg, "Zwischen imperialer Geschichte und Ostmitteleuropa als Geschichtsregion. Oskar Halecki und die polnische 'jagiellonische Idee,'" in *Vergangene Größe und Ohnmacht in Ostmitteleuropa. Repräsentationen imperialer Erfahrung in der Historiographie seit 1918*, ed. F. Hadler and M. Mesenhöller (Leipzig: Akademische Verlagsanstalt, 2007), 99–133; S. Höhne, "Mitteleuropa. Zur konzeptuellen Karriere eines kulturpolitischen Begriffs," *Bohemia* 41, no. 2 (2000): 279–94; F. Hadler, "Mitteleuropa—Zwischeneuropa—Ostmitteleuropa. Reflexionen über eine europäische Geschichtsregion im 19. Und 20. Jahrhundert," *Berichte und Beiträge des Geisteswissenschaftlichen Zentrums Geschichte und Kultur Ostmitteleuropas* 1 (1996): 34–41.
40. See N. Porta, *Auf der Suche nach einer eigenen Identität zwischen Osten und Westen, die Mitteleuropa-Konzeption bei Czesław Miłosz, Jan Patočka und Milan Kundera* (Herne: Gabriele Schäfer Verlag, 2014); O. Tokarczuk, "Fantom Europy

Środkowej przegląda się w literaturze. Czy istnieje powieść środkowoeuropejska?" in *Perspectives on Contemporary East European Literature. Beyond National and Regional Frames*, ed. K. Abe (Sapporo: Hokkaido University, 2016), 17–36; M. Font, "Mitteleuropa—Osteuropa—Ostmitteleuropa? Bemerkungen zur Entstehung einer europäischen Randregion im Frühmittelalter," *Jahrbuch für Europäische Geschichte* 7 (2006): 101–25; J. Kłoczowski, I. Goral, H. Łaszkiewicz, G. Wróblewski, K. Deryło, S. Bylina, et al., eds., *Central Europe between East and West* (Lublin: Instytut Europy Środkowo-Wschodniej, 2005); P. Haslinger, ed., *Grenze im Kopf. Beiträge zur Geschichte der Grenze in Ostmitteleuropa* (Frankfurt a. M.: Peter Lang Verlag, 1999); J. Szűcs, *Les trois Europes* (Paris: L'Harmattan, 1985).

Bibliography

"Eastern Ukrainian City of Donetsk Rallies in Favor of Independence Referendum." 2014. *Russia Today*. 5 April. Retrieved 26 May 2018 from http://rt.com/news/ukraine-donetsk-rally-referendum-601.

B., J. 1998. "Polscy celnicy będą chronić całą Unię Europejską." *Rzeczpospolita*, 24 September. Retrieved 26 May 2018 from http://archiwum.rp.pl/artykul/194367-Przed murze-gospodarcze.html.

Bancroft-Hinchey, T. 2014. "The Incoherence of Western Foreign Policy." *PRAVDA.Ru*. 6 June. Retrieved 26 May 2018 from http://english.pravda.ru/opinion/columnists/06-06-2014/127751-western_incoherence-0/.

Bingen, D., and K. Wóycicki, eds. 2002. *Deutschland—Polen—Osteuropa: Deutsche und polnische Vorüberlegungen zu einer gemeinsamen Ostpolitik der erweiterten Europäischen Union*. Wiesbaden: Harrassowitz.

"Bollwerk gegen Putin. Ukraine flirtet mit den Oligarchen." 2014. *ntv*, 25 March. Retrieved 26 May 2018 from http://www.n-tv.de/politik/Ukraine-flirtet-mit-den-Oli garchen-article12533111.html.

Bömelburg, H.-J. 2007. "Zwischen imperialer Geschichte und Ostmitteleuropa als Geschichtsregion: Oskar Halecki und die polnische 'jagiellonische Idee.'" In *Vergangene Größe und Ohnmacht in Ostmitteleuropa: Repräsentationen imperialer Erfahrung in der Historiographie seit 1918*, ed. F. Hadler and M. Mesenhöller, 99–133. Leipzig: Akademische Verlagsanstalt.

Brzezinski, Z. 2014. "Zbigniew Brzezinski offers support for Ukraine's EuroMaidan (VIDEO)." *Kyiv Post. Ukraine's Global Voice*. 15 January. Retrieved 26 May 2018 from http://www.kyivpost.com/opinion/op-ed/brzezinski-offers-support-for-ukra ines-euromaidan-video-334984.html.

Burniewicz, J. 2013. "Szwejk stawia Polsce diagnose." *Polytikier*. 12 April. Retrieved 15 October 2014 from http://politykier.pl/kat,126154,wid,15490577,wiadomosc .html?ticaid=610d4b.

"By Polska pozostała Polską. Protest przeciw islamskim migrantom z udziałem szefowej niemieckiej PEGIDY." 2016. *TVP Info*. 2 February. Retrieved 26 May 2018 from https://www.tvp.info/23917179/by-polska-pozostala-polska-protest-przeciw-is lamskim-migrantom-z-udzialem-szefowej-niemieckiej-pegidy.

Eisenreich, R. and M. Krupa. 2017. "Sie wollen nicht beißen, nur rauchen. Seit Kurzem regiert in Österreich die rechte FPÖ—und gibt sich ungewohnt handzahm. Hat sich die Partei geändert?" *DIE ZEIT* 53. Retrieved 3 June 2018 from https://www.zeit.de/2017/53/fpoe-oesterreich-heinz-christian-strache-partei-ziele/seite-2.

Erlanger, S. 2000. "Poland Finds Itself the Border Cop of West Europe." *New York Times.* 28 August. Retrieved 26 May 2018 from http://www.nytimes.com/2000/08/28/world/poland-finds-itself-the-border-cop-of-west-europe.html.

Fehlau, B. 2001. "EU-Osterweiterung und die Grenzen," *World Socialist Web Site.* 26 April. Retrieved 26 May 2018 from http://www.wsws.org/de/articles/2001/04/pole-a26.html.

Finkbeiner, F. 2015. "Pegida: Wieder mal die Rettung des Abendlandes." *Blickpunkt WiSo.* 4 March Retrieved 3 June 2018 from https://www.blickpunkt-wiso.de/post/1492/print/.

Font, M. 2006. "Mitteleuropa—Osteuropa—Ostmitteleuropa? Bemerkungen zur Entstehung einer europäischen Randregion im Frühmittelalter." *Jahrbuch für Europäische Geschichte* 7: 101–25.

Gingrich, A. 1998. "Frontier Myths of Orientalism: The Muslim World in Public and Popular Cultures of Central Europe." *MESS. Mediterranean Ethnological Summer School* 2: 99–127.

———. 2010. "Blame It on the Turks: Language Regimes and the Culture of Frontier Orientalism in Eastern Austria." In *Diskurs—Politik –Identität. Festschrift für Ruth Wodak,* ed. R Wodak and R. de Cillia, 71–81. Tübingen: Stauffenburg Verlag.

———. 2015. "The Nearby Frontier: Structural Analyses of Myths of Orientalism." *Diogenes* 60, no. 2: 60–66.

Hadler, F. 1996. "Mitteleuropa—Zwischeneuropa—Ostmitteleuropa. Reflexionen über eine europäische Geschichtsregion im 19. und 20. Jahrhundert." *Berichte und Beiträge des Geisteswissenschaftlichen Zentrums Geschichte und Kultur Ostmitteleuropas* 1: 34–41.

Hafez, F. 2010. *Islamophober Populimus. Moschee- und Minarettbauverbote österreichischer Parlamentsparteien.* Wiesbaden: VS Verlag für Sozialwissenschaften.

Halecki, O. 1937. "Idea jagiellońska." *Kwartalnik Historyczny* 51, nos. 1–2: 486–510.

———. 1950. *The Limits and Divisions of European History.* London and New York: Sheed & Ward.

———. 1952. *Borderlands of Western Civilization: A History of East Central Europe.* New York: Ronald Press.

Hank, R. 2014. "Abendland war stets ein Kampfbegriff." *Frankfurter Allgemeine Zeitung.* 22 December. Retrieved 3 June 2018 from http://www.faz.net/aktuell/wirtschaft/wirtschaftspolitik/pegida-abendland-war-stets-ein-kampfbegriff-13333220.html.

Haslinger, P., ed. 1999. *Grenze im Kopf. Beiträge zur Geschichte der Grenze in Ostmitteleuropa.* Frankfurt a. M.: Peter Lang Verlag.

Höhne, S. 2000. "Mitteleuropa. Zur konzeptuellen Karriere eines kulturpolitischen Begriffs." *Bohemia* 41, no. 2: 279–94.

"Hungary Election. Victor Orban's Fidesz Party Hopes for Third Straight Term." 2018. 8 April. Retrieved 2 May 2018 from http://www.bbc.com/news/world-europe-43687870.

"Jarosław Kaczyński na miesięcznicy: będziemy wyspą wolności i tolerancji w Europie." 2017. *Niezależna.pl.* 10 September. Retrieved 26 May 2018 from http://niezalezna.pl/202885-jaroslaw-kaczynski-na-miesiecznicy-bedziemy-wyspa-wolnosci-i-tolerancji-w-europie-wideo.

"Jarosław Kaczyński: w stulecie odzyskania niepodległości rany powinny się zabliźnić." 2017. 10 November. Retrieved 23 April 2018 from http://www.tvp.info/34771308/jaroslaw-kaczynski-w-stulecie-odzyskania-niepodleglosci-rany-powinny-siezabliznic.

Jenkins, S. 2014. "Crimea: All This Virile Cold War Talk Won't Force Vladimir Putin to Slink Back." *The Guardian*. 25 March. Retrieved 26 May 2018 from http://www.theguardian.com/commentisfree/2014/mar/25/crimea-cold-war-vladimir-putin-russia.

Kaczyński, L. 2005. "Wstęp." In *Polska katolicka w chrześcijańskiej Europie*, ed. Komitet Wyborczy Prawo i Sprawiedliwość. Warszawa: Komitet Wyborczy Prawo i Sprawiedliwość, 7–10.

Kłoczowski, J., I. Goral, H. Łaszkiewicz, G. Wróblewski, K. Deryło, S. Bylina, et al., eds. 2005. *Central Europe between East and West*. Lublin: Instytut Europy Środkowo-Wschodniej.

Konrad, H. and M. Stromberger. 2010. "Der kurze Traum von Selbstständigkeit. Zwischeneuropa." In *Globalgeschichte. Die Welt 1000–2000*, vol. 7: *Die Welt im 20. Jahrhundert nach 1945*, ed. W.L. Bernecker, 54–79. Wien: Mandelbaum-Verlag.

Krause, J. 2009. *Die Grenzen Europas. Von der Geburt des Territorialstaats zum Europäischen Grenzregime*. Frankfurt a. M.: Peter Lang.

Lindner, R. 2002. "Die Ukraine und Deutschland im neuen Europa." In *Die neue Ukraine. Gesellschaft—Wirtschaft—Politik (1991–2001)*, ed. G. Simon, 297–320. Köln, Weimar, and Wien: Böhlau.

"Manifestacje przeciwko imigrantom. W Warszawie pod hasłem 'przeciw islamizacji' Europy." 2016. *Polsatnews*. 6 February. Retrieved 3 June 2018 from http://www.polsatnews.pl/wiadomosc/2016-02-06/manifestacje-przeciwko-imigrantom-w-warszawie-pod-haslem-przeciw-islamizacji-europy/.

Meotti, G. 2016. "Eastern Europe. The Last Barrier between Christianity and Islam." *Gatestone Institute. International Policy Council*. 20 September. Retrieved 3 June 2018 from https://www.gatestoneinstitute.org/8972/eastern-europe-christianity-islam.

"Mocne przemówienie! Jarosław Kaczyński w Sejmie o imigrantach." 2015. *Portal wPolityce*. 15 September. Retrieved 26 May 2018 from https://www.youtube.com/watch?v=fYcVL_CLxRU.

Noskov, V. 2014. "Ukraine Builds a 'European Bulwark' to Separate Itself from Aggressive Russia." *Euromaidan Press. News and Views from Ukraine*. 15 October. Retrieved 26 May 2018 from http://euromaidanpress.com/2014/10/15/ukraine-builds-a-european-bulwark-to-separate-itself-from-aggressive-russia/.

Paruch, W. 2015. "W obronie interesów narodowych i tożsamości politycznej Europy Środkowo-Wschodniej. Eurorealizm w myśli politycznej Prawa i Sprawiedliwości." In *Rodzinna Europa. Europejska myśl polityczno-prawna u progu XXI wieku*, ed. P. Fiktus, H. Malewski, and M. Marszał, 413–24. Wrocław: Uniwersytet Wrocławski.

Piatak, T. 2015. "The New Bulwark of Christendom." *Chronicles. A Magazine of American Culture*. 9 September. Retrieved 9 September 2016 from https://www.chroniclesmagazine.org/the-new-bulwark-of-christendom/.

"PiS: To Polska obroniła Europę przed Turkami i bolszewią. O tym trzeba pamiętać!" 2015. *Fronda—Portal poświęcony*. 10 September. Retrieved 26 May 2018 from http://www.fronda.pl/a/pis-to-polska-obronila-europe-przed-turkami-i-bolszewia-o-tym-trzeba-pamietac,56666.html.

Plichta, V. 2001. "Reich—Europa—Abendland. Zur Pluralität deutscher Europaideen im 20. Jahrhundert." *Vorgänge. Zeitschrift für Bürgerrechte und Gesellschaftspolitik* 154: 60–69.

Porta, N. 2014. *Auf der Suche nach einer eigenen Identität zwischen Osten und Westen, die Mitteleuropa-Konzeption bei Czesław Miłosz, Jan Patočka und Milan Kundera.* Herne: Gabriele Schäfer Verlag.

"Przeciwnicy przyjmowania nielegalnych imigrantów manifestowali w Warszawie." 2016. *wPolitce.pl.* 6 February. Retrieved 26 May 2018 from https://wpolityce.pl/spolec zenstwo/280814-przeciwnicy-przyjmowania-nielegalnych-imigrantow-manifes towali-w-warszawie.

Snowiss, M. 2014. "Poland 'Frontline' in US Effort on Ukraine." *Voice of America News.* 3 June. Retrieved 26 May 2018 from https://www.voanews.com/a/poland-frontline-in-us-effort-on-ukraine/1928449.html.

Snyder, T. 2018. *The Road to Unfreedom: Russia, Europe, America.* New York: Tim Duggan Books.

Sonne, P. 2014. "Rivals Clash on Crimea's Fate." *Wall Street Journal.* 26 February. Retrieved 26 May 2018 from https://www.wsj.com/articles/protests-stoke-fears-over-crimean-separatism-1393415227.

Srodecki, P. 2015. *Antemurale Christianitatis. Zur Genese der Bollwerksrhetorik im östlichen Mitteleuropa an der Schwelle vom Mittelalter zur Frühen Neuzeit.* Husum: Matthiesen Verlag.

———. 2016. "Antemurale-Based Frontier Identities in East Central Europe and Their Ideological Roots in Medieval/Early Modern Alterity and Alienity Discourses." In *Collective Identity in the Context of Medieval Studies,* ed. M. Antonín Malaníková and R. Antonín, 97–120. Ostrava: Filozofická fakulta OU.

———. 2018. "Die Angst vor dem Osten. Europa und die religiöse motivierten Identitäts-, Alteritäts- und Alienitätskonstruktionen im Mittelalter und der Frühen Neuzeit." In *Identitätsentwürfe im östlichen Europa – im Spannungsfeld von Selbst- und Fremdwahrnehmung,* ed. H.-J. Bömelburg, M. Kirchner, M. Koller, and M. Wingender, 11–34. Wiesbaden: Harrassowitz Verlag.

Stark, T. 2015. "Európa és a kereszténység védőbástyája?" *HVG.* 22 September. Retrieved 9 September 2016 from http://hvg.hu/velemeny/20150922_Europa_es _a_keresztenyseg_vedobastyaja.

Szűcs, J. 1985. *Les trois Europes.* Paris: L'Harmattan.

"The Guardian View on Hungary and the Refugee Crisis: Orbán the Awful." 2015. *The Guardian.* 6 September. Retrieved 4 May 2018 from http://www.theguardian .com/commentisfree/2015/sep/06/the-guardian-view-on-hungaryand-the-refu gee-crisis-orban-the-awful.

Tokarczuk, O. 2016. "Fantom Europy Środkowej przegląda się w literaturze. Czy istnieje powieść środkowoeuropejska?" In *Perspectives on Contemporary East European Literature: Beyond National and Regional Frames,* ed. K. Abe, 17–36. Sapporo: Hokkaido University.

"UE zmierza ku przepaści? Andruszkiewicz: My chcemy Europy Ojczyzn, a nie Europy Tuska, Junckera i Timmermansa, pod znakiem półksiężyca." 2018. *wPolityce.pl.* 2 January. Retrieved 26 May 2018 from https://wpolityce.pl/polityka/374605-ue-zmierza-ku-przepasci-andruszkiewicz-my-chcemy-europy-ojczyzn-a-nie-euro py-tuska-junckera-i-timmermansa-pod-znakiem-polksiezyca.

Várkonyi, T. 2015. "A kereszténység védőbástyája." *NSZ. Népszava online.* 20 October. Retrieved 9 September 2016 from http://nepszava.hu/cikk/1073668-a-kereszten yseg-vedobastyaja/.

"W Warszawie odbyła się manifestacja 'Przeciw islamizacji Europy.'" 2016. *Parlamentarny.* 6 February. Retrieved 26 May 2018 from http://www.parlamentarny.pl/wy darzenia/w-warszawie-odbyla-sie-manifestacja-przeciw-islamizacji-europy,5218 .html.

Wehner, M. 2000. "Die Ukraine will nicht aus Europa ausgeschlossen werden. Die Ostgrenze aus östlicher Sicht." *Frankfurter Allgemeine Zeitung,* 11 October, 3.

"Wilders in Wien: Johann Sobieski lebt in uns!" 2015. *PI-NEWS (Politically Incorrect).* 27 March. Retrieved 3 June 2018 from http://www.pi-news.net/2015/03/ wilders-in-wien-johann-sobieski-lebt-in-uns/.

Wirsing, G. 1932. *Zwischeneuropa und die deutsche Zukunft.* Jena: Diederichs.

Załęski, G. 2013. *Eurosceptycyzm.* Rzeszów: Uniwersytet Rzeszowki.

Zandonella, B. 2006. *Pocket Europa. EU-Begriffe und Länderdaten.* Bonn: Bundeszentrale für politische Bildung.

Zuba, K. 2006. *Polski eurosceptycyzm i eurorealizm.* Opole: Wydawnictwo Uniwersytetu Opolskiego.

Index

The letter *f* after a page number denotes a figure.

Adam, Christoph-Michael, 375
Adıvar, Halide Edip, 189
Agaphangel, Metropolitan, 168
Akçura(oğlu), Yusuf, 189
albantsy, 129–30
Alexander III, Tsar, 136
Alexander VII, Pope, 93
Alyosha Popovich, 322, 327
Amvrosii (Lototskii), Archimandrite, 157
Andrew (Pervozvannyi), Apostle, 132
Andruszkiewicz, Adam, 379
Anna Porphyrogenita, 135
antemurale christianitatis, 11–12, 81, 241, 349
antemurale, origin of term, 11–12, 32–33, 103. *See also* bulwark myth
anti-Islamism in Europe, 21st c., 378–84
anti-Ottoman rhetoric
    1450s, 35–39
    18th c., 148–49
anti-Semitism in Central Europe, late 19th c., 110
Antonii (Khrapovitskii), Archbishop, 147, 156, 157
Aptekar, M., 331
Armstrong, John, 6, 347
Aron, Petru Pavel, 70
Atatürk, Mustafa Kemal, 187
Austria
    anti-Islamism, 383
    as bulwark, 383–84
Austro-Hungarian Compromise (1867), 247

Bangha, Béla, 307
Bantysh-Kamenskii, Dmitrii, 222
Barge Haulers on the Volga (*Burlaki na Volge*, painting by Ilia Repin, 1870–73), 319
Barițt, George, 72
Barth, Fredrik, 347
Barvinskyi, Bohdan, 250
Barvinskyi, Oleksandr, 244, 257n21
Barvinskyi, Omelian, 250
Basel, Council of (1431–49), 39
Basil II, Byzantine Emperor, 134
Basilians. *See* Order of St. Basil the Great
Belarus
    Poland and, 356
    Russia and, 355, 356–59
Belinsky, Vissarion, 223–24
Benedict XV, Pope, 298–99
Berezhnaya, Liliya, 6, 9, 320, 376
Berger, Stefan, 208
Bildiriş. *See Message*
Bilenky, Serhiy, 208, 220, 324–25
Black Hundreds, 146–47, 153
Bobola, Andrzej, 302–3
Bogatyri. *See Warriors*
Bolshevism, bulwark myths and, 90
borderland regions, 8, 9–10
Börne, Ludwig, 110
Bowman, Isaiah, 278
Brandenberger, David, 330
Brest, Union of (1596), 164, 296, 302
Brückner, Eduard, 273
Brunson, Molly, 329
Budai, Aron, 72
Bulgarin, Faddei, 222
bulwark myth
    in Austria, 383–84
    in Belarus, 356–59
    as a boundary-defining mechanism, 348, 364–65
    Catholic Europe and, 37–39

civilizing mission element of,
    10–11, 67
  Cold War and, 351–52
  communism and, 114, 349
  contact zones and, 13–14
  Crimea and, 130–31, 168, 376
  as defensive myth, 354–55
  definition, 3, 7–11
  diplomatic correspondence and, 43
  dissemination of, 6–7, 41, 45, 385
  Eastern Europe and, 11–12
  European Union and, 374–75
  in Galicia, 242, 254
  in Georgia, 361–63
  in Germany, 268–70, 383
  ghetto and, 104, 106, 109, 113, 116
  geography and, 265–66, 278–79,
    282–83
  historical mythology and, 208,
    348–50
    in Hungary, pre-19th c., 42–44,
      303–5
    in Hungary, 20th–21st c.,
      279–82, 305–7, 376, 377,
      381–83
  messianism and (see messianism)
  monasteries and, 148
  nationalism and, 14, 242, 364–65
  Ottoman Empire and, 37, 41,
    148–49, 349, 350
  origin of term, 32–33, 36, 40, 349
  in Poland, 15th–18th c., 42–47, 82,
    213, 293–94
  in Poland, 19th–early 20th c.,
    81–84, 86–87, 88, 90–93, 94–96,
    262, 271, 294–95, 308
  in Poland, 20th–21st c., 295–303,
    375, 376, 377–79
  as political device, 350–51
  popularity of, 385–86
  printing press and, 41, 45
  role in society, 9, 10
  in Romania, 61
  secularization of, 10, 149, 349, 376
  sui generis myth and, 348, 349, 356,
    365
  symmetry and, 350

transnational nature of, 15–16,
    17–18
  in Turkey, 8, 10, 186–87, 190–91,
    197–98
  in Ukraine, 208–9, 224–26, 274,
    278, 338n13, 359–61, 375
  Warriors painting and, 320–21, 325,
    329–30, 333, 334–35, 336–37
Buonaccorsi, Filippo. *See* Callimachus
  Experiens
*Burlaki na Volge. See Barge Haulers on
  the Volga*
Burniewicz, Józef, 375, 382
Butsmaniuk, Iulian, 163–64, 165
Byzantine Empire, 33–34

Caferoğlu, Ahmet, 190, 191–92, 197
Callimachus Experiens (pseud. of Filippo
  Buonaccorsi), 44
"Carte Rouge." *See Magyarország
  néprajzi térképe*
Central Europe, definition, 13, 351–53
Chassin, Charles-Louis, 305
cheder schools, 110
Chepa, Andrian, 219
Chikovani, Nino, 363
Chołodecki, Alexander, 89
Ciążyński, Stanisław, 297
Cieszyński, Nikodem, 295
Ciołek, Erazm, 294
Cipariu, Timotei, 69
Constantine VIII, Byzantine Emperor,
  135
Constantinople, capture of (1453),
  33–34. *See also* Istanbul
"Constantinopolitana clades" (speech by
  Enea Silvio Piccolomini, 1454), 37, 40,
  53n69
Cossack Hetmanate, 211, 212, 217–189
Cossacks, 14, 208
  as bulwark, 157, 211–12, 216, 222,
    245–46
  decline of, 214–15
  Hetmanate, 211, 212, 217–18
  in *History of the Home Country*,
    252–53
  in *History of the Rus*, 218

military myth of, 215–16, 222
political states of, 210–11
Sloboda (Slobidska) Ukraine, 211, 212, 217
Zaporozhian Sich, 211–12, 216, 221
Crimea
    Andrew the Apostle in, 132
    baptism of Vladimir (Volodymyr) the Great, 134–35
    as bulwark, 130–31, 168, 376
    Cyril and Methodius in, 133–34
    as "holy ground," 127, 131–35, 168
    Muslim population of, 128, 130, 135, 170
    Orthodox Christianity and, 128–29, 136–37, 168
    Russia and, 125–27
    Russian annexation of, 1783, 129, 130–31
    Russian annexation of, 2014, 127
    "Russian Athos" movement, 166–68
Crimean Tatars, 137
Crimean War, 135–36, 168
Cud nad Wisłą (Miracle on the Vistula). *See* Warsaw, Battle of
culture, defining features of, 347
Cyril (Constantine), Saint, 133–34

Dalbor, Edmund, Cardinal, 298
Deutscher Volks- und Kulturboden. See *German Ethnic and Cultural Lands*
Dianina, Katia, 326
Didytskyi, Bohdan, 245
Divovych, Semen, 215, 219
Długosz, Jan, 44
Dobromyl reform (1882), 161
Dobrynya Nikitich, 322, 327
Dontsov, Dmytro, 359–60
Dositheos, Patriarch of Jerusalem, 65
Dzhokhadze, Avto, 362

Eastern Europe, definition, 13, 351–53
empire, definition, 15
Engel, Johann Christian von, 214
Engin, Âli, 198
Engin, Arın (pseud. of Mehmet Saffet Engin), 195–96

Ercilasun, Ahmet B., 199
Erer, Tekin, 196, 201n35
Ergin, Muharrem, 196–98
Ethnographical Map of Hungary (*Magyarország néprajzi térképe a népsűrűség alapján*, 1918–19), 279–80, 281f
Euroskepticism, 379–84

Farage, Nigel, 380
Fedevych, Klymentii I., 156
Fedevych, Klymentii K., 156
Filelfo, Francesco, 41
First Congress of Christ the King (I Kongres Chrystusa Króla, 1937), 302
Florence, Union of (1439), 34
Foch, Ferdinand, 94
Frankfurt, Diet of (1454), 34, 37, 39, 43
Frederick III, Holy Roman Emperor, 107
Fryling, Zygmunt, 110–11, 120n32

Galicia (Habsburg crownland). *See also* schoolbooks in Habsburg Galicia
    bulwark myth and, 254
    educational policy, 247
    as successor to Rus, 251–52
    Ukrainian language in, 243
Gall, Rudolf, 113
Ganghofer, August von, 273
Ganghofer, Ida von, 273
Ganghofer, Ludwig von, 273
Gardiner, Nile, 377
Gasimov, Zaur, 6, 8, 10, 386
Gasprinskii, Ismail, 189, 195, 197
Gavriil (Rozanov), Archbishop, 136
Geier, Wolfgang, 294
Geographical-Statistical Atlas of Poland (*Geograficzno-statystyczny atlas Polski*, Eugeniusz Romer, 1916), 272
geography
    bulwark myth and, 265–66, 278–79, 282–83
    political motivation of, 264–65
Georgia
    geopolitical identity, 355, 362–63
    Russia and, 355, 361–64
Gerasimov, Alexander, 331, 332

German Ethnic and Cultural Lands (*Deutscher Volks- und Kulturboden,* map by Albrecht Penck, 1925), 269–70
Germany, bulwark myth and, 268–70, 383
ghetto
    anti-Semitism and, 114–16
    bulwark myth and, 104, 106, 109, 113, 116
    in Cracow (1495), 107–8
    as ideological construct, 105, 111–12
    in Frankfurt (1463), 107, 109
    in Galicia (19th c.), 109–14
    origin of term, 103–4
    in Venice (1916), 108–9
    Zionism and, 111–13, 115
Ghisa, Ciprian, 12, 15, 376
Ghitta, Ovidiu, 64
Gilferding, Aleksandr Fedorovich, 323
Gindely, Antonin, 244
Gingrich, Andrei, 383
Giovanni di Castiglione, Cardinal, 35–36
Gogol, Nikolai, 221
Gökalp, Ziya, 189, 197
Gömbös, Gyula, 305
Goscilo, Helena, 319–20
Gregory X, Pope, 294
Grochowski, Stanisław, 45
Grunewald, Battle of (1410), 215
Gudenus, Johann, 383
Gumplowicz, Abraham, 110, 119n26

haidamaky, 220, 223
Halecki, Oskar, 295, 301, 385
Hasenko, Heorg von, 276
Hasenko (Gasenko), Heorhii, 276
Hein-Kircher, Heidi, 7, 386
Herb, Guntram, 268
Herder, Johann Gottfried, 220
Heyde, Jürgen, 6, 376
Hildermeier, Manfred, 154
Himka, John-Paul, 161
historical myths, types of, 348
History of the Home Country (*Istoriia kraiu rodynnoho,* schoolbook, 1895), 249–53

History of the Rus (*Istoriia Rusov*), 215, 216, 217, 218–19
Hofeneder, Philipp, 7, 385
Hoiska, Anna (Hanna), 150
Holovatskyi, Jakiv, 244
Holy Dormition Lavra, Pochaiv, 146–47, 149
    anti-Polish rhetoric, 155
    anti-Semitism and, 154–55
    Basilian period, 151
    as bulwark, 152–59
    ecumenical character of, 159
    founding, 150
    Greek Catholic Church in Galicia and, 157–58
    monarchist rhetoric, 155–56
    printing house, 151
    as a stronghold of Cossack Ukraine, 156
    Theotokos icon, 150–51
    Ukrainian nationalism and, 158–59
Holy Dormition Monastery, Bakhchisarai, 149
    anti-Islam rhetoric and, 169
    as bulwark, 168–70
    Crimean War and, 168–69
    founding, 166
    revival, 166–67
    Theotokos icon, 166
Horvat, Niceta, 71–72
Hosking, Geoffrey, 322
Hrushevskyi, Mykhailo, 137, 226, 274, 359
Hungary. *See also* bulwark myth: in Hungary
    anti-Bolshevik activity, 305–7
    anti-Russian activity, 303–5
    as bulwark against Ottomans, 35–36
    messianism in, 308, 377
    nationalism in, 71, 306
    Red Terror (*vörösterror*), 293, 305
Huntington, Samuel, 348, 353–54
Hunyadi, John (János), Regent of Hungary, 36
Hüseyinzade, Ali Bey, 189

Ianovskyi, Mykola, 216
Iatseniuk, Arsenii, 376

Ignatius (Gosadino), Metropolitan, 166
Ilarion (Ivan Ohienko), Metropolitan, 158–59
Ilia Muromets (film, 1956), 335, 340n75
Innokentii (Borisov), Archbishop, 136, 166–67
integral nationalism, 359, 368n42
Ioseliani, Otar, 362
Iov (Zalizo), Abbot and Saint, 150, 164
Irányi, Dániel, 305
Istanbul, 189–90
Istoriia kraiu rodynnoho. See *History of the Home Country*
Istoriia Rusov. See *History of the Rus*
Ivanov, M. M., 327

Jackson, David, 326
Jan III Sobieski, King of Poland, 82, 87, 92, 160
Janša, Janez, 381
Jews
    assimilationism, 110–11, 113, 117n4
    cheders, 110
    segregation of, 105–7, 109 (*see also* ghetto)
Jobst, Kerstin, 9, 168, 376
John the New of Suceava, Saint, 160

Kaczyński, Jarosław, 379–82
Kaczyński, Lech, 382–83
Kahlenberg, Battle of (1683), 82
Kakowski, Aleksander, Cardinal and Archbishop, 298
Karaosmanoğlu, Yakup Kadri, 187, 200n3
Kasianov, Georgiy, 4
Kelles-Krauz, Kazimierz, 294
Kemal, Yahya, 197
Kenneweg, Anne Cornelia, 31
Khmelnytskyi, Bohdan, Hetman, 87, 88–89, 165, 212, 215, 218
Khoinatskii, Andrei, 150, 157
Kholodovskaia, M. Z., 333
Khotyn, Battle of (1621), 215, 295
Kırmacı, A. N., 196
Kiss-Rigó, László, 383
Kliuchevskii, Vasilii, 129
Koberidze, Nodar, 362

Kohn, Hans, 14
Kolbe, Maksymilian, 302
Koliivshchyna rebellion, 220
Kolstø, Pål, 8, 325, 376, 382, 386
Konarski, Kazimierz, 295
Koneczny, Feliks, 296–97
Konopczyński, Władysław, 295
Konotop, Battle of (1659), 215
Köprülü, Fuat, 192
Kosovo, Battle of (1389), 215
Kossak, Wojciech, 86
Kossuth, Lajos, 303–5
Kovalskyi, Vasyl, 244
Kováts, Edgar, 163
Kozelsky, Mara, 126, 166
Kozlovskyi, Kyprian, 161
Kramskoi, Ivan, 325
Krasiński, Zygmunt, 308
Kraszewski, Józef Ignacy, 294
Kravchenko, Volodymyr, 6, 15, 359, 376
Kuchma, Leonid, 360
Küçük-Kaynarca, Treaty of (1774), 129
Kulikovo, Battle of (1380), 215
Kulish, Panteleimon, 221
Kundera, Milan, 351–52
Kuntsevych, Iosafat, 164
Kurz, Sebastian, 383
Kvitka, Hryhorii, 212
Kvitka, Illia, 212
Kyiv, 88, 132, 136, 165, 249, 251, 276, 302, 323, 325, 328–29, 333–35, 360, 376
    baptism of, 134
    as cradle of the Ukrainian national revival, 252
    historical legacy of, 210
    Saint Vladimir Cathedral, 137, 141n58
    as spiritual symbol of the Rus World, 220
    as stronghold against the Polish and Catholic influences, 301
Kyivan Rus, 129, 132, 137, 168, 171, 224, 322, 323, 326, 329, 331, 336, 338n13

Land of Fire (*Odlu Yurt*, journal), 190–91

Łaski, Jan, the Elder, 294
Lassalle, Ferdinand, 110
Laurian, August Treboniu, 73
Lawaty, Andreas, 149
Lebedev, A. K., 333
Lelewel, Joachim, 262
Lemeni, Ioan, Bishop, 65, 69, 73
Le Pen, Marine, 380
Lewicki, Anatol, 247–49
Lewis, Bernard, 350
Linnaeus, Carl, 220
"Little Russia"
    as cradle of Rus, 219–20, 224
    Russian Empire and, 221–24
    as successor to Cossackdom, 214–17
    as term, 209–10
Lomonosov, Mikhail, 129
Lueger, Karl, 113
Lutosławski, Wincent, 296
Luzhkov, Iurii, 127
Lviv, 85–86
    architecture, 93–94
    as bulwark, 81–82, 88, 90–93, 94–96
    ethnic identity of, 86, 87, 89, 93–94
    Exposition of 1894, 87–88
    Russian occupation of 1914, 89–90, 92
    travel guides, 81–82, 84–85
Lysiak-Rudnytskyi, Ivan. *See* Rudnytskyi, Ivan Lysiak

Magyarország néprajzi térképe a népsűrűség alapján. See Ethnographical Map of Hungary
Maier, Charles, 264
Makovskii, S., 329
Maksymovych, Mykhailo, 220, 221, 222
Mamontov, Savva, 323
Mannheim, Karl, 351
Map of Poland during the Reign of King Jan Sobieski (*Mapa Polski za Panowania Krola Jana Sobieskiego*, J. Szpetkowski, 1883), 262, 263f, 265
Markevych, Mykola, 215, 218, 220, 223, 224
Martin I, Pope, 139n23

Martonne, Emmanuel de, 279
Martos, Olexii, 215
Matejko, Jan, 86, 324
Matiiv, Ivan, 249–53
Matthias Corvinus, King of Hungary, 44
Mazepa, Ivan, 165, 212, 213, 218
Medvedev, Dmitry, 363
Mendelssohn Bartholdy, Felix, 110
Meotti, Giulio, 384
mesoregion, 12–13
Message (*Bildiriş*, journal), 190–91
messianism, 11, 46–47, 149, 350, 385
    in Hungary, 308, 377
    in Poland, 307–8
Methodius, Saint, 133–34
Mickiewicz, Adam, 308
Micu, Samuil, 72
Micu-Klein, Inochentie, 62, 70, 71
Miechowita, Maciej, 294
Military-Political Map of Poland (*Wojenno-polityczna mapa Polski*, Eugeniusz Romer, 1916), 271f, 272
Miller, Alexei, 222, 324
Miller, Gerhard Friedrich, 211
"Miracle on the Vistula." *See* Warsaw, Battle of
Mishkova, Diana, 13
Missionary (*Misionar*, journal), 161–63
monasticism
    bulwark myth and, 148
    nationalism and, 146–47
Morawiec, Małgorzata, 149
Morgunov, N., 331–32
Morgunova-Rudnitskaia, Nataliia, 334
Mościcki, Ignacy, 159
Mucha, Alphonse, 324
Muromets, Ilia, 322, 323
mythomoteur, 6, 366n11

Nadezhdin, Nikolai I., 135, 141n51
Nałęcz-Korzeniowska, Maria Regina, 262
Nathans, Benjamin, 155
national identity
    artists and, 324
    bulwark rhetoric and, 46
    sacralization of, 9, 131, 149, 173n24

nationalism, expression of, 14–15
Nativity Monastery, Zhovkva, 149
    anti-Semitism and, 162
    founding, 160
    murals and paintings, 160, 163–65
    printing house, 161
    Russophile activity, 160–62
    Ukrainophile activity, 160–63, 165
Naumann, Friedrich, 266
Naumovych, Ivan, 159, 177n80
Navoi, Alisher, 192, 197
Neumann, Iver B., 364
Nicholas of Cusa, Cardinal, 35, 40
Niedermüller, Peter, 5
Nopsca von Felső-Szilvás, Baron, 279
Norris, Stephen M., 7, 385
Novorossiia project, 211–12, 223

Odessa, 212
Odlu Yurt. See *Land of Fire*
Ohienko, Ivan. *See* Ilarion (Ivan Ohienko)
Ohladova karta ukrainskykh zemel. See
    Survey Map of Ukrainian Lands
Ohonovskyi, Omelian, 244
Orbán, Viktor, 380, 381
Order of St. Basil the Great, 174n30
Orzechowski, Stanisław, 294
Ostroróg, Jan, 293
Otar, İbrahim, 194
Outline of the History of Poland (*Zarys
    historyi Polski i krajów ruskich z nią
    połączonych,* schoolbook, 1884),
    247–49

Pajgert, Adam, 295
Paris Peace Conference (1919), 295
Partytskyi, Omelian, 244, 245
Pazniak, Zianon, 357–58
Pegida (Patriotische Europäer gegen die
    Islamisierung des Abendlandes), 378,
    383
Penck, Albrecht, 264–70, 274
Peredvizhniki. See Wanderers
Piccolomini, Enea Silvio (Pope Pius II),
    35, 37–42
Pickles, John, 282
Piłsudski, Józef, 90, 92, 293

Pimonenko, Mykola, 324
Pius XI, Pope, 302
Platt, Kevin M. F., 330
Plokhy, Serhii, 4
Pobedonostsev, Konstantin, 147
Pochaiv Lavra. *See* Holy Dormition
    Lavra, Pochaiv
Pogodin, Mikhail, 224
Poland
    anti-Bolshevik activity, 295–303
    anti-Islamic activity, 378–80, 382
    anti-Semitism in, 114–16, 299–300
    anti-Russian activity, 294, 300
    anti-Ukrainian activity, 91
    bulwark myths and, 15th–18th c.,
        42–47, 82, 213
    bulwark myths and, 19th–early
        20th c., 81–84, 86–87, 88, 90–93,
        94–96, 262, 271, 294–95, 308
    bulwark myths and, 20th–21st c.,
        295–303, 375, 376, 377–79
    Euroskepticism in, 379–83
    as German colonial space, 269–70
    in *History of the Rus,* 219
Poletyka, Hryhorii, 219
Polevoi, Nikolai, 224
political myth, 5–7
politics of eternity, 384–85
Poltava, Battle of (1709), 215
Pompilj, Basilio, Cardinal, 298
Popovici, Ioan, 72
Poroshenko, Petro, 360–61
Potemkin, Grigorii, 130
Potocki, Andrzej Kazimierz, Governor,
    86
Potocki, Mikołaj, 151
Pratt, Mary Louise, 13
Primary Chronicle, 132
printing press, 40–42
Psiotis, Argyrios K., 156
Ptushko, Aleksandr, 335
Pushkin, Alexander, 222
Putin, Vladimir, 127, 363, 384
Pütz, Wilhelm, 245

Radziwiłł, Michał Kazimierz "Rybeńko,"
    160

INDEX   *403*

rampart. *See* bulwark myth
Rasulzade, Mahammad Emin, 190, 200n10
Rațiu, Petru, 72
Ravid, Benjamin, 105
Regensburg, Diet of (1454), 34, 37, 39, 41, 43
Rehman, Antoni, 273
religion
    defining civilizations through, 353–54
    nationalization of, 9–10, 149, 173n24
Repin, Ilia, 319, 324, 325, 331, 332
Robakidze, Grigol, 362
Romania. *See* Transylvania
Romer, Adam, 301
Romer, Eugeniusz, 264, 266, 268, 270–73, 278
Rossknecht, Jadwiga, 273
Ruderman, David, 109
Rudnytskyi, Denys, 273
Rudnytskyi, Ivan Lysiak, 209
Rudnytskyi, Lev, 273
Rudnytskyi, Stepan, 264, 273–79
Rumsfeld, Donald, 352
Russia
    anti-Islam rhetoric in, 169
    anti-Semitism in, 155
    art, 326, 330–31
    Church policy, 147
    Crimea and, 125–27 (*see also* Crimea: Russian annexation of)
    definition, 210
    Enlightenment thought and, 213
    as Eurasian, 294, 356
    geopolitical identity, 294, 355–56, 358
    Georgia and, 363–64
    Novorossiia project, 211–12, 223
    as threat to neighboring countries, 354–56
    Ukrainophilia in, 222
"Russian Athos" movement, 166–68
Ruthenian ethnonym, 98n24
Ruthenian national movement, 86–87
Rutkovych, Ivan, 160

Rutowski, Tadeusz, 89
Rutskyi, Iosyf, Metropolitan, 174n30

Saakashvili, Mikheil, 361–62
Saganovich, Genad, 357
Șaguna, Andrei, 73
Sălăjean, Iosif Pop, 70, 72
Sapieha, Adam Stefan, Archbishop, 298
Šarec, Marjan, 381
Schérer, Jean-Benoît, 213, 220
Schiller, Salomon, 111, 120n35
schoolbooks in Habsburg Galicia
    anthologies, 245–46
    bulwark myth in, 245–47, 254–55
    Polish control of, 247
    Russophilism in, 245–46
    Ukrainian-language, 243–45, 248
Schöpflin, George, 5, 10, 11, 215
Scythians, 132
securitization, 7–8, 83–84, 95–96
Seegel, Steven, 7, 385
Senkovskyi, Osip, 223
Seraphim, Peter Heinz, 114–16
Seydahmet, Cafer, 190, 192–95
Shafonskyi, Opanas, 215
Shashkevych, Markiian, 244
Sheptytskyi, Andrei, Metropolitan, 163, 165
Shevardnadze, Eduard, 363
Shevchenko, Taras, 156
Shumlianskyi, Iosyf, 160
Sienkiewicz, Henryk, 294
Simmel, Georg, 8
Singer, Isidor, 110–11, 120n30
Skalkovskyi, Apollon, 222–23
Slovenia, anti-Islamism in, 381
Słowacki, Juliusz, 294, 308
Smith, Anthony, 9, 216
Smoleński, Władysław, 295
Snyder, Timothy, 384–85
Sobalkowski, Szczepan, 303
Sobolev, A., 327
Sofronie of Cioara, Saint, 64
Solzhenitsyn, Alexander, 128
Soysal, Abdullah Zihni, 192
Spinoza, Baruch de, 110
Srodecki, Paul, 6, 9

404   INDEX

Stasov, Vladimir, 319, 327
Staszic, Stanisław, 294
Stebelsky, Ihor, 276
Stender-Petersen, Adolf, 132
Strickland, John, 338n6
Styka, Jan, 86
Stypułkowski, Zbigniew, 114
Surikov, Vasily, 324, 331
Survey Map of Ukrainian Lands (Ohladova karta ukrainskykh zemel, Stepan Rudnytskyi, 1914), 276
Symonovskyi, Petro, 219
Szálasi, Ferenc, 307
Szeged Idea, 305
Székács, Aladár, 306
Szekfű, Gyula, 306
Szelągowski, Adam, 295
Szijarto, Peter, 377
Szporluk, Roman, 208

Taborska, Emilia, 273
Tarnowski, Jan, 295
Tazbir, Janusz, 43, 213
Teleki, Mihály II, 279
Teleki, Pál, 264, 279–82, 307
Tempea, Radu, 72
Teodorowicz, Józef, Archbishop, 298
Teutonic Order, 43
Tevzadze, Gigi, 363
Ther, Philipp, 4
Thon, Ozjasz, 112, 120n37
threat scenario, 7–8, 15, 83–84, 95
Togay, Muharrem Feyzi, 192
Tolstoi, Alexandr, 167
Tomicki, Piotr, 294
Tomkiewicz, Władysław, 301
Tóth Zoltán, Inokai, 64
transnational history, 4, 15–16
Transylvania, 15, 61–62
    anti-union writings in, 65–67
    Hungarian nationalists and, 71, 280
    pro-union writings in, 68–69
    religion in, 62–73
travel literature, 83, 84–85
Trencsényi, Balázs, 13
Trianon, Treaty of (1920), 280, 306
Türk amacı. See *Turkish Target*

Turkey
    anti-communism in, 190–91, 193, 196, 198
    as bulwark, 8, 10, 186–87, 190–91, 197–98
    communism in, 187
    political publications in, 190–98
    relations with Soviet Union, 187–88
    secularism in, 198
Turkish Target (*Türk amacı,* journal), 192
"Turkish Wall." See Turkey: as bulwark
Türk Kültürünü Araştırma Enstitüsü (Institute of Research of Turkish Culture), 196, 202n38
Turks
    ethnonym, 37
    nationalist sentiment, 189, 194–95, 196, 386
    "otherness" of, 37–38, 46
    in the Russian Empire, 188

Uhlig, Karl, 273
Ukraina: Land und Volk. See *Ukraine: Land and People*
Ukraina u svoikh etnohrafichnykh mezhakh. See *Ukraine in Its Ethnographic Borders*
Ukraine
    as bulwark, 18th c., 213–14
    as bulwark, 20th–21st c., 278, 359–61, 375, 376–77
    Crimea and, 137
    Enlightenment views on, 213–14, 215
    as Eurasian, 221
    Euromaidan, 376
    geopolitical position, 212–14, 217–19, 354, 375
    Huntington, Samuel, and, 354
    as "Little Russia," 209–10, 214–17
    in maps, 274–78
    national space of, 207–8
    nation-building process, 207–8
    Romantic views on, 221
    Russia and, 18th–19th c., 214, 219–24

INDEX   *405*

Russia and, 20th–21st c., 355, 359–61, 364, 376–77
    as term, 210, 217, 231n65
    transnational history and, 4
Ukraine in Its Ethnographic Borders (*Ukraina u svoikh etnohrafichnykh mezhakh*, map by Heorg von Hasenko and Stepan Rudnytskyi, 1920), 276, 277f
Ukraine: Land and People (*Ukraina: Land und Volk*, Stepan Rudnytskyi, 1915–16), 274
Ukrainian Autcephalous Orthodox Church, 158–59
Ukrainian Territory in Europe (*Das Wohngebiet der Ukrainer in Europa*, map by Stepan Rudnytskyi, 1914), 275
Union for the Liberation of Ukraine (SVU), 274
Union of the Russian People, 146–47, 153
Urban, Jan, 301–2

Vaida, Dimitrie, 69
Vasile Erdelyi, Bishop of Oradea, 70
Vasnetsov, Viktor
    at Abramtsevo artistic community, 323, 326
    early life, 323–24
    nationalist label and, 325–27, 332–33
    other artistic works, 325–26, 327–29
    post-Soviet biography of, 335–36
    religiosity of, 321, 326, 329
    Soviet biography of, 333–34
    view of *Warriors*, 326
Verchratskyi, Ivan, 244
Vereshchagin, Pavel, 331
Vienna, Battle of (1683), 61, 82, 295, 378, 383
Visarion Sarai (Serbian monk), 63
Vitalii (Maksimenko), Abbot, 147
Vitéz, János, Bishop of Oradea, 35–36, 44
Vladimir (Volodymyr) the Great, 134–35
Voltaire, 211, 213

Vorontsov, Mikhail, 167
Vyntskovskyi, Dmytro, 250
Vyslobotskyi, Iulian, 245, 250

Wanderers (*Peredvizhniki*), 324, 325, 331, 338n14
Warriors (*Bogatyri*, painting by Viktor Vasnetsov, 1898)
    bulwark myth and, 320–21, 325, 329–30, 333, 334–35, 336–37
    description, 321–23
    exhibitions of, 330–31, 333
    historical context, 324–25
    interpretation, post-Soviet, 335–37
    interpretation, Soviet, 332–34
    reception, 319, 320–21, 329, 331
    religion and, 329
Warsaw, Battle of (1920), 82, 293, 298, 378
Warszewicki, Krzysztof, 45, 294
Weiand, Kerstin, 6, 82, 386
Wesselényi, Miklós, 304
Wiener Neustadt, Diet of (1455), 34, 36, 39, 43
Wilde, August de, 272
Wilders, Geert, 380, 384
Wilson, Andrew, 359
Winkelriedism, 308
Winnicki, Robert, 378–79
Wiśniewski, Marian, 300
Witek, Elżbieta, 377–78
Władysław III, king of Poland and Hungary, 34, 39, 44
Wohngebiet der Ukrainer in Europa, Das. See *Ukrainian Territory in Europe*
Wojenno-polityczna mapa Polski. See *Military-Political Map of Poland*
Wrocław, Synod of (1267), 105–6

Zakrzewski, Stanisław, 295
Zaporozhian Sich, 211–12, 216, 221
Zarys historyi Polski i krajów ruskich z nią połączonych. See *Outline of the History of Poland*
Zhovkva Nativity Monastery. See Nativity Monastery, Zhovkva

Zhuravlev, V., 333
Zhvania, Zurab, 362
Ziegfeld, Arnold Hillen, 270

Zionism, 112–13, 117n4
Zipper, Albert, 88
Żółkiewski, Stanisław, 160

www.ingramcontent.com/pod-product-compliance
Lightning Source LLC
Chambersburg PA
CBHW072141100526

44589CB00015B/2030